Y0-GGF-038

FROM THE PARTS TO THE WHOLE

ACTA OF THE 13TH INTERNATIONAL BRONZE CONGRESS

VOLUME 2

JOURNAL OF ROMAN ARCHAEOLOGY

SUPPLEMENTARY SERIES NUMBER 39

Editorial committee:
Carol C. Mattusch, George Mason University
Amy Brauer, Arthur M. Sackler Museum, Harvard University Art Museums
Sandra E. Knudsen, Toledo Museum of Art

This volume is published with the support of Shelby White and Leon Levy

ISBN 1-887829-97-0
ISSN 1063-4304 (for the supplementary series)

Copyright © 2002 The individual authors. Printed by Thomson-Shore, Dexter, Michigan.
This and other supplements to the *Journal of Roman Archaeology*® may be ordered from:
JRA®, 95 Peleg Road, Portsmouth, Rhode Island 02871, U.S.A.
telephone (USA code+) 401 683 1955
telefax (USA code+) 401 683 1975 (fax only)
e-mail: jra@JournalofRomanArch.com
or via our Web site at: www.JournalofRomanArch.com

AN INTERNATIONAL JOURNAL

24619988

FROM THE PARTS TO THE WHOLE

VOLUME 2

Acta of the 13th International Bronze Congress, held at Cambridge, Massachusetts, May 28 - June 1, 1996

edited by

Carol C. Mattusch, Amy Brauer, and Sandra E. Knudsen

DG
11
J68X
Suppl.
No. 39
2000
V.2

MKS 7/23/02

Portsmouth, Rhode Island
2002

WITHDRAWN
OHIO UNIVERSITY
LIBRARY

Abbreviations

Abbreviations are based on the standards recommended by the *Journal of Roman Archaeology* and the *American Journal of Archaeology* 95 (1991) 3-16. Most abbreviations for ancient sources follow the *OCD*. Most monograph abbreviations repeated in the notes follow the form of author plus short title; most articles are abbreviated by author plus year. Only the lead museum name is normally cited for exhibition catalogues.

The following do not appear in the above works:

13th Br. Cong.	*Abstracts, 13th International Bronze Congress* (Cambridge, MA 1996).
Archäologische Bronzen	H. Born (ed.), *Archäologische Bronzen. Antike Kunst, moderne Technik* (Berlin 1985).
Art and technology	S. Doeringer, D. G. Mitten and A. Steinberg (edd.), *Art and technology: a symposium on classical bronzes* (Cambridge, MA 1970).
Bol, *Bronzetechnik*	P. C. Bol, *Antike Bronzetechnik. Kunst und Handwerk antiker Erzbildner* (Munich 1985).
Comstock–Vermeule, *Bronzes*	M. B. Comstock and C. C. Vermeule, *Greek, Etruscan, and Roman bronzes in the Museum of Fine Arts, Boston* (Greenwich, CT 1971).
Comstock–Vermeule, *Sculpture in stone*	M. B. Comstock and C. C. Vermeule, *Sculpture in stone: the Greek, Roman and Etruscan collections of the Museum of Fine Arts, Boston* (Boston 1976)
Due bronzi	*Due bronzi da Riace: rinvenimento, restauro, analisi, et ipotesi di interpretazione (BdA* spec. ser. 3, Rome 1984) (2 vols.).
The fire of Hephaistos	C. C. Mattusch *et al., The fire of Hephaistos: large classical bronzes from North American collections* (Exhib. cat., Arthur M. Sackler Museum, Harvard University Art Museums [Cambridge, MA 1996]).
The gods delight	A. P. Kozloff, D. G. Mitten *et al., The gods delight: the human figure in classical bronze* (Exhib. cat., Cleveland Museum of Art [Cleveland OH 1988]).
Haynes, *Technique*	D. Haynes, *The technique of Greek bronze statuary* (Mainz 1992).
Master bronzes	D. G. Mitten and S. F. Doeringer (edd.), *Master bronzes from the classical world* (Exhib. cat., Fogg Art Museum, Cambridge, MA [Mainz 1967]).
Mattusch, *Classical bronzes*	C. C. Mattusch, *Classical bronzes: the art and craft of Greek and Roman statuary* (Ithaca, NY 1996).
Mattusch, *Greek bronze statuary*	C. C. Mattusch, *Greek bronze statuary: from the beginnings through the 5th c. B.C.* (Ithaca, NY 1988).
Pollitt, *Art of Rome*	J. J. Pollitt, *The art of Rome c.753 B.C.-A.D.337: sources and documents* (Cambridge 1983).
Pollitt, *Art of Greece*	J. J. Pollitt, *The art of ancient Greece: sources and documents* (Cambridge 1990).
Ridgway, *Severe style*	B. S. Ridgway, *The Severe style in Greek sculpture* (Princeton 1970).
Rolley, *La sculpture grecque*	C. Rolley, *La sculpture grecque.* 1: *des origines au milieu du V siècle* (Paris 1994).
Rolley, *Greek bronzes*	C. Rolley, *Greek bronzes* (New York 1986).
Rolley, *Die griechischen Bronzen*	C. Rolley, *Die griechischen Bronzen* (Munich 1984). French edn.: *Les bronzes grecs* (Fribourg 1983).
Small bronze sculpture	M. True and J. Podany (edd.), *Small bronze sculpture from the ancient world: papers delivered at a symposium organized by the Departments of Antiquities and Antiquities Conservation and held at The J. Paul Getty Museum March 16–19, 1989* (Malibu 1990).
Walters, *British Museum Bronzes*	H. B. Walters, *Catalogue of the bronzes, Greek, Etruscan, and Roman in the Department of Greek and Roman Antiquities, British Museum* (London 1899)
The Western Greeks	G. P. Carratelli (ed.), *The Greek world: art and civilization in Magna Graecia and Sicily* (Exhib. cat., Palazzo Grassi, Venice [Milan–New York 1996]).
Das Wrack	G. Hellenkemper Salies, H.-H. von Prittwitz und Gaffron, and G. Bauchhenß (edd.), *Das Wrack: Der antike Schiffsfund von Mahdia* (Kataloge des Rheinischen Landesmuseums Bonn, 2 vols., Cologne 1994).
Zimmer, *Bronzegußwerkstätten*	G. Zimmer, *Griechische Bronzegusswerkstätten: zur Technologieentwicklung eines antiken Kunsthandwerkes* (Mainz 1990).

CONTENTS OF VOLUME 2

[continued overleaf]

Table of contents

Preface

These two volumes represent the distillation of the work of the 13th International Bronze Congress over three intensive days at Harvard University from May 29 to June 1, 1996, during which 90 scholars presented papers about the results of their work on many aspects of Greek, Roman, and Etruscan small bronzes and large-scale bronze statuary. This congress provided a fitting culmination for many years of research into the technologies and styles of classical bronzes at the Fogg Art Museum of Harvard University. Already during the late 1920s, the scientific practice of conservation and analysis of works of art had begun at the Fogg Art Museum under the guidance of E. W. Forbes and P. J. Sachs, co-directors of the Fogg Art Museum until 1944. Soon, important results for the study of ancient bronzes began to emerge, as in R. J. Gettens's pioneering study of mineral incrustation on the interior of a large hollow-cast seated statuette of an Egyptian lion-headed goddess which came to the museum in 1943 as part of the Grenville Winthrop Bequest. Gettens's research also led up to his later fundamental studies of how Chinese ritual bronze vessels were cast, after he moved to the Freer Gallery of Art in Washington, D.C.

During the years following World War II, the energetic efforts of G. M. A. Hanfmann, Curator of Ancient Art, led to major exhibitions of ancient art at the Fogg Museum — *Ancient art in American private collections* (1955-56), followed by the first public exhibition of the Norbert Schimmel collection in 1964. In both of these trend-setting exhibitions, classical bronzes played a prominent rôle. However, the Fogg Museum's involvement with classical bronzes reached a new level of intensity with the comprehensive international exhibition of Greek, Roman, and Etruscan bronzes, *Master bronzes from the classical world,* which was shown in Cambridge, St. Louis, and Los Angeles during 1967 and 1968. The opening of the exhibition in Cambridge was accompanied by an interdisciplinary symposium, "Art and Technology," which set the stage for all future meetings of this kind, including the series of bronze congresses that have been held in Europe (and now the United States) at regular intervals ever since.

In this ground-breaking symposium, which formed a critical beginning for the international effort to publish and study classical bronzes, the underlying emphasis was on how the manufacture of bronzes affects our understanding of their style. This was promoted, above all, by the leadership of the late C. Stanley Smith and H. Lechtmann of the Massachusetts Institute of Technology, which co-sponsored the symposium with Harvard University. In addition, the critical participation of leading European colleagues such as the late H. Menzel of Mainz, already widely recognized as the authority on bronzes from the provinces of Roman Europe, set the stage for the international effort to study classical bronzes that followed. At the initiative of H. Hoffmann, at that time Curator of Ancient Art in the Museum für Kunst und Gewerbe, Hamburg, H. Menzel had secured a number of the finest Roman statuary bronzes found in Western Europe for the exhibition. The proceedings of this symposium were published by Massachusetts Institute of Technology Press in 1970. Together this volume and the exhibition catalogue, *Master bronzes from the classical world,* have served as basic reference works for research in classical bronzes ever since.

Shortly after the exhibition, H. Menzel was host to a small gathering of bronze scholars at the Römisch-Germanisches Zentralmuseum, Mainz. This expanded into the regular series of bronze congresses that has produced a wealth of important scholarship on all aspects of classical bronzes during the decades since. At the same time, a library of definitive catalogues of collections of classical bronzes has steadily appeared from the Netherlands, Belgium, France, Austria, Switzerland, and especially from Germany itself, these last from H. Menzel's own exacting scholarship. In addition, new archaeological discoveries, such as that of the hoard of bronze statuettes from Weissenberg on the Danube in Bavaria, have provided exciting new impetus to this international wave of scholarly interest in classical bronzes. In the United States, interest was heightened by the exhibition of Greek, Roman and Etruscan statuettes, *The gods delight,* which appeared at the Cleveland Museum of Art, the Boston Museum of Fine Arts and the Los Angeles County Museum of Art in 1988 and 1989. The J. Paul Getty Museum, Malibu, sponsored an important symposium of small classical bronzes in 1989, with participants from many countries in Europe as well as North America.

It seemed to the organizers of the 13th International Bronze Congress that, for a fitting accompaniment that would recognize the pre-eminent rôle that technical studies of ancient bronzes had come to play in the laboratories of Cambridge and Boston area institutions, an exhibition should be organized examining and bringing together representatives of large-scale bronze statuary as a focus for the participants' discussions and the scholarly work of the meeting. This exhibition, *The fire of Hephaistos*, supported by a major grant from the National Endowment for the Humanities, was organized by C. C. Mattusch of George Mason University, H. Lie of the Straus Center for Conservation and Research, Harvard University Art Museums, and A. Brauer of the Harvard University Art Museums. S. Hemingway's internship enriched all aspects of the exhibition. As a result, we now know a great deal more about how many of the monumental Greek and Roman bronzes in American collections were cast and assembled. It also seems fitting that presentation of technical research on the casting of large-scale bronze statuary is prominent among the papers which we are happy to present here.

Among the many individuals to whom we owe enduring thanks for making this, the 13th International Bronze Congress, a reality, I must mention S. White and L. Levy for so generously supporting the publication of these papers. J. Cuno, Director of the Harvard University Art Museums, enthusiastically supported and sustained the planning of the congress and accompanying exhibition from the beginning. Without his guidance and support, the achievements of the 13th International Bronze Congress, including its definitive fruits which appear in this volume, would not have been possible.

David Gordon Mitten

Introduction

In 1982 Dorothy Kent Hill came to George Mason University to lecture about ancient bronzes, enthusiastic about having just attended the 7th International Congress on Ancient Bronzes in Székesfehérvár: she was adding names to the mailing list for future congresses. She died not long before the 9th Congress in Vienna in 1986. Had she lived until 1990, when the 11th Congress convened in Madrid, she would certainly have been a member of the committee in whose behalf D. G. Mitten proposed that the Congress meet in the United States in 1996. The members of that newly formed Planning Committee were B. Barr-Sharrar and E. B. Harrison; D. Buitron-Oliver and A. Oliver; C. Houser; J. J. Herrmann, Jr.; D. G. Mitten; and myself as chair. D. G. Mitten, the most experienced American participant in the congresses on ancient bronzes, proposed that our congress be held at Harvard University in Cambridge, MA. J. Cuno, Director of the Harvard University Art Museums, generously agreed to host the congress, and A. Brauer at that institution became our tireless and multi-talented Congress Coordinator. Planning began with a seed grant from G. Ortiz, a regular congress participant, and we benefited frequently from the guidance of S. E. Griffin, conference planner.

The 13th International Congress on Ancient Bronzes was held in Cambridge from May 28 through June 1, 1996. Ninety speakers and more than 200 participants came from Bulgaria, Canada, Denmark, England, France, Germany, Greece, Ireland, Italy, the Netherlands, Poland, Portugal, Russia, Spain, Switzerland, and the United States. One of the most delightful gatherings during the Congress was at the magnificent reception hosted by Dr. and Mrs. Jerome M. Eisenberg at the Museum of Fine Arts, Boston.

The major focus of the 13th Congress was large-scale bronzes, as had been the case in Vienna 10 years before. The papers published here include presentations of recently discovered bronzes, technical studies of statues well-known from the field of stylistic analysis, and a wide range of approaches to the study of ancient bronzes, both traditional and innovative. The organization of the *Acta* is generally chronological, though the papers were originally delivered in the following sessions: Athens; Early Greece; the Roman Provinces; Inscriptions, Coins, and Signatures; Vessels, Tools, and Implements; Post-Antique Bronzes; two sessions on Small Bronzes and two on Large Bronzes; and three sessions on Technology, Analysis, and Conservation. The session Chairs were E. B. Harrison, J. Neils, C. Houser, B. Barr-Sharrar, D. G. Mitten, A. Beale, H. Lie, J. A. Scott, J. H. Kroll, A. Oliver, S. Fabing, J. J. Herrmann, Jr., and myself.

The types and styles of classical bronze statuary, ancient technology, and modern research on the ancient bronze industry were the major themes of the exhibition which was organized to accompany the Congress: *The fire of Hephaistos: large classical bronzes from North American collections.* The Berlin Foundry Cup, one of two objects in the exhibition not made of bronze, set the stage: it shows that technology did not drive sculptural styles and that styles were not dependent upon the medium in which they were produced. Scholarly collaboration was the key to the exhibition, and I worked with H. Lie and with A. Brauer in the conception and implementation of the exhibition. In addition to making extensive observations about the technique by which each bronze was produced, we had the alloy of each bronze analyzed and x-radiographs made of many of the bronzes. Lenders to the exhibition showed great interest in the project, and generously allowed us extended access to their bronzes. In particular, K. T. Luckner at The Toledo Museum of Art gave us expert advice on planning and organization, but, sadly, he did not live to see the results of our work. The exhibition traveled to Toledo and to the Tampa Museum of Art. The exhibition catalogue (Harvard University Art Museums 1996) included essays by B. Barr-Sharrar, A. Beale, B. R. Brown, H. Lie, A. Oliver, A. E. Raubitschek, and B. S. Ridgway. The editor, S. E. Knudsen (Toledo Museum of Art) worked tirelessly to ensure flawless production, and she is also to be credited with the more difficult task of editing both volumes of the *Acta*. N. Luraghi and F. Prado-Vilar edited the Italian and Spanish papers respectively. A. Lilly and C. Schroeder managed manuscript preparation and extensive retyping; S. Kohler assisted with the management and photocopying of manuscripts. A. Brauer has taken on any and all tasks relating to these *Acta* cheerfully and skillfully; K.

Manning has assisted us with the details of volume 2. We are all grateful to J. H. Humphrey for taking on publication of the *Acta* in the *Journal of Roman Archaeology*'s supplementary series, and to S. White and L. Levy for their generous support of the publication.

Carol C. Mattusch

The International Bronze Congresses
and associated publications and exhibitions

1 1970 NIJMEGEN
Tagung über römische Bronzegefäße im Rijksmuseum G. M. Kam in Nijmegen von 20. bis einschließlich 23. April 1970, Hektogr. Niederschrift (Nijmegen 1970).

2 1972 MAINZ
H. Menzel (ed.), "Bericht über die Tagung 'Römische Toreutik' vom 23-26. Mai 1972 in Mainz," *JRGZM* 20 (1973) 258-82.

3 1974 BRUSSELS–MARIEMONT
Actes des IIIe journées internationales consacrées à l'étude des bronzes romains, Bruxelles–Mariemont 27-29 mai 1974 (Bulletin des Musées Royaux d'Art et d'Histoire 46 [1974 (1977)] 5-217). Also printed separately.

4 1976 LYON
Actes du IVe colloque international sur les bronzes antiques, 17-21 mai 1976 (Annales de l'Université Jean Moulin, Lyon 1977) 5-236.

5 1978 LAUSANNE
Bronzes hellénistiques et romains: tradition et renouveau: Actes du Ve colloque international sur les bronzes antiques, Lausanne, 8-13 mai 1978 (Cahiers d'archéologie romande de la Bibliothèque historique vaudoise 17 [1979]).

6 1980 BERLIN
Toreutik und figürliche Bronzen römischer Zeit: Akten der 6. Tagung über antike Bronzen, 13-17 Mai 1980 in Berlin (Staatliche Museen Preußischer Kulturbesitz, Antikenmuseum, Berlin 1984).

7 1982 SZÉKESFEHÉRVÁR
Bronzes romains figurés et appliqués et leurs problèmes techniques: Actes du VIIe colloque international sur les bronzes antiques, Székesfehérvár, 1982 (Alba Regia 21 [1984] 5-136).

8 1984 STARA ZAGORA
Papers unpublished.
Ancient Bronzes (Exhib. cat., District Historical Museum, Stara Zagora 1984).

9 1986 VIENNA
K. Gschwantler and A. Bernhard-Walcher (edd.), *Griechische und römische Statuetten und Großbronzen: Akten der 9. internationalen Tagung über antike Bronzen, Wien, 21-25 April 1986* (Vienna 1988).
K. Gschwantler (ed.), *Guß + Form: Bronzen aus der Antikensammlung* (Exhib. cat., Kunsthistorisches Museum, Vienna 1986).

10 1988 FREIBURG
J. Ronke (ed.), *Akten der 10. internationalen Tagung über antike Bronzen, Freiburg, 18-22 Juli 1988 (Forschungen und Berichte zur Vor- und Frühgeschichte in Baden-Württemberg* 45 [Stuttgart 1994]).
H. U. Nuber, *Antike Bronzen aus Baden-Württemberg* (Exhib. cat., *Schriften des Limesmuseums Aalen* 40 [1988]).

11 1990 MADRID
J. Arce and F. Burkhalter (edd.), *Bronces y religion romana: actas del XI congreso internacional de bronces antiguos, Madrid, Mayo-Junio 1990* (Consejo Superior de Investigaciones Científicas, Madrid 1993).
Los bronces romanos en España (Exhib. cat., Palacio de Velázquez, Madrid 1990).

12 1992 NIJMEGEN
S. T. A. M. Mols *et al.* (edd.), *Acta of the 12th International Congress on Ancient Bronzes, Nijmegen, 1-4 June, 1992 (Nederlandse Archeologische Rapporten* 18, Provinciaal Museum G. M. Kam, Nijmegen 1995).

13 1996 CAMBRIDGE, MA
C. C. Mattusch *et al.* (edd.), *From the parts to the whole: Acta of the 13th International Bronze Congress, Cambridge, MA, 31 May–2 June 1996* (*JRA* Suppl. 39.1-2 [2000-1]).
C. C. Mattusch, H. Lie *et al.*, *The fire of Hephaistos: large classical bronzes from North American collections* (Exhib. cat., Harvard University Art Museums, Cambridge, MA 1996).

14 1999 KÖLN
Antike Bronzen, Werkstattkreise: Figuren und Geräte, 14. internationaler Kongress, Römisch-Germanischen Museums, Köln, 21 bis 24 September 1999.

Times of trouble?
The votive bronzes of Late Iron Age Portugal

Teresa Júdice Gamito

Research on ritual or religious aspects of prehistoric societies, and even on of those of historic times, presents some difficulties unless other features can also be considered. Recent work on the archaeology of cult and the archaeology of mind has brought some progress to these issues, although they are still difficult to comprehend from the archaeological evidence alone.[1] In fact, once the purposes and meanings behind past behaviors have been forgotten or lost, we can only suggest possibilities. Anthropology can then make a contribution toward a better understanding of the problem.

Every religious cult is surrounded by specific rituals and rites, the first more concerned with religious worship, the latter with external ceremonies and acts. E. R. Leach distinguished between *technical actions*, through which the individual tries to change the outside world, and *expressive actions*, through which the individual shows his/her state of mind about the world as it is and the spheres of interaction between this and the other world.[2] Archaeological evidence can reveal both these actions, for it represents the work of individuals facing spiritual or world forces against which they felt they could not, or were unable to, fight.

As C. Renfrew emphasized,[3]

> Religious beliefs assert the existence of some transcendental, supernatural force or power, or of several of these. It is the purpose of cult to bring the participating humans and also sometimes those whom they represent, into some more direct relation with these transcendental realities.

From that action or act an expression of gratitude would be formulated, if the deity seemed to favor the individual's desire. Thus, votive offerings substantiated public gratitude or expressed the individual's intention to bring some change to his or her immediate world. These religious acts usually had a special location, a sacred place that might be a cave, a wood, a fountain, a certain point of a river, a mountain, or a special constructed place — that is to say, a temple. It could even be located at home, in a special place or shrine where the individual or his or her family worshipped the deity.

Recent studies connected with the archaeology of mind have proposed interesting and sometimes rewarding methods of research.[4] Recent archaeological data have contributed to a better

---

1 Already in the preface of his 1985 study of the Mycenean sanctuary of Phylakopi on Melos (*The archaeology of cult: the sanctuary at Phylakopi* [London 1985]), C. Renfrew emphasized the difficulties for the archaeologist when considering past cults and religious places based on material remains alone. What survive are only traces of past behavior, and much information is lost forever. In 1994, more concerned with aspects connected with cognitive archaeology, Renfrew stressed the rôle of symbolism and iconography within religion (C. Renfrew and E. B. W. Zubrow, *The ancient mind: elements of cognitive archaeology* [Cambridge 1994]).

2 In *Culture and communication* (Cambridge 1976) especially 37-82, Leach presented an interesting approach to the problem of considering the attitudes of the individuals when trying to reach or contact the sacred entities they believe will help them. The interaction between this and the other world is then of extreme importance.

3 Renfrew, *Cult* (supra n.1) 16, discussed various aspects of cult, human participation, and rituals connected with the idea of the holy.

4 From the 1980s onward there has been a preoccupation with archaeological research connected to aspects that go beyond the immediate data we possess. It started with a rediscovery of the work carried out by C. Lévi-Strauss on structural anthropology, only then translated into English. The impact of his *Anthropologie structurale* (Paris 1973) was great, beginning among American scholars, as seen in R. A. Rappaport, "The sacred in human evolution," *Annual Review of Ecology and Systematics* 2 (1971) 23-44, among others. It soon appeared in British research, for example, in I. Hodder's pioneering work connected with structural symbolism in *Symbols in action* (Cambridge 1982) or in his *Reading the past*

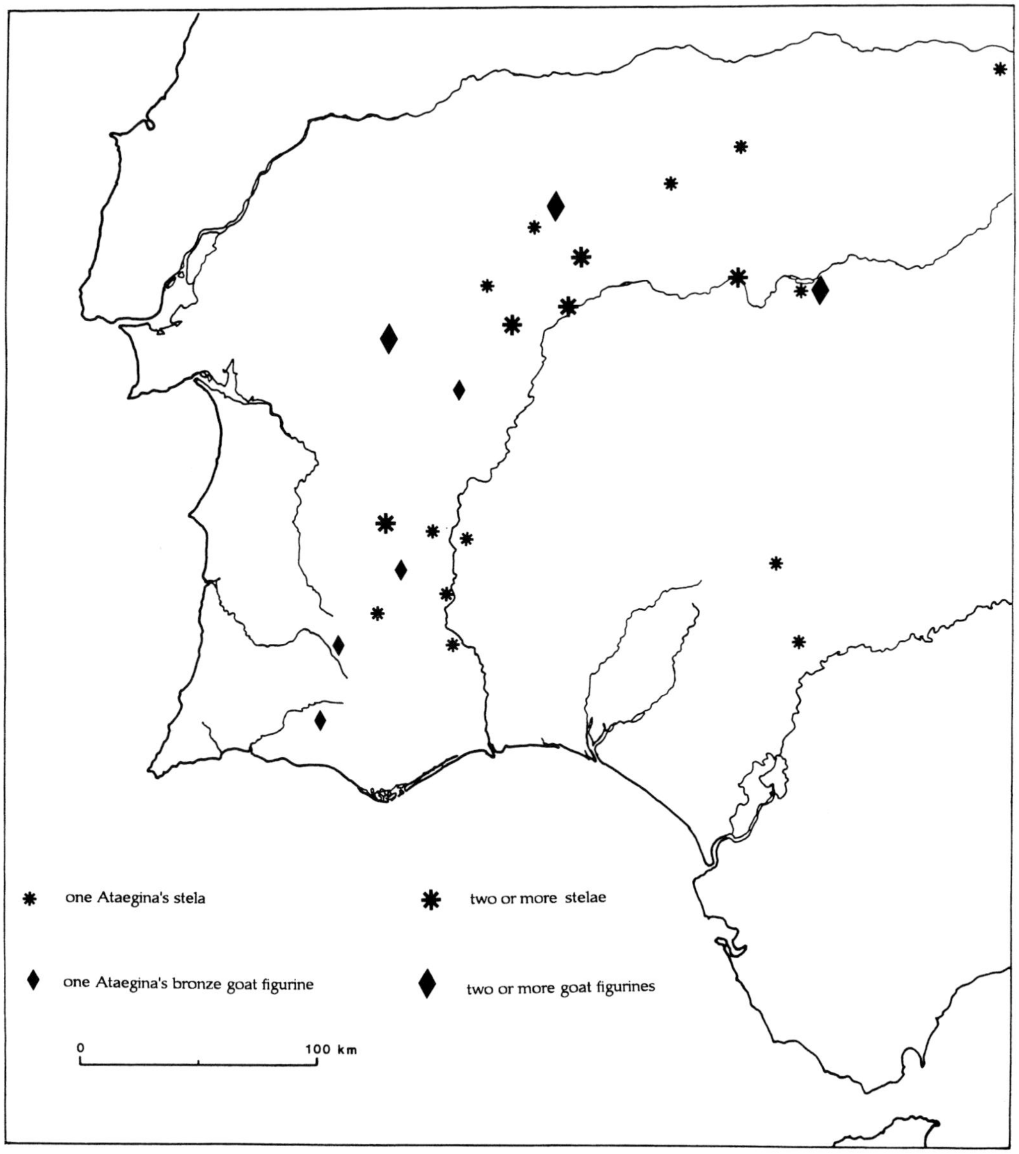

Fig. 1. Map of SW Iberia, showing finds associated with Ataegina. (Author)

understanding of ritual and rite. We know that ritual behavior or display is associated with particular forms, which help us to recognize them as dedicated to a certain deity or as a religious phenomenon. From R. A. Rappaport's definition of ritual as

> conventional acts of display through which one or more participants transmit information concerning their physiological, psychological, or sociological states either to themselves or to one or more participants,[5]

we can infer that this evidence will very probably cluster in a given area. One or more religious centers can thus be expected to be located in a geographic area to serve devotees. This seems to be the situation in the inland part of SW Iberia.

In the south of the Iberian peninsula, a large number of impressive votive deposits have been found. The most commonly referred to are Despeñaperos and Castellar de Santisteban, not

---

(Cambridge 1986), and in the work of C. Renfrew and S. Shennan, *Ranking, resource and exchange* (New York 1982), although here more connected with functionalist ideas. In 1985, Renfrew, *Cult* (supra n.1), gave much more attention to the religious aspects of the human mind, and did so again in 1994 (Renfrew and Zubrow [supra n.1]).

5 Rappaport (supra n.4) 25.

far from the Guadalquivir in the province of Jaen, as well as La Luz, near Murcia (Andalucia).[6] In these ritual places large numbers of small bronze figures of individuals, most probably representing devotees, were offered to a deity. They may reflect troubled times, for they are of the Late Iron Age when constant wars between Punic and Roman peoples were fought in southern Iberia. However, a large number of smaller cult places have also been found, some of them dedicated to important indigenous gods and goddesses such as *Endovellicus* or *Ataegina*. I shall concentrate here on Ataegina's cult.

In these parts of SW Iberia Celtic influences and settlement were strong, and gods, rituals, and rites were naturally of Celtic origin. Ataegina, as her name suggests, was a local pre-Roman indigenous deity of Celtic origin whose cult seems to have been concentrated in the inland areas of eastern Portugal and western Spain (fig. 1).

Most of the information about Ataegina's cult is archaeological, consisting of epigraphic documents and small bronze figurines representing goats.[7] The localization of this evidence suggests that the cult was specific to this area. There are several dedications and votive bronzes in the form of engraved *stelae* and *arae*, and bronze goat figurines. One of these stelae, found at Mérida in the 18th c., is a *devotio* (curse), praying Ataegina to act against a thief.[8] More recently a large number of epigraphic documents were found re-used as stones or building material inside the walls of a rural mediaeval church, Santa Lucia del Trampal (Alcuéscar, Cáceres). It has provided the largest known assemblage of Ataegina's cult inscriptions. During the work of restoration and consolidation of the church, some 31 inscriptions were recovered, and from these 15 were altars dedicated to the goddess. Some examples are illustrated in figs. 2-3. It should be stressed that Ataegina is one of the few local deities referred to as *Dea sancta*, sufficient reason to consider that those inscriptions carrying only this phrase were dedicated to *Ataegina* or *Ataecina*[9] (see the inscriptions below in Appendix A, part 1).

Ataegina's cult seems to have been associated with the annual renewal of nature and vegetation cults, including fertility rituals. As such, it might have evolved from the cult of Hera,

6 In 1969, G. Nicoli was the first to publish the whole corpus of votive bronzes from the Iberian sanctuaries in *Les bronzes figurés des sanctuaires ibériques* (Paris 1969), especially the well-known examples from Despeñaperos, but his attention was centered on the human figurines and their characteristics.

7 The occurrence of these small bronzes and their findspots attracted the attention of several scholars, among them J. Leite de Vasconcellos, *As religiões da Lusitânia* (Lisbon 1905); J. M. Blázquez, *Religiones primitivas de Hispania, fuentes epigráficas* (Rome 1962); id., *Dicionario de las religiones prerromanas de Hispania* (Madrid 1975), id., *Religiones prerromanas* (Madrid 1983). The present author referred to the problems connected with Ataegina in *Social complexity in southwest Iberia (8th-3rd c.* B.C.*) — aspects of evolution and interaction* (Ph.D. diss., Univ. of Cambridge 1986), expanded in *Social complexity in southwest Iberia (800-300* B.C.*) — the case of Tartessos* (BAR 439, Oxford 1988). See also G. Gamer, *Formen römischer Altare auf der hispanischen Halbinseln* (Madrider Beiträger 12, 1989). M. de la P. García-Bellido, "Las religiones orientales en la Península Ibérica: testimonios numismáticos," *ArchEspArq* 64 (1991), wrote from a numismatic point of view. More recently Ataegina's inscriptions and the implications of her cult were discussed by J. M. Abascal Palazón, "Las inscriptiones latinas de Santa Lucia del Trampal (Alcuéscar, Cáceres) y el culto de Ataegina," *ArchEspArq* 68 (1995) 31-105.

8 As we can see in Leite de Vasconcellos (supra n.7) 146-47.

9 Indeed, the large number of Ataegina's inscriptions at Sta. Lucia del Trampal renewed interest in the problem of Ataegina's cult and votive inscriptions and bronzes, although here there are only stone inscriptions. The problem was well summarized by Abascal (supra n.7), although it was also referred to by E. Cerrillo, "Excavaciones en la basilica de Magasquilla de los Donaires en Ibahernando (Cáceres)," *XIII Cong. Nac. de Arq. Huelva, 1973* (Zaragoza 1975) 979 ff. and id., *La basilica de época visigoda de Ibahernando* (Cáceres 1983). On the problem of shorter inscriptions, mentioning only DEA SANCTA, see M. A. Dias and A. Monge Soares, "Inscrição votiva de Vila Verde de Ficalho, Serpa," *FichEp* 18 (1986), also published in *AEpigr* p. 278 and *HEp* 1, p. 661, where this problem is discussed. Dias published it again in *Euphrosyne* 17 (1989) 374. It has 4 little holes on the top, suggesting that a votive bronze, probably a goat, was attached.

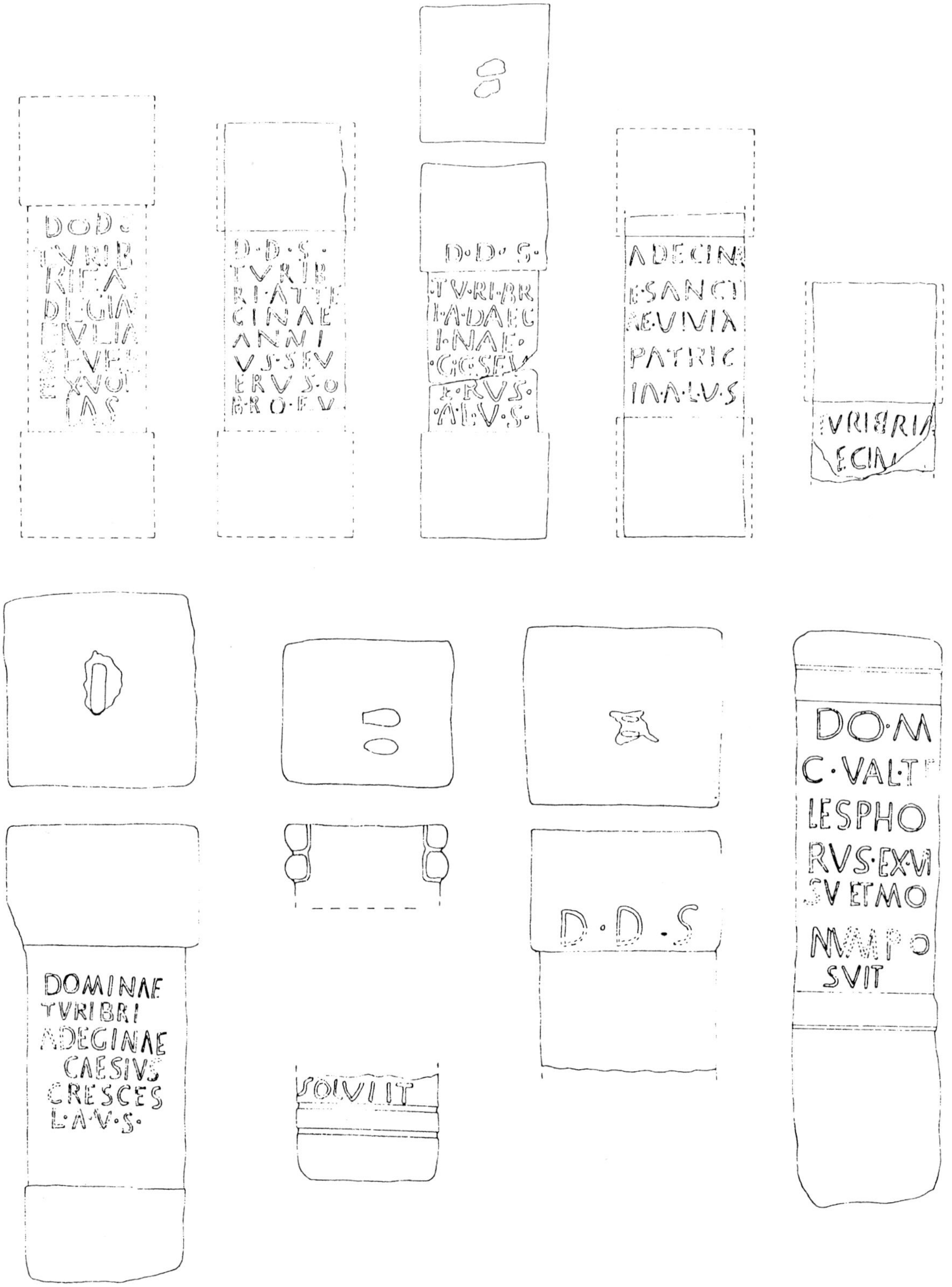

Figs. 2-3. Inscriptions from Sta. Lucia del Trampal. (Author)

which was reported by classical authors to have been well established in southern Iberia in the Iron Age, and later was associated with Juno, mentioned in Pliny[10] and Pseudo-Scymnos.[11] A

10 Pliny, Fr. 4, 120.

11 Pseudo-Scymnos, Fr. 153.

temple was located near Trafalgar, as mentioned by Ptolemy[12] and Mela.[13] A possible assimilation of cults might have occurred.

> The identical attributes of Hera (Juno) and Ataegina, carrying similar meanings and later related to Persephone (Proserpina), facilitated the process of acculturation ....[14]

The importance of the cult is stressed by J. Leite de Vasconcellos: Ataegina is always referred to as *dea, domina, sancta, invicta, servatrix*. On the other hand, three important aspects of the cult, connected with an earlier feminine goddess, relate her to the renewing of nature, the underworld and infernal qualities, and to medical powers. These all emphasize the power of Ataegina as an indigenous deity.

Ataegina's name, **Ate-gena* in Celtic, or *re-genita* in Latin, suggests a reborn deity and the reviving of nature in her cult that is also found in the worship of Proserpina. The medicinal powers of Ataegina may be stressed by the goat figurines, for the goat was a customary offering to Bacchus, or Liber, and his sister Libera, as mentioned by classical authors.[15] The association of Ataegina's cult with this form of worship is strengthened by the occurrence of small bronze figurines of goats dedicated to her. The relation of the goats to medicine is also stressed by Leite de Vasconcellos,[16] but, oddly, most of the goats are pregnant. Some examples illustrated here (figs. 4-8) are in the National Museum of Archaeology, Lisbon.

These figurines were probably related to altars to the goddess, for they appear to have been attached or linked to a stone or plaque. Some still carry a message to Ataegina, as is the case with that from Malpartida (Cáceres).

Another important aspect of this ancient cult is related to the territory of the Turobrigenses (their capital of Turobriga has not yet been located). Both the people and the toponym express their Celtic character through the ending *-briga*.[17] Nineteen bronze goats have been found in this same territory:

1. Malpartida (Cáceres), stuck to a plaque with a dedicatory inscription to Ataegina;
2. Malpartida (Cáceres), with its legs stuck to two bronze plaques, one with a dedication to Ataegina;
3-4. Medellin (Badajoz), two little goats in a parallel position, stuck together through two bronze plaques, which were probably attached to a stone slab;
5-7. Torrejoncillo (Cáceres), three goats, that should be joining their legs in a point, one with broken legs;
8. Torrejoncillo (Cáceres), a standing goat, very well represented;
9-10. Torrejoncillo (Cáceres), two goats in running position;
11-13. Alentejo (Évora Museum), three standing goats;
14. Mina de S. Vicente (Silves), a goat with elongated body and carefully drawn hair beautifully represented (fig. 4);
15. Alentejo (Museu Nacional de Arqueologia, Lisbon), a goat with a realistic representation of hair (fig. 5);
16. Alentejo (Museu Nacional de Arqueologia, Lisbon), a goat in a running position, realistic representation (fig. 6);
17. Redondo (Évora, Alentejo), a realistic representation of a goat (fig. 7);
18. Almodovar (Ourique, Alentejo), a stylized representation of a goat (fig. 8);
19. Alentejo(?), a very stylized representation of a goat (now in the Biblioteca Nacional, Lisbon).

---

12 Ptolemy 2.4, 5.

13 Mela 2.6.9.

14 I discussed this Celtic deity and the implications in the Iberian context in my *Social complexity* (supra n.7) 45.

15 As we can see in Virg., *Geog.* 2.380; Ov., *Met.* 15.114; Hor., *Carm.* 3.18 or 1.14.

16 Leite de Vasconcellos (supra n.7) 170-72.

17 As mentioned by J. Untermann, *Sprachraüme und Sprachbewegungen im vorrömischen Hispanien* (Wiesbaden 1961), as well as K. H. Schmidt, *Geschichte und Kultur der Kelten* (Heidelberg 1986) 14-24. They both discuss extensively the origin of Iberian languages and names.

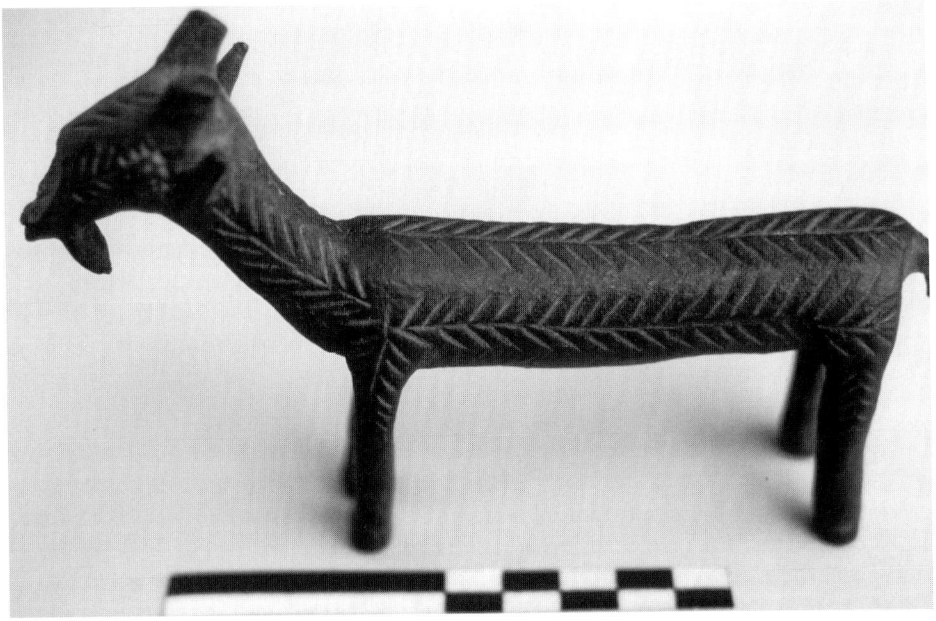

Fig. 4. Little goat from Mina de S.Vicente, precise findspot unknown but certainly by Silves. Lisbon, Museu Nacional de Arqueologia. (Author)

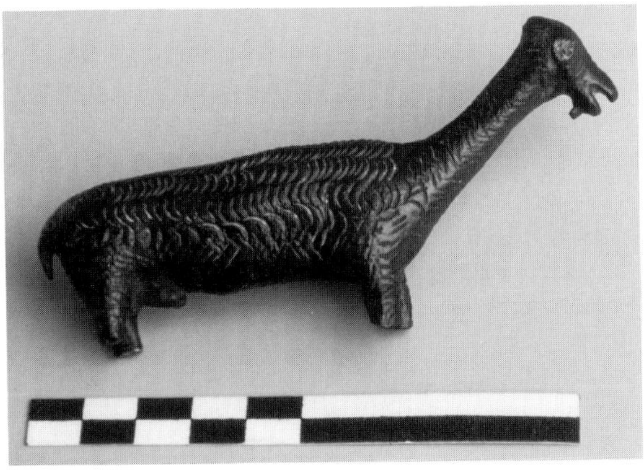

Fig. 5. Little goat from Alentejo, precise findspot unknown. Lisbon, Museu Nacional de Arqueologia. (Author)

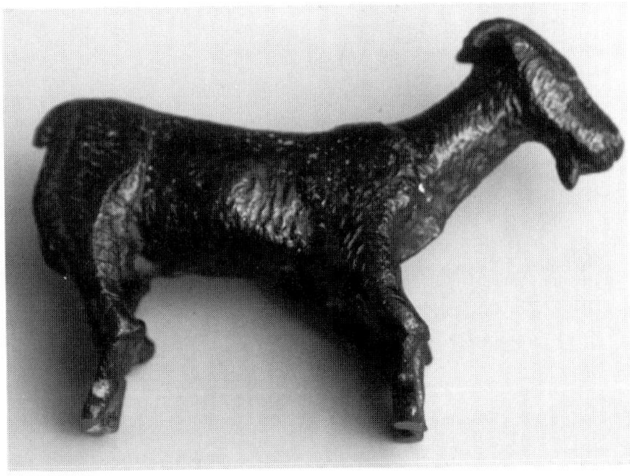

Fig. 6. Running goat from Alentejo. Lisbon, Museu Nacional de Arqueologia. (Author)

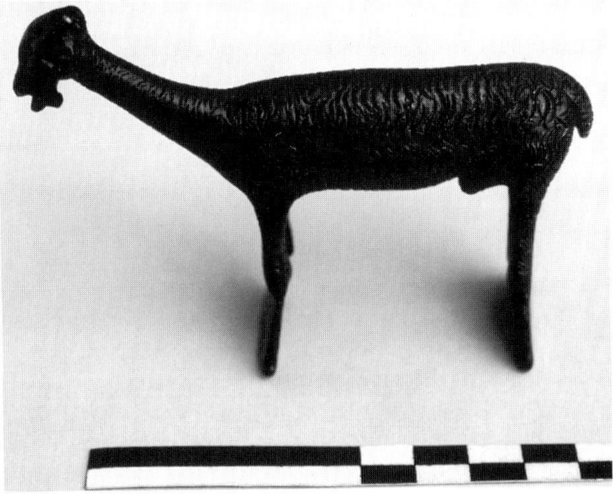

Fig. 7. Running goat from Redondo (Évora).
Both Lisbon, Museu Nacional de Arqueologia. (Author)

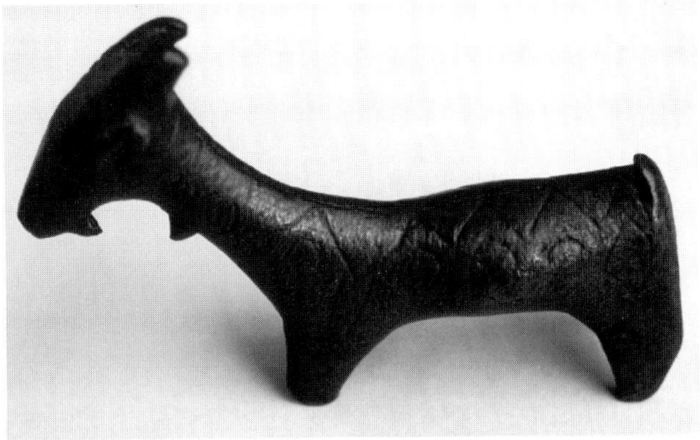

Fig. 8. Stylized goat from Almodovar (Ourique).

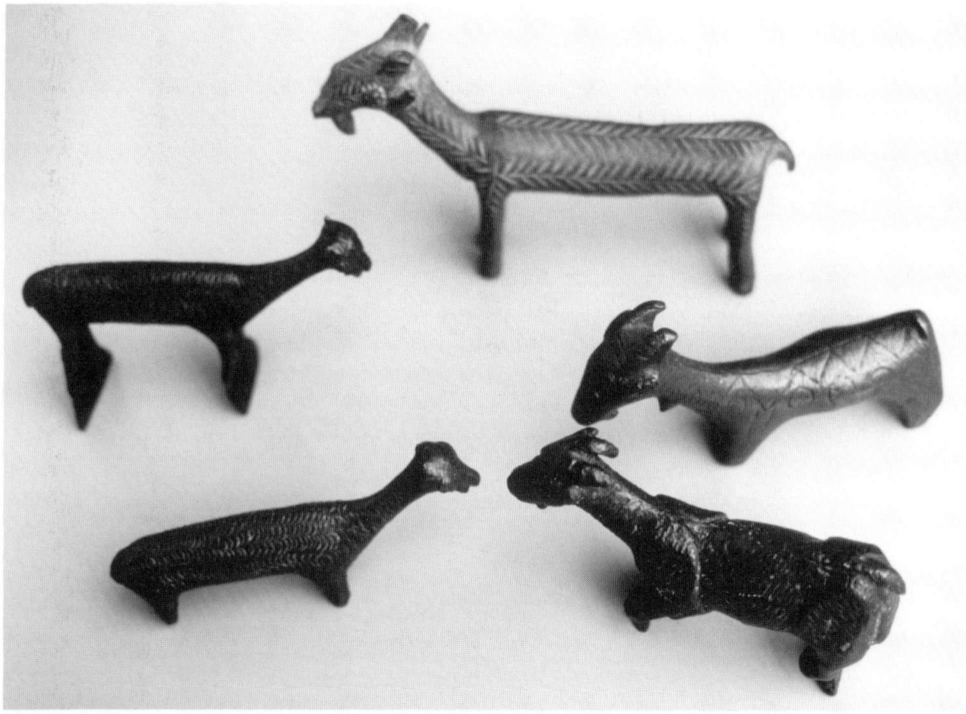

Fig. 9. The same goats shown together. Lisbon, Museu Nacional de Arqueologia. (Author)

Although the cult of Ataegina may have been well established long before the 1st c. A.D., the time-span for these votive offerings seems to lie between the 1st and the 3rd c. A.D. because the inscriptions are all in Latin. These figures express the gratitude of devotees to their deity, *expressive actions* in the sense Leach suggests,[18] and the unification of that transcendental and supernatural power recognized in Ataegina.

Universidade do Algarve, Gambelas, 8000 Faro

APPENDIX A

Ataegina inscriptions on slabs, Part 1

1. *Dea sancta* (Mérida, Badajoz)
2. *Dea sancta* (Mérida, Badajoz)
3. *Dea sancta* (Mértola, Beja)
4. *Dea sancta* (Quintos, Beja)
5. *Dea sancta* (Vila Velho de Ficalho, Serpa)
6. *Dea sancta* (Vila de Chã, Esposende), in a completely different location;
7. *D(ea) s(ancta)* (Ouguela, Campo Maior)
8. *Dea sancta* (Tejada de Tiétar, Cáceres)

Ataegina inscriptions on slabs, Part 2

A large number of inscriptions clearly dedicated to Ataegina are those of a simple *invocatio*:

9. *Ataecina* (Talavera de la Rena, Toledo)
10. *Ataecina* (Careluela, Toledo)
11. *(At)a(e)cina* (Santa Ana, Cáceres)

or more complete:

12. *Adecin(a) Sancta* (Alcuéscar, Cáceres)
13. *Dea Ataecina Turibrig(ensis) Proserpina* (Mérida, Badajoz)
14. *D(ea) At(a)e(cina) Proserpina Tu(ribrigensis)* (Salvatierra, Badajoz)
15. *Dea Ataecina Turobrigae (S)ancta* (Mérida, Badajoz)
16. *D(ea) d(omina s(ancta)* .... (Alcuéscar, Cáceres)

---

18 Leach (supra n.2) 9.

17. *D(ea) d(omina) s(ancta) Turibri(gensis) Attegina* (Alcuéscar, Cáceres)
18. *D(ea) d(omina) s(ancta) Turibri(gensis) Adaecina* (Alcuéscar, Cáceres)
19. *D(ea) d(omina) s(ancta) T(uribrigensis) A(taecina)* (Alcuéscar, Cáceres)
20. *D(ea) d(omina) s(ancta) Turibri(g)e(nsis) Adegina* (Alcuéscar, Cáceres)
21. *D(ea) d(omina) s(ancta)* (Malpartida, Cáceres)
22. *D(ea) dom(i)na Tur(ibrigensis)* .... (Alcuéscar, Cáceres)
23. *D(ea) d(omina) (T)uri(b)ri(gensis)* (Alcuéscar, Cáceres)
24. *D(ea) s(ancta) A(taecina) T(uribrigensis)* (Cagliari, Sardinia)
25. *D(ea) s(ancta) A(taecina) T(uribrigensis) P(roserpina)* (Cardenas, Badajoz)
26. *D(ea) s(ancta) A(taecina) T(uribrigensis)* (Malpartida, Cáceres)
27. *D(ea) s(ancta) T(urobrigensis) Ad(aecina)* (Malpartida, Cáceres)
28. *Dea sanc(ta) Turib(ricensis) L(ucius) Iuventius Iulianus a(nimo) l(ibens) v(otum) s(olvit)* (Mérida)
29. *Dea sanc(ta) Turibrice(nsis)* (Quintos, Beja)
30. *D(ea) S(ancta) Turubrige(nsi) L(ucius) Monius v(otum) s(olvit)* (Quintos[?], Beja)
31. *Dea sancta Turibrice(nsis)* (Herguijuela, Cáceres)
31. *Sancta (sic)* (Herguijuela, Cáceres)
32. *Domina (A)ttaegina (T)urubriga(e)* (La Bienvenida, Badajoz)
33. *Domina Turibr(igensis) Attaec(i)na* (Alcuéscar, Cáceres)
34. *Domina Turibri(gensis) (A)degina* (Alcuéscar, Cáceres)
35. *Domina Turibri(gensis) Addaecin(a)* (Alcuéscar, Cáceres)
36. *Domina (T)uribrig(ensis) Adaegina* (Medellin, Badajoz)
37. *Do(mi)na (T)uribr(igensis) Add(aec)ina* (Salvatierra, Cáceres)
38. *(D)o(mina) s(ancta) Tur(obrigensis) A(taecina)* (Saelices, Cuenca)
39. *Domina* .... (Alcuéscar, Cáceres)
40. *Dom(ina)* (Alcuéscar, Cáceres)
41. *Tur(ibrigensis) Ad(aecina)* (Alcuéscar, Cáceres)
42. *(T)uribri(gensis) A(d)ecin(a)* (Alcuéscar, Cáceres)
43. Text illegible (El Gordo, Cáceres)

Ataegina inscriptions on bronzes

44. *De(ae) S(anctae) A(daegina) T(uribrigensi) Cocceius Modestianus v(otum) s(olvit)* (Medellin)
45. *De(ae) S(anctae) A(daegina) T(uribrigensi)* (local, unknown).

Recipes for Sardinian bronzes

Miriam S. Balmuth and Robert H. Tykot

Sardinia is well known for its indigenous Nuragic culture, *c.* 1800-500 B.C., characterized by the remains of some 7,000 monumental stone towers on an island roughly the size of the state of Massachusetts.[1] The Nuragic culture is also well known for its *bronzetti*, small human, animal, and other figures often found in votive contexts at temples and sacred wells. At the sanctuary of Su Tempiesu in the mountainous Nuorese region, for example, they were found as part of a hoard at a sacred well surrounded by a broad flat pavement that would have been suitable for their display.[2] In their economy of execution some *bronzetti* have an appeal to the modern eye similar to that given by Cycladic marble figurines. More than 500 examples are housed in Sardinian museums, and public and private collections all over the world house a larger number.[3]

What is less well known is that Sardinia is itself rich in copper and other ores and that it has its own metallurgical tradition dating from the 4th millennium B.C.[4] The ore deposits that were worked in historic times are located in the Iglesiente region in the SW part of the island (e.g., Monte Rosas); in the mountainous Barbagia region of east-central Sardinia (e.g., Funtana Raminosa); and near Alghero in the northwest (e.g., Calabona). Recently a Nuragic metal workshop has been excavated at Santa Barbara (Bauladu, Oristano) and supports the evidence for indigenous Nuragic metallurgical activity, which previously had depended on the many finds of stone molds, copper bun ingots, and bronze artifacts in archaeological contexts.[5]

Excavations led by L. Gallin, under the auspices of the Soprintendenza Archeologica per le Provincie di Cagliari e Oristano, focused on the village area adjacent to a multi-towered nuraghe.[6] A number of separate rooms surrounding a central paved courtyard were uncovered and dated to the Italian Late Bronze and Early Iron Ages, from about the 12th to the 8th c. B.C. The SW part of the site contained abundant evidence of metalworking: scrap metal, smithing slag, ceramic crucibles with copper metal residues still attached, ceramic cores used for hollow casting of spearheads, Y-shaped ceramic gates for channeling molten metal into molds and that sometimes formed bases for figurines, and even pieces of the clay molds for the figurines themselves, broken open to release the cast bronzes.[7]

---

1 See most recently G. Webster, *A prehistory of Sardinia 2300-500 B.C.* (Sheffield 1996). Other important sources include M. S. Balmuth and R. J. Rowland, Jr. (edd.), *Studies in Sardinian archaeology* (Ann Arbor, MI 1984) 23-52; M. S. Balmuth (ed.), *Studies in Sardinian archaeology* 2: *Sardinia in the Mediterranean* (Ann Arbor, MI 1986); ead. (ed.), *Studies in Sardinian archaeology* 3: *Nuragic Sardinia and the Mycenaean world* (Oxford 1987); G. Lilliu, *La civiltà dei Sardi dal Paleolitico all'età dei nuraghi* (Turin 1988); id., *La civiltà nuragica* (Milano 1990); M. S. Balmuth, "Archaeology in Sardinia," *AJA* 96 (1992) 663-97; R. H. Tykot and T. K. Andrews (edd.), *Sardinia in the Mediterranean: a footprint in the sea: studies in Sardinian archaeology presented to Miriam S. Balmuth* (Sheffield 1992); E. Contu, *La Sardegna preistorica e nuragica* (Sassari 1997); and M. S. Balmuth and R. H. Tykot (edd.), *Sardinia and Aegean chronology: towards the resolution of relative and absolute dating in the Mediterranean* (Oxford 1998).

2 M. A. Fadda, "Il tempio a pozzo di Su Tempiesu (Orune, Nuoro)," *Rivista di Scienze Preistoriche* 37 (1982) 284 ff.; id., *La fonte sacra di Su Tempiesu* (Sassari 1988); id., "Antichi Sardi purificati," *Archeologia Viva* 15 (maggio/giugno 1996) 78-83.

3 G. Lilliu, *Le sculture della Sardegna nuragica* (Cagliari 1966) is the most comprehensive catalogue available of the Sardinian *bronzetti*.

4 F. Lo Schiavo, "Sardinian metallurgy: the archaeological background," in Balmuth 1986 (supra n.1) 231-50; "Early metallurgy in Sardinia," in R. Maddin (ed.), *The beginning of the use of metals and alloys, Zhengzhou, China, 1986* (Cambridge, MA 1988) 92-103.

5 E.g., M. J. Becker, "Sardinian stone moulds: an indirect means of evaluating Bronze Age metallurgical technology," in Balmuth and Rowland (supra n.1) 163-208.

6 L. J. Gallin and S. Sebis, "Bauladu (Oristano) — villaggio nuragico di S. Barbara: lo scavo: i materiali di età nuragica," *Nuovo Bullettino Archeologico Sardo* 2 (1985) 271-75.

7 C. Atzeni *et al.*, "Bronze metalworking at the Nuragic site of Santa Barbara, Sardinia, Italy," *Historical*

There was also abundant use of metallic lead in Nuragic Sardinia, especially for ceramic repairs.[8] Analysis by R. H. Tykot of the metal residue in a crucible from Nuraghe Santa Barbara indicates that it is composed of *c.* 76% copper, 21% lead, and 3.5% tin. However, of the handful of bronze artifacts from Santa Barbara that has been analyzed, not one contains more than 1% lead. It is possible that the crucible residue is the result of multiple uses with different pure and alloyed metals.

Metallurgical investigation of the Nuragic *bronzetti* themselves was initiated in 1978 by M. Balmuth with the analysis and publication of 4 figurines from American museums.[9] The *bronzetti* were analyzed by L. Stodulski, Center for Conservation and Technical Studies, Fogg Art Museum, Harvard University, under the supervision of A. Beale, and were part of a larger scheme to examine multiple aspects of Sardinian metal production, namely metal sources, manufacturing methods, and chronology.[10] Since that time, collections in the British Museum and the Cagliari National Museum have been examined, as were the figurines in a major exhibition of 1980, *Kunst und Kultur Sardiniens vom Neolithikum bis zum Ende der Nuraghenzeit*.[11] Considerable effort has also been expended on the characterization of Sardinian and other Mediterranean copper sources using lead isotope analysis, which indicates that all of the analyzed Nuragic copper-based ingots and artifacts are consistent with having come from Sardinian ore sources, while all of the ox-hide ingots of Eastern Mediterranean style found in Sardinia are consistent with a Cypriot origin.[12]

We report here on the analysis of an additional 4 *bronzetti* in American collections; they have been prepared for publication by M. S. Balmuth along with two more, as a sequel to her 1978 publication.[13] All had been assigned the standard dates of 9th to 7th c. B.C. without explanation. The controversy concerning the chronology and original introduction of the figure type to Sardinia is still unresolved, the existence of Cypriot iconographic parallels from the

---

Metallurgy 26 (1992) 31-35; L. J. Gallin and R. H. Tykot, "Metallurgical activity at the Nuragic village of Santa Barbara (Bauladu), Sardinia, Italy," *JFA* 20 (1993) 335-45; L. J. Gallin *et al.*, "Attività metallurgica al Nuraghe Santa Barbara Bauladu (OR)," *Quaderni della Soprintendenza archeologica per le provincie di Cagliari e Oristano* 11 (1995) 141-53.

8 C. Atzeni *et al.*, "Notes on lead metallurgy in Sardinia during the Nuragic period," *Historical Metallurgy* 24 (1991) 97-105.

9 M. S. Balmuth, "Sardinian *bronzetti* in American museums," *StSard* 24 (1974 [1978]) 145-56.

10 M. S. Balmuth and R. F. Tylecote, "Ancient copper and bronze in Sardinia: excavation and analysis," *JFA* 3 (1976) 195-201; R. F. Tylecote, M. S. Balmuth, and R. Massoli-Novelli, "Copper and Bronze Age metallurgy in Sardinia," in Balmuth and Rowland (supra n.1) 115-62.

11 J. Riederer, "Metallanalysen sardischer Bronzen," in J. Thimme (ed.), *Kunst und Kultur Sardiniens vom Neolithikum bis zum Ende der Nuraghenzeit* (Exhib. cat., Badisches Landesmuseum Karlsruhe 1980) 156-60; P. T. Craddock, "The metallurgy of Italic and Sardinian bronzes," in J. Swaddling (ed.), *Italian Iron Age artefacts in the British Museum* (London 1986) 143-49; C. Atzeni *et al.*, "Struttura e composizione dei 'bronzetti nuragici' del Museo Archeologico Nazionale di Cagliari," *La metallurgia italiana* 83 (1991) 583-90; C. Atzeni *et al.*, "Some metallurgical remarks on Sardinian bronzetti," in Tykot and Andrews (supra n.1) 347-54.

12 Z. A. Stos-Gale and N. H. Gale, "New light on the provenience of the copper oxhide ingots found on Sardinia," in Tykot and Andrews (supra n.1) 317-46; Z. A. Stos-Gale *et al.*, "Lead isotope characteristics of the Cyprus copper ore deposits applied to provenance studies of copper oxhide ingots," *Archaeometry* 39 (1997) 83-123; E. Angelini *et al.*, "Lead isotope analysis of Nuragic bronzes and copper ores by ICP-MS," in G. Holland and A. N. Eaton (edd.), *Applications of plasma source mass spectrometry* 2 (Cambridge 1993) 165-74. The Gales's conclusions have been challenged because of the possibility that ores from multiple sources may have been mixed, because some sources have not yet been well characterized, and because of the statistical methods employed. Nevertheless, we still find their results convincing in light of present evidence. See P. Budd *et al.*, "Oxhide ingots, recycling and the Mediterranean metals trade," and the comments by the Gales and others in the same issue, *JMA* 8 (1995) 1-75.

13 M. S. Balmuth, "More Nuragic bronzetti in American museums," in A. Moravetti (ed.), *Studi in onore di G. Lilliu per il suo ottantesimo compleanno* (Sassari 2001).

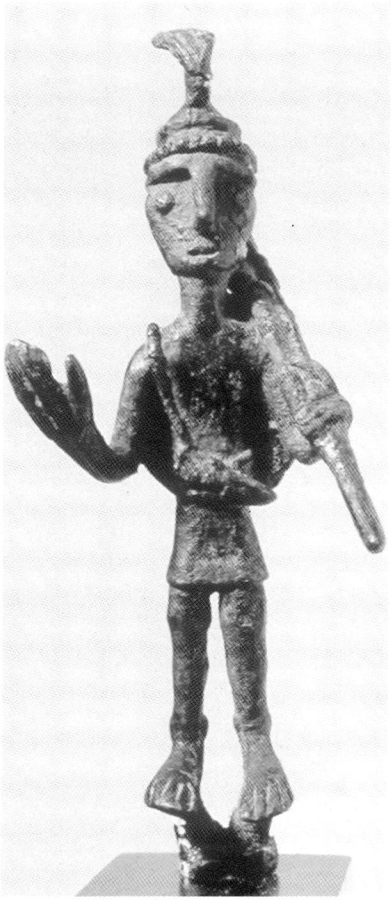

Fig. 1. Warrior. Sardinia. Bronze, h. *c.*11.0 cm. Medford, MA, Tufts University Art Collection 1985.9.3. (Photo: M. S. Balmuth)

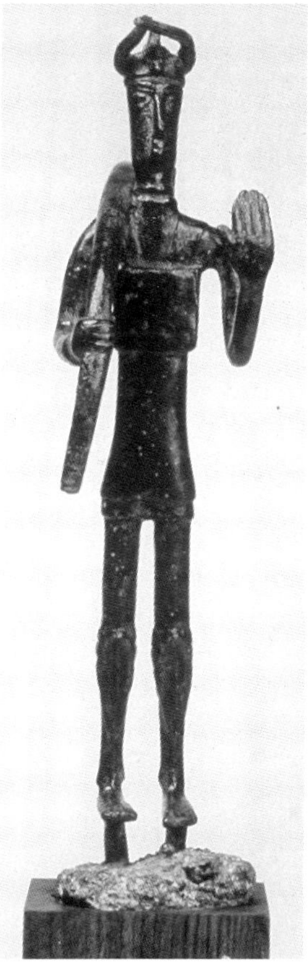

Fig. 2. Warrior. Sardinia. Bronze, h. *c.*24.5 cm. Los Angeles, The J. Paul Getty Museum 75.AK.110. (Photo: courtesy The J. Paul Getty Museum)

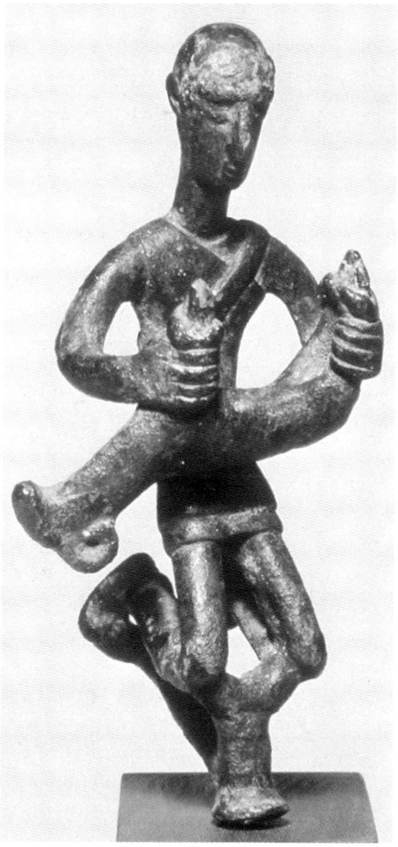

Fig. 3. Kneeling shepherd. Sardinia. Bronze, h. 12.7 cm. Cambridge, MA, Arthur M. Sackler Museum, Gift of Mr. and Mrs. Samuel Lindenbaum 1984.798. (Photo: courtesy Harvard University Art Museums)

11th c. B.C. contrasting with the presence of *bronzetti* in Etruscan tomb contexts of the late 9th through the 7th or 6th c. B.C.[14] Authentication presents another problem and should be dealt with elsewhere.

1. From the Tufts University Art Collection (1985.9.3) comes a warrior figure, carrying a large spear over his left shoulder and a shield strapped to his back, while his right hand is extended slightly upward but with the palm facing down (fig. 1). About 11 cm in height, the figure is wearing a short straight skirt and perhaps a short-sleeved shirt. A plumed helmet on the head and a sheathed dagger at the waist complete the visible accessories. Analysis by Tykot using inductively coupled plasma mass spectrometry (ICP-MS) indicates a composition of 89.4% copper, 8.4% tin, and 1.9% lead (Table 1).[15] No other elements were present in more than trace quantities.
2. The second *bronzetto* is a warrior from the J. Paul Getty Museum (75.AK.110), *c.* 24.5 cm in height (fig. 2). He wears a short skirt, greaves on his legs, and a helmet with curved horns on his head. In his right hand he carries a bow, while his left arm is raised with the palm of the hand facing outward. Analyses by D. Scott of the Getty Conservation Institute using inductively coupled plasma mass spectrometry (ICP-MS)

---

14 F. Barreca, "Phoenicians in Sardinia: the bronze figurines," in Balmuth 1986 (supra n.1) 131-43; A. M. Bisi, "Bronzi vicino-orientali in Sardegna: importazioni ed influssi," in Balmuth 1987 (supra n.1) 225-46; F. R. Serra Ridgway, "Nuragic bronzes in the British Museum," in Balmuth 1986 (supra n.1) 85-101.

15 The ICP-MS technique has been described in detail elsewhere: R. H. Tykot and S. M. M. Young, "Archaeological applications of inductively coupled plasma-mass spectrometry," in M. V. Orna (ed.), *Archaeological chemistry: organic, inorganic, and biochemical analysis* (Washington, D.C. 1996) 116-30.

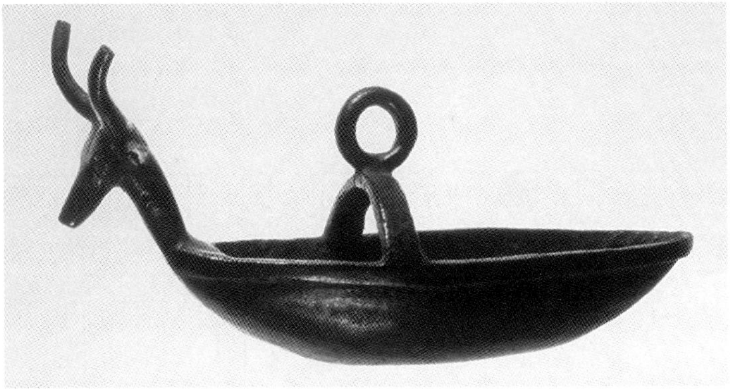

Fig. 4. Boat. Sardinia. Bronze, l. *c.*16.5 cm. Boston, Museum of Fine Arts, J. W. and J. M. Elliot Fund 1976.67. (Photo: courtesy Museum of Fine Arts)

and x-ray fluorescence (XRF) indicate a composition of 81.5% copper, 5.5% tin, 8.9% lead, 2.5% zinc, 0.3% nickel, 0.14% iron, and 0.13% antimony. The exceptionally high zinc content raised significant doubts about the authenticity of this figure, since no previously published example contains more than 1% zinc. Lead isotope analysis using ICP-MS, however, indicates consistency with a Sardinian ore source, and metallographic examination suggests that the corrosion patina displays all of the features anticipated for a genuine ancient bronze.[16]

3. The third figure is a kneeling shepherd from the Arthur M. Sackler Museum, Harvard University Art Museum (1984.798), 12.7 cm in height (fig. 3). The shepherd wears a short skirt, and a tunic is evident on the upper chest and shoulders. With both hands he holds the legs of what appears to be a moufflon (horned sheep). The animal is not rendered with much detail, and the softness in modeling of the whole figure is atypical. Chemical analysis by J. Riederer of the Rathgen Research Laboratory, Berlin, indicates a composition of 78.7% copper, 2.3% tin, 2.9% lead, 15.3% zinc, 0.34% nickel, 0.37% iron, and less than 0.1% each of antimony and arsenic. The excessive presence of zinc is unique and thus problematic.
4. The fourth *bronzetto* is a votive model boat with rather simple decoration from the Museum of Fine Arts, Boston (1976.67; fig. 4). The boat is *c.* 16.5 cm in length and has a deer with antlers as its figurehead. A curved bar with a circular ring spans the middle of the boat. Electron microprobe analysis performed by R. Newman, Department of Objects Conservation and Scientific Research, Museum of Fine Arts, indicates a composition of 69.9% copper, 8.8% tin, 21% lead, and 0.26% arsenic. Zinc, nickel, iron, silver, and antimony were present in only trace amounts.

Comparison of the compositions of the 4 *bronzetti* shows that only the Tufts warrior is similar in composition to previously analyzed figures from American collections. The MFA boat and the Getty warrior contain substantially more lead, while the Sackler shepherd and to some extent the Getty warrior contain significant quantities of zinc.

Such high lead and/or zinc concentrations are in fact unknown in the corpus of analyses currently available (Table 1).[17] Analyses by P. Craddock of 20 *bronzetti* in the British Museum reveal compositionally consistent bronzes with about 9% tin and perhaps 1% lead. Similarly, most of the 80 analyses by Riederer of figurines, boats, and other votives in the 1980 Karlsruhe exhibition are compositionally consistent, with the exception of a boat that contains 5-6% silver and less than 1% tin. Recently, a second example of a high-silver Nuragic object was found among 12 *bronzetti* in the Cagliari National Museum analyzed by P. Virdis and his colleagues at the University of Cagliari. This figurine, from the Teti (Abini) hoard, is clearly genuine and suggests that a precious metal was deliberately used instead of tin, a possibility which must be considered likely in light of the cult or ritual context in which these votive figurines are found.[18] It is unlikely that the high silver content could have resulted from the indiscriminate

---

16 Lead isotope analysis by D. Scott of the Getty archer produced values [2.100 (^{208}Pb/^{206}Pb), 0.861 (^{207}Pb/^{206}Pb), and 17.95 (^{206}Pb/^{204}Pb)] very similar to lead isotope ratios for some Sardinian artifacts of known archaeological context.

17 Riederer (supra n.11); Craddock (supra n.11); C. Atzeni *et al.* 1991 (supra n.11).

18 The Teti figurine with high silver content is no. 116, figs. 277-80 in Lilliu (supra n.3) 217-19; E. Pais, "Il ripostiglio di bronzi di Abini presso Teti," *Bullettino Archeologico Sardo* n.s. I, fasc. V-XII (1884) 67-179.

TABLE 1. CHEMICAL ANALYSES OF NURAGIC *BRONZETTI*

Ref.[1]	Sample[2]	Description	*Cu*	*Sn*	*Pb*	*Zn*	*Fe*	*Ni*	*Ag*	*Sb*	*As*	*Total*
1	Tufts 1985.9.3	Warrior	89.4	8.4	1.89	tr	tr	0.03	0.08	tr	0.26	100.0
1	MFA 1976.67	Boat	69.9	8.8	21.01	0.00	0.00	0.00	0.00	0.00	0.26	100.0
1	Sackler 1984.798	Shepherd	78.7	2.3	2.91	15.30	0.37	0.34	0.02	0.07	0.05	100.0
1	Getty 75.AK.110	Archer	82.5	5.6	9.01	2.53	0.14	0.00	0.14	0.13	0.00	100.0
2	Albright-Knox 65.22	Warrior	92.3	5.9	<0.45	0.26	0.38	<0.10	0.03	<0.06	0.46	100.0
2	RISD 55.030	Warrior	89.0	7.3	2.54	0.32	0.02	<0.11	0.03	0.13	0.51	100.0
2	DIA 49.587	Female figure	89.2	8.7	<0.6	<0.2	0.31	<0.07	0.03	<0.04	0.69	100.0
2	Fogg 1952.30	Warrior	89.3	8.5	<0.68	0.45	0.27	<0.14	0.03	<0.03	0.54	100.0
3	Cleveland 52.258	Warrior	89.3	8.8	0.69	0.37	0.39	0.01	0.03	0.05	0.39	100.0
4	BM 1856.12-23.664	Model sheath	89.1	9.9	0.45	0.03	0.01	0.12	0.07	0.25	0.10	100.0
4	BM 1914.3-18.1	Warrior	88.8	10.8	0.07		0.07	0.05	0.02		0.20	100.0
4	BM 1926.5-11.1	Jug	89.4	9.6	0.12		0.15	0.04	0.30	0.02	0.30	100.0
4	BM 1926.5-11.113	Ring	90.5	6.3	2.47	0.02	0.11	0.03	0.11	0.03	0.43	100.0
4	BM 1926.5-11.11a	Conical button	90.1	9.5	0.22	0.01	0.05	0.03	0.01	0.03	0.07	100.0
4	BM 1926.5-11.11b	Conical button	90.0	9.6	0.27	0.00	0.04	0.04	0.00	0.04	0.01	100.0
4	BM 1926.5-11.12	Stud	90.0	9.1	0.32	0.03	0.04	0.03	0.04	0.03	0.40	100.0
4	BM 1926.5-11.13	Button	88.0	10.7	0.59	0.08	0.17	0.02	0.08	0.05	0.30	100.0
4	BM 1926.5-11.136	Pendant (rod)	93.9	4.3	0.39	0.04	0.85	0.03	0.20	0.03	0.17	100.0
4	BM 1926.5-11.136	Pendant (top)	96.6	2.2	0.50	0.01	0.22	0.02	0.09	0.04	0.30	100.0
4	BM 1926.5-11.137	Rattle (top)	91.1	6.3	0.45	0.04	1.61	0.04	0.09	0.06	0.25	100.0
4	BM 1926.5-11.137	Rattle (rod)	94.3	2.8	0.80	0.04	1.70	0.03	0.07	0.02	0.22	100.0
4	BM 1926.5-11.14	Button	87.5	11.2	0.56		0.17	0.17	0.08	0.05	0.25	100.0
4	BM 1926.5-11.15	Stud	88.3	9.4	1.16	0.03	0.60	0.03	0.13	0.03	0.40	100.0
4	BM 1926.5-11.16	Stud	91.7	6.9	0.50	0.03	0.29	0.02	0.07	0.02	0.45	100.0
4	BM 1926.5-11.2	Cast tripod	91.6	7.6	0.28	0.01	0.14	0.02	0.12	0.04	0.22	100.0
4	BM 1926.5-11.22	Ring	89.8	8.8	0.71		0.03	0.03	0.12	0.04	0.45	100.0
4	BM 1926.5-11.22	Ring	82.5	16.3	0.60		0.07	0.03	0.11	0.05	0.30	100.0
4	BM 1926.5-11.26	Ring	87.5	5.4	6.10	0.02	0.24	0.02	0.15	0.03	0.55	100.0
4	BM 1926.5-11.3.1	Openwork plaque	89.2	9.5	0.61	0.02	0.12	0.03	0.06	0.03	0.42	100.0
4	BM 1926.5-11.3.2	Openwork plaque	86.2	12.8	0.18	0.01	0.08	0.03	0.16	0.02	0.49	100.0
4	BM 1926.5-11.3.3	Openwork plaque	87.5	11.8	0.03	0.00	0.03	0.03	0.02	0.02	0.65	100.0
4	BM 1926.5-11.3.4	Openwork plaque	88.0	11.2	0.21		0.03	0.03	0.09	0.03	0.41	100.0
4	BM 1926.5-11.3.5	Openwork plaque	88.1	11.2	0.02	0.01	0.06	0.03	0.08	0.02	0.41	100.0
4	BM 1926.5-11.4	Boat	85.0	13.8	0.74		0.14	0.05	0.06		0.15	100.0
4	BM 1926.5-11.41	Ring	89.8	9.1	0.46	0.00	0.04	0.02	0.12	0.08	0.37	100.0
4	BM 1926.5-11.44	Ring	89.2	9.5	0.29	0.03	0.27	0.02	0.37	0.03	0.35	100.0
4	BM 1926.5-11.47	Ring	88.7	9.4	0.55	0.03	0.78	0.02	0.06	0.03	0.39	100.0
4	BM 1926.5-11.5	Anchor pendant	86.4	11.3	1.79	0.01	0.02	0.02	0.04	0.03	0.32	100.0

1 Key to analysis references: 1 (this work); 2 (Balmuth [supra n.9]); 3 (Tylecote *et al.* [supra n.10]); 4 (Craddock [supra n.11]); 5 (Riederer [supra n.11]); 6 (Atzeni *et al.* 1991 and 1992 [supra n.11]).

2 Collection accession numbers are given when known; otherwise the published catalogue or laboratory numbers are used.

Ref.	Sample	Description	Cu	Sn	Pb	Zn	Fe	Ni	Ag	Sb	As	Total
4	BM 1926.5-11.6	Votive dagger	88.8	8.8	1.31	0.03	0.81	0.04	0.05	0.03	0.12	100.0
4	BM 1926.5-11.7	Spearhead	86.8	11.0	0.80	0.03	1.10	0.03	0.05	0.02	0.15	100.0
4	BM 1926.5-11.8	Dagger	89.0	9.3	1.10		0.15	0.04	0.24	0.02	0.20	100.0
4	BM 1926.5-11.9	Spear butt	92.2	4.6	0.81	0.02	1.82	0.03	0.09	0.03	0.44	100.0
4	BM 1974.12-1.1	Warrior	88.8	10.1	1.01		0.04	0.03	0.02			100.0
4	BM 1974.12-1.2	Archer	93.6	5.0	0.40	0.20	0.42	0.04	0.07	0.25	0.10	100.0
4	BM 1974.12-1.5	Model sheath	87.8	11.7	0.38		0.09	0.01	0.02	0.01	0.03	100.0
5	Riederer 1	Votive animal	96.7		0.19	0.10	0.17	0.03	0.01	0.24	2.60	100.0
5	Thimme 194-a	Boat (bow)	91.6	0.5	2.31	0.35	0.02	0.03	5.11	0.03	0.05	100.0
5	Thimme 194-b	Boat (mast)	88.8	0.7	3.40	0.01	0.61	0.03	6.30	0.04	0.14	100.0
5	Thimme 161	Moufflon	91.1	2.2	6.31	0.05	0.01	0.05	0.12	0.07	0.08	100.0
5	Riederer 5	Male figure	95.4	2.3	1.93	0.29	0.03	0.01	0.03	0.02		100.0
5	Thimme 213	Disk ornament	94.4	3.3	1.04	<0.01	0.01	0.03	0.18	0.07	0.98	100.0
5	Thimme 256	Axe	94.5	3.5	1.71			0.04	0.06	0.06	0.16	100.0
5	Thimme 179	Boat	95.8	3.7	0.21	0.01	0.16	0.02	0.03	0.02	0.08	100.0
5	Thimme 123	Male figure	95.5	4.0	0.14	0.01	0.31	0.01	0.04	0.04	0.04	100.0
5	Thimme 182	Boat	91.3	4.2	3.95	0.06	0.23	0.03	0.14	0.02	0.15	100.0
5	Thimme 150	Bull	93.6	4.9	0.79	0.16	0.04	0.03	0.11	0.14	0.24	100.0
5	Thimme 174	Boat	87.0	5.5	6.89	0.03	0.02	0.03	0.16	0.02	0.39	100.0
5	Thimme 124	Female figure	93.8	5.5	0.39	0.18	0.03	0.01	0.02		0.09	100.0
5	Thimme 188	Boat	86.6	5.7	7.31	0.01	0.05	0.04	0.08	0.05	0.18	100.0
5	Thimme 270	Bracelet	90.0	6.3	1.68	0.04	1.76	0.04	0.03	0.01	0.19	100.0
5	Thimme 170	Hedgehog	87.7	6.4	4.48	0.01	1.23	0.03	0.03	0.01	0.09	100.0
5	Thimme 191	Boat	67.2	6.7	25.78	<0.01	0.03	0.02	0.03	0.03	0.23	100.0
5	Thimme 288	Boat	91.8	6.9	0.80	0.02	0.24	0.04	0.05	0.06	0.17	100.0
5	Thimme 152	Bull	92.5	7.0	0.08	0.05	0.03	0.03	0.12	0.02	0.16	100.0
5	Thimme 189	Boat	89.6	7.2	1.24	0.43	1.19	0.03	0.06	0.02	0.24	100.0
5	Thimme 145	Mask	89.0	7.6	1.56	0.22	0.39	0.02	0.09	0.22	0.92	100.0
5	Thimme 92	Archer	90.6	7.7	0.97	0.05	0.13	0.03	0.10	0.04	0.34	100.0
5	Thimme 121	Shepherd	90.7	7.7	0.85	0.12	0.17	0.05	0.10	0.03	0.30	100.0
5	Thimme 102	Warrior	88.0	7.8	2.78	0.14	0.10	0.13	0.10	0.25	0.74	100.0
5	Thimme 205	Scepter	91.6	7.8	0.18	<0.01	0.04	0.02	0.04	0.02	0.35	100.0
5	Thimme 120	Shepherd	90.6	7.9	0.85	0.05	0.18	0.05	0.09	0.03	0.31	100.0
5	Thimme 156	Bull	90.3	8.1	1.01	0.01	0.09	0.02	0.11	0.02	0.37	100.0
5	Thimme 262	Chisel	90.4	8.2	0.36	0.02	0.74	0.03	0.09	0.01	0.19	100.0
5	Thimme 163	Votive animal	89.6	8.2	1.50	0.30	0.02	0.02	0.02	0.04	0.33	100.0
5	Thimme 228	Lance point	90.2	8.3	0.77	0.03	0.34	0.03	0.08	0.01	0.34	100.0
5	Thimme 91	Warrior	88.6	8.3	1.86	0.03	0.83	0.03	0.08	0.02	0.31	100.0
5	Thimme 95	Archer	85.0	8.3	5.55	0.01	0.48	<0.01	0.14	<0.01	0.57	100.0
5	Thimme 141	Amphora carrier	89.8	8.6	0.96	0.05	0.16	0.03	0.02	0.04	0.30	100.0
5	Thimme 183	Boat	89.9	8.6	1.02	n.b.	0.03	0.03	0.03	0.02	0.33	100.0
5	Thimme 114	Shepherd	84.3	8.7	6.22	0.03	0.03	0.03	0.03	0.02	0.65	100.0
5	Riederer 36	Male figure	89.5	8.9	0.34	0.03	0.77	0.05	0.07	0.11	0.21	100.0
5	Thimme 173	Handle	89.8	9.1	0.25	0.02	0.44	0.03	0.06	0.02	0.35	100.0
5	Thimme 260	Chisel	90.5	9.1	0.20	0.01	0.02	0.02	0.01	0.02	0.15	100.0
5	Thimme 231	Spearpoint	86.8	9.3	3.36	0.01	0.29	0.03	0.03	0.02	0.14	100.0
5	Thimme 259	Axe	86.9	9.5	3.25	<0.01	0.01	0.02	0.05	0.02	0.27	100.0
5	Thimme 257	Axe	90.1	9.6	0.11			0.05	0.04	0.03	0.07	100.0
5	Thimme 247	Sword frag.	89.9	9.7	0.09		0.01	0.06	0.04	0.03	0.14	100.0

Ref.	*Sample*	*Description*	*Cu*	*Sn*	*Pb*	*Zn*	*Fe*	*Ni*	*Ag*	*Sb*	*As*	*Total*
5	Thimme 118	Shepherd	89.2	9.8	0.23	0.03	0.02	0.08	0.08	0.03	0.53	100.0
5	Thimme 279	Fibula	89.2	9.8	0.41	0.01	0.08	0.16	0.08	0.06	0.17	100.0
5	Thimme 93	Archer	88.3	10.0	1.39	0.03	0.01	0.03	0.02	0.02	0.27	100.0
5	Thimme 195	Boat	88.8	10.1	0.76	0.02	0.03	0.05	0.06	0.08	0.19	100.0
5	Thimme 126	Female figure	87.6	10.3	0.85	0.01	0.97	0.06	0.07	0.13	0.06	100.0
5	Thimme 178	Boat	88.0	10.4	0.40	0.02	0.80	0.01	0.05	<0.01	0.27	100.0
5	Riederer 49	Male figure	88.1	10.9	0.51	0.01	0.04	0.02	0.09	0.02	0.36	100.0
5	Thimme 258	Axe	88.0	11.0	0.43	0.01	0.06	0.03	0.10	0.02	0.43	100.0
5	Thimme 138	Female figure	84.3	11.0	3.98	0.02	0.24	0.02	0.07	0.04	0.33	100.0
5	Thimme 261	Chisel	87.4	11.3	0.64	0.01	0.06	0.03	0.08	0.01	0.47	100.0
5	Thimme 250	Double-axe	86.2	11.4	1.18	0.02	0.80	0.03	0.05	0.01	0.25	100.0
5	Thimme 254	Hoe	87.2	11.9	0.45	<0.01	0.05	0.03	0.05	0.01	0.34	100.0
5	Thimme 132	Praying figure	87.2	12.0	0.31	0.02	0.15	0.03	0.02	0.02	0.21	100.0
5	Thimme 167	Bull protome	86.8	12.2	0.36	0.14	0.02	0.03	0.03	0.02	0.40	100.0
5	Thimme 105	Warrior	86.2	12.2	0.63	0.01	0.61	0.03	0.06	0.02	0.17	100.0
5	Thimme 122	Flute player	84.5	12.4	2.81	0.02	0.05	0.04	0.05	0.05	0.13	100.0
5	Thimme 287	Boat	85.1	12.6	1.55	n.b.	0.30	0.04	0.07	0.04	0.28	100.0
5	Thimme 157	Lid	86.0	12.7	0.47	0.03	0.62	0.02	0.07		0.11	100.0
5	Thimme 277	Bull protome	86.0	12.8	0.47	0.03	0.11	0.06	0.09	0.13	0.37	100.0
5	Thimme 149	Animal group	82.6	12.8	4.21		0.04	0.03	0.04	0.02	0.30	100.0
5	Thimme 278	Bull protome	85.0	13.5	0.98		0.04	0.06	0.03	0.07	0.32	100.0
5	Riederer 64	Votive animal	80.7	18.6	0.08	0.02	0.11	0.06	0.02	0.03	0.38	100.0
5	Thimme 240	Dagger	88.8	8.8	1.31	0.03	0.81	0.04	0.05	0.03	0.12	100.0
5	Thimme 198	Tripod side	91.6	7.6	0.28	<0.01	0.14	0.02	0.12	0.04	0.22	100.0
5	Thimme 243	Votive dagger	87.8	11.7	0.38	0.03	0.09	<0.01	0.02		0.01	100.0
5	Thimme 244	Votive weapon	89.0	9.9	0.45	0.03	0.11	0.12	0.07	0.25	0.10	100.0
5	Thimme 111	Archer	93.6	5.0	0.40	0.20	0.42	<0.04	0.07	0.25	0.10	100.0
5	Thimme 208	Jug	89.4	9.6	0.12		0.15	0.04	0.30	0.02	0.30	100.0
5	Thimme 237	Dagger blade	88.9	9.3	1.10		0.15	0.04	0.25	0.02	0.20	100.0
5	Thimme 129-a	Shepherd	91.5	6.7	0.87	<0.01	0.06	0.51	0.10	0.11	0.13	100.0
5	Thimme 129-b	Shepherd	90.0	8.0	1.20	<0.01	0.06	0.45	0.10	0.09	0.12	100.0
5	Thimme 96-a	Archer	85.3	12.0	0.93	<0.02	0.34	0.59	0.28	0.03	0.51	100.0
5	Thimme 96-b	Archer	87.0	7.4	1.00	0.03	3.50	0.47	0.20	<0.02	0.36	100.0
5	Thimme 96-c	Archer	88.7	8.7	0.87	<0.04	0.49	0.41	0.30	<0.03	0.50	100.0
5	Thimme 96-d	Archer	91.1	6.7	0.73	<0.03	0.80		0.21	0.01	0.39	100.0
5	Thimme 109	Archer	91.3	3.4	5.00	<0.10					0.31	100.0
5	Thimme 104	Warrior	92.5	5.9	<0.45	0.26	0.38	<0.10	0.03	<0.06	0.46	100.0
5	Thimme 98	Warrior frag.	89.1	7.3	2.55	0.32	0.02	<0.11	0.03	0.13	0.51	100.0
6	Lilliu 84	Warrior	88.8	10.3	0.59	0.01	0.20	0.02	0.09	<0.06		100.0
6	Lilliu 110	Warrior	89.4	9.5	0.70	0.02	0.25	0.02	0.07	<0.06		100.0
6	Lilliu 98	Warrior	89.5	9.3	0.99	0.01	0.12	0.02	0.08	<0.06		100.0
6	Lilliu 104	Warrior	90.2	9.4	0.29	0.01	0.04	0.03	0.02	<0.06		100.0
6	Lilliu 121	Female offerer	88.6	10.8	0.31	0.02	0.17	0.02	0.08	<0.06		100.0
6	Lilliu 128	Warrior	87.0	12.4	0.42	0.01	0.05	0.03	0.06	<0.06		100.0
6	Lilliu 116	Praying figure	92.8	0.3	0.29	0.10	0.01	0.04	6.50	<0.06		100.0
6	Lilliu 163	Offerer	86.5	13.1	0.14	0.00	0.23	0.03	0.01	<0.06		100.0
6	Lilliu 207	Cow	89.7	9.4	0.70	0.00	0.03	0.04	0.01	0.12		100.0
6	Lilliu 216	Yoked animal pair	81.4	12.0	6.50	0.01	0.05	0.03	0.00	<0.06		100.0
6	Lilliu 144	Female offerer	89.9	10.0	0.06	0.01	0.03	0.02	0.01	<0.06		100.0
6	Lilliu 145	Priestess	92.3	5.9	0.68	0.01	0.93	0.02	0.14	<0.06		100.0

mixing of recycled silver and bronze scrap metal, since the latter would have contained at least a modest amount of tin, and tin is not lost in the re-melting and casting processes. Nevertheless, recycling of bronze and other metals was probably a common occurrence, and extreme caution should be used in determining the provenance of bronze objects from lead isotope data.[19]

It is difficult to propose a specific recipe for Sardinian bronze at this time. Of the 129 objects that have been analyzed (Table 1), the 6 with high silver (Lilliu 116; Thimme 194), zinc (Sackler 1984.798; Getty 75.AK.110), or nickel (Thimme 129; Thimme 96) are atypical at best. The remaining 123 average 88.9 ± 3.9% copper, 8.8 ± 2.9% tin, 1.6 ± 3.2% lead, 0.3 ± 0.4% iron, and 0.3 ± 0.3% arsenic. Zinc, nickel, silver, and antimony all average 0.1% or less. Tin ranges from 2.2% to 18.6%, and lead ranges from 0.1% to 25.8%, however, suggesting that no single recipe was employed in all the places and at all the times that Nuragic bronzes were produced. Without archaeological provenance for most of the *bronzetti*, it is impossible to determine whether there may have been specific geographic or chronological differences in composition. The physical effects of alloying tin and copper in certain percentages was clearly understood, while the casting and working advantages of leaded bronze were only occasionally taken advantage of in the manufacture of votive objects, despite the otherwise common use of lead. We should note that, in contrast to Sardinia, much of the contemporary metal production in Etruscan Italy and Geometric Greece was in leaded bronze.[20] While this might be used to support a high dating of much of the Sardinian bronze production, it also may be due to the retention by the Nuragic people in Sardinia of a Bronze Age metallurgical tradition at the same time that increased use of metal by mainland city-states led to the debasement of copper-based objects. Authentic copper-silver alloys were occasionally employed in Sardinia, but we must remain highly sceptical of copper-zinc (brass) alloys for this time-period in Sardinia.

Department of Classics & Archaeology, Tufts University, Medford, MA 02155 (M.B.)
Department of Anthropology, University of South Florida, Tampa, FL 33620 (R.T.)

---

19 While bronze objects — already a mixture of ores — may be the result either of recycling or of new metal use, pure copper objects, especially ingots, are far less likely to derive from mixed ore sources.

20 Craddock (supra n.11) 146.

Iberian bronze figurines: technological and stylistic analysis

Robert H. Tykot, Lourdes Prados Torreira and Miriam S. Balmuth

Thousands of votive bronze figurines are known from just three sanctuary sites in the eastern Andalusia region of Spain, where they were clearly an important aspect of Iberian religious practices. Several thousand have been found at the Collado de los Jardines (Despeñaperros, Jaen), the best known of the sanctuaries; another 2,000 at Castellar de Santisteban, *c.* 35 km distant; and several hundred more at Nuestra Señora de Luz (Murcia). Individual figurines have been found at some 30 other sites in Spain.[1]

We report here on a collection of 20 figurines that belongs to the Harvard University Art Museums but is on permanent loan to the Peabody Museum of Archaeology and Ethnology, Harvard University.[2] This collection was donated to Harvard in 1932 by the Spanish Republic, along with some ceramics and other materials.[3] Both the historical provenance of the collection and the typological characteristics of the figurines leave little doubt that they come from the Collado de Los Jardines sanctuary, where many similar figurines have been found.[4]

Unfortunately, their chronology is based primarily on stylistic evidence, since the excavations by Calvo y Cabré were done more than 75 years ago, and many of the other figurines come from clandestine activities. Some of the more detailed figurines are thought to be close to Phoenician models of about 600 B.C., while more schematic types may be later, possibly of Roman age.[5] More recently, the Iberian figurines have been extensively studied by Prados Torreira, who has catalogued nearly 2000 examples in the Museo Arqueológico Nacional in Madrid.[6] We estimate that most of the figurines in the Harvard collection date between the end of the 5th and the 2nd c. B.C.

The figurines in the Harvard collection are a heterogeneous group, both stylistically and compositionally, perhaps as a result of chronological differences (figs. 1-2). Several of the figurines are quite simple and schematic, with little detail executed before or after casting. Only one has breasts to indicate that it represents a female; she also wears a cape which covers her head and flows down below her waist (no. 130). Two are clearly males judging from the genitalia (nos. 135 and 113), while a third (no. 114) carries a dagger, as does one of the males (no. 113).

Half of the Harvard pieces may be described as offerers or supplicants, dedicated to an unknown divinity. Prados Torreira has interpreted this group, as well as the phallic males, as having fertility connotations. She also interprets the figurines as reflecting different social classes, in terms of both who they represent and who acquired and deposited them. Some of the figurines represent women wearing jewelry and expensive garments; the quality of the figurines themselves suggests that some were probably made by specialized artisans.[7]

---

1 R. J. Harrison, *Spain at the dawn of history: Iberians, Phoenicians and Greeks* (London 1988) 126-34.

2 A descriptive catalogue of this collection has already been published: L. Prados Torreira, "La colección de bronces ibericos del Peabody Museum de Harvard," in *Bronces y religion romana: Actas del XI Congreso internacional de bronces antiguos, Madrid, mayo-junio, 1990* (Madrid 1993) 361-67.

3 This was in appreciation for the return of the sarcophagus of Alfonso, son of Count Pedro de Ansúrez de San Benito de Sahagún.

4 P. Paris, *Essai sur l'art et l'industrie de l'Espagne primitive* (Paris 1903-4); J. Calvo y Cabré, *Excavaciones en la Cueva y Collado de los Jardines: Santa Elena* (Memorias de la Junta Superior de Excavaciones y Antigüedades, Madrid 1919); F. Alvarez Ossorio, *Catálogo de los exvotos de bronce ibéricos: Museo Arqueológico Nacional* (Madrid 1941).

5 G. Nicolini, *Les bronces figurés des sanctuaires ibériques* (Paris 1969).

6 L. Prados Torreira, "Exvotos ibéricos de bronce: aspectos tipológicos y tecnológicos," *Trabajos de Prehistoria* 45 (1988) 175-99; id., *Exvotos ibéricos de bronce del Museo Arqueológico Nacional* (Madrid 1992).

7 Prados Torreira considers the Harvard collection to represent the average class of figurines from the

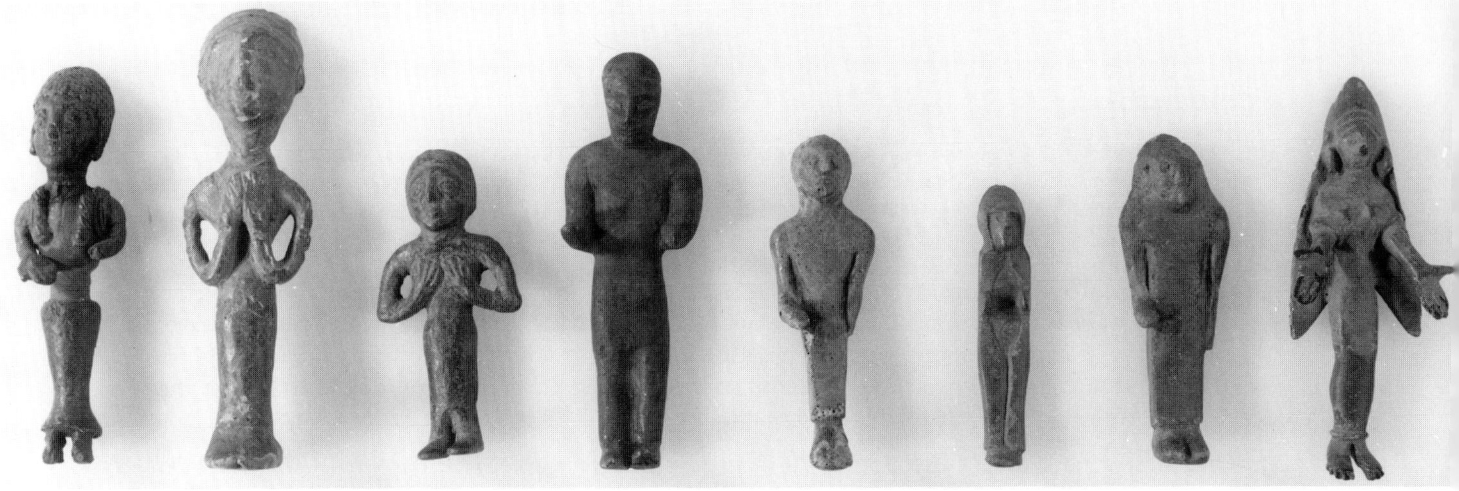

Fig. 1. Female figures. Iberian. Bronze. From left to right: inv. nos. 128, 129, 123, 127, 125, 124, 126, and 130. Cambridge, MA, Harvard University Art Museums. (Photo: H. Burger, courtesy Museum)

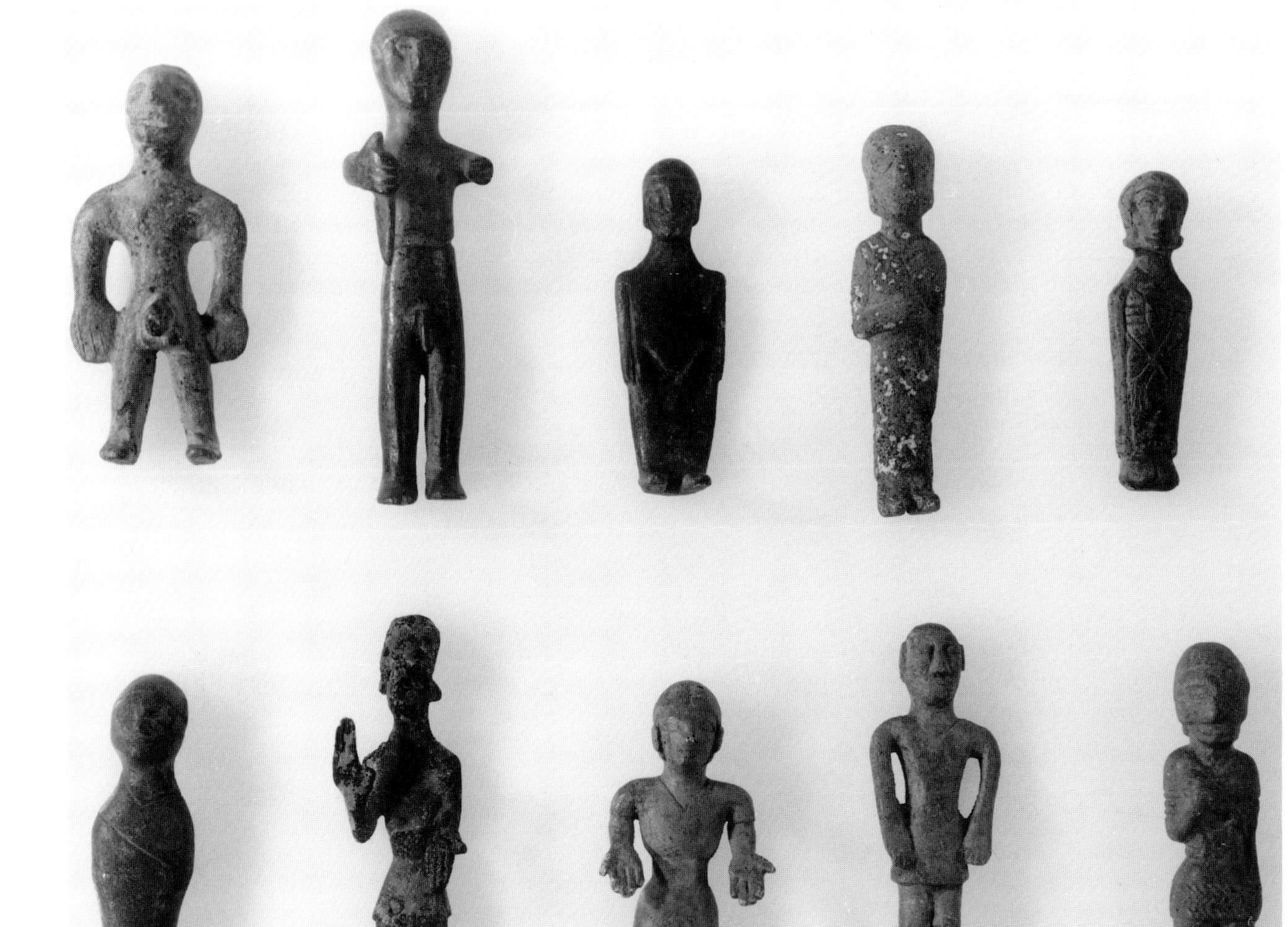

Fig. 2. Male figures. Iberian. Bronze, h. (of tallest) 10 cm. From left to right, top and then bottom row: inv. nos. 135, 113, 118, 121, 120, 122, 119, 136, 134, and 114. Cambridge, MA, Harvard University Art Museums. (Photo: H. Burger, courtesy Museum)

Chemical analysis

Iberian bronze figurines were cast using the lost-wax process in clay molds that were then broken open and discarded. Knowledge of the alloys provides information on the types of ores exploited, as well as on the technological nature of the production process itself. Issues such as the addition of lead to improve casting properties, the use of standardized recipes, and the recycling of scrap metal may then be considered.

A fine drill bit was used to remove approximately 10 mg of clean metal from the interior of one leg from each figurine, with minimal damage to the appearance of each piece. Samples were put into solution and analyzed for major and trace elements by inductively coupled plasma-mass spectrometry, a technique which is increasingly being applied to archaeological materials.[8] ICP-MS has a number of distinct advantages over other analytical techniques, the most important for metal analyses being its simple requirements for preparing the samples, low cost, and the ability to produce isotope ratio data in addition to elemental composition. Although the size of the sample removed from each figurine is small (and metals are notoriously heterogeneous), these samples potentially yield a more representative compositional analysis than that obtained by the analysis of surface material alone (e.g., by X-ray fluorescence, PIXE, or SEM-based analyzers).

TABLE 1. CHEMICAL ANALYSES OF IBERIAN FIGURINES (tr = trace)

Sample no./inv. no.	*Cu*	*Sn*	*Pb*	*Zn*	*Fe*	*Ni*	*Ag*	*As*	*Total*
PM 33-67-40/113	80.45	6.97	10.66	1.31	0.60	0.13	0.06	0.14	100.00
PM 33-67-40/114	83.40	10.54	4.69	1.37	tr	0.03	0.09	0.10	100.00
PM 33-67-40/118	87.97	3.51	7.48	1.04	tr	0.01	0.05	0.02	100.00
PM 33-67-40/120	94.74	2.62	1.53	1.11	tr	0.03	0.06	0.03	100.00
PM 33-67-40/121	94.58	5.16	0.26	tr	tr	0.00	0.03	0.01	100.00
PM 33-67-40/122	83.43	4.63	11.62	0.33	tr	0.06	0.04	0.20	100.00
PM 33-67-40/123	82.90	5.68	10.57	0.84	tr	0.04	0.08	0.08	100.00
PM 33-67-40/124	71.02	5.55	23.11	0.32	tr	0.02	0.06	0.05	100.00
PM 33-67-40/125	95.10	1.41	3.49	tr	tr	0.03	0.05	0.01	100.00
PM 33-67-40/126	92.54	2.81	4.29	0.36	tr	0.01	0.06	0.05	100.00
PM 33-67-40/127	88.92	5.46	5.62	tr	tr	0.02	0.06	0.05	100.00
PM 33-67-40/128	89.07	9.96	0.97	tr	tr	0.01	0.06	0.03	100.00
PM 33-67-40/129	91.61	1.29	6.69	0.41	tr	0.02	0.05	0.09	100.00
PM 33-67-40/130	89.91	5.06	4.65	0.39	tr	0.03	0.05	0.11	100.00
PM 33-67-40/134	76.32	4.17	18.77	0.74	tr	0.03	0.09	0.10	100.00
PM 33-67-40/135	80.31	5.01	13.84	0.85	tr	0.04	0.06	0.09	100.00
PM 33-67-40/136	89.85	6.93	2.85	0.37	tr	0.03	0.06	0.05	100.00

Results were obtained for 17 of the Harvard figurines (Table 1). As a group, these Iberian figurines are extremely variable in their lead content: they average 7.7%, but range from 0.26% to 23.1%. Tin, which averages 5.1%, ranges from 1.3% to 10.5%. Several of the figurines have measurable quantities of zinc (average 0.72%), but never more than 1.4%. There does not appear to be any correlation between our analyses and the type or style of the figurines. For example, the most elaborate figurines (e.g., no. 128), whose casting might have been facilitated by the use of leaded bronze, are not among those with more than 10% lead (nos. 113, 122, 123, 124, 134,

Collado de los Jardines sanctuary. Figurines of higher quality may be found in the Museo Arqueológico de Madrid and in the Museo Arqueológico de Barcelona.

8 R. H. Tykot and S. M. M. Young, "Archaeological applications of inductively coupled plasma-mass spectrometry," in M. V. Orna (ed.), *Archaeological chemistry: organic, inorganic, and biochemical analysis* (Washington, D.C. 1996) 116-30.

135). Our results are largely consistent with those previously reported for figurines from sanctuary sites in Spain,[9] and complement those available for Bronze Age Iberian metalwork.[10]

The extreme compositional variability present in the Harvard collection, and in other collections, implies that a standard recipe was not used in the production of Iberian votive bronze figurines, and that metal production in Iron Age Spain may have been a largely decentralized activity. This variability is also not easily explained by chronological changes in alloy composition, whether for technological, economic, or social reasons. Most likely, the variability present in these collections results from the widespread recycling of scrap metal containing copper, tin, and/or lead in differing proportions. This may have occurred for reasons of convenience, cost, or availability of alternative materials. Further analyses of Iberian bronzes from dated archaeological contexts may help resolve these issues and allow us to connect metallurgical production techniques to socioeconomic factors in prehistoric Iberian societies.

Department of Anthropology, University of South Florida, Tampa, FL 33630 (R.H.T.)
Departamento de Prehistoria y Arqueologia, Universidad Autonoma de Madrid (L.P.T.)
Department of Classics & Archaeology, Tufts University, Medford, MA 02155 (M.S.B.)

---

9 Prados Torreira 1992 (supra n.6) 151-56. XRF analyses of 54 figurines from the same site, Collados de los Jardines, average 9.4 ± 5.2% Sn, 9.7 ± 8.5% Pb, and 0.3 ± 0.3% Zn. Twenty figurines from Castellar de Santisteban average 7.0 ± 4.9% Sn, 13.7 ± 7.1% Pb, and 0.2 ± 0.3% Zn. Eight figurines from La Luz average 9.7 ± 7.4% Sn, 16.5 ± 7.6% Pb, and 0.3 ± 0.2% Zn.

10 R. J. Harrison, P. T. Craddock, and M. J. Hughes, "Study of the Bronze Age metalwork from the Iberian peninsula in the British Museum," *Ampurias* 43 (1981) 113-79.

The Los Angeles–Princeton warriors

Quentin Maule†

Two Etrusco-Italic bronzes in American collections, one in the Los Angeles County Museum of Art (fig. 1)[1] and the other in the Museum of Art, Princeton University (fig. 2),[2] are examined here. They belong to a large class of elongated military figures that have been traditionally referred to as 'Etruscan', although increasingly of late they are being labeled 'Umbrian' warriors. With very little in the nature of reliable information, the class is usually assigned to the general area of central Italy, but no single example has been found under archaeologically controlled conditions.

The two figures share certain physical peculiarities: a long cylindrical neck, narrowing toward the top and flaring at the base; thin arms and legs with a trace of sinuous muscularity; and a prognathous face with weak jaw and bulging almond-shaped eyes, the head tilted pugnaciously upward.

The pose with right arm raised and left arm lowered, standard for the class as a whole, is distinctive here for its stiffness. The advanced left leg, slightly bent, and the straight right leg, in vertical alignment with the body, produce a notable imbalance. In a Greek object of this period (5th or perhaps 4th c. B.C.), such an asymmetrical stance would be carefully counter-poised: the left hip perhaps lowered to allow the left leg (the hypotenuse of the right triangle described by the right leg and the ground line) to meet the right leg. Compounding the unstable effect are the left leg, which is bent, and the right foot, which is placed on a tiny platform. The upper half of the figure makes no accommodation to these strained circumstances: all is level and horizontal — shoulders, waist, and hips. The result is the so-called Etruscan tension.

These figures, like most examples of the class, wear a Greek-style open-faced helmet with raised cheek guards and a high crest, the tail of which extends down the back halfway to the waist. The Los Angeles example wears a bell cuirass, probable of metal, that ends at the waist and is decorated with incised spirals on the chest. The Princeton warrior may be wearing a newer style of leather cuirass as the V-shape engraved on the chest appears to indicate: this would represent the lapel-like flaps that reach over the shoulders from the back and tie to the

---

† [We very much regret to report that Quentin Maule died in March 2000. A native of Oklahoma, he earned a bachelor's degree in archaeology from the University of Oklahoma, a master's degree in English from the University of Chicago, a certificate in art history from the University of Paris, and a doctorate from the University of California, Berkeley. From 1944 to 1945 he served as a volunteer in Italy and India in the American Field Service, where he received the British Bronze Star of Merit. Maule worked as a writer and editor at Time Inc., at Harper & Row, and at the Smithsonian Institution. He taught at the University of Arkansas, Northern Illinois University, Reed College, Rollins College, and Fordham University. He served as the chair of the art department at the University of Arkansas. He was an expert on Etruscan warriors, and this is his last publication on the subject. — The editors]

1 Los Angeles, Los Angeles County Museum of Art A.5832.47-40, h. 0.241 m: E. W. Robinson, *Small bronzes of the ancient world* (Exhib. cat., Detroit Institute of Art, MI 1947) 8, no. 35; S. Cles-Reden, *Das versunkene Volk* (Innsbruck 1948) 107, fig. 8, right; R. S. Teitz, *Masterpieces of Etruscan art* (Exhib. cat., Worcester Art Museum, MA 1967) 56, no. 45, fig. p. 144; G. Colonna, *Bronzi votivi umbro-sabellici a figura umana* (Florence 1970) 83, no. 192.

2 Princeton, University Art Museum 41.27, h. 0.205 m, reportedly from Bologna: D. Levi, *Record of the Museum of Art* 1.1 (Spring 1942) 9 ff., fig. on p.10; F. F. Jones and R. Goldberg, *Ancient art in the Art Museum, Princeton University* (Princeton, NJ 1960) 32-33; E. H. Richardson, *The Etruscans: their art and civilization* (Chicago 1964) 108-9, pl. 27a; Teitz (supra n.1) 65-66, no. 54, fig. p. 160; Colonna (supra n.1) 36, no. 41; M. A. Del Chiaro, *AJA* 80 (1976) 39; G. K. Sams, *Small sculptures in bronze from the classical world* (Exhib. cat., W. H. Ackland Memorial Art Center, Chapel Hill, NC 1976) no. 45, fig.; *Gens antiquissima Italiae dall'Umbria a New York* (Exhib. cat., Grey Art Gallery, New York 1991) 209, no. 4.10, fig. p. 208.

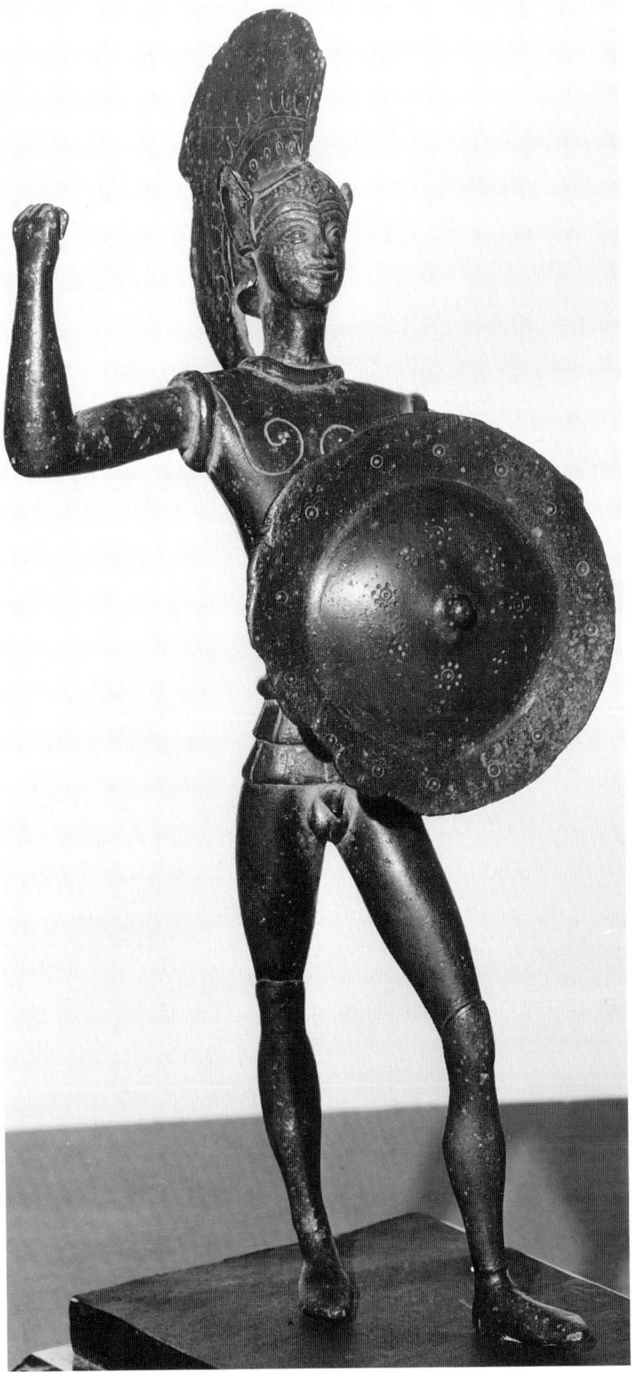

Fig. 1. Warrior. Etrusco-Italic, 5th-4th c. B.C. Bronze, h. 0.241 m. Los Angeles County Museum of Art, Hearst Foundation Fund A. 5832.47.50. (Photo: courtesy Museum)

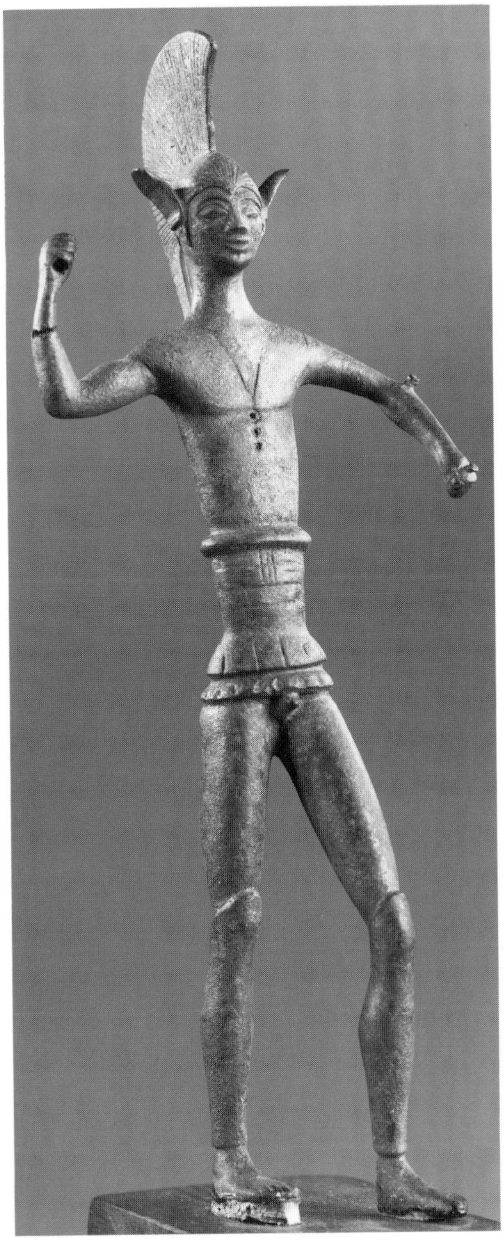

Fig. 2. Warrior. Etrusco-Italic, 5th-4th c. B.C. Bronze, h. 0205 m. The Art Museum, Princeton University, Museum Purchase, Carl Otto von Kienbusch, Jr., Memorial Collection 41.27. (Photo: courtesy Museum)

corselet in front. The belt on this warrior is high up on his body, with the ventral area below treated like a tight girdle, decorated with a few incised lines in straight-line pattern. Two rows of *pteryges* (protective flaps) flare out below the cuirass, with the ruffles of an undertunic indicated beneath them. The genital area is left uncovered in both instances, while greaves protect shins and knees. The raised right fist of the Princeton warrior is tiny, with a hole drilled through it for holding the (missing) lance. The right arm and fist of the Los Angeles piece are slightly more massive. On the lowered left arm of the Princeton example there is a knob at the elbow to which a round shield must have been attached. The Los Angeles warrior grasps his round shield with his left hand.

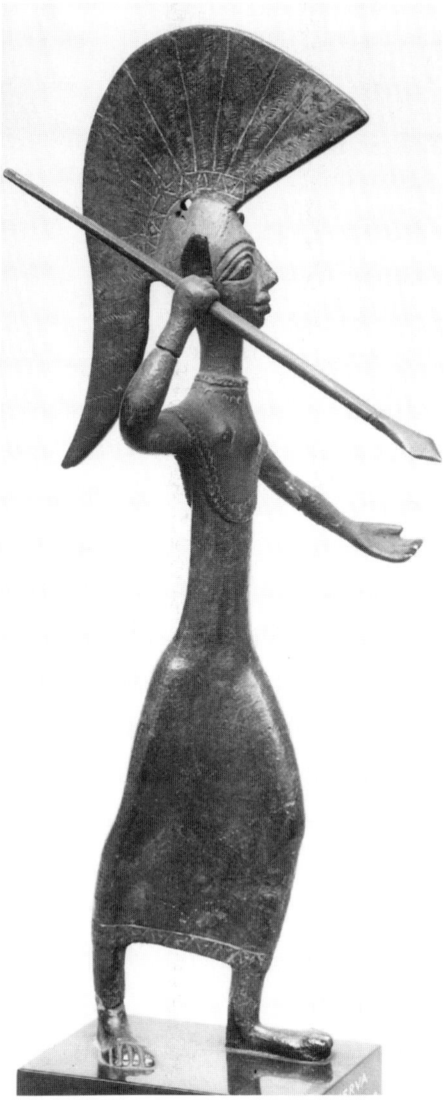

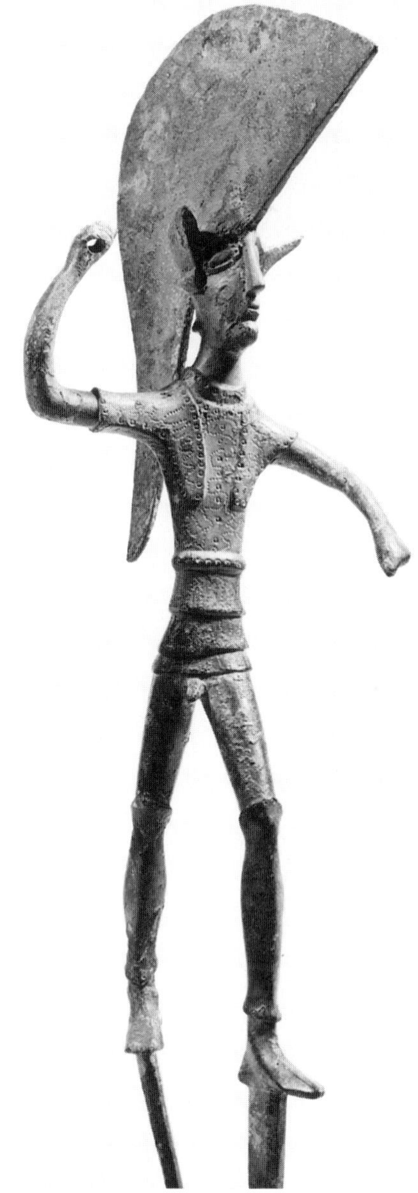

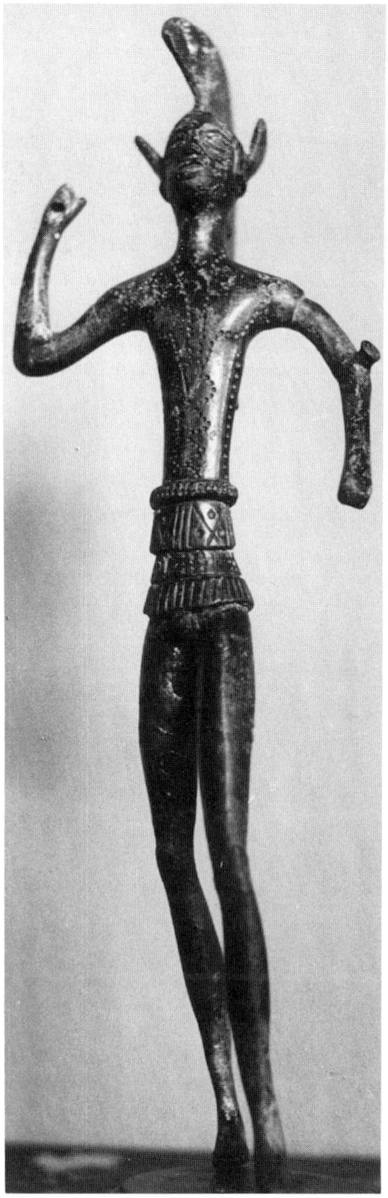

Fig. 3. Minerva. Etrusco-Italic, 5th-4th c. B.C. Bronze, h. 0.209 m. London, British Museum 1824.4.13.3. (Photo: courtesy Trustees)

Fig. 4. Warrior. Etrusco-Italic, 5th-4th c. B.C. Bronze, h. 0.265 m. Cambridge, Ashmolean Museum Fortnum B-7. (Photo: courtesy Museum)

Fig. 5. Warrior. Etrusco-Italic, 5th-4th c. B.C. Bronze, h. 0.26 m. Florence, Museo Archeologico 253/350. (Photo: courtesy Soprintendenza)

The figures are not twins but they belong to the same family, and the same artist may have made them. One sees this in the similar modeling of the ever-so-slightly muscular limbs, the thin waist, and the tensely tilted stance. Details of head and face most strongly betray the kinship: ovoid skull with long conical neck, protruding eyes and lips, wide nose, and small pointed chin with full cheeks.

Very like these figures is a Minerva statuette in the British Museum (fig. 3):[3] the same ultra-thin quality with long neck, large bulging eyes as if pasted to the ovoid head, and flat feet with left leg advanced, bent at the knee. The upper part of the body is too long for the legs.

---

3 London, British Museum 1824.4.13.3, h. 0.209 m: Walters, *British Museum Bronzes* 61, no. 443; G. K. Loukomski, *Art étrusque* (1930) 6, pl. 59; G. Fogolari, *StEtr* 23 (1954) 386, fig. 1; R. Bloch, *L'art et la civilisation étrusque* (Paris 1955) 81, fig. 16; Richardson, *MAAR* 27 (1962) 159, 197, figs. 113-14; W. Zschietzschmann, *Etruskische Kunst* (Frankfurt 1969) pl. 111; Colonna (supra n.1) 66, no. 139, pl. 36; E. H. Richardson, *Etruscan votive bronzes* (Mainz 1983) 358, figs. 846-47 [hereafter *EVB*] ; G. Colonna, *LIMC* 2 (1984) 1056, no. 61, pl. 773.

The spaghetti-thin arms and legs of the Minerva show no signs of the tight muscularity of the Los Angeles and Princeton warriors, but the bulging hips under the skirt lend a certain fleshiness to the figure.

A warrior in the Ashmolean Museum (fig. 4)[4] is almost a brother to the goddess in the British Museum: the same prominently beaked nose, long neck, and pasted-on almond-shaped eyes. But the mouth is different: quite tiny. The high belt with three rows of pteryges spacing out the distance above the genitals reminds one of the Princeton warrior. Overall, the figure is more angular and less fleshy than either the Los Angeles or Princeton warrior, and without the London Minerva it might not be possible to make the connection to this group.

A warrior in the Museo Archeologico, Florence, no. 350 (fig. 5),[5] is very like the Los Angeles warrior: prognathous face, round cheeks, small chin, almond-shaped eyes, tiny hands, high belt, and prominently raised cheek guards. Where the area below the belt of the Princeton figure appears to be merely a sketchy pattern of straight lines with abbreviated flaps below, here the pteryges encroach on that zone, the two lowermost layers fanning out naturalistically over the buttocks and the regular folds of the undertunic emerging below.

A second warrior in Florence, no. 357 (fig. 6),[6] exhibits most of the stylistic attributes of this group, with slight changes: jaw stronger, cheek pieces not as prominent, neck not as long, belt not as high, and waist not as stretched out. There is some attempt to achieve a sort of *contrapposto*, although the artist does not seem to know quite how to adjust the heights of hips, waist, and shoulders to express this essentially foreign concept. He retains something of what we think of as 'Etruscan tension' in spite of himself.

The bronze warrior no. 24553 in the Villa Giulia Museum, Rome (fig. 7),[7] carries this naturalism much further: proportions are more regular and facial details more realistic, with full lips, smaller nose, and fine modeling of cheeks and chin. Most descriptive details are easy to identify: nose piece to helmet, folds of tunic protruding from beneath the cuirass at neck and arms, wide shoulder flaps meeting on the chest. Even the double belt, one high, one lower down, does not appear as abstract as it did on other members of the group. The stance is still flat-footed, however, with the left leg advanced and slightly flexed while the upper body retains its generally horizontal direction. Hands and arms are tiny, and eyes are enormous and almond-shaped (now bordered by strong upper and lower eyelids). The shape of the head is like the others of the group, with broad cheeks and small chin. The raised cheek pieces are slightly curled as they reach out rakishly from the head (as they are also on Florence 350).

A Minerva figure also in the Villa Giulia, no. 24552 (fig. 8),[8] is perhaps a female counterpart of Villa Giulia 24553, much as British Museum Walters 443 can be associated with Oxford Fortnum B-7. It has the same facial features as Villa Giulia 24553 — mouth, nose, cheeks, and eyes — but thinner legs. It has the same ungraceful, flat-footed stance as the Minerva in the

4 Oxford, Ashmolean Museum, Fortnum B-7, h. 0.265 m: C. D. E. Fortnum, *BdI* 1866, 65; Richardson 1962 (supra n.3) 159, fig. 112; Colonna (supra n.1) 66, no. 138, pl. 36; *Treasures of the Ashmolean Museum* (Oxford 1970) no. 22 (R. W. Hamilton).

5 Florence, Museo Archeologico 253/350, h. 0.26 m: J. Martha, *L'art étrusque* (Paris 1889) 502, fig. 336; L. Goldscheider, *Etruscan sculpture* (New York 1941) pl. 75; U. Cristoffel, *Die Kunst und das schöne Heim* 53.9 (June 1955) 326; Colonna (supra n.1) 69, no. 147, pls. 38-39.

6 Florence, Museo Archeologico 254/357, h. 0.18 m: Colonna (supra n.1) 75-76, no. 173, pl. 48.

7 Rome, Museo di Villa Giulia 24553, h. 0.325 m: A. F. Gori, *Museo etrusco* (Florence 1737-43) pl. 110; M. Moretti, *National Museum of the Villa Giulia* (Rome 1963) 128, fig. 94; Richardson, *EVB* (supra n.3) 184, figs. 430-31; M. Sprenger and G. Bartolini, *Die Etrusker: Kunst und Geschichte* (Munich 1977) fig. 186, right.

8 Rome, Museo di Villa Giulia 24552, h. 0.282 m: M. Pallottino and H. and I. Jucker, *Art of the Etruscans* (New York 1955) fig. 203; E. H. Richardson, *Etruscan sculptures* (New York 1966) pl. 21 a, d; Colonna (supra n.1) 37–38, no. 43, pl. 13; Richardson, *EVB* (supra n.3) 352, figs. 843-44; Colonna (supra n.3).

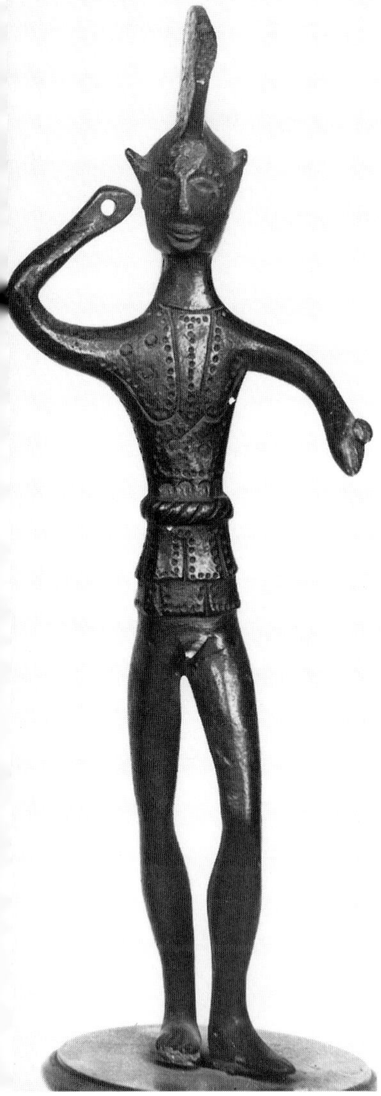
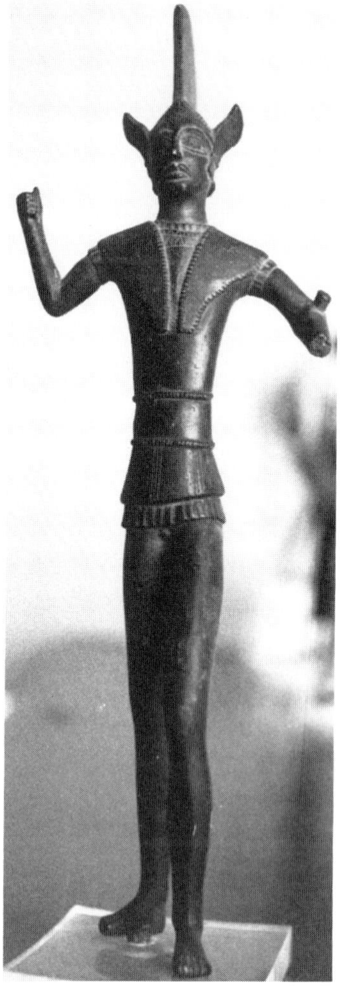
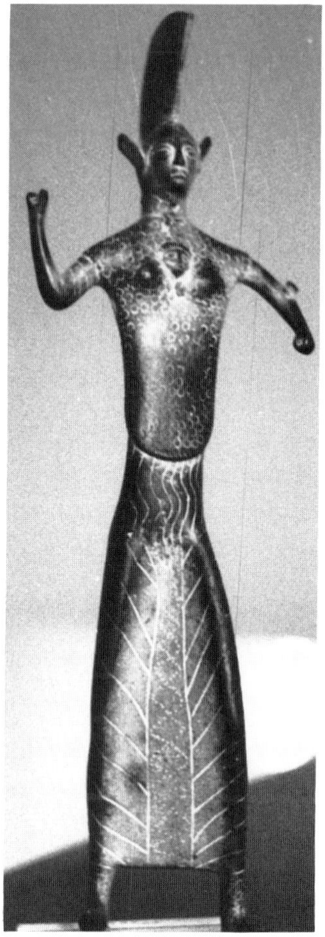
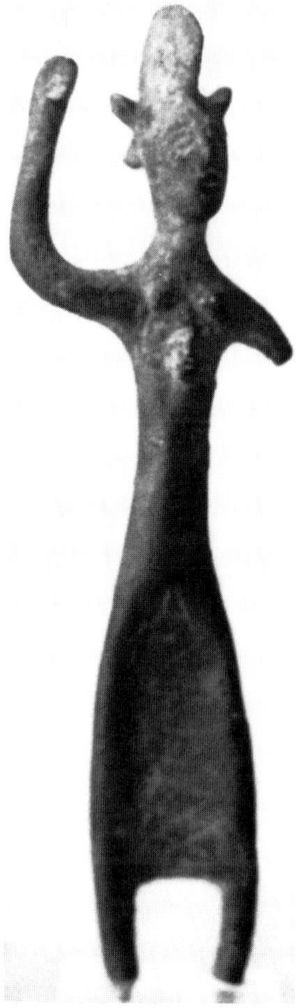

Fig. 6 (left). Warrior. Etrusco-Italic, 5th-4th c. B.C. Bronze, h. 0.18 m. Florence, Museo Archeologico 254/357. (Photo: courtesy Soprintendenza)
Fig. 7 (second from left). Warrior. Etrusco-Italic, 5th-4th c. B.C. Bronze, h. 0.325 m. Rome, Museo di Villa Giulia 24553.
Fig. 8 (second from right). Minerva. Etrusco-Italic, 5th-4th c. B.C. Bronze, h. 0.282 m. Rome, Museo di Villa Giulia 24552.
Fig. 9 (right). Minerva. Etrusco-Italic, 5th-4th c. B.C. Bronze, h. 0.125 m. Rome, Museo di Villa Giulia 24546. (figs. 7-9 photos: courtesy Museo)

British Museum, the aegis draping over the chest with something of the same smoothness; the incised patterning on both upper and lower garments is more precise.

Villa Giulia no. 24546 (fig. 9)[9] is a less carefully executed Minerva, a variation of Villa Giulia 24552. The ungainly legs (both feet are missing) press through the skirt as in 24552. But the raised right arm and elbow are hastily fashioned, a thin rod with a bend in it. The head is tilted pugnaciously upward like the Los Angeles warrior prototype and the lips protrude harshly in the true manner of the Los Angeles and Princeton pieces.

Perhaps we can place these bronze figurines among their numerous fellows from central Italy if we consider the similarities of one of its members — British Museum Walters 443, say — to a

9 Rome, Museo di Villa Giulia 24546, h. 0.125 m: Colonna (supra n.1) 38, no. 45, pl. 15; Richardson, *EVB* (supra n.3) 352, figs. 839-40; Colonna (supra n.3).

warrior in Perugia.[10] One notes the same arrogant tilt to the head, large eyes, prominent nose, broad face, and thin limbs. Perugia 901 is a work by the so-called Fossato di Vico Master, belonging to a group of craftsmen working in the valley of the Esino, a stream that enters the Adriatic a few kilometers above Ancona. The Esino valley school of bronzeworkers produced a distinctive style,[11] a flamboyant version of the more traditional Etrusco-Italic works of SW Umbria (such as those coming from the area around Todi — the well-known Florence 586, for example[12]). But this little group is not by the Fossato di Vico Master: other works by that craftsman reveal an artist using larger, more geometrically abstract forms, not quite as bizarre as the artist we may call the Los Angeles–Princeton Master.[13] The juxtaposition does suggest, however, that the 9 pieces examined probably originated in that area, on the Adriatic side of the Italian peninsula, across the divide from the home of Umbro-Etruscan art as we are accustomed to think of it. The strong Greek overlay in Etrusco-Italic culture (at least when speaking of the more provincial works, such as those described here) was probably stronger in Etruria proper (as Florence 586 splendidly epitomizes) and quickly disintegrated as it spread out from there. By the time Greek influence reached the hills of NE Umbria, we encounter only pale reflections of the Greek panoply — of raised cheek guards, segmented cuirass, round shield — and much less of the physiologically accurate body movements that one would encounter in Greece proper at this time. The works have slipped into the native Italic mode, elongation becoming extreme, distortions broadening, and extravagance bursting out.

---

10 Perugia, Museo Nazionale dell'Umbria 901, h. 0.22 m, from Fossato di Vico: Colonna (supra n.1) 43, no. 61, pl. 19; Q. Maule, *StEtr* 59 (1993) 96, pl. 23a.

11 Maule ibid. 87ff.

12 Maule, *StEtr* 57 (1991) 53 ff., with bibliography.

13 Maule (supra n.10).

Etruskische Sphyrelata

Fritzi Jurgeit

In diesem Rahmen möchte ich auf eine frühe Denkmälergruppe etruskischer Bronzen verweisen, nämlich auf die aus Blech getriebenen lebensgroßen bzw. annähernd lebensgroßen Hände. Von ihnen sind dreizehn Exemplare bekannt, die zuletzt von M. Cristofani zusammengestellt wurden.[1]

Das bekannteste Beispiel, das zwischen 1834 und 1837 in Vulci zutagekam, ist das Paar im Museo Gregoriano Etrusco des Vatikan (Abb. 1).[2] Es zeigt eine linke und eine rechte Hand mit ihrer Außenseite und gerade ausgestreckten Fingern sowie einen Teil der Unterarme. Aus einem einzigen Stück kräftigen Blechs sind die schematisch gebildeten, an ihren Rändern leicht nach hinten gebogenen Finger und die Seitenpartie des Handrückens geschnitten. Für den Puls ist das Blech oval zusammengebogen und mit je zwei Nieten auf der Rückseite verbunden. Es wurde also ein räumliches — im Bereich der Hand allerdings auf der Rückseite offenes — und sich selbst tragendes Gebilde geschaffen. Die Handrücken waren mit mindestens fünf Reihen von mit Goldfolie überzogenen[3] kleinen Bronzehalbkugeln verziert. G. Colonna interpretierte dies als Angabe von verzierten Handschuhen.[4]

Daß der Handrücken[5] dargestellt wird, ist besonders deutlich bei einem Händepaar, ebenfalls aus Vulci, im Museo di Villa Giulia in Rom;[6] dort sind in der ornamentalen Form einer von der Rückseite her getriebenen Raute die Knöchel dargestellt. Das Händepaar stammt gemein-

---

1 G. Colonna, in *La civiltà dei Dauni nel quadro del mondo italico: Atti XIII Convegno di studi etruschi e italici, Manfredonia 1980* (Firenze 1984) 272 Anm. 59; M. Cristofani, *I bronzi degli Etruschi* (Novara 1985) 16, 288, Nr. 108. Das von V. v. Gonzenbach, *JberProVindon* 1951/52, 17 erwähnte Exemplar in der Villa Giulia existiert nach freundlicher Auskunft von Ida Caruso nicht.

2 Inv. 11930 / 11931: H 28.0 / 27.5 cm; B 9.6 / 9.9 cm; Puls H 10.0 / 10.0 cm; B x T 5.4 x 4.9 / 5.6 x 4.7 cm; BlechSt 0.05-0.1 cm; kräftiggrüne rauhe Patina über braunem glatten Bronzegrund. Daumen modern abgeschnitten / Oberer Teil des verdrückten Pulses ergänzt, ebenso der Ansatz des Zeigefingers und die untere Partie des Mittelfingers, Daumen und Ringfinger schräg abgeschnitten. *Musei etrusci, quod Gregorius XVI Pont. Max. in aedibus Vaticanis constituit monimenta: pars prima* (Vatikan 1842) Taf. 72b: "... non sono frammentate le due mani votive"; Helbig[4] I Nr. 685 (T. Dohrn referiert lediglich, die Hände seien "als Bekrönung römischer Feldzeichen oder als Weihgeschenke (mit apotropäischer Bedeutung) erklärt worden", vgl. infra Anm. 30); Colonna (s.o. Anm. 1) Taf. 46b; M. Cristofani (Hrsg.), *Dizionario della civiltà etrusca* (Firenze 1985) 335, Abb. 5 (seitenverkehrt!); F. Buranelli, in ders. und G. Rosati, *Musei Vaticani: Egizi ed Etruschi* (Firenze 1983) 39, Nr. 8; F. Buranelli, *The Etruscans: legacy of a lost civilization from the Vatican Museum* (Ausstellungskat., Wonders, Memphis, TN 1992) 190-91, Nrr. 170-171; F. Buranelli, in *The human body in ancient art from the Vatican Museums* (Ausstellungskat., Toyota 1996). F. Buranelli danke ich herzlich für die Möglichkeit, die Bronzen im Original untersuchen zu können, und M. Sannibale für Informationen zu ihrer Publikation.

3 Bei 11390 sind 9, bei 11391 20 Kügelchen erhalten. An den Stellen, an denen heute gegenüber älteren Photos (wie Abb. 1) Halbkügelchen fehlen, sind keine Niet- oder Lotspuren zu erkennen, es scheint nur die oberste Patinaschicht verändert zu sein; vielleicht waren die Verzierungen nur aufgeklebt. Zur Folienvergoldung W. A. Oddy in H. Born (Hrsg.), *Archäologische Bronzen* (Berlin 1985) 64-67.

4 Colonna (s.o. Anm. 1).

5 Die Handinnenseite, die gewöhnlich bei Votivgaben zur Darstellung kommt, fehlt hier. Zu den verschiedenen Deutungen des Gestus der erhobenen Hände H. Demisch, *Erhobene Hände—Geschichte einer Gebärde in der bildenden Kunst* (Stuttgart 1984): bei Klage- oder Erscheinungsgebärden sind immer die Handinnenflächen, nicht die Handrücken dargestellt.

6 Inv. 84866 / 84865: H 21.0 / 20.5 cm; B 7.6 / 8.6 cm; Puls H 8.1 / 8.4 cm; B x T 5.1 x 3.2 / 4.9 x 3.4 cm; BlechSt 0.05 cm; olivgrüne rauhe Patina mit braunen Flecken. Daumen größtenteils weggebrochen, Mittelfinger mit Ergänzung wieder angesetzt / Vollständig, mit Kunstharz hinterfüllt. Cristofani (s.o. Anm. 1).

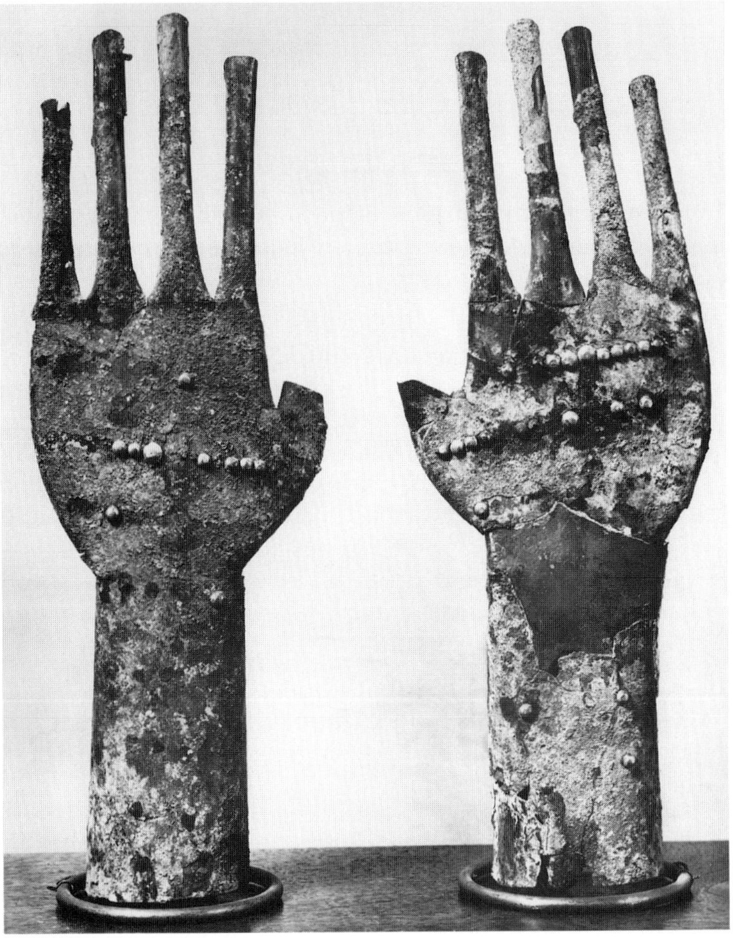

Abb. 1. Händepaar aus Vulci. Bronze, H 28,0/27,5 cm. Vatikan, Museo Gregoriano Etrusco 11930/11931. (Foto: Postkarte A. Egger, Köln)

sam mit einem zweiten, naturnäher gestalteten Paar[7] — doch auch dieses ohne Angabe der Fingernägel — aus demselben ungestörten Kammergrab, dessen Ausgrabung 1965 wissenschaftlich beobachtet wurde, aber leider immer noch nicht endgültig publiziert ist; es muß hier auf den 1967 vorgelegten Vorbericht von G. Scichilone[8] zurückgegriffen werden. Die Tomba del carro di bronzo enthielt neben dem namengebenden, mit Bronze verkleideten Wagen[9] zwei sich gleichende bronzene Aschenurnen sowie etliche Bronzegeräte und -gefäße, alles wohl lokale Erzeugnisse. Das Grab wird einhellig in die 1. Hälfte des 7. Jhs. v.Chr. gesetzt, aufgrund der importierten korinthischen und 'rhodischen' Keramik sogar in das 1. Viertel des Jhs.[10] Wenn die Händepaare zum Kult der beiden wohl männlichen Verstorbenen gehörten, sind sie sicherlich die jüngsten Gegenstände im Grabzusammenhang.

---

7 Inv. 84867 / 84868: H 23.5 / 23.5 cm; B 10.5 / 9.6 cm; Puls H 7.5 / 7,0 cm; BlechSt 0.05 cm; kräftiggrüne rauhe Patina. Daumen bestoßen und mit Ergänzung wieder angesetzt, Ergänzung am Pulsansatz; Niete aus dem elastischen Blech ausgefallen / Daumen und Zeigefinger mit Fehlstellen, innen Kunstharz hinterfüllt; unter dem unteren Niet Geweberest. M. Moretti, *Vulci* (Novara 1982) Abb. 59.

8 G. Scichilone, in *Arte e civiltà degli Etruschi* (Ausstellungskat., Torino 1967) 25-44, bes. Nrr. 35-36. M. Moretti, *Il Museo Nazionale di Villa Giulia* (Roma 1973) 31-34, Abb. 21 zeigt die jeweils rechte Hand beider Paare; unter Nr. 5 des Textes ist versehentlich von einer "terza coppia" die Rede; 34: "Si tratta indubbiamente di oggetti la cui funzione rimane assolutamente oscura, anche se è lecito avanzare l'ipotesi di una destinazione rituale." Ich danke A. M. Sgubini Moretti herzlich für die Erlaubnis, die Bronzen im Original untersuchen zu dürfen, vgl. auch infra Anm. 22-23.

9 Zuletzt A. M. Sgubini-Moretti–G. F. Priori, in A. Emiliozzi (Hrsg.), *Carri da guerra e principi etruschi* (Ausstellungskat., Viterbo 1997-98) 139-53.

10 G. Colonna, *StEtr* 40 (1972) 569.

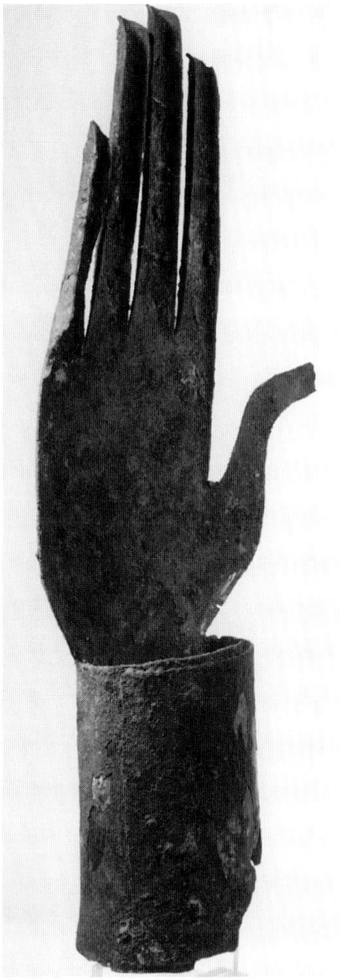

Abb. 2. Hand. Bronze, H 29,0 cm. Ascona, Sammlung Rosenbaum. (Foto: Vermittlung durch W. Hornbostel)

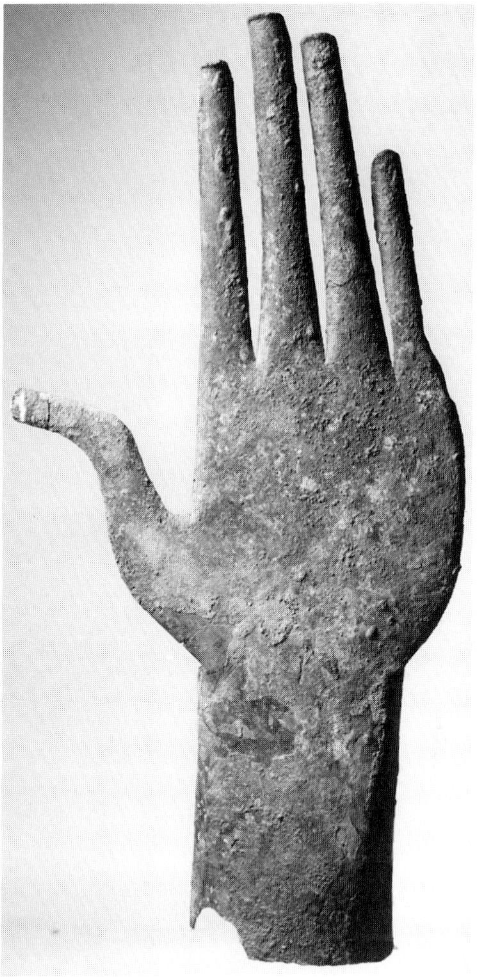

Abb. 3. Hand (Rückseite Abb. 2) (Foto: Vermittlung durch W. Hornbostel)

Die anderen bekannten Bronzehände seien hier kurz vorgestellt.

Aus den Grabungen von Lucien Bonaparte, Principe di Canino, stammt eine bereits 1837 erwähnte rechte Hand im British Museum (Abb. 5); Walters bezeichnet sie als "gauntlet", also als Panzerhandschuh.[11] Aus Pescia Romana kommt eine rechte Hand im Museo della Maremma in Grosseto.[12]

Neben die acht Exemplare mit sicherem Fundort Vulci, bzw. dem ihm zuzurechnenden Gebiet treten weitere Beispiele ohne bekannten Fundort in Privatbesitz.

Auf ein Paar, von dem das Deutsche Archäologische Institut in Rom 1963 ein Photo anfertigte, hat bereits Colonna hingewiesen; nähere Angaben zu Auffindung oder Aufbewahrung der

11 J. De Witte, *Description d'une collection des vases peints et bronzes antiques provenant des fouilles de l'Étrurie* (Paris 1837) 119, Nr. 240; Walters, *British Museum Bronzes* Nr. 2733; *DarSag* IV.2 (1911) 1313, Abb. 6418 (A. J. Reinach); v. Gonzenbach 1952 (s.o. Anm. 1) 17, Abb. 5. Judith Swaddling danke ich herzlich für die Übersendung des Photos. Vgl. auch F. Buranelli in M. Natoli (Hrsg.), *Luciano Bonaparte: le sue collezioni d'arte, le sue residenze a Roma, nel Lazio, in Italia [1804-1840]* (Roma 1995) 81-218.

12 Inv. 1424; erh. H 22,0 cm; bis auf den Daumen alle Finger ab- oder weggebrochen. A. Mazzolei, *Grosseto: il Museo Archeologico della Maremma* (Grosseto 1977) 102. S. Clarke, die das Fundmaterial aus Pescia Romana im Rahmen einer tesi di laurea publiziert, überließ mir freundlicherweise ein Photo des bisher nicht abgebildeten Stückes, wofür ihr herzlich gedankt sei.

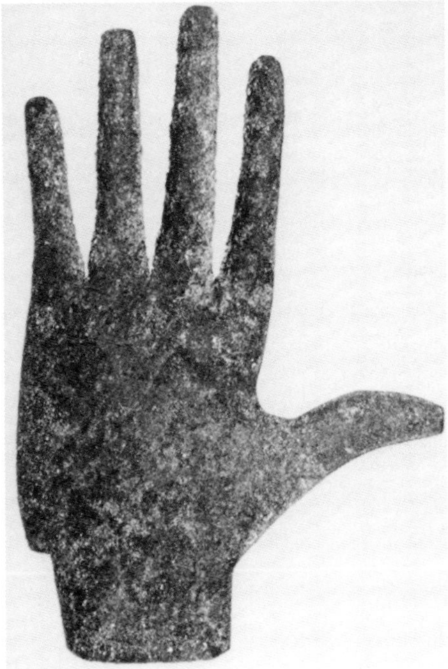

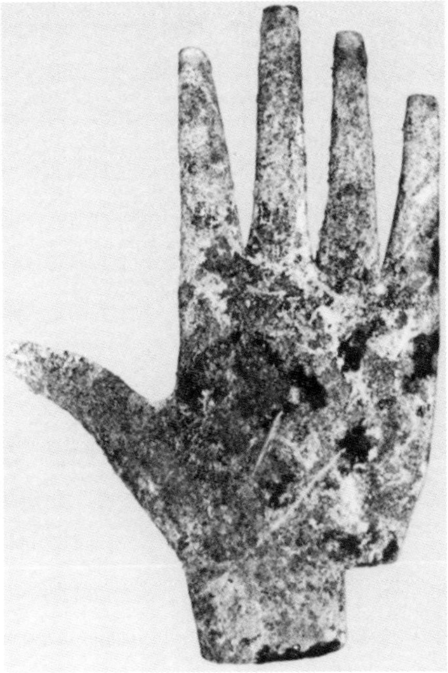

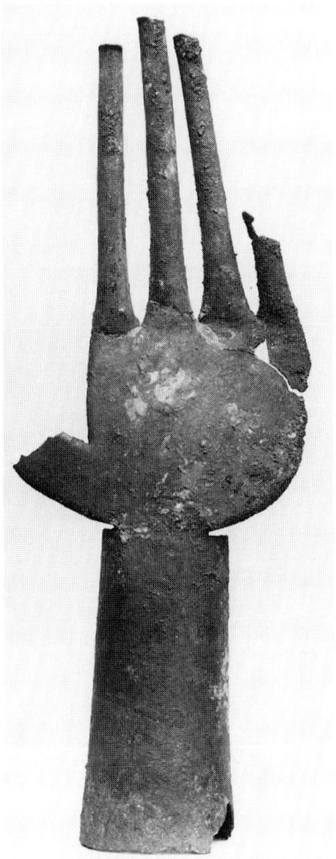

Abb. 4. Händepaar. Bronze, H 23,0 cm. Sammlung Barbier-Mueller. (Foto: nach *Summa Galleries Inc., Catalogue* 1 [1976] Nr. 73)

Abb. 5. Hand aus Vulci. Bronze, H 31,6 cm. London, British Museum. (Foto: Museum XCIII C 35)

Bronzehände liegen nicht vor.[13] Eine rechte Hand, die 1981 bei der Ausstellung *Kunst der Etrusker* in Hamburg gezeigt wurde, befand sich in der Sammlung Rosenbaum in Ascona (Abb. 2-3).[14] In der Schweizer Sammlung Barbier-Mueller wird eine linke Hand mit ausgesprochen kurzem Puls aufbewahrt, für die als Herkunft "Italie centrale" angegeben wird.[15] Sie dürfte mit einem 1976 im Kunsthandel von Beverly Hills angebotenen Stück identisch sein (Abb. 4),[16] das mit einer rechten Hand ein Paar bildete. Doch scheint diese nicht in die Genfer Sammlung gelangt zu sein.

Zum Abschluß sei ein vierzehntes, stark fragmentiertes Exemplar im Badischen Landesmuseum Karlsruhe[17] vorgestellt (Abb. 6). Es stammt aus der 1853 angekauften Bronzensammlung von Friedrich Maler, die dieser vor 1843 in Rom zusammentrug. In dem von ihm selbst verfaßten Verzeichnis von 1854 beschreibt er es gemeinsam mit anderen Fragmenten als "Beschlägstücke". Als "Fragment von einem Gefäßhals" wurde es im Museumsinventar bezeichnet und K. Schumacher nahm das unscheinbare Fragment nicht in seinen Bronzenkatalog von 1890 auf. An dem

---

13 Colonna (s.o. Anm. 1) Taf. 46a. Aus dem Photoinventar des DAI Rom ergibt sich für die Negative 63.812 und 63.813 kein Hinweis auf den ehemaligen Aufbewahrungsort.

14 W. Hornbostel, *Kunst der Etrusker* (Ausstellungskat., Interversa, Hamburg 1981) Nr. 13, vgl. auch Nr. 12. W. Hornbostel danke ich für die freundliche Übersendung von Maßen und Photos des bisher nicht abgebildeten Stückes: H 29.0 cm; B 14.0 cm; Puls B x T 6.6 / 5.5 cm.

15 J.-L. Zimmermann, *Art antique dans les collections du Musée Barbier Mueller* (Paris 1991) 112, 171, Nr. 37, mit "cfr." ist wohl auf die Erstpublikation verwiesen. S. folgende Anm.

16 *The Summa Galleries Inc. Catalogue 1* (Beverly Hills, CA 1976) Nr. 73: H 23.0 cm; "... both are intact". Vielleicht wurde die rechte Hand nur nicht in den Katalog aufgenommen, weil sie zu stark gereinigt und neu patiniert worden war. Oder ist sie modern? Für Anfertigung und Übersendung einer Reproduktion des dort abgebildeten Photos danke ich E. Rehm.

17 Inv. F 252; erh. H 11.9 cm; B x T 6.2 x 5.0 cm; BlechSt 0.07 cm, dunkelgrüne körnige Patina mit kräftiggrünen Partien über rotbraunem Bronzeton: F. Jurgeit, *Die etruskischen und italischen Bronzen im Badischen Landesmuseum, Karlsruhe* (Roma 1999) Nr. 10.

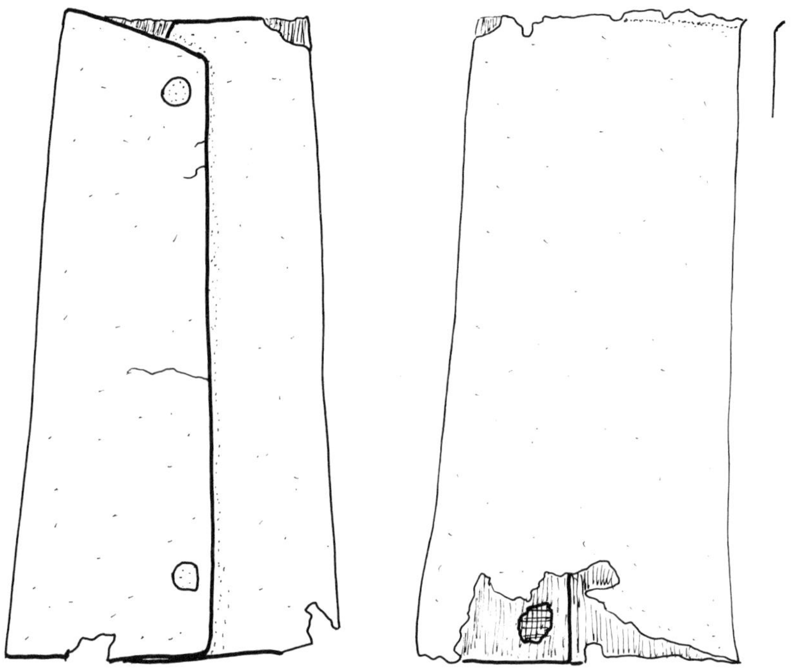

Abb. 6. Handfragment. Bronze, erh. H 11,9 cm. Karlsruhe, Badisches Landesmuseum F 252. (Skizze: Verfasserin)

mit zwei Nieten verbundenen Blech des Pulses hat sich bei ansonsten originaler Kante auf der Vorderseite der Ansatz des im übrigen weggebrochenen Handrückens erhalten. Für viele Bronzen gibt Maler einen Fundort auf "den Ländereien des Prinzen von Canino" an. So ist z.B. auch ein Fragment des nachantik mit der Bronzebüste aus der "Tomba d'Iside" von Vulci in London verbundenen Blechstreifens[18] mit dieser Herkunftsangabe nach Karlsruhe gelangt. Das Karlsruher Handfragment könnte also — auch von den Maßen und der Oberflächenbeschaffenheit her — das linke Gegenstück zu der rechten Hand in London sein.[19]

Die Technik des Vernietens von Bronzeblechen untereinander ohne einen stützenden Kern, die für den griechischen Raum als σφυρήλατον-Technik[20] bezeichnet wird, ist in Etrurien, ebenfalls im Vulcenter Gebiet, auch für Kugelköpfe belegt. Gemeinsam mit den beiden Händepaaren wurde in der Tomba del carro di bronzo auch eine "sfera bronzea su collo cilindrico" gefunden, die Cristofani zusammen mit den Händen als "... una prima realizzazione simbolica di un monumento funerario in materiale nobile ..." bezeichnet.[21] An einer Halbkugel, die mit einer zweiten wohl verlötet ist,[22] ist der aus einem Blechstück gerollte und zusammen-

---

18 S. Haynes, *Etruscan bronzes* (London 1985) Nr. 21 mit Lit.; dies., *StEtr* 57 (1991) 3-9, bes. 6 und Taf. 3. Haynes betont ebd. Anm. 34 entgegen Cristofani 1985 (s.o. Anm.1) Nr. 111, daß die einzelnen Bronzebleche nicht verlötet sondern vernietet wurden.

19 Dafür spricht auch das Überlappen des Bleches bei dem Karlsruher Fragment nach rechts hin, das sich bei den linken Händen aus der Tomba del Carro di Vulci wiederfindet (bei 84867 überlappt das Blech lediglich aufgrund der Restaurierung des senkrecht durchgehenden Bruches im Puls nach links) — bei den rechten Händen überlappt das Blech nach links; dies gilt auch für das Händepaar im Vatikan.

20 J. Papadopoulos, *Xoana e sphyrelata: testimonianza delle fonti scritte* (Roma 1980); dazu Rez. F. Jurgeit, *Gymnasium* 92 (1985) 151-53.

21 Scichilone 1967 (s.o. Anm. 8) Nr. 34; Moretti (s.o. Anm. 8) 33, Nr. 4; E. Woytowitsch, *Die Wagen der Bronze- und frühen Eisenzeit in Italien* (*Prähistorische Bronzefunde* XXVII 1, München 1978) 39-40, Nr. 34, Taf. 6.7: "Deichselkopf"; Cristofani (s.o. Anm . 1) Nr. 107.

22 Inv. 84875: H ges. 19.5 cm; Dm der Kugel 13.7 cm. Braune, z.t. sehr glatte Patina, auf der unteren Kalotte Verlaufspuren in zickzackartiger Anordnung. Der Hals (erh. H 7.8 cm; Dm 7.9 cm; BlechSt 0.05 cm) ist mit drei Nieten auf die untere Kalotte der Kugel genietet, zwei Nietlöcher befinden sich auf jeder Seite seines Bleches. Im Innern sind deutlich Finnenschläge erkennbar; das Blech war wohl wieder nach außen gebogen, ein Nietloch scheint im Ansatz erhalten. Woytowitsch 1978 (s.o. Anm. 21) 40: "Die Kugel ist aus zwei übereinander geschobenen Halbkugeln zusammengesetzt." Bislang schien die Technik

genietete Hals seinerseits vernietet. Er war auch nach unten hin mit einem Gegenstand vernietet. Die heute mit dem Kugelkopf ausgestellte Schale kann mangels Nietspuren nicht mit ihm verbunden werden.[23] Hände und Kugelkopf können nicht zusammen mit den Aschenurnen[24] gesehen werden, da deren M-förmige Henkel und mit Griffen verzierte Deckel eine Kombination mit ihnen verbieten. Ein ähnlicher Kugelkopf befindet sich in der Sammlung Bloch-Diener in Bern in sicher antiker Zusammenstellung mit einem doppelkonischen henkellosen Gefäß; an Deckel und Gefäßkörper haben sich Geweberreste erhalten.[25] Zwei weitere solche Köpfe sind aus Vulci bekannt, wohl jeweils in Verbindung mit Aschenurnen.[26]

Wie von Scichilone beschrieben, haben sich an der rechten Hand des einen Vulcenter Paares Geweberreste erhalten,[27] am anderen Händepaar[28] lassen sich wohl 9 leicht schräg über den Puls geführte Reihen von gravierten Ornamenten erkennen: Es sind sog. phönizische Palmetten und Flechtbänder, getrennt durch eine Kordelzier, wie sie in ähnlicher Weise auf einem Armschmuck aus Vetulonia zu sehen sind.[29] Vielleicht wurden Büsten aus den Bronzeteilen und Holz und Stoff zusammengestellt, wie es die ganz aus Bronzeblech gefertigte Büste aus Marsiliana d'Albegna nahelegt.[30] Eine Zugehörigkeit der Bronzen zu Kanopen wie sie für Chiusi typisch[31] und auch für Vulci belegt sind, scheint nicht vorzuliegen.[32] Vielmehr dürfte es im 1. Viertel des 7. Jhs. v.Chr. in Vulci zur Darstellung des Toten, losgelöst von seiner Aschenurne, gekommen sein. Das durch *tombaroli* ausgenommene Grab in Vulci, bei dem angeblich auf einem Bronze-

---

des Lötens erst für die 2. Hälfte des 6. Jhs. v. Chr. belegt: Haynes (s.o. Anm. 18) 6, Anm. 34. Woytowitsch lagen wohl bei seiner Beschreibung der Auffindungssituation über die publizierten Angaben hinausgehende Informationen vor; vgl. jetzt dazu infra Anm. 9.

23 Inv. 84876: H ca. 3.0 cm; Dm 16.2 cm; BlechSt 0.1 cm; hellgrüne fleckige Patina, in der Mitte glänzend braun; kleinere Fehlstellen im Rand. Scichilone 1967 (s.o. Anm. 8) führt die Schale gesondert als Nr. 33 auf. Die "tre lacune minori ... all'interno" sind nur oberflächliche Bestoßungen und keine Nietlöcher. Lotspuren sind nicht erkennbar. Ich danke T. Porzi (Soprintendenza per l'Etruria Meridionale) für seine Hilfe.

24 Scichilone (s.o. Anm. 8) Nrr. 25-26; Moretti (s.o. Anm. 8) 32, Nr. 1, Abb. 20; Moretti (s.o. Anm. 7) Abb. 56; für die bei Haynes (s.o. Anm. 18) 74 vorgetragene Meinung, daß die Hände dazu dienten, "to anthropomorphize the ash-container," gibt es keine diese stützenden Grabungsbefunde.

25 H. Jucker, in Hornbostel (s.o. Anm. 14) Nr. 12. Die Kanopen wurden in Tücher eingehüllt, vgl. R. D. Gempeler, *Die Etruskischen Kanopen. Herstellung, Typologie, Entwicklungsgeschichte* (Einsiedeln, ca. 1974) 240.

26 G. Colonna, in *La civiltà arcaica di Vulci e la sua espansione: Atti X Convegno di studi etruschi e italici, Grosseto–Roselle–Vulci 1975* (Firenze 1977) 200, Anm. 42, Nr. 2 (scavi di Vulci, soc. Hercle); Nr. 3, Taf. 40b (ehem. Slg. Berman, Rom).

27 S.o. Anm. 7 und 8.

28 S.o. Anm. 6 und 8.

29 M. Cristofani und M. Martelli (Hrsg.), *L'oro degli Etruschi* (Novara 1983) Nr. 96, zum Flechtband ebend. Nr. 95.

30 Cristofani 1984 (s.o. Anm. 1) Nr. 109. Zu weiteren, stärker naturalistischen Resten eines "bustum-sepulcrum", A. Minto, *Marsiliana d'Albegna* (Firenze 1921) 119-21, 211. – Scichilone (s.o. Anm. 8) Nr. 35 schließt grundsätzlich eine praktische Funktion wie z.B. als "manici di ventaglio" nicht aus; vgl. auch das Simpulum aus Populonia, Tomba dei Flabelli mit einer rechten Hand als Griffattasche (S. Bruni, in *Etrusker in der Toskana* [Ausstellungskat., Hamburg 1987] 241, Nr. 38). Zu römischen Feldzeichen in Form von Händen vgl. Dohrn (s.o. Anm.2); *EAA* IV (1961) 163-65 s.v. *insignia militaria* (G. Forni); v. Gonzenbach (s.o. Amn.1) 5-21; A. Leibundgut, *Die römischen Bronzen der Schweiz* 3 (Mainz 1980) Nr. 140; A. Kaufmann-Heinimann, *Die römischen Bronzen der Schweiz* 5 (Mainz 1994) zu Nr. 369. Vielleicht gehören in den Zusammenhang eines möglichen "bustum" auch die beiden Bronzeblechstreifen mit Frauenfriesen aus der Tomba del carro di bronzo (Scichilone (s.o. Anm. 8) Nrr. 37-38), die in gleicher Stärke wie die Pulse der Hände zusammengebogen sind.

31 Gempeler (s.o. Anm.25) 183-84 Armstumpfurnen; 185-86, 188 Urnen mit Henkeln, in die plastisch gebildete Arme mit gestikulierenden Händen gesteckt werden konnten. Zu den Terrakottaarmen: L. Milani, *MusItal* 1 (1885) 316-17, 331-39 (A γ. κ. λ. B σ. τ. ω).

32 Zu dem Kanopus aus Vulci: F. Buranelli, *ArchCl* 43 (1991) 863-71.

thron vom Typ Barberini — wohl dem Exemplar in Paris[33] — eine "colonna di nenfro" stand und auf dieser ein noch unpublizierter mit Goldblech überzogener Holzkopf,[34] der sich im Museo Civico von Mailand befindet, zeigt die nächste Stufe auf dem Weg zur figürlichen Großplastik in Etrurien.

Via Castiglione del Lago, 14, 00191 Roma

Addendum

Zwischenzeitlich konnte ich im Rahmen der Katalogisierungsarbeiten für die Bronzen der Sammlung Castellani im Museo di Villa Giulia eine rechte Hand entdecken (Abb. 7-8); sie dürfte das von v. Gonzenbach erwähnte Exemplar sein.[35] Laut Angabe im Inventar stammt es aus "Norcia" (H 30,0 cm; Inv. 51243). Die Hand ist seit Ende des Jahres 1999 in der Neuaufstellung der Sammlung Castellani wieder ausgestellt.

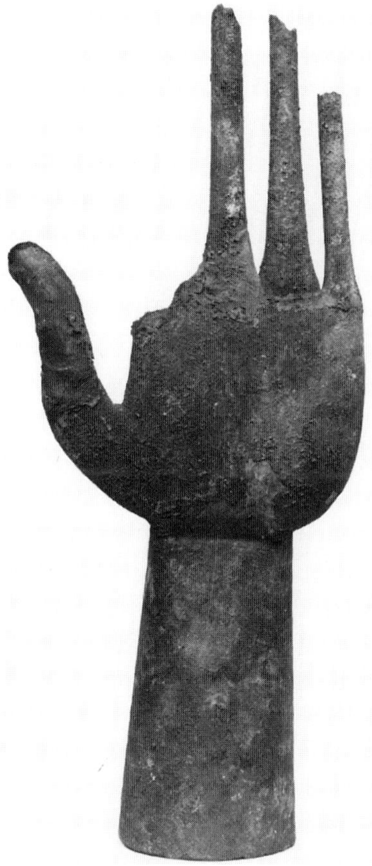

Abb. 7. Hand aus Norcia. Bronze, H 30,0 cm. Rom, Museo di Villa Giulia. (Foto: DAI Rom Inst. Neg. 99.182)

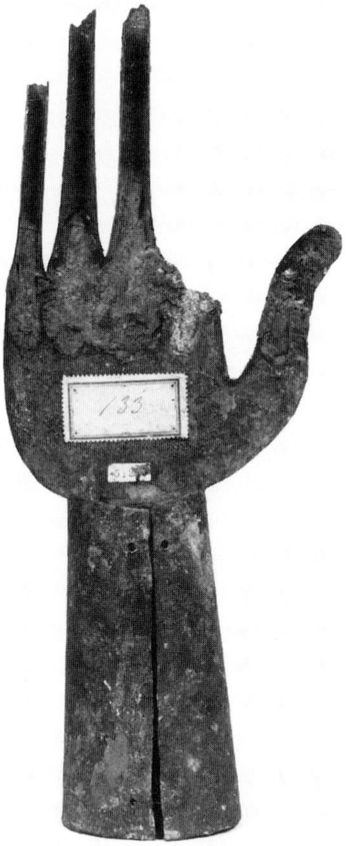

Abb. 8. Hand (Rückseite Abb. 7.) Rom, Museo di Villa Giulia. (Foto: DAI Rom Inst. Neg. 99.183)

33 F. Jurgeit, *RömMitt* 97 (1990) 4, 10-13, Taf. 8; *Die Etrusker und Europa* (Ausstellungskat., Berlin 1992) Nr. 95.

34 G. Tagliaferri und L. Rupi Paci, *Tombaroli si nasce* (Firenze 1992) 26-27; der lebensgroße Kopf wurde 1987 erworben, jetzt abgebildet bei F. Prayon, *Die Anfänge großformatiger Plastik in Etrurien* in *Archäologische Untersuchungen zu den Beziehungen zwischen Altitalien und der Zone nordwärts der Alpen während der frühen Eisenzeit Alteuropas (Regensburger Beiträge zur Prähistorischen Archäologie* 4 [1998]) 205-6 Abb. 14. – Sechs 1963 in Vulci gefundene, zum Einstiften hergerichtete elfenbeinerne Fingerkuppen weisen auf eine vergleichbare Darstellungsweise (M. T. Falconi Amorelli, *StEtr* 37 [1969] 202-11, Nr. 5, Abb. 11, Taf. 39: Grab C).

35 S.o. Anm. 1.

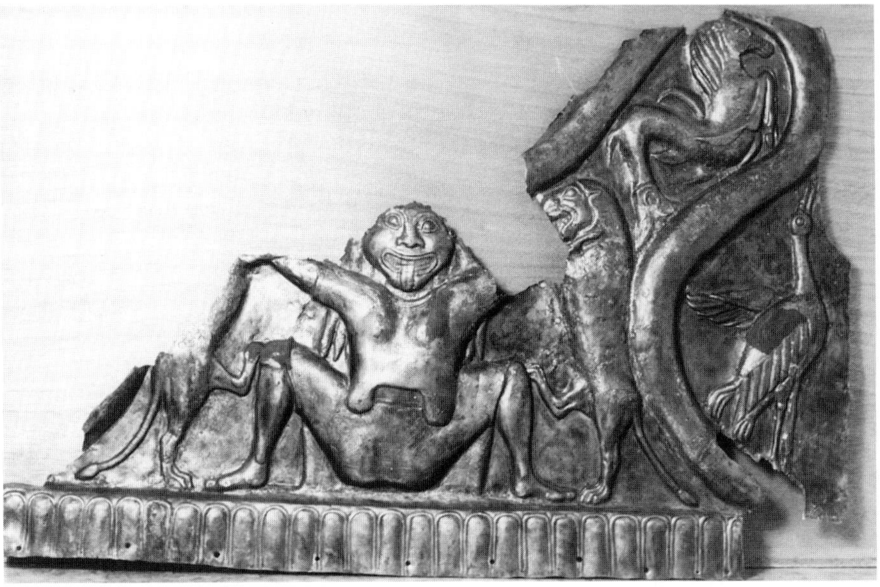

Fig. 1. Bronze gorgon plaque. Munich, Staatliche Antikensammlungen und Glyptothek. (Photo: author, 1971)

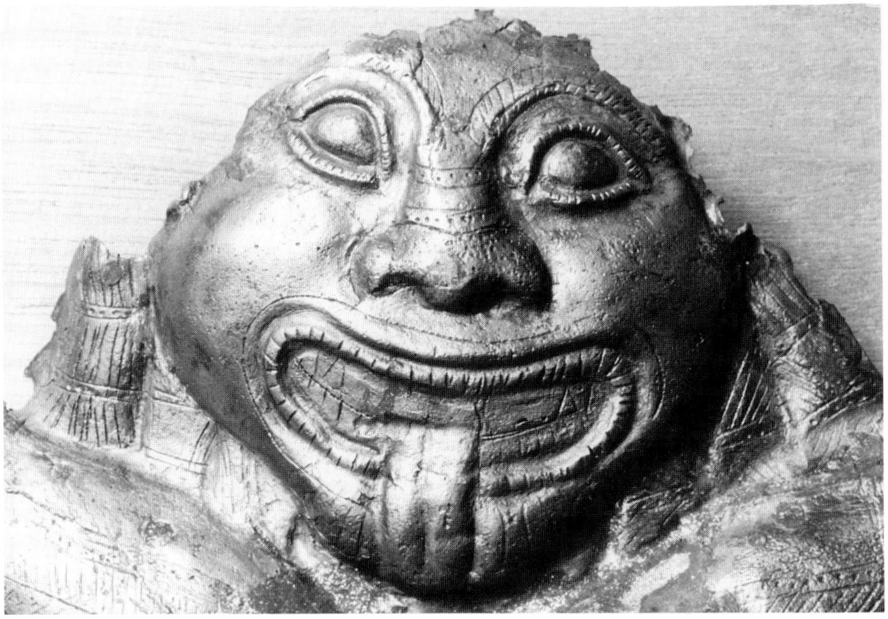

Fig. 1a. Bronze gorgon plaque (detail). Munich, Staatliche Antikensammlungen und Glyptothek. (Photo: author, 1971)

The Etruscan bronze repoussé reliefs at Perugia and their 19th- and 20th-c. companions

Jerome M. Eisenberg

A group of Etruscan repoussé bronze reliefs of the late 6th c. B.C. was found at Castello San Mariano near Perugia in 1812. They were promptly published by G. B. Vermiglioli, *Saggio di bronzi etruschi trovati nell'agro Perugina* (Perugia 1813) and are now in the Museo Archeologico Nazionale dell'Umbria at Perugia. A second group, said to be from the same find, was published several years later by F. Inghirami in *Monumenti etruschi o di etrusco nome* 3 (Fiesole 1825). This new group had already been divided and sold in 1820 in Rome to two dealers, L. Vescovali and J. Millingen, then acquired by a third dealer, E. Dodwell, who sold it to King Ludwig I of Bavaria. The reliefs are now in the James Loeb Collection of the Staatliche Antikensammlungen und Glyptothek in Munich. I was kindly given the opportunity to examine them in the museum laboratory in 1971. I also viewed the reliefs at Perugia in 1971, but was not able to study them out of the vitrines.

I will attempt to demonstrate that most, if not all, of the larger repoussé reliefs in Munich from this second group were created in the second decade of the 19th c., probably soon after the appearance in 1813 of the publication by Vermiglioli. Due to restrictions of space (the paper presented at the Congress was accompanied by 61 illustrations), I have limited my observations here to a few of the more obvious errors by the forger. In this I apply my principles of the "aesthetics of the forger ("The stylistic criteria in the forgery of ancient art," AIA 72nd Meeting, Jan. 1970, abstract in *AJA* 75 [1971] 200; *Minerva* 3 [May/June 1992] 10-15). The chief premise is that a forger commits a number of basic errors in the creation of a forgery that ancient artists would not ordinarily make. Some mistakes may be committed by an unskilled ancient artist or apprentice but normally his lack of skill is reflected in the overall quality of the work. The ancient artist would not deliberately make any of the basic errors I shall list because of his intuitive dislike of stylistic principles foreign to his own culture. Basic errors include misunderstanding the harmony in ancient design, introducing traces of the personal style of the forger, inability to imitate consistently the techniques used by the ancient artist, and copying (often in mirror image) of similar objects. Several of the Munich bronze reliefs exhibit a number of these errors, as well as a disregard for the effect of age/corrosion on ancient surfaces, the surfaces being concealed under artificial patina.

The gorgon

For more than 150 years the bronze gorgon plaque in Munich appeared to be a relatively complete relief. In 1971, after old restorations were removed, it presented a different appearance (fig. 1). The forger had created what appeared to be a genuine but restored antiquity, a common ruse. The surface of the plaque is acid-etched, with rills and depressions all over the surface, especially at the bottom. The drilled holes, made to imitate damage, had been partially masked with an artificial patina. The edges are knife-sharp.

Nor is this an ancient gorgon. Protruding fangs of the gorgon head, essential for its apotropaic effect, are evident in Etruscan terracotta gorgon heads of the late 6th c. B.C. and in Greek bronze reliefs of the same period. On the Greek reliefs, the 4 incised fangs are fully developed and separated from one another, since they are not subject to breaking off as in the terracottas. On the Munich bronze plaque, however, the fangs are indicated by bisected quadrangles above the lower row of teeth (fig. 1). Compare this gorgon to one on the Monteleone chariot in New York (fig. 11): it also has bisected quadrangles as fangs, and in 1968 and 1979 I demonstrated it to be a forgery ("On the authenticity of the 'Etruscan' bronze chariot from Monteleone," AIA 91st Meeting, Jan. 1990, abstract in *AJA* 94 [1990] 342; see also below).

The peculiar, deeply suspended, pendulous breasts with their incised panther heads appear to be a misinterpretation of an animal skin garment hanging over the ancient back sections of

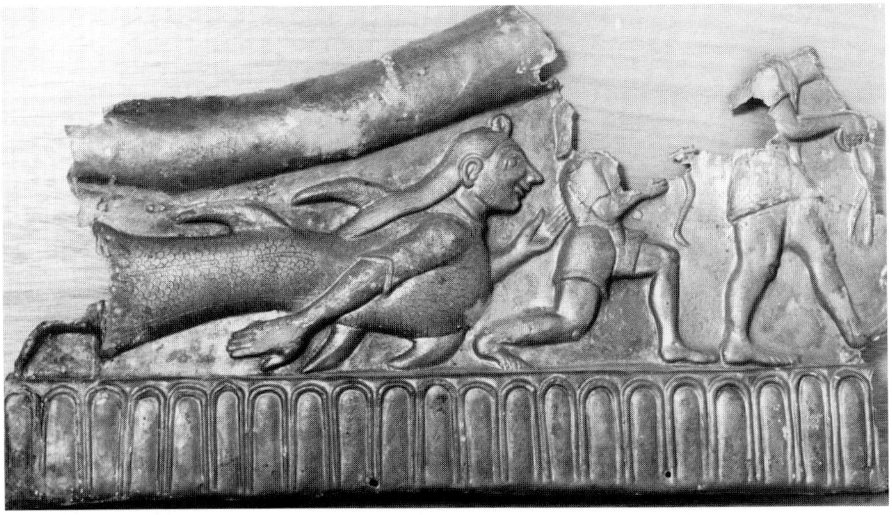

Fig. 2. Bronze chariot section with hunters and merman (detail). Munich, Staatliche Antikensammlungen und Glyptothek. (Photo: author, 1971)

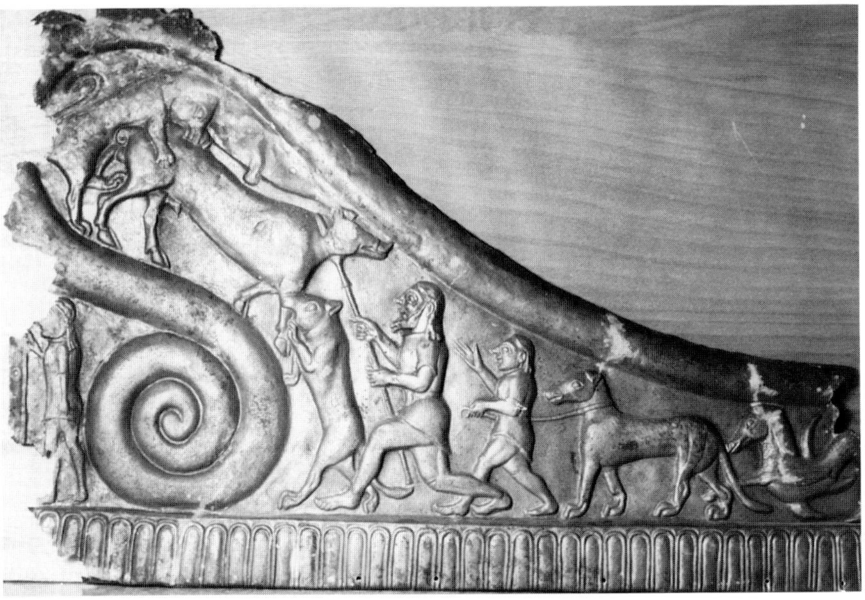

Fig. 3. Bronze chariot section with hunters and merman (detail). Munich, Staatliche Antikensammlungen und Glyptothek. (Photo: author, 1971)

two bronze korai in Munich. (These two korai *are* genuine, as can be seen by the advanced oxidation of the bronze.)

The hunters and the merman

A bronze chariot section (figs. 2-3) in Munich depicting a unique hunting scene and a merman is clearly derived from the volute design of an ancient relief section in Perugia and was intended to complete the Perugia panel. The bearded merman (fig. 2) swimming oddly behind the 4 human figures is based upon two fragments of flying or swimming females in Perugia but the image is reversed. This 'Disneyesque' figure has several aberrant stylistic features, including large and overly realistic hands, exaggerated thumbs, large eyes, exaggerated eyebrows, large fully exposed ears, and disconnected, wig-like hair — all hallmarks of a forgery. The figures, as is typical of the Munich forgeries, are hammered from the back and then engraved with myriad minute details such as the stippled beard, that show off the abilities of the forger but are not in keeping with authentic Etruscan bronzes.

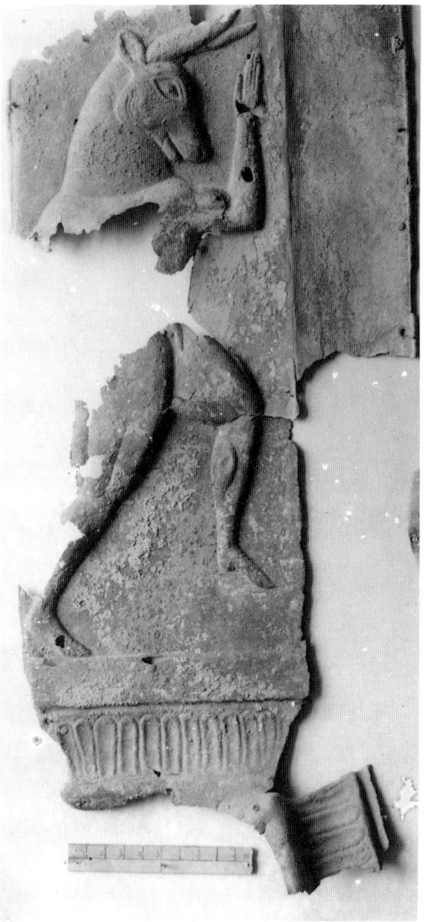

Fig. 4. Etruscan bronze minotaur plaque. Perugia, Museo Archeologico Nazionale dell'Umbria. (Photo: courtesy DAI-Rome, neg. 581)

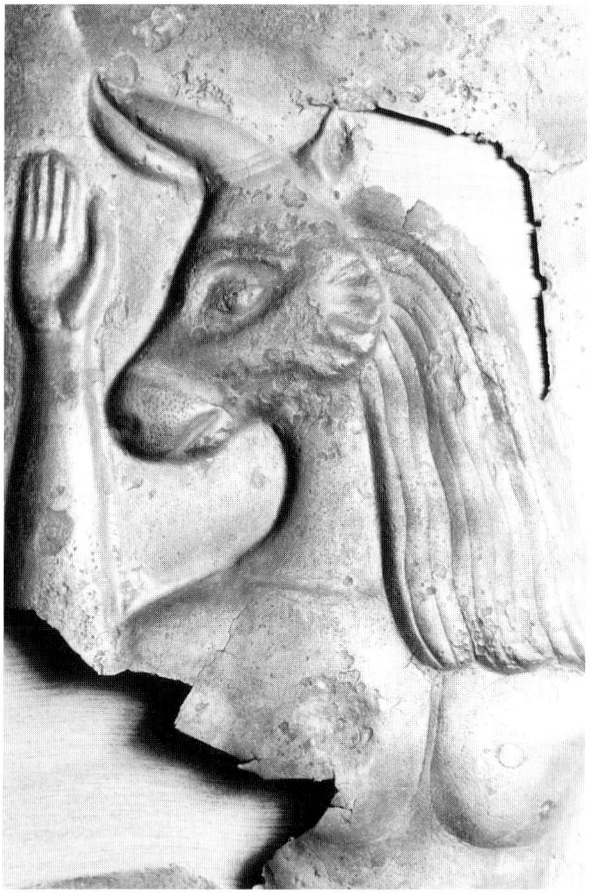

Fig. 5. Bronze minotaur plaque (detail). Munich, Staatliche Antikensammlungen und Glyptothek. (Photo: author, 1971)

On the same plaque the boar being attacked simultaneously by two animals and by a hunter who spears the boar right through the neck (fig. 3), can only be the product of the creative mind of the forger. Equally inappropriate is the man leading an animal by a leash into this hunting scene. Note the giant hands and prominent thumbs. The men also have large eyes, exaggerated eyebrows, large fully exposed ears, and disconnected wig-like hair. The overlapping legs of the hunter and the attacking animal, both raised off the ground, and the other leg of the hunter, which overlaps the leg of the man with the animal on a leash, creating a forward plane, do not conform to Etruscan artistic concepts. The attacking animals are on tiptoe, with their paws elevated. The water-bound hippocamp follows this land scene merely to fill the narrow space, for it has no obvious connection to the rest of the scene — an example of the forger's *horror vacui*.

The minotaur

The genuine Etruscan minotaur on a bronze plaque in Perugia (fig. 4) is typical of the Archaic period; it is lively and has small hands and feet. The plaque has irregular, jagged breaks. The Munich minotaur (fig. 5), a direct elaboration of the Perugia minotaur but in mirror image, sports a full head of human hair, a human neck, a very realistic athlete's body, and realistic hands with over-sized thumbs. The dewlap of the bull has been misinterpreted and turned into an ear-like formation, rather than into the folds of flesh, as clearly seen on another plaque in Perugia which shows a bull being attacked by a panther. The broken areas have been cut away, leaving angular edges, and show extensive filing on the bottom part of the plaque.

The man holding two lions

Another Munich bronze plaque (fig. 6) depicts a man holding two lions on a leash, a scene

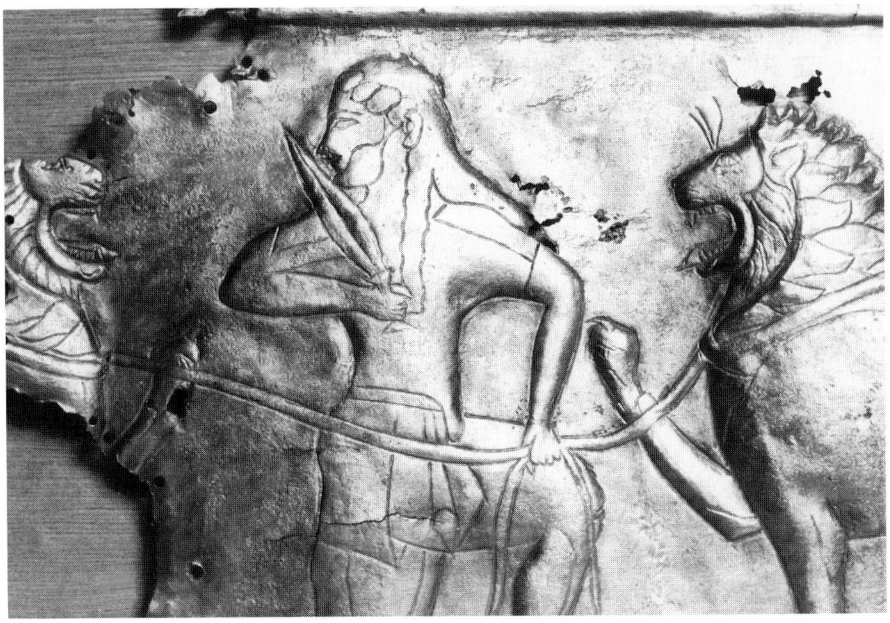

Fig. 6. Bronze plaque with man holding two lions on leashes. Munich, Staatliche Antikensammlungen und Glyptothek. (Photo: author, 1971)

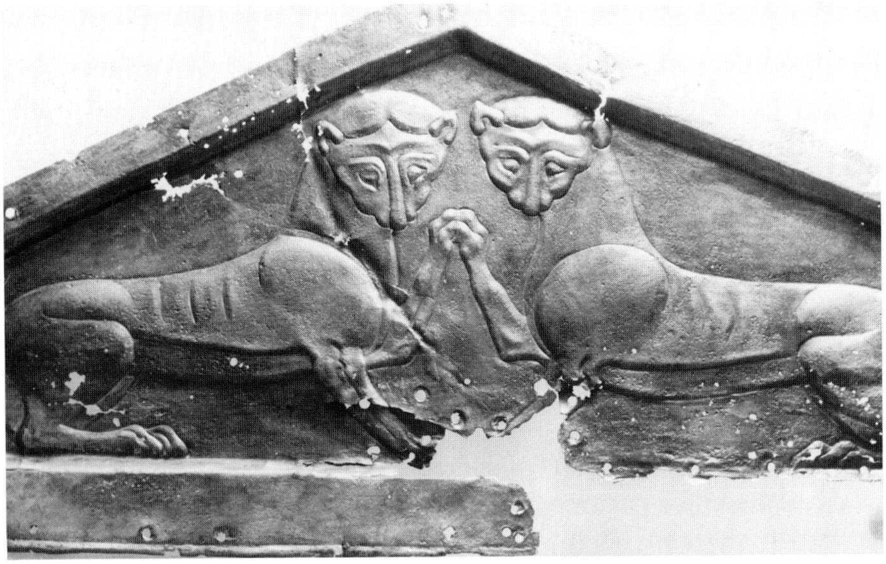

Fig. 7. Bronze gable-shaped plaque with two panthers (detail). Munich, Staatliche Antikensammlungen und Glyptothek. (Photo: author, 1971)

that seems more suited for a circus. The composition may have been derived from the depiction on one of the tripods of a running goddess between two lions. The strange hair styles and the curiously drawn dagger are grave stylistic errors, but even more incriminating are the damaged areas which were created by connecting a series of drilled holes. The surface is etched with rills and round shallow depressions. As usual, the incised lines are sharp with no signs of wear or oxidation. The fractures in the metal were cut with a sharp instrument.

The gable-shaped plaque with two panthers

The bronze gable-shaped plaque, shown here after conservation (fig. 7), is typical of most of the Munich plaques, particularly in the way in which the forger has attempted to emulate wear and corrosion on the surface. By placing a light behind the plaque, I was able to emphasize the effect created by the drilling. The damage consists primarily of a large number of clean-

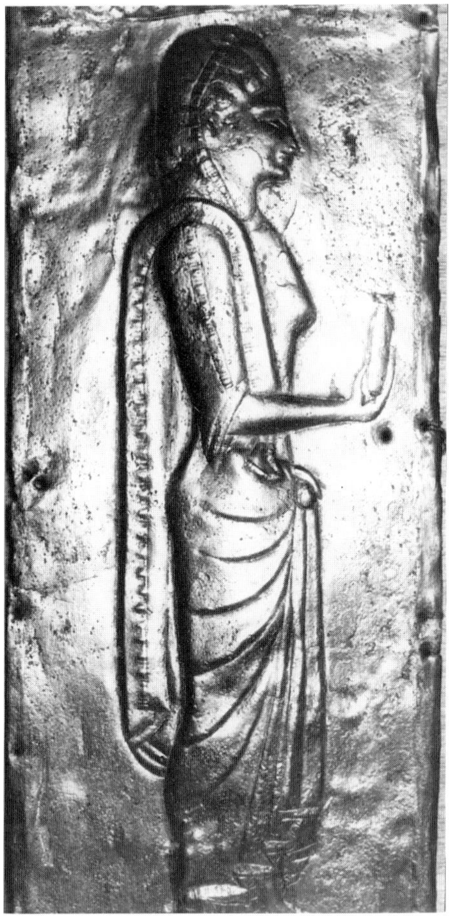

Fig. 8. Bronze plaque with veiled woman (detail). Munich, Staatliche Antikensammlungen und Glyptothek. (Photo: author, 1971)

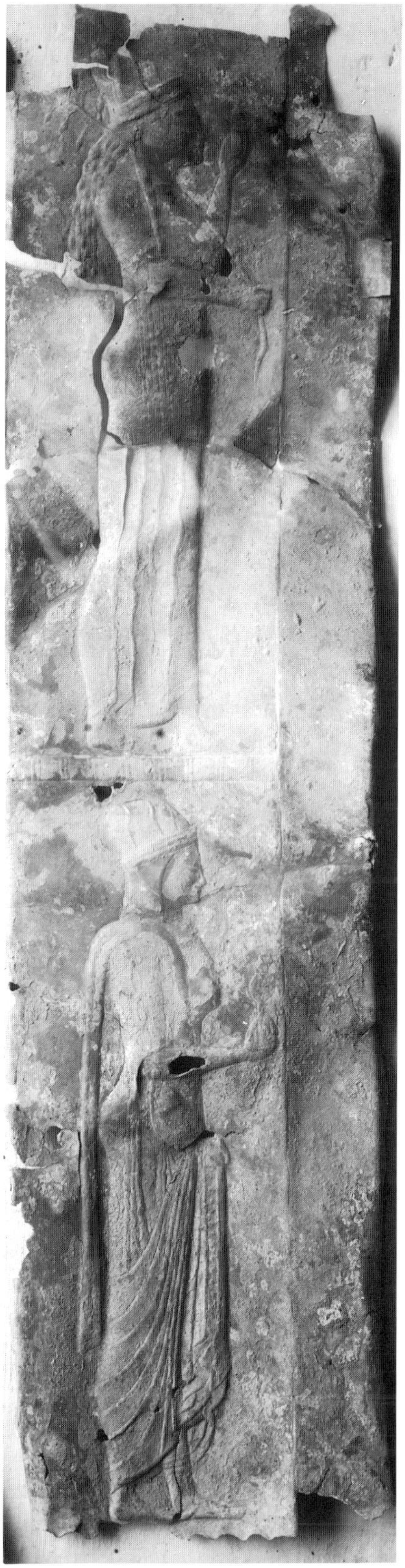

Fig. 9. Etruscan bronze plaque with two women. Perugia, Museo Archeologico Nazionale dell'Umbria. (Photo: courtesy DAI-Rome, neg. 585)

ly drilled holes of varying sizes. The smaller holes were pierced cleanly; the larger holes were drilled from the back and the excess metal filed down. In one hole the fragment of the broken metal is still attached. Some of the holes were joined to create broken areas. Other sections were clipped off. The resulting sharp edges of the drilling were then masked by artificial patination placed on the plaque by the forger, but were revealed when the bronzes were cleaned. The whole surface is covered with shallow circular depressions with holes and rills no doubt created by acid. The panthers themselves vary significantly in style. Compared to a typical ancient panther from Perugia or on one of the Munich tripods, they have exaggerated triangular faces with large brows (straight on one, curved on the other) and disconnected ears, not unlike the panther mask on the central panel of the Monteleone chariot forgery described below (cf. fig. 11).

The veiled woman

The golden bronze plaque in Munich with the veiled woman holding an alabastron (fig. 8) is a crude imitation of the shallow Perugia plaque with two draped women.

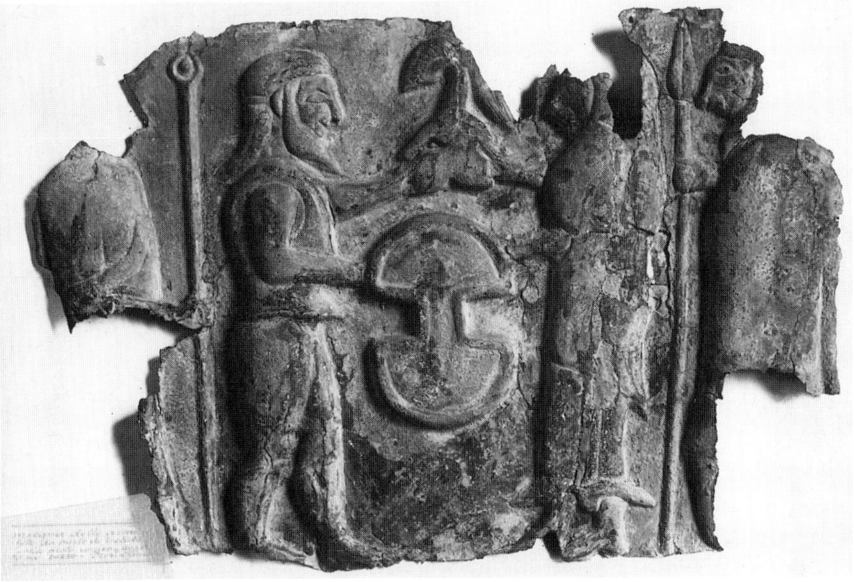

Fig. 10. Etruscan bronze plaque with warrior and woman. Florence, Museo Archeologico Nazionale 84851. (Photo: courtesy Soprintendenza alle antichità d'Etruria)

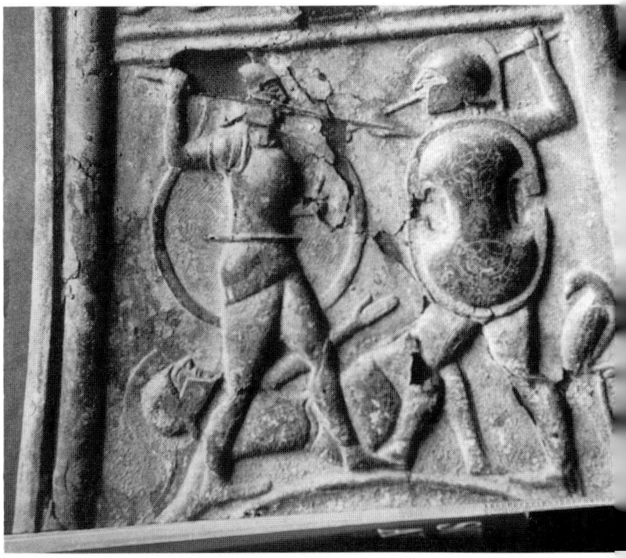

Fig. 12. Etruscan bronze Loeb tripod (detail). Munich, Staatliche Antikensammlungen und Glyptothek. (Photo: author, 1971)

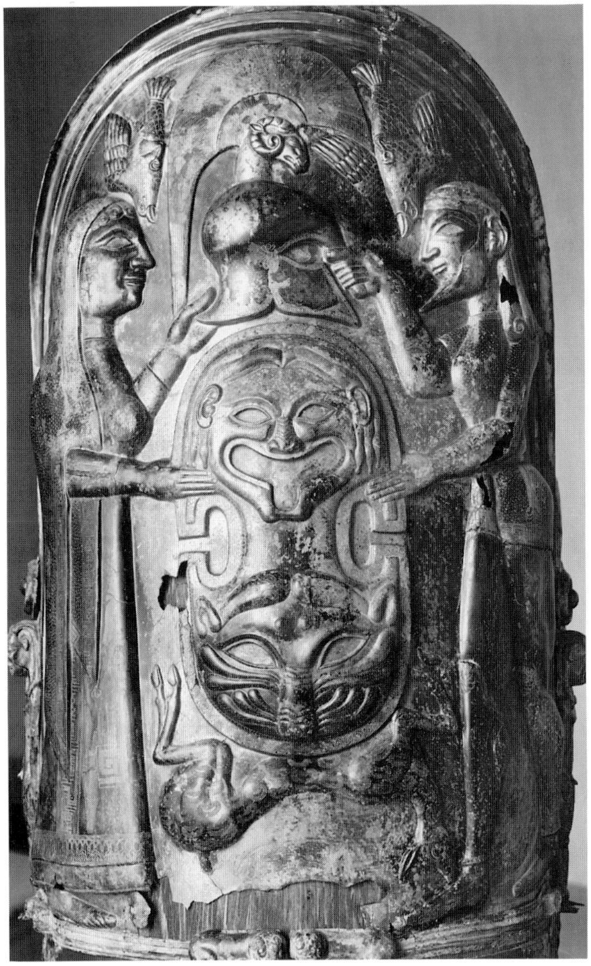

Fig. 11. Monteleone bronze chariot, central panel. New York, The Metropolitan Museum of Art, Rogers Fund, 1903, 03.23.1. (Photo: courtesy Museum)

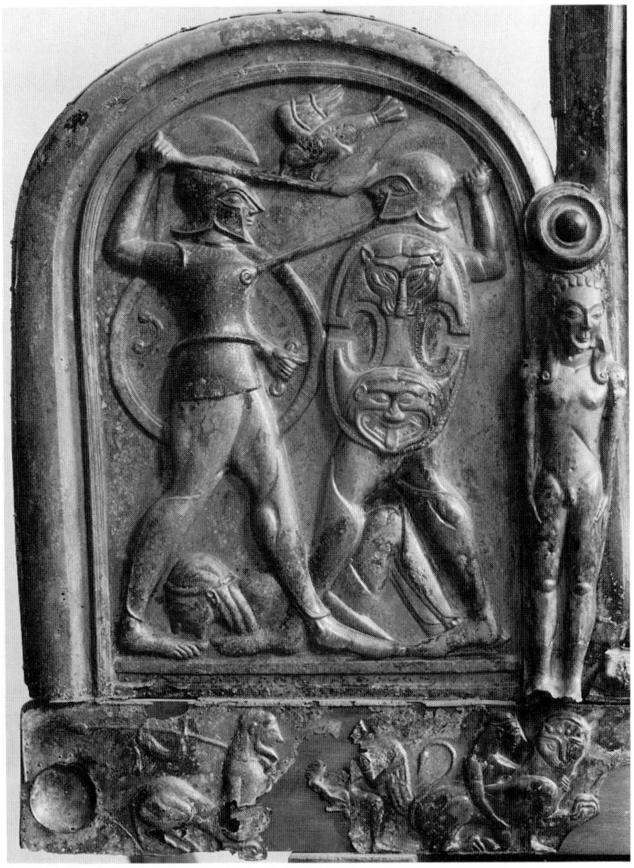

Fig. 13. Monteleone bronze chariot, left panel. New York, The Metropolitan Museum of Art, Rogers Fund, 1903, 03.23.1. (Photo: courtesy Museum)

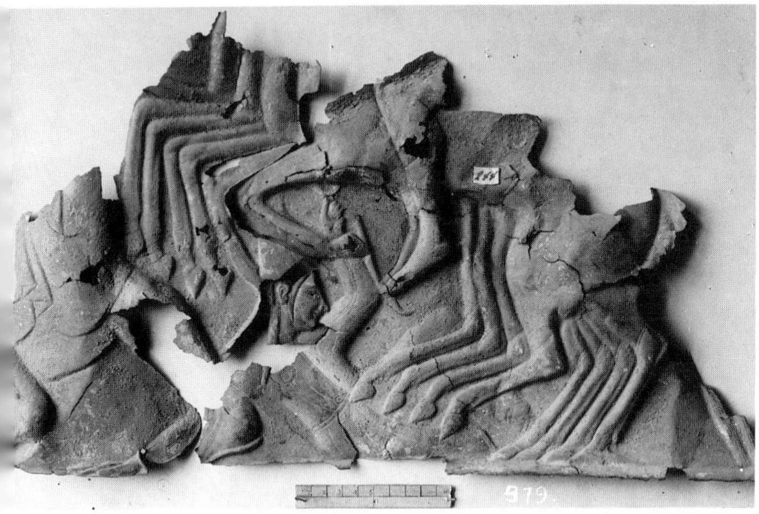

Fig. 14. Etruscan bronze relief with battle scene. Perugia, Museo Archeologico Nazionale dell'Umbria. (Photo: courtesy DAI-Rome neg. 579)

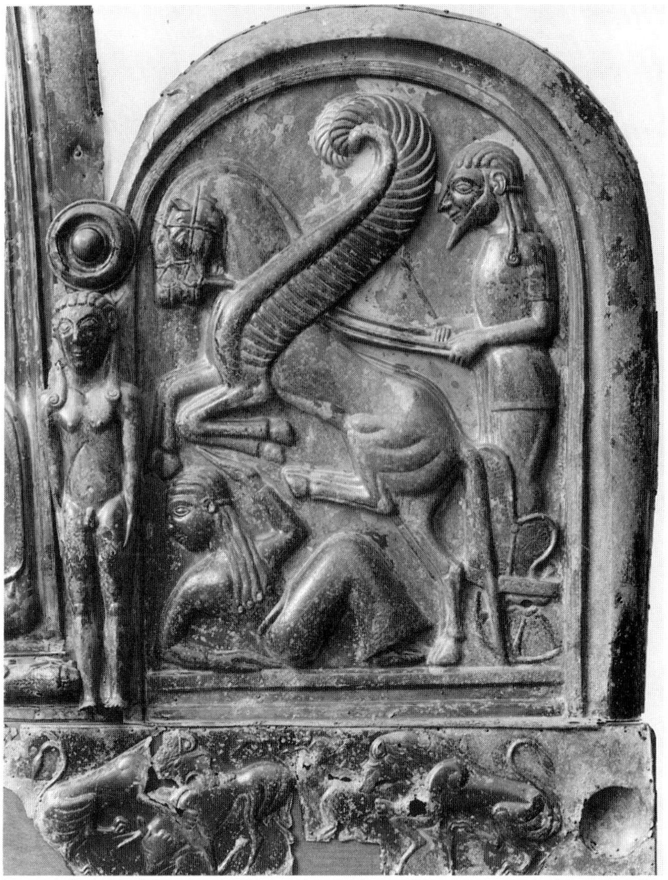

Fig. 15. Monteleone bronze chariot, right panel. New York, The Metropolitan Museum of Art, Rogers Fund, 1903, 03.23.1. (Photo: courtesy Museum)

The latter (fig. 9, below) wears a similar scarf-like fold of garment; the other (fig. 9, above) holds an alabastron-like flower. The elaborate Perugia headdresses have been replaced by a veil and the garment has been greatly simplified. The flower held by the woman at the top has been misinterpreted as an alabastron: the forger omitted the thumb and changed two fingers into a single elongated one. The surface is heavily acid-etched and has tiny pits apparently created by a punch; its edges are also quite sharp.

The candelabrum plaques

The Herakles and Hera bronze candelabrum plaques in Munich were apparently made to match the Perugia plaque with a veiled woman. These golden bronze reliefs were worked in unusually high relief — 1 cm for Herakles, 1.2 cm for Hera — compared to the much shallower Perugia plaque. Their thickness is 1 mm, compared to the average of 0.5 mm for the other Munich plaques. They are sharply cut and lack any signs of wear. The surfaces are acid-etched and pitted, with small rills and drilled holes.

The Monteleone chariot

There is an interesting connection between ancient Etruscan reliefs and their 19th- and early 20th-c. companions. A large bronze chariot, supposedly found at Monteleone, Italy, in 1903, and acquired by the Metropolitan Museum of Art, was demonstrated by the author, in a paper read at the Archaeological Institute of America Annual Meeting in 1989 (cited above), to be a forgery. It is a pastiche of small genuine reliefs of the late 6th c. B.C. (bottom row of reliefs, figs. 13 and 15) which are similar to some of the Perugia bronzes. Above are three large chariot panels (figs. 11, 13, and 15) which, except for part of the rims, are entirely of early 20th-c. manufacture. The forged panels are based upon a variety of ancient sources.

An ancient Etruscan bronze plaque in Florence (fig. 10) was the main source for the central panel of the Monteleone chariot, depicting a woman and a warrior holding a Boeotian shield (fig. 11). A panel on one of the three genuine bronze Munich tripods (fig. 12), said to have been found in the area of Perugia, probably served as the principal inspiration for the left panel (fig. 13); it shows two warriors battling and a fallen warrior below. A genuine Etruscan relief (fig. 14) in Perugia and the enigmatic Perugia silver plaque in the British Museum of the horsemen over the fallen Amazon served as the principal sources for the right panel (fig. 15) of the chariot.

It is my conviction that removing these 19th- and 20th-c. creations from the Etruscan repertoire will help to clarify some problems in attributing Etruscan bronze workshops, without resorting to the excuse of Greek influences to explain the many discrepancies. Unfortunately, it is difficult for many art-historians to deny some of the long-accepted icons of ancient art. A comprehensive monograph on the Perugia bronzes in Munich was published by U. Höckmann, *Die Bronzen aus dem Fürstengrab von Castel San Mariano* (Munich 1982). It illustrates and describes the bronzes from Perugia, as well as the Monteleone chariot, but it does not question the authenticity of any of the bronzes. It is hoped that this paper will lead to a re-examination of the Perugia bronzes in Munich.

153 East 57th Street, New York, NY 10022

Addendum

I have now published a version of this paper as "The Etruscan bronze reliefs from Perugia: their 19th century companions and 20th century relatives," in *Minerva* 12 (March-April 2001) 14-19, alongside my review, "The Etruscan masterworks at the Palazzo Grassi", an exhibition in which the bronze reliefs from both Munich and Perugia were shown and without questioning the authenticity of the former. In my review article I note that two plaques in Munich — the gable-shaped one with two panthers (fig. 7 above) and the Gorgon one (fig. 1 above) — are very like the west pediment of the early 6th-c. B.C. Temple of Artemis on Corfu. The Munich Gorgon is not unlike the Corfu Gorgon, especially in the long locks of hair, and the facing panthers differ only in that the forepaws are raised to meet one another on the Munich plaque. It seems very likely that the Corfu pediment was a primary source for the forger of the Munich plaques.

Forgeries of Etruscan engraved mirrors

Richard D. De Puma

Throughout their history, the Etruscans produced polished bronze (and sometimes silver) hand mirrors. From the end of the 6th c. B.C., large numbers of these mirrors were ornamented with engraved scenes depicting a wide variety of mythological and genre subjects.[1] The period of both highest quality and greatest quantity appears to have been the second half of the 4th c. B.C., but mirrors continued to be an important part of artistic production until *c.*100 B.C., by when the Etruscans had become part of the Roman state. More than 3,500 mirrors are extant; most of these were recovered during the 19th c., when about a thousand examples were recorded in the major corpus published by Eduard Gerhard in 4 volumes between 1840-67, then completed by A. Klügmann and G. Körte in 1897.[2] A century later, an international team of Etruscologists is attempting to publish definitively all known Etruscan mirrors. The *Corpus Speculorum Etruscorum (CSE)* presently consists of 20 fascicules representing more than 700 examples from collections in 10 countries.[3]

Unlike 19th-c. scholars of mirrors, who concentrated primarily on iconography, present researchers are considering many other aspects of mirrors ignored by earlier connoisseurs. For example, totally unengraved mirrors, mirror fragments, the decorative embellishments on the reflecting sides of mirrors, the evolution of mirror sections, discs, and tangs, and various types of handles are all now carefully studied.[4] Perhaps most significantly, modern scholars have incorporated a broad range of hard data, especially weights, measurements, and alloy analyses, into their studies of ancient mirrors.[5] The results have enormous potential for our better understanding of this important class of Etruscan objects.

The ongoing investigations by authors of the *CSE* have renewed interest in another major class of mirrors: forgeries.[6] There are 4 basic types of Etruscan mirror forgeries: 1) complete fakes

---

1 Useful surveys of Etruscan mirrors include J. D. Beazley, "The world of the Etruscan mirror," *JHS* 69 (1949) 1-17; N. T. de Grummond (ed.), *A guide to Etruscan mirrors* (Tallahassee, FL 1982); I. Jucker (ed.), *Italy of the Etruscans* (Mainz 1991) 96-117; R. De Puma, *Corpus Speculorum Etruscorum U.S.A.* 2: *Boston and Cambridge* (Ames, IA 1993) 13-20.

2 E. Gerhard, *Etruskische Spiegel* I-IV (Berlin 1840-67); A. Klügmann and G. Körte, *Etruskische Spiegel* V (Berlin 1897). Henceforth, *ES*.

3 In order of publication, these *CSE* fascicles now include H. Salskov Roberts, *Denmark* 1: *Copenhagen* (Odense 1981); G. Sassatelli, *Italia* 1.I-II: *Bologna* (Rome 1981); L. Bouke van der Meer, *Netherlands* (Leiden 1983); G. Heres, *DDR* 1-2 (East Berlin 1986-87) R. De Puma, *USA* 1: *Midwestern collections* (Ames 1987); U. Höckmann, *BRD* 1 (Munich 1987); R. Lambrechts, *Belgique* 1 (Rome 1987); D. Emmanuel-Rebuffat, *France* 1.I-II: *Paris* (Rome 1988, 1991); U. Liepmann, *BRD* 2 (Munich 1988); B. von Freytag gen. Löringhoff, *BRD* 3 (Munich 1990); J. Szilágyi and J. Bouzek, *Hongrie-Tchécoslovaquie* (Rome 1992); R. De Puma, *USA* 2: *Boston and Cambridge* (Ames 1993); R. V. Nicholls, *Great Britain* 2: *Cambridge* (Cambridge 1993); A. Frascarelli, *Italia* 2: *Perugia* (Rome 1995); G. Cateni, *Italia* 3: *Volterra* (Rome 1995) R. Lambrechts, *Vaticano* 1 (Rome 1995); G. Zimmer, *BRD* 4: *Berlin* (Munich 1995).

4 Major studies of these aspects include D. Rebuffat-Emmanuel, *Le miroir étrusque d'après la collection du Cabinet des Médailles* (Rome 1973); R. Lambrechts, *Les miroirs étrusques et prénestins des Musées royaux d'art et d'histoire à Bruxelles* (Brussels 1978); R. Adam, *Recherches sur les miroirs prénestins* (Paris 1980).

5 Many of the volumes listed supra nn.3 and 4 have lists of alloy analyses, often with comments on their significance. For more on this topic, see I. Wiman, *Malstria–Malena: metals and motifs in Etruscan mirror craft* (Göteborg 1990), and reviews by R. De Puma in *AJA* 98 (1994) 375-76 and L. Bonfante in *AnalRom* 25 (1996) 277-78.

6 For Etruscan mirror forgeries, see R. Noll, "Gefälschte etruskische Spiegel," *ÖJh* 29 (1935) 203-8; J. Szilágyi, "Echte und gefälschte etruskische Spiegel in Ungarn," *ActaAntHung* 10 (1962) 249-71; N. de Grummond, "Forgeries" in de Grummond (supra n.1) 61-68; U. Liepmann, "Des M. A. de la Chausse 'Romanum Museum' als Vorlage moderner Rückseitenbilder etruskischer Spiegel," *Niederdeutsche*

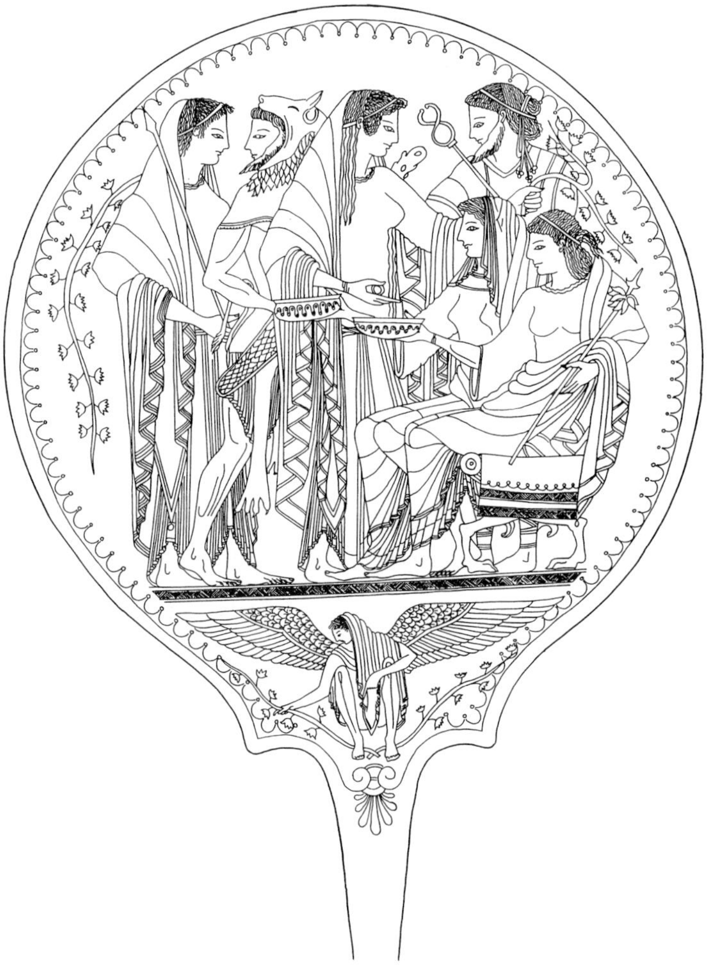

Fig. 1. Engraved mirror. Bronze, diam. 30.0 cm. Philadelphia, University of Pennsylvania Museum 52-35-3. (Drawing: author)

made to look genuine by imitating the style, design, techniques, and patina of ancient engraved bronze mirrors; 2) authentic Etruscan blank (or nearly blank) mirrors to which engravings have been added; 3) pastiches made by joining a number of authentic fragments, often from a variety of unrelated objects of different dates; 4) authentic Etruscan mirrors whose engravings have been extensively retouched or enhanced, sometimes significantly altering the original meaning of the subject. This paper briefly examines the first two of these types.

The complete fake is well represented by a large mirror, acquired on the New York market in 1955, in the University of Pennsylvania Museum, Philadelphia (fig. 1).[7] Today, more than 40 years later, it is hard to imagine that anyone was fooled by such an oddity. At the time, no less an authority than G. Mansuelli expressed uncertainty.[8] He based his opinion on a photograph of the object accompanied by a few measurements; I believe that, if he could have examined the object in person, he would have been convinced of its modern date. Its size is the most obvious problem. The mirror is 30 cm (almost a foot) in diameter. Being practical people, the

---

Beiträge zur Kunstgeschichte 26 (1987) 9-22; J. Szilágyi, "Falschungen etruskischer Kunstwerke," in H. Heres and M. Kunze (edd.), *Die Welt der Etrusker: int. kolloquium, 1988* (Berlin 1990) 393-96.

7 Inv. 52-35-3, ex Collector's Corner, New York, NY, diam. 30 cm; h. 45 cm; weight 1,003 g: de Grummond (supra n.1) 63-64, fig. 68 (photo reversed); R. De Puma, *CSE U.S.A. 4: Northeastern collections* (forthcoming) no. 35.

8 Letter of March 12, 1955, to F. F. Jones. The various criticisms made by Mansuelli are discussed by De Puma (supra n.7). Mansuelli mentioned the possibility that this was an authentic blank mirror to which modern engravings were added.

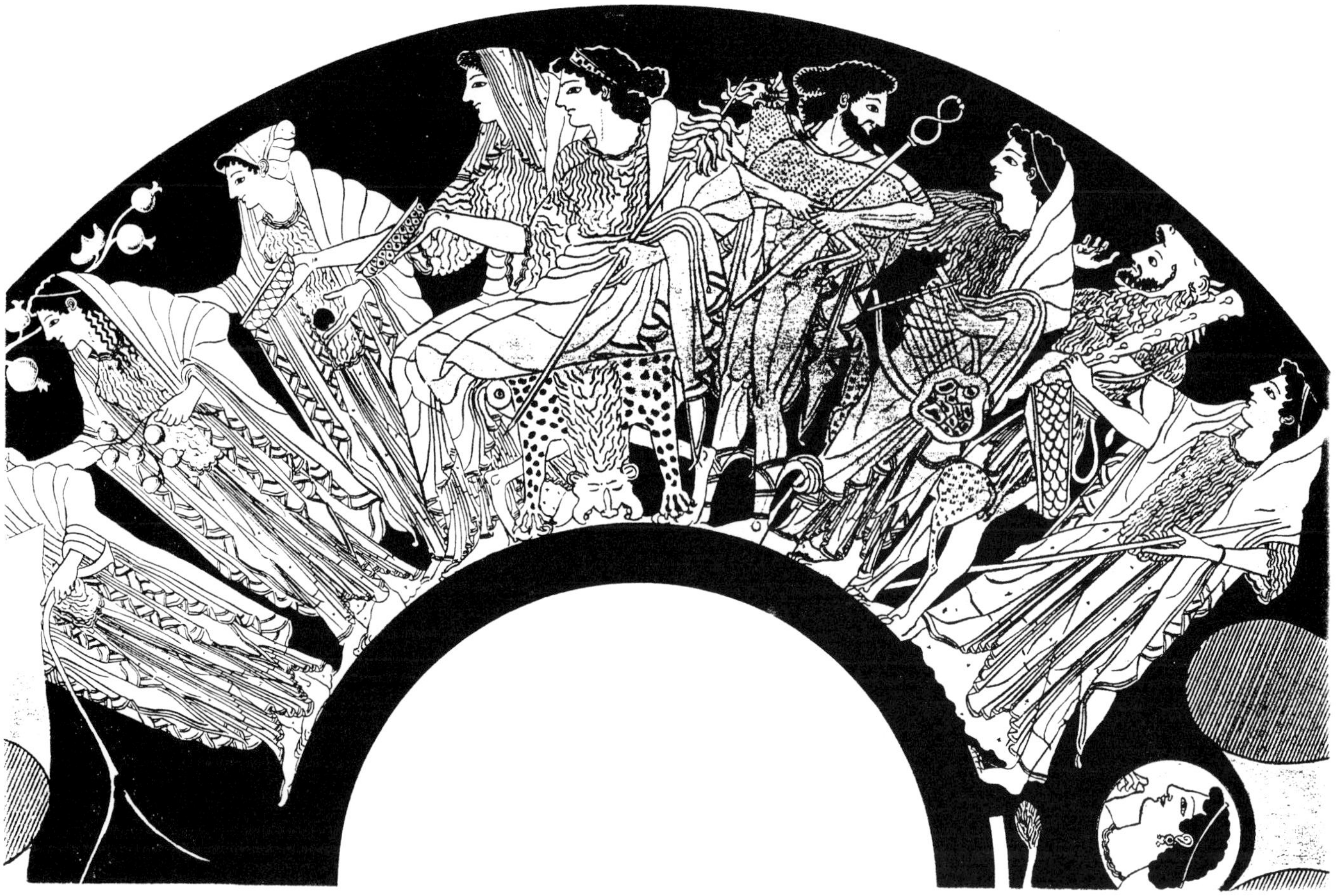

Fig. 2. Drawing of exterior of Attic cup by the Sosias Painter, Berlin F2278. (From *FR* III, pl. 123)

Etruscans never made such huge mirrors. Note also that this is a tang mirror: with its handle, it would be even larger and more unwieldy. The forger was not aware of the difference between tang mirrors and mirrors with disc and handle cast in one piece — two basic types produced by the Etruscans. Instead he mistakenly believed, as do many casual observers, that the tang functioned as a handle. This kind of problem appears on other dubious examples, like a mirror acquired in 1908 by the Museum of Fine Arts, Boston (fig. 8).[9] Here the tang is engraved, something not done on authentic mirrors because most of the tang would be invisible when inserted into a separately made handle of bone, wood, or ivory.[10]

In this necessarily brief overview, a detailed analysis of the specific formats, shapes, and sections of these problematic mirrors and how they diverge from authentic examples is not possible. Instead, let us focus on the engraved design on the Philadelphia mirror (fig. 1). This shows a crowded gathering of 6 figures from Greek myth surrounded by a unique border. If the Archaic figure style and gestures seem vaguely familiar, it is because they were copied from a famous red-figure cup in Berlin, the Sosias Painter kylix, of *c.*500 B.C., from Vulci (fig. 2).[11] Excellent drawings of this cup were published as early as 1829. But a later and more accessible

9 MFA 08.253, Bequest of Charles H. Parker, ex Alfred Greenough Collection, diam. 13.1 cm; h. 21.1 cm: De Puma 1993 (supra n.3) 49-50, no. 30 with earlier bibliography.

10 Several authentic mirrors survive with intact bone handles, e.g., Villa Giulia 2745, from an excavated context at Todi (P. Bruschetti in F. Roncalli [ed.], *Antichità dall'Umbria a Leningrado* [Milan 1990] 337-38, no. 5.4). Compare the unprovenanced examples, Copenhagen 581 (Salskov Roberts [supra n.3] no. 12) and Cambridge GR.10.1972 (Nicholls [supra n.3] no. 11).

11 Berlin F2278: *ARV*^{2} 21.1. The earliest publication is *MonInst* 1 (1829) pls. 24-25. Other early illustrations include, E. Gerhard, *Trinkschalen und Gefässe des königlichen Museums zu Berlin und anderer Sammlungen* (Berlin 1848-50) pls. 6-7; *AntDenk* 1 (1887) pls. 9-10. For recent color photos, see *Euphronios der Maler* (Milan 1991) 244-49, no. 59.

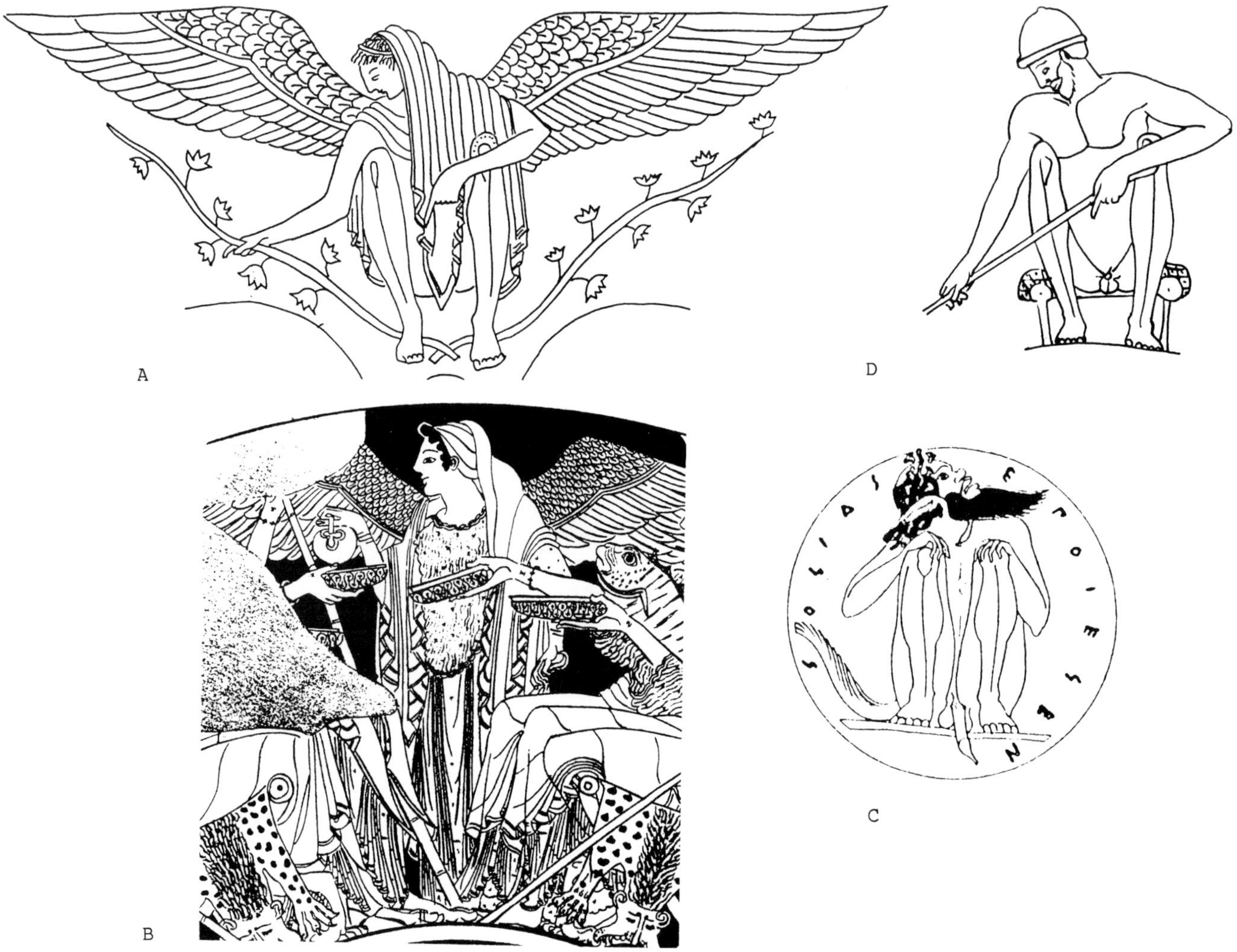

Fig. 3. a) Exergue figure from fig. 1 compared to possible sources; b) winged goddess on Sosias cup; c) satyr on Sosias standlet (*FR* III, p. 13, fig. 6); d) crouching man on the Foundry Painter cup (drawing based on *FR* III, pl. 135: author)

publication, like A. Furtwängler and K. Reichhold's 1932 folio, *Griechische Vasenmalerei*, is also a possible source of inspiration.[12] The forger excerpted some groups directly (e.g., the two seated goddesses) and reversed others (e.g., Herakles) to create a new composition more appropriate for the circular medallion of the mirror. He invented a border, mechanically produced scallops and tiny circles, unlike any known on authentic Etruscan mirrors. The unusual exergue figure (fig. 3a) may have been inspired by a synthesis of the wings on a goddess from the Sosias cup (fig. 3b) and by another vase, a stand signed by Sosias as potter and, significantly, used as the frontispiece to Furtwängler's text (fig. 3c).[13] This depicts a satyr, but his crouching position and, especially, the treatment of his legs are close to the distinctive figure created for the mirror. But perhaps the best candidate for the source of the forger's inspiration is the figure of a crouching man on the famous cup by the Foundry Painter (fig. 3d).[14] On both figures the position of heads, legs (including their distinctive markings), and left arms and hands is virtually identical. Furthermore, both figures squat, but only the Foundry Painter's man sits on

---

12 A. Furtwängler, K. Reichhold *et al.*, *Griechische Vasenmalerei* III (Munich 1932) pl. 123. Henceforth, *FR*.

13 *FR* III (supra n.12) 13, fig. 6: standlet of Sosian type, signed by Sosias as potter, *ARV*^{2} 21. The earliest publication of this painting is *GazArch* 4 (1878) pl. 25.2.

14 Berlin F2294, from Vulci: *ARV*^{2} 400.1. Earliest publication: Gerhard (supra n.11) pl. 9.2 and pls. 12-13. This cup also appears in *FR* III, pl. 135. For a related metalworker in similar position but facing right, see Athens, Acropolis 166 (*ARV* 92, 64), a fragmentary cup by the Euergides Painter.

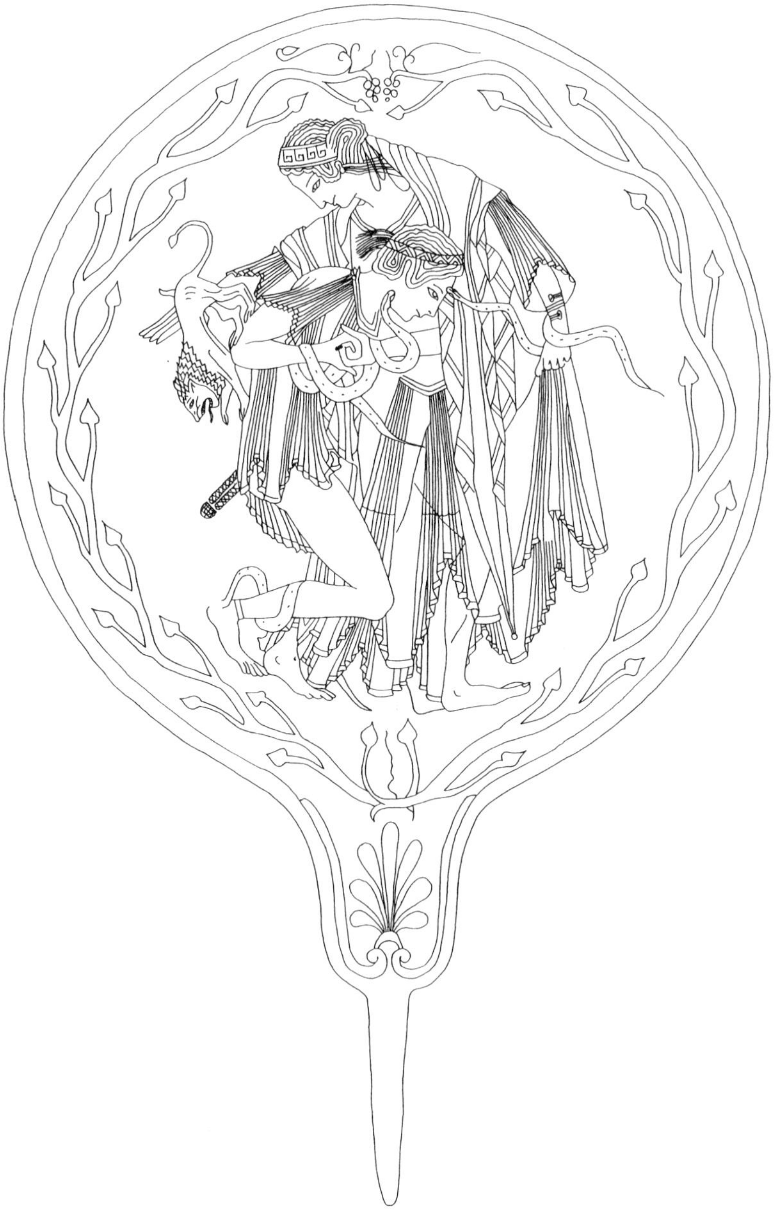

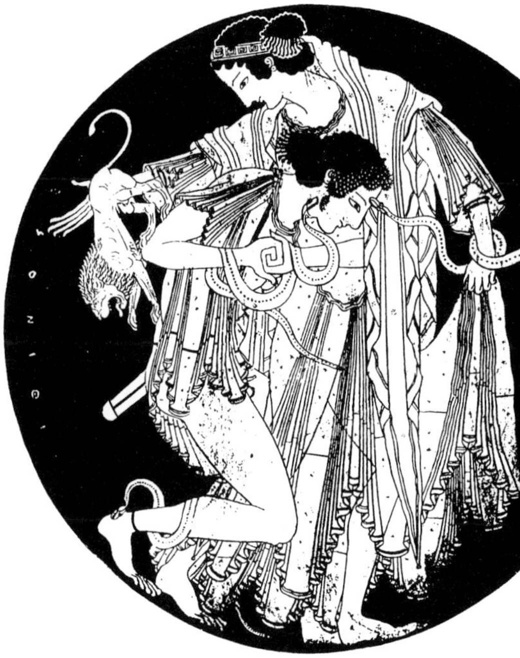

Fig. 4 (left). Engraved mirror. Bronze, diam. 25.0 cm. Los Angeles, The Los Angeles County Museum of Art 50.37.17 (Drawing: B. Forbes)

Fig. 5 (above). Drawing of Attic cup tondo by Peithinos, Berlin F2279. (From E. Pfuhl, *Malerei und Zeichnung der Griechen* [Munich 1923] fig. 417, top)

a low stool. The absence of this stool on the mirror seems all the more telling when we see how effectively it functions on the vase. The intriguing fact that both the Sosias and Foundry Painter cups appear together as early as Gerhard's *Griechische und etruskische Trinkschalen* of 1840 indicates the possibility that the forgery could have been produced as early as the second half of the 19th c., although it will probably never be possible to know what illustrated volumes were available to this anonymous forger.

The Philadelphia mirror is an unusually fine example of 19th- or early 20th-c. engraving. Perhaps the forger hoped that his expertise, combined with the meticulous and vaguely familiar details of his design, as well as the impressive size of the mirror, would ensure its success on the market. Such technical details as the anachronistic border were overlooked — even by experts — because scholarly familiarity with the complexities of Etruscan mirror manufacture and development was still in its infancy.

Another total fake, related to the one in Philadelphia, is now at the Los Angeles County Museum of Art and comes from the William Randolph Hearst Collection.[15] I have been unable to ascertain Hearst's source or date of acquisition for this object. The mirror (fig. 4) is again quite large, almost 10 inches in diameter, and has a tang. The engravings closely follow another Attic red-figure cup in Berlin, the tondo by Peithinos, of *c.*510 B.C., from Vulci (fig. 5).[16]

15 Los Angeles 50.37.17: diam. 25.0 cm; h. 37.8 cm; weight 619 g: unpublished; H. Nagy *et al.*, *CSE U.S.A.* 5: *West Coast Collections* (forthcoming).

16 Berlin F2279: ARV^2 115.2: earliest publication, E. Gerhard, *Griechische und etruskische Trinkschalen*

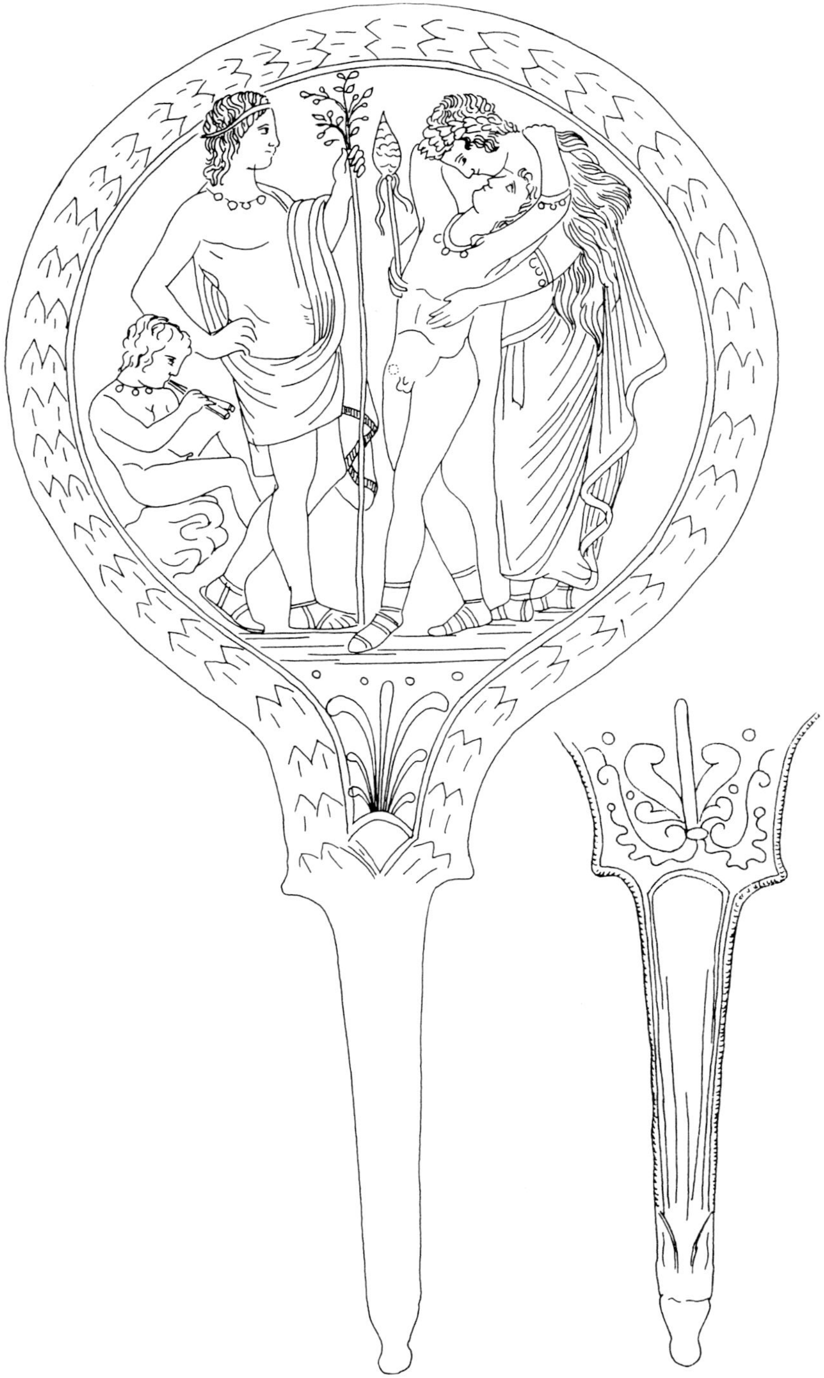

Fig. 6. Engraved mirror (obverse detail). Bronze, diam. 17.0 cm. Kansas City, Nelson-Atkins Museum of Art 56.124. (Drawing: author)

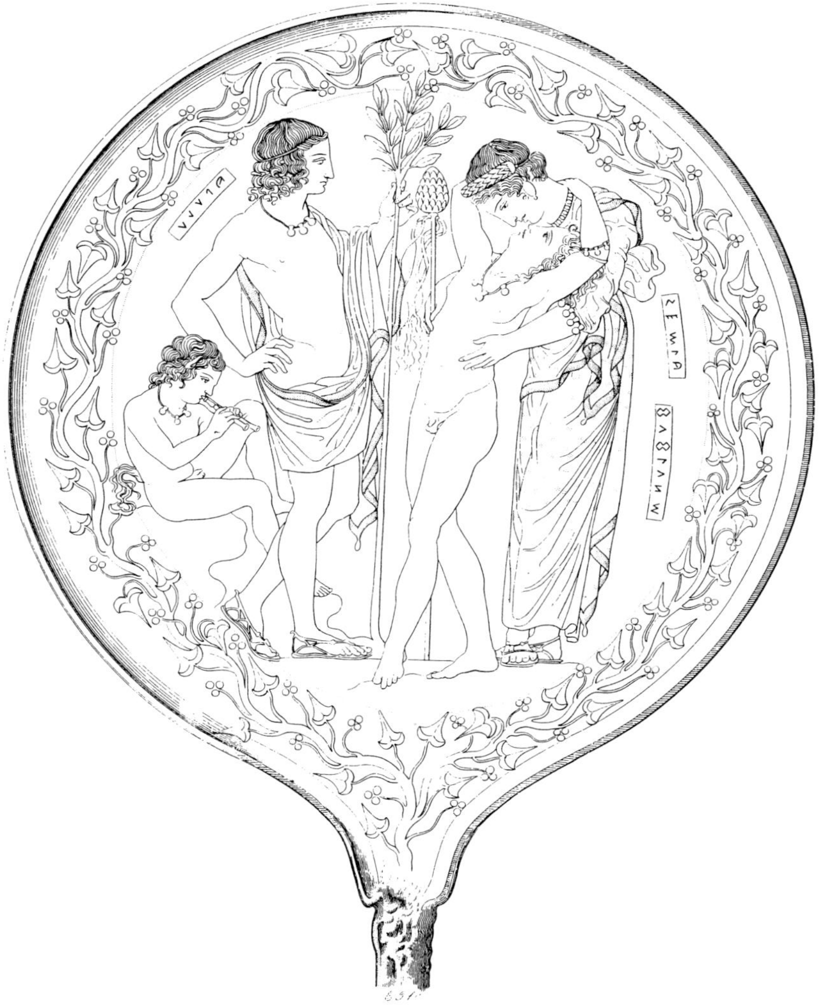

Fig. 7. Engraved mirror. Bronze, diam. 18.6 cm. Berlin Fr. 36 (M.I. 3276). (From *ES* I, pl. 83)

At least the forger realized that a cup tondo offered a more harmonious composition for a circular mirror than a cup's exterior. All he had to do was copy a typical border design[17] and add a generic palmette above the tang to create an imitation that is less innovative but more convincing than the Philadelphia mirror.

Both mirrors share many features: they have large tangs with elaborate engravings only on the reverse. (Etruscan mirrors often have some limited ornament engraved on the reflecting side as well.) Both utilize styles and subjects copied from Attic red-figure vases in Berlin. These vases date from the last decade of the 6th c., but the mirror shapes they decorate are more like those made by the Etruscans in the 4th c. B.C. This discrepancy was not understood until recent refinements in dating the various types of Etruscan mirrors had been developed. However inappropriate they are, the engravings on both mirrors are carefully executed by a skilled and confident artist. Chemical analysis of the Los Angeles mirror shows that its alloy is almost pure copper, unlike authentic mirrors where copper represents between 80 and 90 % of the tin-bronze alloy. Unfortunately, the Philadelphia mirror has not yet been analyzed, but it too appears to have an excessively high copper content. I suspect that both mirrors were made in the same workshop, probably in Italy, and perhaps by the same engraver, as recently as the 1930s.

A much more difficult type of forgery is represented by a mirror in the Nelson-Atkins Museum of Art (fig. 6).[18] The piriform shape of this hand mirror is typical of those associated with the site of Praeneste (Table 1, nos. 7 and 8). The design engraved above the handle on the original reflecting side is also typical of motifs of the 4th c. B.C. (fig. 6, right detail).[19] Everything about this side of the mirror looks perfectly consistent and appropriate. The reverse is a different matter. Here we see an elaborate depiction clearly copied from a famous mirror in Gerhard's private collection until 1859 (fig. 7).[20] This magnificent mirror was published by Gerhard as early as 1832.[21] A comparison of related details on the two mirrors shows that the Kansas City engravings are in every way inferior to those on Gerhard's mirror. First, note that the elegant and complex border on the Berlin mirror has been replaced by a simpler, but unparalleled, one. The little satyr has lost most of his charm as well as his tail, the feet of Dionysos and Semele (or, to use their Etruscan names, Fufluns and Semla) have been treated in a perfunctory manner, and the inscriptions have been omitted. Furthermore, the engraved lines on this side of the Kansas City mirror are very different from those on its reflecting side. On the reflecting side they are firm, deep, and consistent. On the reverse, the engravings are often sketchy, shallow, and hesitant. In addition, a good deal of the medallion's patina has been removed to provide a smoother surface for these new engravings.

These and other features convinced me that the mirror was not entirely ancient when I first studied and published it a decade ago.[22] In 1995, scientific examination of the patina and the engraved lines demonstrated that the engravings on this side are indeed modern. They pene-

---

des königlichen Museums zu Berlin (Berlin 1840) pl. 9, 1 and pls. 14-15.

17 For a likely source, see Vienna 1709: Klügmann and Körte (supra n.2) pl. 138, 2; U. Fischer-Graf, *Spiegelwerkstätten in Vulci* (Berlin 1980) 15-16, fig. 1, V5, and pl. 2, 1.

18 Kansas City 56.124: De Puma 1987 (supra n.3) no. 23 with earlier bibliography.

19 For a similar mirror with related obverse ornament, see Lambrechts 1995 (supra n.3) no. 22, from Capena.

20 Berlin F3276, from Vulci: Heres 1986 (supra n.3) no. 5 with earlier bibliography. For the "backward embrace" in the context of other characters on mirrors and vases, see Frascarelli (supra n.3) no. 17; G. Battaglia, "Lo specchio vulcente con Dionisio e Semele," *RendLinc* 6 (1930) 275-90; G. Pfister-Roesgen, *Die etruskischen Spiegel des 5. Jhs. v. Chr.* (Frankfurt 1975) 76-81, 175-79.

21 *MonInst* 1 (1832) pl. 56A. Gerhard discussed the mirror in three more articles (1833-38) before including it in *ES* I, pl. 83. The mirror was thus quite well known before the mid 19th c. George Dennis used an engraving of it for the frontispiece of his popular book, *Cities and cemeteries of Etruria* (rev. edn., London 1878).

22 R. De Puma, "Engraved Etruscan mirrors: questions of authenticity," in G. Maetzke *et al.* (edd.), *Secondo Congresso int. etrusco. Firenze, 1985: Atti* 2 (Rome 1989) 695-711.

TABLE 1. MIRROR REPLICAS OF THE PELEUS AND THETIS TANG MIRROR IN LONDON
The engravings on all are modern, but a few (perhaps nos. 5-8) are ancient blank mirrors to which engravings were added in the 19th or early 20th c.

Museum/Inventory No.	*Year*[1]	*Provenance*	*Diam.*[2]	*Mirror/Tang type*[3]	*Ins.*[4]	*Border*	*Publications*[5]
London BM 1966.3-28.13	d 1844	Perugia	17	CT/not visible	Yes	ivy	G. Vermiglioli, *La favola di Pelio e Teti* (1846); *ES* IV, 386; Fischer-Graf, *Spiegelwerkstätten* (1980) 83-86.[6]
1. Frankfurt 1984.7	d 1865	Perugia	13.7	CH/no tang	Yes	vine	U. Höckmann, *CSE* BRD 1, no. 42.
2. St. Petersburg V-1806	a 1926	unknown	13.5	CH/no tang	Yes	vine	L. Stephani, *Apollo Boedronios* (1860).
3. Boston, MFA 19.314	a 1919	unknown	12.5	CT/T5	Yes	cymation	R. De Puma, *CSE* USA 2, no. 31.
4.Nijmegen XXI.f/App.I,3	a1920s	unknown	12.4	CT/T5	Yes	cymation	L. Bouke van der Meer, *CSE* Netherlands, no. 33.
5. Upenn, Classics, lost[7]	a 1909	Fidenae?	14.2	CT/missing	Yes	none	J. Rolfe, *AJA* 13 (1909) 3-14, figs. 1-2.
6. Edinburgh, RSM 1136	a 1921	unknown	14.6	CT/T2	No	none	M. Johnstone, *StEtr* 11 (1937) 393, pl. L, 1
7. Vatican 12276[8]	a 1922	unknown	14	PH/no tang	No	none	B. Nogara, *StEtr* 8 (1934) 131, pl. 33, 2.
8. Vatican 12278	a 1922	unknown	15.5	PH/no tang	No	none	B. Nogara, *StEtr* 8 (1934) 131, pl. 33, 1.
9. Geneva, MF 911	d pre-1874	Tarquinia?	12.4	CT/T5	Yes	ivy	W. Fol, *Catalogue du Musée Fol* (1874) I, 195; Pandolfini, *StEtr* 39 (1971) 369, pl. 79
10-13. Perhaps Rome[9]	d 1860s	Perugia					Gerhard, *AA* 1865, 142; *ES* IV, *Paralip.* 334d-f.
14. Lead stele-mirror[10]	d 1853	Perugia		CH/no tang	Yes	none	G. Conestabile, *MonInst* 2 (1855) 57-58, pl. XIII.

1. Year of discovery (d) or year of acquisition (a) by present museum.
2. Horizontal diameter of disc in cm.
3. See R. De Puma, "Notes on terminology and classification," in *CSE USA* 2: *Boston and Cambridge* (Ames, IA 1993) 13-20.
4. This notes only whether inscriptions occur on the disc; it does not take into account the accuracy or placement of inscriptions and how they vary from the prototype.
5. Earliest publication and/or recent, more definitive publication.
6. Vermiglioli's fold-out illustration is correctly oriented, but Gerhard's is reversed. It is instructive to note that only two mirrors (nos. 1 and 2) reverse the image, thus indicating that they were probably based on Gerhard. For reasons clear from the Table, these two forgeries were probably produced by the same person. The same is true for nos. 3 and 4.
7. This fragmentary mirror was purchased by Rolfe in 1909 from a Roman dealer, who claimed it came from Monte Tufello, near Fidenae, just northeast of Rome. It was stolen from a display case in the Classics Department during the 1960s and is still missing.

8. The two Vatican mirrors (nos. 7 and 8) were gifts to Pope Pius XI, who reigned from 1922 to 1939. When Nogara published them in 1934, he mentioned that they came into the papal collection "circa vent'anni fa," but this would place them about 1914, during the pontificate of Benedict XV. Until better information is available, I have placed them at 1922, the beginning of Pius XI's pontificate.

9. Three or 4 additional mirrors with Peleus and Thetis, mentioned as having been discovered at Perugia before 1865, and 1933.611 may have found their way to Roman collections or dealers. Two of these are possibly the mirrors in the Astorri Collection (DAI Rome, neg. 1933.610 and 1933.611); the others are either lost or perhaps among those listed in the table with unknown provenance.

10. This unique object purported to be an Etruscan lead stele with depictions of the deceased (copied from a cinerary urn lid), various vases, and a large mirror displayed prominently at the center. The "engraving" is clearly based on the published illustrations of the London mirror. The fact that the prototype and many of the copies in table 1 come from Perugia strongly suggests that Perugia is the most likely location for the workshop that produced these forgeries.

TABLE 2. MIRROR REPLICAS OF THE DIONYSOS AND SEMELE TANG MIRROR IN BERLIN
The engravings on all are modern, but at least 4 (nos. 1-2, 4, and 6) are ancient blank mirrors to which engravings were added in the 19th or early 20th c.

Museum/Inventory No.	*Year*	*Provenance*	*Diam.*	*Mirror/Tang type*	*Ins.*	*Border*	*Publications*
Berlin Fr. 36 (M.I. 3276)[1]	d 1832 a 1859	Vulci	18.6	CT/R1 or R4	Yes	ivy/berry	Gerhard, *MonInst* 1 (1832) pl. 56A; Heres, *CSE DDR* 1, no. 5.
1. Paris, Cab. d. Méd. 1301[2]	a 1880	Corinth?	14.5	CT/T2	No	scallop	Rebuffat-Emmanuel, *Miroir*, 128-31, 409-11, pl. 19
2. Paris, Cab. d. Méd. 1303	a 1874	unknown	16.6	CT?/missing	No	palmette	Rebuffat-Emmanuel, *Miroir*, 136-38, 411-12, pl. 21.
3. Boston, MFA 08.253[3]	a 1908	unknown	13.1	CT/T1	Yes	leaf/berry	R. De Puma, *CSE USA* 2, no. 30.
4. Rome, Villa Giulia 24875	a 1920s ?	unknown	11.8	CH/no tang	Yes	none	Battaglia, *MemLinc* 6 (1930) 278-79, fig. 2.
5. Syracuse, MA, no inv. no.	a 1920s ?	unknown		PH/no tang	Yes	ivy/berry	Battaglia, *MemLinc* 6 (1930) 276, pl. 2.
6. Kansas City, NA 56.124[4]	a 1956	unknown	17	PH/no tang	No	leaf (unique)	R. De Puma, *CSE USA* 1, no. 23.

1. See fig. 7.
2. See fig. 9.
3. See fig. 8. This mirror and no. 4 are almost certainly by the same modern engraver.
4. See fig. 6. This mirror and no. 5 are almost certainly by the same modern engraver.

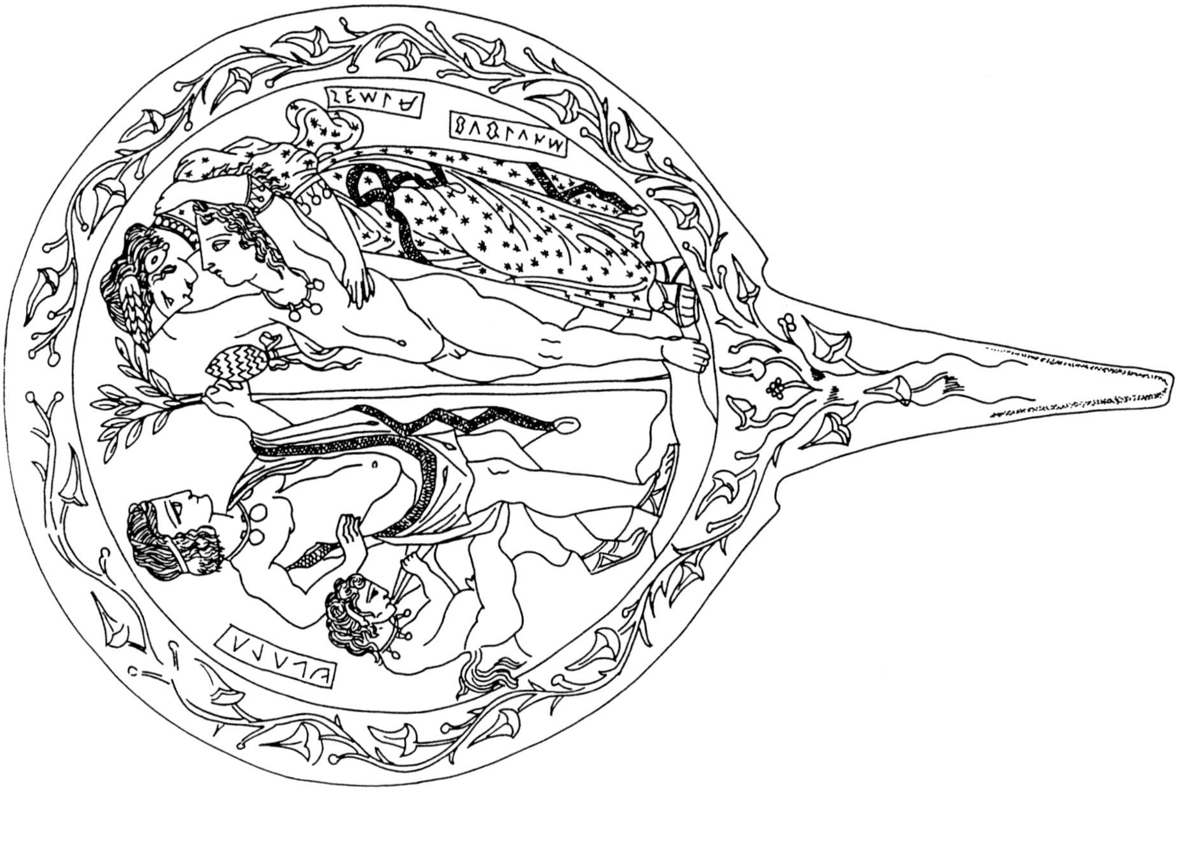

Fig. 8. Engraved mirror. Bronze, diam. 13.1 cm. Boston, Museum of Fine Arts 08.253 (Drawing: author)

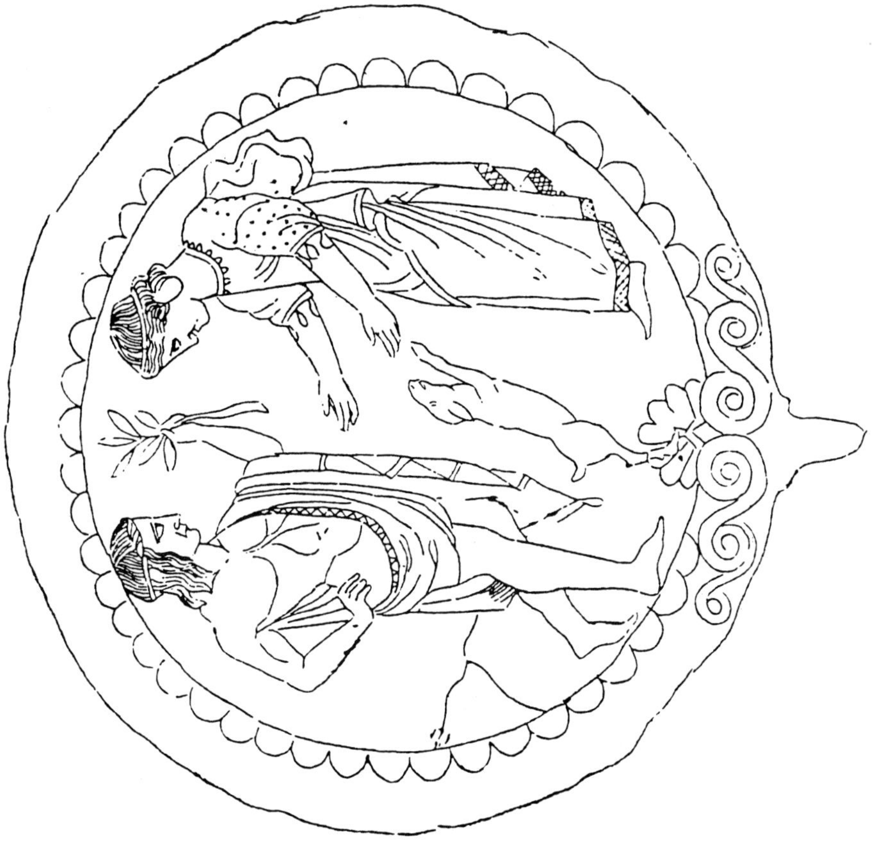

Fig. 9. Engraved mirror. Bronze, diam. 14.5 cm. Paris, Cabinet des Médailles 1301. (From Rebuffat-Emmanuel [supra n.4] pl. 19)

trate the ancient patina and were later filled in with a white paint-like substance. What we have, then, is a Praenestine mirror of the 4th c. B.C. that was originally undecorated except for the handle and minor engravings on the reflecting surface. This bronze mirror was probably discovered in the 19th c., when the cemeteries of ancient Praeneste were heavily exploited. To enhance the object's value, it was engraved with a scene copied from Gerhard's widely published Vulci mirror. This was one of the most popular mirror designs for forgers to copy; at least 5 other modern copies have been added to ancient mirrors (see Table 2). The example in Boston has already been mentioned (fig. 8); the alloy of this mirror has not been analyzed chemically, but it may be entirely modern. Two mirrors in Paris with the same subject make the Kansas City mirror seem refined. One (fig. 9) even has its engravings added to the original reflecting surface, the wrong side of the mirror for engraved scenes. It is significant that the closest stylistic parallel for the engravings on the Kansas City mirror is an example in Syracuse.[23] Here too the mirror is an authentic Praenestine blank to which modern engravings have been added.

The Kansas City mirror was acquired by gift in 1956, but appears to have been purchased in Rome in the 1930s. At this point, it cannot be connected with a specific modern forger, but it is quite possible that it was excavated by Francesco Martinetti (1833-1895), the notorious Roman antiquarian.[24] Martinetti possessed a dangerous combination of talents. He was a skilled engraver and jeweler, a licensed archaeologist in charge of work at Praeneste, a restorer, a collector, and an antiquities dealer. It is possible that he not only excavated this mirror but also had one of his less-talented assistants add the engravings. Perhaps it was a practice piece; his own work is far more competent. Much later the mirror attracted the eye of an American tourist who eventually donated it to the museum in Kansas City. During the 1960s, it appeared in a few exhibitions, accepted as a fine example of Etruscan art.[25] Now it can be recognized as only part of what it seems to be. It represents a growing number of ancient mirrors with modern enhancements provided by 19th-c. "Etruscans" (see Table 1).

It should be noted that the mere fact that a subject is repeated on a number of mirrors does not make all of them modern forgeries. Numerous Etruscan mirrors with secure archaeological provenances show identical subjects and, in several cases, identical stylistic details.[26] Still others have identical subjects and iconography but demonstrate radically different engraving skills.[27] When such mirrors do *not* have secure archaeological contexts, our suspicions should be aroused, and we should examine all details carefully, looking for discrepancies between

---

23 Battaglia (supra n.20) 276, pl. II. See Table 2, no. 5. This mirror was given to the Museo Archeologico by Alfred A. de Pass of Cliffe House, Falmouth, sometime in the 1920s. Its earlier history is unknown.

24 See M. Guarducci, "Il cosiddetto fibula prenestina," *MemLinc* 24 (1980) 413-574, esp. 472-86; ead., "Il cosiddetto trono di Boston," *BdA* 43 (1987) 49-62, esp. 56-58; M. C. Molinari *et al.*, *Il tesoro di Via Alessandria* (Exhib. cat., Milan 1990); L. Pollak, *Römische Memoiren: Künstler, Kunstliebhaber und Gelehrte, 1893-1943* (Rome 1994); T. Hoving, *False impressions: the hunt for big-time art fakes* (New York 1996) 256-78 (where he is consistently called "Marinetti"), with additional bibliography on 344-45.

25 E.g., R. Teitz, *Masterpieces of Etruscan art* (Exhib. cat., Worcester, MA 1967) 88-89.

26 Two subjects are repeated on many mirrors: the so-called Lasa and the Dioskouroi. For the first, see A. Rallo, *Lasa: iconografia e esegesi* (Florence 1974) and almost every fascicule of the *CSE*, the earlier ones conveniently excerpted and collected in Wiman (supra n.5) chapt. 12. For the Dioskouroi, see D. Rebuffat-Emmanuel, "Dioscures à l'amphore en Etrurie," *RA* 1981, 217-26; ead., Typologie générale du miroir étrusque à manche massif," *RA* 1984, 195-226; *LIMC* III (1986) 597-608, s.v. Dioskouri/Tinas Cliniar (R. De Puma). See also U. Höckmann, "Die Datierung der hellenistisch-etruskischen Griffspiegel des 2. Jahrhunderts v. Chr.," *JdI* 102 (1987) 247-89.

27 Cf., e.g., 4 mirrors with Herakles suckled by Hera, listed here in order of descending quality: 1. Florence 72740, from Volterra: *ES* V, pl. 60; 2. Bologna It. 1075, probably from Vulci: Sassatelli (supra n.3) no. 15; 3. Berlin 7769, from Vulci: *ES* V, pl. 59; 4. Tarquinia 68705 (= 4883-17), from Scataglini necropolis, tomb 65, Tarquinia: F. R. Serra Ridgway, *I corredi del fondo Scataglini a Tarquinia* (Milan 1996) I, 79-80, and II, pl. CXL.

engraving style or technique and mirror design (Tables 1-2). Chemical analysis of the alloy and examination of the patina may corroborate our formal (and more subjective) stylistic analyses.

Are such dubious mirrors worth our attention at all? Should we simply relegate them to the lowest depths of museum storage? I am convinced that they have much to tell us, especially about our own understanding and growing awareness of peripheral cultures like that of the Etruscans. We may never have foolproof methods of determining the authenticity of Etruscan mirrors, relatively few of which have anything approximating a firm archaeological context. But by examining carefully every aspect of a mirror's shape and ornament, and by combining traditional art historical methods with scientific analyses, we may be able to separate the completely authentic mirrors from the partially authentic, and from the total forgeries.

School of Art and Art History, University of Iowa, Iowa City

Acknowledgements

For assistance and hospitality during several visits to the University of Pennsylvania Museum of Archaeology and Anthropology, Philadelphia, I am especially grateful to D. G. Romano, K. De Vries, and T. Brennan, all of the Mediterranean Section. Thanks are also due to H. Nagy, University of Puget Sound, and to B. Forbes for information and documentation on the Los Angeles mirror. R. Cohon, Curator, and K. Garland, Objects Conservator, at the Nelson-Atkins Museum of Art have been most generous with assistance and information on the Kansas City mirror.

Observations on archaistic bronzes of Apollo

Mary-Anne Zagdoun

Only a few monumental bronze statues in archaistic style have survived. The small number can be partly explained by the cost of bronze and by the difficulty of the technique. Another reason should also be taken into account: marble became very popular in Roman Imperial times and may sometimes have been preferred to bronze.

Archaistic bronzes are free imitations of Greek Archaic art. They are usually not considered faithful copies of a lost original. Generally archaistic monumental bronzes that survive are unique. There exist very similar bronze herms of Dionysos in archaistic style that probably belong to the same ancient series,[1] but their model is archaistic, not Archaic. Exact copying of Archaic statuary seems limited to a few marble statues,[2] and exact copying is now attested in Classical bronze statuary.[3]

The Piraeus Apollo

I will focus here on three well-known large bronzes that represent Apollo in archaistic styles. They are particularly difficult to date and to analyze. Despite accurate and detailed analysis, there has been much hesitation as to the date of the Piraeus Apollo.[4] Should it be assigned to 520-510 B.C., as is suggested by the downward look and the bent arms? Should it be dated to 150-100 B.C., just before the period of its burial, as is indicated by the loose structure of the body and the solid-cast incised eyes — which certainly seem strange in an Archaic bronze?[5] G. Dontas has dated the statue around 480 and considers it to be archaistic.[6] Two of his arguments seem to me very convincing and corroborate what we know of archaistic art: the Piraeus Apollo reproduces a *kouros* type of the second quarter or middle of the 6th c.,[7] and it seems close to Peloponnesian types.[8] Both features are remarkable and appear exceptional in archaistic art. A late archaistic bronze of the Hellenistic or Imperial periods would normally have reproduced an Attic original of the end of the Archaic period.[9] As for Peloponnesian influences on this bronze statue, even if this geographic argument seems a little tentative,[10] they have to be taken into consideration. Peloponnesian influences on archaistic art are very rare and could well indicate a date in the 5th c.[11] These two peculiarities — the date of the

---

1 Mattusch, *Classical bronzes* 168-90.

2 M. D. Fullerton, *The archaistic style in Roman statuary* (*Mnemosyne* Suppl. 110, 1990) 116-18; M.-A. Zagdoun, *La sculpture archaïsante dans l'art hellénistique et dans l'art romain du Haut-Empire* (BEFAR 269, 1989) 212-13. Copies of Archaic statues are sometimes very difficult to distinguish from archaistic objects.

3 Mattusch, *Classical bronzes* 191-216.

4 Athens, Piraeus Museum: Zagdoun (supra n.2) 229, no. 67.

5 Rolley, *Les bronzes grecs* 36, with all the different chronological possibilities. C. Houser and D. Finn, *Greek monumental bronze sculpture* (London 1983) 52-57, consider the statue Late Archaic. Mattusch, *Classical bronzes* 140, sees the Piraeus Apollo as particularly difficult to date and explains it "as a reflection of the Archaic style."

6 G. Dontas, "Ο Χάλκινος Απόλλων του Πειραιά," in *Archaische und klassische griechische Plastik* 1 (Mainz am Rhein 1986) 181-92, pls. 77-79.

7 Ibid. 186.

8 Ibid. 191.

9 Zagdoun (supra n.2) 29.

10 Dontas (supra n.6) 192 is more interested in chronological comparisons than in their geographical links. Peloponnesian influence does, however, seem to exist in this statue: C. Houser, *Greek monumental bronze sculpture of the fifth and fourth century* B.C. (London 1987) discusses the possibility of Peloponnesian influences here.

11 Zagdoun (supra n.2) 156-57.

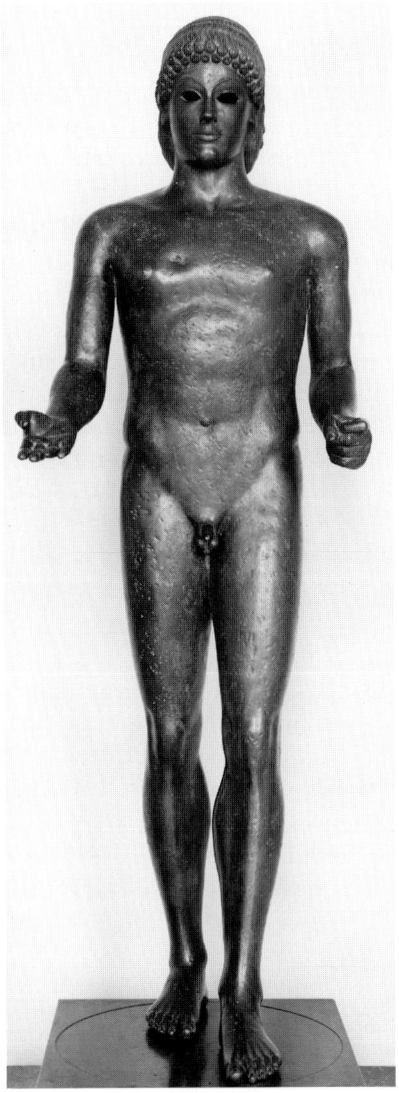

Fig. 1. Piombino Apollo. Bronze, h. 1.158 m. Paris, Musée du Louvre Br. 2. (Photo: courtesy Museum, Département des antiquités grecques et romaines)

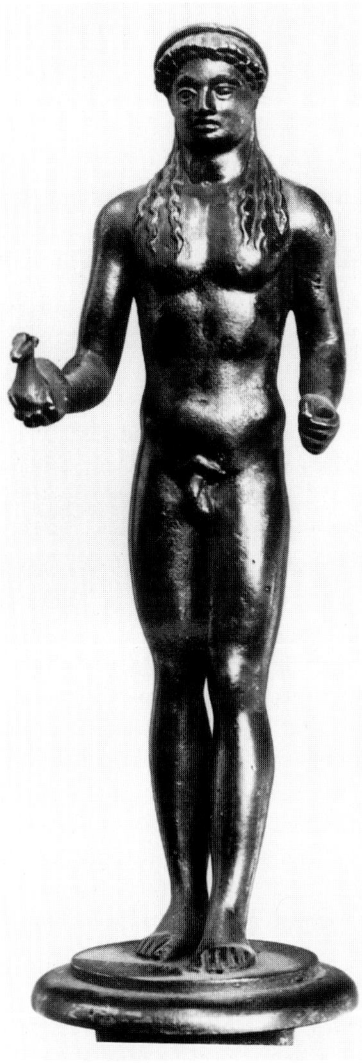

Fig. 2. Payne-Knight Apollo. Bronze, h. 0.18 m. London, British Museum 209. (Photo: courtesy Trustees of British Museum)

model and the Peloponnesian link — are likely to have existed at the beginning of archaistic art, when artists felt free to show a certain liberty and invention in their art.

The Piombino Apollo

The bronze Apollo from Piombino in the Louvre (fig. 1) is much more difficult to analyze and to date. It was considered for a long time to be a sub-Archaic work of *c.*470 B.C.[12] In an important paper, B. S. Ridgway thoroughly studied this statue,[13] which she believes to be an archaistic work of the 1st c. B.C. It would be presumptuous of me to try to impose a definitive date. However, looking through archaistic works, I find that the bronze Apollo discovered in the House of Gaius Julius Polybius at Pompeii in 1977[14] could be of some help, although it is still unpublished and known only through occasional photographs and a few descriptions. The

12 See, for example, D. Willers, *Zu den Anfängen der archaistischen Plastik in Griechenland* (*AthMitt* Beiheft 4, 1975) 17 and n.37.

13 B. S. Ridgway, *AntP* 7 (1967) 43-75, pls. 23-24.

14 This Pompeii statue was briefly presented in *Riscoprire Pompei* (Exhib. cat., Palazzo delle Esposizione, Rome 1993) no. 193; it has been discussed by B. S. Ridgway in *The fire of Hephaistos* 129 and by Mattusch, *Classical bronzes* 139-40, 225, pl. V.

Pompeii Apollo is under life-size, like the Apollo from Piombino. Seen in profile, it also recalls the Apollo from Piombino. The similarity is striking when seen in the two profile views illustrated by C. C. Mattusch.[15] Further study is needed, however, to establish securely the relationship between the two statues.[16]

Perhaps I may add a few stylistic remarks on the Apollo from Pompeii. It has a somewhat ungainly position and its proportions lack harmony. Seen in front view the Apollo from Piombino seems to have a more constructed anatomy. I am struck by the statue's very ornamental aspect. The representation of a diadem, very fashionable in archaistic Greek sculpture of the 1st c. A.D.,[17] gives it a very decorative look, as does the hairstyle, which is similar to that of the Piombino Apollo except that it also has ornamental locks falling upon the chest. If the Apollo from Pompeii really held a wooden tray supported by tendriled shafts and rosettes, its ornamental appearance must have been further enhanced. These ornaments do not appear on the most recent photographs, but one of the earliest reproductions[18] shows the right hand extended and within it the end of a tendriled shaft. This ornamental quality contrasts with the inconsistencies in the rendering of the anatomy, which is neither as exact nor as well-proportioned as the Louvre statue. Finally, the Apollo from Pompeii had a functional use — it probably was a torchbearer.

The Apollo from Piombino (fig. 1), much less ornamental, had no such domestic purpose. Probably it was a votive statue. Even if we admit a late date for the statue, it is surely older than the Apollo of Pompeii, dated in the 1st c. A.D. Although the Apollo from Piombino has no clear parallel, in the present state of our knowledge, it compares favorably with the most recent of the Archaic kouroi and could be attributed to Magna Graecia, along with a few other enigmatic sub-Archaic or archaistic works. It is also possible that the Piombino statue reproduces a model of the early 5th c. but that its actual date is later. Only further comparative study of these statues and technical investigation can produce a definite answer.

The Apollo Philesios by Canachos

The exact appearance of the famous Apollo Philesios by Canachos is a problem.[19] We know from late coins and gems that the god was represented standing, both arms bent, with one hand holding a bow, and with a fawn or a stag on the other, extended hand. Most archaistic large bronzes or bronze statuettes of Apollo show the god holding a bow in one hand and a *phiale* or nothing in the other. Two small bronzes[20] may echo very faintly the statue of Canachos: a small bronze in Naples and the Payne-Knight bronze in the British Museum (fig. 2). Both show the god holding a fawn or a stag, but the Naples statuette also shows him holding a laurel branch. As for the Payne-Knight statuette, whose authenticity, though sometimes questioned, seems assured,[21] it could have been inspired by other models.[22]

There also exist numerous archaistic statuettes of popular types other than Apollos, such as the Athena Promachos and Spes. They are, on the whole, rather easy to date and usually reproduce well-known statuary types. A statuette of Athena Promachos in the British Mus-

15 Mattusch, *Classical bronzes* pls. 5-6.

16 Ibid. 139-40.

17 On these archaistic heads see H. Herdejürgen, *MadMitt* 9 (1968) 213-29, pls. 63-70; id., *JdI* 87 (1972) 299-313.

18 F. Zevi, "Découvertes exceptionnelles à Pompéi," *Archeologia* 136 (1979) 62-64, fig. on p. 63.

19 Zagdoun (supra n.2) 214-15.

20 Ibid. 215.

21 G. De Luca, "Kouroi in italienischen Museen," *AntP* 3 (1964) 55, no. 8.

22 Paus. 9.10.2; 2.10.4, tells us that the Apollo Ismenios of Kanachos in Thebes was very similar in its dimensions and aspect to the statue of Apollo Philesios by the same artist: *LIMC* II, 225-26, s.v. Apollon, no. 333 (W. Lanbrinudakis).

eum[23] belongs to a well-represented series that seems to originate from the Dresden Athena. The Spes Castellani[24] and the Aphrodite Antheia in the Bibliothèque Nationale Paris[25] refer to a type which is well known from quite a few bronze statuettes and also represented in marble statuary.[26]

With a few exceptions, archaistic bronze statuettes can be classified in series and reproduce types well-known from marble statuary, whereas large-scale archaistic (or sub-Archaic) bronzes are unique. Archaistic bronze statuettes illustrate well-known stylistic trends in archaistic art, while archaistic large statues in bronze are eclectic, somewhat a little too refined, with a decorative tendency. Apollo in archaistic style seems to have been a favorite subject in large bronzes that were produced during Greek and Roman times, while bronze statuettes seem to date mostly from Roman times.

10, Place des Vosges, 75004 Paris

Acknowledgements

I would like to thank C. C. Mattusch and B. S. Ridgway for their kind helpp and useful remarks and also to express my gratitude to all those who helped me in the Musée du Louvre (Département des antiquités grecques et romaines) with photographs and documentation: A. Pasquier, Conservateur en chef; S. Descamps, Conservateur; and B. Tailliez (Service photographique).

---

23 Zagdoun (supra n.2) 240, no. 251.

24 Ibid. 240, no. 253. The authenticity of the statue has been questioned: Fullerton (supra n.2) 108 n.17.

25 Zagdoun (supra n.2) 245, no. 315.

26 On the Spes type in statuary, see Fullerton (supra n.2) 108-11.

C'erano delle "serie" toreutiche nell'antichità romana?

Constantin-Adrian Pop

Rispondendo in modo affermativo, almeno in parte, se non categoricamente, a questa domanda, ho cercato di mettere in discussione un'interessante ipotesi di lavoro per quanto riguarda la segnalazione di un aspetto inedito riguardante la realizzazione dei bronzi antichi.

Occupandomi per parecchi anni della toreutica classica greco-romana, ho notato che alcune rappresentazioni figurate di bronzo, provenienti da diverse regioni dell'impero, che si trovano oggi in diversi musei nel mondo o in collezioni private, presentano straordinarie somiglianze, che vanno fino all'identità.

Mi riferirò, in quanto segue, a cinque pezzi toreutici che mi sono sembrati più evidenti (le immagini degli oggetti sono eloquento [vedi le tavv. 1-6]), e che corrispondono ad altre copie del genere. Per mettere in rilievo le loro chiare analogie, ho raggruppato questi bronzetti in coppie, secondo la loro descrizione e il loro ruolo funzionale: statuette votive nn. 1-3; figurina a carattere laico n. 4; e recipiente di uso utilitario n. 5.

Si trata di:

1. Statuetta rappresentante Dionisio, sorpreso nel momento in cui "sta rimproverando la pantera, animale favorito" (tav. 1.1).[1] Alt. 0.586 m, proveniente dalla Colonia Aurelia Apulensis (Alba Iulia, Romania, nelle collezioni del Museo del Banat, di Timişoara). Oggi scomparso. Il pezzo toreutico è considerato un prodotto di importazione nella provincia di Dacia. Un'altro esempio, quasi identico, è stato scoperto, nel 1863, a Pompei (Museo Archeologico Nazionale di Napoli; tav. 1.2).[2] La statuetta, di notevoli dimensioni (alt. 0.59

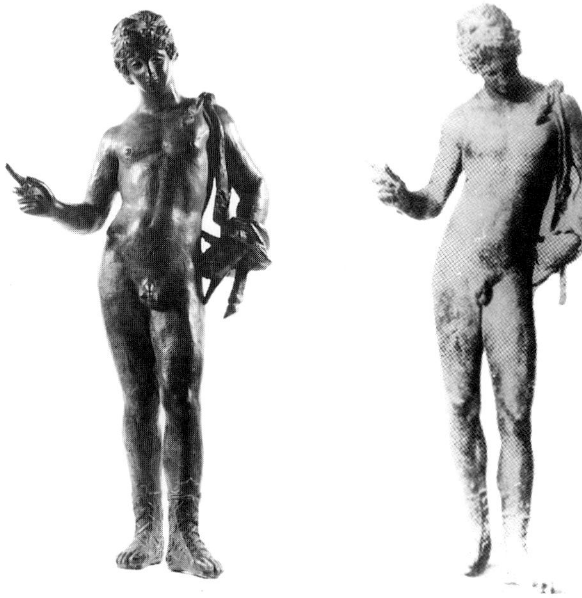

Tav. 1. 1. Dionisio (Alba Iulia). 2. Dionisio (Pompei).

---

1 C. Pop, "O statuetǎ dionysiacǎ în Muzeul Banatului," *Tibiscus* 3 (1974) 137-39, tav. 20; id., "Bronzi votivi di Dacia Romana: una inedita rappresentazione iconografica e tipologica di Dionisio," in J. Arce e F. Burkhalter (edd.), *Bronces y religion romana: Actas del XI Congreso int. de bronces antiguos, Madrid, mayo-junio 1990* (Madrid 1993) 345-48, fig. 1-2.

2 O. Rayet, *Monuments de l'art antique* (Paris 1884) 48; S. Reinach, *RSGR* II.1 (Paris 1897) 121, no. 7; A. Mau, *Pompeji in Leben und Kunst* (Leipzig 1900) 444-45, fig. 263; A. De Franciscis, *Il Museo Nazionale di Napoli* (Cava dei Tirenni 1963) 66, n.5003 ff.

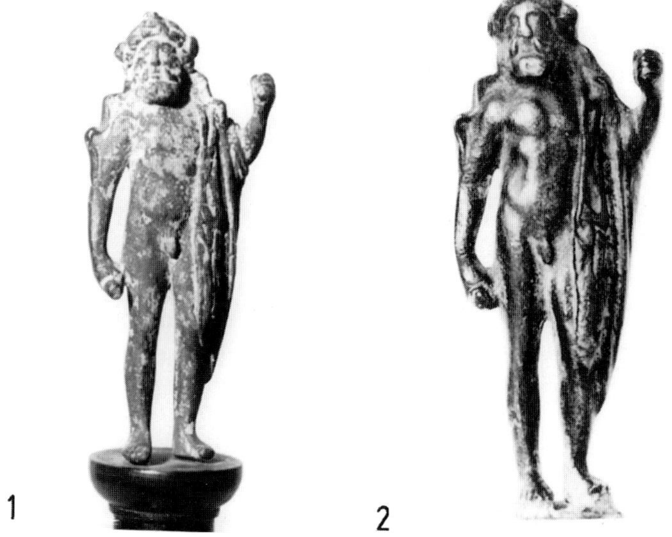

Tav. 2. 1. Giove (Chiusi). 2. Giove (Speyer).

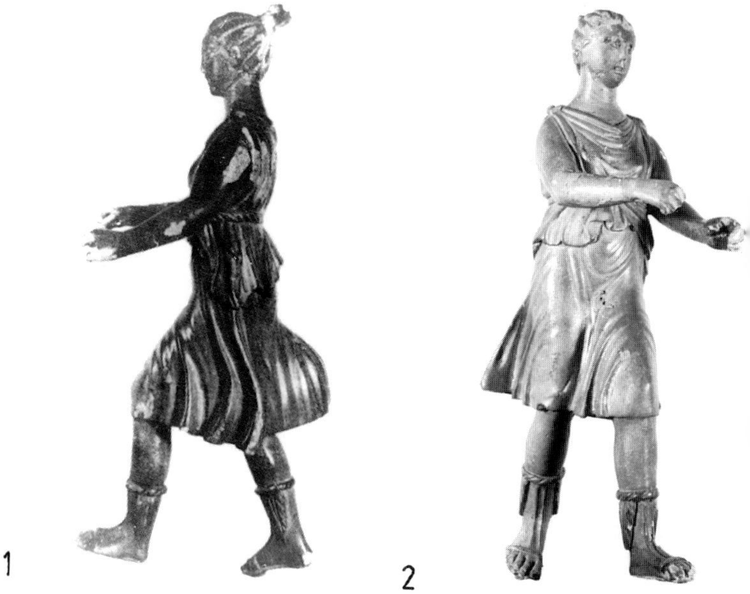

Tav. 3. 1-2. Diana (Ostrov).

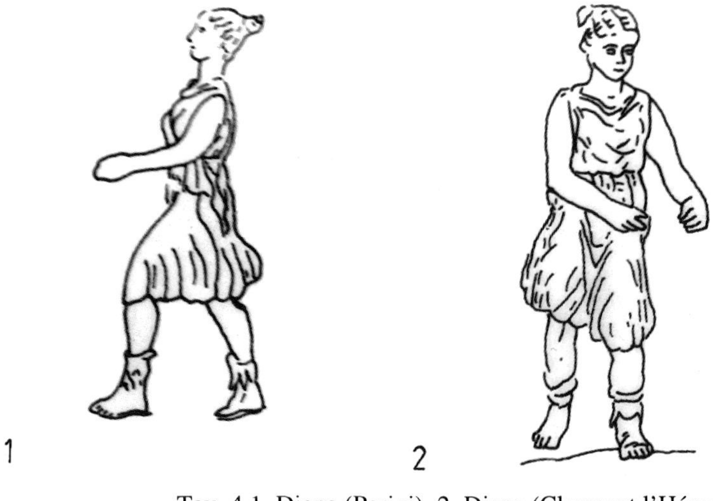

Tav. 4.1. Diana (Parigi). 2. Diana (Clermont l'Hérault).

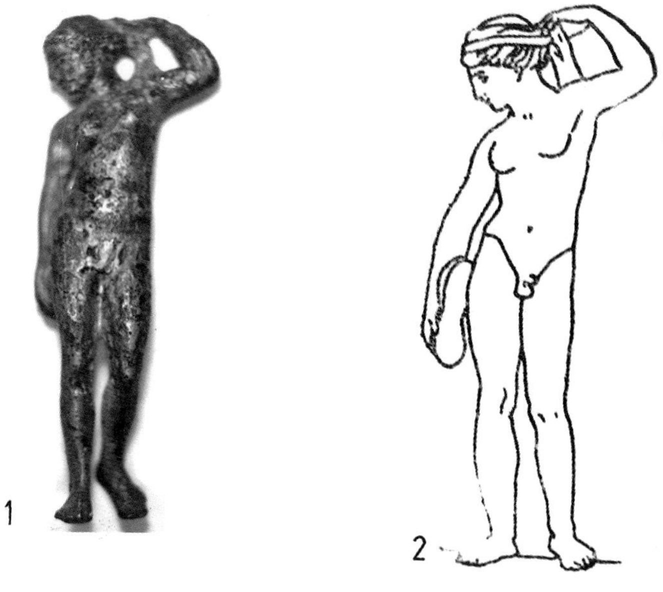

Tav. 5.1. Efebo (Berzovia). 2. Efebo (Londra).

m), è il prototipo del pezzo di Alba Iulia, prototipo ellenistico concepito, senz'altro, sotto l'influenza della scuola di Prassitele.[3]

2. Figurina di Giove nell'ipostasi di *fulminans* (tav. 2.1).[4] Ritrovata probabilmente a Clusium (Chiusi, oggi nel Museo Nazionale di Storia della Transylvania, di Cluj). Alt. 0.105 m. Fa una riuscita coppia quasi identica, con un altro pezzo toreutico,[5] di provenienza sconosciuta, oggi conservato al Museo di Speyer (alt. 0.103 m; tav. 2.2). Considerati al tempo della loro pubblicazione come dei semplici pezzi contraffati[6] (secondo un prototipo antico di bronzo di Châlons-sur-Saône[7]), sono del parere che questa ipotesi — in base alle nuove ricerche — dovrà essere riformulata.

---

3 De Franciscis (ibid.) 66.

4 C. Pop, "Precizări în legătură cu câteva piese sculpturale antice din Muzeul de Istorie Cluj," *Acta Musei Napocensis* 4 (1967) 489-91, figs. 1a-b, 2a-b.

5 H. Menzel, *Die römischen Bronzen aus Deutschland* I (Mainz 1960) 54-55, fig. 94.

6 Menzel (ibid.) 55; Pop (supra n.4) 491.

7 E. Babelon e A. Blanchet, *Catalogue des bronzes antiques de la Bibliothèque Nationale* (Paris 1895) n.9, fig. 5.

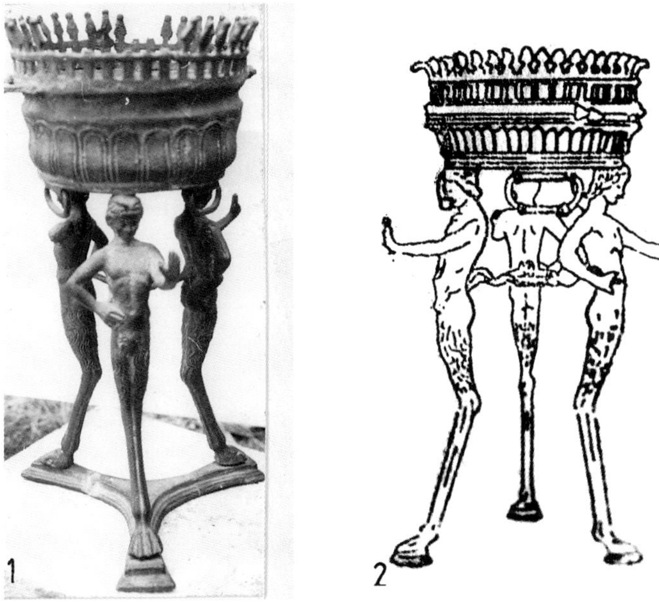

Tav. 6.1. *Turibulum* (Pompei). 2. *Turibulum* (Herculanum).

3. Statuetta rappresentante Diana (tav. 3.1-2).[8] La dea è sorpresa nell'atto di "armare l'arco con la saetta [purtroppo, i due componenti sono andati persi], in una brusca fermata, personaggio alquanto privo di equilibrio, dopo aver seguito di corsa la preda."[9] Luogo della riscoperta: Ostrov (prov. di Hunedoara, Romania), nell'ambito di Ulpia Traiana Sarmizegetusa. Oggi scomparso. Alt. 0.162 m. Anche di questo pezzo si può dire che sia un prodotto di importazione. I bronzi somiglianti (la cui altezza varia tra 0.158 e 0.167 m), uno nella collezione della Bibliothèque Nationale a Parigi (tav. 4.1),[10] gli altri provenienti da Clermont l'Hérault (tav. 4.2),[11] Pagonda[12] ed Efeso,[13] completano l'interessante serie di quest'iconografia. Da notare la pettinatura del personaggio: le ciocche che formano una treccia intorno a una calotta che copre la testa, strettamente attaccata con una *taenia*, nella zona della nuca in una piccola crocchia (tav. 3.1-4.1).
4. Figurina di efebo (tav. 5.1).[14] L'oggetto toreutico, ritrovato nella località civile dell'antica Berzobis (Berzovia, Romania; nel Museo di Caransebeș), rappresenta un efebo (ermafrodito?) che ripulisce il suo corpo con della pomice (*pumex*), dunque appare nella situazione di un 'baigneur' *pumicatus*.[15] Il bronzo, realizzato oltre i confini della provincia di Dacia, ha 0.132 m di alt. Una sorprendente analogia presenta una figurina somigliante riscoperta, insieme ad altre statuette votive, nel 1837, a Londra, all'occasione di alcuni lavori di scavo "in the bed of Thames" (alt. 0.13 m; tav. 5.2).[16] In quel periodo, il pezzo di Londra poteva essere ammirato nella collezione di John Newman.
5. *Turibulum* di Pompei, nella proprietà dell'ex-primo-ministro rumeno fra le due guerre, il poeta Octavian Goga (oggi nella sua Casa Memoriale di Ciucea, prov. di Cluj, Romania) (tav. 6.1).[17] Alt. del recipiente 0.258 m. Un altro *turibulum* (alt. 0.262 m), proveniente da

---

8 C. Pop, "Diana de la Ostrov," *Acta Musei Napocensis* 11 (1974) 85-91, fig. 1.1a-d.

9 Ibid. 88.

10 Reinach (supra n.2) 311, n.3.

11 Ibid. 312, n.1.

12 Ibid. 312, n.2.

13 Reinach, *RSGR* IV (Paris 1910) 186, n.1.

14 C. Pop, P. Bona, e R. Petrowszky, "Bronzuri figurate din Dacia romană: un tip iconografic inedit," *Acta Musei Napocensis* 19 (1982) 307-10, fig. 1.1a-b.

15 Ibid. 310.

16 C. R. Smith, *Archaeologia. Miscellaneous tracts relating to antiquity* 28 (Society of Antiquaries, London 1840) 38-39, tav. IV.

17 C. Pop, Cr. Găzdac, e A. Bud, "Piese pompeiiene în Muzeul Memorial 'Octavian Goga' (Ciucea),"

Herculanum, presenta un analogia con il primo pezzo (tav. 6.2).[18] Il supporto è oggi scomparso.

Purtroppo, non si è potuto stabilire con certezza per nessuno dei pezzi sopra analizzati l'officina di provenienza. Forse si potrebbe avere qualche indizio riguardante le officine di Pompei e di Herculanum, per quanto riguarda i bronzi rappresentanti Dionisio (tav. 1.2) e i due recipienti per bruciare l'erbe (tav. 6.1-2), sono stati riscoperti in Italia.

Alcune piccole differenze nell'aspetto delle coppie di bronzi e nelle loro dimensioni sono dovute, secondo me, soprattutto all'imperfezione della matrice, che ha cambiato le sue particolarità, in seguito ad un lungo uso e ai successivi ritocchi.

Per concludere, sono dell'opinione che l'uso del termine di "serie" toreutica non deve essere considerato troppo moderno e ricercato, per disegnare un metodo di fondere in bronzo più oggetti simili nella stessa matrice, nella nota tecnica antica a cira persa.

Muzeul Național de Istorie a Transilvaniei,
Constantin Daicoviciu St., no. 2, RO-3400 Cluj-Napoca

Acta Musei Napocensis 31.1 (1994) 265-66, n.3, fig. 6a, tav. 15.6b.

18 S. Reinach, *RSGR* II.2 (Paris 1898) 782, n.3.

A 'rediscovered' colossal bronze bull in the Conservatori Museum

Claudio Parisi Presicce and Lori-Ann Touchette

The posterior end of a colossal bronze bull has been displayed in the Sala dei Bronzi of the Conservatori Museum, Rome, for more than a century (figs. 1-3).[1] Dismissed by H. Stuart Jones as a Roman mediocrity, the bull has remained buried in obscurity.[2] Recent restoration and conservation necessitate a re-appraisal of this important statue. Analysis of the bronze has revealed that the statue dates from the 5th or 4th c. B.C.[3] In addition, the restoration has exposed a sensitivity in treatment long concealed beneath the patina of centuries. Thus, a mediocre Roman copy has been transformed into a fragment of a Greek original of high quality. H. von Steuben's earlier suggestion that the bull might be a Greek original, based on the character of the work and its size, has been confirmed by modern scientific techniques.[4]

The bull was discovered during excavations in 1849-50 on the vicolo delle Palme in Trastevere by L. Canina.[5] The earliest finds were perhaps the most spectacular: a marble copy of the Apoxyomenos, now in the Vatican,[6] and a bronze large-scale equestrian statue, of which only the horse survives (fig. 4).[7] The horse was discovered in April 1849 during work on the foundations of the Ospizio di Santa Lucia delle Botteghe Oscura.[8] Recent restorations have also identified this bronze as a Greek original of the 5th or 4th c. B.C.[9] In October of the same year, the Apoxyomenos came to light; several more fragments turned up in excavations through January 1850.[10] In addition to these large-scale statues, other fragments of marble sculpture and architecture, as well as small bronzes and inscriptions, were discovered.[11] All of these excavations were in the street itself. In December 1849 the focus turned to the interior of the building. Almost immediately, the fragmentary colossal bull was found.[12] In January of the next year, a bronze foot said to come from an equestrian group, but of larger scale than the horse mentioned above, was recovered.[13] Finally, another bronze animal, in this case the head of a doe re-figured as a stag, was associated with the excavations by Stuart Jones.[14] An as-yet-unidentified marble Bacchante is also mentioned in the excavation reports.[15]

---

1 The photographs of the bull pre-date the recent restoration.

2 Rome, Museo dei Conservatori 1067: H. Stuart Jones (ed.), *A catalogue of the ancient sculptures preserved in the municipal collections of Rome: the sculptures of the Palazzo dei Conservatori* (Oxford 1926) 170, no. 1, pl. 61.

3 See below. This preliminary report attempts to address some of the implications of the evidence that has come to light. It is hoped that further restoration will provide more precise evidence for the dating of the statue. Fragments of pottery embedded in the surviving core are particularly intriguing in this respect.

4 Helbig[4] II, 382-83, no. 1580 (H. von Steuben).

5 G. Sacchi Lodispoto, "Gli scavi archeologici del vicolo delle Palme in Trastevere," *BollMusCom* 31 (1984) 3-22 with earlier bibliography.

6 Rome, Musei dei Vaticani 1185: Helbig[4] I, 196-98, no. 254.

7 Rome, Museo dei Conservatori 1064: Helbig[4] II, 384-85, no. 1582.

8 Sacchi Lodispoto (supra n.5) 5-12.

9 See below.

10 Sacchi Lodispoto (supra n.5) 12-15.

11 Three of the finds are marked on the map in Sacchi Lodispoto (supra n.5) 6, fig. 2.

12 Ibid. 16-17.

13 Rome, Museo dei Conservatori 2175: Stuart Jones (supra n.2) 297-98, no. 43, pl. 118; Helbig[3] I, 572, no. 1000; Sacchi Lodispoto (supra n.5) 17-18.

14 Rome, Museo dei Conservatori 1071: Stuart Jones (supra n.2) 174, no. 8, pl. 62; Sacchi Lodispoto (supra n.5) 19.

15 Sacchi Lodispoto (supra n.5) 19.

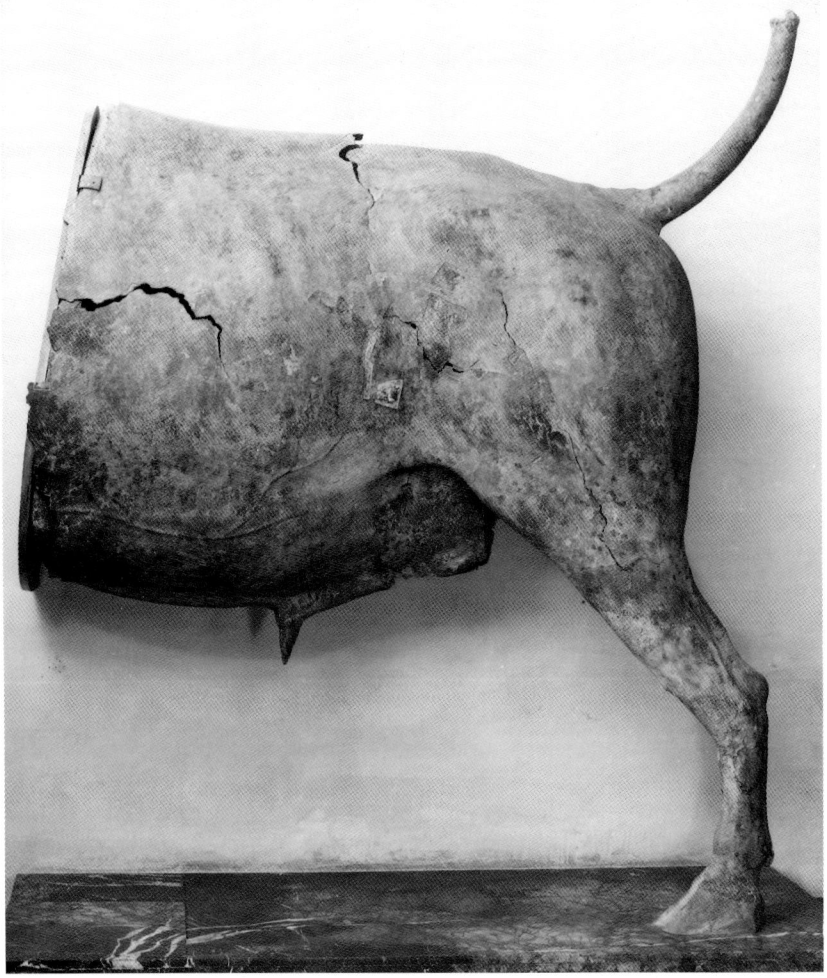

Fig. 1. Bull, from vicolo delle Palme, Rome. Side view. Greek, 5th or 4th c. B.C. Bronze, h. 1.87 m; l. 1.52 m. Rome, Museo dei Conservatori 1067. (Photo: DAI Rome 67.16)

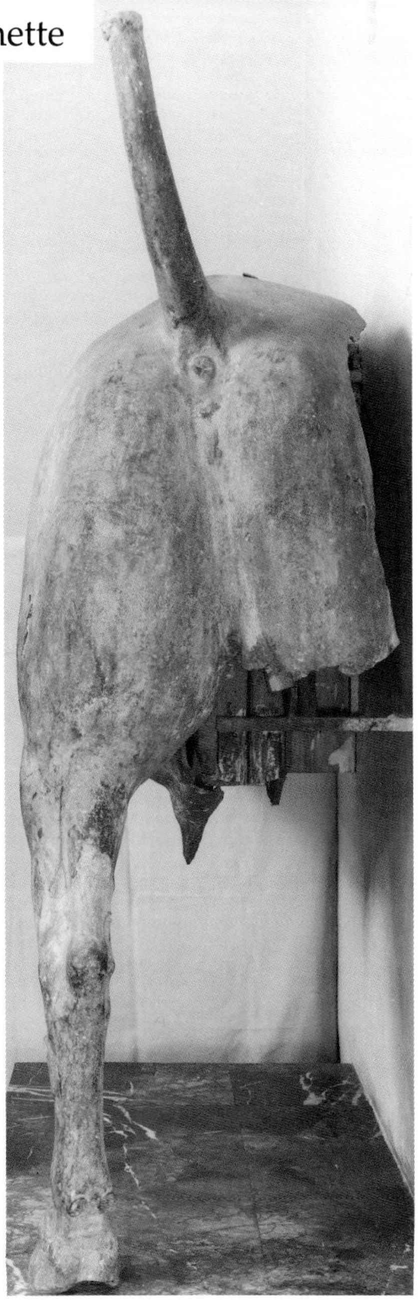

Fig. 2 (right). Rear view. (Photo: DAI Rome 67.17)

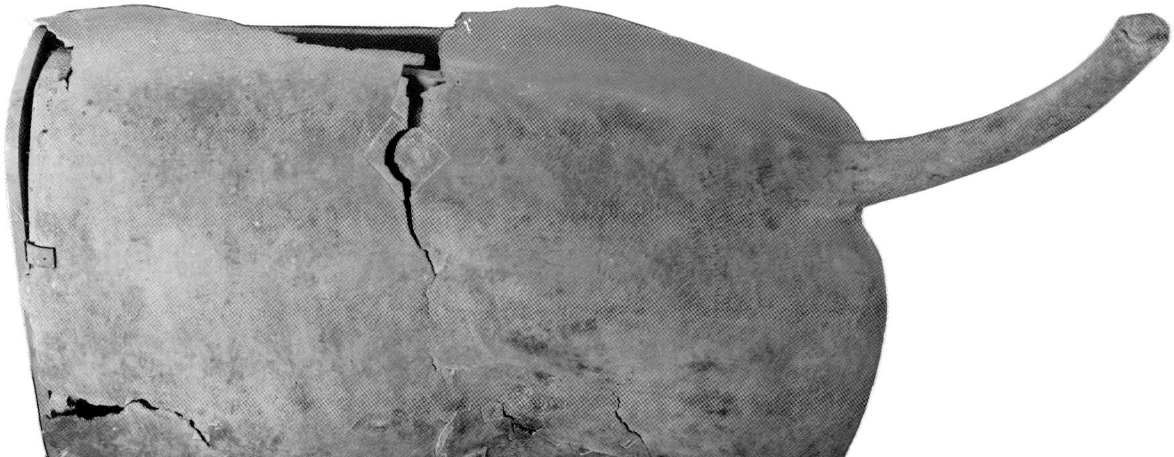

Fig. 3. View from above. (Photo: courtesy Musei Capitolini Archivio Fotografico)

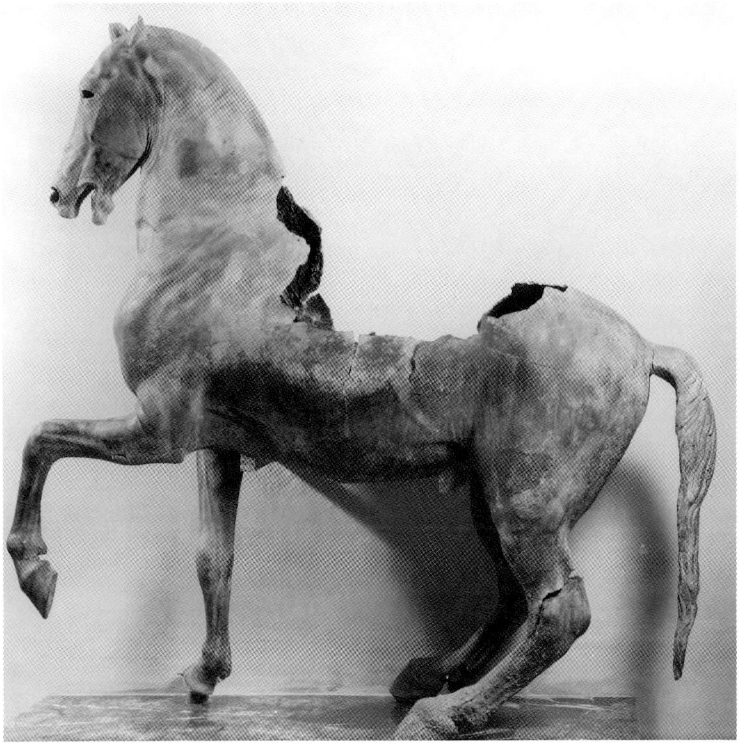

Fig. 4. Horse, from Vicolo delle Palme, Rome. Side view. Bronze, h. 1.95 m. Rome, Museo dei Conservatori 1064. (Photo: DAI Rome 65.1739)

The area of the excavations has been identified as the site of a 2nd-c. bath complex, perhaps either the Thermae Priscidiani or the Thermae di Ampelide, both mentioned in the *Regionary Catalogues*.[16] The Apoxyomenos and the statue of the Bacchante would be quite at home in such a context.[17] More problematic are the large-scale bronzes found in the excavations. In each case, a major portion of the statue has been lost. The evidence of a massive destruction by fire and the presence of fragments of fused bronze suggest that the bath complex was transformed in a later period (late antique or mediaeval?) into a bronze foundry.[18] Perhaps the preserved mass of the bull provides some indication of the dimensions of the furnace.

Restoration and scientific assessment of the bronzes from the site have focused largely on the equestrian statue, which is dated to the mid 5th c. B.C.[19] A new identification of the horse as belonging to one of the Dioscuri by Hegias is proposed here.[20] The vibrant modeling, the extremely short mane, and the skeletal quality of the head position the horse as a transitional piece between Severe style horses and the horses of the Parthenon frieze. According to Pliny (*NH* 34.78), the Dioscuri of Hegias, considered the master of Pheidias, stood in front of the Temple of Jupiter Tonans on the Capitoline. Recent research has confirmed the original presence of a rider. In addition, it is probable that the asymmetrical character of the head

---

16 Ibid. 21-22.

17 For sculpture in bath complexes see H. Manderscheid, *Die Skulpturenausstattung der kaiserzeitlichen Thermenlagen* (Berlin 1981); M. Marvin, "Free-standing sculptures from the Baths of Caracalla," *AJA* 87 (1983) 347-84. For a later example, see R. Stupperich, "Das Statuenprogramm in der Zeuxippos-Thermen. Überlegungen zur Beschreibung der Christodorus von Koptos," *IstMitt* 32 (1982) 210-35; S. G. Bassett, "*Historiae custos*: sculpture and tradition in the Baths of Zeuxippos," *AJA* 100 (1996) 491-506.

18 Sacchi Lodispoto (supra n.5) 21-22.

19 *I cavalli di San Marco* (Exhib. Cat., Convento de Santa M. Apollonia, Venice 1977) 202, no. 94; G. Calcani, *Cavalieri di bronzo: la torma di Alessandro opera di Lisippo* (Rome 1989) 31-34, 110-12, figs. 48, 50, 55 with earlier bibliography (work of Lysippos connected to the Granikos group, following Canina); J. Bergemann, *Römische Reiterstatuen: Ehrendenkmäler im öffentlichen Bereich* (Mainz 1990) 103-5, no. P50, pls. 1a, 3b, 5b, 7c,d,f (100 B.C.). A full publication of the horse by M. Mattei is forthcoming.

20 The hypothesis presented here is that of C. Parisi Presicce.

when viewed from the front resulted from its original conception as part of a group. The later addition of an inscription on the left flank suggests that the statue was moved to a new location in antiquity, perhaps during one of the periodic clearings of the Capitoline.[21]

In 1993, while the bronze horse was under study, a series of tests was carried out on the other bronzes from the Vicolo delle Palme.[22] In the case of the bull, the preliminary investigations yielded sufficient evidence for the assignment of a date. The bull measures 1.87 m in height and 1.52 m in length. The rear left quarter of the bull with the tail and part of the left leg and hoof are preserved. The fragmentary nature of the statue makes it difficult to reconstruct the original pose: on the basis of comparative material, either a passive standing bull or an active charging or butting bull is possible. The removal of the bull from its early 20th-c. wall mount revealed the full extent of the areas restored in stucco and, in particular, that the join between the body of the animal and the leg had been made in stucco.

Close visual examination of the preserved portion of the bull, despite a thick layer of incrustation with the inclusion of heterogeneous elements, failed to reveal any joins in the surface of the bronze. The fragment seems to have been cast from a single mould, with the exception of the tail, which was soldered onto the base of the spine. The tail was re-soldered in antiquity, perhaps in a new position. A small patch soldered to the front flank on the right side was revealed through ultrasound examination;[23] it is of thinner dimensions than the rest of the bull and provides evidence for an ancient repair datable to the Roman Imperial period. The dismantling of the leg revealed the existence of two different lead channels on the interior, attributable to successive mountings of the statue.

The composition of the bronze obtained from metallurgical analysis[24] and evidence from thermoluminescence testing of the clay core[25] verify the date of the statue in the 5th or 4th c. B.C. In addition, the colossal format, the thinness of the bronze walls, and the presence of small rectangular patches used to cover imperfections in the casting process all point to a Classical Greek date. Evidence of its later history is also present on the surface of the bull. A number of bronze patches of polygonal shape, at times overlays of the Greek patches, can be attributed to restoration in the Roman period. The doubling of the lead pouring channel on the foot also points to more than one erection of the statue: first in its original Greek context, then in its new Roman site. Both the colossal bull and the horse were evidently transported to Rome as *spolia*, two examples of the tons of statuary brought to Rome from the Greek world in the course of Rome's acquisition of empire.[26]

Bronze bulls in Greece

The 'rediscovery' of this colossal statue justifies a re-assessment of the evidence for bronze bulls known to have stood in Rome. It is also necessary to reconstruct the possible function and position of the bull in its Greek context. This discussion considers in turn the possible context of the bull in the Greek and the Roman periods. As noted above, the find-spot in the Vicolo delle Palme does not illuminate its display context in Rome, and its removal from its original Greek context and transferral to Rome has obscured the bull's original setting.

---

21 A. La Regina, "*Tabulae signorum urbis Romae*," in M. R. Di Mino (ed.), *Rotunda Diocletiani: sculture decorative delle Terme nel Museo Nazionale Romano* (Rome 1991) 3-8, esp. 6, no. 3.

22 Namely, the two damaged legs of the horse, the head of the doe/stag, the rider's foot, and the colossal bull.

23 The ultrasound tests were conducted by AB2 Art in Rome.

24 The metallurgical analysis was carried out by the Department of Chemistry of the University of Genoa.

25 The thermoluminescence analysis was conducted by the Department of Physics of the University of Milan.

26 On the phenomenon of the transport of Greek art to Rome, see esp. P. Zanker, "Zur Funktion und Bedeutung griechischer Skulptur in der Römerzeit," in *Le classicisme à Rome* (EntrHardt 25 [1979]) 283-306; M. Pape, *Griechische Kunstwerke aus Kriegsbeute und ihre öffentliche Aufstellung in Rom* (Hamburg 1975); O. Vessberg, *Studien zur Kunstgeschichte der römischen Republik* (Lund 1941).

There is evidence for large-scale bull statuary in the Greek world in two contexts: honorific and funerary. At least 7 bronze bulls of Classical date survived down to the 2nd c. A.D., when they were described by Pausanias.[27] They stood as dedicatory monuments in the great pan-Hellenic sanctuaries of the Greek world — Athens, Delphi, and Olympia — where they flanked the sacred ways or altars. The majority were made in the late 6th to early 5th c. B.C. and associated with the Persian Wars. Pausanias also describes the Marathonian Bull monument on the Acropolis, which has been plausibly reconstructed as a single standing bull.[28] The best preserved example recovered archaeologically is the silver and gold bull of the 6th c. B.C. discovered buried beneath the Sacred Way at Delphi.[29]

From the beginning, the emphasis in the literary sources is on verisimilitude. Thus, the bronze bull of Perillus, the earliest bronze bull mentioned in the literary *testimonia*, was said to bellow like a real bull.[30] Pliny reveals the macabre twist to the tale: "No one should praise Perillus, who was more cruel than the tyrant Phaleris, for whom he made a bull, guaranteeing that if a man were shut up inside it and a fire lit underneath the man would do the bellowing." Fittingly, Perillus was the first to experience this torture. That he was not the last is suggested by the references to the bronze bull in the Forum Tauri in Constantinople; as late as the 6th c., a pope is said to have roasted in this manner.

Bronze bulls or heifers have been attributed to the Early Classical sculptor Myron, who was praised for his ability to breathe life into statues. Petronius tells us that 'Myron, who could almost catch the souls of men and beasts and enchain them in bronze, found no heir.'[31] A single epigram from the *Palatine Anthology* demonstrates the literary trope of the lifelikeness of his heifer: 'Myron did not mould me; he lied; but driving me from the herd where I was feeding, he fixed me to a stone base.'[32] The heifer also was said to wish to low.[33]

Another Early Classical sculptor who worked at Delphi and Olympia, Pythagoras of Rhegion, has been associated with a bronze mythological group of Europa and the bull at Tarentum.[34] Again, verisimilitude was his *forte*. According to Pliny, he was 'the first to represent sinews and veins, and to bestow attention on the treatment of the hair.'[35] Pausanias describes Pythagoras as 'a good sculptor if ever there was one.'[36] Mythological representations on vase-paintings include two different versions, with Europa seated on the bull or standing beside it.[37] Several bronze statuettes of Europa seated on a bull survive.[38] A free-standing marble statuette in the Metropolitan Museum of Art, New York, is inscribed on the base with the name 'Europe'; she either stood alone or beside a bull.[39]

---

27 P. Orlandini, "I donari firmati da Kresilas e Dorotheos ad Hermione," *ArchCl* 3 (1951) 94-98; H. A. Shapiro, "The Marathonian Bull on the Athenian Akropolis," *AJA* 92 (1988) 376-82; F. Chamoux, "La génisse d'Herculanum: un aspect de la sculpture animalière chez les Grecs," *MonPiot* 62 (1991) 9-32; G. Nenci, "I donativi di Creso a Delfi," *AnnPisa* 23 (1993) 319-31, pls. 17-20, esp. 325, pl. 18.

28 Paus. 1.27.9-10; Shapiro ibid. 373-82.

29 P. Amandry, "Statue de taureau en argent," *Études delphiques* (*BCH* Suppl. 4) 273-93 (restored h. 1.46 x w. 2.59 m).

30 Pliny, *NH* 34.89.

31 Petr., *Sat.* 88.

32 *Anth. Pal.* 9.719.

33 E.g., *Anth. Pal.* 9.724, 728, 740, 742.

34 Cic., *Verr.* IV.30.135. On Pythagoras's works at Olympia, see also Paus. 6.4.18 (chariot of Kratisthenes), 6.4.3 (statue of Leontiskos).

35 Pliny, *NH* 34.59.

36 Paus. 6.4.3.

37 *LIMC* I, s.v. Europe I, 76-92 (M. Robertson).

38 E.g., Paris, Cabinet des Médailles 32: *LIMC* IV, 88, no. 220.

39 New York, The Metropolitan Museum of Art 24.97.31: G. M. A. Richter, *Catalogue of the Greek sculptures in The Metropolitan Museum of Art* (Oxford 1954) 25-26, no. 30, pl. 29.

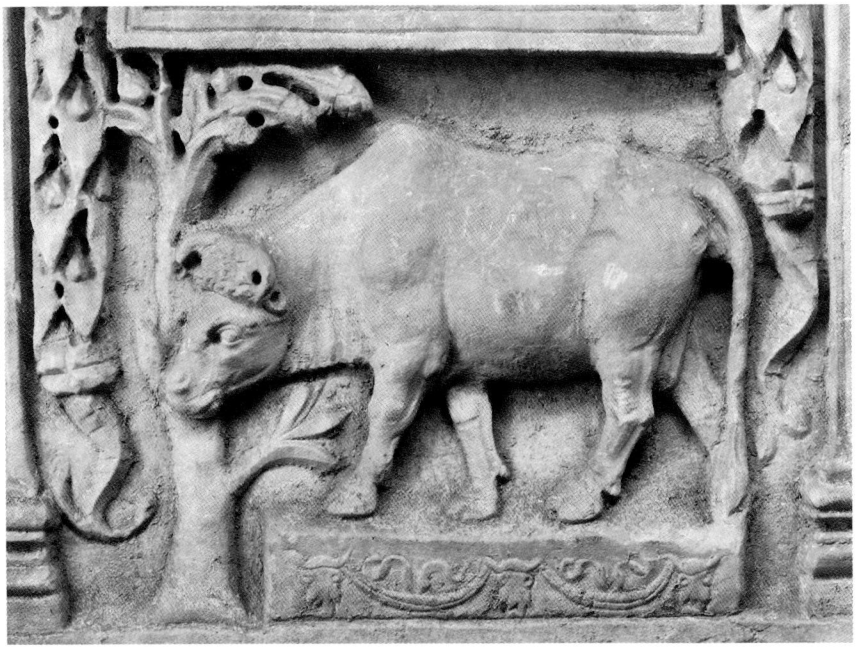

Fig. 5. Ash urn of Claudia Primigenia, detail showing statue of cow on base with *bucrania* and festoons. Roman, late 1st c. B.C. to early 2nd c. A.D. Marble, h. 0.47 m. Rome, Museo Nuovo Capitolino 2826. (Photo: B. Malter; courtesy Musei Capitolini Archivio Fotografico)

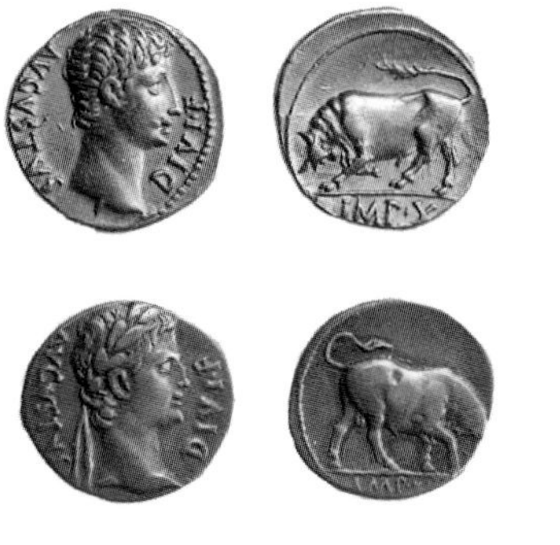

Fig. 6. Two Augustan coins with single bulls on the reverse. London, British Museum. a) BM 28478.40; b) BM 28478.39. (Photos: courtesy Trustees of British Museum)

Several marble funerary bulls of the 5th to 4th c. B.C. survive from the Greek world.[40] Perhaps the best known is a mid 4th-c. B.C. example of a butting or charging bull from the tomb plot of Dionysios in the Athenian Kerameikos.[41] A similar example is now in the Ny Carlsberg Glyptotek, Copenhagen.[42] No Athenian funerary monument in bronze survives; it seems that even the state funerary monuments erected to commemorate the Athenian war dead were of stone.[43] Beyond the Greek mainland, however, it is possible that similar monuments were of bronze. Bull iconography is also attested for material deposited in tombs. An ivory vessel from a tomb of the 4th c. B.C. in the Kerameikos is decorated with a series of animal groups, including a bull confronting a griffin and two lions.[44] In the Roman period, a bronze *patera* with an appliqué of a pawing bull was buried in a tomb of the 2nd c. A.D. at Bois-et-Borsu, Belgium.[45]

Bronze bulls in Rome

For bronze bulls in the city of Rome, we must turn first to the literary and archaeological *testimonia*. Like the Greek examples, the bulls divide into two groups, single bulls and mythological groups. In each case, the bulls were dedicated in fora and temple areas, sometimes flanking the altar. Their placement served as a direct reference to their rôle as sacrificial

---

40 Collected in C. C. Vermeule, "Greek funerary animals, 450-300 B.C.," *AJA* 76 (1972) 56-57; U. Vedder, *Untersuchungen zur plastischen Ausstattung attischer Grabanlagen des 4. Jhs. v. Chr.* (Frankfurt 1985) 121-25.

41 Athens, Kerameikos P 689: Vedder ibid. 284-85, no. T8 (l. 1.84 m).

42 Ny Carlsberg Glyptotek 1567: M. Moltesen, *Catalogue: Greece in the Classical period. Ny Carlsberg Glyptotek* (Copenhagen 1995) 77, no. 21 (h. 0.70 m; l. 1.40 m); Vedder ibid. 293, no. T49.

43 R. Stupperich, "The iconography of Athenian state burials in the Classical period," in W. D. E. Coulson *et al.* (edd.), *The archaeology of Athens and Attica under the democracy* (Oxford 1994) 93-103.

44 W. F. Kovacsovics, *Kerameikos* XIV: *die Eckterrasse an der Gräberstrasse des Kerameikos* (Berlin 1990) 38, tomb 24, no. 21, fig. 26.

45 Liège, Musée Curtius I 7/29, I 7/30: G. Faider-Feytmans, *Les bronzes romains de Belgique* (Mainz 1979) 182-84, pls. 154-55; diam. 25.6 cm; diam. medallion 8.8 cm.

animals.[46] For example, Propertius tells us that around the altar of the Temple of Apollo on the Palatine 'stood the cattle of Myron, four oxen that seemed to live'.[47] A reflection of the monument may appear on an ash urn from Rome (fig. 5).[48] The Temple of Roma and Augustus at Ankara once had two bulls flanking the altar.[49] Single bulls in active or passive poses appear on Augustan coinage; there is some dispute as to whether they refer to the group of Myron or to a victory monument for the Battle of Philippi (figs. 6a-b).[50]

Other images of bulls stood in public spaces in Rome. A bull, said to be of Aeginetan bronze, stood in the Forum Boarium and gave the Forum its name.[51] The Portico of Europa, mentioned by Martial, may also take its name from a statuary dedication, in this case a mythological group of Europa and the bull.[52] There is no evidence to associate this group with a specific sculptor. According to the late-antique historian Procopius, the heifer of Myron stood in the Forum Pacis, along with a bronze bull that he suggests might be the work of Pheidias or Lysippos.[53] What is of interest here is the perversion of the literary trope, since Procopius recounts an incident in which a steer left his herd and mounted this bronze bull, rather than the heifer of Myron.

The latest mention of a bronze bull in Rome comes from Magister Gregorius in the 13th c.[54] (see also the earlier accounts of Petrus Mallius and in the *Mirabilia*[55]). According to Gregorius, the bull stands on the ramparts of the Mausoleum of Hadrian, having been moved from its earlier position in the Basilica of St. Peter. Here the two types of display mesh as the author reports a single bull, yet, in describing its pose, refers the reader to a group of Europa and the bull. Thus the bull is *mugituro et moturo similis*.

Images on historical reliefs of the Imperial period match the literary sources with both single bulls and groups. On the Sorrento base, a static bull and ram stand on pillars beside a round Temple of Vesta (fig. 7).[56] The same image recurs on Julio-Claudian coinage.[57] The precise identification of the temple of Vesta shown is disputed, whether that in the Forum Romanum or the Augustan temple beside the Temple of Apollo on the Palatine.[58] In either case, the numis-

---

46 O. Brendel, "'Immolatio boum'," *RömMitt* 45 (1930) 196-226.

47 Prop., *Carm.* 2.31.

48 Rome, Museo Nuovo Capitolino 2826: S. Panciera (ed.), *La collezione epigrafica dei Musei Capitolini* (Rome 1987) 147-52, no. 71, pls. 3.1, 4.1-3 (P. Sabbatini Tumolesi); F. Sinn, *Stadtrömische Marmorurnen* (Mainz 1987) 194, no. 431, pl. 67a-b; N. Himmelmann-Wildschutz, *Über Hirten-Genre in der antiken Kunst* (Opladen 1980) 123, pl. 40. The ash urn is dedicated to Claudia Primigenia and dates to the end of the 1st/beginning of the 2nd c. A.D.

49 Vermeule (supra n.40) 56.

50 E.g., London, British Museum 28478.39, 28478.40: M. Hofter (ed.), *Kaiser Augustus und die verlorene Republik* (Exhib. cat., Mainz 1988) 488-89, 521, nos. 358-59 (W. Trillmich). See also C. H. V. Sutherland, "Deniers d'Auguste frappés en Orient," *RevNum* 16 (1974) 58-62, pl. 7.56, 61; K. Kraft, *Zur Münzprägung des Augustus* (Wiesbaden 1969) 225-35.

51 The bronze is that which Pliny, *NH* 34.10, tells us was used by Myron. See also Tac., *Ann.* 12.24; Ovid, *Fasti* 6.478-79.

52 Esp. Mart. 2.14.

53 Procop., *BellGoth* 4.21.12-16; K. Gantar, "Procope et les statues du Forum Pacis à Roma," *ArhVest* 19 (1968) 189-93.

54 Master Gregorius 191a.

55 G. McN. Rushforth, "Magister Gregorius de Mirabilibus Urbis Romae: a new description of Rome in the twelfth century," *JRS* 9 (1919) 21, 46 no. 3.

56 Sorrento, Museo Correale: *Kaiser Augustus* (supra n.50) 375-78, no. 208 (T. Hölscher) with earlier bibliography. The fullest treatments remain: G. E. Rizzo, "La base di Augusto," *BullCom* 60 (1932) 7-109; S. Stucchi, *I monumenti della parte meridionale del Foro Romano* (Rome 1958) 39-41, figs. 5, 10. See also the similar relief in Palermo, Museo Nazionale: Stucchi, ibid. 39-41, fig. 11.

57 Rizzo ibid. 29-32, pl. A.1-2; G. Fuchs, *Architekturdarstellungen auf römischen Münzen der Republik und der frühen Kaiserzeit* (Berlin 1969) 98-99; *BMC* I, 140, no. 142, pl. 25.10.

58 Rizzo ibid.; A. Degrassi, "Esistette sul Palatino un tempio di Vesta?" *RömMitt* 62 (1955) 144-54; M. Guarducci, "Vesta sul Palatino," *RömMitt* 71 (1964) 158-69; ead., "Enea e Vesta," *RömMitt* 78 (1971)

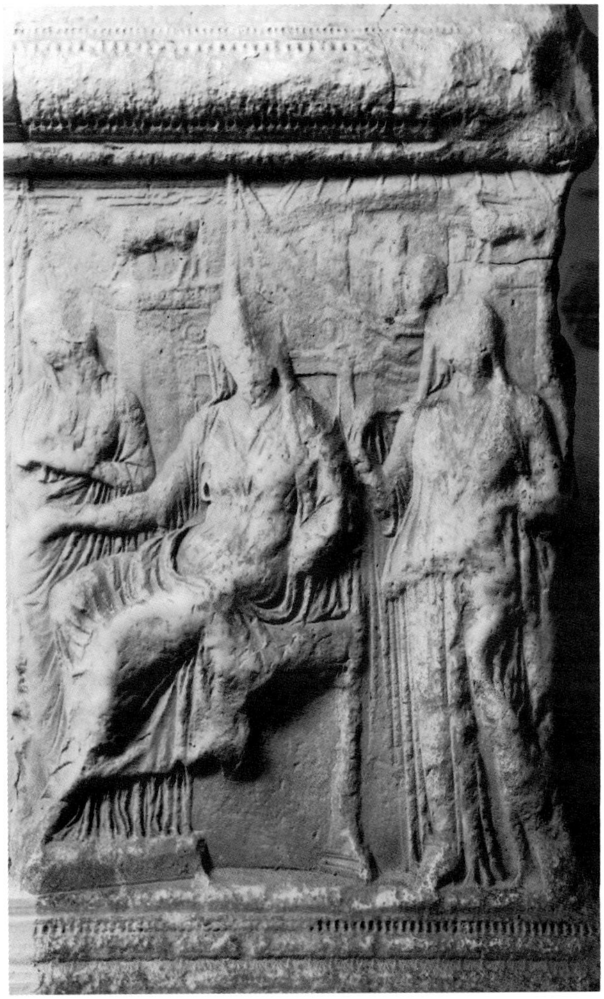

Fig. 7. Sorrento base, detail showing a statue of a bull on a column beside the Temple of Vesta. Roman, late 1st c. B.C. to early 1st c. A.D. Marble, h. 1.17 m. Sorrento, Museo Correale. (Photo: DAI Rome 69.1754)

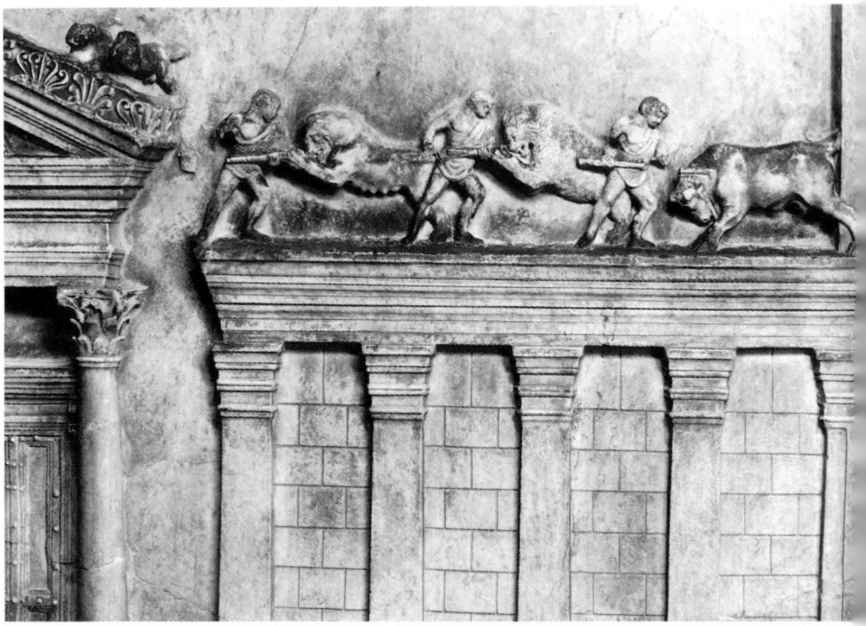

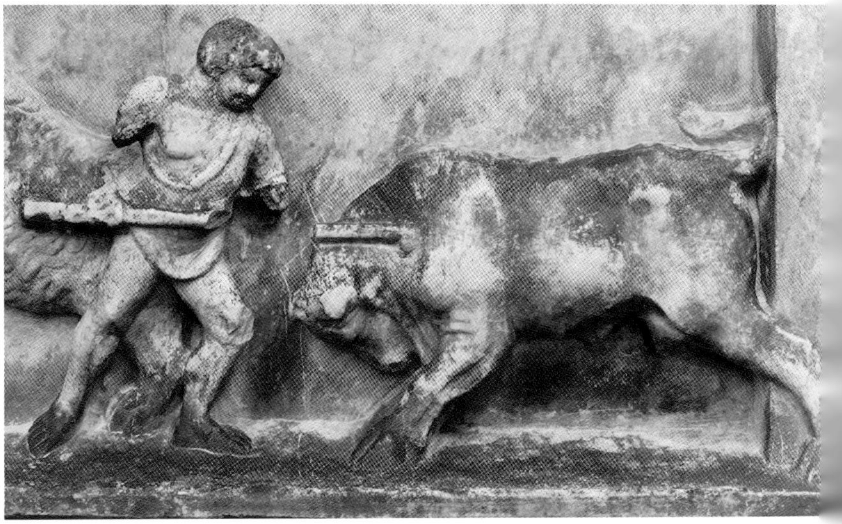

Fig. 8 (above). Aurelianic sacrifice relief, detail showing animal group on top of the Aedes Tensarum. Roman, third quarter of the 2nd c. Marble, h. 3.14 m. Rome, Museo dei Conservatori 807. (Photo: courtesy Museum)

Fig. 9 (below). Aurelianic sacrifice relief, detail showing hunter and bull. (Photo: Rome, Museo dei Conservatori, museum photo).

matic and artistic evidence situates the image of a colossal bull within a sanctuary in the very center of Rome. Also of interest is the representation on the sacrificial scene of the Aurelianic reliefs of statuary groups of hunters and animals; individual hunters are paired with a bull, a lion, and a bear (figs. 8-9).[59] The three groups are poised beside the Capitolium on top of a por-

89-118; H. G. Kolbe, "Noch einmal Vesta auf dem Palatin," *RömMitt* 73-74 (1966-67) 94-104; N. Degrassi, "La dimora di Augusto sul Palatino," *RendPontAcc* 39 (1966-67) 97-116.

59 Rome, Museo dei Conservatori 807: E. La Rocca (ed.), *Rilievi storici capitolini: il restauro dei pannelli di Adriano e di Marco Aurelio nel Palazzo dei Conservatori* (Rome 1986) 40, pls. 37 and 40.1.

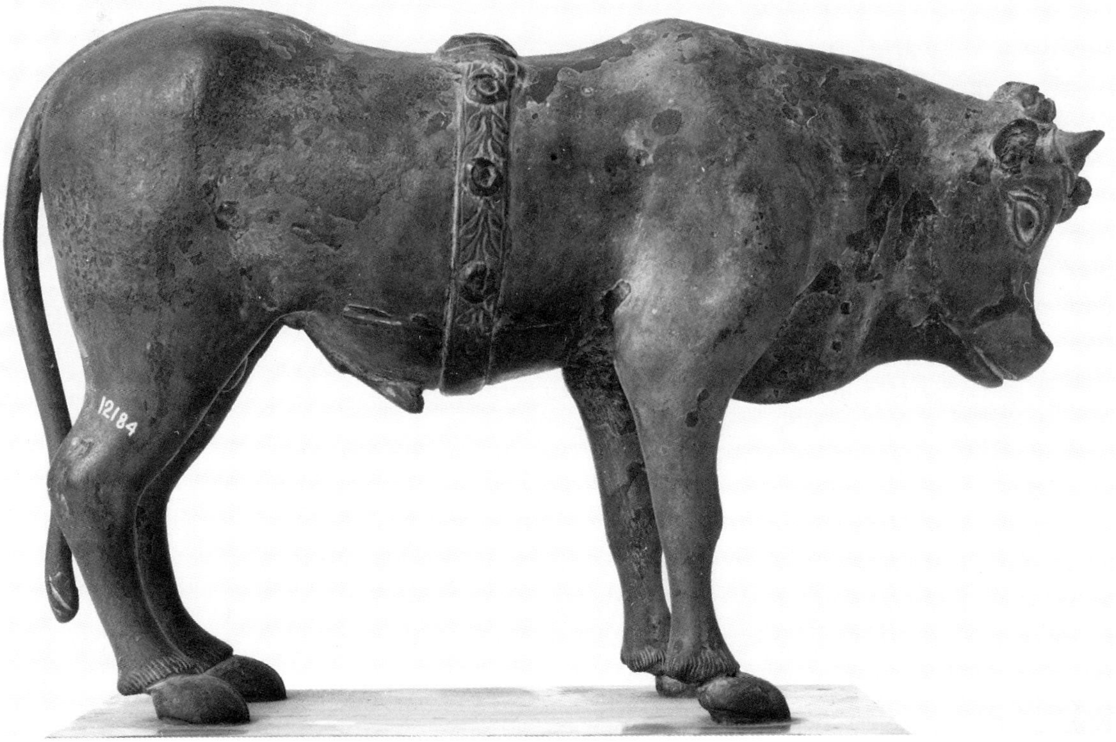

Fig. 10. Statuette of bull with a *dorsuale*. Roman, 1st c. A.D. Bronze, l. 0.25 m. Rome, Musei dei Vaticani 12184. (Photo: courtesy Musei dei Vaticani.)

tico identified as the Aedes Tensarum.[60] Scenes of animal combat that include a lion and bull pair are sculpted on the base of the Farnese Bull.[61]

A more sinister group was acted out in the Flavian amphitheater. The re-enactment of the myth of Pasiphae and the bull was one of the mythic charades with which the Roman audience was entertained.[62] Suetonius relates: '[a]mong the plots of the Pyrrhic performances there was the bull that penetrated Pasiphae, hidden — so many spectators believed — inside a wooden replica of a heifer.'[63]

Proposed identifications of the Conservatori bull

We have presented a straightforward exposition of the literary and archaeological evidence for colossal bulls in the Greek and Roman periods. The question remains: Is the Conservatori bull recognizable as one of the bulls recorded in the literary or artistic record? As we venture into the area of interpretation, we present two variant readings of the evidence.

One possibility is to interpret the ancient restoration to the flank as an indication that a figure was once seated on the bull.[64] Thus, the bull might be linked to the bull from the group of Europa and the bull by Pythagoras at Tarentum. The treatment of the veins of the belly speaks in favour of this interpretation. There is no evidence, however, that this group was ever transferred to Rome, although Strabo records the almost full-scale stripping of the site.[65]

Another possibility would be the bull's identification as a sacrificial dedication in a temple or forum.[66] The restoration might then be the result of the removal of a *dorsuale*, such as that

60 *LTUR* vol. 1 (Rome 1993) 17 (G. Pisani Sartorio).

61 *Il toro Farnese: la 'montagna di marmo' tra Roma e Napoli* (Exhib. cat., Museo Archeologico Nazionale, Naples 1991) esp. pl. 3.

62 K. M. Coleman, "Fatal charades," *JRS* 80 (1990) 63-64.

63 Suet., *Nero* 12.2. See also Mart., *Spect.* 5.

64 The hypothesis presented here is that of C. Parisi Presicce.

65 Strabo 6.3.1; see also Cic., *Verr.* 4.60.135.

66 The hypothesis presented here is that of L.-A. Touchette.

traditionally sported by sacrificial bulls on historical reliefs.[67] A small-scale version of what might be envisaged as the original state of the bull is preserved in the Vatican Museums (fig. 10).[68] Alternatively, a chalchedon signed by the artist Hyllos might prove instructive.[69] There, the bull's dedication to Dionysos is marked by the addition of an ivy vine around his belly. The removal of a similar attribute marking the dedication of our bull to a specific deity might have necessitated the ancient repair to the flank.

It is hoped that further restoration will enhance our understanding of the iconography and various display contexts of this colossal bull. Its 'rediscovery' has been made possible through modern technical advances. This preliminary report also demonstrates the potential for the re-interpretation and rehabilitation of other sculptures, using a combination of new scientific approaches and more traditional scholarly methodology.

Musei Capitolini, Rome (C.P.P.); The British School at Rome (L-A.T.)

---

67 E.g., the Vicomagistri relief, Rome, Musei dei Vaticani 1156, 1157: Helbig^4 I, 203-6, no. 258 (E. Simon). See also the numerous examples in G. Koeppel's articles in *BJb* 185 (1985) 142-213; 186 (1986) 1-90.

68 Rome, Musei dei Vaticani 12184: Helbig^4 I, 608-9, no. 832 (E. Simon), l. 25 cm.

69 Paris, Cabinet des Médailles: M. L. Vollenweider, *Die Steinschneidekunst und ihre Künstler in spätrepublikanischer und augusteischer Zeit* (Baden-Baden 1966) 118-19, pl. 78.1-2, 4; h. 22 mm, w. 41 mm.

Types of Herakles statuettes in Copenhagen that reflect large classical sculptures

Helle Salskov Roberts

In 1820 the Crown Prince of Denmark, later King Christian VIII, took a grand tour to Italy, where he met the Archbishop of Taranto, Msgr. Capecelatro, who had an extensive collection of South Italian vases and some minor bronzes, all of which the Prince acquired. The collection was clearly formed in S Italy, but none of the objects has a more precise indication of provenance. The bronzes included at least 18 statuettes representing various types of Herakles.[1]

One type shows a bare-headed attacking Herakles brandishing a club in his right hand, while his left hand is extended, sometimes holding a bow, with lion-skin hanging from the lower arm. An example of this type is seen in fig. 1;[2] the type is also represented by a finer statuette with a very prominent lion-skin in the Bibliothèque Nationale, Paris, also without provenance.[3]

The cultural ambience to which these statuettes belonged is indicated by the well-known example with an Oscan dedication to Herakles found at Venafro.[4] Another representative of

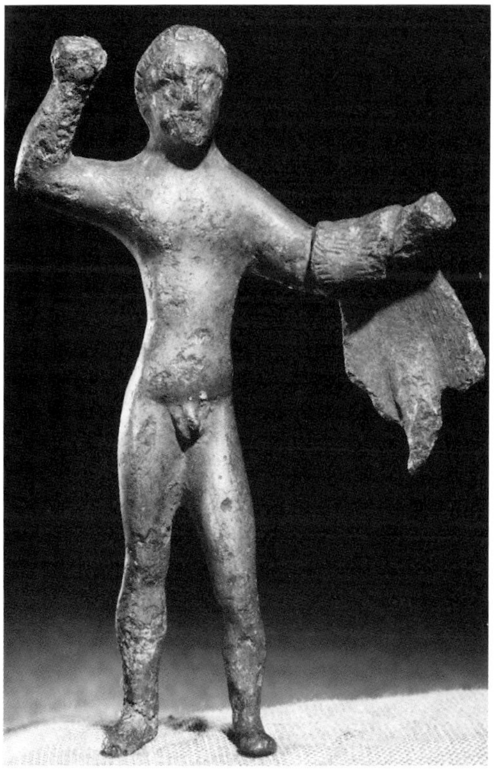

Fig. 1. Statuette of bare-headed, attacking Herakles. Italic, 200-150 B.C. Bronze, h. 10 cm. Copenhagen, Danish National Museum ABa 227. (Photo: N. Elswing; courtesy Museum)

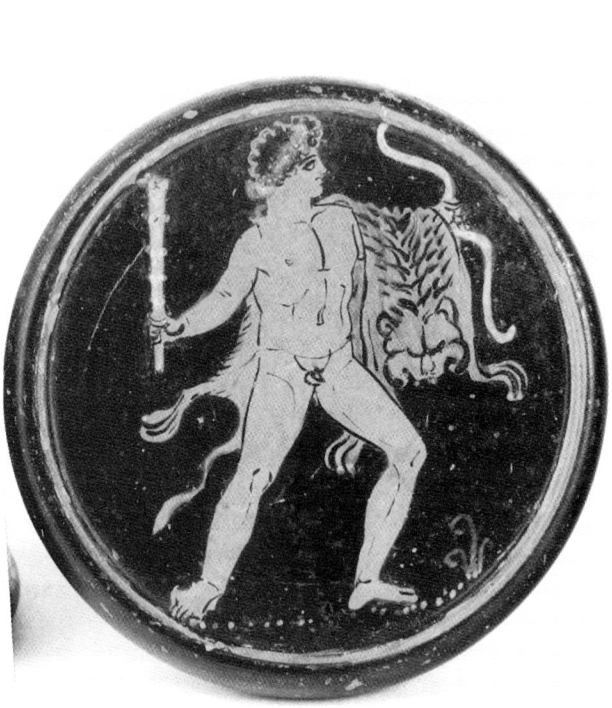

Fig. 2. Red-figure pyxis lid. Italiot (Apulian), *c.*370 B.C. Stadtmuseum Oldenburg. (Photo: courtesy Museum)

1 N. Breitenstein, "Christian VIII's Vasecabinet," in *Antik-Cabinettet 1851 udgivet i Hundredaaret af Nationalmuseet* (Copenhagen 1951) 62-76.

2 Copenhagen, Danish National Museum ABa 227, h. 10 cm.

3 A.-M. Adam, *Bronzes étrusques et italiques* (Paris 1984) no. 272.

4 A. La Regina, "Le iscrizioni osche di Pietrabbondante," *RhM* NF 109 (1966) 270, no. 17, pl. IV, inscription facsimile pl. VIII.

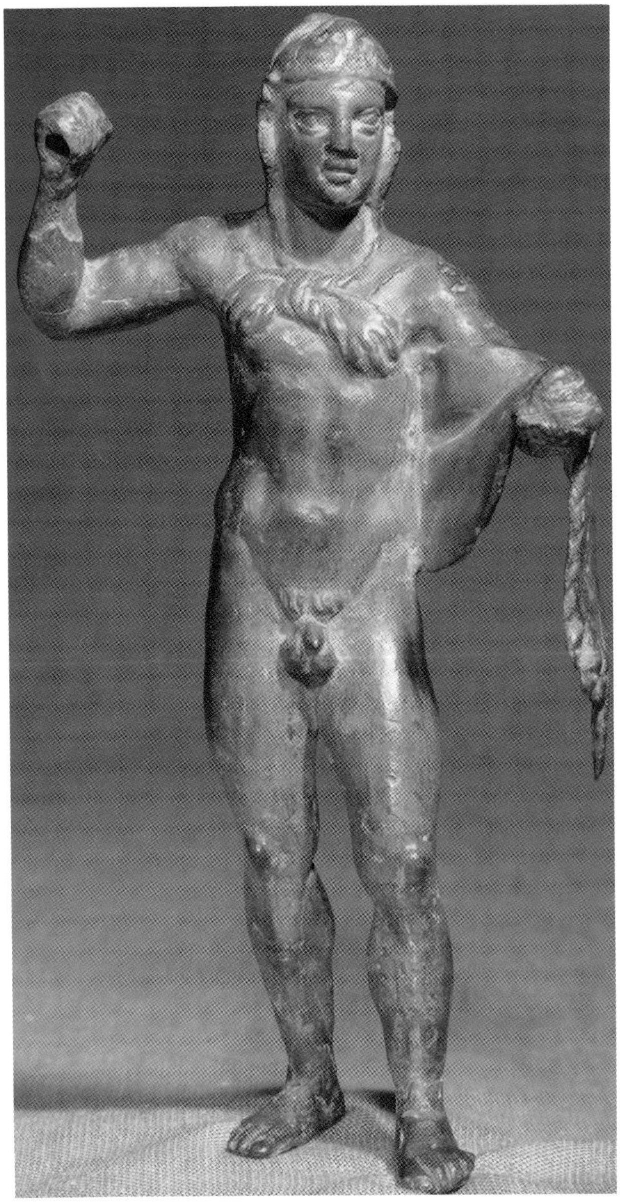

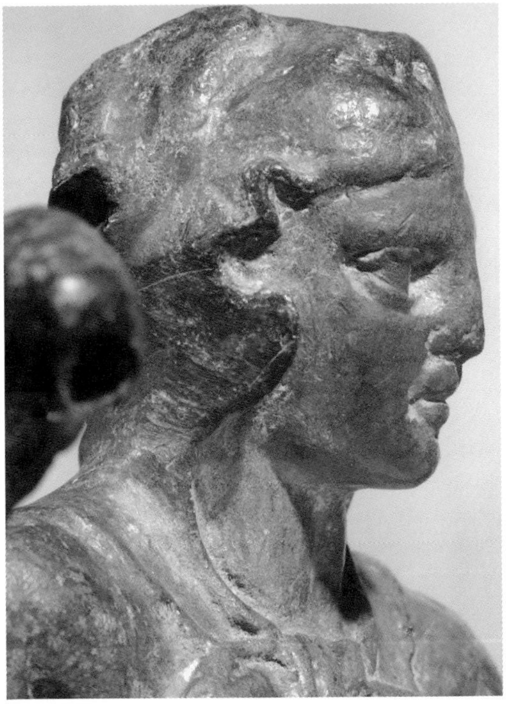

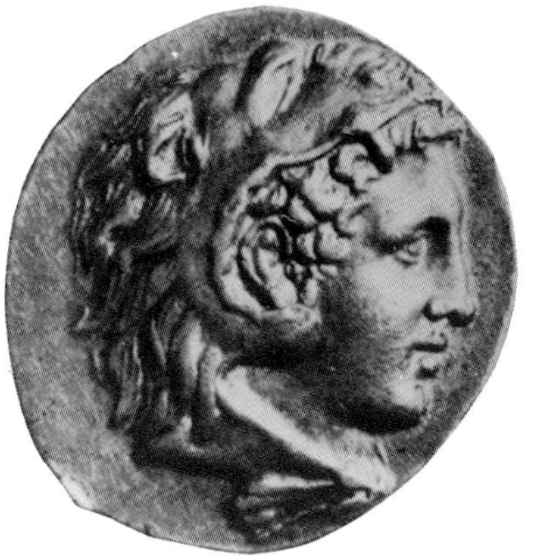

Fig. 3. Statuette of attacking Herakles wearing lion-skin helmet. Italic, late 4th c. B.C. Bronze, h. 15 cm. Copenhagen, Danish National Museum ABa 219. (Photo: N. Elswing; courtesy Museum)

Fig. 4 (above). Detail of fig. 3. (Photo: N. Elswing; courtesy Museum)

Fig. 5 (below). Stater minted in Tarentum *c.*315 B.C., showing beardless Herakles with lion helmet. (Photo: after Jenkins [infra n.8] fig. 452)

this type comes from Trivento, on the left bank of the Trigno.[5] This is an unusually large statuette, 24 cm tall, whereas the common height ranges from 8 to 10 cm.

The inspiration for this native production of statuettes is the type of Greek or Italiot statue of larger size that can be seen on the Apulian bell krater in the British Museum by the Eton-Nika Painter of *c.*370 B.C. The Herakles figure on top of a column is having a sacrifice prepared for him.[6] Another example is painted on an Apulian red-figure pyxis lid now in Oldenburg (fig. 2).[7] Characteristic of this type is the dynamic stance and the prominent lion-skin. Herakles is

5 S. Capini and A. Di Niro (edd.), *Samnium: archeologia del Molise* (Rome 1991) 190, d48e, pl. 8d and cover ill.

6 London, British Museum E 505: A. D. Trendall and A. Cambitoglou, *The red-figured vases of Apulia* (Oxford 1978) 78 no. 88; *LIMC* IV, no. 1097.

7 R. Stupperich, *Antiken in westfälischen Museen* (Oldenburg 1984) 67.

beardless and bare-headed apart from a wreath or fillet. From Lapethus in Cyprus comes a coin dated by the inscription in the name of King Demonikos to 380-360 B.C., that shows the statue of Athena Promachos on one side and, on the other, a Herakles in forward movement brandishing the club and holding the bow — probably also a reference to a statue.[8]

A different — and much more common — type in the Archbishop's collection shows Herakles in the same forward attacking stance, but with the head of the lion-skin worn as a helmet and the body of the lion-skin wrapped around his left arm. The largest example (figs. 3-4)[9] has torso modeling and facial features that are fairly close to the Greek — or Italiot —sculptural prototype, as can be seen when compared to a coin showing a beardless Herakles who has some resemblance to the features of Alexander, minted in Tarentum in *c.*315 B.C. (fig. 5)

In this type great interest is also taken in the details of the lion-skin (fig. 3), of which there are various kinds of stylization. The Louvre possesses a large, well-known specimen with the provenance "Abruzzi".[10] British Museum 1245 is another example.[11] Both are classified by G. Colonna as being of the Caramanico type, as they show characteristics of many of the statuettes in the large deposit of about 50 (smaller) pieces found in 1940 at Caramanico *c.*15 km north of Sulmona.[12]

A bearded Herakles in the attacking stance and wearing the lion-skin helmet is known in Greece from Archaic times, illustrated frequently in red-figure vase-painting.[13] Some representations seem to refer to a sculpture.[14] Many of the great sculptors of the Classical period are also credited with having made versions of Herakles. Lysippos in particular is said to have created two statues for Tarentum, but none can be identified as the likely prototype for a beardless attacking Herakles wearing the lion-skin helmet reproduced so frequently by Italic examples of reduced scale.[15] The beardless lion helmet type can, however, be seen in Cypriot limestone sculpture from Kition-Bamboula throughout the 5th c. B.C.[16] The same type, with bow held high, appears on a coin from Kition struck by Pumayyaton, a local king who died in 312 B.C. This may be a Cypriot version influenced by the iconography of Melqart, but it may, of course, refer to a 4th-c. sculpture from the Greek mainland.[17] A frontal view of an Alexander-like head appearing under the jaws of the lion figures on a rare terracotta medallion from Kakopetria,[18] and a few other frontal heads can be found from the 4th and 3rd c. B.C.[19]

Both types of Italic Herakles statuettes discussed so far seem to reflect larger-scale works from the 4th c. B.C. Scholars commenting on some of the more prominent examples have noted

---

8 G. K. Jenkins, *Ancient Greek coins* (London 1972) figs. 324-25.

9 Copenhagen, Danish National Museum ABa 219, h. 15 cm.

10 A. de Ridder, *Les bronzes antiques du Louvre* 1 (Paris 1913) no. 283, pl. 25; R. Bianchi Bandinelli and A. Giuliano, *Etruschi e Italici prima del dominio di Roma* (Milan 1973) fig. 122.

11 Walters, *British Museum Bronzes* no. 1245.

12 G. Colonna, "Problemi dell'arte figurativa di età ellenistica nell'Italia adriatica," in *Atti del I Convegno di studi sulle antichità adriatiche* (Chieti 1979) 176. On the Caramanico deposit: *AA* 1941, 630-31, fig. 123; R. Papi, "Testimonianze archeologiche della valle dell'Orte: il deposito votivo di Caramanico," *Quaderni di Abruzzo* 14 (1979) 123-48.

13 E.g., Arezzo 1465, krater by Euphronios: *ARV*^{2} 15.6. *Euphronios der Maler* (Ausstellungskat., Berlin-Dahlem 1991) no. 13, ill. p. 132.

14 E.g., *ARV*^{2} 18.1; 1619; *LIMC* IV, s.v. Herakles no. 16. The stance is very similar to that on the Arezzo krater (supra n.13), but the head is not preserved.

15 The identification of the Herakles Alexikakos is still a matter for discussion: *LIMC* IV, s.v. Herakles no. 1282.

16 M. Yon, "Héraklès à Chypre," in C. Bonnet and C. Jourdain-Annequin (edd.), *Héraclès: d'une rive à l'autre de la Méditerranée* (Brussels–Rome 1992) 145-63, fig. 3a, b.

17 Yon ibid. fig. 3d.

18 Yon ibid. fig. 3c.

19 *LIMC* IV, s.v. Herakles no. 124, silver-gilt bronze plaque said to be from Tarentum; no. 125, bronze medallion.

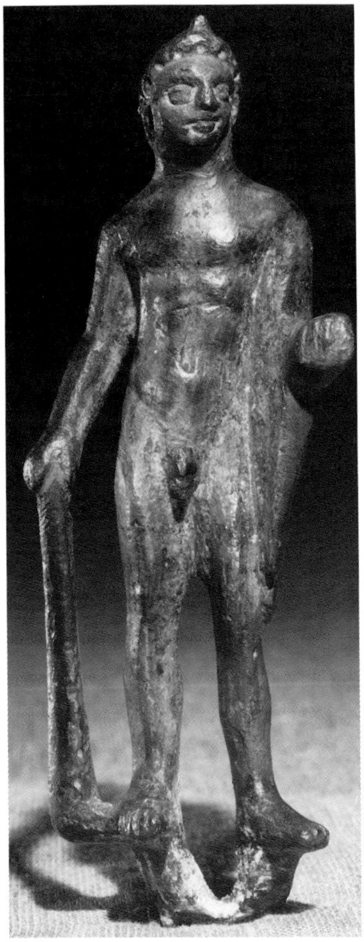

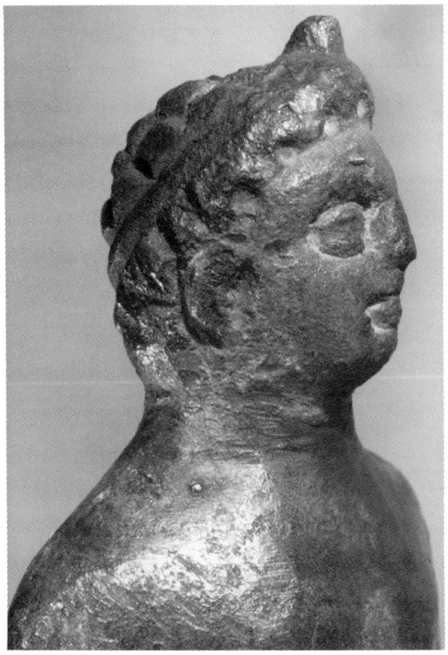

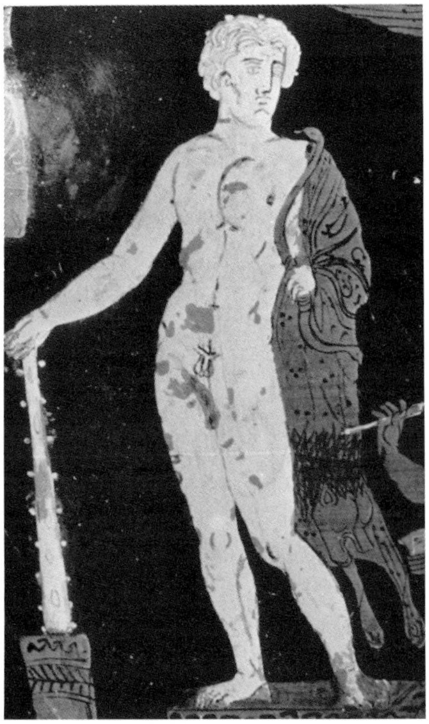

Fig. 6. Statuette of resting Herakles. Italic, mid 3rd c. B.C. Bronze, h. 11.2 cm (without tang). Copenhagen, Danish National Museum ABa 234. (Photo: N. Elswing; courtesy Museum)

Fig. 7. Detail of fig. 6. (Photo: N. Elswing; courtesy Museum)

Fig. 8. Detail of a red-figure Apulian column krater. Italiot, *c.*360 B.C. New York, The Metropolitan Museum of Art, Rogers Fund, 50.11.4. (Photo: after *BMMA* [Feb. 1951] 157)

echoes of Lysippan style,[20] and the apparent resemblance to Alexander iconography is certainly not incompatible with such an inspiration, although Apulian vases show that possible prototypes existed already in the first half of the century.

A third type of Herakles statuette is represented in the Archbishop's collection by only one complete specimen (figs. 6-7).[21] The hero is in a quiet pose, supporting himself on the club with his right hand. The left hand is extended, originally holding upright a thin object (now missing). A semi-cylindrical hollow indicates that this object was his bow.

Herakles' stance is that seen on the Apulian statue vase in New York (fig. 8),[22] where the club rests on a pedestal. The statue of Herakles holds the bow in his left hand, while a prominent lion-skin hangs from his left lower arm. An artist is busy, presumably painting it, which means a marble statue is represented. Herakles himself, in Archaic attire with lion helmet, is critically inspecting his novel image. This vase, from *c.*360 B.C., is likely to represent a Herakles statue erected in Tarentum or its nearby colony Herakleia, where it was chosen as the design on a coin issued in *c.*380 B.C. and was in use until 281 B.C.[23]

---

20 E.g., statuette from Campodipietra near Campobasso: Capini and Di Niro (supra n.5) 166d, 48a, colour pl. XIV.

21 Copenhagen, Danish National Museum ABa 234, h. 11.2 cm without tang.

22 D. von Bothmer, "*Enkaustes Agalmaton*," *BMMA* (Feb. 1951) 157; *LIMC* IV, s.v. Herakles no. 271.

23 E.g., *SNG* Copenhagen I, 1106 (Herakleia, 380-281 B.C.); 1110 (Herakleia, 281-272 B.C.); 1130 (Herakleia, 380-281 B.C.).

The head of this statuette (fig. 7) suggests, however, a slightly later date. The large eyes with their very prominent lids, the mouth with the full lower lip, and the small fat chin, as well as the hairstyle, find their inspiration in the iconography of Ptolemy II Philadelphos, as seen on the coin of this ruler together with Arsinoe II, issued by his son Ptolemy III Euergetes after his ascension in 246 B.C.,[24] and on a stone head in Alexandria.[25]

A certain resemblance can also be observed to a head in Copenhagen tentatively identified as Ptolemy III Euergetes,[26] whose features, not unnaturally, are rather like those of his predecessor. The diadem is standard for royal portraits, whereas the conical ornament (fig. 7) frequently adorning bare-headed types of the hero, is indubitably inspired by the headband of a victorious athlete, such as that worn by the Marathon youth of Praxitelean style[27] or the bronze from Fano,[28] which also has affinities to the iconography of a Hellenistic ruler.

A large number of Herakles statuettes have been found over a wide area, with a concentration in Abruzzi and Molise. They are also present at the Sicilian sanctuary of Erice, at Trieste, and at Celje (former Yugoslavia), and, perhaps, as far away as France. Many are stray finds, but some appear in quantity in deposits like that at Caramanico. When this deposit was found, the Italian archaeologists tried to locate the sanctuary it presumably belonged to but without success.

A number of other small sanctuaries, however, have been located. One is Campochiaro at the *tratturo* Pescasseroli-Candela on the road that connected Bovianum with Saepinum. The small sanctuary (21.30 x 15.30 m) is now thought to be that of Herculi(s) Rani mentioned on the *Tabula Peutingeriana*. Stamped tiles giving the names of Samnite magistrates indicate the official character of the building, which was prostyle tetrastyle. It can be dated to *c.*140-130 B.C., but there are architectural remains from earlier building phases, possibly as early as the 3rd c. B.C.[29] Recent excavations have produced fragments of bronze statuettes representing Herakles and the torso of a Roman copy of a Hellenistic marble showing the hero wearing a lion-skin with the paws tied in front.[30] There is evidence of activity from the middle of the 4th c. B.C., when there was possibly only a wooden structure of modest size, the cult concentrating around altars.[31] Campanian, Apulian, and Lucanian coins of the 4th and 3rd c. B.C. show the contacts of those who frequented the sanctuary from its early stages, before the more permanent building of the 2nd c. B.C.[32]

Another prostyle tetrastyle building of modest dimensions (17.92 x 10.81 m), located near the *tratturo* Foggia-Celano and near the source of the Trigno, is that of Vastogirardi, also datable to *c.*130 B.C.[33] Very few ex-votos were found in the actual temple area. There were, however, a couple of terracotta fragments of oxen from the filling of the podium and a terracotta showing a nose and two eyes, indicating that the deity protected cattle and the health of the devotees. Statuettes of the attacking Herakles[34] — like that of fig. 1, found a few kilometers away from

---

24 G. M. A. Richter, *The portraits of the Greeks* (3rd edn., London 1965) fig. 1781.

25 Ibid. figs 1792-94.

26 Ibid. figs. 1818-19.

27 Athens, National Archaeological Museum 15118: J. Boardman *et al.*, *Die griechische Kunst* (Munich 1984) fig. 235.

28 Los Angeles, The J. Paul Getty Museum 77.AB.30: A. Viacava, *L'atleta di Fano* (Rome 1994); P. Moreno (ed.), *Lisippo: l'arte e la fortuna* (Exhib. cat., Rome 1995 [Monza 1995]) 68 ff., no. 4.10.1, figs. pp. 72-73.

29 S. Capini, "Il santuario di Ercole a Campochiaro," in Capini and Di Niro (supra n.5) 115-19; F. Coarelli and A. La Regina, *Abruzzo, Molise* (Guide archeologiche Laterza 9, Bari 1993) 202-9.

30 Capini and Di Niro (supra n.5) 285; 306 pl. 5e, e43.

31 Ibid. 119.

32 Ibid. 165-66.

33 J.-P. Morel, "Le sanctuaire de Vastogirardi (Molise) et les influences héllenistiques en Italie centrale," in P. Zanker (ed.), *Hellenismus in Mittelitalien* 1 (Göttingen 1976) 255-66; id., "Gli scavi del santuario di Vastogirardi," in *Sannio: Pentri e Frentani dal VI al I sec. a.C.* (Rome 1980) 35-41.

34 Morel ibid. 266, fig. 8.

the sanctuary — point more specifically to Herakles as the deity of Vastogirardi.

A third prostyle tetrastyle *sacellum* of the second half of the 2nd c. B.C. at Schiavi d'Abruzzo has even more modest measurements (7.40 x 13.30 m). In this case, part of the base of the cult statue is extant,[35] but neither here nor in other sanctuaries is the cult statue — or statuette — preserved in context. It is, however, not unlikely that some of the larger bronze statuettes, e.g., the Trivento Herakles (h. 24 cm) or the Campodipietra bronze (h. 27 cm), were the cult images in modest rural sanctuaries, where one should hardly expect life-size or even half life-size statues.

The vast majority of the small Herakles statuettes are, of course, ex-votos, and the donors were most likely herdsmen practicing transhumance,[36] which would account for the wide range of places where they have been found.[37] Another explanation may be suggested for some of the very distant find-spots such as France. Small bronzes of the attacking Herakles might have appealed to Italic soldiers serving further north and could easily have been carried with them on campaign during Roman expansion into Europe.[38]

This brings us back to the difficult question of the date of many of the statuettes. The three examples from the Archbishop's collection (figs. 1, 3, and 4) discussed here have been shown to be reflections of Greek or Italiot creations of the 4th and 3rd c. B.C. The buildings of the sanctuaries with which they can be connected are largely from the latter half of the 2nd c. B.C., although coins show that the sanctuaries were frequented in the 4th and 3rd c. The life-spans of the sanctuaries vary, but it seems that activity at small Italic sanctuaries was allowed to continue by the Romans after the end of the *bellum sociale*, in contrast to large centers where it was stopped. The monumental temple of Pietrabbondante, which could fairly be suspected of harboring anti-Roman attitudes, is a striking example of this. As mentioned above, there are important finds from the Roman period at Campochiaro, and the *sacellum* at Schiavi d'Abruzzo also seemed to continue.[39] The deposit of S. Agata, Castelvecchio Subequo, which held at least two specimens of the bare-headed attacking Herakles similar to that of fig. 1, also included two other types of Herakles and a coin of the 1st c. B.C., as well as a *cippus* with a Latin dedication to Hercules Victor.[40] Unfortunately, the coin can not be used for dating any particular figure in the deposit. Of the 32 extant Herakles figurines in the Caramanico deposit, 31 are in the dynamic attacking stance, some bare-headed and some wearing the lion-skin helmet, while only one represents the resting hero.[41] The large bronze found in the sanctuary of Hercules Curinus at Sulmona shows a bearded Herakles in a resting position. This is now thought to be an original work from the 3rd c. B.C., produced in the tradition of Lysippos and with the reduction of size made by him.[42] It has, however, the later dedication by Peticius Marsus of the early Empire, showing the preference of that period.

Dating individual statuettes still depends on stylistic criteria. The choice of the attacking Herakles may reflect the attitude of mind of the native population of Samnium in the 4th and 3rd c. B.C. Later, Herakles was still venerated at the sanctuaries near the springs with waters beneficent to grazing flocks and to man, but quieter aspects of the hero were perhaps felt to be more appropriate, although among the Samnites the resting Herakles could never compete in popularity with the more aggressive type.

Eivindsvej 36, DK 2920 Charlottenlund

35 A. La Regina, "Il Sannio," in Zanker (supra n.33) 232, fig. X.

36 F. Van Wonterghem, "Le culte d'Hercule chez les Paeligni: documents anciens et nouveaux," *AntCl* 42 (1973) 36-48, esp. 45 ff.; E. Mattiocco and F. Van Wonterghem, "La Fortuna di Ercole tra i Peligni," in E. Mattiocco (ed.), *Dalla villa di Ovidio al santuario di Ercole* (Sulmona 1989) 47-70, esp. 48-51.

37 See distribution map I with *tratturi:* La Regina in Zanker (supra n.33) 220.

38 Cf. Papi (supra n.12) 126.

39 La Regina in Zanker (supra n.33) 237.

40 G. Bendinelli, *NotSc* 46 (1921) 284-90.

41 Papi (supra n.12) 139-48, figs. 1-32.

42 Moreno (supra n.28) 103, no. 4.14.1.

Two Gallo-Roman bronze portraits of sacrificial assistants in the Getty Museum

John Pollini

In The J. Paul Getty Museum are two life-size bronze portrait busts of high quality that represent two different adolescents (figs. 1-2). These portraits formed part of a cache of 8 remarkable bronzes (also including three warrior figures, a statuette of a stag, a money chest, and a *situla*) of Gallo-Roman workmanship that reportedly comes from east-central Roman Gaul. From internal evidence (including inscriptions), it appears that the 8 objects once belonged to a shrine of a hitherto unknown, syncretistic, Romano-Celtic warrior god named Cobannus, who is represented in the group of warrior figures. This shrine may have been associated with the *Iuventus*, a provincial youth organization that also included the imperial cult. The two Getty portraits (the focus of the paper given at the Bronze Congress) represent sacrificial assistants who most likely participated in the cult of Cobannus and date to about the third quarter of the 1st c. A.D., while the other 6 bronzes date from about the mid 1st to the 3rd c. A.D. All of these objects from the cache, including the two portraits discussed here, are the subject of my comprehensive monograph now in press: *Studia varia: occasional papers on antiquities of The J. Paul Getty Museum* (2001).

The two Getty portraits were part of the exhibition *The fire of Hephaistos* and were briefly discussed in a catalogue entry by C. Mattusch.[1] Contrary to her conclusions, the iconographical

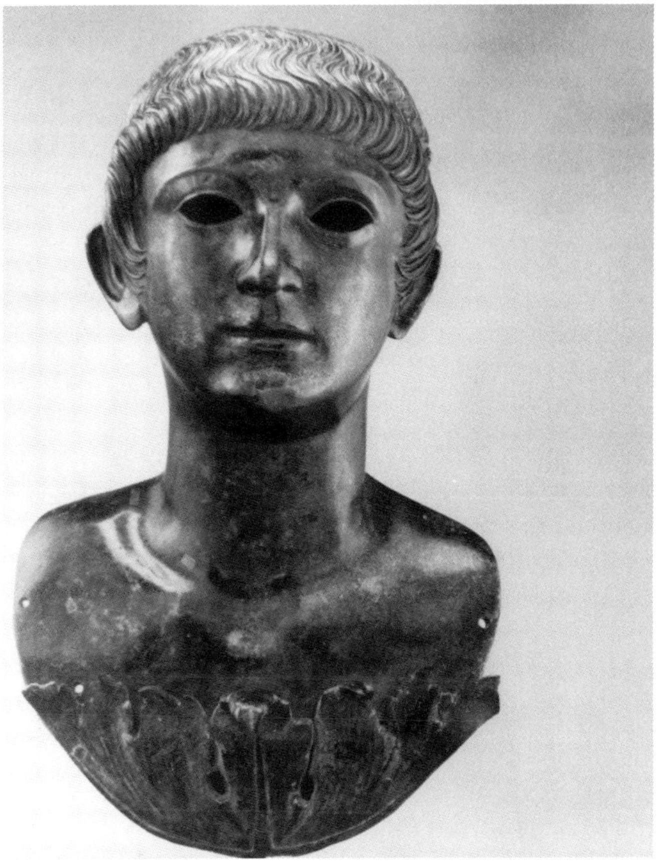

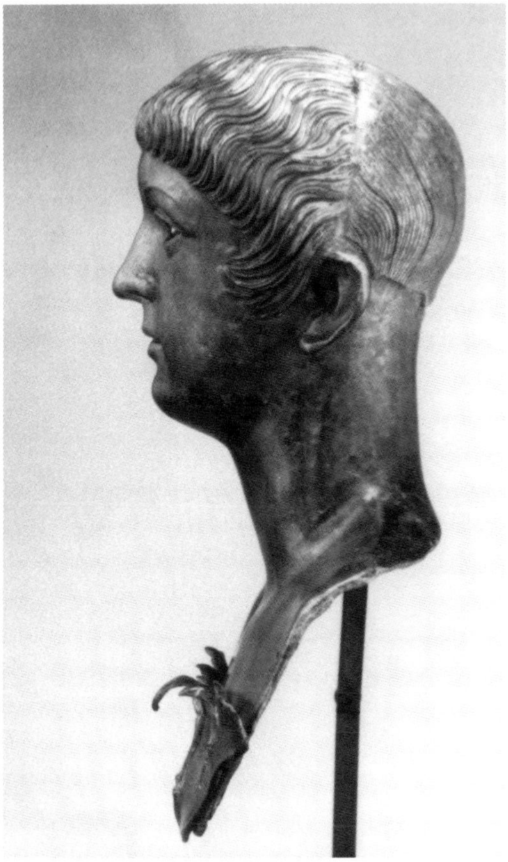

Fig. 1. Portrait bust of male adolescent with calyx of acanthus leaves (portrait A). Gallo-Roman, third quarter of 1st c. A.D. Bronze, h. 0.40 m. Los Angeles, The J. Paul Getty Museum 89.AB.67.1. (Photo: courtesy Museum)

---

1 *The fire of Hephaistos* 325-30, nos. 48 and 49.

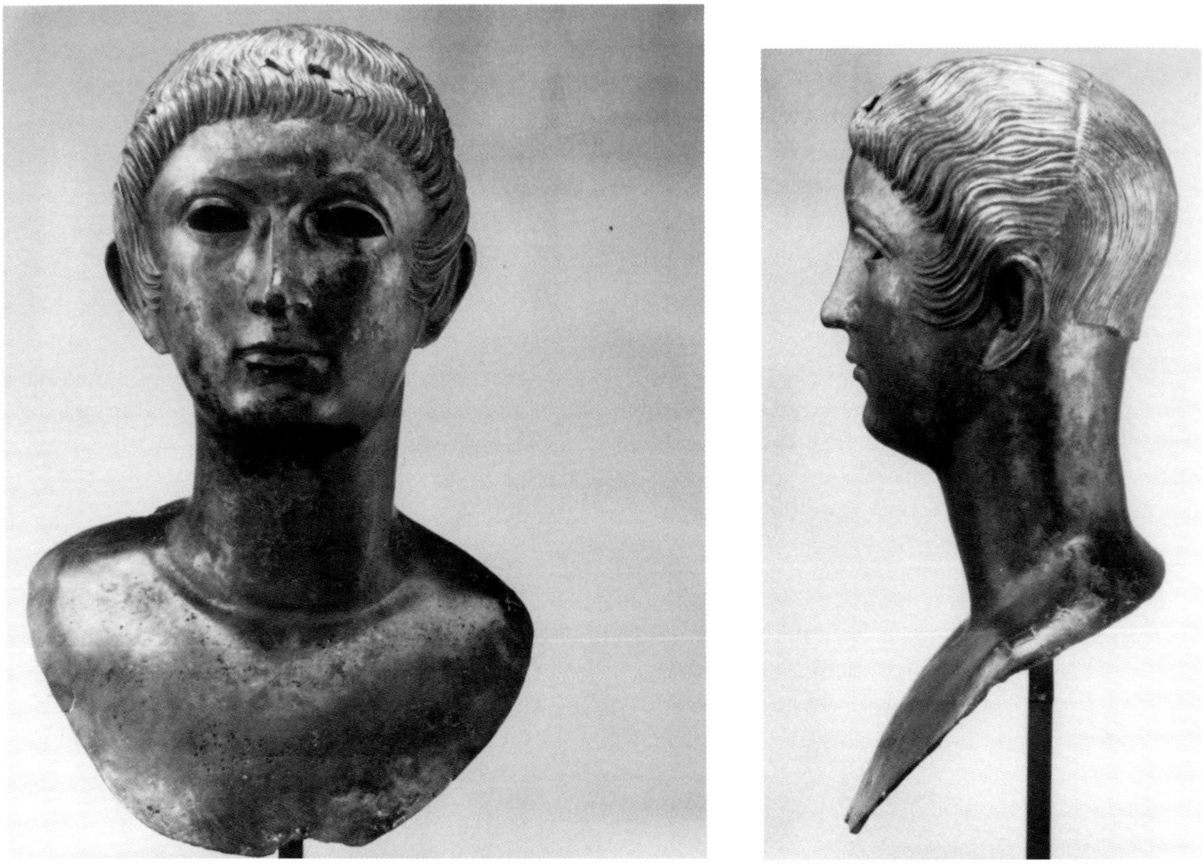

Fig. 2. Portrait bust of male adolescent (portrait B). Gallo-Roman, third quarter of the 1st c. A.D. Bronze, h. 0.406 m. Los Angeles, The J. Paul Getty Museum 89.AB.67.2. (Photo: courtesy Museum)

coiffures of the two adolescents have nothing to do with Gallic hairstyles, other than in the obvious linear emphasis in the treatment of hair. The distinctive hairstyle, parted from ear to ear over the top of the head and brushed forward over the forehead and down behind the head, is typically worn by servile ministrants. The now missing long tresses of both Getty portraits were once separately-fashioned bronze sections attached by solder (traces extant) to zigzag cut hairlines at the backs of both heads. In my full study, I term this feminized coiffure the "long-tressed sickle-lock" type. Visual evidence for similar feminized hairstyles worn by slave 'boys', as well as corroborating literary evidence, in my view conclusively indicates that the Getty adolescents belonged to a particular class of slaves who functioned as priestly sacrificial assistants (cf., e.g., fig. 3).[2] Among their other servile functions, these adolescents may have been *delicati*, favorite sex-slaves, like the pedicated 'boy' on the Warren Cup (fig. 4).[3] The master of the 'boys' represented in the Getty busts (and presumably the dedicant of these portraits) may even have served as a priest in the cult of Cobannus.

---

2 Cf., e.g., A. Giuliano (ed.), *Museo Nazionale Romano: le sculture* I.1 (Rome 1979) 260-64, no. 161 (P. Rendini); cf. F. Fless, *Opferdiener und Kultmusiker auf stadtrömischen historischen Reliefs* (Mainz 1995) esp. pls. 21 and 31.

3 J. R. Clarke, "The Warren Cup and the contexts for representations of male-to-male lovemaking in Augustan and early Julio-Claudian art," *ArtB* 75 (1993) 280-81, figs. 8 and 9 (detail of head). Clarke does not interpret this boy (or the other youth represented on the cup) as a master's pet sex-slave 'boy', nor does he make any connection between sex-slave 'boys' and sacrificial assistants. See further id., *Looking at lovemaking: constructions of sexuality in Roman art, 100 BC to AD 250* (Berkeley, CA 1998) 61-78 and passim, figs. 16-22, color pls. 1-2; J. Pollini, "The Warren cup: homoerotic love and symposial rhetoric in silver," *ArtB* 81 (1999) 21-52. Since acquisition by the British Museum, the Warren Cup has been published by D. Williams, *Minerva* 10.4 (July/August 1999) 33-35; id., *British Museum Magazine* 35 (Autumn/Winter 1999) 25-28.

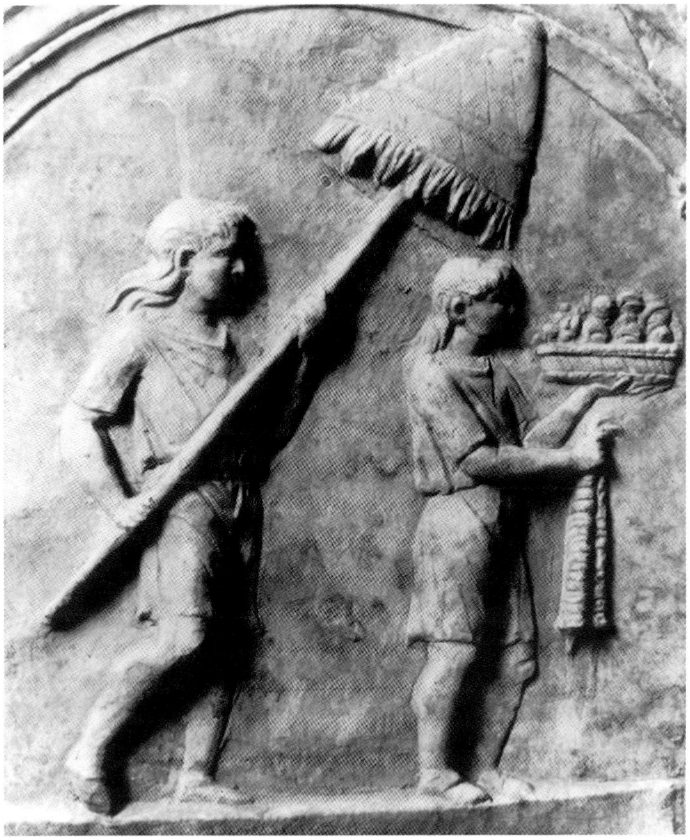

Fig. 3. Relief on the right side of a funerary altar. Roman, middle of the 1st c. A.D. Marble, h. 0.94 m. Rome, Museo Nazionale Romano 124514. (Photo: from A. Giuliano [ed.], *Museo Nazionale Romano: le sculture* I.1 [Rome 1979] 263)

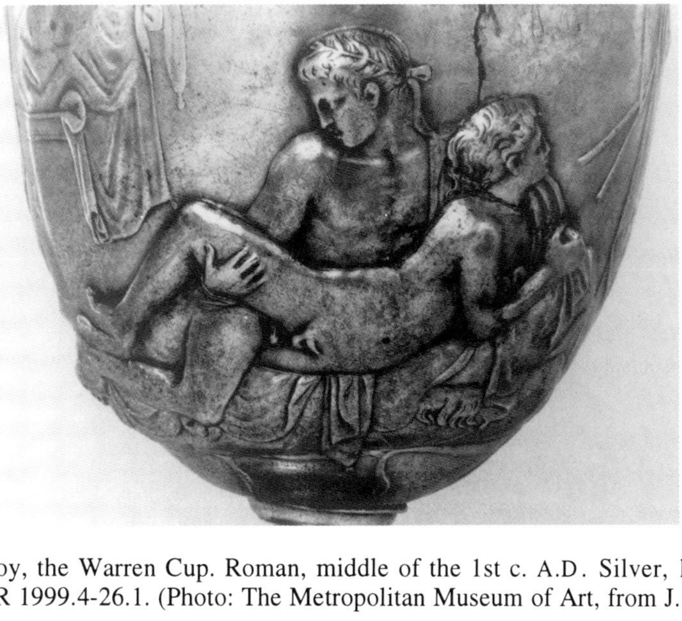

Fig. 4. Detail of boy, the Warren Cup. Roman, middle of the 1st c. A.D. Silver, h. 13.5 cm. London, British Museum GR 1999.4-26.1. (Photo: The Metropolitan Museum of Art, from J. R. Clarke in *ArtB* 75 [1993] fig. 8)

Department of Art History, University of Southern California, Los Angeles

TABLE 1. RESULTS OF ICP ANALYSIS (PERCENT BY WEIGHT)

The results have a precision of *c.* ± 1-2% for Cu, ± 5% for elements present at levels greater than 1%, but deteriorate to ± 50% at the respective limits of detection (Table: author)

Statue	*part*	*Cu*	*Sn*	*Pb*	*Zn*	*Ag*	*As*	*Au*	*Bi*	*Co*	*Fe*	*Ni*	*Sb*
horse	strap	55.6	7.9	24.1	0.46	0.05	0.93	0.19	1.66	0.033	0.45	0.06	0.37
"	r. side	45.0	8.3	23.7	0.57	0.02	-	0.12	1.04	0.01	0.55	0.03	1.04
"	l. ear	62.8	4.2	26.0	0.50	0.05	0.01	0.01	0.23	0.007	0.28	0.03	0.15
"	r. ear	51.4	6.6	23.6	0.41	0.02	0.20	0.03	0.15	0.006	0.30	0.02	0.16
"	hair	63.2	4.8	27.7	0.45	0.05	0.42	0.01	0.84	0.035	0.25	0.08	0.14
"	rivet	54.1	8.1	26.6	0.74	-	2.30	0.03	1.85	0.009	0.42	0.03	0.05
"	join	60.3	8.6	27.3	0.45	0.05	0.32	0.02	0.91	0.020	0.55	0.05	0.12
"	repair	58.0	18.0	22.0	0.30	-	0.07	0.01	0.50	0.010	0.20	0.01	-
"	filling	52.0	13.0	29.0	0.20	-	0.20	0.01	0.50	0.010	0.10	0.01	-
arm	arm	73.0	11.0	1.50	0.30	0.18	0.08	0.06	0.03	0.002	0.05	0.02	-
"	"basin"	54.7	14.1	29.3	0.41	0.02	-	0.06	0.07	0.03	0.20	0.70	-
"	hand ins.	75.2	8.2	16.1	0.40	0.17	0.15	0.01	0.18	0.010	0.06	0.03	-
"	ind. 1 ph.	76.4	7.3	15.1	0.41	0.02	0.17	0.03	0.04	0.010	0.09	0.03	0.03
"	index, tip	65.0	12.1	22.1	0.30	-	0.20	0.03	0.03	0.030	0.12	0.09	-
"	thumb tip	67.3	12.2	19.2	0.31	-	0.20	0.05	0.05	0.014	0.07	0.03	-
"	filling	56.5	12.3	25.0	0.60	-	0.07	0.06	1.0	0.005	0.60	0.03	-
hoof 1	edge	68.2	11.0	19.1	0.30	0.01	0.30	0.01	0.03	0.010	0.10	0.02	-
"	patch	60.6	14.3	24.4	0.51	-	0.11	0.01	0.05	0.022	0.31	0.02	-
hoof 2	edge l.	66.2	8.2	25.1	0.45	0.04	0.08	0.05	0.02	0.005	0.12	0.04	-
hoof 3	edge l.	52.0	15.0	30.1	0.45	-	0.22	0.15	0.01	0.051	0.27	0.04	-
"	leg	55.3	15.2	27.0	0.40	-	0.20	0.11	0.12	0.022	0.30	0.04	-
"	patch	65.0	9.1	24.2	0.41	-	0.02	0.04	0.09	0.020	0.20	0.01	-

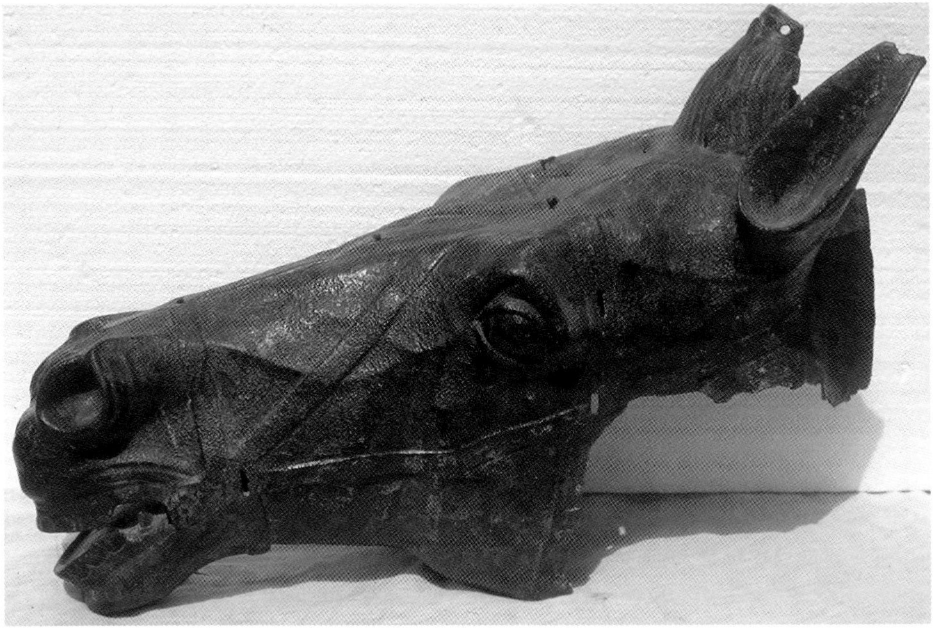

Fig. 1. Horse's head, found in the river Wertach (*Virdus*) at Augusta Vindelicorum. Augsburg, Römisches Museum VF164. The head consists of 7 sections assembled by different methods and was foil gilded. (Photo: author)

Technique and composition of equestrian statues in Raetia

Alessandra Giumlia-Mair

Five large fragments of equestrian statues found in the Roman province of Raetia have been scientifically examined. The study has revealed that the working techniques used for some of the statues differ in several details not only from the techniques used for Greek statuary but also from those used for other Roman statues studied up to now. The composition of the metal was analyzed by inductively coupled plasma-emission spectrometry (ICP), and the results (Table 1) compare well with analyses of other Roman statuary, which generally contains more lead and less tin than Greek statuary.[1] The Raetian examples contain up to 30% lead in the alloy, but the composition depends on the joining techniques employed for the various pieces of a statue. The tin content ranges from 7% in some pieces up to 18% in the case of repairs or solder. The differences in composition suggest that a fresh batch of alloy was prepared in a relatively small crucible for each casting. Piece castings require smaller furnaces, smaller casting pits, and the use of relatively small and simple moulds. This simplifies and speeds up the casting process and the assembling of the statue. The use of alloys with higher amounts of tin and lead for repairs and joins is advantageous because of their lower melting point. Working at lower temperatures reduces the risk of spoiling the sections while assembling them.

The largest and best known of the fragments studied is a horse's head (fig. 1) found at Augusta Vindelicorum in the river Wertach.[2] The sculpture is dated to the Hadrianic period. The head consists of 7 sections: the muzzle, the head, the left and right ears, the knotted forelock, the free strands of the forelock over the knot (now lost), and part of the short mane. Numerous castings of moderate size are typical of Roman casting technique. In this case they were assembled in various ways, but the method employed was always the simplest and the quickest for each section. The separate ears, the forelock, and the small piece of mane were welded on the head by pouring on the join the same alloy used to cast the sections. The outer surface has been worked and polished to render the seam less visible. The muzzle was inserted over the headpiece and adheres to it only over the nose. No metal is visible between the two sections, and there is a large fissure under the chin. The join is probably only mechanical, not metallurgical, and the muzzle has been socketed to the rest of the head. The free strands of hair were inserted into the open section underneath and kept in place by a strip of metal or a rod pushed through the two holes near the edge of the forelock section and fixed by bending it. Even the join between head and neck was mechanical. On the intact front side it can be seen that the edge of the head has been bent inward, as probably was also the upper edge of the neck section, and that the two pieces were riveted to each other. The casting is very thin, in some areas decreasing to a thickness of less than 2 mm. It is evident that thin wax sheets were pressed into the moulds, because on the inner surface there are unmistakeable traces left by a spatula-like tool. The existence of such a tool in antiquity has often been denied, but the impressions left in the wax and reproduced in the bronze of the horse's head cannot be mistaken for traces left by fingers, as is the case with some other statues. Traces of a tool are also visible

---

1 A. Giumlia-Mair, "Il caso di industria: la metallurgia del bronzo e Plinio," *QuadAPiem* 11 (1993) 61, 65.

2 Augsburg, Römisches Museum VF164: K. Kluge and K. Lehmann-Hartleben (edd.), *Die antiken Grossbronzen* 2 (Berlin 1927) 86; H. Menzel, *Die römischen Bronzen aus Bayern* (Mainz 1969) 33, N. 46, Taf. N. 15, 1; G. Gamer, "Fragmente von Bronzestatuen aus den römischen Militärlagern an der Rhein- und Donaugrenze," *Germania* 46 (1968) 53 ff.; L. Bakker, "Reste monumentaler Kaiserstatuen und der Pferdekopf aus der Wertach," in *Die Römer in Schwaben* (Exhib. cat., Augsburg 1985) 104-5; J. Bergemann, *Römische Reiterstatuen: Ehrendenkmäler im öffentlichen Bereich* (Mainz 1990) 59-60, P6; A. Giumlia-Mair, "Studi tecnici sulla testa di cavallo romana da *Augusta Vindelicum*," in E. Formigli (ed.), *I grandi bronzi antichi* (Siena 1999) 255-70.

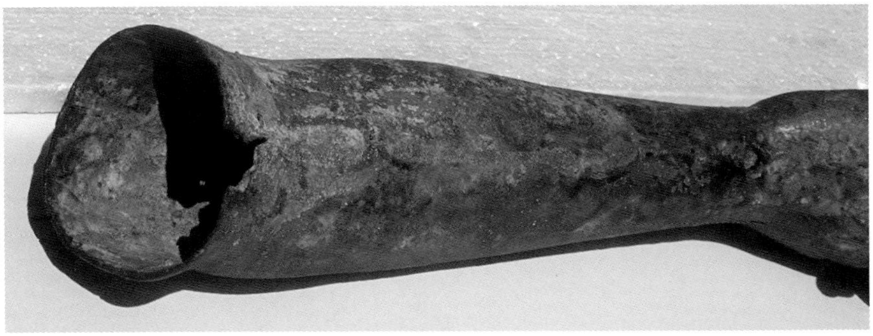

Fig. 2. Right hand and forearm of a rider, found in the river Lech (*Licus*) at Augusta Vindelicorum, detail of the inside. Augsburg, Römisches Museum 428. The arm consists of 9 variously assembled sections. The two methods employed for attaching the two longitudinal sections of the arm are of interest. On this side the "basin method" was used. (Photo: author)

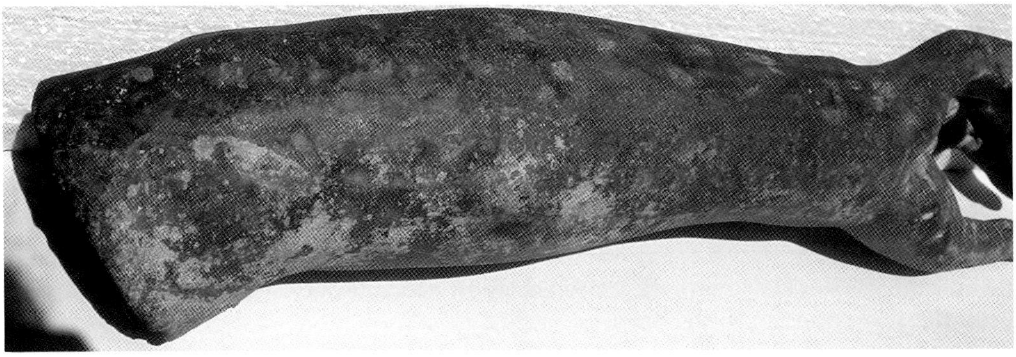

Fig. 3. Outside of the rider´s arm in fig. 2, showing "tongue and hole" join. This technique has been dated to the Renaissance until now, but this example and an arm from Bubon demonstrate that it was already used in Roman times. (Photo: author)

inside the Chatsworth head[3] and on one of the fragments of the Brindisi bronzes, illustrated in the paper delivered by De Palma, Fiorentino and Marabelli at this Congress (see below p. 175).

On the horse's head section there are several repairs of casting flaws, all carried out by pouring on from the inside, using the same alloy as for the castings, probably after summarily lining the outside with clay. No trace of cold working is visible on the outer surface; the details are rather dull, particularly the execution of the hair of the forelock. Any visible casting flaw, uneven join, or difference in the texture of the surface would have been disguised by a layer of gilding, substantial remains of which are to be seen all over the surface, particularly in the deeper details. The very high lead content of the metal (average 25%) led to the supposition that the gilding method was foil gilding. However, as caution is always advisable when dealing with ancient metallurgy, a tiny sample of gilding was taken from under the chin and analyzed by emission spectroscopy. No traces of mercury could be detected, and we can safely conclude that the horse was indeed foil gilded.[4]

The forearm of a rider, also found at Augsburg but in the river Lech, has also been examined (figs. 2-3).[5] The hand is in the position of holding reins, but it is now impossible to determine who the rider was or the date of the statue. However, the alloy (with an average content of 17% lead and 10% tin), the thickness (*c.* 2-3 mm), the shape, and the finishing of the details

3 Haynes, *Technique* 36, pl. 4.

4 Cf. A. Oddy, "Gilding of metals in the Old World," in S. La Niece and P. Craddock (edd.), *Metal plating and patination* (Oxford 1993) 171-81, with further bibliography.

5 Augsburg, Römisches Museum 428: Menzel (supra n.2) 34, N. 51; Bakker (supra n.2) 104, Abb. 69; Bergemann (supra n.2) 60, P7.

allow without doubt a date in the Roman Imperial period.[6] The forearm was attached to the statue by a socket hidden under a fold of a garment or in a sleeve and fixed with a rivet. The way in which the sections were positioned is unusual: there is a join, visible because of its lighter colour, that runs parallel to the arm from the inside of the elbow to the hollow between thumb and forefinger (fig. 2). The pieces were joined by the widely used method of cutting half ovals from either side of the seam and filling the resulting ovals (and in Roman times also the connecting channel, as here) with molten metal.[7] The bronze used for this join contains 29% lead and 14% tin and has a much lower melting point than the bronze of the arm. Dark rings due to the formation of a different phase in the metal around the edges of the basins can be distinguished on the surface. This technique is well known from famous statues such as the Riace bronzes[8] and many others, but the joins are normally positioned at the wrist and over the elbow and not lengthwise down the arm. The joining technique at the opposite side of the forearm is even more unusual (fig. 3). In this case, several holes were opened on both sides along the seam. The molten bronze was poured from inside along the junction and into the holes to obtain a strong hold between the two sections. The metal employed for this sort of "tongue and hole" join can be distinguished on the surface because of its lighter colour. Similar joins are known from earlier times,[9] but it has been claimed that this technique was not used in classical times, nor in the Middle Ages until the Renaissance.[10] There can be no doubt, however, that the arm fragment from Augsburg is Roman and that this is a join and not a repair. The composition, the texture, and colour of the metal of the join compare well with the metal used to fill the holes left by the rods that held the core in place during the casting process. It could not have been restored in this way during the Renaissance, because there are no traces of oval basins and this is clearly the original join. Furthermore, there is another instance of a statue fragment with a similar seam down the length of the arm, from the Sebasteion in Bubon, that was used by J. Riederer to illustrate scientific methods employed in archaeology.[11] In that case the join was hidden with many patches of different sizes. Patches were also employed to hide the joins on the wrist and under the shoulder where the arm was attached to the body. The seam line down the arm has been interpreted as a repair, because the corresponding seam on the other side was different and not very evident. However, computer tomography carried out on the arm showed a thicker ridge on the inner surface, roughly on the same line as that on which the join runs on the arm from Augsburg.[12] Several lighter spots and a hole in the area of the almost imperceptible seam are visible on the illustration that Riederer kindly sent to the author. It is difficult to distinguish the exact position of the junction, but the lighter spots and the hole seem to be in the positions where one would look for them in the case of a "tongue and hole" join on the line revealed by the tomography. The metal poured into the holes along the seam seems to have fallen out of one of them, but to be certain of this one should closely examine the arm. Nevertheless, the existence of the same type of joins down the length of the arm and, at least in one case, the use of a "tongue and hole" join in Roman times is now established, and these examples are probably not the only instances of the use of this technique.

---

6 Cf. Bergemann ibid. 60.

7 E. Formigli *et al.*, "Indagini sulle tecniche di esecuzione di un torso bronzeo romano dei Musei Vaticani," *BMusPont* 10 (1990) 5-24.

8 E. Formigli, "La tecnica di costruzione delle statue di Riace," in *Due Bronzi* 107 ff.

9 E. Formigli, "Tradizioni ed innovazioni nella metallotecnica etrusca," in *L'Etruria mineraria: Atti del XII Convegno di studi etruschi e italica, 1979* (Florence 1981) 66 ff.

10 E. Formigli, "Tecnica e cronologia dei grandi bronzi antichi," in S. T. A. M. Mols *et al.* (edd.), *Acta of the 12th int. congress on ancient bronzes, 1992* (*NAR* 18, Nijmegen 1995) 155.

11 J. Riederer, "Die naturwissenschaftliche Untersuchung eines römischen Bronzearmes," in K. Gschwantler and A. Bernhard-Walcher (edd.), *Griechische und römische Statuetten und Großbronzen: Akten der 9. Tagung über antike Bronzen in Wien 1986* (Vienna 1988) 158-64.

12 Ibid. 160, Abb. 6.

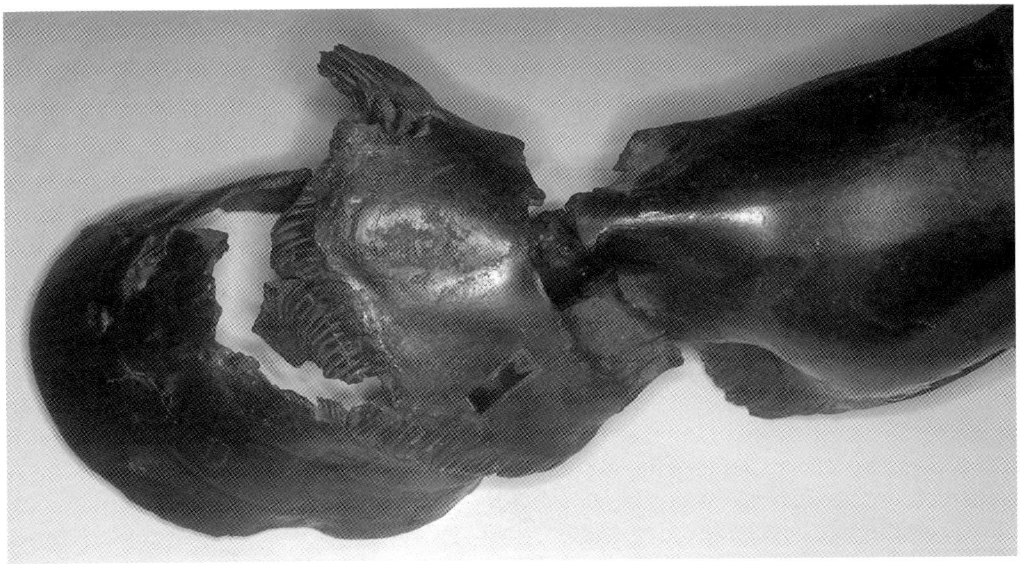

Fig. 4. Horse's hoof from Cambodunum. Kempten, Römisches Museum 0.316.2. Typical Roman polygonal patches. (Photo: author)

The sections of the hand are divided in one of the customary ways, with a join in the middle of the hand and the middle finger as a separate casting, attached by pouring into the gap an alloy with a lower melting point. The fingertips were also made separately to avoid undercutting; but no welding or soldering metal is visible, and the composition of the alloy used for these parts (with tin and lead content higher than that of the other sections, but lower than in the metal used for the joins and the fills) suggests that they were simply cast on the second phalanges. On the first and second phalanges of the index finger there exist a hole left by an iron nail and part of a nail which held the reins in place.

Three horse hooves of bronze found in Cambodunum (mod. Kempten) were also examined. Two of them come from a Flavian layer;[13] the third is gilt and cannot be more precisely dated than to the Roman Imperial period.[14] The casting and finishing of the three hooves, which are all of different sizes and surely belonged to different statues, diverge slightly from those of the fragments discussed above. The reason for the diversity could be change of taste and of working habits over time, but only further studies on well-dated material could prove this hypothesis. The casting sections are generally thicker than later examples, and the casting flaws are repaired with well-finished patches of different sizes, depending on the extent of the flaws underneath. Some of the patches are of the typical Roman polygonal shape, but all of them, even those under the gilding (which is foil gilding), were carefully hammered into the keying and are almost invisible. The hair above the hooves at the coronet and the fetlock of the largest example (fig. 4) is accurately depicted; the hair was drawn on the wax model and is not cold worked.

The details of the horse's head and the finishing of the details on the forearm of the rider are, in contrast to the hooves, rather indistinct. This observation, and the carelessness of the repairs, contrasts sharply with the skill shown in producing the extremely thin casting of the horse's head without any waste of metal. An incised Roman numeral 'X' (10) on one of the hooves (Kempten 0.316.1) and a Roman numeral 'V' (5) on the arm from Augsburg can be seen on the surface of the fragments. Apparently these statues were not put together where they were made, and the various pieces were numbered to facilitate their assembly. The arm from

13 Kempten, Römisches Museum 0.316.1 and 0.316.2: W. Krämer, "Cambodunumforschungen 1953 I," *Materialhefte zur bayerischen Vorgeschichte* 9 (1957) 61, Taf. 10.7-8; Bakker 1985 (supra n.2) 104-5, Abb. 69.

14 Kempten, Römisches Museum 0.316.3: Bakker (supra n.2) 104; G. Weber, "Ein neuentdeckter römischer Siedlungsplatz in Ursularied," in *Das archäologische Jahr in Bayern 1994* (Stuttgart 1995) 116-18.

Augsburg consists of 9 pieces, but only one number is visible on the fragment, so it seems that some statue sections were assembled in the workshop and parts that were awkward to transport were left separate. It is difficult to imagine mounting the parts of the statue in the wrong way, for example by attaching a left arm onto the right side. It seems more probable that the numbers were perhaps not just used for checking if all parts of the statue were present, but also to give the order in which they could be mounted with the fewest problems and with the greatest speed. (This is perhaps also the case with the alphabetic signs on the crater from Vix and the crater in Munich.[15]) Workshops produced the different parts of official portraits of emperors and other notables in many copies to be sent to all the larger towns of the empire, perhaps with instructions for assembling them. In the cases of these 5 statue fragments we are evidently dealing with Roman mass production of monuments representing public figures, for which cheapness and speed in the casting and finishing processes were important. Gilding was employed not only to give the impression of wealth but also to hide patches and differences of colour. Only the final effect was important: these statues were intended to make an impressive political statement and to express Rome´s power, but with the least possible expense and with no waste of time.

Università di Udine, Centro Polifunzionale, Palazzo Alvarez, Via Diaz 5, 34170 Gorizia

Acknowledgements

The author wishes to thank L. Bakker, Römisches Museum Augsburg, and G. Weber, Römisches Museum Kempten, for their interest in this project; A. Fuganti and A. di Corrado, Institute of Material Science, University of Trento, for their practical help with the analysis of the bronze and the gilding; J. Riederer for providing illustrations of the Roman arm which he presented in 1986; and S. La Niece, British Museum, for emission spectrometry analysis of one sample of the gilding on the horse's head from Augsburg.

15 Bol, *Antike Bronzetechnik* 84.

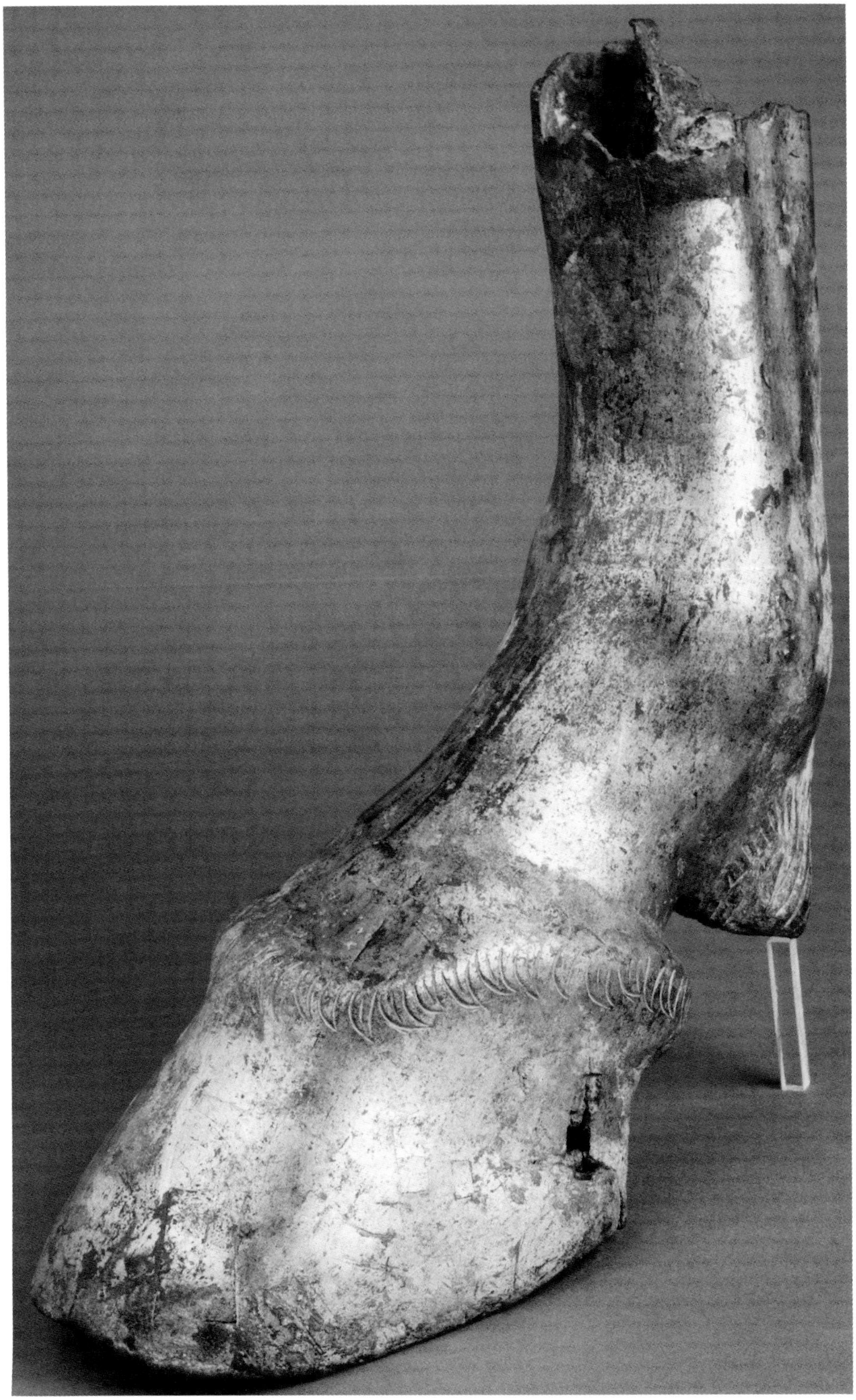

Fig. 1. Horse's hoof. Gilded bronze, max l. 38.2 cm. London, The British Museum GR 1856.12-26.624. (Photo: © Trustees of the British Museum)

The technology and conservation of two fragments of life-size gilt bronze Roman statuary

Andrew Oddy

The gilding of large-scale bronze sculptures seems to have been distinctly uncommon in the Hellenistic world, and it was not particularly common in Roman times. A recent investigation of surviving fragments of life-size, gilded bronze statues listed component parts from about 33 statues or statuary groups, all of which are thought to be Roman in date (where dating is possible on art-historical or archaeological grounds).[1] Since this list was assembled, more fragments have been seen in the Museo Nazionale Romano and reported from other collections. Indeed, a gilded bronze finger and a fragment of gilded bronze drapery have been located in the British Museum.[2] Doubtless other fragments survive in the storerooms of museums in Europe, North America, Turkey, and the Near East; but in comparison with surviving fragments of ungilded bronze statues, gilded pieces are rare.[3]

Investigation has shown that bronze statues were usually gilded in one of two ways: sticking gold leaf to the surface of the bronze (leaf-gilding) or spreading a gold amalgam (solution of gold dissolved in mercury) onto the surface and then heating to evaporate the mercury (fire-gilding). Leaf-gilded statues were usually cast in leaded bronze (copper 65-90%, tin 3-10%, lead 5-28%), while fire-gilded ones were usually cast in impure copper (copper >94%, tin <3%, lead <3%).

The purpose of this paper is to make more widely known two fragments of leaf-gilded statuary in the British Museum.[4] Both are hitherto unpublished, apart from being included in the list already mentioned[5] and in an earlier published version of the same project.[6] One of them (the arm) has been illustrated in colour in a general account of gilded bronzes.[7]

Gilded bronze horse's hoof (fig. 1)

The hoof was bequeathed to the British Museum in 1856 by Sir William Temple, who had been British ambassador in Naples during the first half of the 19th c. His collection consisted of many types of antiquities, most of which appear to have been found in Italy, although no provenance is given in the case of the hoof.[8]

---

1 W. A. Oddy *et al.*, "The gilding of bronze sculptures in the classical world," in *Small bronze sculpture* 103-24.

2 Finger: GR 1814.7-4.789; drapery: PRB 1982.1-3.170. Analysis of the gilding has shown that both objects contain mercury in the gold and must therefore have been fire-gilded. The bronze of the finger has not been analyzed, but the fragment of drapery is, surprisingly (because of the technique of gilding), a leaded tin bronze (*c.*82.1% Cu, 3.3% Sn, and 12% Pb).

3 The author would appreciate receiving information about fragments of large gilded bronzes in museums or from excavations in the area of the former Roman Empire.

4 The author is very grateful to D. Williams, Keeper of the Department of Greek and Roman Antiquities in the British Museum, and to J. Swaddling, Curator of Metalwork, for permission to publish and for access to departmental records.

5 Oddy *et al.* (supra n.1).

6 W. A. Oddy, "Gold in antiquity: aspects of gilding and of assaying," *Journal of the Royal Society of Arts* 130 [5315] (1982) 730-43.

7 W. A. Oddy, "Vergoldungen auf prähistorischen und klassischen Bronzen," in Born, *Archäologische Bronzen* 64-71.

8 GR 1856.12-26.624. The Department of Greek and Roman Antiquities in the British Museum possesses a manuscript catalogue of the Temple Collection by R. Gargiulo, entitled *Catalogo delle diverse collezioni di oggetti antichi di sua Eccellenza il Cavaliere Temple, Ministro Plenipotenziario di Sua Maesta Brittannica presso la Real Corte del Regno delle Due Sicilie*, in which the hoof is no. 11 and is described as "Porzione di gamba con piede di cavallo piu grande del naturale."

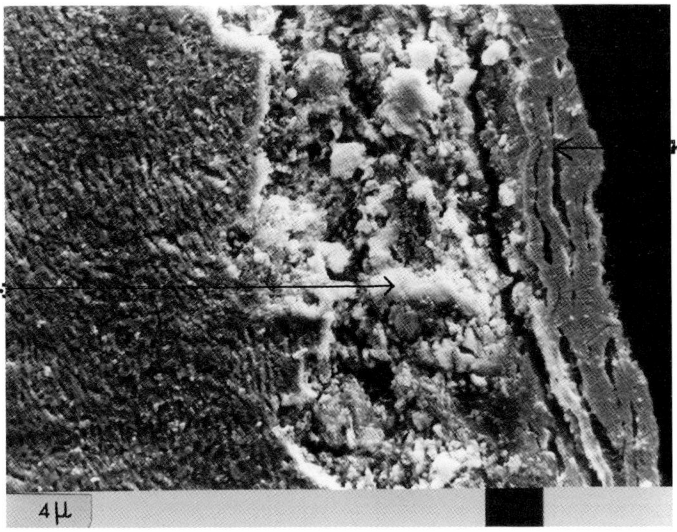

Fig. 2. Cross-section of gilding from fig. 1. (Photo: © Trustees of the British Museum)

The hoof is from a hind leg, approximately life size, broken above the fetlock. It has a maximum length of 38.2 cm (from the front of the hoof to the broken back of the leg) and a maximum height (when the underside of the hoof is flat on a surface) of 29.8 cm. The underside of the hoof measures 14.9 cm front to back and 11.4 cm in maximum width. The hoof is hollow, and the thickness of the casting around the rim of the hoof varies from *c.*5 to 9 mm and around the broken-off leg from *c.* 2 to 6 mm. The fragment weighs *c.*5.2 kg.

At least 6 rectangular repair patches have been let into the bronze to hide (presumed) casting flaws. Three of these patches are now missing; two on the actual hoof and a third at the break in the leg. The patches measure 34 x ? mm (broken), 9 x 6.5 mm, 17 x 7.5 mm, 9 x 5.5 mm, 16 x 8 mm and 32 x 19 mm.

At the point where the leg is broken, the thickness of the casting has undergone an abrupt change. Excess metal within the cavity of the leg preserves the shape of a rectangular (wooden?) strut that was part of the core. It is difficult to interpret this excess metal, although it may represent a flow weld used to join separately cast parts of the statue. However, another ring of excess metal is visible about halfway up the existing fragment of leg, and this does look as if it represents a join between two separately cast pieces. If both rings of excess metal represent flow welds, they indicate that the statue may have been cast in a large number of separate pieces.

Once casting was complete, chasing took place to indicate hair around the coronet band (the upper edge of the hoof) and over the fetlock. The chasing is fairly crude and does not attempt to give a detailed representation of hair, but it bears a close similarity to the hooves of the horses on the Basilica di San Marco in Venice.[9]

Finally, the hoof was gilded, and the gilding now hides any evidence for flow welds that might originally have been visible on the outer surface. Analyses have shown that the bronze contains 87.5% copper, 2.8% tin, and 8.2% lead,[10] with traces of other metals, and that there is no mercury in the gold.[11] This is a leaded tin bronze, although both lead and tin are at the bottom of the usual range for Roman statuary. The absence of mercury in the gold indicates that fire-gilding was not used. Hence, the statue was gilded by attaching gold leaf to the surface with an adhesive, possibly the white of an egg.[12]

---

9 See J. and V. Wilton-Ely (transl.), *The horses of San Marco* (Exhib. cat.; Milan–New York 1979) pls. 189-91.

10 This analysis was carried out by P. Craddock, who has generously allowed me to quote the results in advance of his own definitive publication.

11 The gilding of both objects was analyzed by M. Cowell using emission spectroscopy.

12 Pliny, *NH* 33.20.64-65.

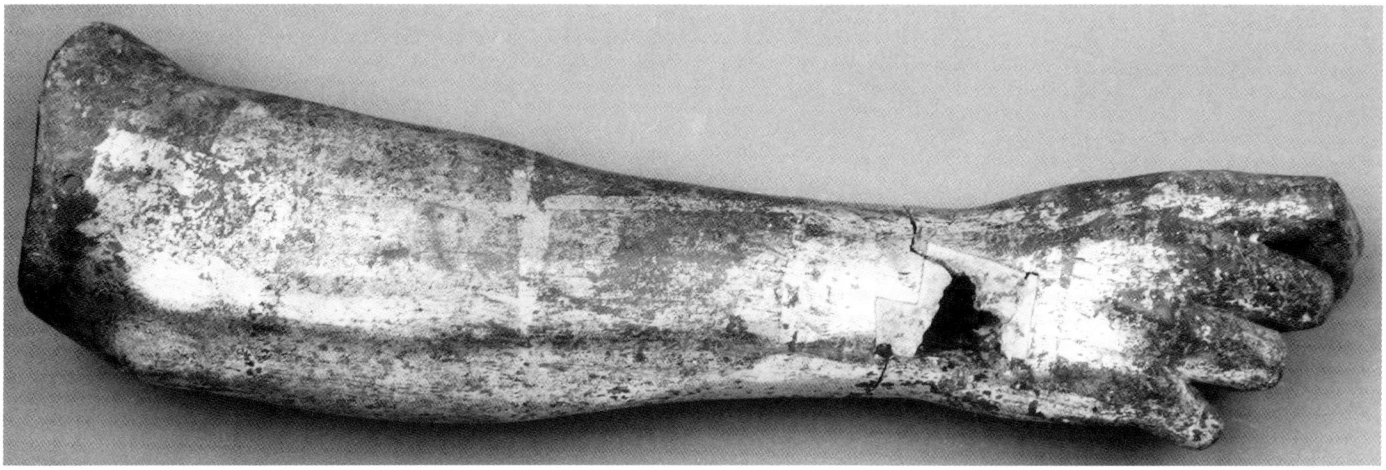

Fig. 3. Right forearm of a man. Gilded bronze, length (from tip of thumb to crease of elbow) 44.2 cm. London, The British Museum GR1904.2-4.1249. (Photo: © Trustees of the British Museum)

The gilding of the hoof is unusual in that it is quite thick, and it is almost impossible to detect the edges of the sheets of gold leaf. This suggests that more than one layer of gold leaf was applied, and this has been confirmed by the examination of a cross-section of a sample of metal taken from the broken edge of the leg (fig. 2). There are at least 4 (and possibly 5) layers of gold leaf, each of which is 1 to 2 mm thick.[13] This may represent one original gilding when several layers were applied to give a rich gold appearance to the surface, but it is possible that the various layers represent successive restorations of the statue over time as the gilding wore rather thin.

With so little of the statue remaining, it is difficult to suggest a date. The technology, particularly of the gilding, does, however, suggest a date in or before the 3rd c. A.D.

Gilded bronze right forearm of a man (fig. 3)

The arm was part of the Morel collection, purchased by the British Museum in 1901.[14] It was found in a well at Clairmarais, Rheims, in 1876. Léon Morel (1828-1909) was a tax collector, amateur archaeologist, and collector. His collection, which was formed in the Champagne region, was exhibited several times in Paris between 1878 and 1900; Morel then decided to sell it.[15] After being turned down by the Musée des Antiquités Nationales, Paris, the collection was bought by the British Museum.

The arm is an unclothed right forearm, slightly larger than that of an average modern man. It measures 44.2 cm from the tip of the thumb to the crease of the elbow along the inside of the arm and is broken off just above the elbow. The maximum circumference of the forearm is 34.1 cm, and the circumference of the wrist is 22.5 cm. The arm is hollow, and the thickness of the casting varies between *c.*2 and 6 mm. It weighs *c.*7.0 kg.

The arm is in two pieces, being broken just above the wrist at the point where there was a major casting flaw. There is no evidence that this represents a failed flow weld, although a ring of excess bronze inside the arm, just above the existing break, may indicate where a separately cast hand and forearm were joined. This ring of excess metal preserves three of four chaplets that protrude into the hollow arm. The index finger exhibits minor casting flaws.

An irregularly shaped repair patch (now missing) was let into the surface to cover the casting flaw. Its maximum dimensions were 45 x 61.5 mm. Two other repair patches are still in place

13 The metallography of both objects was carried out by N. Meeks.
14 GR 1904.2-4.1249.
15 I. Stead, *The Gauls: Celtic antiquities from France* (London 1981) 13.

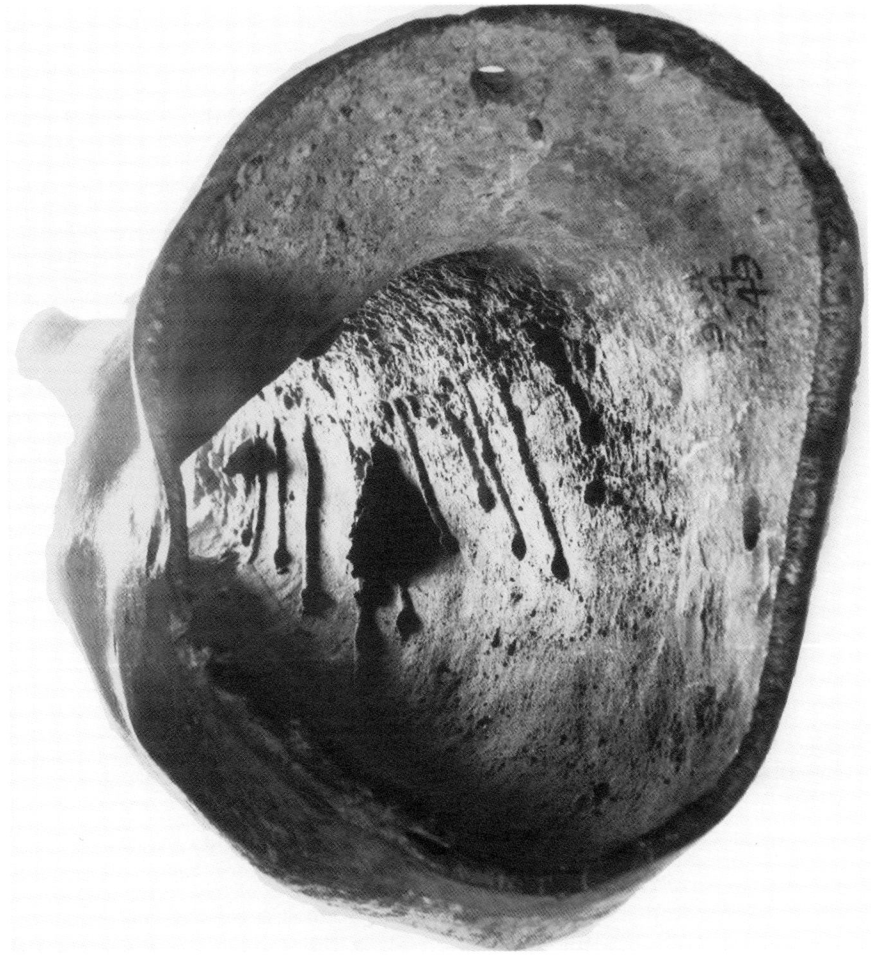

Fig. 4. Interior of fig. 3, showing drips of molten wax preserved in bronze. (Photo: © Trustees of the British Museum)

near the knuckles of the second and third fingers (dimensions 12 x 6 mm and 11 x 6 mm), and a third can be seen near the elbow (25 x 21 mm).

There can be no doubt that the arm and hand were cast by the indirect process, as the interior surface of the bronze preserves a flow pattern of runs of molten wax (fig. 4) that could only occur if molten wax was used to coat the inside of a mould of the arm.

The upper end of the arm, just above the elbow, has a finished look (rather than a broken edge). Three holes represent fixing positions, and (if they are ancient, which they appear to be) they suggest a mechanical attachment to the rest of the figure rather than a flow weld. Presumably the arm slotted into a hole within drapery.

Rather crude chasing was done to indicate knuckles, and more careful chasing elaborated the fingernails. The hand forms a gripping position, having presumably held a weapon or piece of regalia.

Analysis of the bronze has shown that it contains 76.5% copper, 4.9% tin, and 17.4% lead, with traces of other metals, and that there is no mercury in the gold.[16] This is a leaded tin bronze, more typical of Roman bronze statuary than the horse's hoof.

Examination of the arm shows clearly that it was gilded by sticking sheets of gold leaf onto the surface. These vary in size but on average are 90 to 110 mm x 50 to 70 mm. This is reasonably

16 P. T. Craddock, *The composition of copper alloys used in the classical world* (Ph.D. diss., Institute of Archaeology, Univ. of London 1975) analysis no. 32.

consistent with the statement in Pliny that gold leaf was hammered into sheets four fingers square.[17] These would be in the range 80 to 100 mm square, depending on the size of the fingers.

Over much of the surface the gold is probably only one leaf thick; hence the pattern of overlapping leaves is revealed by the double thickness of gold round the edges. However, in some areas the gold appears to be thicker and the pattern of overlapping leaves is not visible. A small sample for metallography was removed from one of these areas at the edge of the break at the wrist. This showed that the gold here is 4 to 6 microns thick and shows no evidence for more than one layer having been applied. However, repeated applications of gold leaf to a clean surface, followed by burnishing, would cause the separate leaves to join together imperceptibly.

Once again, dating is difficult, but the technology of the gilding suggests a date in or before the 3rd c. A.D.

Conservation

These fragments of gilded bronze have both been conserved in recent years, as corrosion of the bronze during burial had partially covered the surface with a layer of green oxidation products that obscured the gilding. As is normal with gilded bronze, the corrosion of the base metal also meant that the gilding is no longer attached to the bronze surface but is now separated from it by a layer of oxidation products identical to those on top of the gilding. It was thus impossible to clean the bronze by soaking it in a bath of one of the solvents usually used to dissolve bronze corrosion products.

Instead, cleaning was carried out by a combination of softening the visible corrosion with 30% formic acid on a cotton-wool swab and then picking or scraping it off with a scalpel. The process is simple, but the practice is very difficult. Excessive use of formic acid or too vigorous application of the scalpel will lift the gold leaf. Hence, the process is slow and painstaking and must be carried out by observing the surface down a binocular microscope at a magnification of x5 to x20. The surface must be frequently swabbed with distilled water to ensure that the formic acid dissolves only the corrosion products on top of the gilding. The conserved objects are a tribute to the skill of the conservators involved.[18]

Department of Conservation, The British Museum, London

---

17 Pliny, *NH* 33.19.61-62.

18 Conservation was carried out by H. Newey, P. Winsor, and C. Enderly.

An undignified end: the bronze Severan empress from Sparta

Lee Ann Riccardi

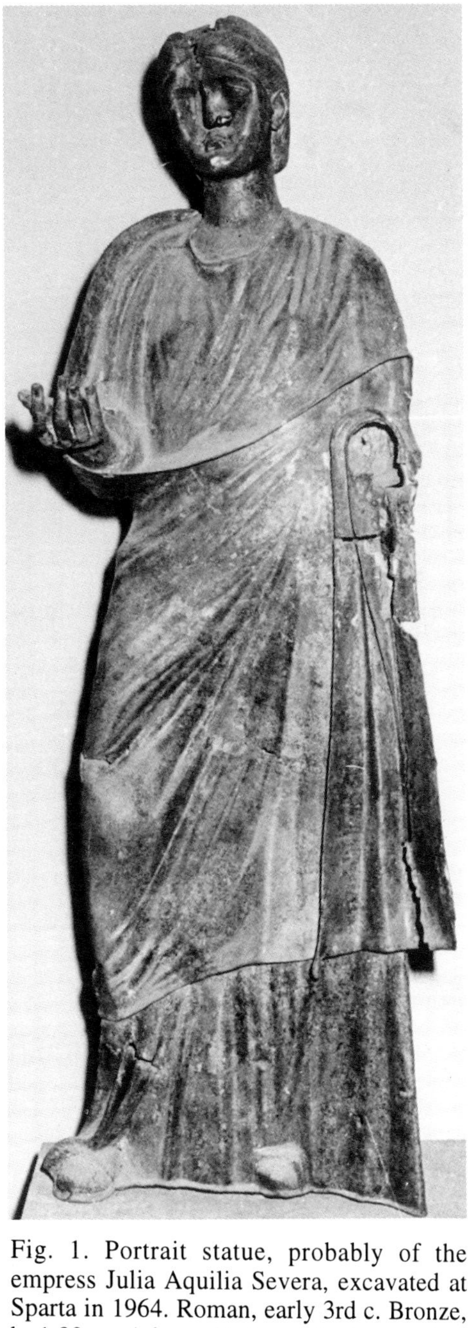

Fig. 1. Portrait statue, probably of the empress Julia Aquilia Severa, excavated at Sparta in 1964. Roman, early 3rd c. Bronze, h. 1.83 m. Athens, National Archaeological Museum 23321. (Photo: courtesy Museum)

A full article on this piece has now appeared: "The mutilation of the bronze portrait of a Severan empress from Sparta: *damnatio memoriae* or Christian iconoclasm?" *AthMitt* 113 (1998) 259-69.

During the 1964 excavations on the acropolis of Sparta, an almost intact life-size bronze sculpture of a woman was found in the so-called Round Building.[1] The hairstyle is distinctive for late Severan women, and the statue was mutilated in antiquity before it was deposited. Based on its date and the fact of its defacement, the portrait was first identified as Julia Mamaea,[2] the mother of Alexander Severus, both of whom were the victims of occasional, unofficial *damnationes memoriae*. An identification as Plautilla, the wife of Caracalla, who also suffered *damnatio*, has been suggested as well.[3]

Stylistically, the statue fits comfortably into the late Severan period. Its attribution to Julia Mamaea or Plautilla rests on the fact of its defacement. Yet an attack by angry Romans is unlikely to be responsible for the destruction and burial of this statue. The particular style of this statue's mutilation and concealment was typical of Christian zealots but not of provincial Romans attempting an unofficial *damnatio*. *Damnatio* was not usually carried out with such vigor in the provinces, whereas Christian defacement of pagan statues was common.

With Christian iconoclasm the motive for the destruction of the statue, identification of the figure as Julia Mamaea or Plautilla is no more likely than any of the other late Severan empresses. The hairstyle is most closely paralleled by portraits on the coinage of Julia Aquilia Severa, and she is the most likely wife of Elagabalus to have been part of a late Severan dynastic monument. If the statue was faithful to a Roman model, it would most likely have been intended as a representation of her.

Department of Art, College of New Jersey,
P.O. Box 7718, Ewing, NJ

---

1 K. O. Orlandos, "Τῆς αρχαιολογικῆς Εταιρεῖας κάτα το 1964," *Ergon* (1965) 110-11; A. H. S. Megaw, *Archaeological reports 1965*, 12; C. Christos, "Ανασκαφὴ ἀκροπόλεως Σπάρτης," *Prakt* 1964 [1966] 115-19.

2 A. Datsoule-Stavridi, "*Damnatio memoriae*," *AAA* 9 (1976) 224-28; S. N. Koumanoudes, "Ιουλία Μαμαία ἐκ Σπάρτης," *AAA* 3 (1970) 260-62.

3 O. Palagia, "Seven pilasters of Herakles from Sparta," in S. Walker and A. Cameron (edd.), *The Greek renaissance in the Roman empire* (*BICS* suppl. 55, 1989) 125 n.23.

The Toledo bronze youth and a classicizing movement during the Severan period

Susan C. Jones

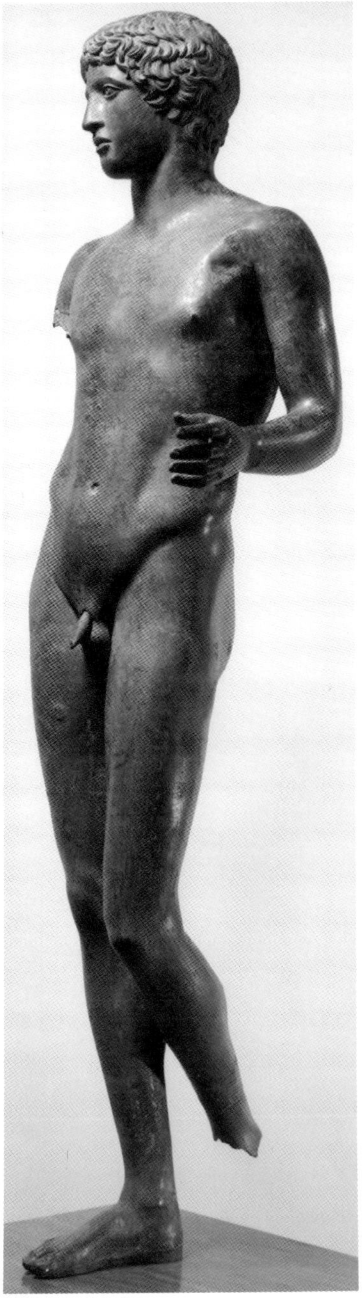

Fig. 1. Youth. Roman, early 3rd c. Bronze, h. 1.43 m. Toledo, Ohio, The Toledo Museum of Art, purchased with funds from the Libbey Endowment, Gift of Edward Drummond Libbey, 1966. 126. (Photo: courtesy Museum)

The large bronze statue of a youth in the Toledo Museum of Art[1] is the product of a Severan bronze workshop. Examination of the technical details demonstrates how such observations may establish a work's chronology and place of origin with a methodology that is analogous to that used in stylistic analysis.[2] The output of the proposed workshop included over life-size imperial portraits, portraits of private individuals, and large decorative ideal works such as the Toledo sculpture. Specific items include statuary from the Sebasteion at Bubon in SW Asia Minor and from Kythrea and Soloi on Cyprus. The portraits of Septimius Severus and his son Caracalla that belong to this group strongly suggest that the workshop was in existence during the very late 2nd and early 3rd c. A.D.

Comparison of the Toledo bronze with Polykleitos's *Doryphoros* reveals the stylistic influence that this artist of the 5th c. B.C. had on the creator of the Toledo sculpture. The two figures share overall body proportions, a chiastic stance, a coiffure with layers of wavy strands radiating from the crown to frame the face and ears, the shape of the cranium, and a relatively flat face. It is equally obvious that the Toledo youth is not an attempt to copy the *Doryphoros*. It has many particularly Roman stylistic traits that do not occur in any existing Roman copy of Polykleitan works — for example, the incised irises and lunate highlights of its eyes. Another reflection of Roman aesthetic sensibilities is the presentation of the idealized male as younger and without the mature athletic body of the *Doryphoros*. Indeed, the Toledo bronze youth is an original conception that mirrors both the continuing influence of Polykleitos and contemporary Roman tastes. Since it is a classicizing creation of an early 3rd c. workshop from the Greek-speaking, eastern Roman Empire, it can be concluded that such works continued to be popular after the Antonine period, and, most importantly, that it can no longer be assumed that a sculpture that exhibits strong stylistic influence from Classical Greece must be dated to the Augustan or the Hadrianic era.

Roosevelt, NJ

1 Acc. no. 1966.126: *The fire of Hephaistos* 232-36, no. 24 (C. C. Mattusch, with previous bibliography).

2 For a more complete exploration of these technical details and their implications, see ibid. and S. Jones, "The Toledo bronze youth and East Mediterranean bronze workshops," *JRA* 7 (1994) 243-56.

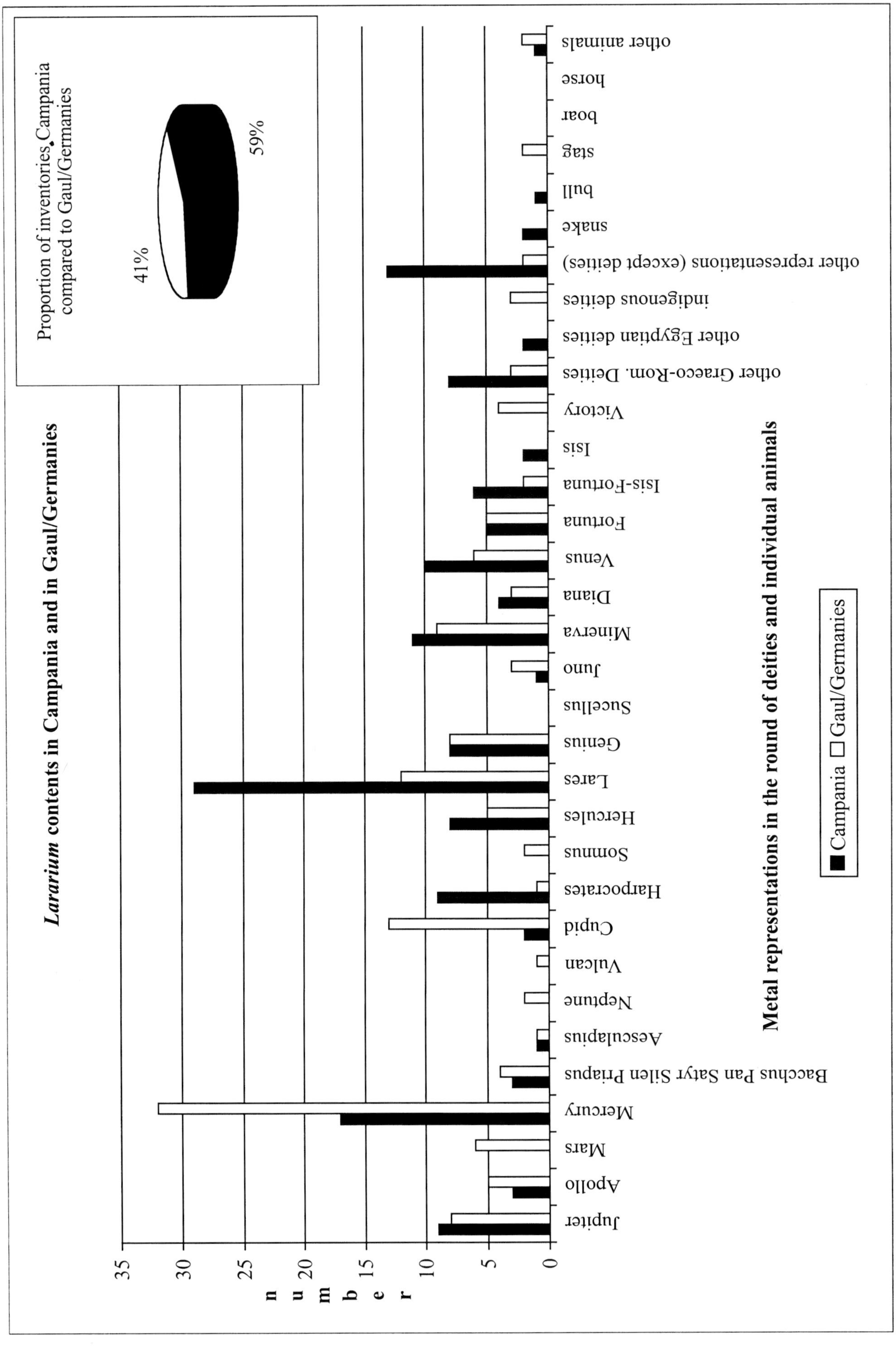

Fig. 1. *Lararium* contents in Campania and in Gaul and the Germanies: metal representations in the round of deities and individual animals. (Chart: author)

The evidence of statuettes in closed finds for private and public cults

Annemarie Kaufmann-Heinimann

Private cult

The main archaeological source of information on Roman *lararia* and their contents are the Campanian *lararia* preserved *in situ* by the eruption of Mt. Vesuvius in A.D. 79.[1] A number of house shrines have been excavated with their contents intact: statuettes, a lamp and maybe an incense burner, a jug for libations, and a small altar. A few examples can be used to illustrate the variety of *lararium* statuettes. Seven rather small bronze statuettes — Jupiter, both standing and seated, a Genius, the Dioscuri, and two Isis-Fortunas — were found in a room near the kitchen of a house in Boscoreale.[2] In the *lararium* niche of house I 2.20,21 at Pompeii, used as a tavern (*caupona*), there were two bronze statuettes of Diana and a rider, a terracotta statuette of a seated woman with child, a female terracotta bust, a green-glazed clay head of Medusa, and a marble Bacchic head.[3] The *lararium* in the Casa degli Amorini dorati (VI 16.7,38) contained 6 rather large bronze statuettes: the Capitoline triad (Jupiter, Juno, and Minerva), a seated Mercury of nearly double their size, and a pair of *lares*.[4]

Another phenomenon is documented *in situ* as well: a house shrine did not have to be installed in a separate niche or *aedicula* but could be integrated into a cupboard used for domestic purposes. The wooden cupboard in the Casa del sacello di legno in Herculaneum (V 31) has two levels: the upper one used as a shrine, the lower one used for storage of terracotta and glass vessels.[5] Here, of course, we do not have any problems distinguishing between the different types of objects and their intended use, but under normal archaeological circumstances it would be impossible to reconstruct the original setup of the cupboard.

There is also another kind of evidence for the contents of Campanian house shrines. In a corner of the peristyle of house IX 6.5-7 lay the bodies of two victims of the eruption; next to them were found gold and silver coins, some pieces of jewelry, and three statuettes of the *lares* and of Mercury.[6] Obviously the inhabitants, when trying to flee, took their most valuable and cherished belongings with them. The same situation seems to account for 4 statuettes — Mercury, a pair of *lares*, and a genius — buried in the Strada di Nola in Reg. V.[7]

---

1 For an early survey see G. K. Boyce, *Corpus of the lararia of Pompeii* (*MAAR* 14, 1937); also S. Adamo-Muscettola, "Osservazioni sulla composizione dei larari con statuette in bronzo di Pompei ed Ercolano," in U. Gehrig (ed.), *Toreutik und figürliche Bronzen römischer Zeit* (Berlin 1984) 9-32 figs. 1-25 (detailed study with ills.); D. G. Orr, "Roman domestic religion: the evidence of the household shrines," in *ANRW* II.16.2 (Berlin 1978) 1557-91; T. Fröhlich, *Lararien- und Fassadenbilder in den Vesuvstädten, Untersuchungen zur 'volkstümlichen' pompejanischen Malerei* (*RömMitt* Ergh. 32, 1991) (both with main focus on the paintings). The whole topic of closed finds with statuettes is dealt with more thoroughly in my study *Götter und Lararien aus Augusta Raurica: Herstellung, Fundzusammenhänge und sakrale Funktion figürlicher Bronzen in einer römischen Stadt* (*Forschungen in Augst* 26, 1998). I owe much to discussions with E. Künzl.

2 H. *c.*7-10 cm: D. Kent Hill, *Catalogue of classical bronze sculpture in the Walters Art Gallery* (Baltimore 1949) nos. 12, 18, 27, 51, 138, 222-23, pl. 5; Kaufmann-Heinimann (supra n.1) 210, fig. 145.

3 H. *c.*3-12 cm: Fröhlich (supra n.1) 250-51, L3; I. Baldassarre (ed.), *Pompei, pitture e mosaici* I.1 (Roma 1990) 47; Kaufmann-Heinimann (supra n.1) 212, fig. 150.

4 H. *c.*16-37 cm: Adamo-Muscettola (supra n.1) 12-13, figs. 3-4; Kaufmann-Heinimann (supra n.1) 220, figs. 165-66.

5 A. Maiuri, *Ercolano, i nuovi scavi (1927-1958)* (Rome 1958) 254, fig. 202; Kaufmann-Heinimann (supra n.1) 212, fig. 149.

6 Adamo-Muscettola (supra n.1) 25-26, fig. 23; Kaufmann-Heinimann 1998 (supra n.1) 223, fig. 170.

7 Boyce (supra n.1) 109, no. 10.

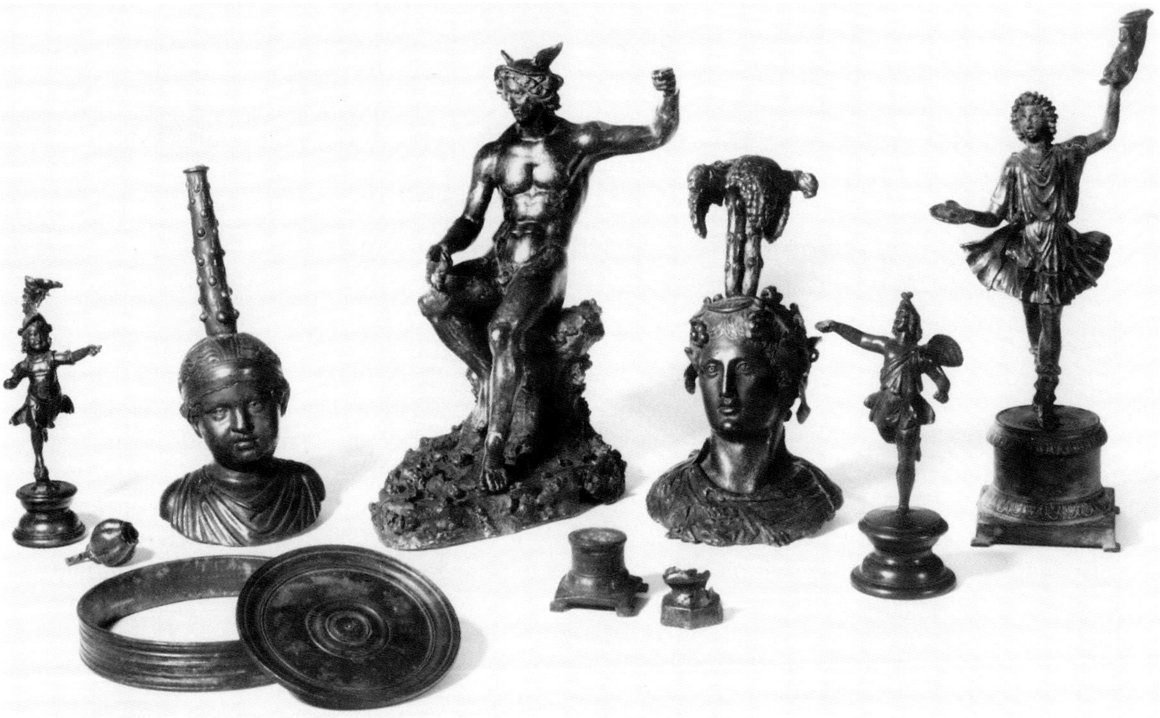

Fig. 2. Group of bronze statuettes and household goods from Augst (Baselland). (Photo: U. Schild; courtesy Römermuseum Augst)

The approximately 40 groups of *lararium* statuettes found in the Vesuvian cities show some common features (see fig. 1). The number of statuettes may vary; figurines of different deities are present, among them very often one or two *lares*; more than one statuette of the same deity may be present;[8] and statuettes of different size, material, quality, and style may be assembled in one shrine. Roman domestic religion in the form we encounter in the Vesuvian cities goes back to Augustus's re-organization of the household cult.[9] The practice of assembling statuettes of various deities in a private shrine, according to the needs and taste of the family, with the new rôle of the genius and the *lares*, seems to have spread quickly from Italy to the provinces, most probably by means of the Roman army.

Despite the less favourable conditions of preservation outside the Campanian cities, a few *lararia* have been preserved with their contents *in situ* in the NW provinces as well. In a Roman villa in NE Spain at Vilauba, three bronze statuettes of Mercury, a *lar*, Fortuna, and the socle of a fourth statuette were found in a room next to the kitchen.[10] They seem to be 1st- or 2nd-c. works, perhaps imported from Italy, and inhabited the household shrine until the whole villa was destroyed by fire in the late 3rd or early 4th c.

A very fine group of 1st-c. *lararium* statuettes, imported from Campania, was buried with some household goods in a house in Augusta Raurica (Augst/Kaiseraugst), most probably in the 3rd c. (fig. 2).[11] The owner seems to have made a deliberate choice of high quality objects for

8 The number of deities seems to be fixed only for the genius and the *lares*, the two being connected with the imperial cult (see below). In one shrine there could not be not more than one genius and two *lares*: see H. Kunckel, *Der römische Genius* (*RömMitt* Ergh. 20, 1974) 29-32 and her forthcoming monograph on the *lares*.

9 Basically still G. Wissowa, *Religion und Kultus der Römer* (2nd edn., Munich 1912) 161-73; see also Kunckel 1974 (supra n.8) 22-28 and esp. id., forthcoming (supra n.8); Orr (supra n.1) 1559-60, 1562-67.

10 J. Tremoleda, P. Castanyer, and A. Roure, "Vilauba: estudi preliminar del larari de la vil.la," *Cypsela* 7 (1989) 49-69; P. Castanyer and J. Tremoleda, "La villa de Vilauba: resultados de las últimas campañas de excavación (1990-93)," *JRA* 8 (1995) 275-77; Kaufmann-Heinimann (supra n.1) 228, fig. 175.

11 Statuettes of Mercury and a *lar*, two busts (one of Bacchus and one of Hercules as a child), two cupids carrying poppy-like torches (h. 13-29 cm), fragments of furniture, iron nails: Kaufmann-Heinimann (supra n.1) 143-47, figs. 40, 105.

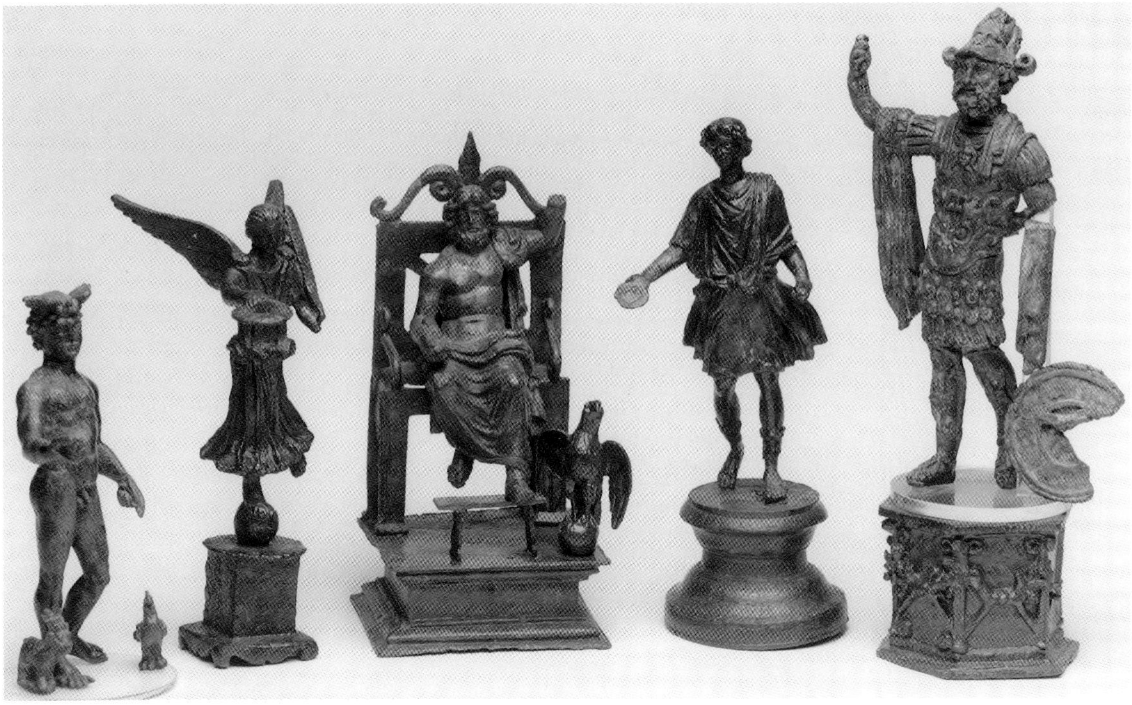

Fig. 3. Group of bronze statuettes from Rouen (Seine-Maritime). (Photo: courtesy Musée des antiquités, Rouen)

his *lararium*, which met not only religious but also artistic requirements.[12] We can assume that the objects had originally been stored on different shelves of the same cupboard, as was the case in the Casa del sacello di legno in Herculaneum, and that the items got mixed up when the house was destroyed.

Situations of imminent danger arose not only in the Vesuvian cities but also in provincial towns, especially in connection with the invasions of the later 3rd c. At Rouen (Seine–Maritime), 5 bronze statuettes of Jupiter, Mars, Mercury, a *lar*, and Victory were found lying in the ditch of a road, within a layer of burnt débris dated shortly after 250 (fig. 3).[13] Obviously an inhabitant of the Roman town lost his precious household gods while trying to save them.

A wooden crate, packed with 40 bronze kitchen and table vessels and three statuettes of Mercury, Hercules, and a *lar*, and then hidden under a plank in a house at Kaiseraugst, testifies to a situation of imminent danger, perhaps the Germanic invasions during the years around 270.[14] The difference between the find in house IX 6.5-7 in Pompeii (see above) and this find seems to be slight: in both cases, the stress lies on the special value the items had for their owners, not on a presumed common use.

In some cases, it was obviously not the legal owner who put a group of *lararium* statuettes and other items in a safe place. Near a Roman villa at Detzem (Rheinland-Pfalz) four statuet-

12 In this respect we may compare the group of *lararium* statuettes found at Montorio near Verona, which consists mostly of exceptionally fine statuettes, including a seated philosopher and a pair of slaves or peasants used probably as lamp-carriers (Kaufmann-Heinimann [supra n.1] 293, fig. 257) or, on a much bigger scale, the works of art being kept in the *sacrarium* of C. Heius at Messana (Cic., *Verr.* II 4.3-7; cf. G. Zimmer, "Das Sacrarium des C. Heius: Kunstraub und Kunstgeschmack in der späten Republik," *Gymnasium* 96 [1989] 493-520).

13 H. *c.*11-16 cm: G. Sennequier and P. Halbout, in *De l'Egypte ancienne à la Renaissance rouennaise* (Exh. cat., Rouen 1992) no. 44; Kaufmann-Heinimann (supra n.1) 260, fig. 216; G. Sennequier and A. Kaufmann-Heinimann, "Un ensemble de statuettes en bronze trouvées à Rouen en 1990," *BAC* 26 (1998) 65-84.

14 H. statuettes *c.*8-19 cm: T. Tomasevic-Buck, "Ein Bronzedepotfund aus Augusta Raurica (Dorfstrasse 1, Kaiseraugst, Kt. Aargau)," *BayVgBl* 49 (1984) 143-96; Kaufmann-Heinimann (supra n.1) 140-41, figs. 101-3.

tes — Mercury, a *lar*, a genius, and Fortuna(?) — and a large quantity of metal parts of furniture, vessels, tools, and horse trappings, were found together.[15] The fact that there are all sorts of iron and bronze fragments indicates that here the metal value was the focus of interest, not the statuettes as such. Germanic invaders must have plundered the villa with the object of collecting as much metal as possible to be re-used, and then hid their loot in a temporary spot.[16]

Thus, the contents of *lararia* in the NW provinces may be inferred not only by statuettes preserved *in situ* but also by groups stored in secondary connections. If we look at the composition of provincial *lararia*, basically the same rules are valid as for the Campanian ones (cf. fig. 1): an indefinite number of statuettes of different size, quality, and style can be combined, with the exception that, in contrast to Campania, only statuettes of the same material were gathered in one shrine.[17] As to the deities present, there seem to be no strict rules either; priority is given to the Roman gods, and a clearly indigenous deity is only exceptionally combined with them. A feature that cannot be explored in the Vesuvian cities because of their short period of existence is the life-span of *lararia*. In general, a *lararium* lasted as long as the house to which it belonged, i.e., 200 years or longer, and during this period new statuettes could be added to the venerable old ones, some of which had been imported from Campania, and could have been in the house for generations.

Public cult

Bronze statuettes were used not only in house shrines but also as votive offerings in public sanctuaries. Yet votive offerings are hardly ever preserved *in situ*, not even in the Vesuvian cities, because restoration work was still going on there after the damage of the earthquake of A.D. 62, and most temples were not yet fully functional.[18] Still, we can gain an insight into at least the more valuable kinds of votive offerings from temple treasures, of which quite a number have survived, especially in the NW provinces.[19] By 'temple treasures' I mean all types of intentional safe-keeping — as opposed to accidental conservation — of votive offerings. There may be different reasons leading to such safe-keeping, but they are usually obscure for us.

The hoard from Champoulet (Loiret) must be seen in connection with a rural sanctuary not yet identified. Unfortunately, only half of the hoard has survived: 5 statuettes or bases of statuettes — Apollo, Mercury, Rosmerta, Epona, and a bull — and a few dishes (fig. 4).[20] The items were dedicated by four individuals to the deities of the local sanctuary of the estate of *Dubnocaratiacus* (or *-um*?). The dedications on the bases and on the vessels make clear that these are not the contents of a private shrine but of a public sanctuary.

Apart from inscriptions, there may be other indications as to the original public use of a hoard. The find from La Comelle-sous-Beuvray (Saône-et-Loire) consists of 8 statuettes — Apol-

---

15 *Trierer Jahresberichte* N.F. 9 (1916) 11-12, 14-15, pls. 1, 2.1-2; Kaufmann-Heinimann (supra n.1) 268, fig. 227.

16 Their yield was quite modest compared to other hoards, e.g., the loot loaded on an Alamannic boat and sunk with it near Neupotz (Rheinland-Pfalz), which contained *c.*500 kg of iron, 200 kg of copper alloy, and 10 kg of silver objects, all stolen from at least one *villa rustica* and a sanctuary: E. Künzl *et al.*, *Die Alamannenbeute aus dem Rhein bei Neupotz: Plünderungsgut aus dem römischen Gallien* (Mainz 1993).

17 *Lararia* consisting of terracotta statuettes must certainly have existed but are rarely preserved. Cf. J. Santrot, "Le petit monde du 'laraire' gallo-romain de Rezé (Loire-Atlantique)," *REA* 95 (1995) 265-94.

18 For restoration work after A.D. 62: P. Zanker, *Pompeji: Stadtbilder als Spiegel von Gesellschaft und Herrschaftsform* (*TrWPr* 9, 1988) 41, fig. 18.

19 For a survey on the topic: E. Künzl, "Römische Tempelschätze und Sakralinventare: Votive, Horte, Beute," in *L'argenterie romaine de l'Antiquité tardive* (*AnTar* 5, 1997); id., "Anmerkungen zum Hortfund von Weissenburg," *Germania* 74 (1996) 453-76.

20 H. statuettes *c.*23-50 cm: R. Joffroy, "Découverte d'une cachette de bronzes gallo-romains à Champoulet (Loiret)," and M. Lejeune, "Note sur les dédicaces de Champoulet," *CRAI* 1978, 795-814; Kaufmann-Heinimann (supra n.1) 245, fig. 196. The other half of the hoard seems to be in private hands.

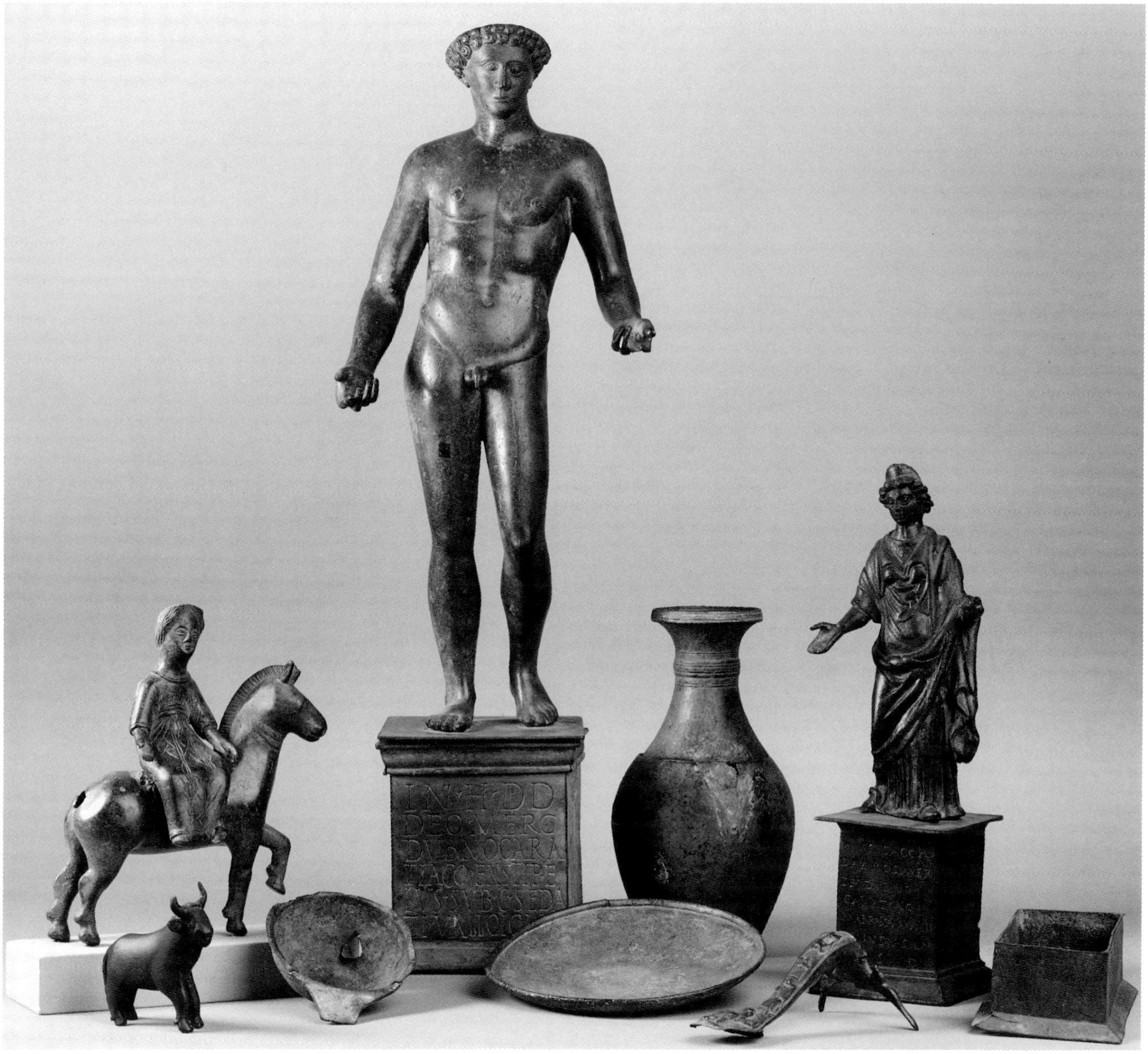

Fig. 4. Group of bronze statuettes and vessels from Champoulet (Loiret). (Photo: L. Hamon; courtesy Musée des Antiquités Nationales de Saint-Germain-en-Laye)

lo, three Mercurys, Hercules, Atlas, Minerva, Fortuna — a bowl, a rattle, four geometrically decorated sticks, and a silex knife.[21] There is no indication of the statuettes having been used in anything other than a domestic context, but as they were hidden in a safe place together with utensils used in public cult activities, such as the rattle and possibly the knife, it seems likely that they all came from a public sanctuary.

There is a similar find more to the south, at Clermont-Ferrand (Puy-de-Dôme) (fig. 5).[22] Rather intriguingly, the hoard was found in a dwelling house, yet the nature of the objects suggests that they must originally have been used in a public context. There is a mixture of straightforward Roman and clearly indigenous deities: two Campanian statuettes of Fortuna (with silver head, arms, and feet) and a genius, 6 probably locally-made statuettes of Mars,

---

21 H. statuettes *c.*5-12 cm: H. de Fontenay, "Notice des bronzes antiques trouvés à la Comelle-sous-Beuvray, arrondissement d'Autun," *Mém. Soc. Éduenne* N.S. 9 (1880) 275-95; Kaufmann-Heinimann (supra n.1) 249, fig. 200.

22 *Gallia Informations* 1989.1, 36-39, figs. 20-23; Kaufmann-Heinimann (supra n.1) 248, fig. 199.

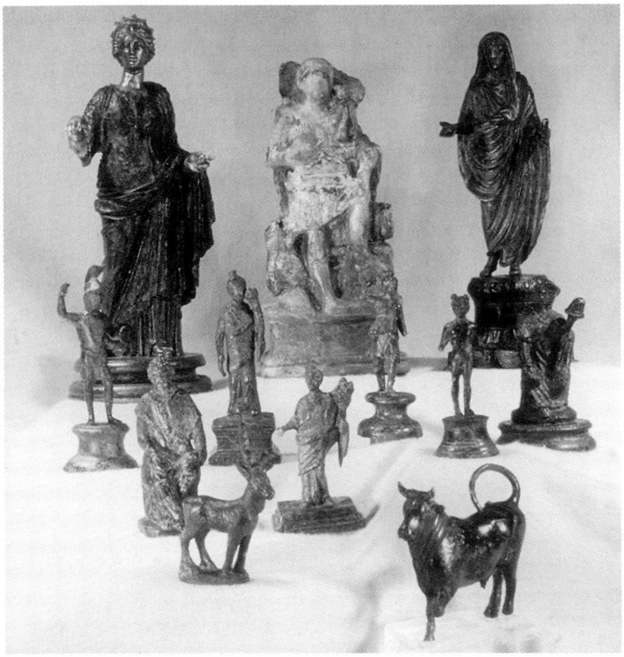

Fig. 5. Group of stone, bronze, and bronze/silver statuettes from Clermont-Ferrand (Puy-de-Dôme). (Photo: Y. Duterne; Service régional de l'archéologie d'Auvergne)

Mercury, Cernunnos, Diana, and three other Fortunas, a stone statuette of Sucellus and, again, a rattle used during cult activities. We must conclude that for some reason this valuable temple equipment had temporarily to be kept safe in a private house.

Indigenous elements are much stronger in another, well-known temple treasure, the one from Neuvy-en Sullias (Loiret).[23] In a pit there were some vessels and a large quantity of bronze votive offerings: a big statue of a horse, dedicated to the otherwise unknown deity *Augustus Rudiobus,* three statuettes of Mars, Aesculapius, and the infant Hercules, 10 human figurines (dancers? worshippers?), 8 animals, especially boars, and a trumpet. The vessels do not bear votive inscriptions; they were probably used in the sanctuary, as the trumpet certainly was.

Conclusion

We have looked at a selection of closed finds containing statuettes from a total of around 160 known complexes,[24] in order to see what their characteristics are in view of distinguishing the private and the public spheres in which they were used.

As finds preserved *in situ* are quite rare, at least outside the Vesuvian cities, the mostly secondary find-spots do not offer decisive information for answering these questions. More reliable and meaningful hints are gathered from inscriptions and from the composition of the finds. Basically, the same statuettes could be put into a household shrine and dedicated in a sanctuary, with the difference that the bases of statuettes standing in a *lararium* did not bear votive inscriptions because the household shrine remained within the scope of the family.[25] As

23 H. statuettes *c.*9-23 cm, h. horse 1 m: S. Reinach, *Antiquités Nationales: description raisonnée du Musée de Saint-Germain-en-Laye* [2]: *bronzes figurés de la Gaule romaine* (Paris 1894) 241-61; Kaufmann-Heinimann (supra n.1) 257, fig. 211.

24 All details to be found in Kaufmann-Heinimann (supra n.1) 181-318.

25 The only two exceptions I know of are the statuette of Minerva found in house I 13.2 at Pompeii dedicated by a certain Theodorus *magister* (Kaufmann-Heinimann [supra n.1] 215, figs. 154-55) and the pair of *lares* in Mainz dedicated by the *libertus* Bello; both individuals obviously donated the statuettes to their *familia* or the *dominus* (G. Behrens, "Zwei neue Laren-Statuetten aus Bronze", and A. Oxé, "Die neue Mainzer Laren-Inschrift," *Germania* 1 [1917] 68-70, 143-46). The inscriptions on the bases of the *lararium* statuettes from Mâlain (Côte-d'Or) are not votive but indicate the deities represented (Kaufmann-Heinimann [supra n.1] 255-56, fig. 208). The same is true for the inscription on the base of

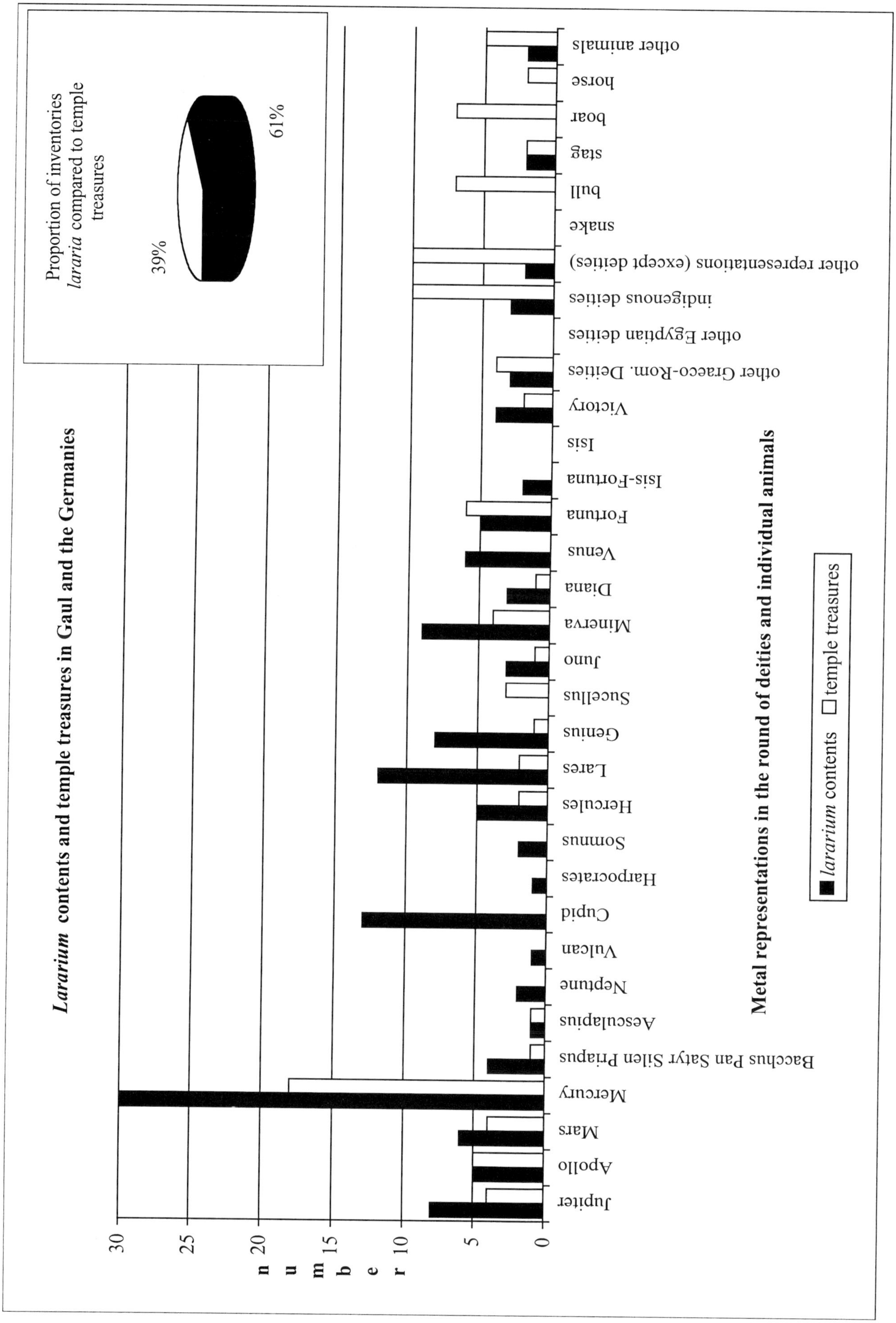

Fig. 6. *Lararium* contents and temple treasures in Gaul and the Germanies: three-dimensional metal representations of deities and individual animals. (author)

for statuettes dedicated in a sanctuary, the donor could choose whether to remain anonymous or not.

When there are no votive inscriptions, the composition of a find may indicate whether it was originally used in a private or a public sanctuary. Implements such as different kinds of vessels and musical instruments (trumpets, rattles, bells) indicate a sanctuary, so statuettes found with such items are likely to come from the same context.

It is quite interesting to compare the range of deities represented by *lararium* statuettes with that of statuettes used in sanctuaries (see fig. 6).[26] Even in Gaul and Germany, besides the central figures of the household cult — the *lares* and the genius — mainly classical Roman deities are assembled in a household shrine.[27] Obviously the household cult was understood as an imported institution, and people tried to stick to its rules. On the other hand, the indigenous element is strongly represented in provincial temple treasures; here we find different kinds of indigenous deities — Cernunnos, Sucellus, Rudiobus, Rosmerta — both human-shaped and animals. We may assume that people felt less restrained in their choice of votive offerings for sanctuaries than in their choice of statuettes to be put into a *lararium*.

Archäologisches Seminar der Universität Basel, Schönbeinstrasse 20, CH-4056 Basel

---

one of the statuettes from the Weissenburg hoard, all of which seem to have been taken out of household shrines (H. J. Kellner and G. Zahlhaas, *Der römische Tempelschatz von Weissenburg in Bayern* [Mainz 1993] no. 7, pls. 21.3, 22-24; Künzl [supra n.19] 457-58, chart 1).

26 As there are hardly any temple treasures known from Italy, the comparison includes finds from the NW provinces only in order to keep a numeric balance.

27 Even in the case of Mercury, it cannot be his indigenous counterpart only that accounts for his popularity, as he rates very highly in Italy too (see fig. 1). The rather high number of Cupids can be explained by the fact that they very often served as a pair of torch holders.

El brasero romano de Hinojosa de Jarque (Teruel)

Romana Erice Lacabe

El brasero, procedente del yacimiento de Hinojosa de Jarque, Teruel, fue objeto de hallazgo casual por el propietario del terreno. El asentamiento no ha sido excavado, pero los restos documentados indican la existencia de un centro amurallado. La aparición de monedas con la leyenda *Damania* ha llevado a situar en el cerro, aunque no existe unanimidad, dicha ciudad ibero-romana. El brasero se encuentra depositado en el Museo de Zaragoza.

El brasero

Mide 51 cm de largo, 39.1 cm de ancho, y 24 cm de alto, es rectangular y está formado por una base superior lisa que configura un marco rectangular a cuyo borde interior se soldaron las diferentes piezas del remate almenado. Estas piezas se fundieron por separado, uniéndose posteriormente de dos en dos, precisamente por la parte en la que se sitúan los apéndices, para acomodarse a su posición. Todas ellas presentan la huella de apoyo al cuerpo del *foculus* en una de sus caras y en la otra algunas muestran restos, producto del contacto con hierro y, quizá, la arcilla refractaria. Su altura es relativamente similar, entre 4.6 y 5.1 cm, salvo una de ellas de mayor tamaño, 5.6 cm, mientras que el grosor varia entre 0.45 y 0.70 cm. Los extremos de cada una de las piezas terminan en unos pequeños apéndices enfrentados que conforman unas aberturas rectangulares siempre paralelas, tres en los lados largos y una central en cada uno de los cortos. La finalidad de los apéndices debe de estar en relación con la bandeja que soportaba la materia refractaria y las brasas.

El cuerpo lo forman cuatro placas o chapas de 0.5 cm de grosor, soldadas en ángulo recto, cuya parte inferior está adornada por tres molduras. Sobre estas placas se situan, en los lados más cortos, las asas macizas de bronce, cuyos extremos girados representan cabezas de ánades. Éstas se sujetan a través de dos pasadores de bronce macizo acabados en una anilla, de la que cuelgan las asas. Por la parte exterior atraviesan dos discos moldurados, mientras que el resto del pasador atraviesa la lámina y queda inmovilizado con unas piezas rectangulares de hierro introduci-

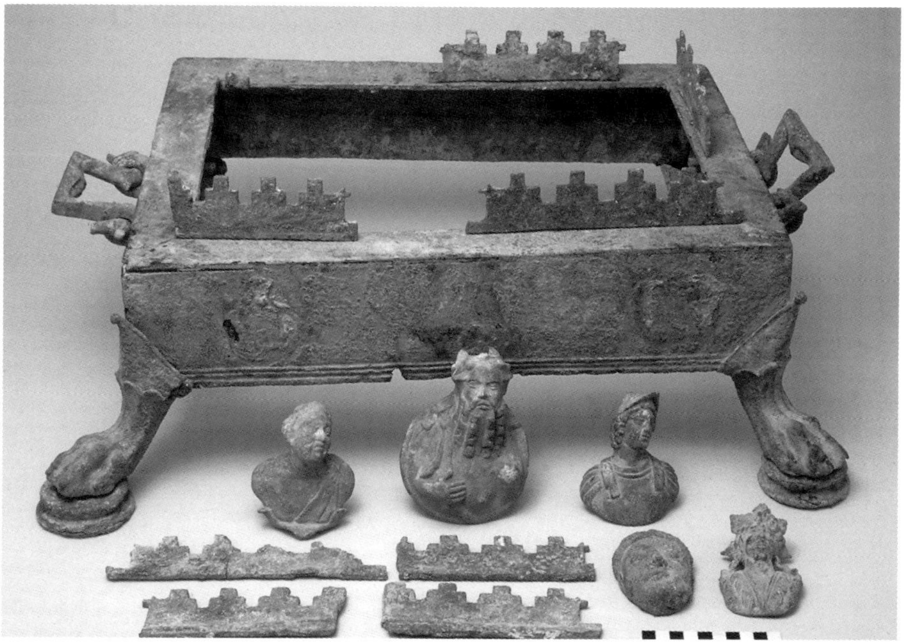

Fig. 1. Brasero de Hinojosa de Jarque, Teruel. (Foto: J. Garrido, Museo de Zaragoza)

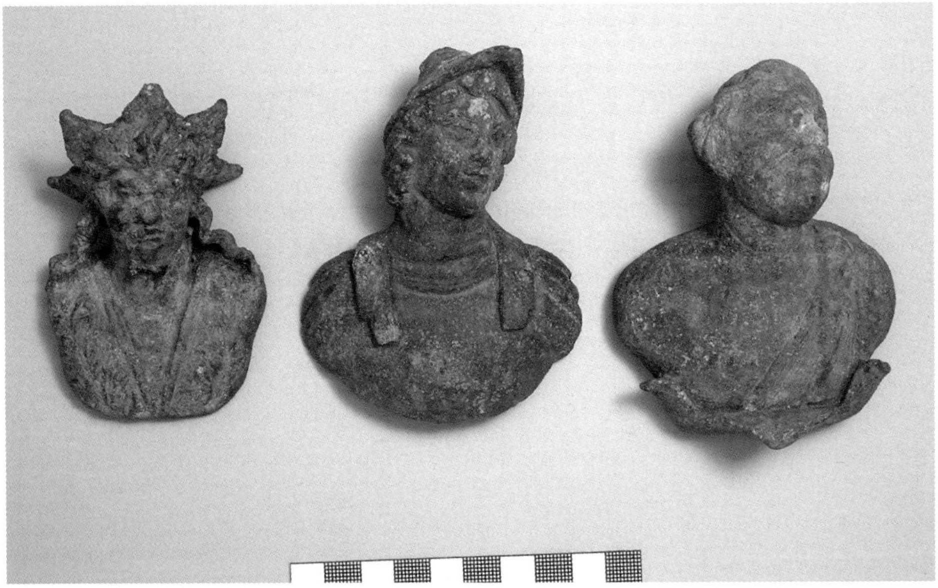

Fig. 2. Figuras del lado 1. De izda. a dcha: sátiro, Marte y sátiro niño (Foto: J. Garrido, Museo de Zaragoza)

das en las aberturas del propio pasador. Tanto las asas como los pasadores se fundieron a molde.

El mueble es sostenido por cuatro garras huecas fundidas a la cera perdida, que se prolongan, cubriendo las aristas de la caja, en un cono abierto rematado por una hemiesfera maciza. El cuerpo se encaja en el interior de las garras desde la parte posterior de las mismas, donde está unido a través de dos puntos de soldadura en cada una de ellas. Cada garra estaba soldada a una base circular moldurada, torneada y hueca.

Todas las piezas del brasero están soldadas unas a otras, salvo las espigas que sujetan las asas que, al atravesar la lámina, quedan inmovilizadas por los topes de hierro.

Son escasos los ejemplares de *foculi* de bronce conservados hasta hoy día. Los braseros portátiles conocidos, que son circulares, cuadrangulares o rectangulares, se circunscriben al área occidental mediterránea (Argelia, España, Francia, e Italia),[1] donde pervive su uso en el tiempo. Estos objetos de lujo, de fácil traslado, han sido hallados tanto en termas públicas como en los *triclinia* de las viviendas privadas. El brasero de Hinojosa mantiene las mismas características estructurales que se observan en los muebles procedentes de Vienne, Pompeya y Herculano, aunque con una menor esbeltez y ligereza, indicio, posiblemente, de que se trata de un trabajo provincial. Sin embargo, presenta la particularidad de las aberturas en el remate almenado, hecho que no se repite en ninguno de los muebles conocidos hasta ahora y que tiene seguramente relación con la bandeja, posiblemente de hierro, que se adaptaría al interior de las almenas, profundizando apenas por debajo del marco superior, a la vez que la arcilla refractaria, sobre la que se situaban las brasas, se apoyaría en la parte superior del interior de las almenas.

Las figuras

Se han conservado cinco de las seis que adornaban los lados largos del brasero; cuatro son bustos, mientras que la quinta, y probablemente la sexta, son rostros. Salvo el dios Marte, todas

---

1 B. Barr-Sharrar, "Rolling brazier," en *Das Wrack* 1, 657-61; J. L. Argente, *La villa tardorromana de Baños de Valdearados (Burgos)* (ExcArqEsp 100, 1979) 112-14, fig. 21D; S. Boucher, G. Perdu, y M. Feugère, *Bronzes antiques* 2: *instrumentum aegyptiaca* (Lyon 1980) 43-44, no. 262; A. Maiuri, *La casa del Menandro e il suo tesoro di argentaria* (Roma 1933) 432-33, fig. 164, inv. 4326; *Le collezione del Museo Nazionale di Napoli* (Roma 1986) 182-83, no. 68, inv. 73014 (de Herculano); E. Pernice, *Die hellenistische Kunst in Pompeji* 4: *Gefässe und Geräte aus Bronze* (Berlin 1925) 4-5, fig. 5-6, inv. 72991; L. Eschebach, "Die Forumsthermen in Pompeji, Regio VII, Insula 5," *AntW* 22.4 (1991) 269, figs. 34-35.

ellas tienen relación con la iconografía dionisíaca, como es habitual en los muebles de este tipo, ya que suelen estar decorados con cabecitas de leones, ménades, sátiros y el propio Dionisos.

Sátiro

Mide 9.3 cm de largo. Es un busto masculino joven con una abundante melena que mira al frente. Su corta barba se compone de dos mechones puntiagudos paralelos. La caricaturización del personaje se acentúa con las líneas de sus pómulos y de la frente. Las orejas son puntiagudas. Está tocado con una corona con cinco grandes hojas de vid triangulares extendidas, sujeta por dos largos lazos ondulados visibles sobre cada uno de los hombros. El joven se cubre únicamente con una piel de animal dispuesta en escote en pico.

Por detrás, la figura es hueca y se encuentra rellena de plomo desde la cabeza hasta la mitad del busto con la intención posiblemente de ajustar peso. El centro de la cabeza lo ocupa un pequeño orificio circular, como el que aparece en los bustos convertidos en pesas de balanza. Junto a la nuca se concentran restos férricos pertenecientes a un posible vástago.

Marte

Mide 10.3 cm de largo. Es un busto vestido con coraza y cubierta con casco, al que le falta la cimera. Tiene la cabeza ligeramente inclinada hacia su izquierda. Porta una corta melena rizada que sobresale del casco y cubre sus orejas y nuca.

El personaje viste una túnica, de la que se observa el cuello, cubierta por una coraza lisa con ptéryges sobre los hombros, y los dos humerales de cuero que vienen hacia el pecho. Sobre su hombro derecho llevaba quizá un pequeño disco o una flor.

En su parte posterior, la figura es hueca y conserva el resto de un vástago de hierro en la cabeza. Del centro del busto, coincidiendo con el pecho, emerge el resto de una espiga de sección rectangular, que ha sido seccionada para no entorpecer su soldadura al brasero. La espiga es propia de figuras que van a decorar una superficie de madera.

Su identificación se hace difícil al faltarle atributos complementarios definitorios. El único personaje que se muestra con este tipo de vestimenta es el dios Marte,[2] que, no obstante, no aparece frecuentemente representado. Se descarta Artemisa, la Diana romana, que se encuentra con cierta frecuencia en el repertorio de bustos helenísticos y romanos, pero que, sin embargo, no viste en ningún caso el tipo de coraza que porta esta figura.[3]

Sátiro niño sobre cáliz

Mide 10.6 cm de largo. Es un busto infantil masculino, con los hombros redondeados y apoyado en un cáliz tripétalo. El niño tiene la cabeza ligeramente girada hacia su izquierda y hacia arriba. Es un personaje de cara redondeada y mofletudo. Tiene los rasgos faciales caricaturizados. Las orejas, poco claras, podrían ser puntiagudas. El pelo se compone de grandes mechones de rizos y caracoles. El busto se cubre únicamente con una piel de animal anudada sobre su hombro izquierdo, de cuya lazada le cae por delante una cabecita de animal.

Hueca en la parte posterior, la figura tiene una gran abertura rectangular y dos orificios menores y circulares que se corresponden con los hombros, junto a un tercero ubicado en su nuca. Esta particular forma plantea la posibilidad de que en origen se fabricara como adorno de un carro.

La ausencia de atributos, de nuevo, dificulta reconocer con claridad si se trataba de un Dionisos niño, de un Sátiro niño o, incluso, de un Eros. Estos últimos llevan la piel cruzando su busto,

---

2 *LIMC* II.1 523, s.v. Mars (E. Simon). El busto llamado de Minerva procedente de Besançon, varias veces publicado como tal (*Bronzes antiques découverts à Besançon* [Besançon 1981] 106, inv. 852.2.9) y nombrado de la misma manera en otras publicaciones, ha sido erróneamente interpretado, ya que no se conoce ninguna Minerva con este tipo de coraza (*LIMC* II.1 1074-1109, s.v. Minerva [F. Canciani]). Lo mismo se puede decir del paralelo de Velleia citado en el mismo texto, que también fue dado como de Minerva.

3 B. Barr-Sharrar, *The Hellenistic and Early Imperial decorative bust* (Mainz 1987) 91-96.

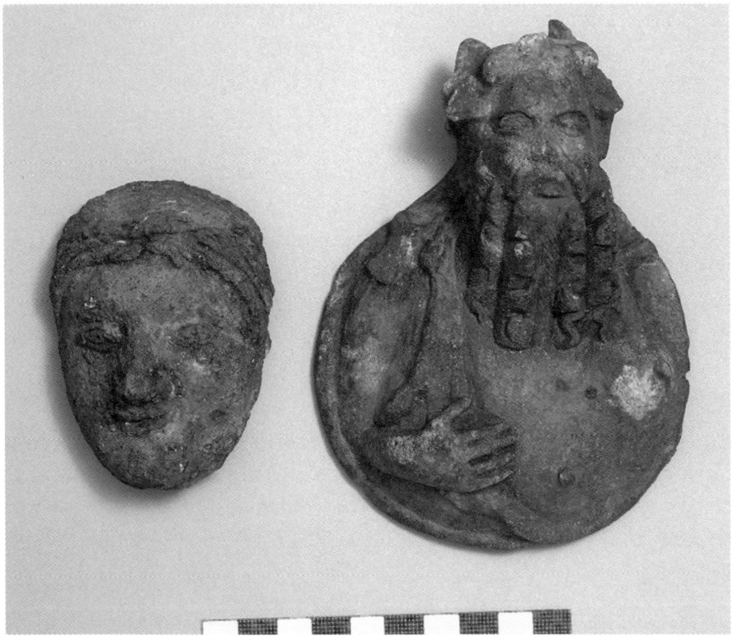

Fig. 3. Figuras del lado 3. Ménade y Sileno. (Foto: J. Garrido, Museo de Zaragoza)

coronas de hiedra, una especie de moño sobre la frente y unas alitas. El Dionisos niño, por su parte, representado estáticamente expresa de esta manera la dignidad del dios de corta edad. Los Sátiros niños pueden tener las orejas puntiagudas, una corona de hiedra en la cabeza, unos corimbos o unos cuernecillos, rasgos faciales caricaturizados y una piel de animal cruzando su cuerpo desde un hombro hasta el costado contrario. Se podría pensar que se trata de un Dionisos niño al que el artesano haya considerado que no necesitaba más atributos para ser identificado como tal. Sin embargo, los Dionisos niños no suelen llevar una piel cruzando su cuerpo,[4] ni los rasgos faciales caricaturizados. Debido a estas dos razones pensamos que debe ser un Sátiro niño.

La figurita del brasero emerge de un cáliz tripétalo. Este motivo de origen egipcio se adopta en el arte helenístico y se transmite al romano, donde en los temas dionisíacos encontró un importante eco y el que, a la vez, ha sido interpretado con un sentido de Fertilidad y de Vida después de la Muerte.[5]

Ménade o Ariadna

Mide 8.1 cm de largo. Es una cara femenina ovalada con las pupilas vacías. Su pelo se encuentra recogido en la parte posterior, es liso y está parcialmente cubierto por un casquete circular o velo que deja un fino mechón sobre la frente a la vista. Unos mechones o, quizá, unos pendientes pueden situarse en las orejas, pero su estado de conservación impide una interpretación segura.

La parte posterior de la cara está totalmente hueca y todo su contorno se apoyaba sobre la superficie del brasero, sin sobresalir, como ocurre con los bustos. Es la única figura concebida originalmente para decorar el brasero.

Se propone su identificación como ménade o Ariadna por ser ambos personajes femeninos asiduos acompañantes de Dionisos.

Sileno

Mide 14 cm de largo. Es el busto de un personaje anciano masculino adaptado a un disco bron-

---

4 I. Manfrini-Aragno, *Bacchus dans les bronzes hellénistiques et romains: les artisans et leur répertoire* (CahArchRomande 34, 1987) 140, 144. Tampoco lo hace en la gran estatuaria, los relieves y la cerámica, aunque sí aparece esta característica en sus acompañantes (E. Pochmarski, *Dionysische Gruppen: Eine typologische Untersuchung zur Geschichte des Stützmotivs* [Wien 1990]).

5 H. Jucker, *Das Bildnis im Blätterkelch: Geschichte und Bedeutung einer römischen Porträtform* (Biblioteca Helvetica Romana 3, Olten 1961) 216.

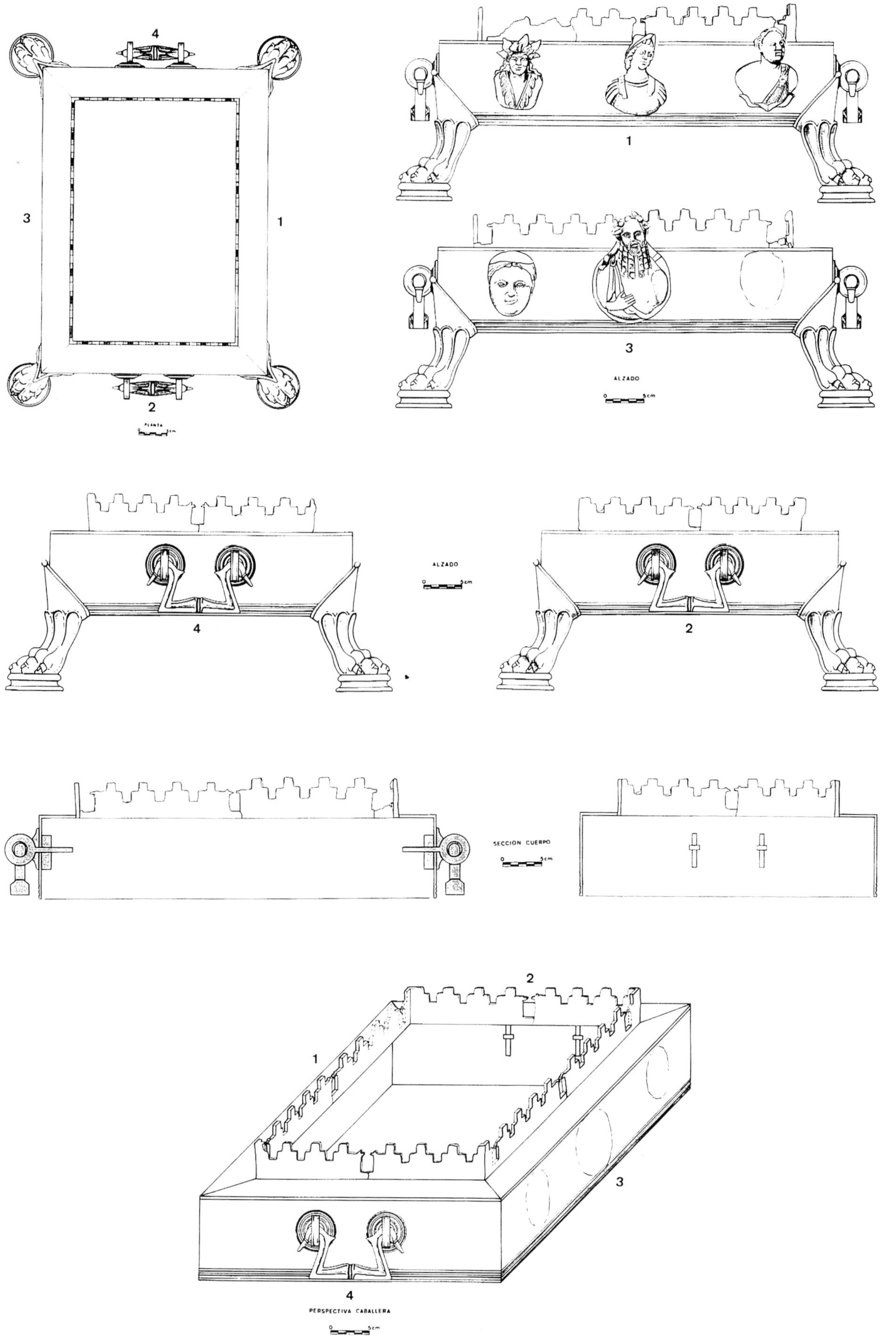

Fig. 4. Planta, alzado, sección, y perspectiva caballera del brasero. (Dibujos: B. del Rincón, Museo de Zaragoza)

cíneo rayado. Tiene la cabeza ligeramente girada hacia su izquierda y hacia arriba. La cara es alargada. Tiene huecas las pupilas. La nariz es puntiaguda y pequeña. La barba es abundante, larga y se compone de seis grupos de tirabuzones con un rayado interior oblícuo y ondulado. Es un personaje calvo, adornado con una corona de seis hojas de hiedra y dos corimbos sobre la frente, además de una cinta o banda que sobresale en la nuca y recorre con una suave ondulación parte del hombro derecho. Sólo se distingue la oreja izquierda, que tal vez sea apuntada.

Su cuerpo semidesnudo porta una piel o nébrida que se anuda en su hombro derecho y baja cubriendo ese lado. El brazo derecho está doblado en ángulo recto y apoya la mano sobre el pecho. Su hombro izquierdo esta considerablemente caido con respecto al derecho.

En la parte posterior tiene dos asientos cónicos de bronce paralelos, y vacios en la zona correspondiente a los hombros. En ellos se introducirían unas espigas de sección rectangular, de las que, quizá, quedan restos visibles en la herrumbre que impregna uno de ellos. Es posible que, por estar la figura adaptada a un disco, la intención con que fue fabricada fuese decorar un *fulcrum*.

El busto del Sileno tiene un aspecto de serenidad, solemnidadp y estatismo, además carece del aspecto regordete y ebrio, que le aleja de la expresión de *pathos* tan característica en los bustos de Silenos de tipo helenístico. Sin embargo, mantiene rasgos de los mismos, como ser un anciano calvo — coronado y con corimbos — con larga y poblada barba rizada y con una vestimenta simi-lar. El Sileno de Hinojosa es una obra que no muestra gran interés en la fidelidad a los patrones artísticos.

Existe un grupo de bustos de Silenos que representan los brazos.[6] Generalmente sostienen odres de vino, en menor medida frutos y, excepcionalmente, un racimo de uva. La similar posición del busto del brasero respecto de uno de estos bustos podría explicar alguno de sus detalles. El Sileno conservado en el Museo del Louvre[7] tiene el brazo derecho doblado en ángulo recto y la palma de la mano se apoya sobre la piel. Sobre el hombro izquierdo descansa un odre de vino sostenido con la mano de ese mismo lado. Esto permite pensar que, tal vez, el desequilibrio en el hombro izquierdo del busto del brasero se debía a que, sobre él, tenía que haberse situado un odre con vino. Sin embargo, por razones desconocidas, el artesano no copió fielmente la obra original.

Conclusiones

Los bustos de tipo helenístico y sus derivaciones romanas adornan una serie concreta de muebles y objetos, como son los *fulcra* de los lechos, el centro de *pyxis* o *phialai*, los carros y las arquetas. También se les reconoce un uso secundario como pesas de balanzas. Sin embargo, hasta ahora, no se había detectado su utilización o reutilización sobre un brasero portátil.

Otro hecho de interés lo constituye el que las figuras del brasero, fabricadas a la cera perdida, adolecen de atributos definitorios para el reconocimiento de los personajes. A la vez, no todos pertenecen al mismo ciclo mitológico, lo cual permite pensar en una pérdida de la simbología intrínseca al tema original. Esto vuelve a manifestarse en el lado en el que se conservan las tres figuras del brasero, ya que dos de ellas miran hacia un lado y la tercera hacia el frente, sin formar una composición conjunta. Otro argumento más apoya la ausencia de intencionalidad en expresar simbología concreta al comprobar que, las partes posteriores de las figuras, se fabricaron originalmente con distintas funciones y, posteriormente, se arreglaron para adaptarse, junto a la cara femenina, a la superficie del *foculus*.

Solamente se ha comprobado la copia de una obra de tipo helenístico en el Sileno anciano, pero es muy probable que el resto de los bustos lo fueran también.

---

6 A. Greifenhagen, "Bronzekline im Pariser Kunsthandel," *RömMitt* 45 (1930) lám. 40a; Barr-Sharrar (supra n.3) C19; C. Boube, "Les lits de bronze de Maurétanie Tingitane," *BAMaroc* 4 (1960) 196.

7 Louvre MNC 1741: Barr-Sharrar (supra n.3) 37, C 19.

Por lo expuesto se puede afirmar que las figuras, y seguramente también el brasero, son obra de un taller provincial, cuyo maestro broncista habría fabricado los bustos para diferentes muebles, copiando con más o menos fidelidad los patrones ampliamente difundidos, y en este caso los habría adaptado al brasero a gusto del comprador.

En un intento de aproximación cronológica, sobre la base de su similitud con el busto del Museo del Louvre, fechado a fines del s. I a.C. "o un poco más tarde,"[8] y debido al hecho de que los bustos de *fulcra* de tipo helenístico se fabricaron hasta finales del s. I d.C., con reservas, se propone fechar este brasero, que no presenta arreglos ni huellas de haber sido adornado con anterioridad, en algún momento del s. I d.C.

Servicio de Cultura (Unidad de Museos Arqueológicos), Torreón Fortea, C/- Torrenueva 25, 50003 Zaragoza

---

8 Ibid. 37.

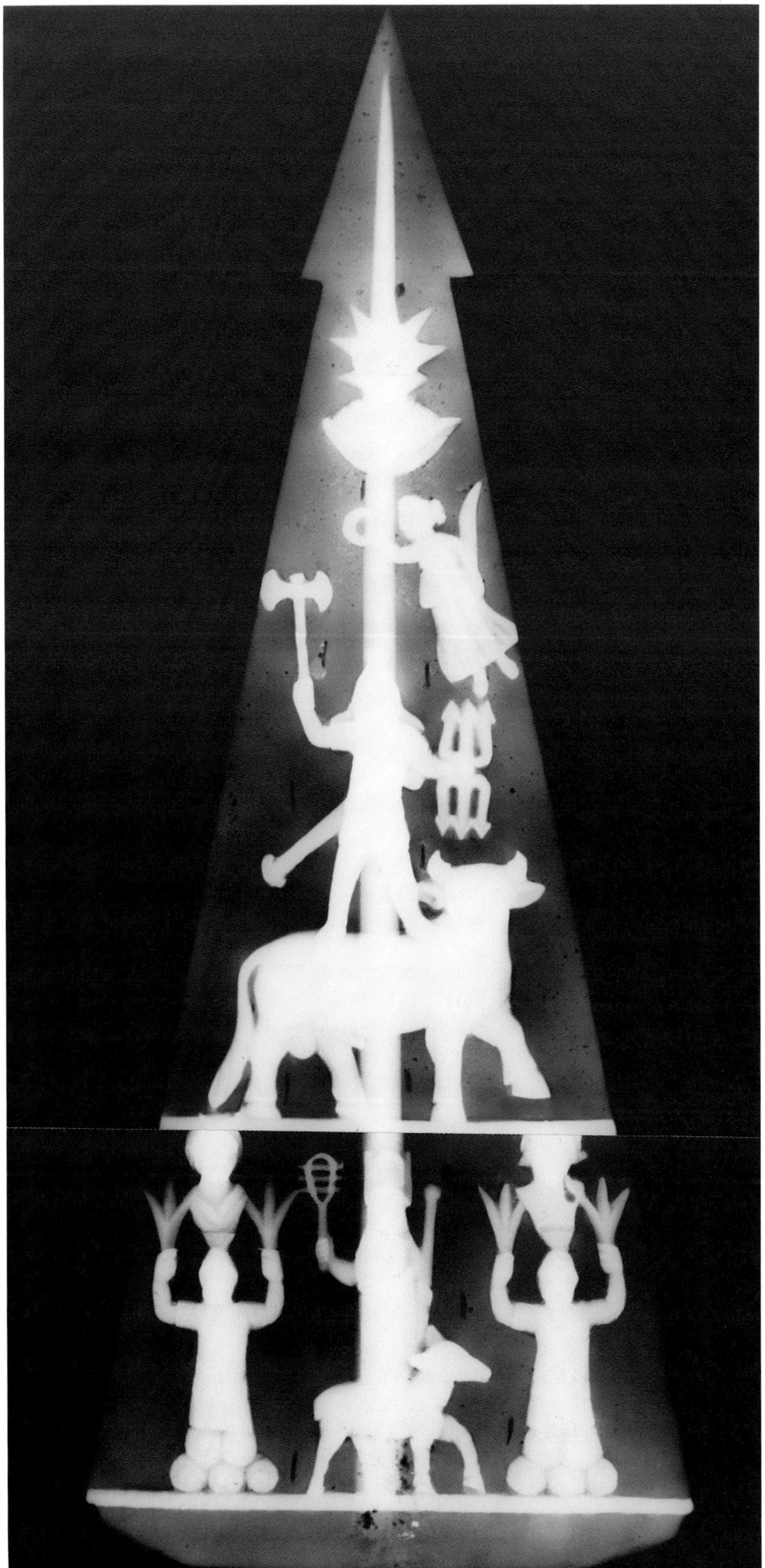

Abb. 1. Votivplatte des Iupiter Dolichenus: Röntgenaufnahme. Römisch, beginnendes 3. Jhs. n. Chr. Bronze, H. 0.49 m. Wiesbaden, Museum Wiesbaden, Sammlung Nassauischer Altertümer 6775. (Röntgenaufnahmen: Römisch-Germanisches Zentralmuseum, Mainz R 93/112-113)

Iupiter Dolichenus und der Regen

Maria Kohlert-Németh

Die dreieckige bronzene Votivplatte[1] aus Nida-Heddernheim in Ober-Germanien, die wahrscheinlich aus einem Dolichenum stammt, ist bereits im vorigen Jahrhundert entdeckt und seitdem in der Literatur oft besprochen worden.[2] Umso erstaunlicher ist es, daß einige wichtige Details bisher unbemerkt geblieben sind.[3] Da sich die Platte zur Zeit als Leihgabe des Wiesbadener Museums im Frankfurter Museum für Vor- und Frühgeschichte befindet, konnte ich durch Autopsie neue Erkenntnisse gewinnen und sie im Labor des Römisch-Germanischen Zentralmuseums in Mainz überprüfen lassen.[4] Hier sollen diese Resultate knapp referiert werden.

1. Ein neu entdecktes symbolhaftes und repetitives Element, das die ganze Komposition überzieht, hilft uns bei der Dechiffrierung der Inhalte. Kleine, längliche, vertikale Metallstreifen, die sich durch Farbe vom Untergrund absetzen, übersäen die gesamte Oberfläche der lederfarbigen, dunkelbräunlich schimmernden Votivplatte, die das dolichenische Götterpaar übereinandergeordnet zeigt (Abb. 1). Die durchschnittlich 6 bis 7 mm bzw. maximal 8 bis 9 mm langen und 1 bis 1.5 mm breiten Streifen sind als Einlagen aus andersfarbiger Metalllegierung gearbeitet. Sie durchdringen die etwa 3 bis 4 mm starke, gegossene Platte und kommen auf deren Rückseite zum Vorschein. Sie beginnen in der oberen Ecke, unterhalb der Solbüste, aufzutreten und verteilen sich — ungeachtet der horizontalen Zweiteilung der Komposition — regelmäßig auf der gesamten Bildfläche. Auf die obere Bildzone entfallen acht, auf die untere sieben Streifen. Sie sind manchmal auch an Stellen angebracht, wo sie schlecht oder kaum sichtbar sind: z.B. unmittelbar neben plastisch hervortretenden Figurenkonturen, wie neben dem Stierhals und dem Stierhorn oder am Hals der unteren Solbüste. So entsteht der Eindruck, daß man beabsichtigte, eine bestimmte Anzahl von diesen Symbolen an der Bildfläche unterzubringen, bzw. in das Kultobjekt "hineinzusetzen": folglich haben wir es mit magischer Bedeutung und wahrscheinlich auch mit Zahlensymbolik zu tun.[5]

---

1 Museum Wiesbaden, Sammlung Nassauischer Altertümer 6775: gegossene Bronze, H. 0.49 m, Br. 0.195 m, T. 0.003 m; Reliefhöhe 0.005 bis 0.015 m, max. 0.019 m.

2 M. Hörig und E. Schwertheim, *Corpus Cultus Iovis Dolicheni* (*EPRO* 106, Leiden 1987) 320-21, Nr. 512, Taf. 108 rechts, mit Zusammenstellung der älteren Literatur.

3 In meinem 1988 erschienenen Katalog des Frankfurter Museums für Vor- und Frühgeschichte (M. Kohlert-Németh, *Römische Bronzen* 1, *aus Nida-Heddernheim: Götter und Dämonen* [Frankfurt am Main 1988] 55-56) habe ich selbst noch nach Fotografie bzw. nach einer Kopie des Stückes gearbeitet und habe deswegen wichtige Einzelheiten ebenfalls nicht erkennen können.

4 An dieser Stelle bedanke ich mich herzlich bei den Frankfurter Kollegen, besonders bei I. Huld-Zetsche, für die tatkräftige Unterstützung meines Vorhabens; ebenfalls U. Seitz-Gray für die Anfertigung fotografischer Aufnahmen und M. Piehl für die Röntgenaufnahmen. Gleichfalls bin ich zu Dank verpflichtet E. Künzl im Römisch-Germanischen Zentralmuseum, Mainz, für fruchtbare Anregungen und Diskussionen. Er hat meine Arbeit stets mit Interesse begleitet und ermöglicht, daß im Mainzer Labor Materialuntersuchungen und Röntgenaufnahmen gemacht werden konnten: sie wurden von D. Ankner durchgeführt, dem ich hiermit ebenfalls danken möchte.

5 Am Hals der kleinen Solbüste, unter der schlecht sichtbaren Einlage, beträgt der Plattendurchmesser sogar 10 mm: trotzdem wurde Wert darauf gelegt, daß auf der Rückseite der Platte das Zeichen zum Erscheinen kommt. Zur Zahlensymbolik, vgl. F. C. Endres und A. Schimmel, *Das Mysterium der Zahl: Zahlensymbolik im Kulturvergleich* (Köln 1984, Sonderausgabe 1995) 142-59, 172-74. Die magische Zahl Sieben deutet möglicherweise auf die sieben Planeten, die glückhafte Acht, eine göttliche Zahl, auf das kosmische Gleichgewicht hin: Es ergeben sich wahrscheinlich gedankliche Verbindungen zu den Mithrasmysterien, wo über der Opferszene oft sieben Sterne angebracht waren. (Zu Mithras in Nida, vgl. I. Huld-Zetsche, *Mithras in Nida-Heddernheim* [Frankfurt am Main 1986] 7, 78-79.) Es sind noch weitere Forschungen notwendig, um die magische und zahlenmystische Seite dieses besonderen Kultobjektes zu erhellen.

Solche ungewöhnlichen Zeichen sind innerhalb dieser Denkmalgattung bisher erstmalig entdeckt worden und ich interpretiere sie als Regendarstellung. Wenn wir uns vergegenwärtigen, daß Iupiter Dolichenus ursprünglich eine uralte kleinasiatisch-syrische Wettergottheit ist, so ist dies verständlich. Die Darstellung des Regens macht den Fruchtbarkeitsaspekt des Gottes relevant: als Heilbringer und Erhalter des gesamten Kosmos.[6]

Die energiedispersive Röntgenfluoreszenzanalyse im Rasterelektromikroskop, durchgeführt von D. Ankner im Labor des Römisch-Germanischen Zentralmuseums in Mainz, hat folgendes Ergebnis gebracht: "Die Kupferlegierung des Dreiecks besteht aus etwa 65% Kupfer, 17% Blei, 10% Zink, und 8% Zinn. Die schmalen Einlagefelder enthalten dagegen nur Kupfer (etwa 83%) und Zink (etwa 17%). Die schwarze Farbe der Kupferlegierung könnte auf eine Oberflächenbehandlung zurückzuführen sein."[7]

E. Künzl im Römisch-Germanischen Zentralmuseum bestätigte mir nach der technischen Untersuchung die Richtigkeit meiner Vermutung: "Durch D. Ankners Analyse entpuppte sich der 'Regen' als goldglänzendes Messing, während das Dreieck selbst wegen des geringen Kupfergehaltes und der starken Blei-, Zink-, und Zinnbeimischungen sicherlich viel weniger goldene Farbe aufwies. Hinzu kommt die Frage, ob nicht ein dunkler Farbton absichtlich erzielt wurde, von dem sich der goldene Regen gut abgehoben hätte."[8] Ich ging diesem Hinweis nach und prüfte die Beziehung dieser schwarzen Bronzen zum *aes Corinthium.* In der Tat sprechen mehrere signifikante Kriterien dafür, die Votivplatte unter dem Begriff *aes Corinthium* einzureihen.[9] Es sind jedoch weitere Analysen notwendig, um diese Hypothese zu erhärten. Meine Untersuchungen werden sich weiterhin damit beschäftigen.

2. Zweitens geht es um neue ikonographische Beobachtungen zur Göttin Iuno Dolichena, die *en face* auf einer Hirschkuh steht (Abb. 2-3). Zum Unterschied zu vielen anderen Darstellungen, wo die Göttin im gleichen Bildstreifen Iupiter Dolichenus nach links blickend gegenübergestellt wird, steht sie hier ohne den Gott im Bildfeld auf ihrem nach rechts schreitenden Tier. Es besitzt merkwürdige Proportionen: kurzen, dicken Hals, großen Kopf, und nach hinten gelegte Ohren. Sein leicht geöffnetes Maul mit Andeutungen von Zähnen ist befremdlich: wohl eine Assoziation zur wilden, ungebändigten Natur.

Die Göttin trägt ein langes Gewand, darüber einen faltenreichen Mantel, der um die Hüfte geschlungen und über den Hinterkopf gezogen ist. In ihrer rechten Hand hält sie ein Sistrum. Dieser Umstand hat die Forscher bewogen, in ihrer Kopfbedeckung eine Isiskrone — eine Sonnenscheibe zwischen zwei Federn — zu sehen. Bei genauer Betrachtung kann man jedoch eine große Mauerkrone mit einem leicht konkav ausgehöhlten Mittelbogen erkennen; darunter kommt ein mit Ähren und Blüten geschmücktes Diadem zum Vorschein (Abb. 2).[10] Der Kopf der

---

6 In diesem Zusammenhang ist aber auch zu überlegen, in wieweit diese Vorstellungen mit religiösen Ideen der einheimisch keltischen Bevölkerung in Nida im Einklang waren und deshalb auf fruchtbaren Boden fielen. Den keltischen Iupiter, dessen bevorzugte Aufenthaltsorte Berge oder Anhöhen waren, wie die Berggötter des Orients, assoziierte man mit natürlichen Erscheinungen des Himmels: man brachte ihn mit Wetterphänomenen und mit Fruchtbarkeit durch Sonne und Regen in Verbindung, vgl. M. Green, *The gods of the Celts* (Stroud 1993) 47, 67-68. Auf ähnliche Affinitäten verweist auch H. Kenner, "Die Götterwelt der Austria Romana," *ANRW* II.18.2 (1989) 147, Taf. VIII.18.

7 D. Ankner, *Untersuchungsbericht des Römisch-Germanischen Zentralmuseums, Werkblatt-Nr. 93/146* (vom 2.9.1993).

8 Kommentar E. Künzl zum Untersuchungsbericht des Römisch-Germanischen Zentralmuseums (s. o. Anm. 7).

9 Vor allem die polychrome Wirkung und die besondere Legierung des Kultobjektes: A. Giumlia-Mair und P. Craddock, "Corinthium aes, das schwarze Gold der Alchimisten," *AntW Sonderheft* 3 (1993) 50.

10 Obwohl der allererste Bericht über die Platte 1844 zutreffend von einer mit Diadem und Mauerkrone geschmückten weiblichen Figur sprach, fand diese Meinung in der späteren Forschung keine Beachtung: F. G. Habel, "Nassauische Annalen," *Jahrbuch des Vereins für Nassauische Altertumskunde und Geschichtsforschung* 3 (1844) 178.

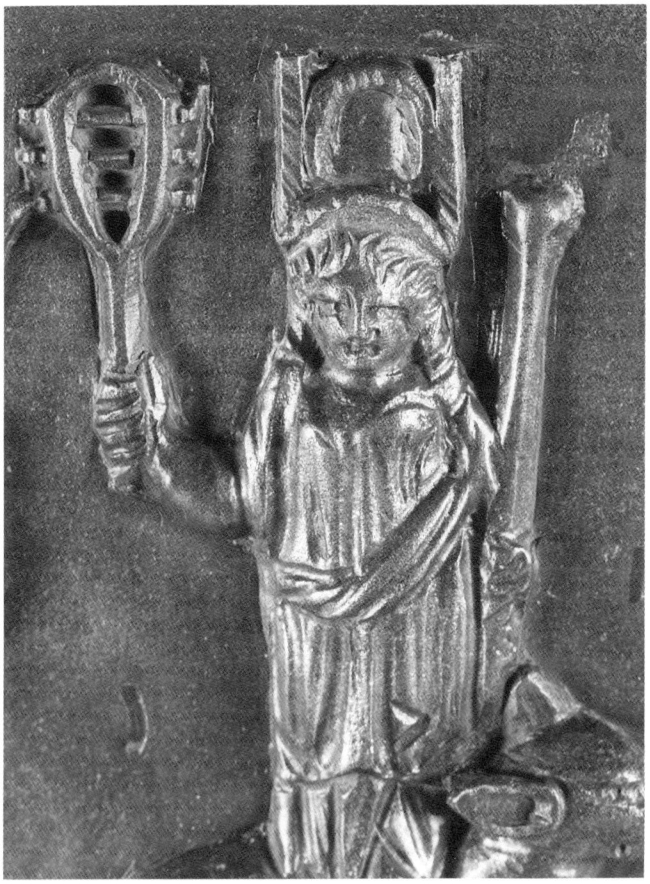

Abb. 2. Detail der Votivplatte des Iupiter Dolichenus. (Foto: U. Seitz-Gray; Museum für Vor- und Frühgeschichte Frankfurt am Main)

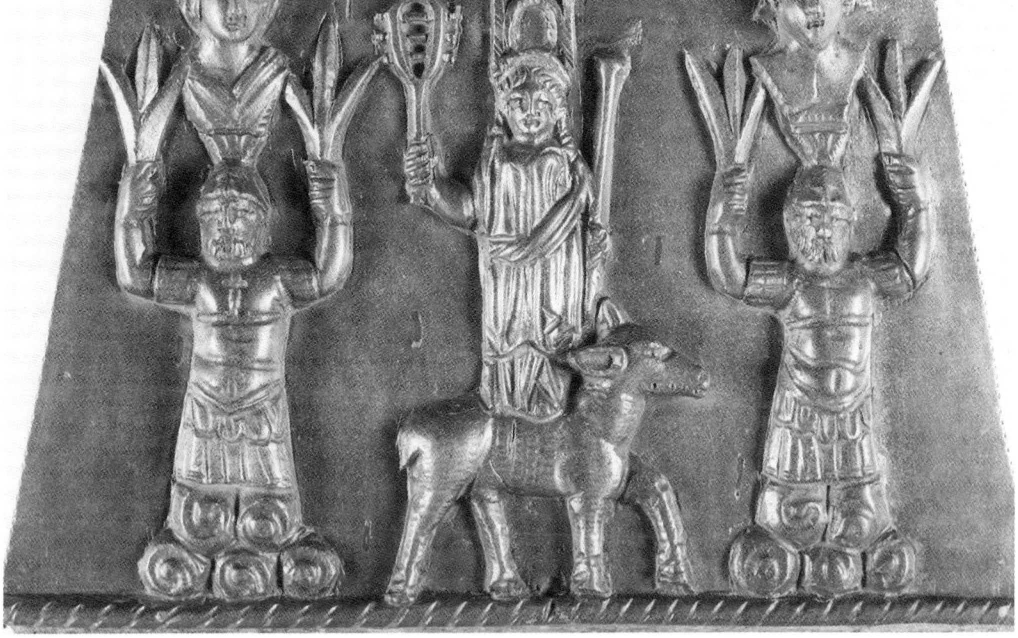

Abb. 3. Detail der Votivplatte des Iupiter Dolichenus. (Foto: U. Seitz-Gray; Museum für Vor- und Frühgeschichte Frankfurt am Main)

Göttin ist leicht nach rechts gewandt, die Augen waren einst mit silbrig glänzendem Metall ausgelegt; die Einlage ihres linken Augensterns ist noch erhalten.

In der linken Hand hielt die Göttin einen langen stabähnlichen Gegenstand, der sich nach oben leicht verbreitet und abgerundet ist: nach bisheriger Interpretation ein Szepter. Nun ist etwas schräg über dessen Ende eine leicht erhabene Stelle zu bemerken, und auf der Rückseite der Platte wird ein kleiner rechteckiger Ausschnitt sichtbar, mit andersfarbigem Material, nämlich rötlichem Metall, ausgefüllt.[11] Wahrscheinlich handelt es sich um die Darstellung der Flamme einer Fackel. Eine Fackel wäre als Attribut gut vorstellbar in der Hand einer synkretistischen Göttin mit Mauerkrone, die offenbar Aspekte der Magna Mater besitzt. Die Repräsentation des Feuers im Kontext von Opferhandlungen ist üblich, sie tritt häufig als Flamme eines brennenden Altars im unteren Bildstreifen dolichenischer Votivdreiecke in Erscheinung.[12]

Auf den chthonischen Charakter der Göttin weist vermutlich die Verzierung der Bodenlinie und die der oberen Abschlußleiste des Relieffeldes hin, die erhaben gearbeitet und schräggestrichelt sind: Sie sind vielleicht als schematische Darstellung von Schlangenleibern zu verstehen.[13]

Hirsch oder Hirschkuh ist, wie schon erwähnt, oft das Begleittier der Iuno Dolichena, auf dem sie steht. Der Hirsch ist aber als attributives Tier jener Natur- und Muttergottheiten nachgewiesen worden, deren Prototyp die alles beherrschende Große Mutter der Frühzeit gewesen ist. Die ursprünglichen Eigenschaften der aus dem kleinasiatisch-syrischen Raum stammenden Göttin als Herrin des Gebirges und gleichzeitig auch als Muttergöttin, haben sich über Jahrtausende hindurch erhalten und kommen durch die Zuordnung des Hirsches zu Iuno Dolichena erneut zum Ausdruck.[14]

Auch die Kompositionsart des unteren Bildfeldes, wo die in hieratischer Haltung frontal stehende Göttin von streng symmetrisch-antithetisch angeordneten Castores Dolicheni flankiert wird, ruft Assoziationen zum uralten Motiv der Potnia Theron wach. Die Unterkörper der Castores sind aus spiralförmig gewundenen Buckeln gebildet, die Felsen symbolisieren. Dadurch ähneln sie Bergdämonen und gleichen sich damit dem Charakter ihrer Herrin an. Sie tragen aber Brustpanzer und Helm und halten Zweige oder Bäume in ihren Händen, aus denen unmittelbar die Büsten der Luna und Sol herauswachsen. Lebensbaum oder Blüte sind auch Symbole der alten lebensspendenden Göttin. Es sind also mehrere Symbole und kompositorische Elemente miteinander verwoben, die an das ursprüngliche Erscheinungsbild der Göttin erinnern.

Iuno Dolichena, mit Sistrum, Mauerkrone, und Fackel ausgerüstet, mit Aspekten einer uralten Erd- und Berggöttin, Muttergöttin, und Fruchtbarkeitsspenderin wird hier mit ihren Bäume tragenden Helfern, inmitten einer mystisch-rituellen Opferhandlung dargestellt, die sicherlich mit Erneuerungs- und Wiedergeburtsvorstellungen in Zusammenhang stehen.[15]

Zusammenfassend läßt sich feststellen, daß Iupiter Dolichenus und seine Gemahlin auf der Votivplatte aus Nida-Heddernheim als Himmel und Unterwelt beherrschendes Götterpaar dargestellt werden. Sie sind Fruchtbarkeitsspender, Lebensbewahrer und halten die kosmische Ordnung aufrecht. Mit allen Mitteln wird die Naturkraft des ursprünglich altorientalischen

11 Wahrscheinlich eisenhaltig, spezielle Untersuchungsergebnisse dazu liegen noch nicht vor.

12 Feueraltar, als Sinnbild des Opfers, gehört zum dolichenischen Bildkanon; dazu Hörig und Schwertheim (s. o. Anm.2) 8, 16.

13 Vgl. Dekorationsschema an Schlangenkrateren und Räucherkelchen; vgl. Huld-Zetsche (s. o. Anm.5) 13-14. An einer dolichenischen Dreieckplatte ist diese erhaben gearbeitete Leiste, die die Komposition horizontal trennt, geschuppt wiedergegeben; von Noll als Blattkranz interpretiert: R. Noll, *Das Inventar des Dolichenusheiligtums von Mauer an der Url (Noricum)* (Wien 1980) 45, Taf. 16.

14 So auch Hörig und Schwertheim (s. o. Anm.2) 40-41, 267-68.

15 Auf weitere Ausführungen dieser Gedanken muß hier wegen der Kürze der Darstellung verzichtet werden: dies wird einer Publikation, die ich zu diesem Thema vorbereite, vorbehalten.

Wettergottes wiederbeschworen. Dazu gehören die ausgesprochene Blitzform des Kultobjektes,[16] vor allem die Darstellung des Regens, aber auch die der Bäume, aus denen Gestirne herauswachsen, die von "felsenfesten" Helfern der Göttin in römischer Soldatentracht getragen werden.

Die Macht der Göttin ist potenziert: sie vereinigt Iuno Dolichena, Isis und Kybele in sich. Interessant wird es, der Frage dieser Synkretismen des beginnenden 3. Jhr. n. Chr. nachzugehen. Wir wissen, daß Nida ein wichtiger Ort für orientalische Kulte war, nicht nur für Mithras, sondern auch für Iupiter Dolichenus und Kybele.[17]

Abschließend soll die Frage zumindest angeschnitten werden, ob die Regendarstellung auf dieser Platte möglicherweise auch einen aktuellen historischen Bezug haben könnte. Ich denke dabei an das sogenannte Regenwunder, das sich auf ein historisches Ereignis bezieht und auf der Markussäule seinen bildlichen Niederschlag gefunden hat. Es wird berichtet, daß im Krieg, den Marc Aurel gegen die Quaden geführt hatte, die von Feinden eingeschlossene römische Heeresabteilung durch ein Blitz- und Regenwunder gerettet wurde. Bei Carnuntum, wo eine wichtige Basis für diese militärische Operation lag, entdeckte man zahlreiche Denkmäler, die bestätigen, daß dort der siegreiche Abschluß der römischen Offensive gegen die Quaden und speziell das im Laufe der militärischen Ereignisse als heilig empfundene Rettungswunder religiöse Verehrungsform gefunden haben.[18] Ein Kopffragment des Iupiter, z.B., in das eine dreizinkige Eisengabel — eine Art halbiertes Blitzbündel — hineingelassen wurde, zeigt ihn wahrscheinlich in seiner ursprünglichen Form, als Blitz- und Wettergott, als Iupiter Fulgurator, als Retter in höchster Not.[19]

Schaumainkai 99, D-60596 Frankfurt am Main

---

16 Die Betonung der Dreieckspitze in dieser Form bei dieser Denkmalgattung ist einmalig. Sie wird zuweilen als lanzenförmig, so Hörig und Schwertheim (s. o. Anm.2) 320, oder auch blitzförmig gedeutet. Angesichts der Aussage der Gesamtdarstellung und der einmaligen Repräsentation des Regens auf der Votivplatte bin ich der Meinung, daß es sich hier um die Andeutung der Spitze eines Blitzes handelt, wie ihn Iupiter Dolichenus selbst in Form eines sechsstrahliges Blitzbündels auf der Platte in der Hand trägt.

17 Die Berührungspunkte und die Verflechtungen zwischen den oben genannten orientalischen Kulten sind bisher wenig untersucht worden. Vgl. dazu E. Schwertheim, "Orientalische Religionen in Deutschland," *ANRW* II.18.1 (1986) 795-97, 801-5.

18 W. Jobst, "Der Pfaffenberg als Sacer Mons Karnuntinus," *ANRW* II.6 (1977) 716, Taf. VIII.16; vgl. dazu auch Kenner (s. o. Anm.6) 949, Taf. VIII.18.

19 Vgl. oben Anm.18. Weiterhin zum Problem des Regenwunders zur Zeit Marc Aurels, seine Verbindungen zu ägyptischen Kulten, zur Magie des Orients und zu der Verbreitung dieser Vorstellungen in der Donau-Region sowie seine Rolle im Kaiserkult, siehe S. A. Takács, *Isis and Serapis in the Roman world* (Leiden 1995) 107-12, und I. Tóth, "Marcus Aurelius' miracle of the rain and the Egyptian cults in the Danube region," in *Az Eötvös Lóránd Tudományegyetem ókori történeti tanszékének kiadványai* 17 (*Studia Aegyptiaca* 2, Budapest 1976) 101-13. Den freundlichen Hinweis verdanke ich S. Takács.

Roman provincial bronzes in the Hilprecht collection, University of Pennsylvania Museum

P. Gregory Warden

The Hilprecht collection of classical and Near Eastern bronzes in the Museum of Archaeology and Anthropology, University of Pennsylvania, Philadelphia, contains more than 300 objects collected by Prof. H. V. Hilprecht between 1894 and 1914. Hilprecht was one of the giants of Near Eastern archaeology at the turn of the century.[1] A native of Germany, he came to the University of Pennsylvania to assist with the university's new expedition at Nippur and eventually became curator of the museum's Babylonian section. When finished excavating at Nippur at the beginning of the 20th c., he announced the discovery of a Temple Library of over 23,000 tablets, a discovery that was hailed as one of the most far-reaching Assyriological discoveries of the century. Hilprecht was a talented and productive scholar, although not a modest man. He was awarded the Drexel Medal for "the best archaeological excavation or publication by an English-speaking scholar" at a time when other Drexel medallists were William Flinders Petrie and Arthur Evans.

By 1904 Hilprecht had conquered the academic world, but his dramatic rise led to an even more dramatic fall. Scandal broke in 1905 when he was accused of having appropriated some of the Nippur finds and of having deliberately misrepresented evidence in his publications on that site. Hilprecht asked for a board of inquiry and was absolved, but his reputation was ruined. In fact he had doctored the evidence, pretending that finds bought from dealers had been excavated by him. He had also appropriated two bronze stag's heads from Nippur and possibly some other finds as well.

Hilprecht was an avid collector. He bequeathed a collection of Oriental art to the Philadelphia Museum of Art, a collection of Near Eastern material to the University of Jena, and the Hilprecht bronzes to the University Museum.[2] Fortunately, Hilprecht's careful notes have been preserved. Written in his own tight handwriting, the cards provide evidence for provenance, down to the day of purchase, the name and address of the dealer, and even anecdotes connected to the purchase. Most of Hilprecht's collecting took place between 1894 and 1912 in Istanbul, where he was a frequent visitor to the bazaar. Hilprecht became well known to the antiquities dealers there; eventually, when a fresh shipment of antiquities arrived, they would send runners to bring choice pieces to him in his hotel. He kept careful track of this process in his notes.

Hilprecht's collection is large. Because of his training as an archaeologist, he bought objects for their cultural rather than aesthetic interest. He seems to have been as fond of the curious, of the culturally interesting object, as of the beautiful. He was fond of animal as well as of human figurines, of implements and ornaments and other archaeological curiosities, and thanks to his strict note-keeping, the collection documents an entire cross-section of bronzes that made their way to the bazaars of what was then Constantinople.

---

1 For Hilprecht's career in Philadelphia, see C. H. Gordon, *The Pennsylvania tradition of Semitics: A century of Near Eastern and Biblical studies at the University of Pennsylvania* (Atlanta 1986) 13. For a more detailed assessment of Hilprecht: B. Kuklick, *Puritans in Babylon: The ancient Near East and American intellectual life, 1880-1930* (Princeton 1996).

2 The Hilprecht collection was first studied by C. Brodkey Moore, *Description and analysis of the bronze and lead objects in the Herman V. Hilprecht collection, the University Museum of the University of Pennsylvania* (Ph.D. diss., Univ. of Pennsylvania 1969). For a complete study of the collection, see P. G. Warden, *The Hilprecht collection of Greek, Italic, and Roman bronzes in the University of Pennsylvania Museum* (Philadelphia 1997). I am grateful to the University Museum and its director, J. Sabloff, for permission to publish this material. I also wish to thank D. G. Romano, keeper of the Mediterranean Section.

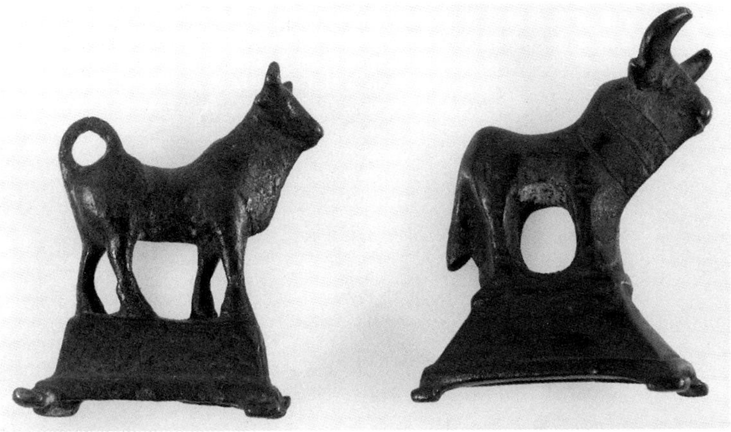

Fig. 1. Bulls. Philadelphia, University of Pennsylvania Museum inv. nos. 48-2-96 (h. 0.047 m) and 48-2-103 (h. 0.051 m).

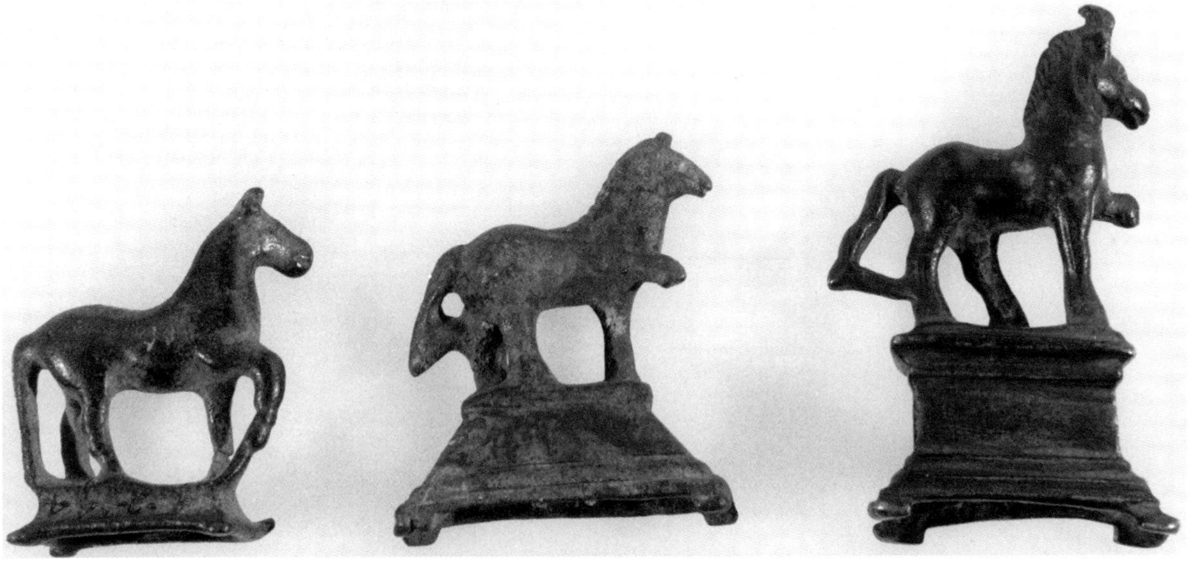

Fig. 2. Horses. Philadelphia, University of Pennsylvania Museum inv. nos. 48-2-110 (h. 0.045 m), 48-2-115 (h. 0.048 m), 48-2-117 (h. 0.064 m).

A characteristic group of Hilprecht's collection is made up of animals, and 16 bulls, probably ex-votos, attest to the popularity of taurine imagery in Anatolia.[3] Some are set on small plinths (fig. 1) or even on pedestals that suggest altars. Bull figurines may have been considered appropriate dedications because the animal itself was the quintessential animal of sacrifice,[4] or because bulls were considered appropriate for specific cults, such as those of Dionysos or Jupiter.

A very fine group of 11 horses,[5] many of which seem to have come from Samsoun or at least from the Pontic coast, has good Anatolian parallels (fig. 2). In the western provinces the popularity of horse figurines can be explained by the animal's connection with the cult of Epona,[6]

3 All inventory numbers refer to the University of Pennsylvania Museum, Philadelphia. Bull standing: 48-2-87, 48-2-88, 48-2-91, 48-2-95, 48-2-98; on plinth: 48-2-85, 48-2-86, 48-2-89, 48-2-99, 48-2-101, 48-2-102; on pedestal: 48-2-96, 48-2-103 (both fig. 1). Originally the Hilprecht collection included another bull (48-2-97), sold to the Florida State University in 1962.

4 For discussion, with bibliography: V. Galliazzo, *Bronzi romani del Museo Civico di Treviso* (Rome 1979) 119.

5 Inv. nos. 48-2-106, 48-2-107, 48-2-108, 49-2-109, 48-2-110 (fig. 2), 48-2-112, 48-2-113, 48-2-114, 48-2-115 (fig. 2), 48-2-116, 48-2-117 (fig. 2). All were bought in Istanbul. A twelfth figurine (48-2-211) was sold to Florida State University in 1962.

6 For a single horse figure in bronze, possibly associated with Epona: A. Leibundgut, *Die römischen*

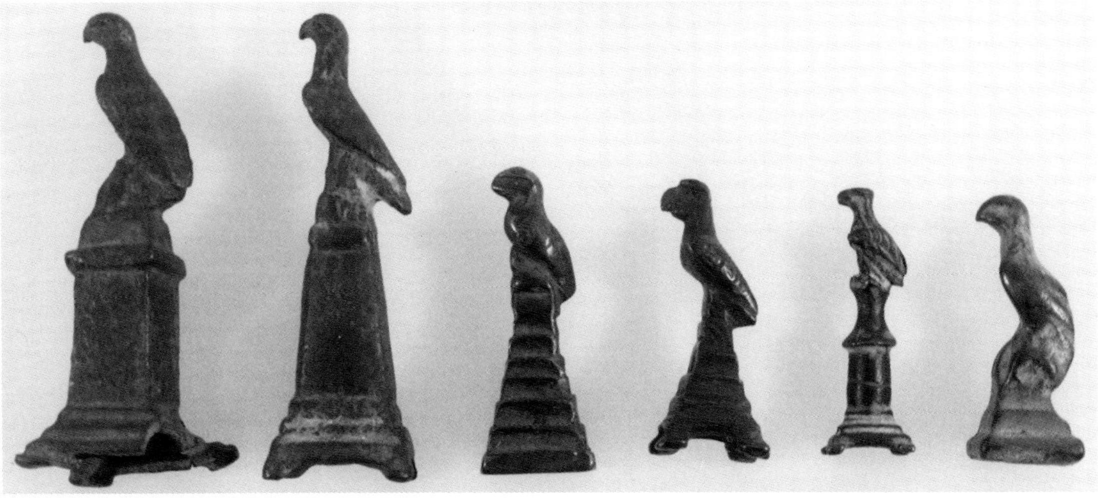

Fig. 3. Eagles. Philadelphia, University of Pennsylvania Museum inv. nos. 48-2-53 (h. 0.083 m), 48-2-54 (h. 0.081 m), 48-2-55 (h. 0.053 m), 48-2-56 (h. 0.048 m), 48-2-58 (h. 0.046 m), 48-2-59 (h. 0.046 m).

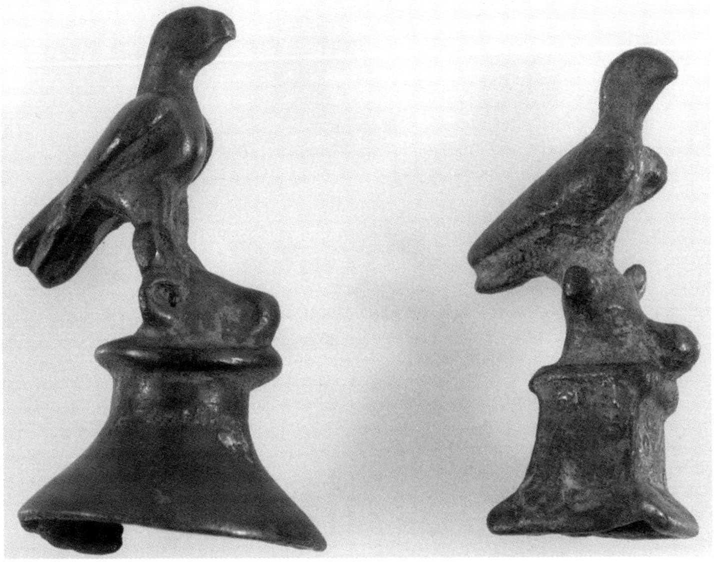

Fig. 4. Eagles on bull's heads. Philadelphia, University of Pennsylvania Museum inv. no. 48-2-63 (h. 0.052 m) and 48-2-64 (h. 0.036 m).

but the votive horses of the eastern empire are another matter. The relative popularity of horses in this part of the world (other examples no doubt exist in museums in central and north-central Turkey[7]) suggests that they may have been appropriate for a specific cult, and they should probably be associated with the popular rider figurines that were also used as ex-votos. They can be associated with the "Thracian Rider" cult that proliferated in the Balkans, the Black Sea region, and Anatolia.[8] Hilprecht's horses are shown with an articulated topknot, walking with right foreleg raised. The impression here is of show horses, of horses on display, which are thus connected to the "Thracian Rider," where the horse is shown with a topknot

Bronzen aus Schweiz 2: *Avenches* (Mainz 1976) 61, no. 41, pl. 46. For the imagery of a horse with foreleg raised, connected to Epona: H.-J. Kellner and G. Zahlhaas, *Der römische Tempelschatz von Weissenburg in Bayern* (Mainz 1993) 89, fig. 11.

7 See, for instance, the horses on display in the Archaeological Museum at Kaiseryi (Caesarea) in Cappadocia. I am grateful to D. White of the University Museum for providing me with a photograph of these pieces.

8 J. M. C. Toynbee, *Animals in Roman life and art* (Ithaca 1973) 175.

and a raised foreleg.[9] We may consider these horses, with topknot and foreleg raised, set on a base or altar, to be an Anatolian type.[10]

Various types of animal figures set on tall bases seem to have been an Anatolian favorite. Represented in the Hilprecht collection are eagles, sometimes sitting on pedestals or altars (fig. 3), or on top of other animals, or both[11] (fig. 4). The latter is also a typical Anatolian combination: the eagle perched atop a ram, goat, bull, or stag. The best known of these combinations, the eagle and stag, has been associated with the cult of Jupiter Dolichenus.[12] The Dolichenus cult gained wide popularity in the 2nd and 3rd c., spread by legionaries who were transferred around the empire. The association of these figures with Jupiter Dolichenus, however, has been disputed,[13] because the cult is Syrian in nature while the figures seem Anatolian in iconography — figures perched atop one another combining various types of human and animal symbolism have a long history in Asia Minor. The ones with known provenance, of which there are only a few, come from central and north-central Anatolia.

Nonetheless, it is hard to believe that any other interpretation is possible. Even single eagles seem to have been associated with Jupiter Dolichenus,[14] and the combination of Jupiter and bull is clearly a fundamental part of the imagery of the cult. Important evidence for this association comes from a group of bronzes from a Dolichenus shrine at Mauer an der Url (Austria), now in Vienna. The centerpiece of the group is an exceptional bronze statuette[15] of Jupiter in the standard Dolichenus pose, wearing a Phrygian cap, standing on a bull. The base is inscribed and the top line reads *IOMD*, a dedication to Iovis Optimus Maximus Dolichenus. Another bronze shows variations on the divinity and animal combination: atop a large rectangular base are another Jupiter Dolichenus figure, on the back of a bull, and a separate figure of Juno Regina standing on the back of a donkey.[16] The imagery is further developed on another bronze from the Mauer cache, a relief that decorated the top of a staff or standard.[17] On one side are Jupiter and Juno astride the same two animals; above them are Sol and Luna, topped by an eagle. The human-animal combination is further reinforced in the lowest register where the Dioskouroi are shown, in strongly classicizing poses, standing in front of their horses.

---

9 For topknot: L. Ognenova-Marinova (transl. D. Karakostov), *Statuettes en bronze du Musée National Archéologique à Sofia (statuettes de culte)* (Sophia 1975) 46, no. 26 (and 47, no. 27, for the pose).

10 The Hilprecht collection includes three figures (inv. nos. 48-2-214, 48-2-215, 48-2-237) of the so-called Thracian Rider type, which was usually set on a horse. Only rarely are both the horse and rider preserved as an ensemble. For recent discussion: T. Kanceva, "Bronzestatuetten des thrakischen Reitergottes im Museum Nova Zagora," in K. Gschwantler and A. Bernhard-Walcher (edd.), *Griechische und römische Statuetten und Grossbronzen: Akten der 9. int. Tagung über antike Bronzen in Wien 1986* (Vienna 1988) 411-12. For a full range of figures: Ognenova-Marinova (supra n.9) 47-57; see also: G. von Bülow (ed.), *Antike Bronzeplastik aus Bulgarien* (Exh. cat. Sofia; Berlin 1990) 82-83, nos. 34-35. The popularity of these rider divinities in Anatolia is attested by a series of stelae and altars with images of riders and inscriptions naming the rider god, sometimes called Sozon: *MAMA* 9 (London 1988): altar from Yenice, no. 246, pl. 91; *MAMA* 6 (London 1939) 14, no. 34.

11 Eagle standing: 48-2-43, 48-2-47, 48-2-79. Eagle on plinth or base: 48-2-44, 48-2-45, 48-2-48, 48-2-49. 48-2-50, 48-2-51. Eagle on earth mound: 48-2-46. Eagle on altar: 48-2-52, 48-2-53 (fig. 3), 48-2-54 (fig. 3), 48-2-55 (fig. 3), 48-2-56 (fig. 3), 48-2-57, 48-2-58 (fig. 3), 48-2-59 (fig. 3), 48-2-75.

12 For the cult of Jupiter Dolichenus: A. H. Kan, *Juppiter Dolichenus* (Leiden 1943); P. Merlat, *Répertoire des inscriptions et monuments figurés du culte de Jupiter Dolichenus* (Paris 1951); and M. Speidel, *The religion of Iuppiter Dolichenus in the Roman army* (Leiden 1978).

13 See Brodkey Moore (supra n.2) 146-47, and A. Roes, "Un bronze d'Asie Mineure du Musée de Leyde," *Syria* 26 (1949) 120.

14 A bronze eagle figurine was found in the Dolichenum at Dura: *The excavations at Dura-Europos: preliminary report of the ninth season of work 1935-1936* (New Haven 1946) pt. III, pl. 23.1.

15 Vienna, Kunsthistorisches Museum M1: R. Fleischer, *Die römischen Bronzen aus Österreich* (Mainz 1967) 34-36, no. 18, pls. 10-12.

16 Vienna, Kunsthistorisches Museum M2: ibid. 36-38, no. 19, pls. 13-15.

17 Vienna, Kunsthistorisches Museum M4: ibid. 98-99, no. 119, pls. 63-67.

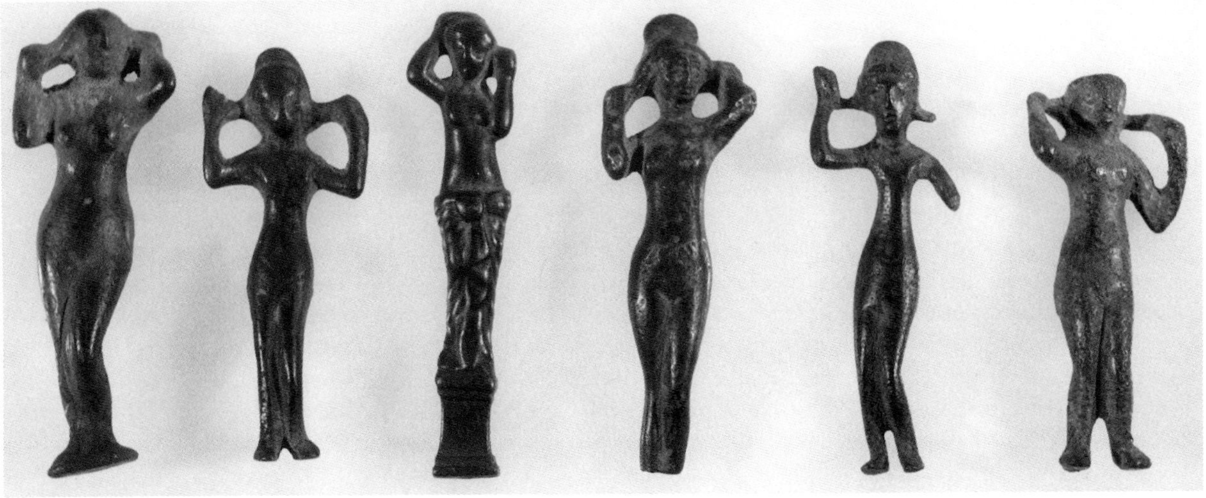

Fig. 5. Venus figures. Philadelphia, University of Pennsylvania Museum inv. nos. 48-2-204 (h. 0.070 m), 48-2-207 (h. 0.064 m), 48-2-208 (h. 0.071 m), 48-2-209 (h. 0.070 m), 48-2-210 (h. 0.065 m), 48-2-211 (h. 0.060 m).

On the reverse are paired peacocks and eagles around the central motif of a hand that holds a thunderbolt. The key elements of Dolichenus iconography are all here: eagles combined with Jupiter imagery, and a succession of human-animal combinations. Our eagle pendants, and the eagle-animal combinations, are part of the same iconography, except that the eagle-animal figurines seem to have been especially popular as ex-votos in central Anatolia.

Four of the Hilprecht pieces combine the eagle with the head of a bull,[18] the combination most appropriate for Jupiter Dolichenus and symbolic of the combined forces of celestial and chthonic religion. Three bronzes combine eagles with goats, twice with the goat head, once with the whole animal.[19] Another shows an eagle perched on a ram's head,[20] while two figurines show another combination, eagles and deer, one an eagle on a stag's head, the other an eagle atop a full stag.[21] The latter combination has a long tradition in Anatolia, documented in Bronze Age and Hittite iconography.[22] The combination may eventually have found its way into the imagery of the cult of Jupiter Dolichenus[23] and it surfaces in various media during the Roman period. Here, once again, we find the emergence of age-old local traditions, this time iconographic, in vernacular small-scale statuary.

The human figures include the ubiquitous provincial Mercurys[24] that are common throughout the empire. Hilprecht also liked Venuses, especially those of the Anadyomene type (fig.

18 Inv. nos. 48-2-63, 48-2-64, 48-2-65, 48-2-160.

19 Inv. nos. 48-2-60, 48-2-61, 48-2-125. Other examples of eagle and goat combinations are known from Anatolia (Cappadocia): F. Cumont, "L'Archevêché de Pèdachtoé et le sacrifice du faon," *Byzantion* 6 (1931) 528. See also A. Andrén, "Classical antiquities in the Zorn collection," *OpArch* 5 (1948) no. 5427. A bronze recently on the art market, part of a group of bronzes from Anatolia but loosely labeled "eastern Mediterranean", shows the same eagle and goat combination: *Münzen und Medaillen Antiken, Auktion no. 181, 22-25 February 1994* (Münzhandlung Gerhard Hirsch, Munich) no. 1247. Another example: ibid. *Auktion* 177 (1992) no. 1783.

20 Inv. no. 48-2-66.

21 Inv. nos. 48-2-62 and 48-2-68.

22 On the numerous examples, from Alaça Hüyük, Malatya, and elsewhere: Brodkey Moore (supra n.2) 144-45 nn.127-29. For the importance of the deer in Hittite mythology: S. Prezeworski, "Notes d'archéologie syrienne et hittite 4: le culte du cerf en Anatolie," *Syria* 21 (1940) 66, 71.

23 A. H. Kan, *De Iovis Dolicheni cultu* (Groningen 1901) 59. Bronze eagles standing on the heads of stags can be found in Berlin: K. A. Neugebauer, *AA* 1922, no. 66, 118-19; and in the Liebmann collection, Munich: *Tierbronzen aus dem vorchristlichen Mittelmeerraum, Sammlung Professor Dr. Sr. h. c. Hans Liebmann, München* (Exh. cat., Kassel 1971) pl. 23, no. 168, said to be from Anatolia.

24 There are 5 Mercury figurines in the Hilprecht collection, all but one bought in Istanbul: inv. nos. 48-2-221, 48-2-222, 48-2-223, 48-2-224, 48-2-227. The latter may have been bought in Florence. For the type,

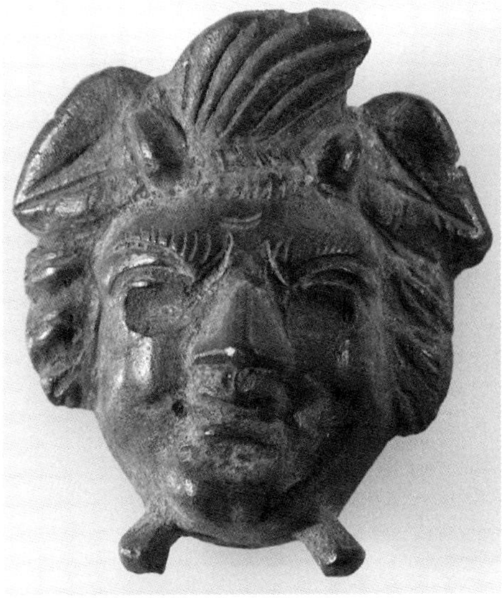

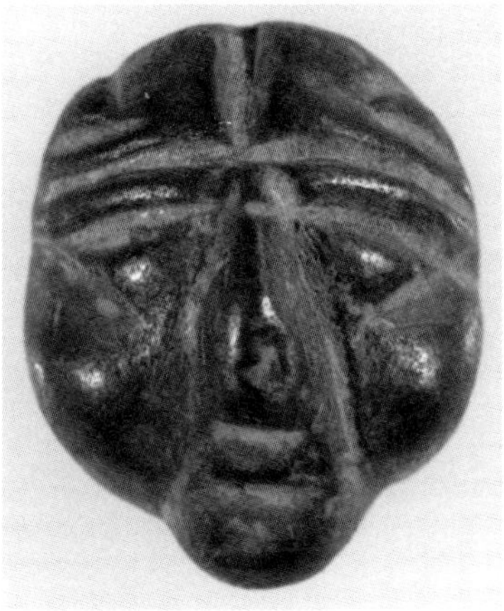

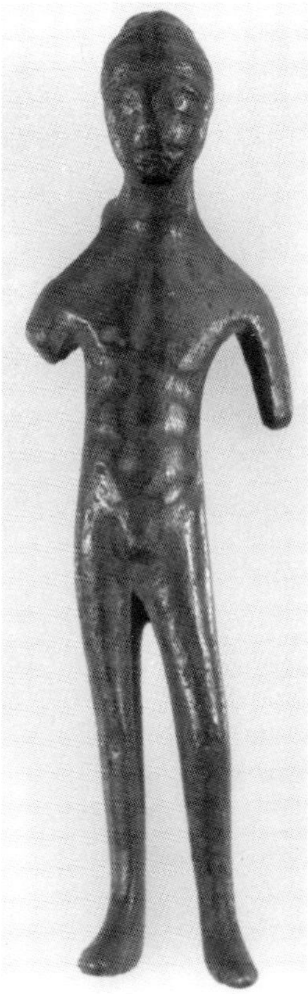

Fig. 6 (top left). Satyr mask attachment. Philadelphia, University of Pennsylvania Museum inv. no. 48-2-265 (h. 0.055 m).

Fig. 7 (center). Human head attachment. Philadelphia, University of Pennsylvania Museum inv. no. 48-2-261 (h. 0.025 m).

Fig. 8 (right). Archer (Apollo?). Philadelphia, University of Pennsylvania Museum inv. no. 48-2-234 (h. 0.072 m).

5); all 8 have an Anatolian provenance.[25] None is of exceptional quality, but even within this unprepossessing group there are strong stylistic differences that attest to the dominance of vernacular approaches. Provincial Venuses will often take on looser forms, becoming elongated or attenuated, losing the sense of anatomical integrity that underlies classical structure. This phenomenon has been studied in the western provinces by C. Lindgren,[26] but the phenomenon is not restricted to the Celtic world. What we are witnessing is the dominance of vernacular, a lack of interest on the part of provincial metalworkers and their patrons in the 'high' traditions of classical art.

Hilprecht could occasionally be seduced by figures in a strongly Greek style. The numerous figural attachments in his collection range from a standard but beautifully rendered satyr mask (fig. 6), bought from a New York dealer in 1909,[27] which may date to the 2nd or 3rd c. A.D.,[28] to a more unusual and unclassical human mask (fig. 7), whose visage is a study of segmentation and abstraction.[29] The satyr is listed as having an Anatolian provenance on Hilprecht's note-card and does indeed seem to belong to the eastern empire.[30]

---

see *LIMC* VI, 507-8, s.v. Mercurius (E. Simon).

25 Inv. nos. 48-2-204, 48-2-205, 48-2-207, 48-2-208, 48-2-209, 48-2-210, 48-2-211, 48-2-272. The latter is not a figurine but part of a lock plate used for boxes, doors, and other wood paraphernalia: W. Deonna, *Delos* XVIII: *Le mobilier délien* (Paris 1938) 250, fig. 287, pl. 669.

26 C. Lindgren, *Classical art forms and Celtic mutations: Figural art in Roman Britain* (Park Ridge, NJ 1978) 68-87 for Romano-British Venuses.

27 Inv. no. 48-2-265, h. 0.055 m: "Bought of Kelekian, antiquity dealer in New York, 19 March, 1909."

28 Brodkey Moore (supra n.2) 197, n.270, based on a private conversation with Menzel.

29 Inv. no. 48-2-261: said to be from Phrygia and bought from an antiquity dealer, Eskişehir, May 24, 1907.

30 A good parallel is provided by a collection of bronze attachments from Stara Zagora which decorated wooden cosmetic boxes: H. Bujukliev, "Serrures et applications en bronze des coffrets de toilette du territoire d'Augusta Trajana (Ville de Stara Zagora, Bulgarie)," in *Griechische und römische Statuetten* (supra n.10) 416-20. The attachments include two satyr masks, as well as other heads and busts of Erotes, bacchants, and women in Phrygian costume. The style and function of the figures is paralleled on other decorated boxes from Bulgaria.

There are also figures of decidedly eastern type, for instance a seated male who wears trousers and a pointed cap, perhaps a Mithraic genius,[31] but most interesting are those figures whose style (rather than their attributes) marks them as provincial. These figures are provincial not because they are misunderstood copies of classical prototypes, but because their style is deliberately non-classical. One such piece is an attenuated nude male,[32] possibly an Apollo (fig. 8). Its provenance is again Anatolian. Here we have moved into an area where the term 'provincial' has come to mean an indigenous response to, or even rejection of, the classical ideal.

It was Hilprecht's training as an archaeologist that made him choose pieces far from the mainstream of classical idealization that was the norm in his day. We should be grateful that he chose to collect and document objects that now interest us because of their marginality. It is difficult, however, to be precise about the specifically Anatolian qualities of the Hilprecht collection when so little comparable material has been published. There is a need for further study of Roman bronzes from the eastern empire. Unlike the objects from the West, the material from Roman Asia remains virtually unpublished. In his summary of the state of research on Roman bronzes and implements, H. Menzel could devote only a few paragraphs to bronzes from Asia Minor or Syria.[33] In her study of the distribution of Roman figural types, S. Boucher was rarely able to include material from SE Europe or Asia in her distribution maps.[34] New evidence has emerged recently from the Balkans, yet anyone who has visited the smaller museums in Turkey knows that many small bronzes are awaiting publication. It is ironic that some of the best parallels for the Hilprecht bronzes, particularly the characteristically Anatolian figurines, are to be found in auction catalogues. Small bronzes of this type only see some kind of publication, it seems, when illicitly excavated and exported, but by then they are deprived of any geographical or cultural context. For this reason alone, the Hilprecht collection deserves to be better known.

Division of Art History, Southern Methodist University, Dallas

---

31 Inv. no. 48-2-213: Hilprecht's notation reads: "Place of Discovery: Asia Minor. Price paid: 6 Frcs. Bought in Constantinople, Sept., 1909 (sent from Samsoun)." This is a modest version of a well-known type: cf. *The gods delight* 288-95, no. 51, with bibliogaphy. For another example in the Bibliothèque Nationale, Paris: E. Babelon and J. Adrien Blanchet, *Catalogue des bronzes antiques de la Bibliothèque Nationale* (Paris 1895) 284-89, nos. 664-74. Brodkey Moore (supra n.2) 100.

32 Inv. no. 48-2-234: h. 0.072 m, bought in Istanbul in 1903.

33 H. Menzel, "Römische Bronzestatuetten und verwandte Gërate," *ANRW* II.12.3 (1985) 127-69.

34 S. Boucher, *Recherches sur les bronzes figurés de Gaule pré-romaine et romaine* (Rome 1976).

Apliques de carros de época romana hallados en Hispania

Salvador F. Pozo

Una terminología abundante designa en las fuentes literarias latinas los diversos vehículos, claramente diferenciados entre ellos por su forma y uso. El término de carro (*currus*) es un vocablo genérico que evoca la imágen del carro de guerra o del carro de triunfo (*currus triumphalis*). Los carros pueden ser divididos en tres categorías: los vehículos consagrados a usos religiosos, los vehículos de viaje, y los de carga. Sólamente las dos primeras categorías llevaban adornos de bronce. Los vehículos de carga (*plaustrum, sarracum, carrus*) estaban desprovistos de cualquier ornamentación.

Entre los vehículos de transporte recordamos el antiquísimo *plaustrum*, de dos ruedas, y el *carrus*, de cuatro ruedas. Se ven vehículos de este tipo representados en los bajo-relieves de las columnas de Trajano y Marco Aurelio.

Entre los vehículos de viaje están: el *carpentum*, de orígen etrusco; la *reda* y la *carruca*, de cuatro ruedas; y el *cisium*, de orígen británico, con grandes ruedas, ligero y cómodo.

Entre los vehículos de ceremonia, la *tensa* tenía función sagrada. Es un carro en forma de templo, cuya caja es rectangular y cerrada, adornada con bajo-relieves y, a menudo, cerrada por un frontón rectangular. Llevaba el *exuvias deorum* y transportaba las imágenes de las divinidades en los *ludi circenses*.

El *pilentum*, provisto de cuatro ruedas, estaba originariamente destinado al transporte de sacerdotes y objetos sagrados. Este tipo puede ser reconocido en el vehículo que aparece en un relieve vaticano. Igualmente la denominada *tensa capitolina* podría ser identificada como un *pilentum*.

Otro vehículo de lujo era el *carpentum*, de dos ruedas, rematado en un baldaquino. A partir del s. III d.c. se convierte en uno de los atributos de los personajes de alto rango. La *carruca*, mencionada por Plinio El Viejo (*NH* 33.140), era un vehículo de cuatro ruedas con adornos de plata, oro, marfil, o apliques de bronce damasquinados. Durante mucho tiempo fue reservado para el uso del emperador y miembros de la familia imperial.

El carro de guerra (*currus triumphalis*), que aparece en múltiples representaciones, es similar a una biga griega pero con la caja semicircular. Como ejemplos, tenemos el relieve de la bóveda del arco de Tito en Roma y el relieve con Marco Aurelio triunfante en el Palazzo dei Conservatori.

Los carros de carrera, que repiten fundamentalmente los tipos griegos y etruscos, muestran estructuras ligerísimas. Los vehículos utilizados para viajes eran el *essedum* y el *cisium*, por ser rápidos y ligeros.

El análisis de los monumentos nos permite precisar el emplazamiento de los diversos apliques y elementos de bronce aparecidos, generalmente por pares, en las excavaciones arqueológicas.

La mayoría de los hallazgos de apliques de carros han sido encontrados en el Sur y Este de Bulgaria, en el Sur de Hungría, y a lo largo del río Danubio: las antiguas provincias de Tracia, Panonia, Mesia, Dacia, asi como en Macedonia, Dalmacia, y Bitinia. También se han producido hallazgos en las provincias de Occidente: Galia, Italia, Germania, Hispania, y Mauritania Tingitana.

La mayor parte han sido hallados en enterramientos de túmulos. La costumbre de enterrar carros, o modelos reducidos de ellos, en las tumbas de personajes importantes remonta a época prehistórica.

El carácter religioso de algunos carros es unánimemente reconocido por los historiadores. No obstante, sólamente los carros descubiertos en enterramientos de túmulos en Europa central (Tracia, Panonia, y Dacia) tenían una función funeraria.

Algunas piezas no tenían ningún significado religioso, sino que eran meros elementos de adorno, tal vez con cierto carácter supersticioso, fetichista, para prevenir accidentes y otros males.

Estos vehículos plantean una serie de problemas e interrogantes: reconstrucción del armazón, emplazamiento y función de los apliques, datación, etc.

A. Alföldi fue el primero en calificar a estos vehículos como carros báquicos, al asociar su decoración (temas báquicos) con la creencia en el Más Allá de la religión de Bacchus-Liber.[1] G. Seure realiza una recopilación de estas piezas y propone varias hipótesis de reconstrucción. Suponía que se trataban de objetos fabricados en uno de los grandes centros helenísticos, como Alejandría o Antioquía.[2] E. von Mercklin elabora un excelente catálogo de los principales apliques de carro.[3] Recientemente, A. Radnoti, entre otros, e I. Venedikov, a propósito de los enterramientos (túmulos) de Tracia, ha realizado un análisis completo de los diferentes elementos del carro romano, y ha propuesto una reconstrucción.[4] C. Boube-Piccot analiza los hallazgos de Marruecos y en unos apéndices recopila todos los carros conocidos en las diversas provincias del Imperio.[5]

Los apliques usualmente denominados "pasarriendas", "Radabweiser" en la terminología alemana, elementos de la suspensión del carro, no son objeto de estudio en el presente trabajo, pues una recopilación de los ejemplares hispanos ha sido realizada recientemente por M. Molin.[6]

El chasis de estos vehículos tenía forma de un cuadrado rectangular de madera, revestido de bronce. Según los descubrimientos de Tracia y Panonia, la parte frontal del chasis es semicircular y, a veces, estaban rematados por estatuillas y apliques de bronce, e iban flanqueados por dos figurillas laterales sobre una base semicircular, provista de orificios para su fijación.

El tema decorativo central está constituido por un grupo de dos o tres personajes: Baco entre Pan y un Sátiro; Baco y Ménade; Sátiro raptando una Ninfa; Venus y su cortejo. Un dato a resaltar es la reiterada presencia de Bacchus o de miembros de su cortejo — ménades, bacantes, sátiros y silenos, panteras — en la ornamentación de los carros. También están representadas otras deidades. Las más frecuentes son Hércules y Mercurio y, más raramente, aparecen Apolo, Minerva, Eros, Eros Báquico, Venus, la Victoria, Pan, y personajes mitológicos como Bellerofonte, los Centauros, Ninfas, o Hércules y Télefo.

Las figurillas laterales suelen ser representaciones de divinidades: Hércules, Mercurio, Tyché, Isis-Fortuna, Hércules, y Amazonas; de personajes relacionados con la mitología, tales como Amazonas heridas, la personificación del dios Río, o guerreros heridos; de personajes femeninos; y, muy frecuentemente, animales (leones, panteras, tigres, toros, perros, o leopardos).

---

1 A. Alföldi, "Allatdíszes kerekvetö-fejek kelta-romai kocsirol," *ArchErt* N.F. 48 (1935 [1936]) 190-213 (resumen en alemán: Zoomorphe Bronzeaufsätze als Radabweiser auf keltisch-römischen Wagen), ibid. 263-70; id., "Chars funéraires bacchiques dans les provinces occidentales de l'empire romain," *AntCl* 8.2 (1939) 347-437.

2 G. Seure, "Un char thraco-macédonien," *BCH* 28 (1904) 210-37; id., "Chars thraces," *BCH* 49 (1925) 347-437.

3 E. von Mercklin, "Wagenschmuck aus der römischer Kaiserzeit," *JdI* 48 (1933) 84-175.

4 A. Radnoti, "Eine römische Pantherstatuette aus Straubing," *BayVgBl* 28 (1936) 67-96; id., "Der Fund von Geinshein-Böbingen," *Mitteilungen des Historischen Vereins der Pfalz* 67 (1969) 87-109.

5 C. Boube-Piccot, *Les bronzes antiques du Maroc* 3: *les chars et l'attelage* (Rabat 1980).

6 M. Molin, "La suspension des voitures: une invention diffusée en Hispanie romaine," *MélCasaVelazquez* 25 (1989) 55-79.

Estos apliques laterales, que están provistos de orificios para su fijación al carro, descansan sobre un soporte semicircular y están abiertos en el reverso.

Los flancos de la caja del carro estaban formados por paneles de madera. La mayoría de las veces hay un aplique de bronce de sección rectangular en su parte superior, el cual está provisto de dos muescas, una en el reverso y otra en la base. La parte anterior del aplique va ornada con bustos de divinidades: Baco, Sileno, Bacante, Sátiro, Fauno, Hércules, Minerva, Paris, Diana Lucífera, Attis, y guerreros; o bien sobre una moldura que sirve de pedestal para una figurilla en bulto redondo: Baco sobre un trono, Eros, personajes sentados, diosa protectora de la ciudad, caballos, etc.

La mayoría de los hallazgos son aislados y es difícil la reconstrucción total del carro, sin embargo algunos se conservan casi intactos. Entre ellos destaca el carro hallado en Nicomedia y conocido como "carro de Karapanos"; otro, que se conserva en Museo de Colonia, fue hallado en el valle de Vardar y comprado en un anticuario de Tesalónica; otros han aparecido en Stara Zagora, en Zagreb, y en Somodor. En las provincias danubianas hay representaciones de vehículos de viaje en relieves del s. II d.c., donde son visibles algunos prótomos de animales como los que decoraban los apliques de carro.

C. Röring ha recopilado varios ejemplos, como el *cisium* (vehículo rápido) de Tök y de Intercissa, la *carruca dormitoria* (vehículo de viaje cerrado) de Virunum, y la *carruca* (vehículo de viaje descubierto) de Intercissa.[7]

Los apliques de carro de época romana descubiertos en Hispania son numerosos tipológicamente. Excepcionalmente,[8] el aplique conservado en el Museo Arqueológico Nacional de Madrid, de procedencia andaluza, decora la parte frontal semicircular de la caja del carro. Los demás apliques estaban ubicados en la parte posterior, a ambos lados de la caja del carro.

Los temas representados son muy variados iconográficamente. Son muy abundantes aquellos que representan a Bacchus o miembros de su *thiasos*. Entre ellos destacan: el aplique con busto de Bacante procedente de la provincia de Toledo, que se encuentra actualmente en la Hispanic Society of America, New York (no. 12); y una pareja de apliques con bustos de Bacantes del Museo Arqueológico Nacional de Madrid (nos. 10-11), sin procedencia conocida.

Entre los ejemplos de apliques decorados con otras deidades podemos señalar: el aplique de Morón de la Frontera (Sevilla), con representación de un busto de Diana Lucífera (no. 9); aplique decorado con una figurilla de Isis-Tyché recostada, procedente de Sotos del Burgo, Soria (no. 3), y otro similar con una estatuilla de Tyché-Fortuna, hallado en Ubeda (Jaén), de la Colección Fontaneda, Palencia (no. 2).

Otros apliques desarrollan algún tema relacionado con personajes mitológicos. Este es el caso de la pareja de bronces que representan el mito de Bellerofonte sobre Pegaso y la Quimera (nos. 4-5). Estos bronces, hallados en La Lentejuela, término municipal de Écija (Sevilla), pertenecieron a la Colección Calzadilla (Badajoz) y, en la actualidad, se supone que están en el mercado de antigüedades de U.S.A. Otro grupo lo forman apliques que aluden a motivos iconográficos relacionados con la plástica griega y helenística, como el aplique con representación de un "filósofo" sedente, hallado en Cañizo, Zamora (no. 13).

---

7 C. Röring, *Untersuchungen zu römischen Reisewagen* (Coblenza 1983); id., "Rekonstruktion des Wagens aus dem Wardartal," *Kölner Römerillustrierte* 1 (Colonia 1974) 319; id., "Bemerkungen zum römischen Wagen aus Frenz, Kreis Düren," *AKB* 8 (1978) 92.

8 A. Fernández-Avilés, "Pasarriendas y otros bronces de carro romanos, hallados en España," *ArchEspArq* 31 (1958) 3-63; A. García Bellido, "Nuevas piezas pertenencientes a atalajes de carros romanos hallados en España," *ArchEspArq* 29 (1956) 206-11; I. Manfrini, "Chars bacchiques: problèmes d'interprétation," in *Actes du IVe Colloque int. sur les bronzes antiques* (Lyon 1977) 117-20; L. Rousseva-Slokoska, "Appliques de bronzes antiques de chars provenant de Pautalia: sur le problème de la reconstitution," in J. Ronke (ed.), *Akten der 10. int. Tagung über antike Bronzen, Freiburg* (Stuttgart 1994) 388-89.

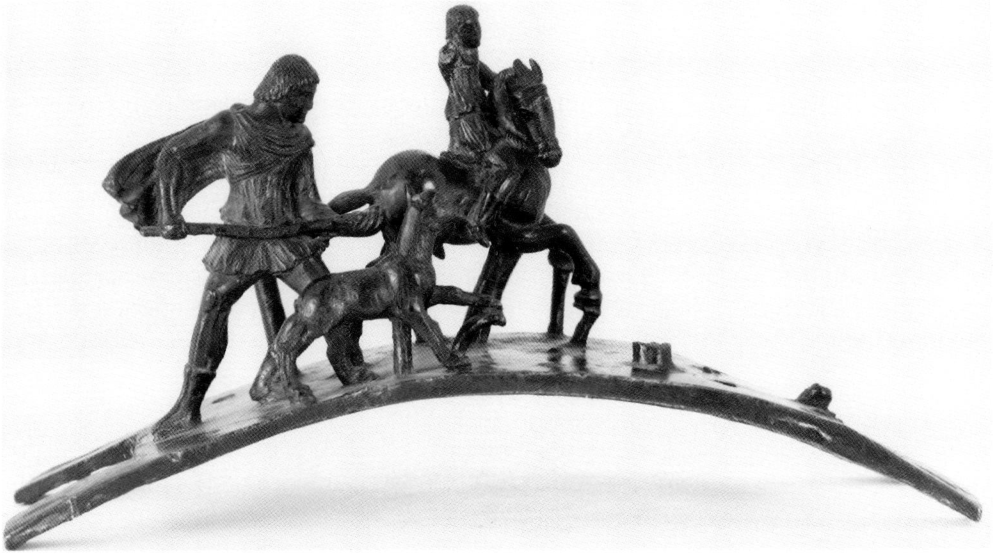

Fig. 1. Escena cinegética (no. 1). Bronce, h. 10.5 cm. Madrid, Museo Arqueológico Nacional 1935/113/1 (Fot.: Cortesía Museo)

Un aplique de carro, que está decorado con una escena cinegética, procede de Andalucía y se conserva en el Museo Arqueológico Nacional de Madrid (no. 1).

También son abundantes los apliques que reproducen motivos zoomorfos. Entre ellos cabe destacar: el aplique del Museo Arqueológico de Córdoba con representación de un toro (no. 6); el aplique del Museo Diocesano de Solsona, Lleida (no. 8) con representación de un perro y un jabalí; un aplique hallado en la villa de Carmo, Carmona, Sevilla (no. 7), que representa un león; un aplique hallado en Varea, Logroño (no. 15), que reproduce una pantera; y un eje de rueda de carro procedende de Augusta Emerita, Mérida, Badajoz (no. 16), decorado con una máscara de león.

Un aplique del Museu Nacional de Arqueología e Etnología de Lisboa (no. 14), originario de Obidos (norte de Portugal), reproduce una cuadriga de caballos.

Catálogo

I. Aplique ubicado en la parte frontal semicircular de la caja del carro

1. Aplique de carro: escena cinegética (Museo Arqueológico Nacional de Madrid) (fig. 1)

Bronce de fundición plena, la pátina de color verde oliva. No se conoce el lugar preciso del hallazgo, sólamente sabemos que procede de algún lugar de Andalucía. Ingresó en el Museo Arqueológico Nacional de Madrid en 1935. L. 28.5 cm; h. 10.5 cm. Número de inventario: 1935/113/1.

El grupo escultórico descansa en una base rectangular muy convexa. Decoraría la parte central semicircular de la caja del carro. La basa presenta dos muescas cuadrangulares en ambos lados menores, junto a ellas, y simétricamente hay cuatro agujeros, seguramente para su inserción en el carro.

El grupo está formado por un jinete sobre caballo al galope, viste túnica con manga larga, *braccae* o pantalones, y *endromides* (botas altas); ha perdido el brazo derecho en el que empuñaría una jabalina para atacar a un jabalí u oso que iba delante del grupo. Sólamente quedan vestigios de los cuatro puntos donde se apoyaría.

Detrás del jinete, otro cazador de pie, de tamaño mayor que el jinete, viste túnica y *chlamys* levantada por la acción figurada del viento. Empuña una jabalina que dirige hacia la fiera desaparecida. A su lado está representado un perro de gran tamaño.

El tema de la caza gozó de la predilección de los artistas del bajo imperio. Es un tema muy representado en sarcófagos, mosaicos, etc. Datamos la pieza en el s. III d.c.

II. Apliques ubicados en la parte frontal semicircular de la caja del carro, a ambos lados del motivo decorativo central

2. Aplique de carro: Tyché-Fortuna (Colección Fontaneda, Palencia)

Bronce de fundición hueca, la pátina de color verde, presenta concreciones terrosas. Fáltale a la diosa el brazo izquierdo y los atributos que llevase. Buen estado de conservación; se dice que fue hallado en Ubeda (Jaén). H 24.5 cm. Pertenece a la Colección Fontaneda (Palencia).

Tyché recostada, según el tipo de Tyché de Afrodisias y Alejandría — época helenística — que seguía modelos iconográficos del s. IV d.c. La figura apoya su antebrazo derecho en un pequeño soporte, adquiriendo una postura elegante y relajada. Viste manto con numerosos pliegues; lleva el pelo recogido atrás en un moño, a la altura de la nuca. Va ceñida la melena con una diadema. Probablemente llevàse la cornucopia en la mano izquierda y el timón de la nave en la derecha. La figura descansa en un soporte semicircular, abierto en el reverso y provisto de tres orificios para su fijación al chasis del carro. Está ornado con nielados de plata formando cuadrados pareados.

Un paralelo muy similar es el aplique de Soto del Burgo (Soria), igualmente con representación de una deidad femenina recostada (Isis-Fortuna). Datamos la pieza en el s. II d.c.

3. Aplique de carro: Isis-Fortuna (colección particular)

Bronce de fundición plena, fue hallado en el paraje de la Cruz del Santo, cerca de Las Paredejas, en el término municipal de Sotos del Burgo (Soria). Buen estado de conservación. H. 4.5 cm; l. 8.5 cm. Pertenece a una colección particular.

Figura femenina, se nos ofrece de perfil y recostada en un *kliné*, decorado con incisiones paralelas en sentido transversal, parecido al de los sarcófagos orientales. Viste túnica sin mangas y manto que envuelve la figura. Lleva el timón de la nave en la mano derecha, extendida junto al cuerpo; la izquierda le sirve para apoyar la cabeza. Lleva el cabello ceñido por una diadema ornada con flores de cuatro pétalos. En el centro se conservan vestigios de la flor de loto, elemento característico de Isis; dos largos tirabuzones caen por la espalda y hombros.

4-5. Apliques de carro (pareja): Bellerofonte y la Quimera; tigresa atacando a una gacela (mercado de antiguedades de U.S.A.; Museo Arqueológico Provincial de Badajoz) (fig. 2)

Bronce de fundición plena, el grupo de Bellerofonte y la Quimera hállase completo a falta tan sólo del antebrazo y del arma que empuñase el heróe. El segundo aplique ha perdido la basa o pedestal, la tigresa fragmentada en su parte trasera, igualmente la gacela tiene roturas y de un tercer animal sólo se conservan las garras que posa sobre el trasero de la gacela. Estos apliques de carro fueron hallados en 1943 en tierras del Cortijo de la Rabia (Écija), al realizar obras en el camino de La Lentejuela a Écija (Sevilla). Perteneció a la Colección Calzadilla (Badajoz); hoy en día al parecer está en el mercado de antigüedades de U.S.A., salvo la tigresa atacando la gacela (Museo Arqueológico Provincial de Badajoz). H. 14.5 cm; l. 17.5 cm. Número de inventario: 12123.

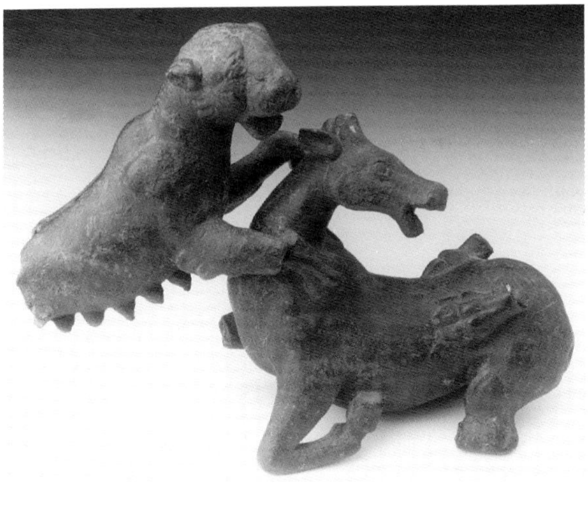

Fig. 2. Tigresa atacando a una gacela (no. 5), de La Lentejuela (Écija, Sevilla). Bronce, h. 14.5 cm Badajoz, Museo Arqueológico Provincial 12123. (Fot.: Cortesía de la Junta de Extremadura)

El grupo escultórico representa a Bellerofonte sobre el caballo alado (Pegaso) que mata a la Quimera; descansa en un soporte semicircular provisto de un orificio para su fijación en el carro. El aplique decoraría la parte frontal semicircular de la caja del carro; el tema central ha desaparecido y se conservan los dos apliques laterales.

El heróe viste sólamente la *chlamys*, alrededor del cuello, levantada por la acción figurada del viento; cabalga sobre Pegaso, representado con las patas delanteras (mutiladas) al aire, la cabeza retrospicente: dirige la mirada hacia atrás, donde la Quimera vencida, yace tras ser matada por Bellerofonte.

No hay paralelos broncíneos donde se represente la leyenda; un mosaico de la villa de Puerta Oscura (Málaga) reproduce dicho mito.

El segundo aplique, pareja del anterior, se ha conservado muy deteriorado. Representa una escena de cacería: una tigresa ataca — con sus garras colocadas en el cuello — a una gacela o cérvido, recostado y sentado en sus cuartos traseros; dirige la cabeza atrás para apartarla del ataque de la fiera. En su parte anterior es visible las garras de otra fiera, desaparecida.

Dicha escena cinegética es similar a la desarrollada en el pasarriendas de carro procedente de Emerita Augusta (Badajoz).

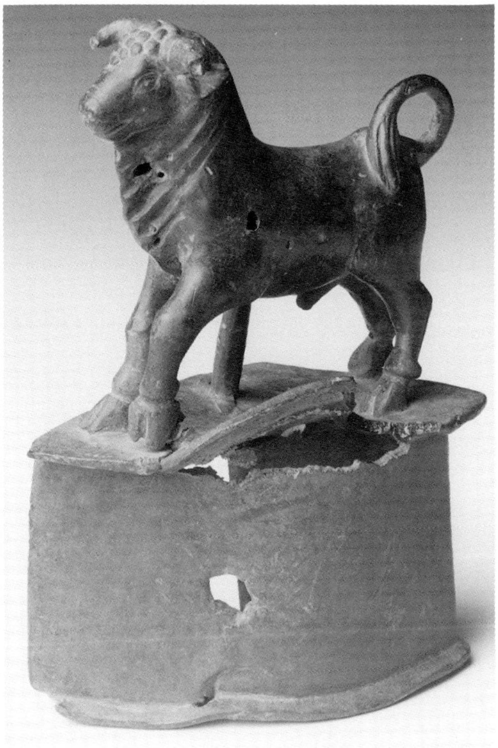

Fig. 3. Toro al paso (no. 6). Bronce, h. 19 cm. Córdoba, Museo Arqueológico Provincial 29766. (Fot.: M. Cuenca; Cortesía de la Junta de Andalucía)

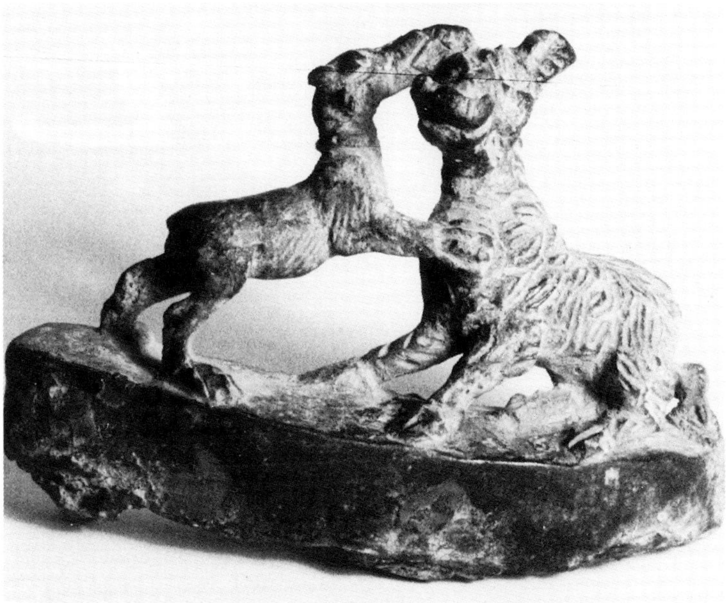

Fig. 4. Escena animalística (no. 8), de Can Sotaterra (Solsona, Lleida). Bronce, h. 6.0 cm. Fot.: Solsona, cortésia Museu Diocesà i Comarcal 2121)

6. Aplique de carro: toro al paso (Museo Arqueológico Provincial de Córdoba) (fig. 3)

Bronce de fundición hueca, la pátina verde clara, regularmente repartida. El toro presenta cuatro orificios y el cuerno izquierdo está mutilado (desperfectos o roturas antiguas). La lámina superior del pedestal está levantada. Tiene un agujero central y otro frontal para su inserción en el carro. Se desconocen el lugar, fecha y circunstancias del hallazgo. H. 19.0 cm; l. 13.0 cm; w. 7.5 cm. Número de inventario: 29766.

El toro se nos ofrece al paso, de perfil, según un esquema iconográfico de toro clásico, conocido en Italia, sobretodo en Pompeya y Herculano: la pata delantera algo levantada, la cabeza fieramente expresada con todos los detalles anatómicos modelados de forma muy naturalista — ojos, cuernos, orejas. Entre los cuernos hay un rosetón de 6 pétalos. Esta particularidad igualmente se observa en el toro de Azaila (Teruel); la cola dirigida hacia arriba, formando un pequeño círculo.

En uno de los flancos del animal hay una columnita o soporte adosado al vientre de la bestia; las pezuñas están indicadas.

A. Furtwängler estudió un tipo de toro clásico, considerando que eran toros isiácos. Relacionamos ésta representación zoomorfa con el culto dedicado a Tavros Trigaranos. En el carro de Jambol (Bulgaria), conservado en el Museo de Sofía, el tema decorativo representado es otro toro.

7. Aplique carro: león al paso (Museo Arqueológico Provincial de Sevilla)

Bronce de fundición plena, la pátina verde oliva. Hállase completo, buen estado de conservación. Se dice haber sido hallado en una villa de Carmona (Sevilla) durante unas excavaciones arqueológicas efectuadas en fecha reciente.

León al paso descansa en un pedestal semicircular, ornado con motivos nielados de plata: una línea de orlas y hexágonos intercalados entre motivos vegetales (rosa de cuatro pétalos) en la parte superior presenta dos orificios circulares para su fijación al carro.

El león representado de perfil, de largas crines; las guedejas cuelgan sobre el cuello y ambos lados del lomo de la fiera. Las fauces están abiertas, los rasgos anatómicos bien modelados, muy naturalistas. Delante de las patas anteriores reposa la cabeza de su víctima, un bóvido; éste detalle puede observarse en el aplique de carro del Musée des Beaux Arts de Lyon.

Otro aplique de carro con representación zoomorfa (león) es el conservado en la Bibliothèque Nationale de Paris, originario de Roma.

8. Aplique de carro: escena animalística (Museu Diocesà i Comarcal de Solsona [Lleida]) (fig. 4)

Bronce de fundición plena, la pátina verde oscura, uniformemente repartida en toda la superficie; buen estado de conservación. Fué hallado en el verano del año 1912 en la finca "Pallarés," en el lugar conocido como "Can Sotaterra", en el término municipal de Solsona (Lleida), al realizar J. Saqués algunos sondeos en los que encontró un silo lleno de escorias de hierro, entre las cuales halló el bronce aquí descrito. Después fué comprado por el Museo Diocesano de Solsona a A. Carulla (Barcelona). H. 6.0 cm; l. 8.5 cm. Número de inventario: 2121.

El grupo escultórico descansa en una peana semicircular (hueca), donde aún quedan vestigios para suponer que iría engastada o insertada al carro. Se trata de una escena animalística: un perro levanta las patas anteriores, para posarlas en el cuerpo de un jabalí, al que muerde la oreja derecha; éste cae hacia atrás y descansa el cuerpo en sus cuartos traseros.

El motivo iconográfico es frequente en la plástica tardorromana hispana; el grupo denota ser obra de un taller provincial bajo imperial. El modelado de las fieras es defectuoso y en general es poco naturalista. No guarda la escala o proporción entre las diversas figuras: el jabalí es muy grande en relación al perro. S. III-IV d.c.

Un pasarriendas del Museo Nacional de Arte Romano de Mérida reproduce el mismo esquema plástico: un perro o lobo muerde a una liebre y un león ataca a una gacela. El tema procede de Oriente y pasa a Occidente donde tendrá vigencia en plena Edad Media. Su sentido prístino es el del poder destructor de la muerte. También vemos reproducido el motivo en un pasarriendas de la Colección Isenberg (Alemania).

III. Apliques ubicados en cada una de las extremedidades de la parte posterior de la caja del carro

9. Aplique de carro: busto de Diana Lucífera (Museo Arqueológico Provincial de Sevilla) (fig. 5)

Bronce de pátina verdosa, regularmente repartida, el interior es hueco y presenta numerosas concreciones terrosas. El brazo izquierdo de la diosa está mutilado; buen estado de conservación. Es originario de Morón de la Frontera (Sevilla), ingresó en el Museo de Sevilla el 16 de octubre de 1950, en calidad de depósito de Doña Concepción Candau. H. 12.0 cm; l. 6.0 cm; diam. 10.7 cm. Número de registro 6.621.

Según C. Boube-Piccot, este tipo de aplique forma parte de los paneles laterales e iría localizado en uno de los ángulos de la parte posterior del carro. El aplique es de sección cilíndrica y su zona posterior es circular. La cara anterior va decorada con un busto de Diana Lucífera, cuya cabeza queda exenta.

La diosa viste túnica sin mangas, sujetada en los hombros mediante pequeñas fíbulas circulares; detrás de ellas dos crecientes lunares. La vestimenta se adapta al cuerpo, dejando entrever los senos, presenta numerosos pliegues realizados con gruesas y profundas incisiones, modelados de forma tosca y poco naturalista. La cabeza es muy voluminosa en relación al resto del busto, se nos ofrece girada de tres cuarto a la izquierda. Los rasgos faciales son muy acusados y geométricos. La melena está sólamente expresada por una línea gruesa de mechones ondulados que enmarcan el rostro. Sobre la parte superior de la testa lleva al modo de una divinidad hathórica un segundo creciente. En la parte inferior del busto hay una zona con rica decoración de motivos vegetales, estilizaciones de hojas.

Otros bustos broncíneos de Diana Lucífera: uno procedente de Higuer (Fuenterrabía, Guipúzcoa) y sendos bustos conservados en la Bibliothèque Nationale de Paris y en el Museum of Fine Arts, Boston.

10-11. Apliques de carro: bustos de bacantes (Museo Arqueológico Nacional de Madrid) (fig. 6)

Bronce de fundición hueca, la pátina de color verde, muy bien conservada. No se conoce su procedencia, aunque su origen hispano es seguro. Ingresó en el Museo Arqueológico Nacional de Madrid en 1935. H. 10.5 cm; l. 11.5 cm. Números de inventario: 35/113/2 y 3.

Las dos piezas son idénticas, salvo los bustos que sirven de remate, son parejas de apliques de un mismo carro e irían colocadas en cada una de las extremidades de la parte posterior de la caja del carro. De un vástago de sección prismática-octogonal, cuya superficie está parcialmente dorada y presenta decoración con nielados de plata: hojas lobuladas de cuatro pétalos, motivos geométricos (espirales, círculos), la decoración viene delimitada por finas molduras. Los bustos simulan emerger de una córola de pétalos, esculpidos desde la línea de los pectorales, con los brazos representados en su totalidad.

Uno de los bustos viste *chlamys* anudada al hombro derecho, dispuesta en diagonal, dejándole al desnudo parte del torso, presenta numerosos pliegues. Levanta el ropaje con la mano izquierda, sujetando en el regazo numerosos frutos. El brazo derecho aparece ligeramente levantado, con la mano abierta en gesto de ofrecer una flor.

El segundo busto emerge de una córola vegetal, viste *chlamys*, dejándole al descubierto los hombros. El brazo derecho sostiene un martillo que apoya en el hombro; el izquierdo sujeta por las patas a un ave que picotea la córola vegetal.

No son muy frecuentes los apliques de carro cuyo engarce o vástago tenga forma prismático-octogonal. Igualmente excepcional es la rica decoración de nielados de plata y damasquinados. Iconográficamente los bustos de Bacantes sí suelen adornar los carros, tal y como aparecen en numerosos ejemplares, entre ellos el carro de Somodor, dos apliques de Volubilis, y un aplique conservado en los Museos Vaticanos, de procedencia desconocida.

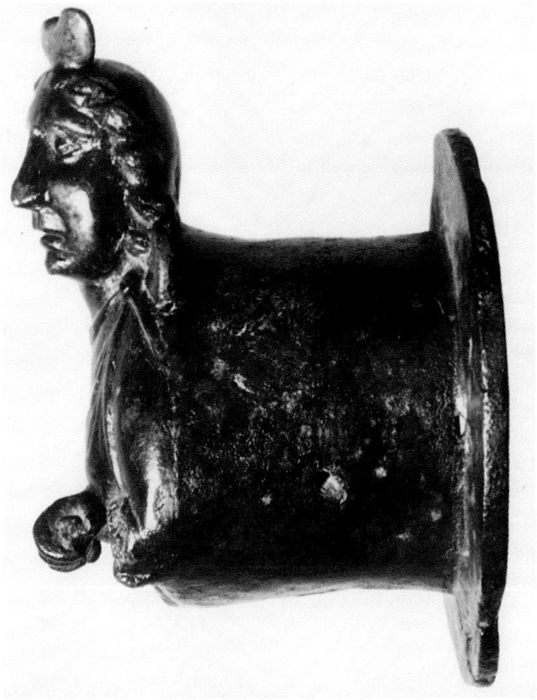

Fig. 5. Busto de Diana Lucífera (no. 9), de Morón de la Frontera (Sevilla). Bronce, h. 12 cm. Sevilla, Museo Arqueológico Provincial 6.621. (Fot.: Cortesía de la Junta de Andalucía)

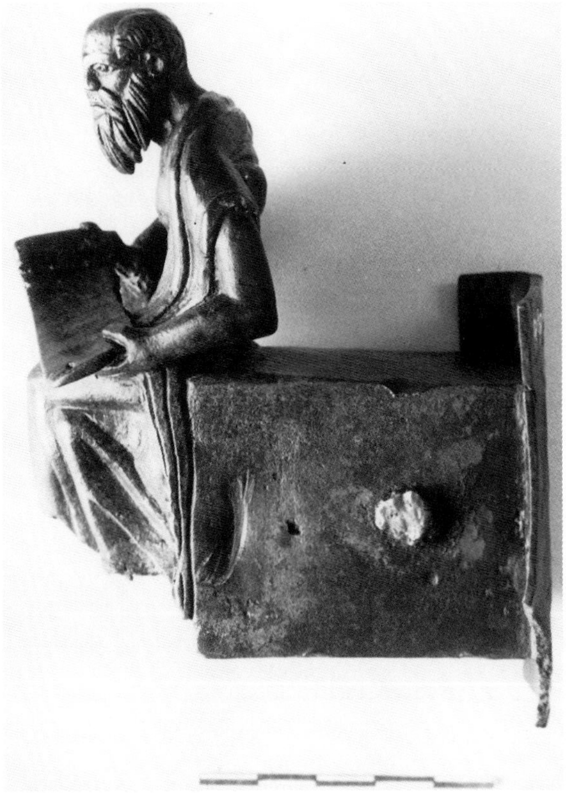

Fig. 7. Figura sedente (no. 13), de Cañizo de Campos (Zamora). Bronce, h. 9.6 cm. Zamora, Museo de Zamora 82/13/1. (Fot.: Joyco; Cortesía de la Junta de Castilla y León)

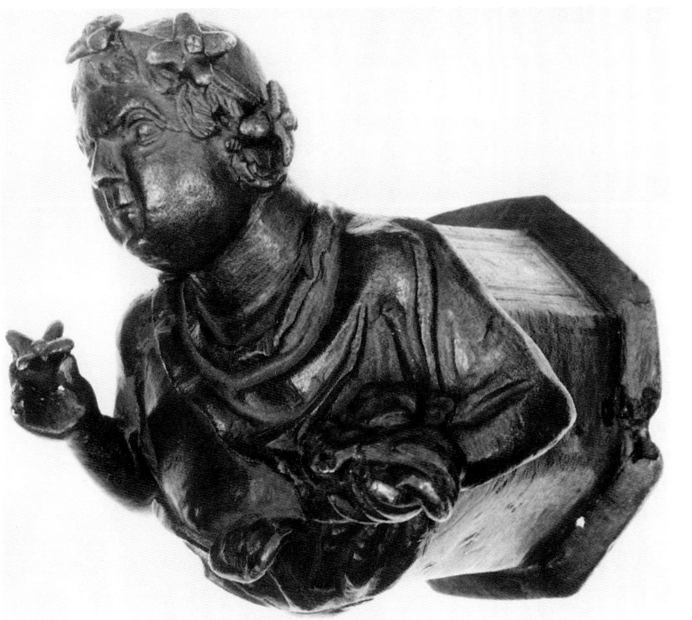

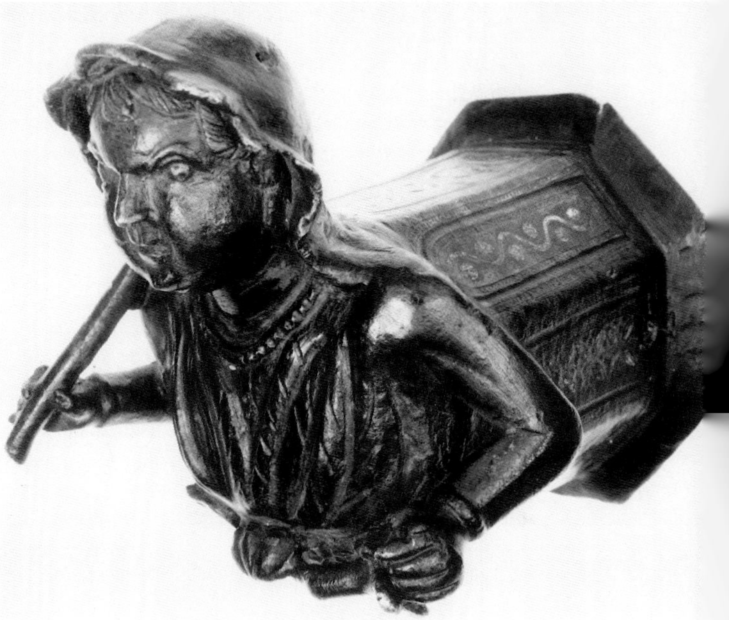

Fig. 6. Bustos de bacantes (nos. 10 [izq.] y 11). Bronce, h. 10.5 cm. Madrid, Museo Arqueológico Nacional 35/113/2 y 3. (Fot.: Cortesía Museo)

12. Aplique de carro: busto de bacante (Hispanic Society of America, New York)

Bronce de fundición hueca, perteneció a la Colección Vives (Madrid), vendida parcialmente al anticuario de G. Meunier (Paris). Ingresó en 1913 en la Hispanic Society. Se dice haber sido hallado en algún lugar de la provincia de Toledo, donde lo compró M. Simancas. H. 5.1 cm; l. 8.8 cm. Número de inventario: R 4427.

El vástago es de sección rectangular, ligeramente prismático; presenta unos agujeros para fijar la pieza en el carro, tiene una abertura en el reverso para ir engastado a la madera del carro. Este tipo de aplique, muy frequente, iría colocado en cada una de las extremidades de la parte posterior de la caja del carro, formando pareja con otro (desaparecido), tal y como vemos, por ejemplo, en los dos apliques anteriores del Museo de Madrid (nos. 10-11).

En la parte anterior del vástago hay representado un busto de bacante, de rasgos muy geométricos y arcaizantes, que denotan una cronología claramente bajo imperial. Lleva la cabeza ceñida por una diadema.

Los apliques de carro procedentes de Volubilis ofrecen un paralelo formal.

13. Aplique de carro: figura sedente (Museo de Zamora) (fig. 7)

Bronce de fundición hueca, la pátina de color verde oliva; presenta concreciones terrosas y oxidaciones. Fáltanle sólamente los pies a la figura masculina y presenta algunas roturas en la zona dorsal del aplique; buen estado de conservación. Fué hallado casualmente en fecha reciente por S. Raposo, en el pago denominado Fuentemiro o Pozo de Airón, en el término municipal de Cañizo de Campos (Zamora), quién lo donó al Museo de Zamora. H. 9.6 cm; l. 8.5 cm; w. 5.5 cm. Número de inventario: 82/13/1.

Aplique de carro que iría engastado en la extremidad de la parte posterior, en uno de los paneles laterales del carro.

El vástago es de sección rectangular, tiene un perno de hierro que permitiría su fijación; su cara posterior es abierta.

En la cara anterior está representada la figura de un personaje masculino con barba, sedente, que sujeta un *volumen*. Se nos ofrece frontalmente, la cabeza girada de tres cuarto a la izquierda; viste *pallium* (manto) que envuelve la figura salvo el torso (desnudo). El rostro barbado, la cabeza calva, en general denota los rasgos faciales de un anciano; sostiene entre ambas manos un *volumen* abierto.

La creación del tipo iconográfico del "filósofo", con el que relacionamos la figura del aplique de Cañizo, está ligada a la creación del retrato fisionómico, y se produjo en ambiente ático en la segunda mitad del s. V a.c. Se crea un tipo iconográfico bien definido, que presenta raras excepciones. El tipo figurativo del filósofo está destinado a representar no sólo a la categoría de los hombres de pensamiento sino, en sentido general, a poetas, literatos, oradores, sacerdotes, a las personas que desarrollan una actividad intelectual. Tal vez sea obra de Lisipo la creación de una figura sedente de filósofo: el cuerpo del personaje está cubierto de un *himation* de forma que deja al descubierto el torso; tiene sus antecedentes en algunas esculturas del s. V a.c., como el Sófocles del Teatro de Dionisos.

Un aplique de carro similar es el hallado en una villa d'Al Rec (Francia) y otro conservado en el British Museum.

14. Aplique de carro: cuadriga de caballos (Museu Nacional de Arqueología e Etnología, Lisboa) (fig. 8)

Bronce de fundición hueca, procede de Obidos (norte de Portugal), no se conocen la fecha y circunstancias del hallazgo. Se conserva en el Museo de Lisboa en calidad de depósito de Doña Maria Coelho. H. 11.2 cm; w. 9.0 cm.

El vástago es de sección rectangular, provisto de dos aberturas, en el reverso y en la base, destinadas a la fijación en cada una de las extremidades de la parte posterior de la caja del carro. El vástago va ornado con hojas (incisiones) en su cara anterior hay una máscara de león, de un estilo tosco y geométrico, muy primitivo.

Sobre el vástago hay un pedestal cuadrangular, decorado con hojas, donde está representada una cuadriga de caballos, al paso, unidos entre sí por las riendas. Todo ello denota ser obra de un taller provincial de época bajo imperial (s. III-IV d.c.).

IV. Elemento en forma de herradura fijado a cada extremidad del yugo del carro

15. Aplique de carro: pantera (Museo de la Rioja, Logroño) (fig. 9)

Bronce de fundición hueca, la pátina de color verde oliva; la superficie se nos ofrece con algunas concreciones terrosas y numerosos focos de oxidación y corrosión. El aplique ha perdido parte del soporte, y la pantera su pata anterior izquierda y la derecha está fracturada desde su inicio. Fue hallado en fecha reciente (principio de los años 80) en un lugar indeterminado de la ciudad romana de Varea (Logroño). Se conserva en el Museo de La Rioja. H. 6.1 cm; w. 6.1 cm. Número de inventario: 11365.

Este elemento del yugo del carro se componía primitivamente de un vástago plano, en forma de herradura, unido a otro vástago plano, horizontal, terminado en cada uno de sus extremos por un medallón circular decorado con una máscara de Medusa en alto-relieve.

Para el emplazamiento en cada extremo del yugo A. Radnoti elabora un inventario y establece una tipología de tres grupos (A, B, y C), según los temas decorativos. El bronce de Varea pertenece al grupo C, que reune las piezas decoradas de figuras de animales de bulto redondo: pareja de leonas o de panteras que posan su pata anterior sobre un aplique circular donde figura un morro de animal, una máscara báquica, una máscara de Attis, de Júpiter-Ammon, de Minerva, femenina, o de Medusa.

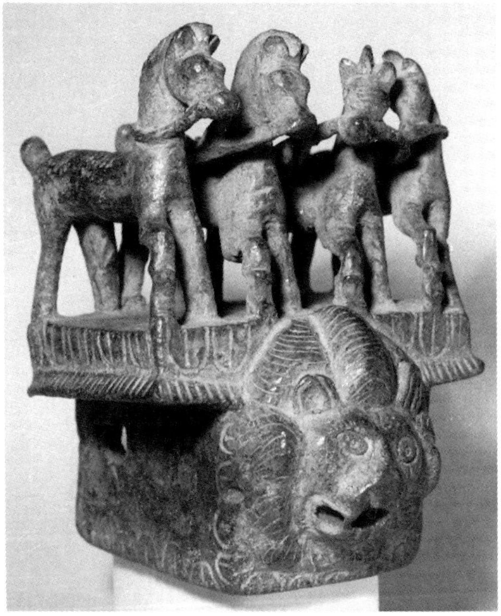

Fig. 8. Cuadriga de caballos (no. 14), de Obidos (norte de Portugal). Bronce, h. 11.2 cm. Lisboa, Museu Nacional de Arqueologia e Etnologia. (Fot.: Cortesia Centro Fotografico de Belém)

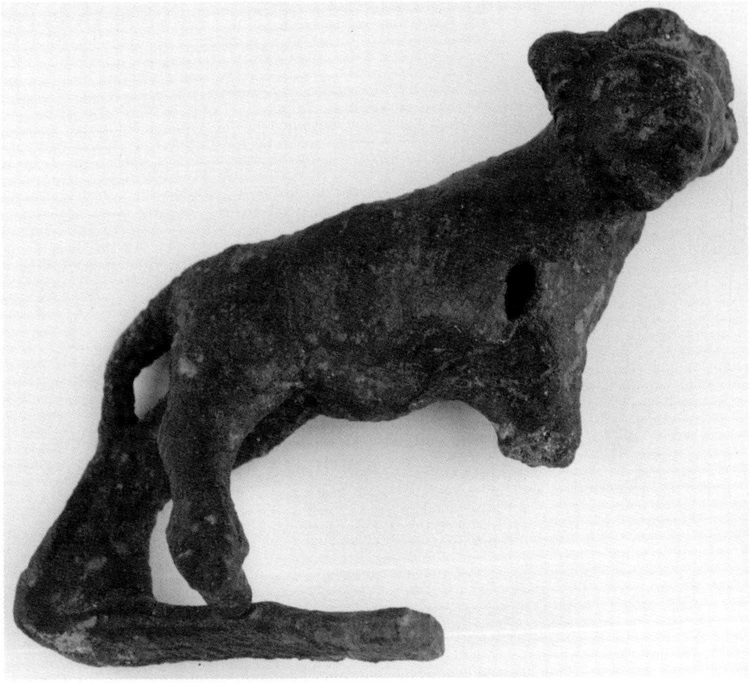

Fig. 9. Pantera (no. 15), de la ciudad romana de Varea (Logroño). Bronce, h. 6.1 cm. Logroño, Museo de La Rioja 11365. (Fot.: Cortesía Gobierno de La Rioja)

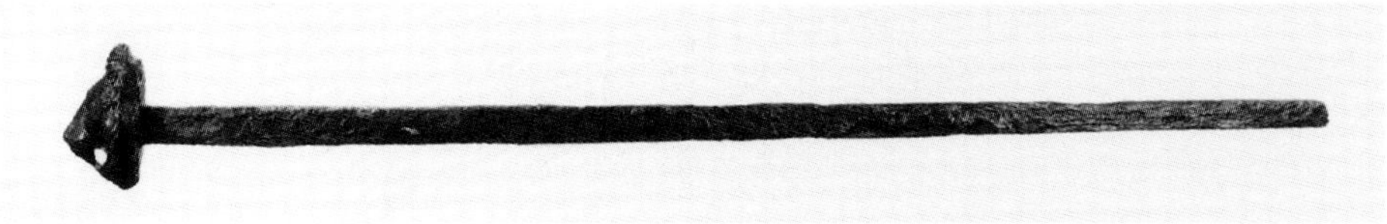

Fig. 10. Máscara de león (no. 16), de origen emeritense. Bronce, l. 19.4 cm. Mérida, Museo Nacional de Arte Romano 30.173. (Fot.: J. L. Barrera; Cortesía de la Junta de Extremadura)

Similar al aplique de Varea es el descubierto en Volubilis, que representa una pantera reposando la pata en un medallón con Medusa en alto relieve. Otros bronces análogos son los recopilados por H. Menzel, procedentes de Alemania, y R. Fleischer hallado en Carnuntum.

V. Tipos diversos

16. Eje de rueda de carro. máscara de león (Museo Nacional de Arte Romano de Mérida) (fig. 10)

Bronce de fundición plena, la pátina verdosa, hállase completo; buen estado de conservación. No se conoce su procedencia precisa, aunque es seguro su origen emeritense. Ingresó en el Museo de Mérida con anterioridad a 1943. L. 19.4 cm. Número de inventario: 30.173.

Eje de rueda de un carro; en uno de sus extremos hay una máscara de león, con las fauces abiertas, según el tipo convencional para estas representaciones zoomorfas.

Un carro procedente del valle de Vardar, conocido como el carro de Salónica, en su reconstitución, que puede verse en el Römisch-Germanisches Museum de Colonia, uno de los ejes de la rueda va ornado también con otra máscara de león.

Universidad de Málaga, Málaga

Bronze appliqués of wood caskets from the site of the *valetudinarium* at Novae

Piotr Dyczek

The legionary fortress of Novae lies on the bank of the Danube in the Roman province of Moesia Inferior. It is currently being explored by Polish and Bulgarian archaeologists. The excavations of Warsaw University's Center for Archaeological Research are concentrated in two sectors: the center of the fortress and the *praetentura,* where two chronologically superimposed structures were discovered — the Flavian legionary baths and the *valetudinarium* (fig. 1). The military hospital building was erected in the early 2nd c. A.D. and remained in operation until the time of Caracalla. It occupied all of one *scamnum* lying at the intersection of the *via praetoria* and the *via sagularis.* About two-thirds of the structure have been uncovered so far, allowing the plan to be reconstructed and the functions of most of the hospital rooms to be identified.[1]

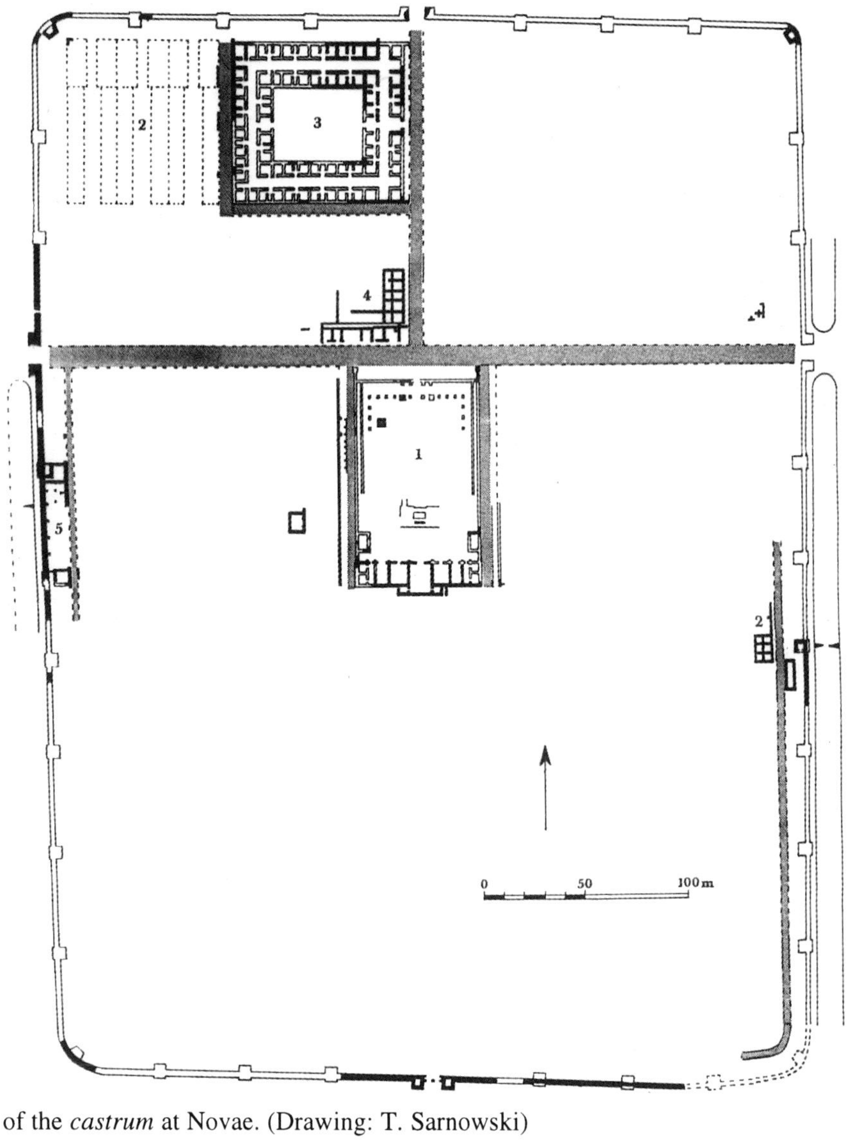

Fig. 1. Plan of the *castrum* at Novae. (Drawing: T. Sarnowski)

1 P. Dyczek, "Valetudinarium at Novae — new components," in W. Groening-van Waateringe (ed.), *Rom-*

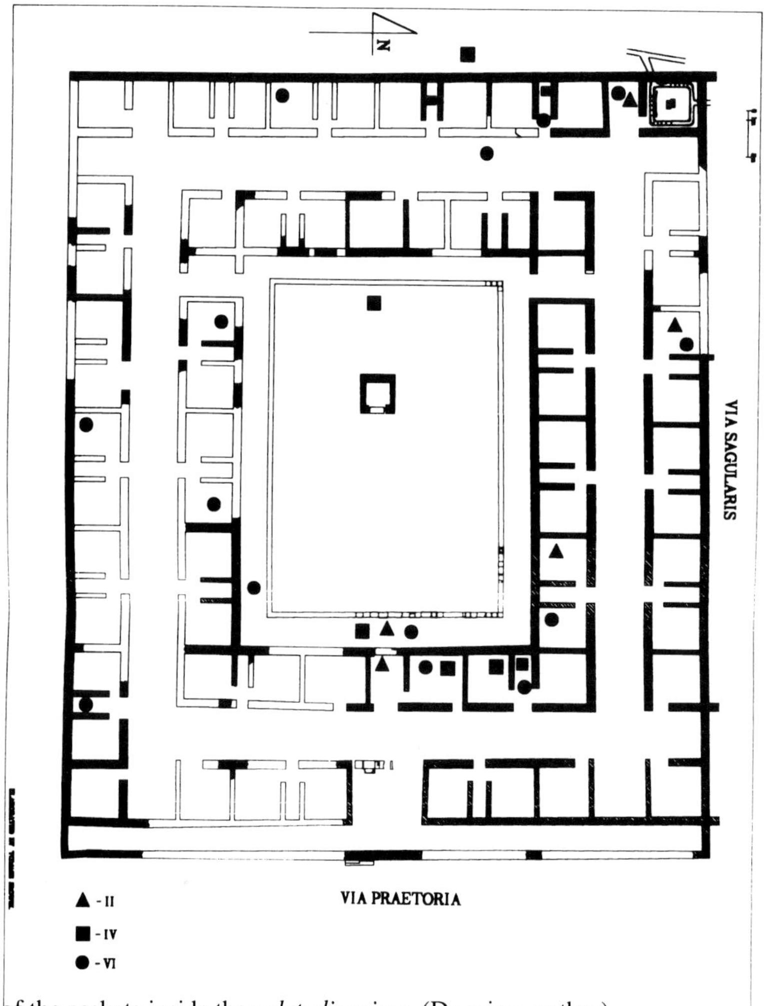

Fig. 2. Findspots of the caskets inside the *valetudinarium*. (Drawing: author)

Fragments of bronze fittings, small bronze handles, bronze nails, rivets, and locks were discovered in many of the rooms (fig. 2). Some of the bronze fittings even had pieces of wood adhering to them. The shape of the fittings and the size of the locks and handles suggest unequivocally that they belong to small caskets. All the fragments come from the débris that filled the *valetudinarium* after its abandonment. The layer is well dated thanks to coins of Caracalla, some of which were struck in Nicopolis ad Istrum just 60 km to the south.[2] Taking into consideration the fact that the caskets could have been in use for some length of time, they should be dated to the late 2nd and early 3rd c.

On the basis of finds, mostly from Pannonia, it has been possible to distinguish 7 types of caskets.[3] Despite the passage of time, their form and decoration underwent only slight, almost indiscernible, modifications. In spite of minor differences (obviously related to the building's function), the caskets from the legionary hospital fit well into the typology for Pannonia proposed by D. Gáspár.

Three types of caskets are found at Novae. With the exception of one group, they are decorated rather modestly. The bronze elements were more for reinforcing the edges and the lock than for appearance. In the *valetudinarium* the caskets were used to store objects used in heal-

---

an frontier studies 1995: Proceedings of the XVIth int. Congress of Roman frontier studies (Oxford 1997) 199-204.

2 A. Poulter, *Nicopolis ad Istrum: a Roman, Late Roman, and Early Byzantine city* (*JRS* Monograph 8, 1995) 269-79.

3 D. Gáspár, *Römische Kästchen aus Pannonien* (*Antaeus. Mitteilungen des Arch. Inst. der Ungarischen Akad. der Wiss.* 15, 1986) 54-58.

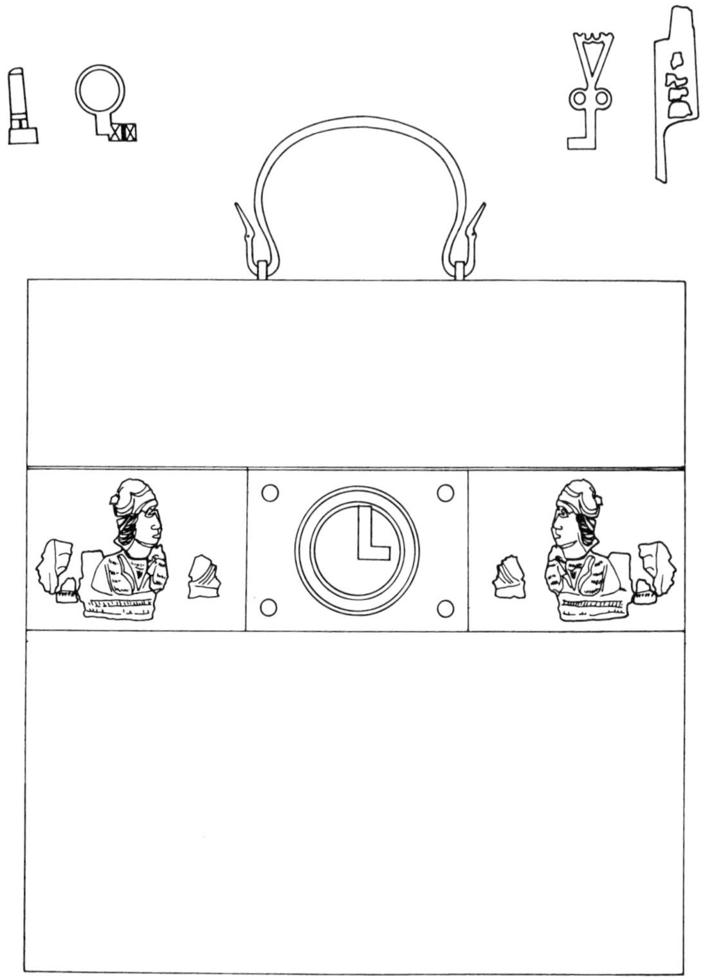

Fig. 3. Reconstruction of Type II casket. (Drawing: author)

ing and thus were presumably part of the hospital equipment. There is no evidence to justify the notion that at least some of them belonged to the patients. The caskets are usually found with fragments of glass — shattered bottles and *unguentaria*.[4] In one case, bronze fittings were found with fragments of bronze instruments: spatulas and tweezers.[5]

1. The first type of casket found at the military hospital corresponds to Type II from Pannonia (fig. 3).[6] Fragments of bronze fittings were found near the exit into the hospital courtyard,[7] next to a room identified as a first-aid room (room 35),[8] and in a niche (room 58) that served as a pottery and lamp storeroom. Remains of locks (keys and bolts) were also discovered in three of the rooms for patients (rooms 16, 17c, and 60) and may be attributed to this type of casket with a high degree of probability. All in all, fragments of 5 caskets were discovered. The wooden box was presumably not larger than 0.6 x 0.6 x 0.6 m. Analogies indicate that this type of casket had a simple and functional handle on the top — a shaped bronze rod, the ends bent to form bird's heads. The bronze fittings covered the entire front of the box and were set in bands. In one of the square panels there is a representation of a goddess, presumably Minerva.[9] The lock was protected by a bronze plaque decorated with a concentric circle motif around an L-

4 P. Dyczek, "Novae — western sector, 1992-1995," *Archeologia* (Warszawa) 46 (1996) 55-62; G. Dankova, "Kieliszki i unguentaria z Novae, materialy do katalogu," *Novensia* 6 (1993) 81-130.

5 Dyczek (supra n.4).

6 Gáspár (supra n.3) 54 ff.

7 Dyczek (supra n.4).

8 Dyczek (supra n.1).

9 H. Buschhausen, *Die spätrömischen Metallscrinia und frühchristlichen Reliquaire* 1 (Vienna 1971) 103.

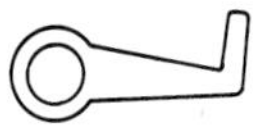

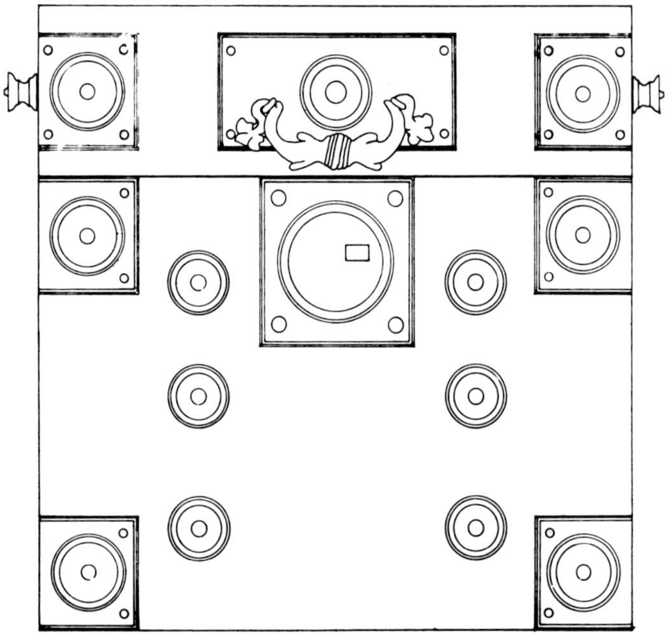

Fig. 4. Reconstruction of Type IV casket. (Drawing: author)

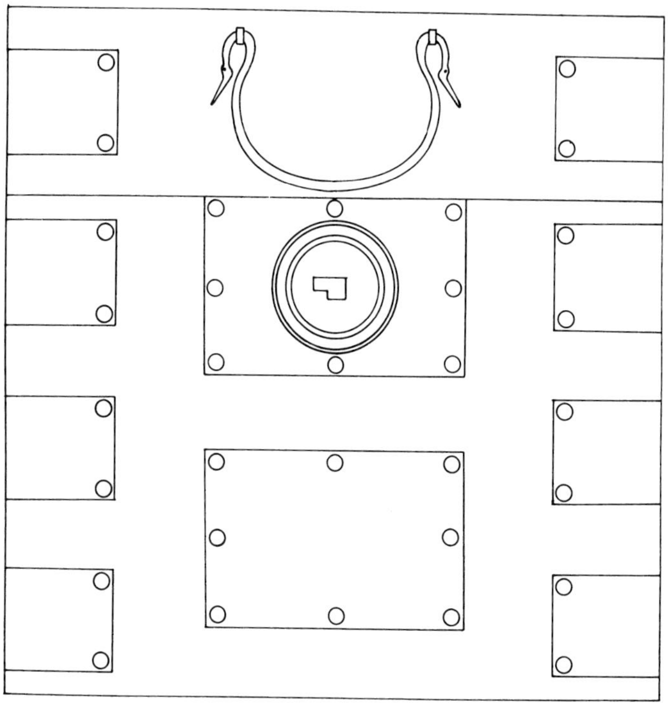

Fig. 5. Reconstruction of Type VI casket. (Drawing: author)

shaped opening cut in the center. The fittings were attached to the wood with small bronze nails (3 cm long, with a round head 8-10 mm in diameter).

The keys and bolts are an indication of the kind of lock used. It probably belonged to Type IV known from Pannonia.[10] These locks were opened with small keys usually ending in a ring. Openwork tops are also known. The mechanism of the lock itself was complicated to the extent that it could not be opened by any other kind of key. Some caskets of this type in Pannonia can be dated to the 2nd c.[11] Analyses of the wood have shown that the Panonnian caskets were made of pine and beech: *Pinus nigra L.* and *Fagus silvatica L.*[12] The Novae casket was made of maple.

The decorative motif of a goddess is found in Pannonia, as are Muses and personifications of the seasons.[13] This richly decorated casket from Novae probably contained medical instruments, and some were found nearby. The value of the contents is reflected in the richness of the decoration.

2. The next type of casket from Novae corresponds to Type IV from Pannonia (fig. 4).[14] Fragments from the legionary fortress reveal some similarity with the casket from Sopianae, which is dated, however, to the time of Carinus and Diocletian.[15] Nonetheless, identical caskets are dated to the 2nd and 3rd c.;[16] in one case it was possible to determine a more exact

10 Gáspár (supra n.3) 48 ff.

11 Ibid. 71-72.

12 Ibid. 376.

13 Buschhausen (supra n.9) 26; D. Gáspár, *Spätrömische Kästchenbeschläge in Pannonia* (Szeged 1971) no. 45, fig. 79; id., "Ein spätrömischer Kästchenbeschlag-Fund von Fenékpuszta," *ActaArchHung* 31 (1979) fig. 18.

14 Gáspár (supra n.3) 48-49.

15 S. Fülep, *The history of Pécs during the Roman era and the problem of the continuity of the Late Roman population* (Budapest 1984) 87, fig. 30.

16 Gáspár (supra n.3) 192.

date in the second half of the 2nd and first half of the 3rd c.[17] It can be assumed that these wooden caskets from Novae measured *c.*0.6 m to the side. Surviving fragments can be attributed to 8 separate caskets of this type. They were found in the first-aid room (room 35) and in its vicinity, in the courtyard near rooms 38 and 51, in one of the rooms for patients (room 31), but mostly in the small vestibules 1a, 3a, and 30. This confirms the tendency, recognized at Novae, that the vestibules served to store pottery, lamps, and food for legionary patients lying in the rooms on either side.[18] This observation leads to the conclusion that the caskets contained medicine. Thus the modesty of the decoration in the case of this type of box is hardly surprising. The round bronze plaque (3 to 6 cm in diameter) was attached to the casket's front with a series of small bronze nails closely spaced around the circumference. In the center of the plaque there was one bigger nail. Depending on the plaque's position, it was either a nail with a biconically shaped head or a large decorative knob used to open the cover. The handle was located in the middle of the side wall of the cover. It generally took the form of two dolphins set mouth to mouth, as in the case of the Novae examples. No fragments of wood were preserved at Novae in association with this type of casket, but there is evidence that spruce (*Picea excelsa L.*) was used in Pannonia.[19]

The lock used in these caskets belonged to Pannonian Type IVa2,[20] which differs from the one described above by an additional hook meant to keep the bolt in the metal slide. Since the caskets seem to have been kept in the vestibules and presumably contained medicine for more than one patient, they could not have been accessible except to hospital staff. Presumably depending on the illness, the caskets were filled with the necessary medicines to avoid constant distribution. It is equally difficult to imagine each patient having uncontrolled access, since the caskets seem to have contained medicines for different illnesses. The complicated lock made access difficult. Hospital staff was presumably charged with giving out the medicines and so was equipped with the necessary keys.

3. The third casket type from the Novae *valetudinarium* is equivalent to Type VI from Pannonia (fig. 5).[21] The dimensions of the boxes were the same as in the above two types. Fragments of 14 caskets were discovered. Their sides were covered with rectangular bronze plaques, either plain or with the motif of concentric circles. Other fittings were meant as reinforcements of the edges. They were attached to the wood by small bronze nails with small heads. This is undoubtedly the least ornamental of all the types. In front there was a simple handle ending in a faintly modeled bird's(?) head on either side.[22] Caskets of this type in Pannonia are dated to the second half of the 2nd c.[23] They were made of poplar (*Populus tremula L.*), a species of tree more common in Pannonia,[24] more rarely of beech (*Fagus silvatica L.*).[25] At Novae casket fragments of this type were found in the first-aid room (room 35), in the vicinity of rooms 38 and 51, and in the niche that served as a pottery and lamp storeroom (room 58), as well as in the small vestibules 1a and 70. But most of the fragments came from the large rooms for patients: 5, 15b, 30, 60, 75, 86, and 93.

The lock used in these caskets is a very complicated mechanism.[26] What attracts attention

---

17 Ibid. 275.
18 P. Dyczek, "Novae — western sector, 1989," *Archeologia* (Warszawa) 42 (1991) 129.
19 Gáspár (supra n.3) 376.
20 Ibid. 61.
21 Ibid. 55-56.
22 A. Rádnoti, *Gefässe, Lampen und Tintenfässer aus Bronze. Intercissa* 2 (Archaeologia Hungarica 36, 1957) 217, no. 15, fig. 39.7; Gáspár (supra n.3) fig. 302.
23 D. Gabler and É. Koczur, "Terra sigillata Depotfund aus Gorsium," *Alba Regia* 15 (1977) 68; Gáspár (supra n.3) 270.
24 Gáspár (supra n.3) 376.
25 Ibid. 302.
26 Ibid. 110, 185.

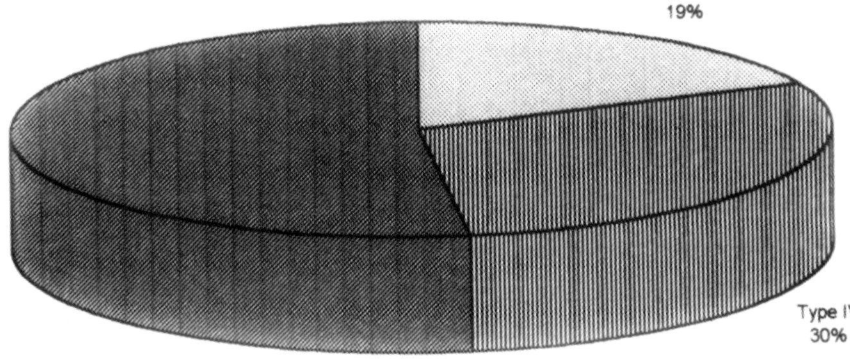

Fig. 6. Occurrence of different types of caskets inside the *valetudinarium* at Novae. (Chart: author)

is the fact that the locks are found mainly in rooms occupied by patients. Not one key has been found, and there is no evidence of the contents. It can be suggested that the caskets were used to store the patients' more valuable belongings and were emptied when they left the hospital. As investigations of the *valetudinarium* have proved, hospitalized soldiers brought their armor and other private belongings that required security. The fact that these caskets dominate among the types discussed here suggests that they were part of the hospital's equipment.

The caskets were made of wood planks, the boards chosen in sizes that allowed each side to be made of one piece. The edges were joined by bronze plaques attached with bronze nails that penetrated the thickness of one board and into the length of the adjacent one. The edges of boards were profiled to allow for exact fitting. A different kind of nail was used to attach the bronze plaques to the casket sides, and bronze rivets were used for the handles. Taking into account the length of these latter two forms of attachment, the sides of the caskets from Novae can be estimated at 1.5 cm thick at most. This agrees with data from Pannonia.[27]

Conclusions

The scattering of different types of caskets in the *valetudinarium* at Novae leads to a number of conclusions in reference to this particular building (fig. 6). The most richly ornamented caskets of Type II presumably served physicians as chests for their medical instruments and special medicines. Caskets of Type IV presumably served as handy containers for medicines; their contents would have been filled up or changed by hospital staff according to need. Finally, caskets of Type VI may have contained the personal belongings of legionaries.

The concentration of caskets of Types II and IV in a room (room 35) identified on other grounds as a first-aid room supports that identification. The room was presumably used for first examinations and for minor operations that required the use of surgical instruments and medicines. The occurrence of caskets of all types in the pottery and lamp storeroom (room 58) may suggest that caskets temporarily not in use may have been kept there, thereby indicating that they were part of the hospital's basic equipment.

Statistical analysis of the occurrence of different types of caskets supports these suggestions. Taking into account the area of the *valetudinarium* that has so far been excavated, it is possible to extend the results to the whole building with considerable probability. Analysis of the types and distribution of caskets with bronze fittings, along with other finds, gives not only a better understanding of the organization and rules of operation of the military hospital at Novae but also contributes to a study of the operation of the entire fortress.

Osrodek Badan Archeologicznyck UW, Ul. Zwirki i Wigury 97/99, Warszawa

---

27 D. Gáspár, "Besondere Metallfunde aus Fenékpuszta," *Mitteilungen des Archäologisches Instituts* 8-9 (1977/78) fig. 6; id. (supra n.3) 144, fig. 63.

Eine Büste der Dea Roma in Köln

Renate Thomas

Das Römisch-Germanische Museum Köln erhielt 1996, zu seinem 50jährigen Bestehen als Geschenk von der Stadtsparkasse Köln, die 1995 im Kunsthandel erworbene 26.5 cm große Bronzebüste einer Dea Roma, charakterisiert durch den attischen Helm und die nach dem Vorbild von Amazonen-Darstellungen entblößte rechte Brust (Abb. 1-5).[1] Die Büste befand sich seit dem vergangenen Jahrhundert in Privatbesitz und stammt nach Angabe des früheren Besitzers aus Les Fins d'Annecy, dem antiken vicus Boutae,[2] einem Ort, an dem bereits vom 17. Jh. an Bronzestatuetten und Statuenfragmente zu Tage traten.[3] Zu den bedeutendsten Funden gehören der Bronzehort der Sammlung Dutuit, im Pariser Petit Palais[4] sowie mehrere umfangreiche Münzschätze, die aus Furcht vor Barbareneinfällen im 3. Jh. vergraben worden sind.[5] Auch für

---

1 W. H. Roscher, *Ausführliches Lexikon der griechischen und römischen Mythologie* 4 (Leipzig 1897-1902) 130-63, s.v. Roma (F. Richter); R. Mellor, "The goddess Roma," *ANRW* II.17.2 (1981) 950-1030.

2 Von dem Fundort, der seit Anlage des Straßennetzes durch Agrippa einen Kreuzungspunkt wichtiger römischer Fernstraßen darstellt, ist aus der Überlieferung wenig bekannt. Durch Ausgrabungen sind neben dem Straßennetz und der Wohnbebauung, ein nördliches Forum mit einer Basilika sowie ein südliches Forum mit einem Theater und möglicherweise einem dem Merkur geweihten Tempel bekannt, außerdem 49 Brunnen, Töpfereien, aber auch metallverarbeitende Betriebe. C. Marteaux und M. Le Roux, *Boutae: vicus gallo-romain de la cité de Vienne* (Annecy 1913); P. Broise, "Genève et son territoire dans l'antiquité," *Latomus* 129 (1974) 69-71, 196-99, Taf. XIV, XV; id., *Le vicus gallo-romain de Boutae et ses terroirs* (Annecy 1984).

3 Marteaux und Le Roux (s. o. Anm.2) 25-35, bes. 33; Broise (s. o. Anm.2) 9-15. Leider blieben die Funde nicht in Annecy, sondern wurden an verschiedene Museen oder Privatsammler verkauft, bevor erst 1842 ein Museum in Annecy eingerichtet wurde, mit einem verantwortlichen Kustos, der bemüht war Zeugnisse der Geschichte von Boutae zu sammeln und zu erhalten.

4 Trotz der Bemühungen des damaligen Konservators L. Revon wurden die Funde von dem Grundstückseigner Bonetto an einen Genfer Kunsthändler verkauft. Auf dem Flurstück 359, heute Place des Romains, das in römischer Zeit im Bereich eines älteren Handwerkerviertels südöstlich des Theaters lag, fanden sich in einer schmalen, mit einem Dachziegel bedeckten Grube dicht zusammengedrängt und z.T. ineinander gestapelt: ein Bein von einer lebensgroßen Statue, darin steckten eine 63 cm große Jünglingsstatuette, eine Büste des Antoninus Pius, sowie zwei hadrianische Privatporträts als Fragmente von lebensgroßen Statuen. L. Revon, "Le nouveau trésor des Fins d'Annecy," *Revue Savoisienne* 12 (1867) 109-11; Marteaux und Le Roux (s. o. Anm.2) 43 ff.; J. Petit, *Bronzes antiques de la collection Dutuit* (Paris 1980) 88-93, Nr. 32, 112-17, Nr. 45-47 (mit älterer Lit.); P. Broise, *Boutae* (s. o. Anm.2) 64-66, Abb. 24-28.

5 Der unbefestigte *vicus* brannte in den Jahren 259 und 277 infolge von Überfällen durchziehender Barbarenheere vollständig ab, wurde jedoch teilweise wieder aufgebaut. Weitere Zerstörungen durch Barbaren sind für das 4. Jh. nachgewiesen. Unweit vom Fundort der Statuette und der Büsten wurden in einem Brunnen weitere Fragmente der Statuen geborgen (Marteaux und Le Roux [s. o. Anm.2] 40). Ein Jahr vorher war auf demselben Grundstück ein Münzschatz mit 10.700 Bronzeprägungen zutagegetreten (Marteaux und Le Roux, *Boutae* (s. o. Anm.2) 42; L. Revon, "Bustes de bronze découverts auprès d'Annecy," *GazArch* 1875, 114-16). Die meisten Stücke waren gallienisch, die älteste Münze stammte von Caracalla, die jüngste von Probus. Ganz in der Nähe wurde 1867 ein zweiter Münzschatz ausgegraben, der mindestens 4.000 Münzen enthielt, von denen die jüngste unter Aurelian geprägt war. Allem Anschein nach wurden die Münzen anläßlich des zweiten Barbareneinfalls im Jahre 277 n. Chr. vergraben. In der Folgezeit wurden im Bereich des südlichen, an das Theater anschließenden Forum weitere Fragmente von Großbronzen geborgen: ein Bein eines überlebensgroßen Pferdes sowie ein Daumen von einer vielleicht zugehörigen überlebensgroßen Statue. Die Großbronzen und die Kaiserbüste, von denen nur noch die Fragmente zeugen, scheinen bei einem Barbareneinfall zerstört worden zu sein. Möglicherweise konnten diese Bruchstücke von den Bewohnern des *vicus* bei ihrer Flucht vor weiteren Barbarenüberfällen sichergestellt und vergraben werden. Marteaux und Le Roux (s. o. Anm.2) 37-50, bes. 41-42; Broise 1974 (s. o. Anm.2) 69-71, 196-99; id., *Vicus* (s. o. Anm.2).

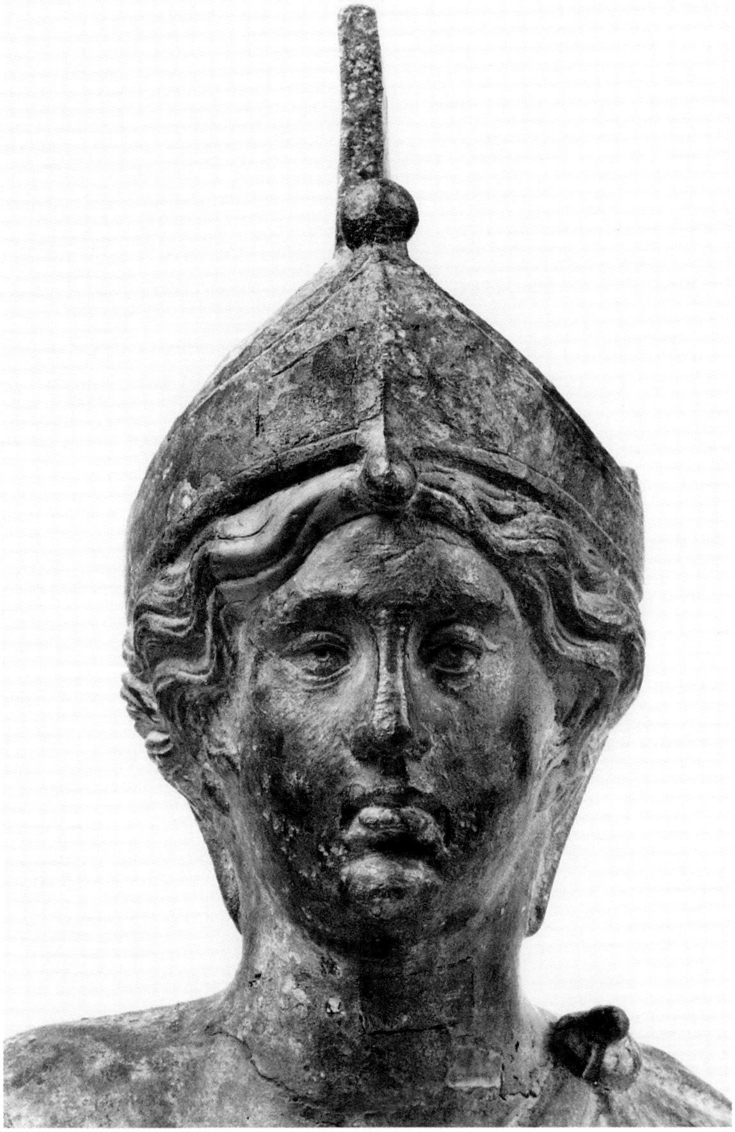

Abb. 1. Dea Roma Büste, Kopf, Detail. Aus Les Fins d'Annecy (antiker vicus Boutae). Bronze, H. 26.5 cm. Köln, Römisch-Germanisches Museum Inv. 95,1. (Foto: G. Dettloff; Forschungsarchiv für Römische Plastik am Archäologischen Intitut der Universität zu Köln)

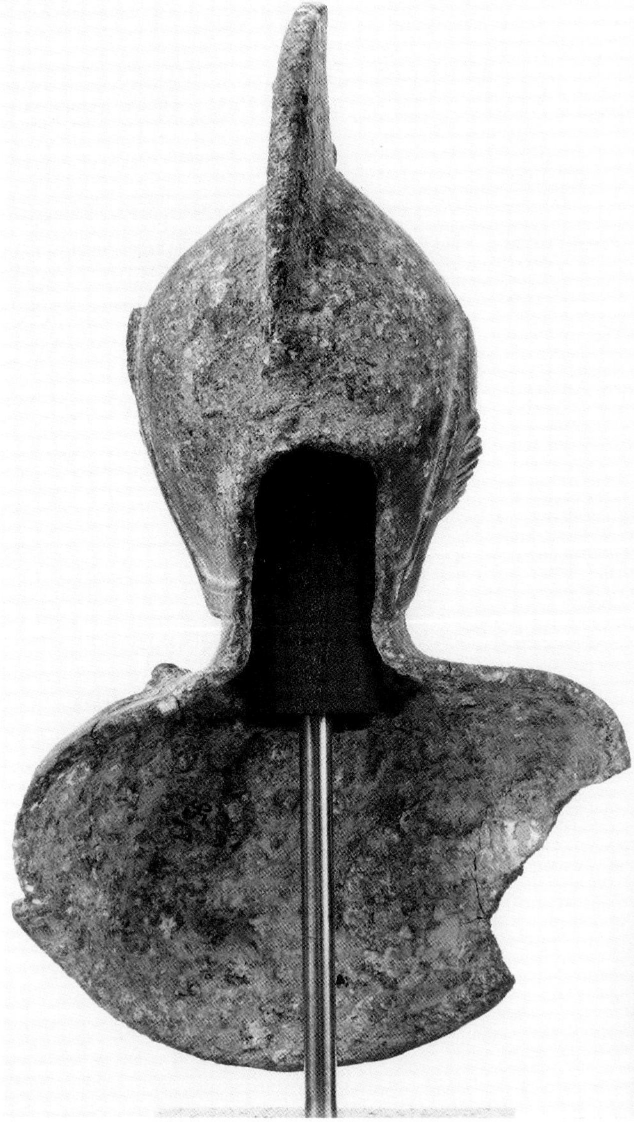

Abb. 2. Wie Abb. 1, Rückseite. (Foto: G. Dettloff; Forschungsarchiv für Römische Plastik am Archäologischen Intitut der Universität zu Köln)

die Dea Roma-Büste liegt aufgrund ihres verhältnismäßig guten Erhaltungszustands nahe, daß sie Teil eines Hortes ist, der möglicherweise ebenfalls bereits im 3. Jh. versteckt worden ist.

Der größte Teil des Gesichts, des Haares und des Gewandes der Büste bewahrt noch die originale Oberfläche. Leicht korrodiert und verkrustet ist lediglich die linke Seite des Helms. Der rechte untere Büstenrand ist weggebrochen. Die rechte Lockensträhne über der Stirn ist modern in Kunststoff ergänzt. Außerdem weist der Hals mehrere Risse auf, die ebenfalls modern mit Kunststoffmasse geschlossen und hinterlegt wurden. Darüber hinaus zeigt die Büste Reparaturen von Gußfehlern, die noch während des Herstellungsprozesses durch Bronzeflicken ausgebessert worden sind. Ein größeres Bronzepflaster sitzt links von der Mittelkante des Stirnschutzes des Helms, ein kleinerer längsrechteckiger Flicken am Hals.

Das schmale Gesicht der Göttin ist streng frontal angelegt mit starr geradeaus gerichtetem Blick. Die asymmetrisch ausgebildeten Augen sind im Vergleich zur Nase relativ klein und liegen unter annähernd geraden Augenbrauen eng beieinander. Die Augenlider sind über ein Drittel des Augapfels heruntergezogen. Das linke überschneidet deutlich das Unterlid und ist

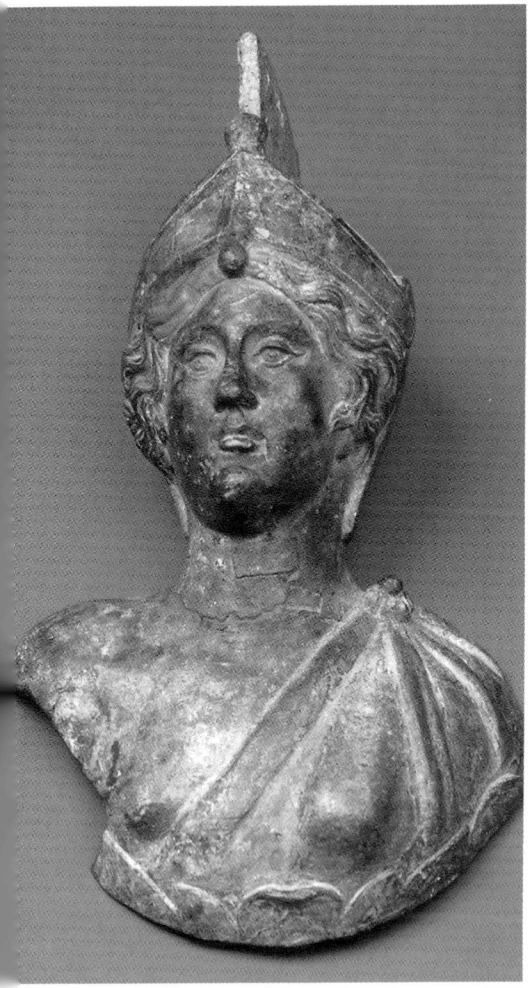

Abb. 3. Wie Abb. 1, Gesamtansicht vor einer Rückwand.

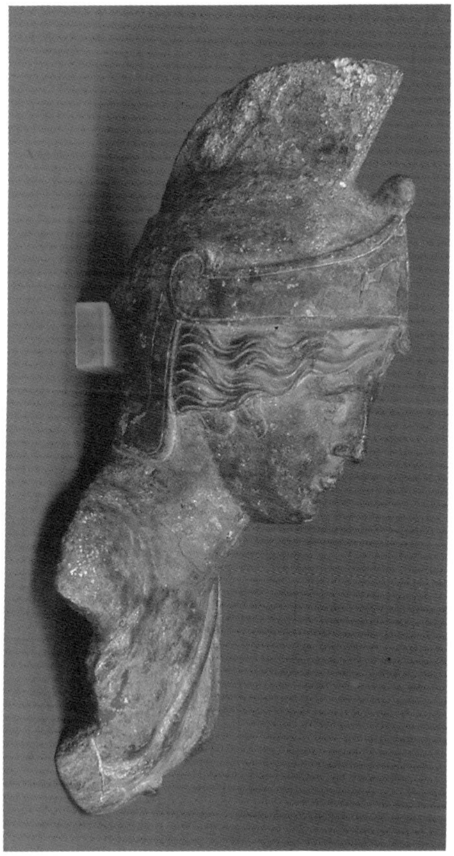

Abb. 4. Rechte Seitenansicht.

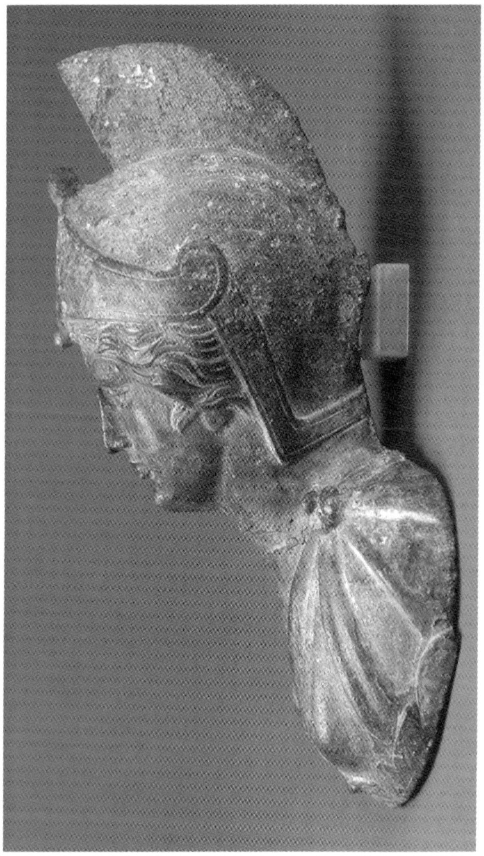

Abb. 5. Linke Seitenansicht.

(alle Fotos: S. Siegers; Römisch-Germanisches Museum Köln)

leicht noch oben geschwungen. Das rechte Unterlid wird von einer scharfgratigen Falte begleitet. Die von den Augenlidern überschnittenen Pupillen sind kreisförmig ausgehöhlt, jedoch sind die Ränder der Iris nicht eingraviert. Durch die leicht geschlossenen Lider und den Ring unter dem rechten Auge, verbunden mit dem starren Blick, erhält das Gesicht einen eigentümlich 'müden' und gleichzeitig 'entrückten' Ausdruck. Der Mund ist auffallend schmal und wird von tiefen nach unten gezogenen Furchen begrenzt. Das vorspringende, kräftige Kinn gibt dem Gesicht einen harten, fast männlich strengen Charakter. Das Haar ist über der Stirnmitte gescheitelt und in weichen voluminösen Wellen zur Seite gekämmt. Eine einzelne kurze Locke liegt vor dem Ohr, von dem nur das Ohrläppchen unter den Strähnen sichtbar wird. Der attische Helm hat einen hochgeschobenen Stirnschutz, dessen Mittelkante oben und unten durch einen runden Knauf verziert ist und der über den Scharnieren in Voluten endet. Der Helmbusch ist als ungegliederter, steil aufragender sichelförmiger Grat stilisiert. Insgesamt macht die Roma den Eindruck einer provinziellen gallo-römischen Arbeit von solider Qualität.

Die Büste weist an der Rückseite (Abb. 2) eine hochrechteckige Öffnung auf. In der Seitenansicht wird erkennbar, daß der Helm an der Stelle der Öffnung leicht nach oben gewölbt ist und sich dort zusammen mit dem Hals unorganisch stark nach hinten verbreitert (Abb. 3-4). Offensichtlich war die Büste ursprünglich an einer hakenartigen Vorrichtung aufgehängt und lag mit dem Büstenausschnitt flach an einer senkrechten Fläche an. Rekonstruiert man die Roma etwas erhöht hängend, machen sich in der Unteransicht bei vorgestrecktem Kopf die Unregelmäßigkeiten im Aufbau des Gesichts, die bei der Montage mit aufrechter Kopfhaltung stören, nicht bemerkbar (Abb. 5). Zu diesen gehören die stark verdickte rechte Wangen- und Kinnpartie sowie der kurze und breite Hals.

Es handelt sich also nicht, wie man zunächst aufgrund der Größe vermuten könnte, um eine freistehende Büste, sondern um eine Applik. Die an Wagen, als Fulcra oder an Möbeln bzw. Kästen befestigten Bronzeappliken sind in der Regel nur 7-8 und höchstens 10 bis 12 cm groß.[6] Am Schiffsbug oder an Ruderkästen befestigte Bronzebüsten zeigen eine andere Montagevorrichtung an der Rückseite.[7] Möglicherweise war die Applik auf einem Clipeus an einem größeren Altar oder an der Wand in einem öffentlichen Gebäude, einem Heiligtum bzw. Tempel angebracht.[8]

Die Roma-Büste zeigt einen halbrunden Büstenausschnitt, der die Schultern mit den Armansätzen sowie die Brust umfaßt. Den unteren Büstenrand, bis in Höhe der Achseln säumt ein Kranz von glatten lanzettförmigen Blättern. Diese Form des im Halbrund begrenzenden Blattkranzes stellt eine Sonderform dar, die vor allem in den nordwestlichen Provinzen verbreitet ist und die offensichtlich nicht in derselben Tradition steht, wie das von H. Jucker von orientalischen Vorbildern abgeleitete Bildnis im Blätterkelch.[9] Besonders beliebt ist dieser Blätterkranz bei Büsten des gallischen Hauptgottes Merkur[10] sowie der personifizierten gallischen Stadtgöttin Tutuela.[11] Auffallend ist die Tatsache, daß der Blätterkranz in den nordwestlichen Provinzen vorrangig in Verbindung mit lokalen Schutzgottheiten Verwendung findet.[12] Bezeichnenderweise zeigt auch ein ungewöhnlicher Büstentypus den rahmenden Blätterkranz, von dem sich ein besonders qualitätvolles Beispiel aus Orange im Cabinet des Médailles in Paris befindet, bei welchem in einer eigenwilligen Form der *interpretatio Romana* die Merkurbüste mit den kleineren Büsten von Jupiter, Juno und Minerva verbunden ist.[13] Aufgrund der von der Büste herabhängenden Glocken vermutet man, daß die inklusive der Glocken 34 cm große Applik an einer Haustür angebracht war, um Böses abzuwenden.

Gerade im gallo-römischen Gebiet lassen sich eine Anzahl von ungewöhnlich großen Bronzebüsten aus Gerät- oder architektonischem Zusammenhang nachweisen. So z.B. die mit 40 cm

---

6 B. Barr-Sharrar, *The Hellenistic and Early Imperial decorative bust* (Mainz 1987).

7 Ibid. C 139, Taf. 42; *Master bronzes* 270, Nr. 26; H. G. Horn, "Dionysos und Ariadne: zwei Zierbeschläge aus dem Schiffsfund von Mahdia," in *Das Wrack* 1, 451-67.

8 Vgl. eine Victoria-Statuette aus Augst, die einen *Clipeus* hoch hält, vor dem eine Jupiterbüste befestigt ist: A. Kaufmann-Heinimann, *Die römischen Bronzen der Schweiz* 1: *Augst* (Mainz 1977) 73-75, Nr. 75, Taf. 77-83. Vgl. eine Bronzetafel mit einer Sol-Büste in London, British Museum: H. Jucker, *Das Bildnis im Blätterkelch* (Lausanne 1961) Abb. 84. Zur Anbringung von *imagines clipeatae* an Wänden, vgl. die Darstellungen auf römischen Wandmalereien des 2. Stils, z.B. in Oplontis: A. de Franciscis, *Die pompejanischen Wandmalereien in der Villa von Oplontis* (Recklinghausen 1975) Abb. 4, 11.

9 Jucker (s. o. Anm.8) 164-70, 216-17; ders., *MusHelv* 16 (1959) 275-77. Zur Interpretation des Blätterkelchs einschränkend: K. Schauenburg, "Zum Sarkophag der Avidia Agrippina," *JdI* 78 (1963) 294-317, bes. 302-9. Zu den gallischen Büsten mit 'Blätterkelchen,' s. a. S. Boucher, *Recherches sur les bronzes figurés de Gaule pré-romaine et romaine* (Rom 1976) 214-15.

10 Vgl., z.B.: a) Sammlung Belloris, ehemals Berlin: Jucker (s. o. Anm.8) Abb. 43; b) Paris, Cabinet des Médailles 363, Fundort angeblich Orange: Jucker (ibid.) Abb. 42; c) Enns, Museum ohne Inv., FO Enns: R. Fleischer, *Die römischen Bronzen aus Österreich* (Mainz 1967) 68, Nr. 71, Taf. 39.

11 Boucher (s. o. Anm.9) 214-15. Vgl. a) Büste einer Göttin mit Diadem, Dôle Museum, Fundort Choisey (Jura): Jucker (s. o. Anm.8) 204-5, Abb. 143-44; Boucher (s. o. Anm.9) Abb. 89; M. Gschaid, "Die römischen und die gallo-römischen Gottheiten in den Gebieten der Sequaner und Ambarrer," *JbRGZM* 41 (1994) 323 ff., 452, Taf. 96.2; b) Stadt-Genius Sammlung Gréau, Fundort Anse: Espérandieu IX 271, Nr. 7060; W. Fröhner, *Collection Julien Gréau: les bronzes antiques* (Paris 1885) 236, Nr. 1108, Taf. 43.

12 In Noricum treten auch Satyr- und Minervabüsten im Blätterkranz auf. Satyrbüsten im Blätterkelch: a) Burgenländisches Landesmuseum 5386, Fundort Deutschkreuz: Fleischer (s. o. Anm.10) 134, Nr. 178, Taf. 94; b) Tiroler Landesmuseum Ferdinandeum, Fundort Wilten (Tirol): Fleischer (s. o. Anm.10) 134-35, Nr. 179, Taf. 95. Minervabüsten: a) Museum Carnuntinum, Fundort Carnuntum: Fleischer (s. o. Anm.10) 44, Nr. 27, Taf. 23; b) Burgenländisches Landesmuseum 24,638, Fundort Winden am See: Fleischer (s. o. Anm.10) 45, Nr. 29, Taf. 24.

13 Jucker (s. o. Anm.8) 161, Abb. 42; H. Rolland, *Bronzes antiques de Haute Provence* (*Gallia* Suppl. 18, Paris 1965) Kat. 65.

lebensgroße Büste einer Stadtgöttin in Dôle, die ebenfalls den charakteristischen halbrunden Büstenausschnitt und den Blattkranz aufweist.[14] Aus Anse, im Rhonegebiet, stammt die 20 cm hohe Bronzeapplik eines Stadtgenius, dessen Büste von einem fächerförmigen Akanthusblatt gesäumt wird.[15] Der auf der Schulter zusammengehaltene Chiton zeigt die gleiche rosettenförmige Gewandnadel wie die Dea Roma aus Annecy.

Zwischen 19 und 23 cm messen drei zusammengehörige Bronzeappliken aus Vienne, die sich heute in Lyon befinden.[16] Die im Ausschnitt ebenfalls mit der Dea Roma vergleichbaren Büsten stellen Jupiter, Mars und Neptun dar. Den unteren Büstenabschluß säumt wiederum ein Kranz von lanzettförmigen Blättern. Während W. Froehner bei den aus der Sammlung Gréau stammenden Appliken zunächst vermutete, daß sie zu einer Dreifußbasis gehörten, wurden sie von S. Boucher überzeugender der Ausstattung eines Altars zugerechnet.[17]

Eine sehr enge, unmittelbare Parallele für die Büstenform und den Blattkranz der Dea Roma stellt eine mit 16 cm etwas kleinere Applik einer Vulkanbüste aus Sens, im Pariser Louvre dar.[18] Wie bei der Roma besteht der Blattkranz aus einem lappigen, nach außen gebogenen Mittelblatt sowie drei schmaleren lanzettförmigen Blättern, rechts und links davon. In gleicher Weise sitzt dieser Blätterkranz leicht aus der Mittelachse der Figur nach links verschoben. Obwohl dem Vulkan ein hellenistisches Vorbild zugrundeliegt und der Roma ein klassisches, lassen sich in Einzelheiten stilistische Gemeinsamkeiten erkennen, die zusätzlich zu den ikonographischen Übereinstimmungen für die Entstehung in derselben Werkstatt sprechen könnten. Beispielsweise ist das Haarvolumen in vergleichbarer Art angelegt. Größere zusammenhängende Locken liegen voluminös um den Kopf; sie werden nur an der Oberfläche durch flache Rillen in einzelne Haare gegliedert. Es trennen keine tiefen bis auf den Kopf heruntergeführten Furchen die einzelnen Strähnen ab. Wo diese Werkstatt angesiedelt gewesen sein könnte, ist bei nur zwei Stücken, die zudem von verhältnismäßig weit auseinanderliegenden Fundorten stammen, nicht zu entscheiden.

Da es sich bei der Roma um eine Applik handelt, kann die Form der Brustbüste mit dem Armansatz nicht ohne weiteres als Datierungskriterium herangezogen werden. Während dieser Büstenausschnitt bei freistehenden Porträtbüsten erst im Laufe des 2. Jhs. entsteht,[19] ist er bei Gerätappliken schon in Pompeji und Herculaneum nachweisbar.[20] Letztendlich ist dieser den Oberkörper einschließende Büstenausschnitt schon durch hellenistische dekorative Büsten vorgegeben.[21] Ein wesentlicher Unterschied zu den antoninischen Porträtbüsten besteht darin, daß die Arme an den Seiten nicht ausgearbeitet sind und auch die Schultern und der Rückenansatz fehlen. Ebensowenig kann die punktförmige Bohrung der Pupillen als Kriterium für die Datierung herangezogen werden, da diese sowohl bei Bronzen als auch in der Glyptik mindestens seit dem 1. Jh. v. Chr. geläufig ist.[22] Auch die klassizistische Merkurstatuette aus dem

---

14 S. o. Anm.11 a). Die Göttin trägt die gleiche stilisierte Mauerkrone einer Stadtgöttin, die auch einen provinziellen, aus Marmor gearbeiteten Göttinnenkopf aus Genf ziert, der als Genava oder Tutuela gedeutet wird. Genf, Museum C 1095, Fundort Genf im linken Seitenarm der Rhone: J. Chamay und J.-L. Maier, *Art romain: scultures en pierre du Musée de Genève* 2 (Mainz 1989) 49, Nr. 63, Taf. 68.

15 S. o. Anm.11 b)

16 Espérandieu IX 140-41, Nr. 6794; Fröhner (s. o. Anm.11) 14, Nr. 47, Taf. 1-3; S. Boucher und S. Tassinari, *Bronzes antiques du Musée de la civilisation gallo-romaine à Lyon* (Lyon 1976) 49, Nr. 40; 57, Nr. 44; 65, Nr. 55.

17 Boucher und Tassinari (s. o. Anm.16) 49.

18 Paris, Louvre 39, Fundort Sens: S. Boucher (s. o. Anm.9) Abb. 418; A. de Ridder, *Les bronzes antiques du Louvre* 1 (Paris 1913) 13, Nr. 39, Taf. 7.

19 Vgl. M. Wegner, *Hadrian* (Berlin 1956) 113-14, Taf. 19, 22, 26, 39, 40, 44.

20 Vgl. unter den zahlreichen Büsten aus Herculaneum und Pompeji beispielsweise Barr-Sharrar (s. o. Anm.6) C 147, Taf. 45.

21 Vgl. die Athena-Büste aus dem Schiffsfund von Mahdia: Barr-Sharrar (s. o. Anm.6) C 184, Taf. 56; ders., "Five decorative busts," in *Das Wrack* 1, 551-58.

22 Zu den Augenbohrungen bei Bronzeköpfen, s. jetzt G. Lahusen und E. Formigli, "Der Augustus von Mer-

Hortfund von Annecy, die ins 1. Jh. v. Chr. datiert wird, hat diese Pupillenbohrung.[23] Darüber hinaus zeigt die Roma aus Annecy nicht die auf eine starke Licht-Schattenwirkung angelegte Durchmodellierung des Haares, ebensowenig die tief in ihren Höhlen liegenden und von den Brauen überschatteten Augen, die man bei antoninischen Arbeiten erwarten würde.[24] Aufgrund des strengen Klassizismus der Romabüste, der verbunden ist mit einer unklassischen, schmalen Proportionierung des Gesichts, den eng beieinanderliegenden kleinen Augen und dem kleinen Mund, welcher an späthellenistische Gesichter wie beispielsweise das des Fechters Borghese[25] oder pasitelische Köpfe wie den des Stephanosathleten und den Orest in Neapel und im Louvre erinnert,[26] glaube ich, daß die Roma in frühaugusteischer Zeit entstanden sein könnte. Ich halte diese Datierung auch gerade deshalb für wahrscheinlich, weil sie aus historischer Sicht, bei einer Entstehung der Büste im gallo-römischen Raum, am meisten Sinn macht.

Die Dea Roma hat ihre wichtigste Bedeutung als Personifikation der Hauptstadt und des römischen Staates in den Provinzen des Imperium Romanum, wo sie dazu dient der imperialen Macht Gestalt zu verleihen.[27] Im Osten werden der Dea Roma bereits im frühen 2. Jh. v. Chr. Tempel erbaut.[28] Durch einen Erlaß Oktavians wird in den Provinzen im Jahre 29 v. Chr. offiziell der Kaiserkult mit dem der Dea Roma verbunden. In Ephesos und Nikaia entstehen für den Divus Iulius und die Dea Roma gemeinsame Tempel.[29] Die im Jahre 12 v. Chr. in Lugdunum für den Kaiserkult der Tres Galliae errichtete Ara Lugdunensis war der Roma und dem Augustus geweiht; das gleiche gilt höchstwahrscheinlich für die etwas später als zentraler Altar für Germanien errichtete Ara Ubiorum.[30] Zahlreiche municipale Altäre für Roma und Augustus im gesamten Bereich der nordwestlichen Provinzen folgten.[31] Unter anderem ist ein solcher Altar in unmittelbarer Nähe von Annecy, in Genf inschriftlich zu erschließen.[32] In hadrianischer Zeit änderte sich die Bedeutung der Roma. Durch den von Hadrian der Venus und Roma errichteten Doppeltempel wird sie erstmals in Rom selbst verehrt, damit ist sie nicht mehr allein Personifikation der Staatsmacht in den Provinzen, sondern wird zur eigenständigen Göttin erhoben.[33]

Die Ikonographie der Roma ist nicht einheitlich.[34] Sie wird entweder thronend in langem Chiton und Mantel dargestellt wie die Athena Polias[35] oder stehend in der Gestalt der kriegerischen Amazone mit dem kurzen Chiton, der eine Brust freiläßt,[36] daneben kommen auch Mischformen vor.[37] Sowohl der Athenatypus als auch der Amazonentypus sind bereits seit dem

---

oë und die Augen der römischen Bronzebildnisse," *AA* 1993, 655-74. Wenn die Augäpfel nicht in anderem Material eingelegt sind, werden bei Bronzeporträts immer die Iris graviert und die Pupille eingetieft.

23 Petit (s. o. Anm.4) 91, Abb. 32.

24 Vgl. M. Wegner, *Die Herrscherbildnisse in antoninischer Zeit* (Berlin 1939) Taf. 13, 15.

25 M. Bieber, *The sculpture of the Hellenistic age* (New York 1981) Abb. 33. Vgl. auch den späthellenistischen Alexanderkopf aus Kos in Istanbul: J. J. Pollitt, *Art in the Hellenistic age* (Cambridge 1986) 29, Abb. 16, oder die Gesichter der Söhne des Laokoon: ibid. 121, Abb. 124.

26 Bieber (s. o. Anm.25) Abb. 686, 688, 784, 786; Pollitt (s. o. Anm.25) 175-77, Abb. 183, 185, 186; P. Zanker, *Klassizistische Statuen* (Mainz 1974) 49-68, Taf. 42-56.

27 Roscher (s. o. Anm.1) 130-45; Mellor (s. o. Anm.1) 984-97, 998-1004.

28 Tac., *Ann.* 4.56; Roscher (s. o. Anm.1) 131-32; Mellor (s. o. Anm.1) 956, 958-60, 998; ders., *ΘΕΑ ΡΩΜΗ: The worship of the goddess Roma in the Greek world* (Göttingen 1975).

29 Cass. Dio 51.20; Tac., *Ann.* 4.37. Vgl. Roscher (s. o. Anm.1) 136; Mellor (s. o. Anm.1) 977-79.

30 Roscher (s. o. Anm.1) 139; Mellor (s. o. Anm.1) 987-88.

31 Mellor (s. o. Anm.1) 998-1002.

32 Für Genf ist ein *flamen Romae et Augusti* überliefert: *CIL* XII 2600; Roscher (s. o. Anm.1) 143.

33 Mellor (s. o. Anm.1) 1018-23.

34 Roscher (s. o. Anm.1) 145-61; G. Calza, "La figurazione di Roma nell'antica," *Dedalo* 7 (1926) 663-68; Mellor (s. o. Anm.1) 1011-17.

35 Roscher (s. o. Anm.1) 152-54; C. C. Vermeule, *The goddess Roma in the art of the Roman empire* (Cambridge, MA 1959) 104-5; Mellor (s. o. Anm.1) 1011-13.

36 Roscher (s. o. Anm.1) 145-46; Vermeule (s. o. Anm.35) 101-3; Mellor (s. o. Anm.1) 1013-15.

37 Roscher (s. o. Anm.1) 153-54; Vermeule (s. o. Anm.35) 103-6; Mellor (s. o. Anm.1) 1015-16.

2. Jh. v. Chr. in Griechenland überliefert.[38] Der häufigste aber nicht notwendigerweise früheste Typus ist derjenige der thronenden Stadtgöttin, wie ihn die Gemma Augustea[39] und auch noch das Kultbild im Venus und Roma-Tempel zeigen.[40] Auch der stehende Amazonentypus, zunächst noch ohne Helm, ist auf Münzen seit sullanischer Zeit belegt.[41] Auf den Prägungen unter Galba und den flavischen Kaisern erscheint Roma mit Helm, in kriegerisch kurzem Amazonengewand stehend, mit der Linken die Lanze aufstützend, auf der vorgestreckten Rechten eine Nike tragend. Über der linken Schulter liegt der Bausch eines Schultermantels.[42]

Die wenigen gesicherten Roma-Büstenappliken, die als Vergleich zu der Büste aus Annecy in Frage kämen, zeigen einen vollkommen anderen, an einem hellenistischen Vorbild ausgerichteten Typus. Ein Beispiel dieses Typus ist aus Annecy selbst erhalten.[43] Auf einem 14 cm großen Clipeus, der an einer schweren Bleifassung befestigt ist, sitzt die 12.6 cm hohe Protome, die die Dea Roma bis zur Taille mit entblößter rechter Brust und dem Mantelbausch auf der linken Schulter zeigt. Auf dem zur Seite gedrehten, deutlich erhobenen Kopf mit aufwärts gerichtetem Blick trägt sie den attischen Helm mit hohem Helmbusch. Sie zieht mit der Rechten das Schwert aus der in der Linken gehaltenen Scheide. Denselben Typus geben auch zwei der von B. Barr-Sharrar zusammengestellten Roma-Appliken wieder, mit dem Unterschied, daß diese diagonal über der Brust einen Schwertgurt tragen. Eine der Appliken, das 12 cm große Stück in Brescia, wird von Barr-Sharrar in augusteisch-frühtiberische Zeit datiert,[44] während sie die andere, die 14 cm große Büste im Pariser Cabinet des Médailles, in trajanisch-antoninische Zeit setzt.[45] In einer leichten Variation mit weniger stark gedrehtem Hals und zur rechten Seite gewendetem Kopf stellt eine zweite, nur 9.6 cm große Roma-Büste im Cabinet des Médailles diesen Typus dar.[46] Das Schwertband und den Schulterbausch sowie den nach rechts gedrehten Kopf tradieren auch zwei weitere kleine Roma-Büsten, von denen die eine aus Casteleone di Suasa stammt und sich in Baltimore befindet[47] und die andere unbekannter Herkunft im British Museum verwahrt wird.[48] Auch die Londoner Applik wird von Barr-Sharrar in augusteische Zeit datiert. Für eine stilistische Bewertung bzw. Datierung der großen Roma aus Annecy bieten die genannten Büsten keine Vergleichsmomente, zumal auch deren Datierungen nicht unbedingt als gesichert gelten dürfen.

Ein anderer Typus, ohne Arme, wird von einer Reihe kleiner Appliken überliefert, die ebenfalls den attischen Helm und den Gewandbausch auf der linken Schulter aufweisen, jedoch nicht die entblößte Brust.[49] Wahrscheinlich handelt es sich hier um Virtus–Darstellungen.[50]

---

38 Mellor (s. o. Anm.1) 1012. Im Fries des Hekataion von Stratonikeia erscheint eine amazonengestaltige Roma. Im Collegium der Poseidoniasten auf Delos ist eine Statue der Roma erhalten, die aus dem späten 2. Jh. v. Chr. stammt und einen stehenden Athenatypus wiederholt.

39 Roscher (s. o. Anm.1) 157 Abb. 18.

40 Vermeule (s. o. Anm.35) 107; Mellor (s. o. Anm.1) 1016-17.

41 Roscher (s. o. Anm.1) 146, Abb. 4.

42 Vermeule (s. o. Anm.35) Taf. V, 19-22.

43 Annecy, Musée 129, gefunden in Fins d'Annecy 1960/62 im Bereich der reichen Wohnhäuser, die sich an das nördliche Forum anschließen: Broise (s. o. Anm.2) 67, Abb. 29; 100, Nr. 126, 149; R. Chevallier, "Note sur un bronze d'Annecy," *Annesci* 21 (1978) 134-45.

44 Brescia, Museo Civico, Fundort Brescia: F. Braemer, *L'art dans l'occident romain: trésors d'argenteries: sculptures de bronze et de pierre* (Paris 1963) 42, Nr. 149 Taf. XIV; Barr-Sharrar (s. o. Anm.6) 81-82, C 192, 113, Taf. 59; C. Stella in B. M. Scarfi (Hrsg.), *Studi di archeologia della X Regio in ricordo di M. Tombolani* (Rom 1994) 414-15, Abb. 2.

45 Paris, Cabinet des Médailles 621: Barr-Sharrar (s. o. Anm.6) 83, C 198, 113, Taf. 61.

46 Paris, Cabinet des Médailles 139: Barr-Sharrar (s. o. Anm.6) 83, C 199, Taf. 61.

47 Baltimore, Walters Art Gallery 54.892: D. Kent Hill, in *Actes des IIIe journées internationales consacrées à l'étude des bronzes romains, 1974* (Brussels 1977) 161-62, Abb. 9; E. R. Knauer, "Bruckstück einer bronzenen Satteldecke in Bonn," *BJb* 192 (1992) 255, Abb. 14-15.

48 London, British Museum GR 1867.5-8.818: Barr-Sharrar (s. o. Anm.6) 82, C 193, Taf. 59.

49 Köln, Römisch-Germanisches Museum 2, Fundort unbekannt: N. Franken, "Die antiken Bronzen im Römisch-Germanischen Museum Köln: Fragmente von architektonischen Monumenten und Inschriften:

Einen Anhaltspunkt für die Datierung der Kölner Dea Roma liefert jedoch möglicherweise eine 33.1 cm große Bronzeapplik, die zusammen mit weiteren Appliken, die u.a. Togati aus einem Opferfries zeigen, wohl zu den Beschlägen eines Prunkwagens gehörte, und sich im J. Paul Getty Museum befindet.[51] Sie zeigt die Dea Roma in klassischem Standmotiv mit entlastetem linken Bein, mit der erhobenen Rechten die Lanze aufstützend und in der vorgestreckten Linken die Nike haltend. Die zugehörigen Togati erlauben anhand der Frisur und der Form der Toga eine Datierung der Appliken in die Zeit um 40-68 n. Chr. Die Roma-Applik im Getty Museum entspricht weitgehend dem Typus der Amazonen-Roma, den die flavischen Sesterzen zeigen, jedoch fehlt der über der Schulter liegende Mantelbausch. In diesem Detail stimmt sie mit der Kölner Roma aus Annecy überein, mit der sie auch die Form des Helms gemeinsam hat. Es ist also nicht auszuschließen, daß auch die Roma aus Annecy auf einen klassizistischen Typus zurückgeht, der älter ist als derjenige, den die flavischen Münzen wiedergeben.

Faßt man die vorgestellten Überlegungen zur Roma-Büste aus Annecy zusammen, so läßt sich festhalten, daß es gut vorstellbar ist, daß sie zu einem der in augusteischer Zeit in den nordwestlichen Provinzen errichteten Monumente für den Kult des Augustus und der Dea Roma gehörte und beispielsweise an einem dem Kaiserkult geweihten municipalen Altar auf einem der Fora von Butae angebracht war.

Römisch-Germanisches Museum, Köln

Hausausstattung, Möbel, Kultgeräte, Votive, und verschiedene Geräte," *KölnJb* 29 (1996) 7-203, hier 27-29, Abb. 23-25.

50 Vgl. Vermeule (s. o. Anm.35) 40-41, 105-6, 108-12; Mellor (s. o. Anm.1) 1014-15.

51 Los Angeles, The J. Paul Getty Museum 84.AB.671, Fundort unbekannt: *The gods delight* 333-36, Nr. 64 (J. J. Herrmann, Jr.); *Small bronze sculpture* 36.

The goddess on the shield-boss from Bonn

Hans-Hoyer von Prittwitz und Gaffron

The numerous bronze medallions found in the northern provinces of the Roman empire have been termed, because of their round or oval form and their size, bosses from parade shields. Some of these medallions or roundels have indeed been found in military bases; they depict Minerva, Hercules, or Ganymede. Shield-bosses in J. Garbsch's catalogue *Römische Paraderüstungen* include an example from the Rheinisches Landesmuseum Bonn (figs. 1-3).[1] It was found in 1873 in the northern part of Bonn where a Roman cemetery of the 2nd and 3rd c. A.D. is located. Subsequently, in his catalogue of Roman bronzes in Bonn, H. Menzel included the medallion with other military objects and described it as a shield-boss[2]; he regards the female bust as the goddess Ceres and dates it to the early 3rd c. Shortly thereafter, H. G. Horn identified the bust as the empress Julia Domna, establishing its date as *c.*195.[3]

The roundel is a thin bronze disc with a diameter of 26.7 cm. It is embossed with a central female bust flanked by two erotes standing next to baskets of grapes, rendered in low relief. Both figures stand on a ledge above the bust's shoulders, holding a garland over her head. The

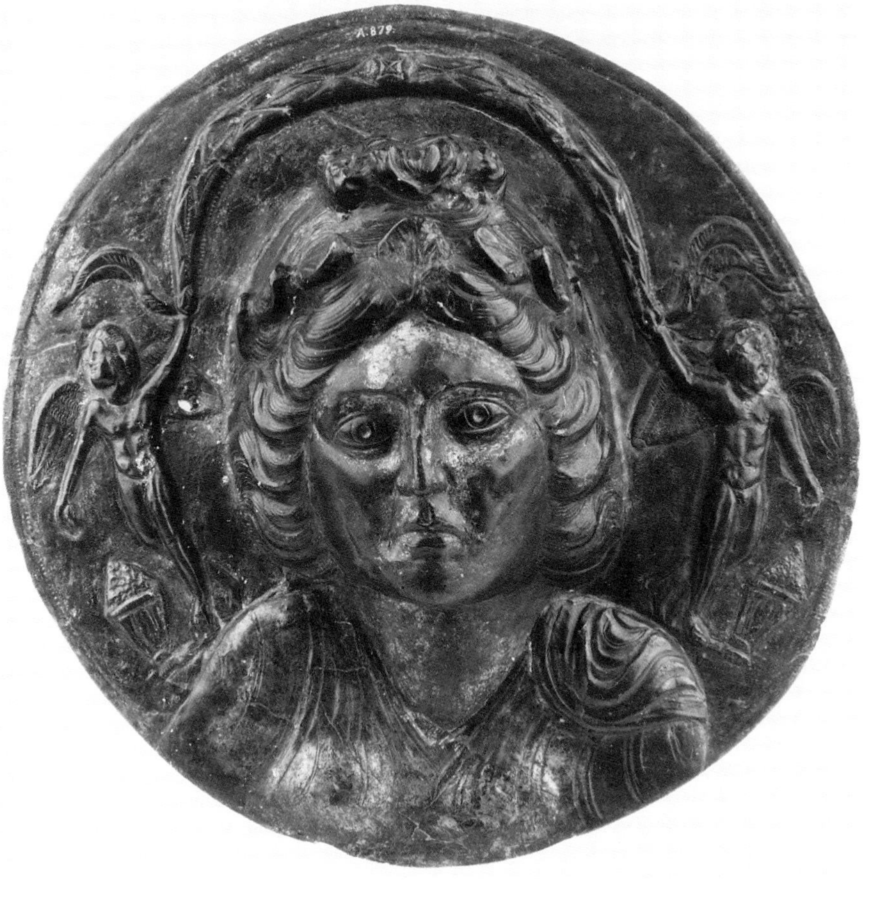

Fig. 1. Roundel, excavated at Bonn, *c.*A.D. 200-225. Bronze, diam. 26.7 cm. Bonn, Rheinisches Landesmuseum A 879. (Photo: H. Lilienthal; courtesy Museum)

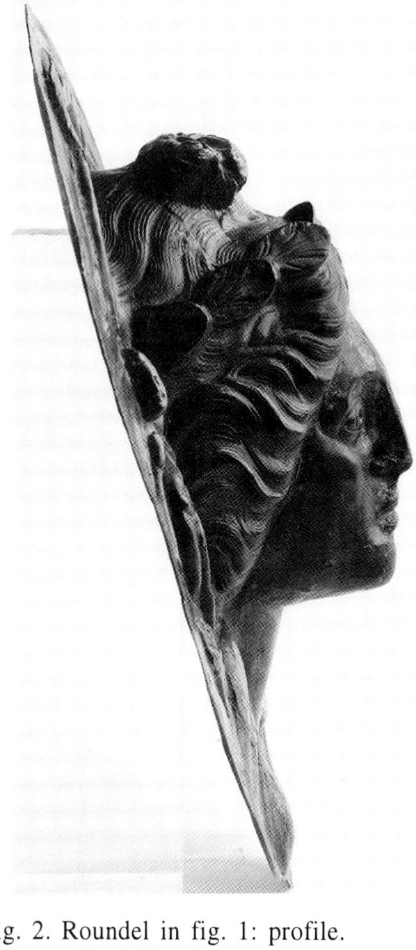

Fig. 2. Roundel in fig. 1: profile. (Photo: H. Lilienthal; courtesy Museum)

1 J. Garbsch, *Römische Paraderüstungen* (Munich 1978) 84, no. 8, pl. 42.

2 H. Menzel, *Die römischen Bronzen aus Deutschland* 3: *Bonn* (Mainz 1986) 81, no. 201, pls. 90-93.

3 H. G. Horn (ed.), *Die Römer in Nordrhein-Westfalen* (Stuttgart 1987) 267, fig. 220.

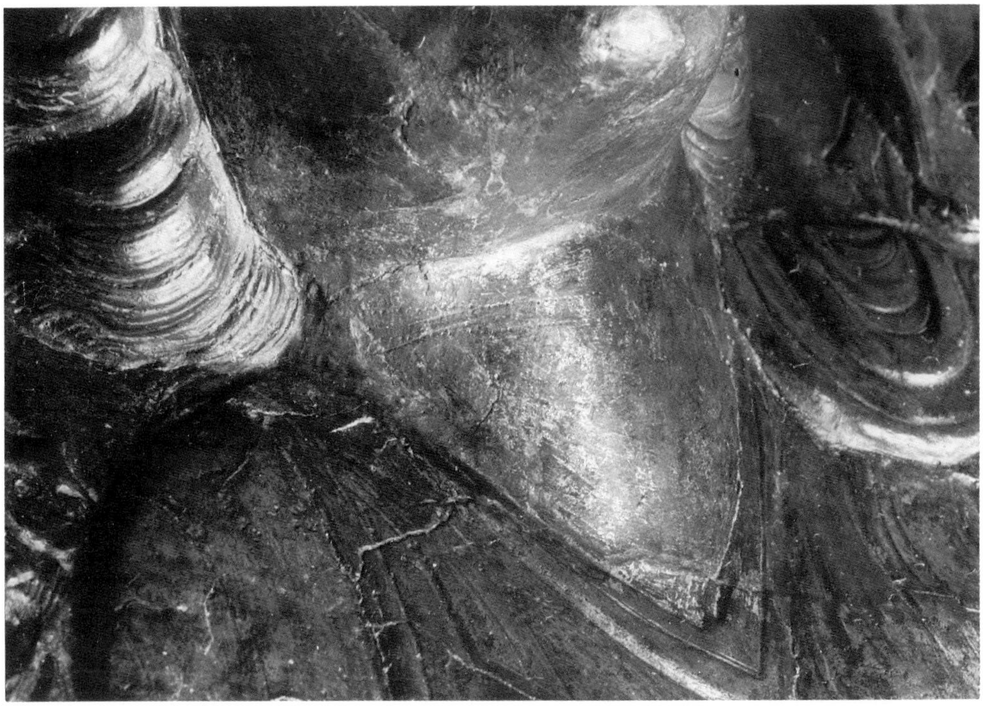

Fig. 3. Roundel in fig. 1: close-up of double-strand necklace. (Photo: H. Lilienthal; courtesy Museum)

woman wears a *tunica*; the end of her *palla* falls over her left shoulder. Her hair, drawn up with care to a *krobylos*, is fashioned in the style of the Severan period and decorated with a silver-plated wreath of leaves. Her face and neck, as well as the flat background of the roundel, are also silver-plated. Examination of the silver plating by U. Sobottka-Braun, at the Rheinisches Landesmuseum Bonn, revealed a double row of very fine indentations around the neck of the bust, indicating a double-strand necklace with a large pendant in the middle and two smaller ones on each side (fig. 3).[4]

The subject represented on the roundel differs greatly from those on other shield bosses. Unlike their motifs of Minerva or Hercules, the Bonn roundel does not relate to military themes. Instead, the woman with her wreath of leaves, rich necklace, and the erotes with their baskets of fruits, suggesting seasons of the year, refers to a more peaceful context.

Other technical details confirm a distinction between this roundel and bosses on parade-shields, such as its larger diameter (22 cm) compared to that of shield bosses, and the unusual attachment-hole next to the head,[5] in contrast to shield bosses which were nailed around the rim. One would also have to find an explanation for the deposit of a weapon in a grave.

A considerably older medallion of clay, from the collection at the University of Leipzig, provides a remarkable comparison for the roundel from Bonn, in its size as well as its theme (fig. 4).[6] The tondo, which dates to the 4th c. B.C., displays a female bust wearing earrings in the form of two erotes and with two winged erotes standing next to candelabra. H. Herdejürgen has shown that such tondi of clay are from graves in Tarentum or Campania.[7] Identification of the woman, whether as Aphrodite, a human bride, or a companion of death, is difficult.[8]

Despite their great difference in date, the busts from Bonn and Leipzig share one important feature: their sepulchral character. The funerary character of the roundel from Bonn finds confirmation in the scene from the lid of the Achilles sarcophagus in Paris, which is dated some-

4 I am grateful to U. Sobottka-Braun for undertaking this examination.
5 On the X-ray picture the quadrangular shape can be seen.
6 *50 Meisterwerke: Antikenmuseum Universität Leipzig* (Leipzig 1994) 25, no. 50.
7 H. Herdejürgen, *Tarentinische Terrakotten der Sammlung Schwitter* (*AntK* 16, 1973) 105, no. 95, pl. 23.
8 Herdejürgen (ibid.) 106 n.26.

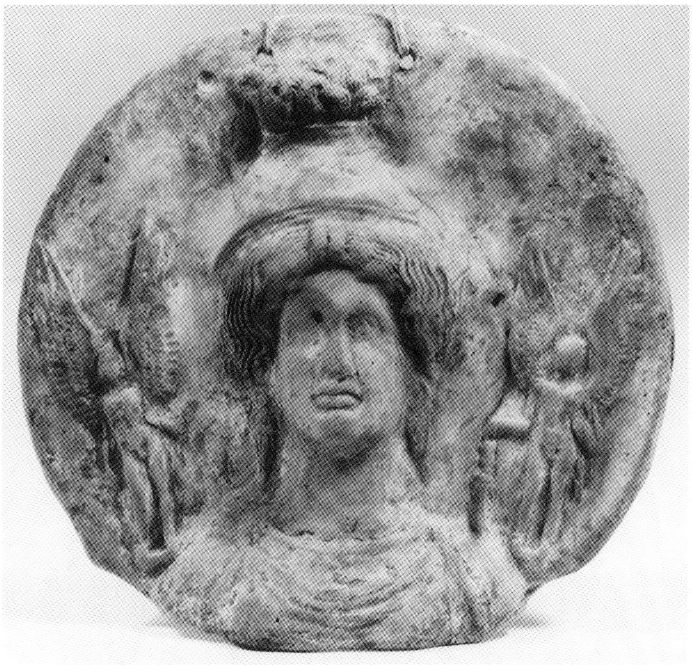

Fig. 4. Roundel, 4th c. B.C. Terracotta, diam. 22.5 cm. Leipzig, Antikenmuseum der Universität T 3157. (Photo: K. Kranich; courtesy Museum)

what later.[9] Here the individual motifs of the tondi from Bonn and Leipzig appear in the same scene: two erotes beside a *thymiaterion* (incense burner), holding a garland over the heads of a deceased couple.

How is the discrepancy of six centuries between the roundel in Bonn and that in Leipzig to be explained? Are there links between them that extend beyond form or motif? Can we consider a continuity of some kind? An answer of yes or no is not possible. Large medallions representing deities date as early as the 4th c. B.C. The above-mentioned clay roundels from Campania are among the oldest. The form of a roundel with a bust in relief was used repeatedly throughout the subsequent periods. Thus, the Bonn roundel stands more or less at the end of a long tradition.

Another special feature of the Bonn roundel is the hairstyle, which is very typical for the period in which it was made. There are some analogies for it, for example on the well-preserved figure of a half-nude Aphrodite in the Ludwig collection, found in a sepulchral context, perhaps in Asia Minor, that displays a hairstyle of the middle of the 3rd c. A.D.[10] The naturalistic rendering of the head stands out in contrast to the schematic modeling of the body. This discrepancy is noticeable on the bust from Bonn as well.

From the middle of the 2nd c. A.D., heads of deities having a likeness to portraits were made.[11] E. Berger interprets this phenomenon as an assimilation of the goddess to the deceased; H. Wrede suggests, in contrast, that the representation of a goddess with a contemporary hairstyle is an attempt to create an up-to-date effigy of a deity.[12] The small size of the Aphrodite's head in the Ludwig collection makes a decision impossible; it could just as well be a portrait of the deceased, modified to incorporate well-known features of Aphrodite.[13]

Interpretation of the symbolism of the roundel in Bonn is equally inconclusive: we have here either a curiously restrained characterization of a deity or, more probably, an image of the deceased. Although many details of the roundel in Bonn can be explained, the depiction of erotes on the shoulders is without parallel in Roman times,[14] and in this respect the roundel remains unique.

Rheinisches Landesmuseum, Colmantstr. 14-16, D-53115 Bonn

Acknowledgements

For translation I would like to express my sincere thanks to E. Schalk; M. Carroll-Spillecke has kindly provided help concerning archaeological terminology.

---

9 Paris, Louvre 3570 (Ma 655): P. Kranz, *Jahreszeiten-Sarkophage* (*ASR* 5.4, Berlin 1984) 252, no. 363, pls. 103.1 and 3.

10 E. Berger and R. Lullies, *Antike Kunstwerke aus der Sammlung Ludwig* 2: *Terrakotten und Bronzen* (Antikenmuseum Basel Veröffentlichungen 4, 1982) 194-203, no. 214.

11 H. Wrede, *Consecratio in formam deorum* (Mainz 1981) 133.

12 Ibid. 185.

13 Ibid. 184-85.

14 Although the motif of the closest relief in Rome (F. Sinn, Museo *Gregoriano Profano ex Lateranense: Katalog der Skulpturen* 1: *Reliefs, Altäre, Urnen* [Berlin 1991] 41, no. 16, figs. 43-45) shows two Erotes floating toward the shoulders of a deceased person, it has a completely different theme.

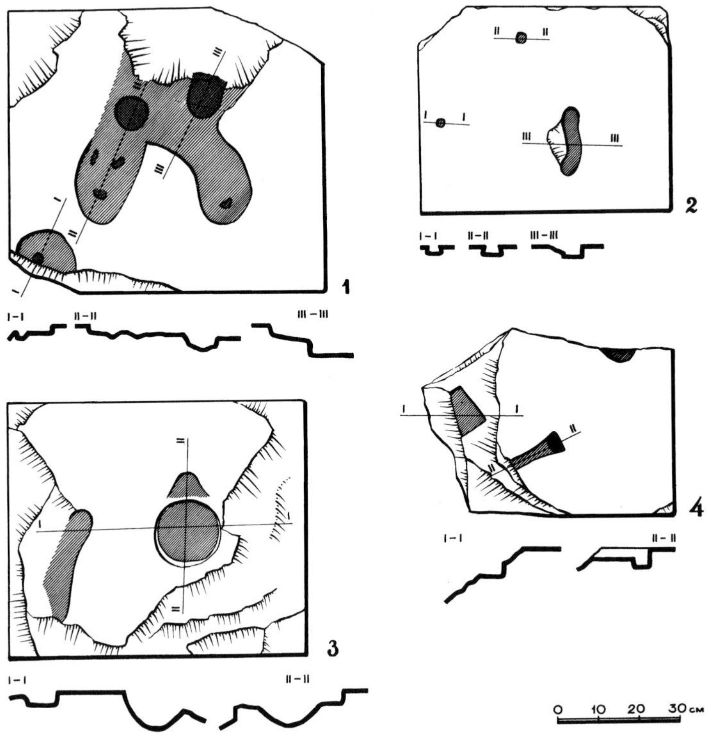

Figs. 1a (above) and 1b (below). Stone bases for bronze statues from **Leuke**: *IPE* I^2 326 - fig. 1a1; **Tyras**, excavated 1987, unpubl. – fig. 1a4; **Olbia**: *IPE* I^2 25+31 – fig. 1a3; O-81, R-19/720 – fig. 1b1; O-81, R-19/723 – fig. 1b2; O-81, R-19/719 – fig. 1b3; O-81, R-19/721 – fig. 1b4; O-81, R-19/722 – fig. 1b5; and **Neapolis**: *IPE* I^2 670 – fig. 1a2. (Drawings: author)

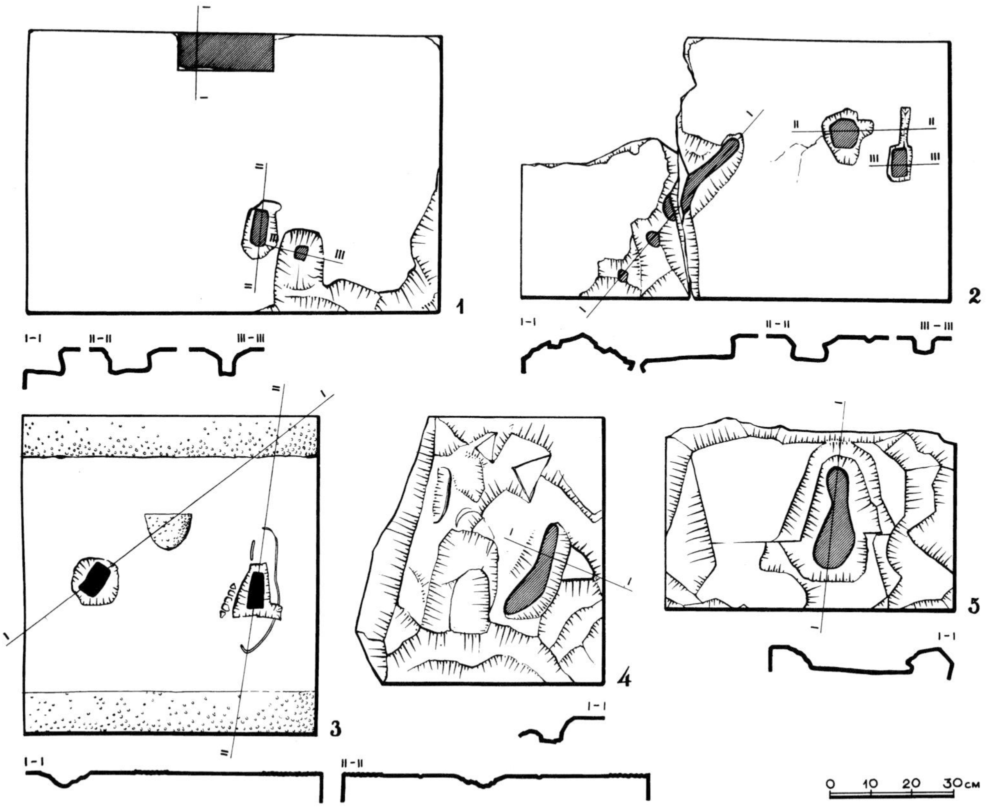

Large-scale bronzes and their installation in the North Pontic area

Mikhail Yu. Treister

Since this subject was introduced at the 9th Congress in 1986,[1] remains of life-size bronze sculpture have been unearthed in 6th-c. B.C. contexts on the island of Berezan, and the list of large-scale bronze fragments should be augmented with a piece in the Archaeological Museum, Odessa. There is now archaeological evidence of the existence of large-scale bronze sculptures in the North Pontic area during the period soon after the cities of Berezan, Olbia, and Phanagoria were established, and for the Hellenistic period (Panticapaeum, Olbia, and Scythian Neapolis).

In 1986 I compiled a list of 43 statue bases from the North Pontic area with sockets for attaching the feet of bronze sculptures (the so-called "Zapfentechnik," or dowel method, which spread throughout the Greek world after *c*.500 B.C.[2]) and I discussed their chronological and geographical distribution as well as the problems of what kinds of statues were set up and who were the sculptors. The list has been augmented (including new finds) and corrected, and it now includes 50 bases dating from the 4th c. B.C. through the 3rd c. A.D. from the island of Leuke (2 pieces), and from Tyras (1), Olbia (12), Scythian Neapolis (5), Chersonesos (11), Nymphaeum (2), Panticapaeum (12), Phanagoria (2), Hermonassa (2), and Gorgippia (1). In general, the bases were made for free-standing sculptures of deities or private persons or for equestrian statues.

The first group of bases, for free-standing figures, can be subdivided into three Types according to the number of sockets for the feet and their positions:

Bases that belong to **Type 1** are characterized by complete sockets for both feet. The sculptures that were installed on them stood firmly on both feet. They may have additional holes to support attributes. At least 12 bases belong to this type.

Type 1a comprises bases without additional sockets for attributes. At least 8 bases belong to this type. They have been found at Chersonesos (fig. 2b.2: *c*.107 B.C., *IPE* I² 422[3]; fig. 2b.3: mid 2nd c. A.D.), Neapolis,[4] Panticapaeum[5] (fig. 3b.2: second half of the 4th c. B.C.), Phanagoria (fig. 3a.1: 304-284 B.C.), and Hermonassa (fig. 3b.3: second quarter of the 4th c. B.C.). The right foot was usually advanced, at an angle to the front of the base, while the left foot remained slightly turned. Only the base on fig. 2b.3 has the socket for the left foot advanced.

Type 1b includes bases with additional sockets for attributes. Three bases came from Leuke (fig. 1a.1), Olbia (fig. 2a.2), and Panticapaeum[6] and are dated to the 4th c. B.C. On the bases from Olbia and Panticapaeum, the additional holes are in the front right edge of the base, while on the base from Leuke it is in the front left. On the base from Leuke there are additional

---

1 M. Yu. Treister, "Bronze statuary in the antique towns of North Pontic area," in K. Gschwantler and A. Bernhard-Walcher (edd.), *Griechische und römische Statuetten und Großbronzen: Akten der 9. int. Tagung über antiken Bronzen, Wien 1986* (Vienna 1988) 152-57. See also M. Yu. Treister, "Materials for the corpus of the bases of bronze statues of North Pontic area," in M. Zolotarev (ed.), *Khersonesskij Sbornik* 10 (Sevastopol 1999) 121-58 [in Russian].
Treister 1988 (supra n.1) 152-57.

2 See Treister 1988 (supra n.1) 152-57 n.13; K. Kissas, *Die statuarischen Basen der archaïschen Zeit in Attika* (Diss., Univ. Salzburg 1986) 13, 246 n.68.

3 Treister 1988 (supra n.1) fig. 6d: A.D. 89/90-92/93.

4 V. Latyshev (ed.), *Inscriptiones antiquae orae septentrionalis Ponti Euxini* (Petropoli 1890-1916) (hereafter *IPE)* I² 671: 2nd c. B.C.

5 Treister 1988 (supra n.1) fig. 5c.

6 Ibid. fig. 5a.

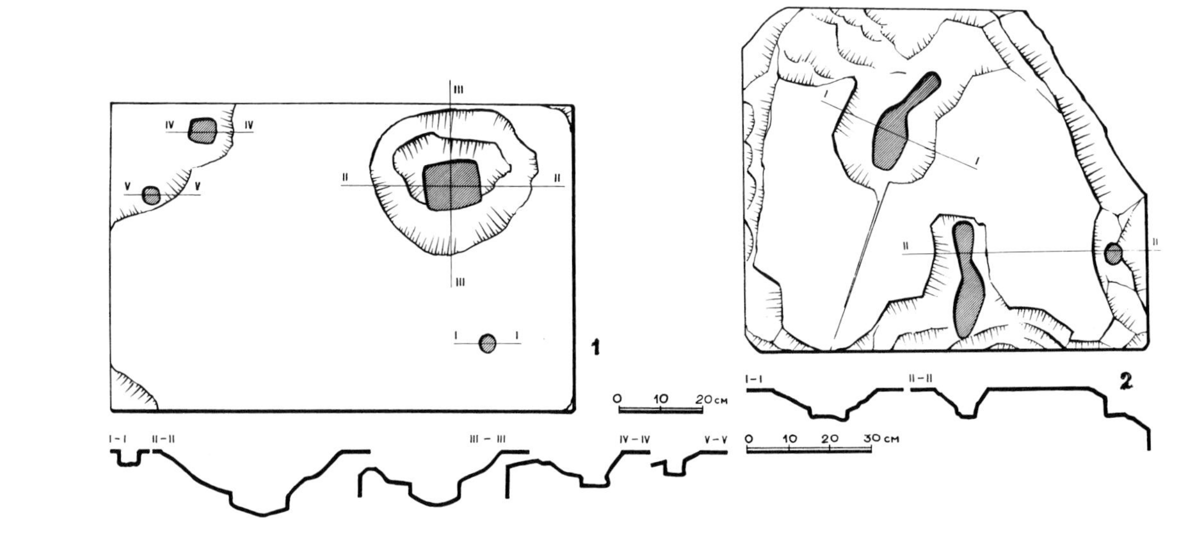

Figs. 2a (above) and 2b (below). Stone bases for bronze statues from **Olbia**: *IO* 65 – fig. 2a2; **Chersonesos**: *IPE* I² 418 – fig. 2a1; *IPE* I² 424 – fig. 2b1; *IPE* I² 406 – fig. 2b2; *IPE* I² 423 – fig. 2b3; *IPE* I² 415 – fig. 2b4; *IPE* I² 410 – fig. 2b5; NW quarter, unpubl. – fig. 2b6. (Drawings: author)

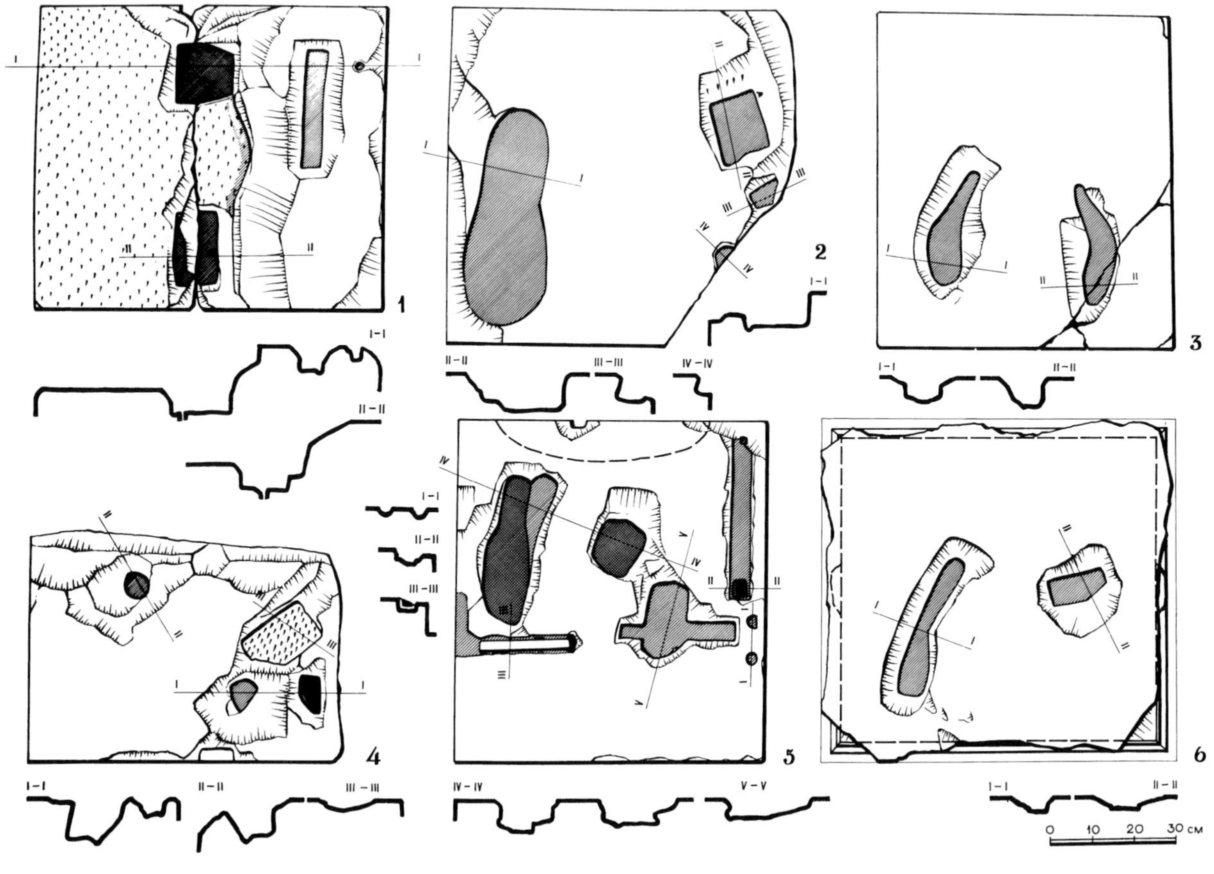

sockets for toes and heels. The positions of the sockets for feet vary on all the bases. A unique variant of Type 1b is represented by the base from Panticapaeum (fig. 3a.2: second half of the 4th c. B.C.), with the complete socket for the left foot and separate sockets for the toe and heel of the right foot.

Bases of **Type 2** are characterized by a complete socket for the right foot and a socket for the front of the left foot of various shapes. There may be additional holes for attributes. Eleven bases are subdivided into three groups. Statues installed on these bases stood with the weight on the right foot, while the left rested on the ball of the foot or on the toe. In comparison with bases of Type 1, more of these date to the 1st c. A.D.

Bases of **Type 2a** have no additional holes for attributes. Four examples come from Olbia (fig. 1a.3: *c*.330-320 B.C.; fig. 1b.1: late 3rd c. B.C.), Chersonesos[7] (fig. 2b.6), and Panticapaeum.[8]

Type 2b includes similar bases with additional holes for attributes. Five bases come from Olbia (fig. 1b.2: 2nd c. B.C.), Neapolis,[9] Chersonesos (figs. 2b.2 and 2b.5: 4th c. B.C.), and Panticapaeum (figs. 3b.4; 4.1,3: A.D. 250).

Type 2c is represented by a single base from Olbia.[10] It has a complete socket for the right foot and a 4-part socket for the left foot.

Bases of **Type 3** are characterized by a complete socket for the left foot and a socket for the front of the right foot of various shapes. They may have additional holes for attributes. Statues installed on these bases stood with the weight on the left foot, while the right rested on the ball of the foot. This type of base was less widespread than the first two. Only three bases definitely belong to this type.

Type 3 includes one base each from Neapolis (fig. 1a.2: 2nd c. B.C.), Olbia (figs. 1b.3; 4.4,6: 2nd c. B.C.), and Panticapaeum (figs. 3b.1; 4.2: A.D. 14-37). The characteristic feature of the two latter bases is the use of anathyrosis on the upper surface. The base from Olbia is also peculiar for its treatment of the socket for the foot; the contour is marked on the surface, in the center of which there is a trapezoidal socket with the remains of lead (fig. 4.6). The small rectangular socket probably served for attaching the toe, while the heel was probably supported by a semicircular projection of the upper part of the base (fig. 4.4).

It seems that the earliest bases for bronze statues using the "Zapfentechnik" had separate sockets for the toes and heels of each foot, like the bases from Olympia dated to the second half of the 5th c. B.C.[11] In Olympia, complete sockets for feet appeared in the second quarter of the 5th c., e.g., on the base of a group of statues dedicated by Mikythos and cast by the Argive founder Glaukos,[12] although on the same base there are feet which have separate cuttings for heels and toes. Complete sockets on bases from Olympia are also attested in the last quarter of the 5th to the first half of the 4th c.[13] Thus, by the time of the earliest known bases for bronze statues, the "Zapfentechnik" had already had a rather long development. It seems that during the 5th c. B.C. Types 1a, 1b, 2a, and 3, the most typical North Pontic sockets on bases, already existed. The combination of sockets characteristic for bases of Types 1a, 1b, and 3 are represented on the bases dedicated by Mikythos.[14] Bases of Types 1a, 1b, and 2a existed in Lindos *c*.400 B.C.[15] There, Types 1a and 2a are especially characteristic of the 4th[16] and 3rd c.,[17] although they continued into the 2nd and one is also attested at each of Delphi,[19] Eretria (2nd c. B.C.),[20]

---

7 Ibid. fig. 6c: A.D. 74/5-78/9.

8 Ibid. fig. 5d: A.D. 221.

9 Ibid. fig. 6a: 2nd c. B.C.

10 *IPE* I^2 188: first half of the 3rd c. B.C.

11 W. Dittenberger and K. Purgold, *Die Inschriften von Olympia* (Berlin 1896) nos. 146-48.

12 F. Eckstein. *ΑΝΑΘΗΜΑΤΑ · Studien zu den Weihgeschenken strengen Stils im Heiligtum von Olympia* (Berlin 1969) 33 ff., fig. 6: bases A, C.

13 Dittenberger and Purgold (supra n.11) nos. 155, 158-59, 164-65.

14 Eckstein (supra n.12) no. 4, figs. 5-7.

15 C. Blinkenberg, *Lindos: fouilles de l'acropole 1902-1914*, II: *Inscriptions* (Berlin 1941) nos. 27, 31, 18.

16 Ibid. nos. 29, 41, 43, 47, 52, 56, 60, 62.

17 Ibid. nos. 73a-b, 74, 78, 110, 113, 127, 133, 142a.

18 Ibid. nos. 164, 344, 383b.

19 E. Bourguet. *Inscriptions de l'entrée du sanctuaire au Trésor des Athéniens* (Fouilles de Delphes III.1, Paris 1929) nos. 63, 67, 70 ff.

20 P. Ducrey, I. R. Metzger, and K. Reber, *Le quartier de la Maison aux mosaiques* (Eretria VIII, Lausanne 1993) 176 f., figs. 293-95.

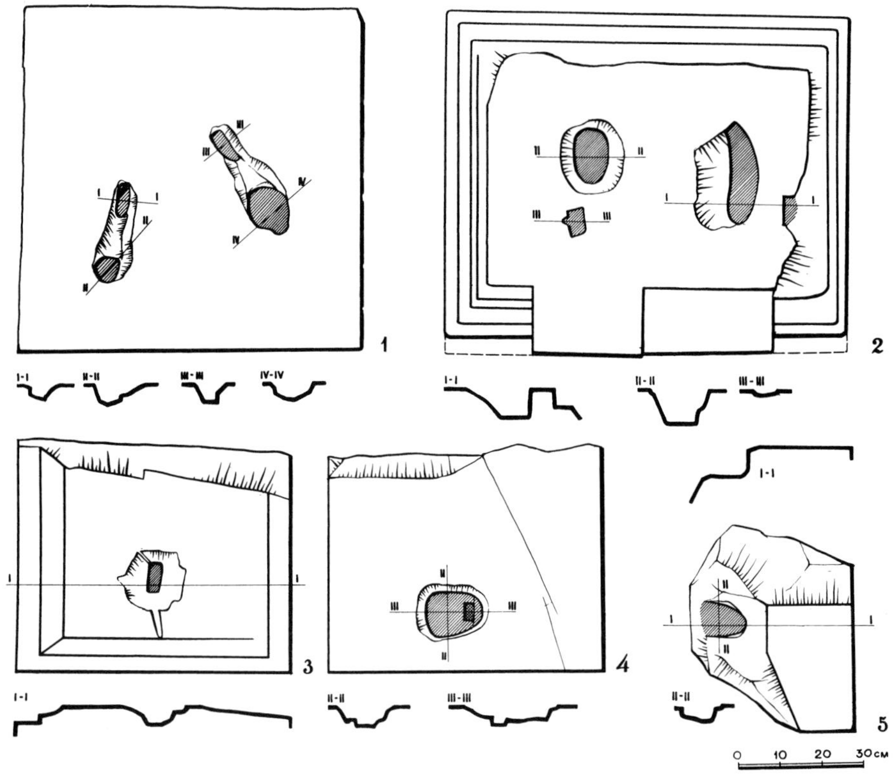

Figs. 3a (above) and 3b (below). Stone bases for bronze statues from **Nymphaeum**: *Tskhaltubo* III, 595 ff. – fig. 3a5; **Panticapaeum**: *CIRB* 9 – fig. 3a2; unpubl. – fig. 3a3 and fig. 3a4; *CIRB* 40 – fig. 3b1; *CIRB* 10 – fig. 3b2; *CIRB* 59 – fig. 3b4; **Phanagoria**: *CIRB* 974 – fig. 3a1; and **Hermonassa**: *CIRB* 1037 – fig. 3b3. (Drawings: author)

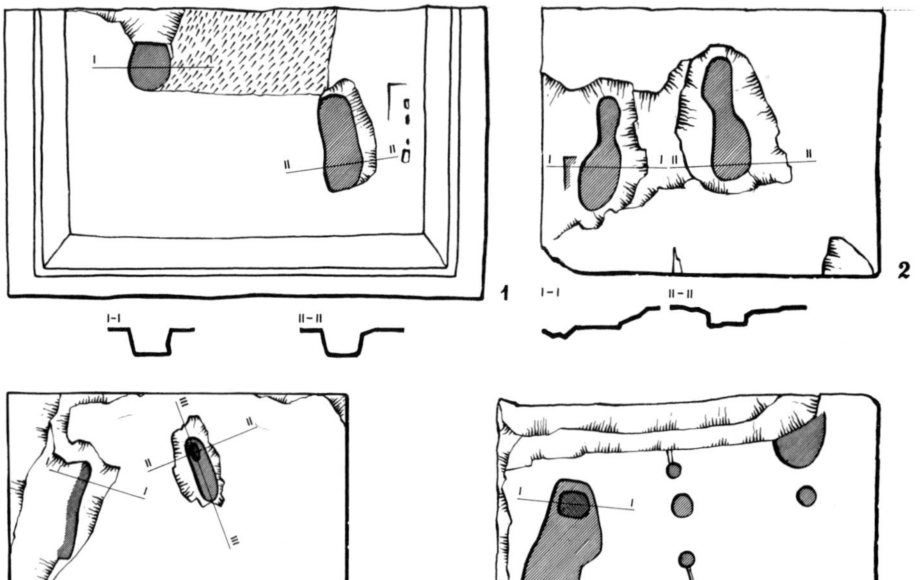

Pergamon (3rd-2nd c. B.C.),[21] and Priene (2nd c. B.C.).[22] In contrast, bases of Type 2a in Lindos are well attested for the 4th c. B.C.[23] but unknown in the 3rd c., when bases of Type 2b spread,[24] but re-appear in the 2nd c. B.C. and later.[25]

Bases of Type 1b were evidently less popular, to judge from finds in both the North Pontic area and in the Mediterranean. On 3rd-c. B.C. bases from Lindos, an additional hole was made behind the right foot socket or to the right of it,[26] while the single example of the 1st c. B.C. has the additional hole in the right rear edge[27]. Similar to the 3rd c. B.C. bases from Lindos is the base of the Lacedemonians and the kings of Argos from Delphi.[28] However, on the 3rd-c. B.C. bases from Pergamon, the additional hole is made to the left of the socket for the left foot.[29] Two of the bases of this type served for statues of Apollo Ietros, including the one from Olbia with the signature of Stratonides of Athens.[30] Of special interest, therefore, is a very similar base from the West Pontic site of Histria, also for a statue of Apollo Ietros, dedicated by Theoxenos, son of Hippolochos, of approximately the same date. The problems of the proximity of both sculptures and their reconstructions have been debated for a long time.[31]

There are parallels to the quadrate sockets on the bases, like that on the base of Type 2c. However, the mid 3rd-c. B.C. base of Type 1 from Lindos[32] has an additional socket in the left rear corner of the upper surface. Another variant, with an additional rectangular socket, exists on a base from Lindos dated to the late 2nd c. B.C.[33]

Although bases of Type 3 were already known in the Early Classical period,[34] they occur rarely and are known in the Eastern Mediterranean in the 2nd and 1st c. B.C. in Lindos[35] and in Priene.[36] This corresponds well to the chronology of such statue bases in the North Pontic area. Anathyrosis, attested on the bases from Olbia and Panticapaeum, was also used on a base of the same type from Lindos dating to *c.*25 B.C. [37]

In some cases, the foot sockets have additional holes inside for heels and toes, as on bases from Leuke (fig. 1a1), Neapolis,[38] Phanagoria (fig. 3a1), Panticapaeum (fig. 3b4; 4.1,3),[39] and Hermonassa (fig. 3b3). There are chronological or geographical regularities in the distribution of this feature. Similar construction of the foot socket is known on bases from Kos of the Augustan period[40] and from Balboura in A.D. 158-161.[41]

---

21 M. Fränkel, *Die Inschriften von Pergamon* (AvP VIII.1, Berlin 1890) nos. 138, 164.

22 F. Hiller von Gaertringen, *Inschriften von Priene* (Berlin 1906) no. 237.

23 Blinkenberg (supra n.15) nos. 33, 45, 54, 57a, 64.

24 Ibid. nos. 83, 109.

25 Ibid. nos. 153, 172, 414.

26 Ibid. nos. 68, 101, 109.

27 Ibid. no. 308.

28 Bourguet (supra n.19) I, 37; VIII, no. 64; I, 43, fig. 21.

29 Fränkel (supra n.21) nos. 4, 137.

30 T. N. Knipovich and E. I. Levi (edd.), *Inscriptiones Olbiae (1917-1965)* (Leningrad 1968) (hereafter *IO*) no. 65.

31 See, e.g., M. Alexandrescu Vianu, "Die Steinskulptur von Histria," in P. Alexandrescu and W. Schuller (edd.), *Histria: eine Griechenstadt an der rumänischen Schwarzmeerküste* (*Xenia* 25, 1990) 185 ff., fig. 3.

32 Blinkenberg (supra n.15) no. 100.

33 Ibid. no. 250.

34 See above.

35 Blinkenberg (supra n.15) nos. 155, 350.

36 Hiller von Gaertringen (supra n.22) no. 186.

37 Blinkenberg (supra n.15) no. 403.

38 Treister 1988 (supra n.1) fig.6a.

39 Ibid. fig. 5c.

40 K. Höghammar, *Sculpture and society: a study of the connection between the free-standing sculpture and society on Kos in the Hellenistic and Augustan periods* (*Boreas* 23, 1993) no. 53, fig. 19; no. 54, fig. 21.

41 J. J. Coulton, N. P. Milner, and A. T. Reyes, "Balboura survey: Onesimos and Meleager II," *AnatSt* 39

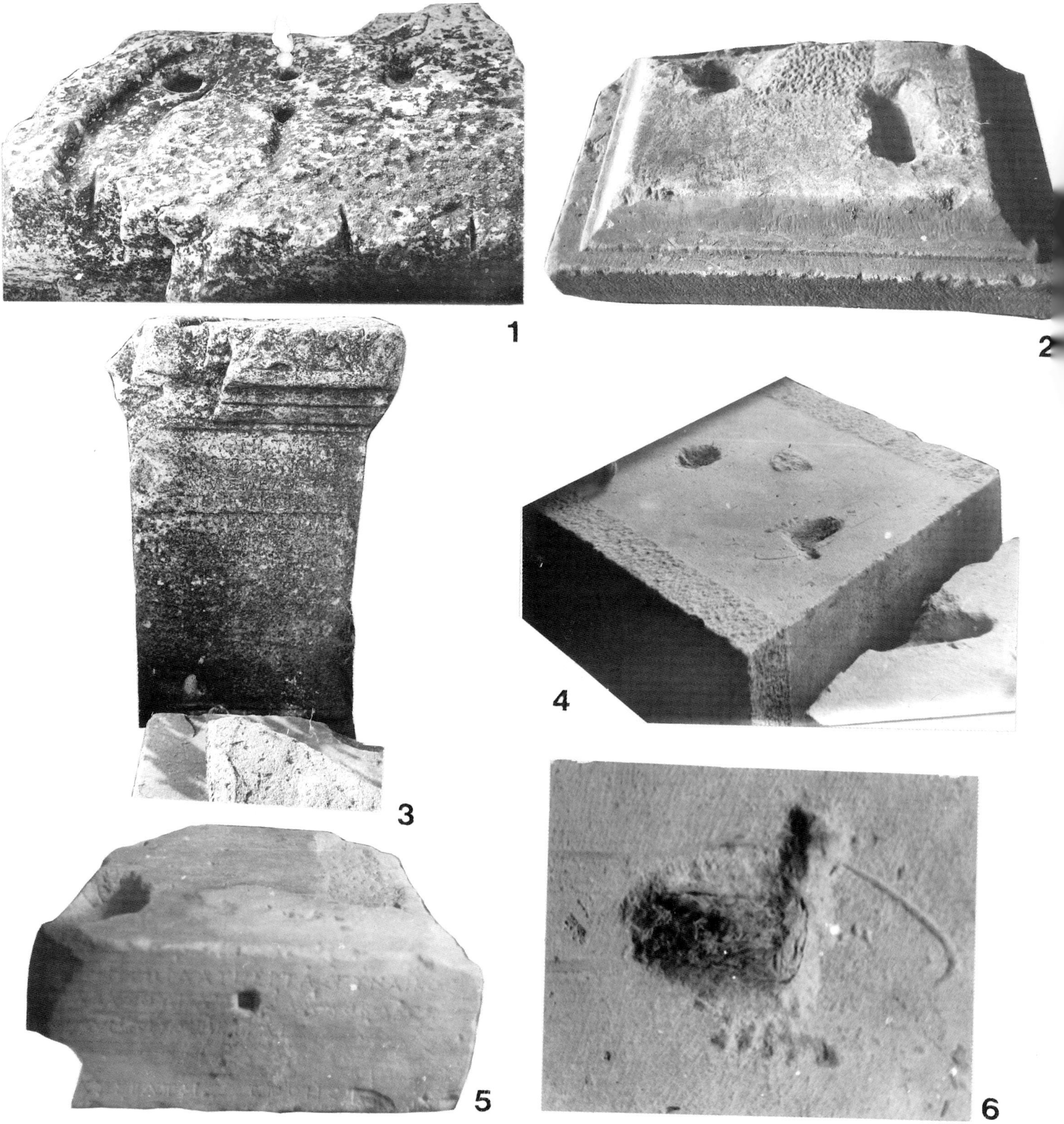

Fig. 4. Stone bases for bronze statues from **Panticapaeum**: *CIRB* 59 – fig. 4.1 top and 3 front; *CIRB* 40 – fig. 4.2; **Olbia**: O-81, R-19/719 – fig. 4.4 top and fig. 4.6 detail; **Chersonesos**: *IPE* I^2 406 – fig. 4.5. (Photos: author)

Also noteworthy is the fact that some bases were used two or three times. The base from Chersonesos (fig. 2b5) was used three times. First, it was used to display stelae: there are three long, narrow sockets with the remains of lead — two sockets parallel to the front edge, and one to the right; there may also have been a fourth socket along the left edge of the base, afterward cut off. Later, the base was reduced to a statue plinth, and one of the front sockets was carefully filled with a piece of white marble. It was used twice to display bronze statues, in both cases with complete sockets for the right foot and for the heel of the left, with additional holes for attributes. The second time, the statue on top was rather large, exceeding life size. According to the inscription,[42] the statue of Bion was dedicated to the Chersonesos virgin. Thus, the practice of the secondary use of bases for bronze statues known, for example, in Kos by the Augustan period,[43] is already attested in Chersonesos in the 4th c. B.C.

Some of the bases belonged to a second group, of equestrian statues, with characteristic sockets for fixing of hoofs,[44] like the base found on Leuke,[45] with three sockets, or the pedestal from Chersonesos for the figure of Agasiklos son of Ktesios (fig. 2a.1) with 4 sockets, or the base with the statue of the Scythian king Skiluros with 5 sockets found in the late Scythian capital.[46] Probably to the same type belonged a fragmentary base with the decree in honor of Autokles from Tyras (fig. 1a.4). Based on the finds of bases in the North Pontic area, bronze equestrian statues constituted *c.*8% of all bronze statues. They were, however, especially characteristic of the late 4th to early 3rd c. B.C., and have not been found in the kingdom of Bosporus.

Statues were usually approximately life-size or somewhat smaller. In several cases, for instance the 4th-c. B.C. base of Athena dedicated by Polykrates (figs. 2b.2; 4.5) at Chersonesos, the statue was taller than 3 m (the socket for the left foot is 49 cm long). Somewhat smaller, but also exceeding life-size, were the statues of Achilles from Leuke (fig. 1a.1) and that of the Bosporan king Rhescuporis IV found in Panticapaeum (figs. 3b.4; 4.1, 3) (the foot sockets are *c.*35-36 cm long). Such a size distribution corresponds well with the results of studies of the bases of bronze statues from Kos.[47]

Some of the statues were installed with the inscriptions on the backs. This is the case with the bases from Chersonesos[48] (figs. 2b.2; 4.5) and from Nymphaeum (fig. 3a.5) that supported statues of Diophantes from Chersonesos and Nymphaeum, and with the colossal figure of Athena in Chersonesos. It may be that the statues were installed facing the sea on the capes or in some high points on the coast, so that they could be seen from ships, while the inscriptions on the bases were intended for those who would read them on land.

Akad. Tchelomeja St. 4, App. 4, 117630 Moscow

(1989) 47, fig. 10a-b.

42 *IPE* I^2 410.

43 Höghammar (supra n.40) 51-52, 69, nos. 53 and 54.

44 Cf. H. B. Siedentopf, *Das hellenistische Reiterdenkmal* (Waldsassen 1968) 65 ff.

45 *IPE* I^2 325.

46 *IPE* I^2 668.

47 Höghammar (supra n.40) 70-71.

48 Treister 1988 (supra n.1) fig. 6b.

A Roman bronze lamp in the form of a barbarian prisoner

Katerina Rhomiopoulou

In 1961, some villagers from Kephalari in the nomos of Drama found a number of objects by chance near some ruins on a mountain called Panayia, not far from their village. The objects were a bronze lamp in the form of a barbarian prisoner, a clay lamp (now lost), and two bases of glass vessels. The finds were delivered to the National Archaeological Museum, Athens, from which they were returned to the Archaeological Museum, Kavala.[1]

The mountainous area to the north of the village of Kephalari, known as Panayia (Panagir Dag), is mentioned by P. Collart in his book on Philippi. Collart also cites all of the observations made by L. Heuzey, who visited the area in the middle of the 19th c. (1861), with which Collart professes himself in agreement.[2] Heuzey compared the descriptions by Appian (historian of the battle of Philippi, fought in 42 B.C.) and Plutarch and presented his own view as to the sites at which the various events connected with the battle of Philippi were played out, identifying the area of Panayia with the site on which Brutus's camp was established.[3] Plutarch states that after the battle Brutus crossed the marshes and the river and ascended the mountain: 'he fled to the mountains, crossing a marshy stream with steep banks.' Appian gives the name of the river as the Gangites. Bounar-bashi, the modern village of Kephalari, is probably the site mentioned by Plutarch. The descriptions in the ancient authors and the survival of remains of Roman buildings and Byzantine fortifications suggest that there was a fort or similar structure which also served to protect the acropolis[4] of the Roman colony of Philippi, later an important Early Christian city.

Over the centuries, a strongly defended site like Panayia hill would have been visited and used as a headquarters by a variety of Roman military units. This accounts for the discovery of objects reflecting the presence and the daily life of military personnel. To this category of finds belongs the suspended metal lamp in the form of a kneeling barbarian prisoner (figs. 1-4).[5]

This is a rare find in terms of its shape, the excellent quality of its workmanship, and its good state of preservation. Indeed, it is the only one of its kind found in Greece. It is 14 cm high and roughly the same width. The chain, together with the hook by which it was suspended, is 35 cm long.[6] The system of chains is connected by rings and is attached to 4 different points of the barbarian's body to ensure correct balance and to prevent the oil from spilling. The lamp (*lucerna*, or *lychnus*) consists of the body (*infundibulum*), which was filled with oil poured in by means of a hole in the barbarian's neck, and the head, which is movable and was attached by a hinge at the back of the neck to serve as a lid.[7] The right leg also acts as the nozzle (*rostrum, nasus*, or *myxus*) from which protruded the wick (*ellychnion* or *verbascum*). Wicks were made of a natural substance and were called *flommos* or *thryallida*, according to the plant used.

---

1 The correspondence on this is kept in the archive of the Kavala Museum (XVIII Ephorate) nos. 428/22.4.61 and 444/26.4.61.

2 L. A. Heuzey and H. Daumet, *Mission archéologique de Macédoine* (Paris 1876) 53-57, 97; P. Collart, *Philippes* (Paris 1937) 175, 207-8, 217-18, *ADelt* 33 (1978) B' 2, p. 292.

3 Appian, *BCiv* 4.113, 106; Plut., *Vit. Brut.* 51; Heuzey and Daumet (supra n.2).

4 *BCH* 62 (1938) 18.

5 Kavala Museum M392. Dark green-brown patina. Slight flaking of the surface, and almost imperceptible corrosion. The chain was broken but has been repaired. It is not known if the finds came from a grave or from within the ruins of a building.

6 The type of chain with a hook is first found in the 1st c. B.C.: S. Loeschke, *Lampen aus Vindonissa* (Zurich 1919) no. 1060.1.

7 C. Grandjouan, *Agora* VI: *Terracottas and plastic lamps of the Roman period* (Princeton 1961) 32; lamp no. 904 has a similar hole and moveable head.

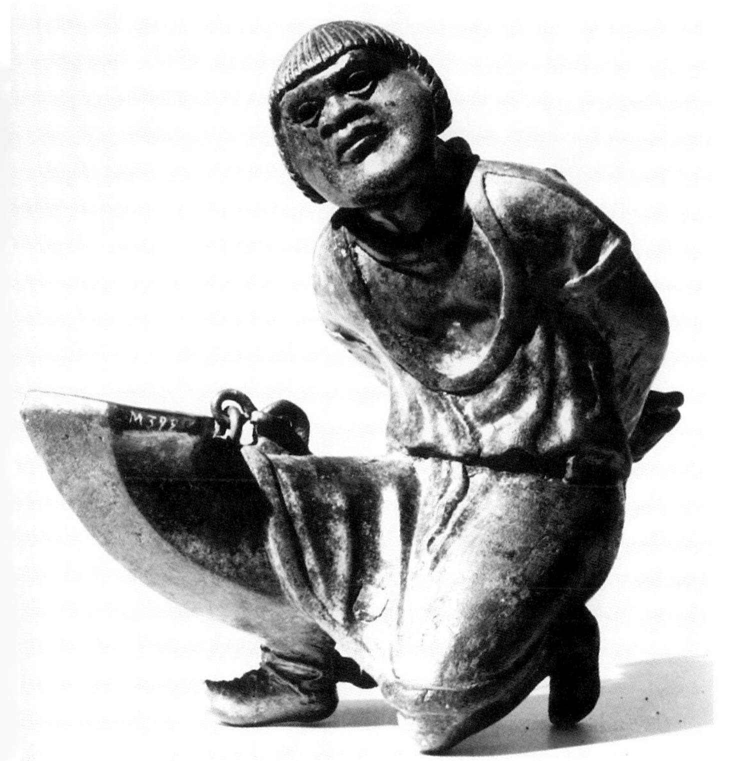

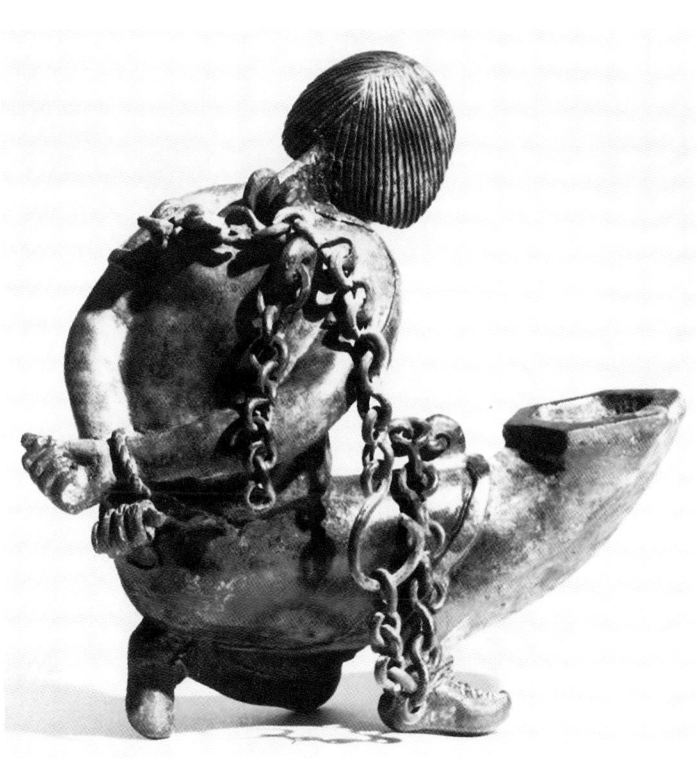

Fig. 1. Lamp in the form of a barbarian prisoner; found at Kephalari (near Philippi). Roman, 4th c. A.D. Bronze, h. 14 cm. Drama, Archaeological Museum M392. (Photo: courtesy Kavala Museum);
Fig. 2. Back of fig. 1.

The lamp was very carefully made, with the body and the head separately cast and the sections of the chain hammered. The alloy is brass. The alloy for the chain contains 73.70% copper, 21.36% zinc, and no appreciable admixture of lead, which confirms that the chain was made by hammering, since the presence of lead hinders the hammering of copper alloys (both copper-tin and copper-zinc) while it facilitates the procedure of casting.[8] The alloy used to cast the body and head contains 74.18% copper, 23.49% zinc, 2.88% lead, 0.59% tin, and traces of other metals.

The earliest Roman lamps were made in Campania (in the area of Naples), and usually copied or were inspired by Greek types. The lamps of the Roman period have anthropomorphic or zoomorphic shapes (slaves, negroes, actors, grotesques, shepherds, soldiers, and various animals).[9] In Greek lamps, on the other hand, decorative figures are worked in relief on the disc of the lamp or at the handle (*ansa, manubrium*). These motifs include griffins, volutes, and swan's heads. Even in the case of anthropomorphic lamps produced by Roman workshops, the figure normally has a purely decorative character and is attached to the main body of the lamp. It very rarely forms a functional component, most commonly acting as a support for the lamp, a tradition that continued into the Middle Ages, when, in Franco-Flemish art and in Italian art of the Renaissance and later, slaves-prisoners hold or support lamps.

The theme of the kneeling barbarian prisoner or slave made its debut at an early date, in ancient Egyptian and Near Eastern art. It became quite common in Greek art from the 4th c. B.C.

---

8 See also P. T. Craddock (ed.), *2000 years of zinc and brass* (BritMusOccPap 50, 1990). I wish to thank E. Mangou, chemist at the National Archaeological Museum, for analysis of the material and for other useful technical information.

9 Loeschke (supra n.6) nos. 345-47, fig. 24, pl. XXIII nos. 1083a-b; K. Weitzmann (ed.), *Age of spirituality* (Exhib. cat. New York 1977 [Princeton 1979]) 339-40, nos. 319 (K. R. Brown) and 320 (M. C. Ross): R. H. Howland, *Agora* IV: *Greek lamps and their survivals* (Princeton 1958) 5 and 72 ff.

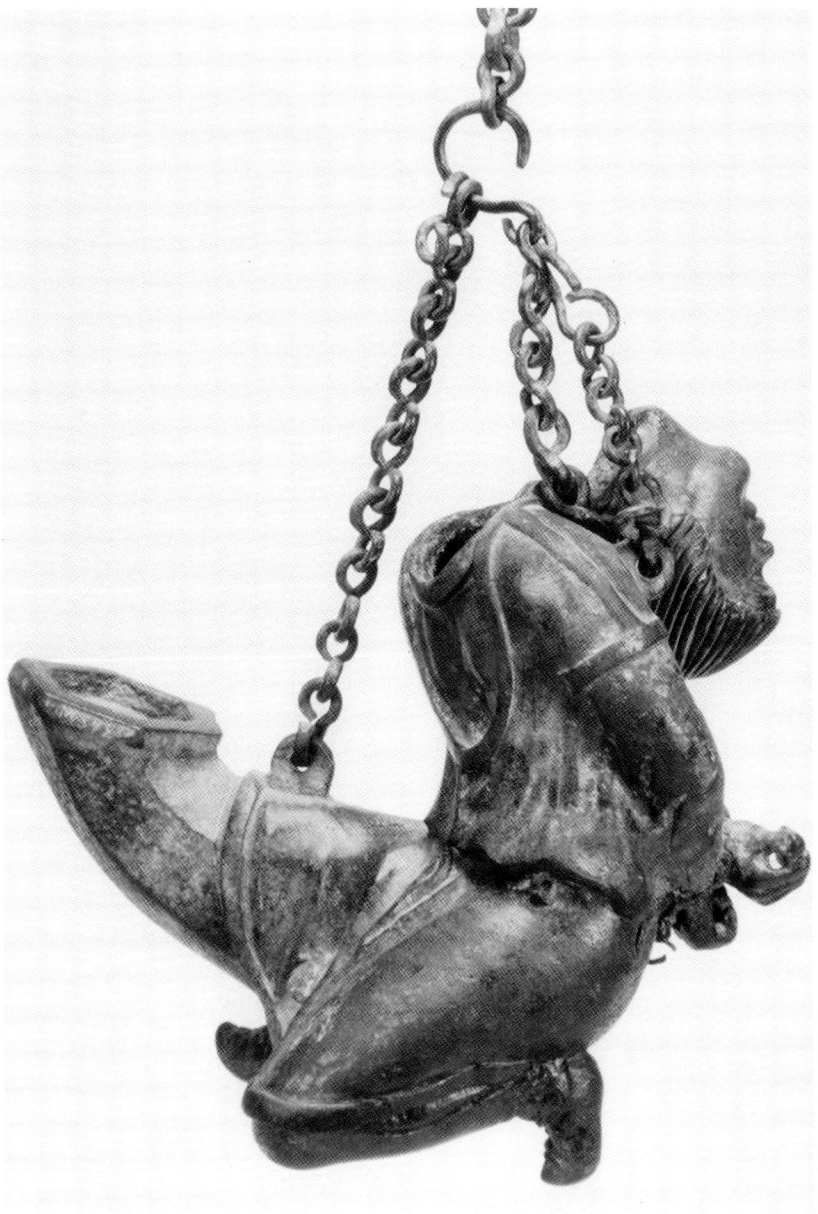

Fig. 3. Profile of fig. 1, with the lid hinged open.

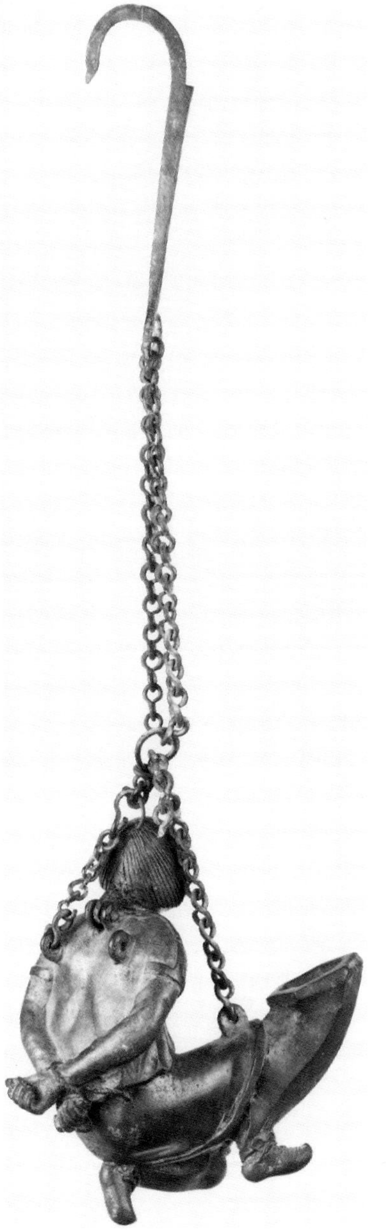

Fig. 4. Back of fig. 1, with the hanging chains and hook extended, total length 35 cm.

to the period of the Roman conquest (cf. the Alexander sarcophagus and other examples).[10] Kneeling prisoners are either being forced to kneel, or are bound, or kneel in an act of veneration (*proskynesis*). In Greek art, this "veneration" is invariably associated with barbarians, since it is a barbarian custom known from the 5th c. B.C. The first occurrences of kneeling figures in Roman art date from the Republic, mainly toward its end, on coins issued by Sulla.[11]

Although figures of barbarians are rare in the form of lamps, barbarian types were used in other objects, such as furniture supports or decorative architectural members (columns) — a phenomenon that continued in later periods.[12] The material used was marble or a combination of different coloured marbles.

---

10 R. M. Schneider, *Bunte Barbaren* (Worms 1986) 180 ff.

11 A. C. Levi, *Barbarians on Roman imperial coins and sculpture* (Numismatic Notes and Monographs 123, New York 1952) 25 ff.

12 Schneider (supra n.10) 22 ff. n.43, pl. 17.

The motif of the bound or subjugated barbarian was popular in Roman Imperial times and helped to form the Roman attitude to their relations with the people who lived within the boundaries of the empire. It also symbolized the victory of the Roman emperor and, in general, alluded to his most famous virtue (*virtus*): his power to bring victory. The barbarian thus became a kind of symbol for the emperor and the goddess Victory. This accounts for the frequent depiction of barbarians on historical reliefs (arches, altars, columns) and on coins: the barbarian, humbled and bound, represented the power of the emperor. The prisoner's nationality was indicated by facial features and hairstyle, and in some cases also by dress. These elements by which the nationality of barbarian prisoners could be recognized and identified are found from the time of Trajan's Column to the time of the Obelisk of Theodosius in Constantinople (end of the 4th c.). The man on this lamp has a broad, fleshy face, round, slightly jutting, powerful jaw, short nose, and forehead covered by straight hair; according to the typology established for barbarians, he probably belonged ethnically to the German or Gothic group, against which various Roman emperors waged war, particularly from the end of the 3rd to the 5th c.[13] The typically "barbarian" coiffure, with short, straight hair covering the forehead, is found as the normal, fashionable hairstyle in portraits of Roman citizens and dignitaries from the end of the 4th c. onward (e.g., obelisk of Theodosius). During the same period there are examples of clean-shaven barbarians and others with small beard, mustache, and even short sideburns.

The individualized features of this prisoner suggest that the artist probably had in mind some specific model or a personal recollection. This makes the statuette unique. The barbarian prisoner is kneeling in an oblique position, his left leg sharply bent, while the right, also bent (and acting as the nozzle), rests firmly on the ground. His arms are bound behind him, with a rope tied at the wrists. He is dressed in a short, sleeved tunic (*tunica*), belted at the waist in such a way as to form a deep overfold. The ends of the belt can be seen falling between the legs. The sparse drapery suggests a roughly woven cloth. There is a kind of border (*seirition*) along the edges of the top part of the tunic, the bottom of the tunic, and the sleeves. He wears a closed leather shoe, fastened with a lace, with slightly upturned toes[14] — a type of shoe commonly worn by slaves and country people. The collar (*torquis*) indicates ownership[15] and was also a kind of badge distinguishing slaves from free men, to prevent them from escaping from their owners. The elongated shape helps to date the lamp to the 4th c. or later.

The kneeling posture is also of interest and reveals the artist's skill. The position is not rendered in the simplest manner, with both knees bent: instead, use is made of *contraposto*. In this way, the figure is opened up toward the viewer and is made broader; its location in space is emphasized through strongly contrasting axes (head to knee, back of knee to head). Two contrasting elements are thus indicated: the highly mobile stance of the body competes with the static quality of the 'simple-minded' barbarian in his coarse dress. This complicated posture possibly indicates that, despite the realism, the artist who made the lamp may also have had in mind similar motifs in Classical and Hellenistic works of art.

Between the period of Trajan and that of Theodosius a difference can be observed in the way barbarians were portrayed, both in reliefs and in works in the round. As the centuries passed, they became more humbled, more degraded. This may have been necessary to promote the image of the emperors, especially in the last centuries when the empire was severely harassed.

---

13 H. Wrede, *Die spätantike Hermengalerie von Welschbillig* (Berlin 1972) 68-72, pls. 33, 41; G. Mansuelli, *La fine del mondo antico* (Turin 1988) 106-7. Cf. a weight bust in the Museum of Fine Arts, Boston: Comstock–Vermeule, *Bronzes* 97, no. 125; B. Kiilerich, *Late fourth century classicism in the plastic arts* (Odense 1993) 238, figs. 14, 16.

14 Cf. the clay shoes in Mansuelli (supra n.13) 189, fig. 2; and the barbarian shoes on the Carrand diptych (A.D. 400?) (see W. F. Volbach *Elfenbeinarbeiten der Spätantike and des Frühmittelalters* [Mainz 1952] no. 108, pl. 30.4).

15 Wrede (supra n.13) 85-97.

The facial features of the prisoner of our lamp, despite the grotesque element in them, may be compared with the barbarian heads on the Welschbillig herms (Villa of Gratianus[?] near Trier), especially heads 82, 90, and 99, which depict Germans; with portraits of prisoners from the base of the obelisk of Theodosius in Constantinople; and with figures on ivory diptychs of the first half of the 5th c. — compare the Halberstadt diptych (early 5th c.) and the Carrand diptych (*c*.400) in Florence.[16] The problem of the workshop is more difficult. Generally speaking, it may be said to be the product of a western workshop (major centers were at Milan, Rome, and Trier). However, during the last centuries of the empire styles and craftsmen, like emperors, traveled widely and frequently changed their production center.[17] As a result, the provenance of the lamp may not be of great significance. Private portraiture at this period, depicting ordinary men, both free and slave, may be said to be more realistic than imperial portraiture. The influence of official imperial portraits was no longer so important. Imperial portraits, moreover, hinted at immortality and therefore tended to idealization, whereas private portraits depicted the immediate present, which would soon vanish, and contained strongly realistic elements. Perhaps this small masterpiece illuminated the tent of a Roman officer and brought back memories of his military career and of the various campaigns in which he had fought.

National Archaeological Museum, Tositsa 1, Athens 106-82

---

16 *Spätantike und frühes Christentum* (Exhib. cat., Frankfurt 1983) 649, no. 229. On the Carrand diptych: see above n.13; Kiilerich (supra n.13) fig. 107.

17 Kiilerich (supra n.13) 196-219.

Conserving and restoring the Brindisi bronzes

Giovanna De Palma and Paola Fiorentino

In July 1992, while diving off Punta del Serrone, just north of the port of Brindisi, Major Robusto of the Italian Carabinieri found a life-size bronze foot. In 1972 in the same area, although the lack of points of reference has obscured the exact location, a foot much larger than life-size, belonging to a draped statue of a woman attributed to the Late Imperial age, had been found. Underwater excavation, promptly instituted in 1992 by the Soprintendenza Archeologica per la Puglia in collaboration with the S.T.A.S. (Underwater Archaeological Technical Service), brought to light about 130 fragments of bronze statues of various types and sizes, as well as more than a hundred smaller fragments. The sculptures were concentrated in a small area of the seabed, 400 m from shore. The close typological connection between the foot found in 1972 and some fragments of draped statues found in 1992 gives credence to the hypothesis that it belonged to the same load. No trace has been found of a wreck.[1]

Observation of the finds shows that the statues had all been completed, erected, and subsequently demolished. Thus, the load was destined for re-melting. What have been found are disjointed fragments from various statues of different periods, with very few chances of joining these fragments. The fragments are mostly open pieces, whose internal walls are easily studied and have given access to a wide range of technological information. For the same reason, only a few fragments have retained substantial parts of their casting cores. The chronology seems to embrace a time span between the 4th c. B.C. and the 4th c. A.D.

The Istituto Centrale per il Restauro (hereafter I.C.R.) was involved from the outset in evaluating the state of conservation of the finds and deciding on the restoration strategy.[2] This necessitated the planning of a broad program of work, based on the uniform observation and documentation of all data that could be gathered during restoration.

The state of conservation of the bronzes varied enormously. The pieces showed different types of strong corrosion and of patinas, primarily crusts consisting of a thick black layer of copper sulfides and Schoenfliesite over another thick inner greenish-white layer of tin dioxide. The core metal lay beneath these layers of corrosion (fig. 1), and what remained of it was much smaller than the original metal mass would have been. These types of loose and crumbling patinas are commonly found on fragments recovered under sediments of decomposed seaweed.[3] There were also present dense adhesive green crusts of atacamite (basic copper chloride) and brownish-yellow or reddish-purple corrosion patinas (copper oxide) adhering to the metal or patinas of reddish-purple corrosion over whitish powdery tin dioxide. It is important to preserve the corrosion layers during restoration because in many cases they contain evidence about the technological processes involved during manufacture (figs. 2-3). In more general terms, most of the Brindisi bronzes present a wide variety of casting defects, such as shrinkage cracks, flaws, widespread porosity, and joints or internal recastings in bronze or lead. The great variety of repair patches provides information about the finishing of the surfaces of all the statues.

---

1 For the discovery and a list of the finds, see G. Andreassi and A. Cocchiaro, "Bronzi di Punta del Serrone: ricerche archeologiche subacquee a Brindisi 1992," *BdA Suppl.* 1992, 3-16; *EAA Suppl. 2* (Rome 1994) 509-10, s.v. Esplorazione Archeologica, figs. 568-70 (id.); A. Cocchiaro, "I bronzi di Punta del Serrone," *Andar per mare* (Exhib. cat. Bari 1997) (Bari 1998) 221-22.

2 The immediate priority seemed to be to carry out intensive baths in running water to desalinize the bronzes as they were removed from sea water. The finds were soaked in fresh running water for at least 48 hours. Dehydration was performed by means of acetone baths and jets of hot air. These operations were carried out at the Museo Provinciale "F. Ribezzo", Brindisi, by restorers of the Soprintendenza Archeologica per la Puglia and by V. Caiulo, a restorer employed by the Province. This treatment proved to be valid, as finds yet to be restored do not show new signs of corrosion.

3 This could confirm the biological origin of this condition, which occurs after contact with hydrogen sulfide in a reducing environment: see P. Fiorentino, M. Marabelli, and M. Micheli, "Indagini ed intervento di conservazione sui reperti bronzei di Porticello," *BdA* 24 (1984) 18.

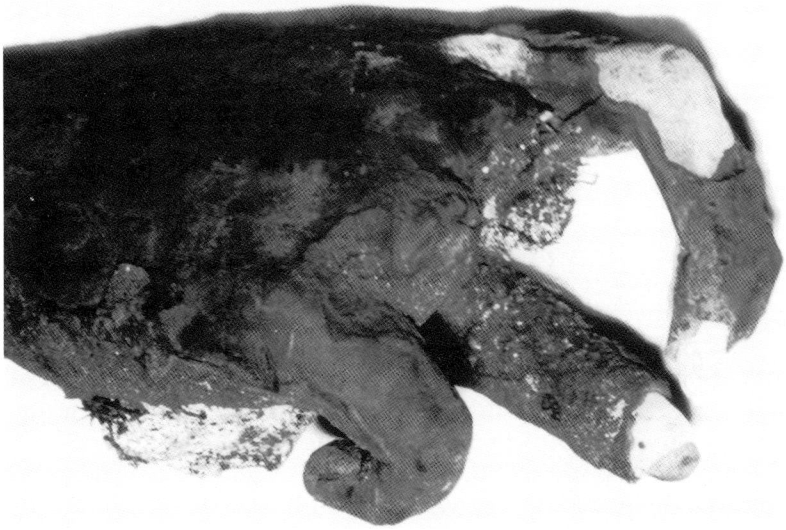

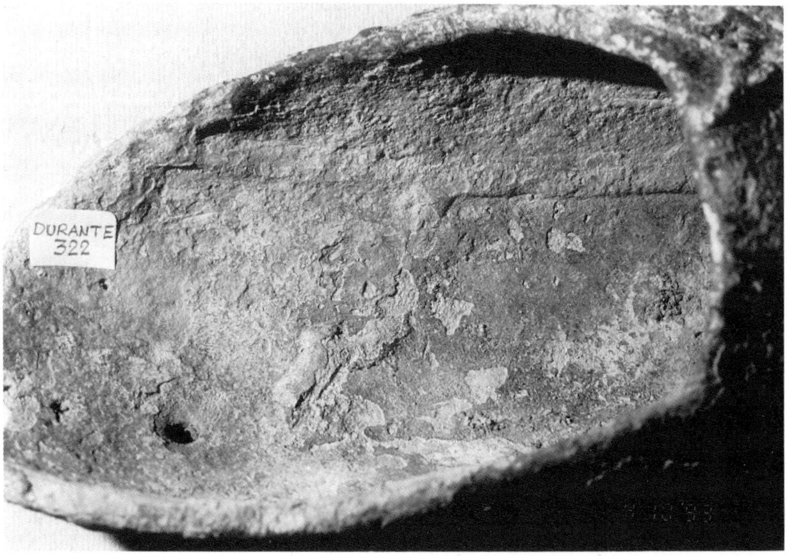

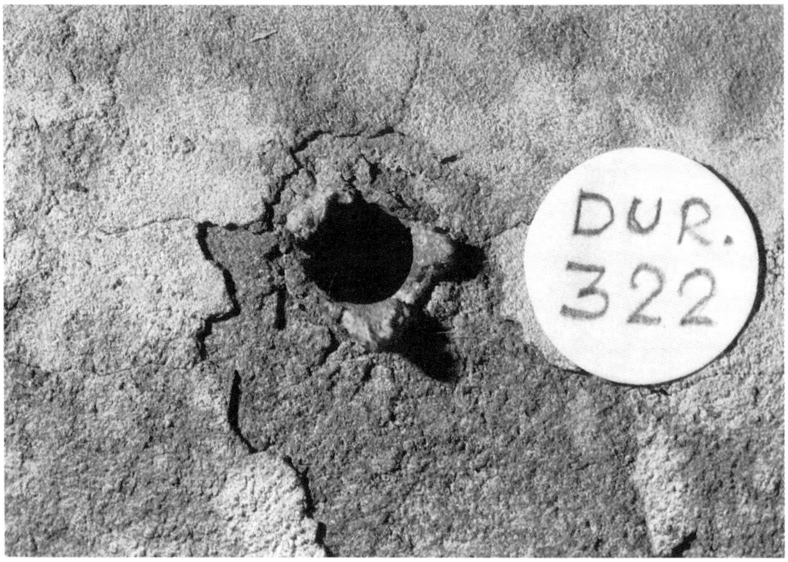

Fig. 1 (top). Hand no. 20, before restoration. The strong corrosion is clearly visible: a thick crust of black copper sulfides over a white inner layer of tin dioxide. At the end of the finger can be seen the metal core. There are also calcareous concretions. (Photo: Archivio I.C.R.)

Fig. 2 (middle). Hand no. 322, during restoration; interior. Relief bands represent wax-to-wax joins. (Photo: Archivio I.C.R.)

Fig. 3 (below). Hand no. 322, during restoration. The opening in the wall was made after casting to attach the arm to another part of the statue. The burring of the metal also indicates the direction in which the attachment was inserted. (Photo: Archivio I.C.R.)

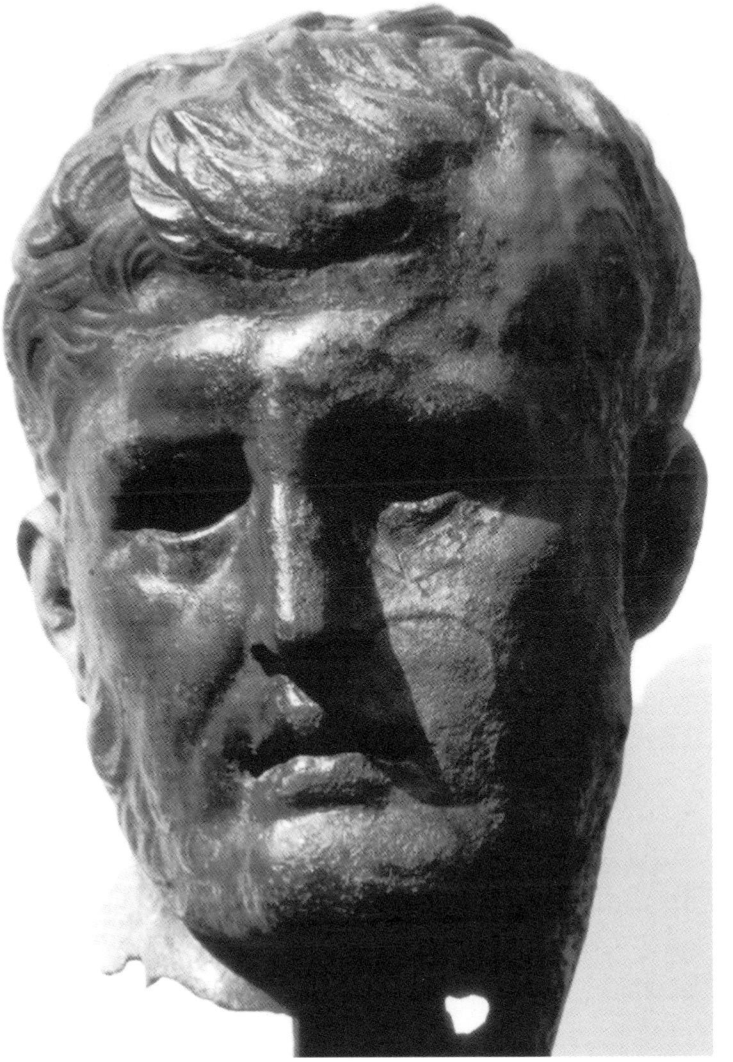

Fig. 4. Head of a man no.19, the so-called Hellenistic Prince, after restoration. The left side of the face was severely abraded by the mechanical action of the sand. (Photo: Archivio I.C.R.)

These different conditions and the typology of the alloys suggested various approaches to conservation. Finds with a high content of lead in either the alloy or the internal supporting cast were excluded from the immersion baths. The work, both of conservation and of analysis, is still under way.[4] To date, a broad spectrum of analyses has been conducted.[5] Examination with the naked eye also immediately supplied information on the technical procedures used in manufacture.

Attracting a great deal of attention is the so-called Hellenistic Prince. On the basis of convincing comparisons, P. Moreno identified the statue as Aemilius Paullus, victor of the celebrated battle of Pydna in 168 B.C.[6] The I.C.R. restored the head (fig. 4),[7] while the torso that has since been identified as belonging to it was treated at the Centro di Restauro of the Soprintendenza Archeologica per la Toscana in Florence. The relative technical and analytical data are still being studied, and they will be the subjects of a joint publication.[8]

---

4 The following finds have so far been restored: the head of the so-called Philosopher no. 17; the head of a man no. 13; the girl's head of the Faustina type no. 424 and the small arm no. 418, probably related to it; the right foot no. 1 and the left foot no. 18, belonging to the same statue; the right hand no. 20 (here fig. 1); the right hand with a pointing forefinger no. 301; the fragment of a right foot no. 340; the fragment of a left foot no. 345; the right wing no. 350; the colossal left arm no. 315; the Julio-Claudian male head no. 366; the right arm no. 383; the fragment of a right foot no. 396; the hand with ring no. 322 (here fig. 2); and many fragments of drapery.

5 Analyses of the patinas and of the alloys of a large number of samples have been conducted by the Chemistry Laboratory of I.C.R. Elemental and trace analyses using inductively coupled plasma-mass spectrometry (ICP-MS) of the elements present in the alloy have been conducted by C.S.M. (Centro Sviluppo Materiali). The examination with scanning electronic microscope (SEM) was carried out by the Department of Chemical Engineering of the University of Rome. Radiographic tests and gammagraphies were conducted by the I.C.R. Physics Laboratory and by ENEA, while it is envisaged that the observations will be broadened by targeted sampling for lead isotope examination and, when appropriate, with computerized axial tomography (CAT scan).

6 P. Moreno, *Scultura ellenistica* 2 (Rome 1994) 661-63, figs. 790-96; "Statua di Emilio Paolo," *Andar per mare* (Bari 1998) 222-24.

7 The restoration was carried out by E. Lantos, restorer of I.C.R.

8 The statue, after re-assembly, was presented during the exhibition *Beni Nascosti* during the XI Settimana

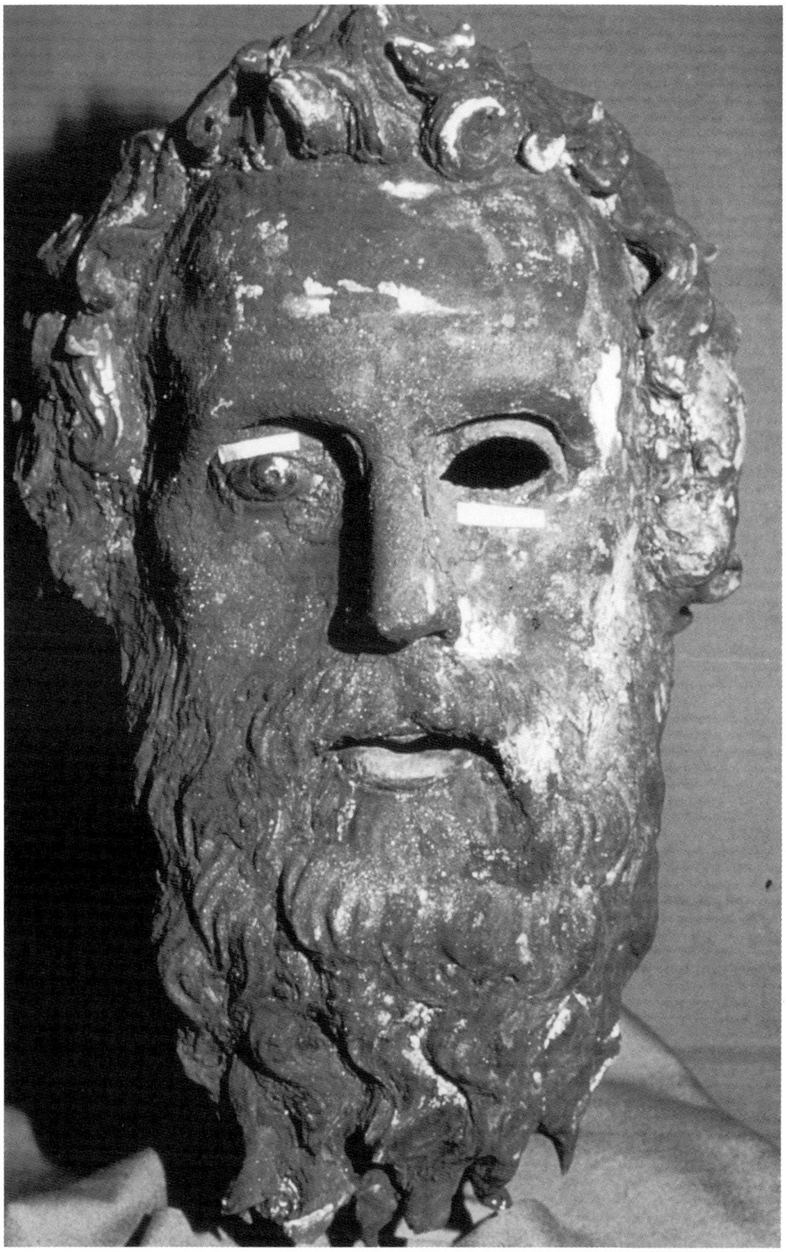

Fig. 5. Head of a man no. 368, before restoration. (Photo: Archivio I.C.R.)

The head of a man no. 368 is probably the oldest member of the group. At the time of discovery, its state of conservation was rather precarious. The bronze had been affected by deep corrosion, with alterations of amorphous black copper sulfides and tin dioxide, cassiterite, and schoenfliesite (fig. 5). This patina was cracked and crumbling, tending to come off in layers. This corrosion process brought about a notable thinning in the bronze and the loss of the finished surface, which survived only in some deep undercuts, where it had been protected by marine sediments. The restoration was conducted by P. Fiorentino, chief restorer of I.C.R. (figs. 6-7).

The face of this old man has a strong bone structure and a wide forehead, furrowed by three long parallel wrinkles. The eyebrows, slightly frowning, follow the line of the eye sockets, with the eyelids well defined and an accurate rendering of the eyes. The nose is slightly curved. The mouth is slightly open and surrounded by a thick mustache. The beard begins halfway

---

per i Beni Culturali ed Ambientali, Rome, December 4-13, 1995: see A. Cocchiaro *et al.*, "I bronzi di Punta del Serrone: un recupero dal mare di Brindisi," *Beni nascosti: Giornale della mostra* (Rome 1995) 2-4.

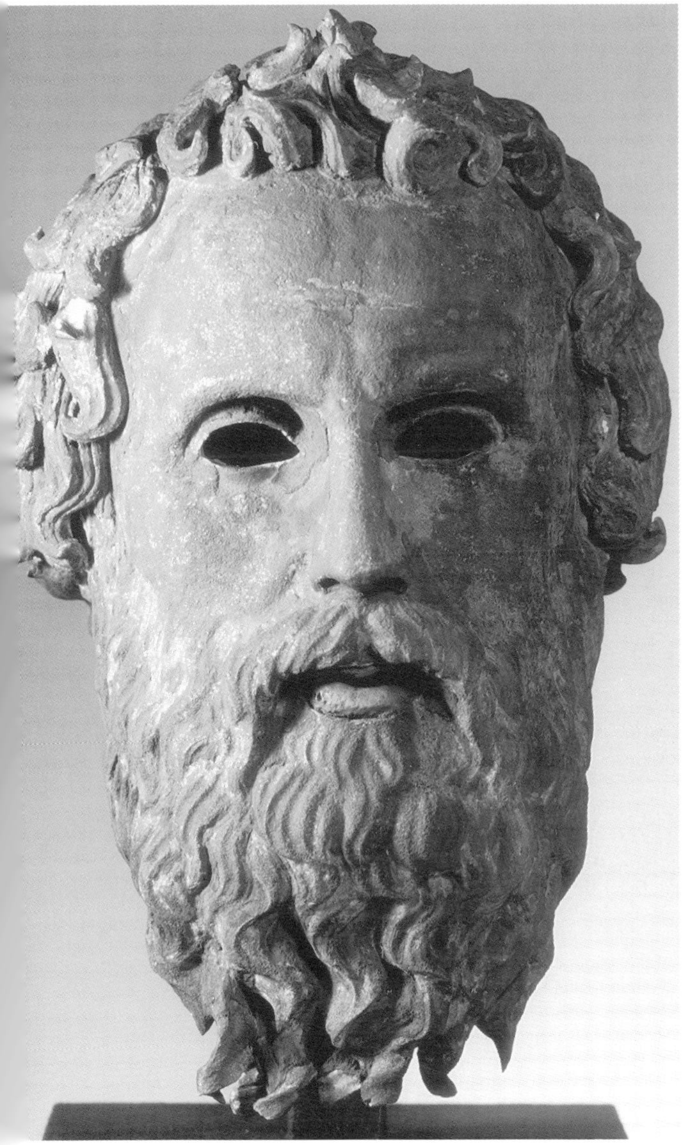

Fig. 6. Head of a man no. 368, after restoration but before re-insertion of the right eye. (Photo: Lorenzo De Masi; Archivio I.C.R.)

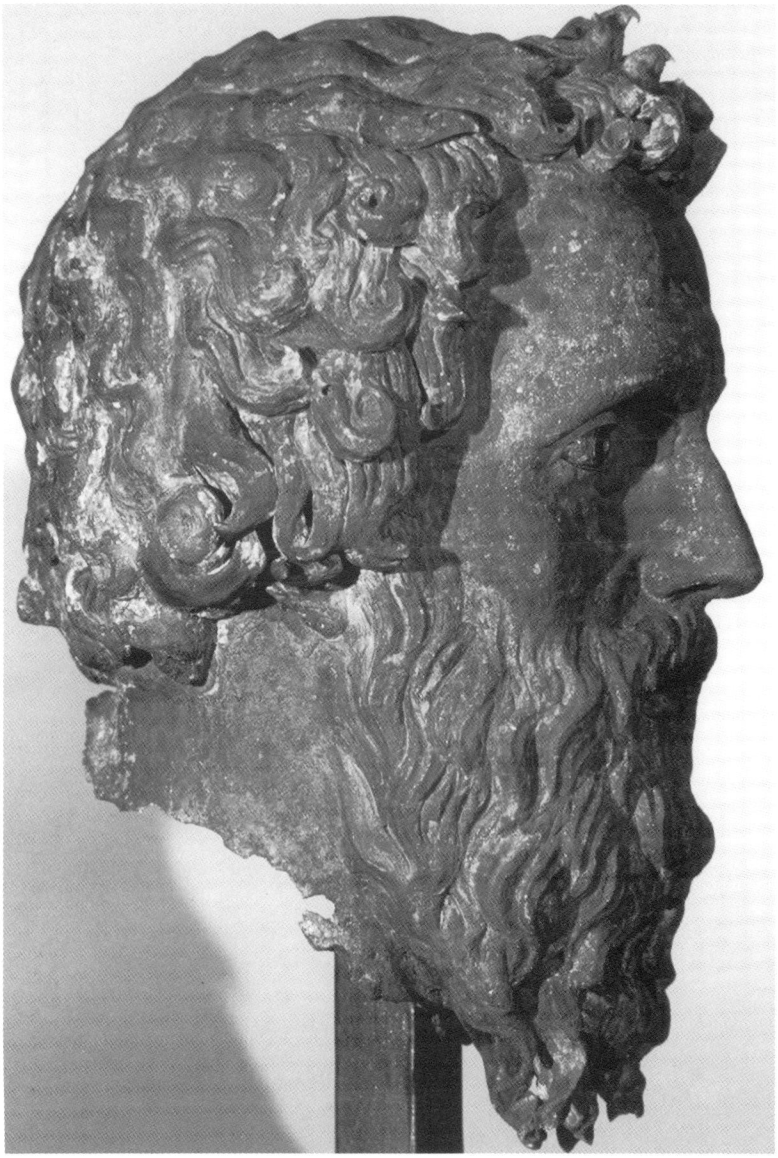

Fig. 7. Head of a man no. 368, profile, after restoration. (Photo: Archivio I.C.R.)

up the face and is prolonged in flame-like locks. The hair, divided on the forehead into tight curls, descends to frame the face with elongated, deeply carved locks that cover the ears. The portrait fits the well-known type of the philosopher as a Late Classical introduction. Lack of specific comparisons prevents us from identifying the individual portrayed;[9] the construction of the face, the expression, and the absence of details tending toward a precise physiognomic characterization suggest that we are dealing with an imaginary portrait. Without other precise points of reference, the features of this excellent casting, the composition of the alloy, and stylistic data place it around the second half of the 4th c. B.C. The alloy, on the basis of elemen-

9 It must not be forgotten that there are many copies of unidentified portraits that clearly derive from 4th-c. originals. The existing identifications cover only part of the surviving record. Furthermore, in the 4th c. the remembrance of the great men of the distant past existed before individualized portraiture had been conceived in Greece and become common, as indicated by the portraits of the Seven Wise Men: see G. M. A. Richter (abridg. and rev. R. R. R. Smith), *The portraits of the Greeks* (Oxford 1984) 18.

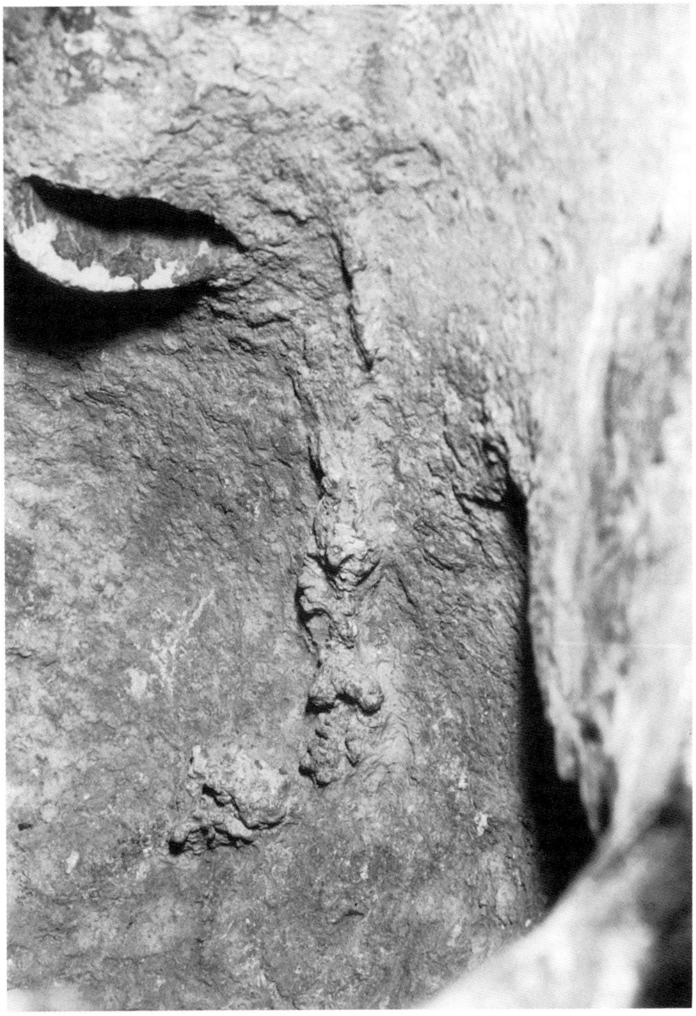

Fig. 8. Head of a man no. 368, interior. A casting spill marks the junction between wax slabs. We can hypothesize 4 piece-molds. The eye socket is clearly visible. (Photo: Archivio I.C.R.)

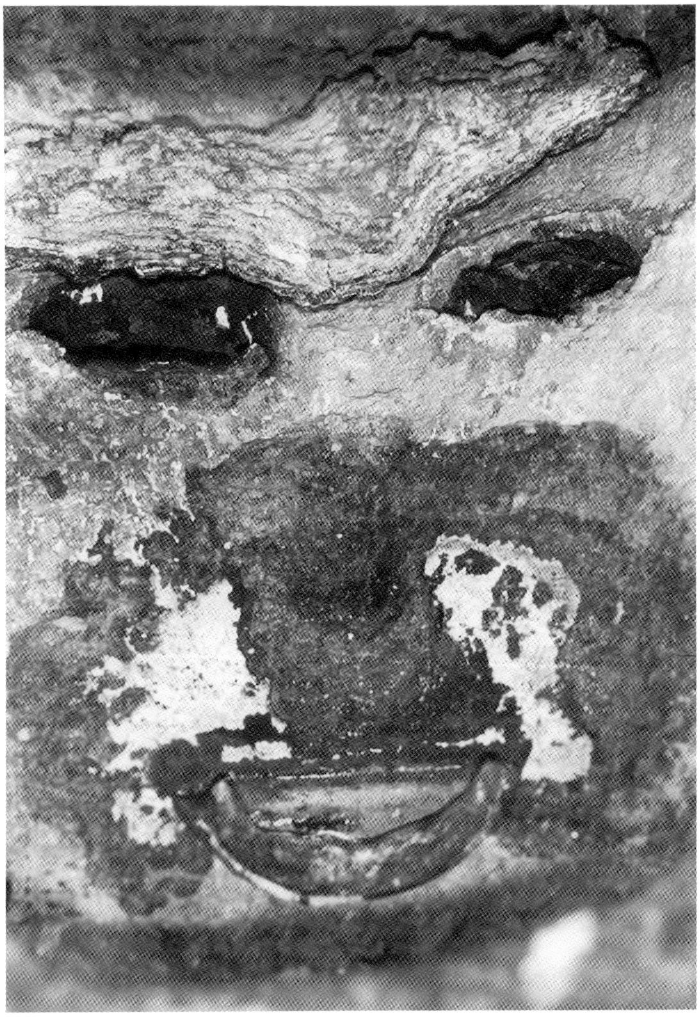

Fig. 9. Head of a man no. 368, interior: the mouth is welded in the socket with the aid of soldering material. (Photo: Archivio I.C.R.)

tal and trace analysis, reveals a binary copper-tin composition.[10] The head was made in a single casting, while the hair and the beard were cast on. There are no repairs, and the thickness of the metal, in spite of the serious decay, is about 6 mm.

The edge of the neck is the finished edge of the casting. A metal drip mark from the casting-on of the beard has fallen onto this edge. On the other hand, the total absence of traces of welding joints on the neck raises interesting questions about the type of statue to which the head may originally have belonged[11] and about whether the pieces were mechanically jointed together, perhaps with the aid of a rectangular projection corresponding with the gap now present in the back of the neck.

An iron chaplet that does not pass through the bronze wall has been preserved on the interior of the head at the nape of the neck. A second chaplet was probably located symmetrically with the first, where there is presently a gap in the bronze. The openings of the eyes and the mouth provided links between the core and the outer mould. The head was emptied of the

10 Percentages: Cu 88.9; Sn 10.4; Pb 0.23; Fe 0.04; Zn 0.13; Sb 0.03; As 0.02; Si 0.01; Ni 0.32; Co 0.01; Ag 0.01.

11 Greek portraits, until late in the Hellenistic period, were full-length portraits, not simply portrait busts, and the composition of the body was as important for expressing the nature of the subject as were the details of the face.

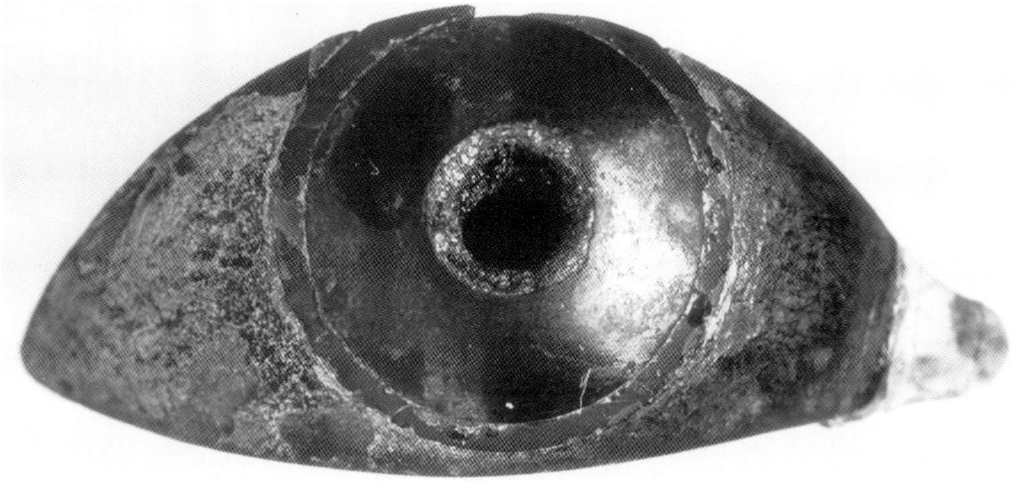

Fig. 10. Head of a man no. 368: the eye before re-assembly. (Photo: Archivio I.C.R.)

core in ancient times, except for one surviving layer, 2 cm thick, covered by marine deposits. On some points of the inner wall, the clay still bears traces of the spatula used to spread it. The sample analyzed shows a weakly stratified structure with homogeneous and widespread oxidization. Iso-oriented traces of hairs are visible macroscopically.[12]

The clay core was submitted to thermoluminescence analysis.[13] The results, even considering the limits to the range of accuracy of this technique, offer a quite convincing chronological picture. The dating falls between 333 and 220 B.C. with an uncertainty of 10%.

The inner wall of the casting still bears, recorded in the metal, clear traces of the application of wax with brushes. On the interior of the face there are drip marks (fig. 8). These seem to be wax spills at the junctions between the wax slabs used to construct the head. Overall, the evidence shows that the head was manufactured with the indirect lost-wax casting process.

The mouth was made separately of a copper alloy, cast in two sections and then welded into its socket with soldering material (fig. 9). The eyes, of which only the right one remains, were inserted from the exterior into their slightly tapering sockets (fig. 10). The white of the surviving eye is composed of limestone, now blackened on the surface from absorption of copper sulfides. A notch that corresponds to the lachrymal gland must have facilitated the insertion of the eye. The iris is made of a barrel-shaped element in brown stone, worked on a lathe, surrounded by a ring of translucent stone. Although only remnants of the eyelashes survive, the sheet-bronze plates of the insertions are clearly visible on the interiors of the sockets.

The beard and the hair were separately cast and attached. The ears are still perfectly modeled below the curls. Behind the beard on the left side are the remains of a sawed-off casting gate. Another sawed-off gate, from the casting of the face, although very corroded, seems to be recognizable on the right side, at the base of the neck (fig. 7).

Following the methods initiated by the I.C.R., similar technical investigations will accompany the ongoing restoration of the whole group of bronze fragments. After such operations are completed, we will have significant new evidence for understanding the evolution of casting techniques in the Mediterranean basin over a period of eight centuries.

Istituto Centrale per il Restauro, Piazza S. Francesco di Paola, 9, I-00184 Roma

12 The mineralogical composition has been determined by reading stratigraphic thin-sections under a polarizing microscope and by means of X-ray diffraction (XRD). The measurements were executed by the I.C.R. Material Testing Laboratory. The matrix contains a homogeneous temper of quartz granules and lithic inclusions of a metamorphic nature of the mica-schist type and a finer micaceous fraction. Calcite is absent both in the clay matrix and in the temper.

13 The thermoluminescence analysis was conducted by the Department of Physics, University of Milan. This was done keeping in mind the fact that none of the finds was X-rayed prior to the analytical tests.

Zur Bedeutung der Anstückungstechnik bei hellenistischen und römischen Bronzestatuetten

Norbert Franken

Durch eine enge Zusammenarbeit von Archäologen, Restauratoren, und Naturwissenschaftlern hat die Erforschung antiker Bronzetechnik in den vergangenen Jahrzehnten einen enormen Wissenszuwachs erfahren. Gleichwohl bleiben noch viele Fragen offen. Zu den dringendsten Desideraten der Forschung zählt zweifellos eine umfassende Untersuchung der Anstückungstechnik bei Bronzestatuetten.[1] Zwar mangelt es in der Literatur nicht an gelegentlichen Erwähnungen des Phänomens, doch fehlt vor allem eine kritische Zusammenstellung der überaus verschiedenartigen Erscheinungsformen,[2] was dazu führt, daß die an den Objekten zurückgebliebenen Spuren dieser Technik häufig nur unzulänglich beschrieben, in ihrer Bedeutung oftmals verkannt und als normale Beschädigungen oder Reparaturen mißverstanden werden.[3]

Auch im folgenden erlaubt der begrenzte Rahmen eines Aufsatzes zwangsläufig keine umfassende Darstellung des Phänomens, statt dessen soll hier aus der Sicht des Archäologen ein einzelner Aspekt herausgegriffen werden, der für das Verständnis der Gesamtproblematik von grundsätzlicher Bedeutung ist. Dabei handelt es sich um die Frage nach dem eigentlichen Sinn und Zweck des Anstückungsverfahrens bei hellenistischen und römisch-kaiserzeitlichen Bronzestatuetten. Ein Blick in die Literatur zeigt, daß in dieser Frage noch kein überzeugender Konsens erreicht ist. Zudem erweisen sich die bisher vorgebrachten Erklärungen des Phänomens insgesamt als zu einfach. Im folgenden glaube ich zeigen zu können, daß es für die Verwendung von Anstückungen bei Bronzestatuetten nicht nur einen einzigen Grund, sondern mehrere Erklärungsmöglichkeiten gibt.

Besonders aufschlußreich für unsere Fragestellung ist zunächst die Betrachtung einer Larenstatuette aus Bonn (Abb. 1).[4] Die Statuette vom Typus des sog. *Lar familiaris* ist bis auf kleinere Beschädigungen sehr gut erhalten und von hoher künstlerischer und handwerklicher Qualität. Angesichts dessen überrascht eine merkwürdig rauh und unbearbeitet wirkende Stelle am Unterkörper, die sich in der Mitte der Vorderseite zwischen den Beinen, als ein senkrechter Streifen von der Gürtung bis zum unteren Saum der Tunika entlangzieht. In der oberen Hälfte dieses Streifens befindet sich ein annähernd ovales Loch, das Einblick ins Innere der hohlgegossenen Statuette gibt.

Der Bonner Bronze lassen sich 12 weitere Larenstatuetten an die Seite stellen, die an derselben Stelle gleichfalls einen entsprechenden unbearbeiteten Streifen aufweisen.[5] Die auffällige

---

1 Wesentlich erschwert wird eine solche Untersuchung durch die weite Streuung der Objekte. Dadurch steht jedem potentiellen Bearbeiter zum genaueren Detailstudium stets nur eine relativ begrenzte Zahl originaler Denkmäler zur Verfügung, was gerade für eine technische Fragestellung wenig ideal ist. Zum technischen Hintergrund, vgl. H. Lechtman und A. Steinberg, "Bronze joining: a study in ancient technology," in *Art and technology* 5-35.

2 Dazu gehört auch eine gründliche Untersuchung der Frühformen von Anstückungen an altorientalischen und altägyptischen Bronzestatuetten.

3 Hierzu zählt z.B. eine schmale Furche, die bei einigen Statuetten am Kontur des ehemals angestückten Gewands entlangläuft und möglicherweise eine Art Markierung darstellt, die dem Künstler helfen sollte, beim Zusammensetzen die richtige Positionierung des anzustückenden Körperteils zu finden. Besonders gut sichtbar ist eine solche Furche bei zwei Statuetten in Malibu und München: *Small sculptures in bronze from the classical world* (Ausstellungskat., Chapel Hill, NC 1976) Nr. 63; V. von Graeve, *MüJb* 36 (1985) 191, Abb. 9.

4 Bonn, Rheinisches Landesmuseum 10496: C. von Veith, *BJb* 59 (1876) 34; H. Lehner, *Führer durch das Provinzialmuseum in Bonn* 1: *Die antike Abteilung* (Bonn 1915) 61; H. Menzel, *Römische Bronzen: Rheinisches Landesmuseum Bonn* (Düsseldorf 1969) 18, Nr. 6; ders., *Die römischen Bronzen aus Deutschland* 3: *Bonn* (Bonn 1986) 22-23, Nr. 48, Taf. 22-23.

5 Berlin, Antikensammlung Inv. 32565: unveröffentlicht; Karlsruhe, aus Pompeji?: K. Schumacher, *Beschrei-*

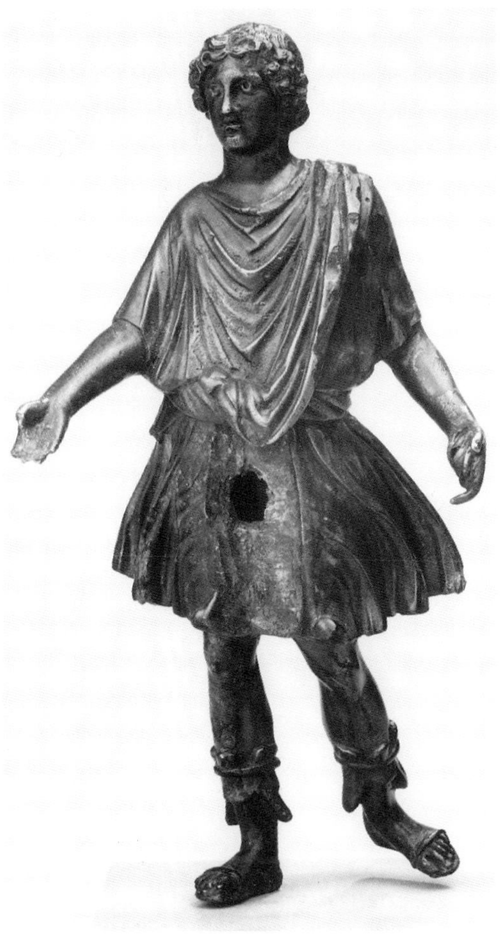

Abb. 1. Larenstatuette aus Bonn. Bronze, H. 12,4 cm. Bonn, Rheinisches Landesmuseum 10496. (Foto: Museum)

Übereinstimmung der 13 Statuetten macht deutlich, daß es sich um eine beabsichtigte technische Zurichtung handeln muß. Ein Vergleich mit anderen Figuren desselben Typs erhellt den Zweck dieser Bearbeitung. Die überaus zahlreichen Vergleichsstücke zeigen alle an der fraglichen Stelle einen über den unteren Saum der Tunika bis etwa in Kniehöhe herabhängenden Mantelzipfel mit Zickzacksäumen. Bei dem Bonner Fundstück und seinen Parallelen wurde der herabfallende Mantelzipfel also zunächst separat gegossen und erst später an die übrige Figur angefügt.

Wie mir freundlicherweise F. Jurgeit-Blanck mitteilte, ist es im Falle der Statuette in Karlsruhe jüngst gelungen, den unter einer anderen Inventarnummer inventarisierten Mantelzipfel wiederzufinden und neu anzusetzen (Abb. 2-3). Zusätzliche Bestätigung findet die beschriebene Vorgehensweise durch die an der Bonner Figur noch deutlich erkennbaren Lotreste und einen einzeln erhaltenen Gewandzipfel in Rabat, der von C. Boube-Piccot in überzeugender Weise einer großen Larenstatuette zugeschrieben wurde.[6]

Wir haben es also im Falle der Bonner Larenstatuette mit einer nur wenig bekannten und noch nie ausführlicher gewürdigten Form der Anstückungstechnik zu tun.[7] Besser bekannt sind die häufigeren Anstückungen einzelner Arme mit oder ohne Gewand. Ganz allgemein fällt dabei auf, daß sich die Hersteller dieser Statuetten stets bemühten, die Nahtstellen der Anstückungen nach Möglichkeit unter Armreifen, Ärmelsäumen oder Attributen zu verbergen.[8]

---

bung der Sammlung antiker Bronzen (Karlsruhe 1890) 189, Nr. 992; Ostia 3535, aus Ostia: G. Calza, *JRS* 5 (1915) 170-71, Abb. 44; ders., *NSc* (1915) 254, Abb. 16; Microfichekatalog DAI Rom, Fiche 1880 E 5-E 14; Ostia 3536: unpubliziert; Microfichekatalog DAI Rom, Fiche 1880 F 1-F 10; Palermo: C. A. di Stefano, *Bronzetti figurati del Museo Nazionale di Palermo* (Rom 1975) 24, Nr. 37, Taf. 10; Paris: Microfiche DAI Rom. Fiche 1894 E 14 links (= Foto Giraudon 9637); Rennes, aus Corseul, Dep. Côtes-du-Nord: F. Braemer, *L'art dans l'occident romain* (Ausstellungskat., Paris 1963) 98, Nr. 430; ders., "Bronzes romains — problèmes de géographie," in *Toreutik und figürliche Bronzen römischer Zeit: Akten der 6. Tagung über antike Bronzen 1980* (Berlin 1984) 67 Anm. 56, Taf. 2.2; Rouen, aus Rouen: A. Kaufmann-Heinimann, *Götter und Lararien aus Augusta Raurica* (Forschungen in Augst 26, 1998) 260 f., Nr. GF 42, Abb. 216; Veszprém/Ungarn, aus Nagydém: E. B. Thomas, *FolArch* 15 (1963) 21 ff.; dies., *Römische Villen in Pannonien* (Budapest 1964) 283-84, Taf. 180; dies., *AntW* 6 (1975) 29 ff.; *Römische Bronzeindustrie in Pannonien* (Ausstellungskat., Székesfehérvár 1982) Nr. 24; Kunsthandel Frankfurt am Main: *Katalog der Sammlung C. A. Milani* (Auktion F. A. C. Prestel, Frankfurt 4.6.1883) 132-33, Nr. 461; Kunsthandel London: Christie's, London (Versteigerung 10.12.1981) Nr. 86; Privatbesitz: A. Garcia y Bellida, *Esculturas romanas de España y Portugal* (Madrid 1949) 105, Nr. 99, Taf. 81 Mitte.

6 C. Boube-Piccot, *Les bronzes antiques du Maroc* 1 (Rabat 1969) 207-8, Nr. 223, Taf. 156.2.

7 Für die Kenntnis dieser Technik, vgl. auch A. Leibundgut, *Die römischen Bronzen der Schweiz* 2: *Avenches* (Mainz 1976) 30 ff., Nr. 15; *The gods delight* 326-29, Nr. 62 (J. J. Herrmann); S. Boucher und H. Oggiano-Bitar, *Le trésor des bronzes de Bavay* (*Revue du Nord, Coll. Archéologie* 3, 1993) 34 ff., Nr. 8-9; dies., in J. Arce und F. Burkhalter (Hrsg.), *Bronces y religion romana: Actas del XI Congreso int. de bronces antiguos 1990* (Madrid 1993) 87-88, Nr. 18-19.

8 Wo dies nicht möglich war, griff man zu anderen Lösungen, vgl. z.B. die ptolemäische Hermesstatuette in Bonn: N. Himmelmann, *Herrscher und Athlet* (Ausstellungskat., Bonn 1989) 234-35, Nr. 19, Farbtaf. S.

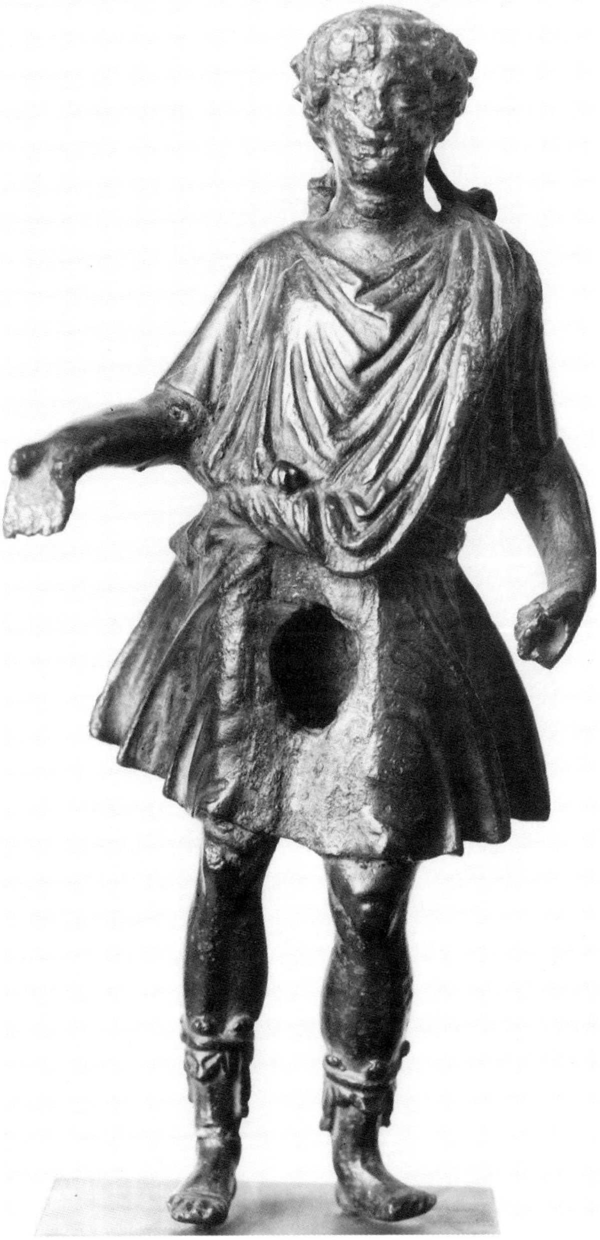

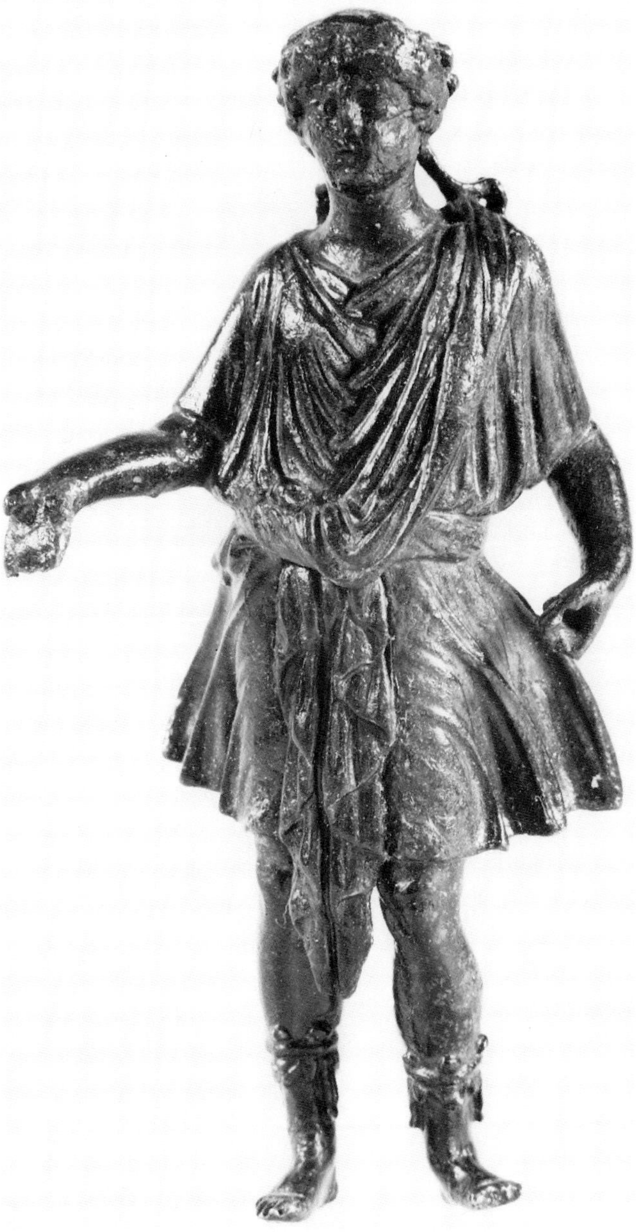

Abb. 2 (links). Larenstatuette aus Pompeji(?). Bronze, H. 12 cm. Karlsruhe, Badisches Landesmuseum F 1179. (Foto: Museum) Abb. 3 (rechts). Wie Abb. 2, mit zugehörigem Gewandzipfel. (Foto: Museum)

Auch an der hier betrachteten Bonner Larenstatuette war die Anstückung ursprünglich mit bloßem Auge kaum erkennbar, da sie oben von dem um die Taille gegürteten Teil des Mantels und dem herabhängenden Gewandbausch verdeckt wurde und sich nach unten hin optisch in den vertikalen Faltenfluß der Tunika einfügte. Bei vollständig erhaltenen Bronzestatuetten ist es darum allein nach Fotografien in vielen Fällen nicht möglich zu entscheiden, ob eine Anstückung vorliegt oder nicht.[9]

Um die Gründe für die Verwendung von Anstückungen genauer zu analysieren, gilt es zunächst zu klären, bei welchen Arten von Statuetten die Technik auftritt. Anhand der genannten Laren und anderer in der gleichen Technik hergestellter Figuren ist festzustellen, daß die An-

233 (mit einer technischen Parallele).

9 Durch eine gründliche Untersuchung unter dem Vergrößerungsglas ließ sich aber feststellen, daß die nackten Teile der Arme an der Bonner Bronze mitgegossen und nicht angestückt sind, wie dies bei anderen Laren zu beobachten ist.

stückungstechnik offenbar vornehmlich bei qualitätvolleren Bronzen Anwendung findet. Ein weiteres wichtiges Kriterium ist zweifellos auch die Größe der Statuetten. Zwar sind die Anstückungen nicht, wie man vielleicht erwarten könnte, allein auf größere Figuren beschränkt, doch gibt es offenbar so etwas wie eine Mindesthöhe. Diese beträgt bei den Laren rund 12 cm.[10] Über dieses Maß hinaus kommen Anstückungen bei Statuetten unterschiedlichster Größe vor.[11]

Einige der Larenstatuetten sind untereinander so ähnlich, daß man in einigen Fällen an die Entstehung in einer gemeinsamen Werkstatt denken könnte.[12] Insgesamt aber überwiegen die Unterschiede. Es scheint deshalb ausgeschlossen, daß alle Statuetten mit Anstückungen Produkte einer einzigen Werkstatt gewesen sein könnten. Dies bestätigt auch die Verbreitung entsprechender Statuetten. So zeigen die bekannten Fundorte eine überaus weite Streuung in Gallien, Germanien, Pannonien, Italien und Mauretanien. Das Vorherrschen von Fundorten im Westen des Imperiums ist aber, mitbedingt durch den unterschiedlichen Stand der Forschung, ein allgemeines Phänomen römischer Kleinbronzen und wohl eher ein besonderes Charakteristikum der Laren als der an ihnen festgestellten Anstückungstechnik.[13]

Was aber war der Sinn solcher Anstückungen? D. Kent Hill, die sich als einzige ausführlicher mit einer besonderen Erscheinungsform des Gesamtphänomens auseinandersetzte, sah in den von ihr untersuchten Anstückungen eine Hilfe zur einfacheren und schnelleren Massenproduktion von Bronzestatuetten.[14] Nach ihrer Vorstellung ließ sich mit Hilfe des Anstückungsverfahrens z.B. ein und derselbe, mit einer bestimmten Gewanddrapierung verbundene Armtypus mit Körpertypen verschiedener Götter verbinden.[15] Was für Arme mit einer wenig spezifischen Gewandangabe wie auch für nackte Arme vielleicht einleuchten mag, kann aber bei eindeutig zuweisbaren Attributen, wie etwa dem Löwenfell des Herkules, nicht überzeugen und muß aus demselben Grund letztlich auch im Falle der Laren bezweifelt werden. Es fällt nämlich schwer sich vorzustellen, daß der separate Guß und die spätere Anstückung eines einzelnen Mantelzipfels tatsächlich irgendeine Arbeitsersparnis bedeutet hätten, zumal man für diesen Gewandzipfel bei keinem anderen Statuettentypus, als dem des *lar familiaris*, Ver-

---

10 Zu diesen kleinsten Beispielen zählen die Laren in Bonn, Karlsruhe und im Londoner Kunsthandel.

11 Die Statuetten im Frankfurter Kunsthandel und in Palermo messen 15,5 bzw. 16,2 cm, die Statuette in Privatbesitz 16,5 cm. Die Statuette in Rennes mißt ohne Füße noch 17 cm und war damit etwa gleichgroß wie der 20,2 cm hohe Lar in Bavay (s. o. Anm. 7). Mit 24 cm Höhe doppelt so groß wie die kleinsten Laren ist die Bronze in Veszprém. Zu den größten Exemplaren zählen schließlich der 31,8 cm hohe Lar in Bavay (s. o. Anm. 7) und das Fragment in Rabat (s. o. Anm. 6), das zu einer Statuette von ursprünglich rund 33-35 cm Höhe gehört haben muß.

12 Dies gilt z.B. für die Laren in Bonn und im Londoner Kunsthandel.

13 Das zeigt eine Reihe im Osten gefundener Statuetten mit verschiedenen Anstückungsformen: G. Mendel, *BCH* 26 (1902) 231, Nr. 1, Abb. 8 (aus Konya); C. Rolley, *Musée de Delphes: Bronzes* (Athen um 1979) 47, Abb. 60 (aus der Nähe von Delphi).

14 D. Kent Hill, "Note on the piecing of bronze statuettes," *Hesperia* 51 (1982) 277-83 (mit richtigen Beobachtungen zur weiten Verbreitung des Phänomens und zum gewöhnlichen Format der Statuetten). Zur Anstückungstechnik, vgl. auch S. Boucher, *Recherches sur les bronzes figurés de Gaule pré-romaine et romaine* (Rom 1976) 280-82.

15 Insgesamt sind aber Typenklitterungen bei in Stückungstechnik hergestellten Bronzestatuetten viel zu selten, um hierin eine regelmäßige Praxis zu sehen. Als eines der wenigen Beispielen, vgl. die mit einem von Gewand bedeckten, linken Arm des Jupitertypus Florenz versehene Merkurstatuette aus der Sammlung Cook in Toronto (*Master bronzes* 257, Nr. 247 [J. A. Scott], für die allerdings schon Boucher, *Recherches* (s. o. Anm. 14) 283-84, Taf. 98, Abb. 496, eine moderne Reparatur nicht ausschließen konnte. Ob nun antike oder moderne Veränderung, in jedem Fall zeigt die unnatürlich verbreiterte linke Schulter, daß beide Teile zumindest von der ursprünglichen Konzeption her nicht zusammengehören können. Gegen die freie Austauschbarkeit von den mit Gewand bedeckten linken Armen spricht ferner der Umstand, daß trotz gelegentlich ähnlicher Drapierung die Bronzestatuetten des Merkur gewöhnlich eine Chlamys mit runder Schließe, Jupiter dagegen stets nur einen einfachen Mantel ohne Verschluß trägt. Eine moderne Montage zeigt ein Merkur in Straßburg: B. Schnitzler, *Bronzes antiques d'Alsace* (Paris 1995) 32, Nr. 4.

wendung gehabt hätte.[16] Für ein Zusammensetzen von Statuetten aus verschiedenen Einzelteilen wäre der Vorgang der Anstückung während der sogenannten Kaltarbeit aber allein schon deshalb nicht notwendig, weil bereits ein früherer Arbeitsschritt, nämlich die Herstellung des Wachsmodells mittels Hilfsnegativen, hierzu wesentlich bessere Möglichkeiten geboten hätte.[17] Der hauptsächliche Grund für die Anstückungen muß darum, nicht nur bei den beschriebenen Laren, ein anderer gewesen sein.

Für die Lösung dieses Problems könnte das schon erwähnte unregelmäßige Loch unter der verlorenen Anstückung von Bedeutung sein. Es ist sicher nicht zufällig, da es sich außer an der Bonner Statuette auch noch bei wenigstens vier weiteren Exemplaren desselben Typs findet.[18] Es diente mit hoher Wahrscheinlichkeit dazu, nach dem Guß die Entfernung des Tonkerns aus dem Inneren der Statuette zu ermöglichen.[19] Demzufolge hatte die Anstückung also wohl die Aufgabe, diese für den beschriebenen Zweck notwendige Öffnung auf möglichst elegante Weise zu verstecken. Dies kann aber nicht der alleinige Zweck der Anstückung gewesen sein, was sich schon allein daran zeigt, daß bei einigen der genannten Larenstatuetten ein entsprechendes Loch fehlt.

Nach den bisher gehörten Argumenten stellt sich nun die Frage, ob sich die hier behandelte Form von Anstückungen nicht konkret aus gußtechnischen Gründen erklären läßt. In der Tat erscheint es sehr viel plausibler anzunehmen, daß die Hersteller der Larenstatuetten für den Guß möglichst einfache Formen anstrebten und deshalb mit Hilfe der Anstückungen versuchten, einen besonders kritischen Bereich, an dem sich beim konventionellen Verfahren erfahrungsgemäß immer wieder Gußfehler einstellten, dadurch zu entschärfen, daß sie den Gewandzipfel separat gossen und erst zum Schluß an die Statuette anlöteten. Dasselbe kann sinngemäß wohl für fast alle Arten von Anstückungen an hellenistischen und römischen Kleinbronzen gelten. Entgegen der Vorstellung D. Kent Hills bot das Anstückungsverfahren so nur eine indirekte Erleichterung bei der seriellen Produktion von Bronzestatuetten, indem es lediglich dabei half, die Zahl von Fehlgüssen zu verringern.[20] Gewissermaßen als Nebeneffekt bewirken die Anstückungen allerdings auch eine ästhetische Verbesserung. Denn durch die tiefen Unterschneidungen und die dadurch hervorgerufenen Verschattungen zwischen Körper und Gewand entsteht ein realistischer Kontrast, der anders als bei geringerwertigen, in einem Guß hergestellten Statuetten den Eigenwert beider Komponenten in natürlicher Weise unterstreicht.

Zum Schluß möchte ich noch einen überraschenden anderen Zweck von Anstückungen zur Diskussion stellen. Ausgangspunkt meiner Überlegungen ist die Statuette eines mit einem Mantel bekleideten Negerknaben in Augst,[21] zu der noch zwei weitere Repliken in Saint-Germain-en-

---

16 Ein entfernt ähnlicher Gewandzipfel begegnet lediglich bei dem sehr viel selteneren Statuettentypus des Silen mit Cista. Vgl., z.B., Statuetten in Paris und London: E. Babelon und J.-A. Blanchet, *Catalogue des bronzes antiques de la Bibliothèque Nationale* (Paris 1895) 170-71, Nr. 378-79; Walters, *British Museum bronzes* Taf. 30.

17 Daß die Bronzegießer die Möglichkeit der Herstellung von Wachsmodellen aus verschiedenen Hilfsnegativen auch tatsächlich ausgiebig nutzten, ist entgegen anderslautender Stimmen inzwischen ausreichend nachgewiesen. Zu diesem Themenkomplex zuletzt: C. C. Mattusch, "The production of bronze statuary in the Greek world," in *Das Wrack* 1, 789-800.

18 Verschiedene, teilweise unpublizierte Abbildungen lassen ein solches Loch außerdem noch an den Statuetten in Karlsruhe und im Londoner Kunsthandel sowie je einer der Statuetten in Bavay und Ostia erkennen.

19 Darüber hinaus sind durch die direkte Verbindung von Gußkern und Gußmantel auch gußtechnische Vorteile gegeben (freundl. Hinweis F. Willer).

20 Eine ähnliche Ansicht vertraten bereits J.-J. Hatt, *RAE* 12 (1961) 217, der das von ihm an einer Merkurstatuette in Straßburg beobachtete Anstückungsverfahren "une simplification technique, en vue de faciliter la coulée" nannte, und A. Kaufmann-Heinimann, *Die römischen Bronzen der Schweiz* 1 (Mainz 1977) 96, Nr. 120.

21 J. Vercouter *et al.*, *L'image du noir dans l'art occidental* 1 (Fribourg 1976) 26, Abb. 293; Kaufmann-Heinimann, ibid. 81, Nr. 83, Taf. 88; Boucher (s. o. Anm. 14) 281, Taf. 94, Abb. 477-78; Kaufmann–Heini-

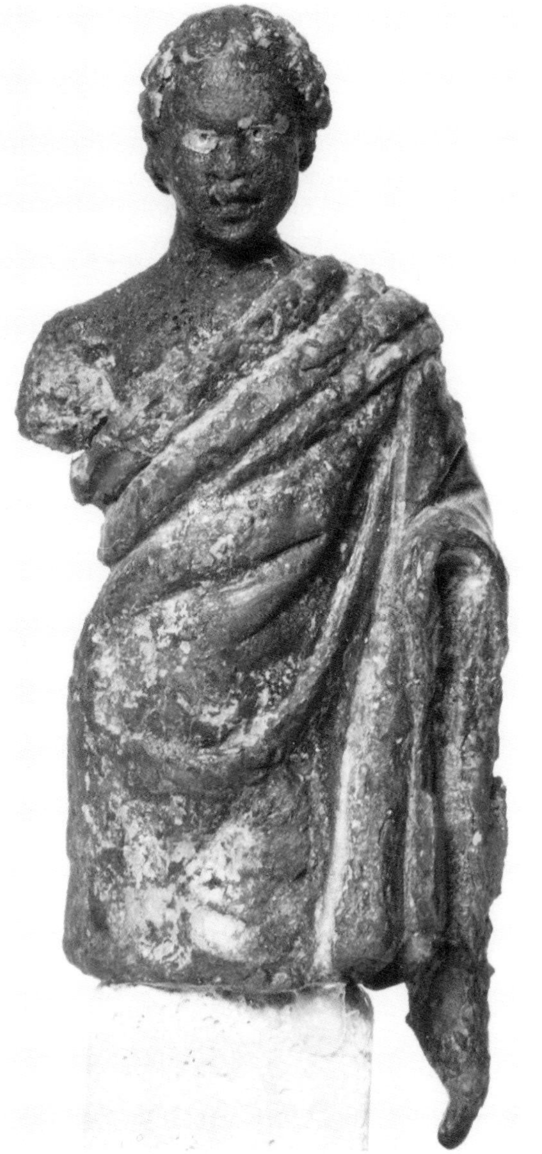
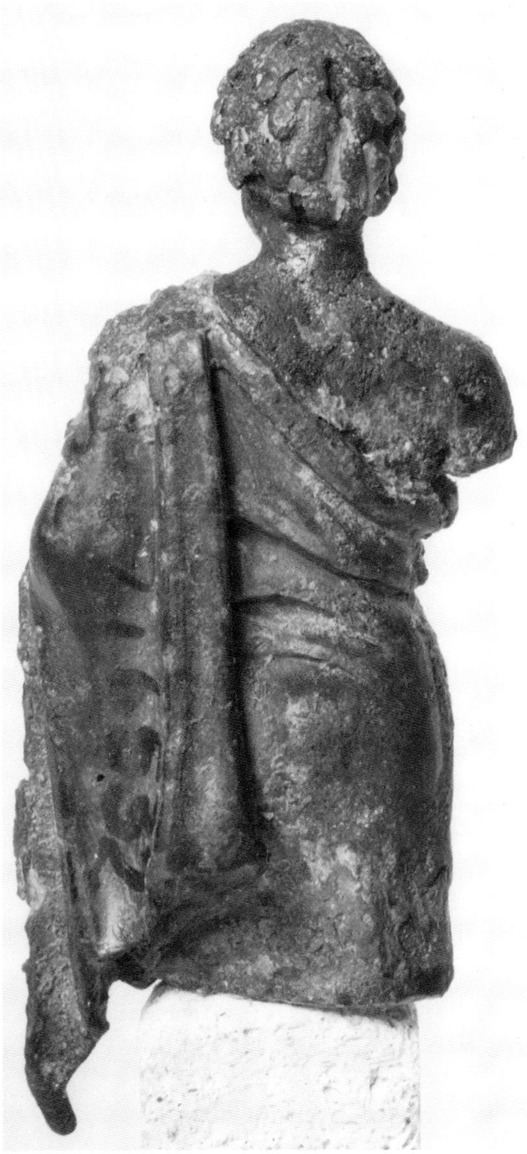

Abb. 4 (links). Negerknabe aus Augst. Bronze und Kupfer, H. 6,6 cm. Augst, Römermuseum 1961.6532. (Foto: RGZM Mainz) Abb. 5 (rechts). Wie Abb. 4: Rückseite. (Foto: RGZM Mainz)

Laye[22] und Boston[23] bekannt sind. Zumindest die beiden erstgenannten Figuren, die beide nicht vollständig erhalten sind, waren ursprünglich gleich aus mehreren separat gegossenen Teilen zusammengesetzt. Bei der am besten bekannten Figur in Augst (Abb. 4-5) handelt es sich dabei im einzelnen um: a) den vom Mantel bedeckten Teil des Körpers, b) den Kopf mit der rechten Schulter, c) den rechten Arm, d) den linken Unterarm, und e-f) die Beine. Besonderes Interesse verdient die Replik in Augst durch die an ihr vor kurzem durchgeführten Materialanalysen.[24]

---

mann (s. o. Anm. 5) 103, Abb. 63.

22 *Catalogue de la Collection Hoffmann* (Hôtel Drouot, Paris, Vente 16.6.1891) Nr. 232 (mir nicht zugänglich); S. Reinach, *Antiquités nationales: Description raisonnée du Musée de Saint-Germain-en-Laye: Bronzes figurés de la Gaule romaine* (Paris 1894) 213, Nr. 199; H. Rolland, *Bronzes antiques de Haute Provence* (*Gallia* Suppl. 18, 1965) 103-4, Nr. 191, Taf.; Vercouter *et al.* (s. o. Anm. 21) 226, Abb. 294.

23 *Collection H. Hoffmann* (Hôtel Drouot, Paris, Vente 28-29.5.1888) 137, Nr. 500; F. M. Snowden, *Blacks in antiquity* (Cambridge, MA 1970) 89, Abb. 64; Comstock-Vermeule, *Bronzes* 78-79, Nr. 82; Vercouter *et al.* (s. o. Anm. 21) 204 ff., Abb. 259.

24 A. Kaufmann-Heinimann und D. Liebel, "Legierungen figürlicher Bronzen aus der Colonia Raurica,"

Insgesamt wurden drei Proben genommen, zwei im Gewand und eine am Kopf. Während die beiden Proben im Gewand untereinander sehr ähnliche Resultate erbrachten, zeigen diese im Vergleich mit der am Kopf entnommenen Probe eine deutliche Abweichung. Bei dem Material des Gewands handelt es sich abgesehen von geringen Mengen anderer Stoffe um über 80% Kupfer mit etwa 8% Zinn und 7-10% Blei, also um echte Bronze. Der Kopf und die rechte Schulter hingegen bestehen, wie die Messung ergab, mit einem extrem hohen Anteil von 97,5% aus fast reinem Kupfer. Es erscheint nun im höchsten Maße wahrscheinlich, in diesem auffälligen Materialunterschied zwischen Körper und Gewand eine besondere Absicht des Herstellers zu sehen. Ich möchte deshalb vermuten, daß sich der Einsatz der Anstückungstechnik in diesem Fall nicht oder nicht nur aus technischen Zwängen erklärt. Vielmehr ging es dem Künstler offensichtlich darum, die Realistik der Kleinbronze zu steigern und zur ethnischen Kennzeichnung des Dargestellten einen farblichen Kontrast zwischen dem blaßbräunlichen Farbton des Gewands und dem stärker rötlichen Inkarnat herzustellen.[25]

Die hier in Kurzform dargelegten Überlegungen zur Bedeutung der Anstückungstechnik im allgemeinen und zur konkreten Bedeutung in einem bislang unbeobachteten Sonderfall konnten nur einen kleinen Ausschnitt des zweifellos sehr vielschichtigen Themas beleuchten. In Anbetracht der unterschiedlichen Ausprägungen des technischen Verfahrens erscheint es unbedingt notwendig, in Zukunft die Frage nach der Bedeutung für jede einzelne in Stückungstechnik hergestellte Statuette neu zu stellen. Eine gezielte kritische Untersuchungen anderer Statuetten dürfte somit sicher noch weitere interessante Aspekte dieses Phänomens zutage bringen.[26]

Römisch-Germanisches Museum, Köln

Die Vorbereitung dieses Artikels wurde maßgeblich erleichtert durch die freundliche Unterstützung zahlreicher Kollegen und Institutionen. Für die Überlassung bzw. Beschaffung von Fotos und hilfreiche Auskünfte danke ich B. Bollmann, H. Gregarek, U. Heimberg, O. Höckmann, F. Jurgeit-Blanck, A. Kaufmann-Heinimann, sowie dem Rheinischen Landesmuseum Bonn, dem Badischen Landesmuseum Karlsruhe, und dem Römisch-Germanischen Zentralmuseum Mainz. Nicht zuletzt gilt mein Dank F. Willer, Restaurator am Rheinischen Landesmuseum, für seine Diskussionsbereitschaft und dem Fotografen des Akademischen Kunstmuseums Bonn W. Klein, für technische Hilfe. Einen Teilaspekt des hier untersuchten Phänomens hat der Verfasser früher bereits an anderer Stelle behandelt: N. Franken, "Eine bronzene Larenstatuette aus Bonn" in *Das Rheinische Landesmuseum Bonn, Berichte aus der Arbeit des Museums 3* (1995) 73-77.

JberAugst 15 (1994) 225 ff. (A. Kaufmann-Heinimann danke ich für einen Sonderdruck und freundliche Auskünfte.)

25 Anders als die sehr viel häufigeren Metalleinlagen sind Anstückungen zur Darstellung farblicher Effekte ein offenbar bislang übersehendes technisches Phänomen. F. Willer machte mich im Gespräch darüber hinaus auf die Möglichkeit aufmerksam, daß das fast reine Kupfer auch als bessere Unterlage einer möglicherweise einst vorhandenen Schwarzpatina gewählt worden sein könnte. Ob die verkrustete Oberfläche hiervon noch Spuren zeigt, wäre gegebenenfalls einmal am Original zu überprüfen.

26 Um beispielsweise herauszufinden, in welchem Umfang die Stückungstechnik zur Darstellung farblicher Gegensätze an Bronzestatuetten eingesetzt wurde, bedarf es in Zukunft verstärkter Materialanalysen. Als mögliche 'Kandidaten' kommen vor allem einige sehr qualitätvolle Statuetten in Frage, bei denen der Körper und das Gewand bzw. ein entsprechendes Attribut separat gearbeitet und angepaßt wurde. Dies gilt z.B. für eine Herculesstatuette in Wien und die bekannte Statuette des Veiovis aus Monterazzano in Rom, Villa Giulia: K. Gschwantler u.a., *Guß + Form: Bronzen aus der Antikensammlung* (Ausstellungskat., Wien 1986) 126-27, Nr. 187, Farbtaf. 7; R. Bartoccini, *BdA* 44 (1959) 311 ff.

Roman copper-based artifacts from Emona

Irena Sivec

Emona (mod. Ljubljana, Slovenia) was founded at the beginning of the 1st c. A.D., when the Roman empire expanded into the Balkans. The town was located on the Via Postumia, connecting Aquileia with Carnuntum and part of the so-called Amber Route to the Baltic. Emona was also along the routes on which other luxury items (glass, terra sigillata, etc.) from Italy were brought to the Panonnian plain. The town was at the crossing of important commercial arteries and became an important trade centre.

The opinions of scholars on Emona's origin are still divergent: it is not clear whether the city was first a military camp or a civilian settlement (Colonia Iulia Emona).[1] In Roman times the area was inhabited by autochthonous tribes, but the inhabitants of Emona were of various ethnic origins. There were N Italic merchant families, veterans, and slaves, but the majority of the middle stratum seems to have consisted of native inhabitants.[2]

The material from excavations dated to the early period (1st c. A.D.) shows mainly Roman elements (terra sigillata, glass, Aucissa *fibulae*, but there are also some local products (particularly pottery of La Tène tradition and some bronze objects). *Fibulae* with a wide perforated triangular foot and an animal-mouth bow (fig. 1.1, Garbsch A 236 C, Almgren 67) are a good example of local tradition. They are characteristic of the Adriatic littoral and can be dated to the first decades A.D.

Some wide elbow *fibulae* (Almgren 68, 69) with applied animal protomes are also dated to the 1st c. A.D., but their origin is to be found in local prehistoric art (graves NM 551, NM 214, and NM 149).[3] A group of boat-shaped bracelets shows the same characteristics: their decoration is entirely prehistoric (graves NM 41 and NM 239), but they are dated to the Claudian period (fig. 1.5).[4]

The bronze belt sets (fig. 1.6)[5] together with the *fibulae* (with a trapezoid foot, decorated with perforation technique and winged bow [fig. 1.4] or a trapezoid foot and knobbed bow [fig. 1.3]) completed the attire of the typical Norico-Pannonian woman of the 1st-2nd c. A.D. The parts of the belts, now in the National Museum of Slovenia (NM), were found out of stratigraphic context in cemetery areas.[6] The examples from the excavations carried out by the City Museum of Ljubljana (MM) were only from settlement strata. Not one of the more than 1,000 graves excavated during the last 30 years contained these kinds of belts.[7] There appeared to be found only knobbed *fibulae*. This may well be due to the fact that Emona was located at the periphery of Noricum and Pannonia, the regions where this type of clothing artifact was connected with Celtic tradition.

---

1 *RE* Suppl. X (1965) 540-77, s.v. Emona (J. Šašel); L. Plesničar-Gec, "The urbanism of Emona," *Mestni musej in Znanstveni inštitut Filozofske fakultete Ljubljana* (1999) 173.

2 The central part of modern-day Slovenia was populated by the Celtic tribe of the Taurisci: M. Šašel-Kos, "Nauportus, literary and epigraphical sources," in J. Horvat (ed.), *Nauportus (Vrhnika)* (Opera SAZU 33, Ljubljana 1990) 157 ff.

3 V. Šribar, "Contribution à la chronologie absolute des fouilles de l'Emona de 1er siècle," *ArhVest* 19 (1970) 451; S. Demetz, *Fibeln der Spätlatène- und frühen Römischen Kaiserzeit in den Alpenländern* (Frühgeschichtliche und Provinzialrömische Archäologie, Materialien und Forschungen 4, Rahden 1999) 137-47.

4 M. Budja, "Metallarmreifen in den Römergräbern Sloweniens," *ArhVest* 30 (1979) 233-53.

5 J. Garbsch, *Die norisch-pannonische Frauentracht* (*MünchBeitr* 11, 1965) 100, Abb. 54, Typ E.f.

6 S. Petru, *Emonske nekropole* (Narodni Muzej v Ljubljani, Katalogi in monografije 7, 1972) pl. 94, 11-21.

7 City Museum of Ljubljana, unpublished. I am grateful for all unpublished items to L. Plesničar-Gec: see id., *The northern necropolis of Emona* (Narodni muzej v Ljubljana, Katalogi in monografije 8, Ljubljana 1983) pl. 29.2, pl. 36.13.

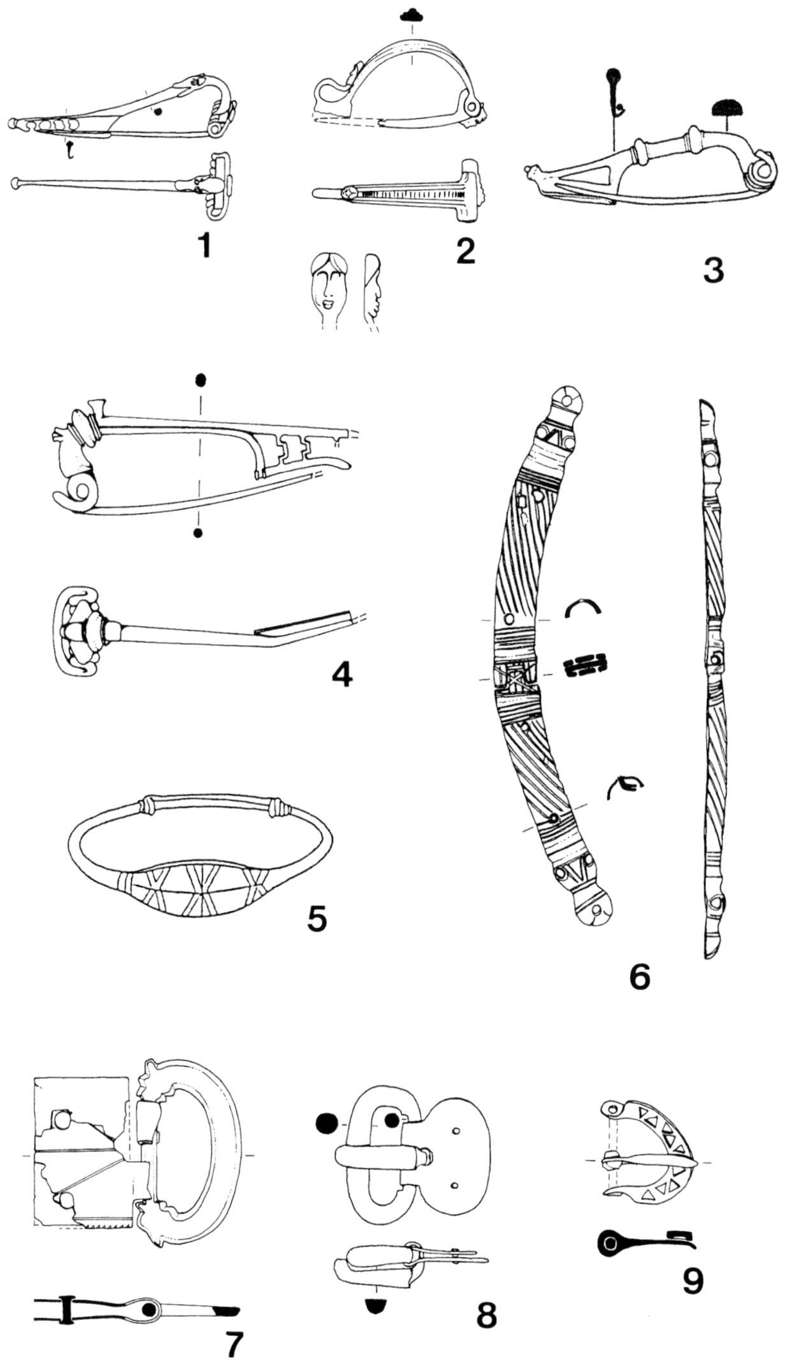

Fig. 1. Bronze finds from Emona of the 1st c. A.D. and later: 1.1 Dog-mouth bow *fibula*, early 1st c. A.D.; 1.2 Aucissa *fibula*, date uncertain; 1.3 Aucissa *fibula*, 1st c. A.D.; 1.4 Norico-Pannonian *fibula* with winged bow, late 1st c. A.D.; 1.5 Boat-shaped bracelet, Claudian; 1.6 Norico-Pannonian belt set, 1st c. A.D.; 1.7 oval belt buckle with animal heads, Late Roman; 1.8 Silver belt buckle, perhaps early 5th c. A.D.; 1.9 Oval belt buckle with incised triangles, second half of 4th c. or early 5th c. A.D. Scale 1 : 2.

Aucissa *fibulae*, frequently found at Emona, are doubtless harbingers of Romanization. One of them, found in an early stratum in the Old Christian complex (fig. 1.2), has a foot shaped like a human face and reflects a high degree of creative craftsmanship.[8] I believe that metal ob-

8 I. Sivec, "Die Bronze- und Beinkleinfunde," in L. Plesničar-Gec *et al.* (edd.), "Old Christian center in

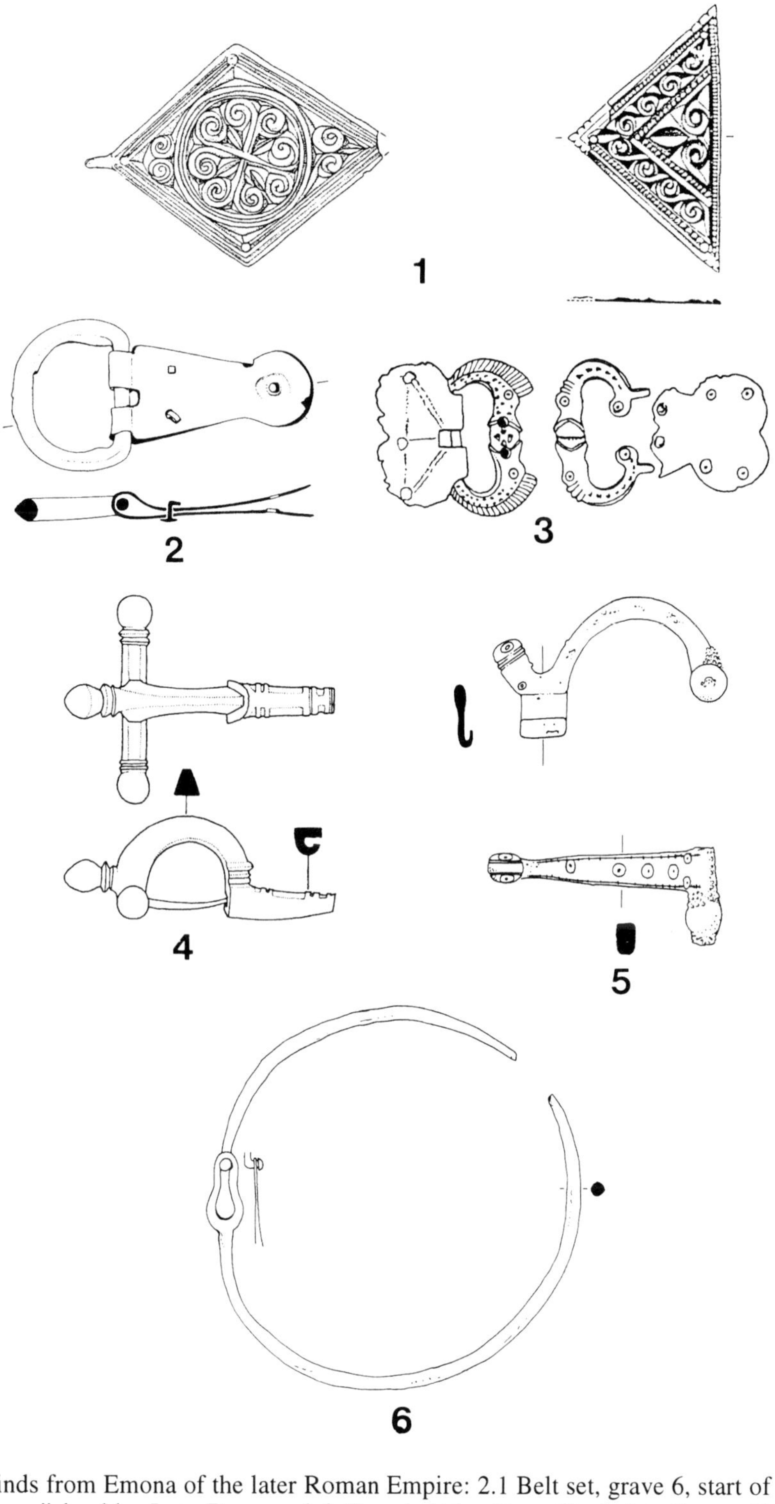

Fig. 2. Bronze finds from Emona of the later Roman Empire: 2.1 Belt set, grave 6, start of 5th c. A.D. 2.2 "Mediterranean" buckle, Late Roman; 2.3 Two belt buckles, Chadwick Group 11A, 5th c. A.D.; 2.4 Crossbow *fibula*, Late Roman; 2.5 Gurina-type *fibula*, second half of 5th c. A.D.; 2.6 Metal necklace, first half of 5th c. A.D. Scale 1 : 2.

objects, which often arrived in Emona unfinished, could be finished there with individualized social, religious, or purely aesthetic features.

Wood cosmetic caskets, paneled with variously shaped and decorated bronze mounts, are characteristic of a wide area from Panonnia to N Italy. Those found at Emona have additional

---

Emona," *Narodni Muzej v Ljubljani, Katalogi in monografije* 21 (Ljubljana 1983) T. 4.1,1a.

rings for fastening the chain, thus combining Roman and local details.[9]

There were almost two centuries of intensive Romanization and relative peace in the area, reflected by Emona's urban plan with its impressive buildings, water supply and discharge networks, and by the remains of its material prosperity (imported pottery, glass, and bronze items). Although Emona itself was not directly affected, a first crisis occurred during the last decades of the 2nd c. with the Quado-Marcomannian incursions. Diocletian's reforms of the army after 286 had a strong influence on the region. Foreign elements, particularly German, appear among the military remains and also in the civilian area. In addition to the legions along the Danube, Diocletian created several defense lines in towns or at strategically important points in the interior and equipped them with military garrisons. The third defense line ran through Slovene territory and encompassed the Alpine passes from the Adriatic (Rijeka) to pre-Alpine regions in the Carinthia.[10]

Traces of foreign influence can be noted in belt buckles of different types found in excavation. An oval belt buckle (fig. 1.9) found in the Jakopič garden is decorated with incised triangles. According to Bullinger and Böhme, it should be dated to the second half of the 4th or the beginning of the 5th c.[11] There is also an oval belt buckle with animal heads (fig. 1.7). Its rectangular plate, partly damaged, consists of two parts belonging to the Spontin type.[12] It was found in a Late Roman settlement stratum near Emona's N Gate. A bronze buckle of so-called Mediterranean shape (fig. 2.2) was found in inhumation grave 128 of the Late Roman cemetery near Metalka, along with an egg-shaped pottery jug (no other significant goods were found in the grave).[13] The oval belt buckles are also typical for this late period. A silver belt buckle (fig. 1.8) was found in the garden of the National Museum, Ljubljana, and another made of bronze came to light in an inhumation grave of the north cemetery of Emona.[14] Several more have been discovered in other sites around Slovenia. These belt buckles may be associated with the presence of Visigoths in 408-9, when they spent the winter in the vicinity of Emona's town walls. The Visigoths came from Epirus under Alaric and waited here for Honorius's permission to occupy Noricum. Emona's inhabitants cautiously provided food for the invaders and also paid a considerable ransom.[15]

Three more belt buckles (fig. 2.3), now in the National Museum,[16] belong to Chadwick's 11A Group and were still in use in the 5th c. A.D.[17]

This region was part of the military frontier and was the actual battlefield in the civil wars between pretenders to the throne in the second half of the 4th c. (*Atrans*–Trojane, *Poetovio*–Ptuj, battle at the Frigido river, near *Castra*–Ajdovščina).[18] This explains the presence of German elements among the finds from Emona. The armies were largely composed of

---

9 I. Sivec, "Die Kästchenbeschläge aus Emona," in S. T. A. M. Mols *et al.* (edd.), *Acta of the 12th int. Congress on Ancient Bronzes, 1992* (Nijmegen 1995) 423 ff.

10 P. Petru, "Recenti ricerche archeologiche della claustra Alpium Iuliarum e delle fortificazioni tardo antiche in Slovenia," *ArhVest* 23 (1972) 362 ff.

11 H. Bullinger, *Spätantike Gürtelbeschläge* (Diss. Archaeologicae Gandenses 12, Brugge 1969) Abb. 47.6; H. W. Böhme, *Germanische Grabfunde des 4. bis 5. Jahrhunderts* (*MünchBeitr* 19, 1974).

12 L. Plesničar and I. Sivec, "Emona at the beginning of Great Migration period," in *Problemi seobe naroda u Karpatskoj kotlini* (Novi Sad 1978) 61 n.18.

13 Cemetery grave 128: unpublished; R. M. Swoboda, "Zu spätantiken Bronzeschnallen mit festem, dreieckigem Beschlag," *Germania* 64 (1986) 91-103.

14 D. Vuga, "Männergrab 1885 aus dem Garten des Narodni Muzej in Ljubljana," *ArhVest* 36 (1985) Abb. 1.2, 254; Grave 232 MM: L. Plesničar-Gec, *The northern necropolis of Emona* (Narodni Muzej v Ljubljani, Katalogi in monografije 8, 1972) T. 64.8, 188.

15 J. Šašel, *K zgodovini Emone v rimskih napisih in literaturi* (Zgodovina Ljubljane, Kronika, 1984) 45.

16 Petru (supra n.6) gr.633, pls. 41.3a, 76.31, 32.

17 S. Chadwick-Hawkes, "Krieger und Siedler in Britannien während des 4. und 5. Jhr.," *BerRGK* 43-44 (1962-63) 212.

18 S. Ciglenečki, *Polis Norikon* (Podsreda 1992) 4.

German and Gothic soldiers who still wore characteristic personal ornaments. The military workshops also produced semi-finished artifacts, which could easily be adapted to the taste and the wishes of the buyer. However, in the Late Roman period, the production of military equipment, which had been in the hands of private companies, became a state monopoly. The equipment became more uniform and individual details disappeared.[19] In this period characteristic belt sets with wedge-shaped ornamentation appear, as well as crossbow *fibulae* decorated with onion-shaped ends (fig. 2.4) for fastening military *chlamydes*.[20] Later, these were also worn by important state officials.

At the end of the 4th and in the first half of the 5th c., civil wars and economic and social decline consumed the western Roman empire. Emona was destroyed in 452 by a plundering raid of the Huns led by Attila on their way back from Italy. The layers of burning found in settlement excavations show that the town was pillaged and burned.[21] Eastern, i.e., Hunnic elements among the material remains of this period are rare. A metal necklace (fig. 2.6) from Emona's cemetery, dated to the first half of the 5th c., is a rare example. This type of jewelry is known from male graves of Germanic or Hunno-Alanic ethnic groups and is found mainly in the central Danube area.[22]

To date, only one example of a Gurina-type *fibula* (fig. 2.5) has been found, but it is worth mentioning since it could perhaps be evidence for Emona's survival into the second half of the 5th c.[23]

Mestni Muzej Ljubljana

19 J. Oldenstein, "Zur Ausrüstung römischer Auxiliareinheiten," *BerRGK* 57 (1977) 71; M. Sagadin, "Antike Gürtelschnallen und -garnituren in Slowenien," *ArhVest* 30 (1979) 294-338.

20 I. Sivec, "Late Roman armory in Slovenia," *ArhVest* 48 (1997) 143-52.

21 L. Plesničar-Gec, "Urban characteristics of Emona," *ArchIug* 13 (1972) 48.

22 T. Knific, "Traces of the Huns in Slovenia?" *Ptujski arheološki zbornik* (Ptuj 1993) 537.

23 Excavated by J. Šašel, *ins.* XII: unpublished; C. Gugl, *Die römischen Fibeln aus Virunum* (Klagenfurt 1995) 41, T. 32.214, 215.

Technical appendix

Alessandra Giumlia-Mair

A number of copper-based objects from Emona were selected for analysis in order to answer specific questions, such as the use of brass, relationships between alloys, working techniques, local traditions, and imports. Several classes of items of different usage were chosen to include as many types of alloys as possible: small objects for personal adornment (such as *fibulae*, pins, and bracelets), decorative elements of different kinds (such as horse trappings and casket or furniture fittings), vessels, statuettes, personal objects of everyday use (such as belt fittings and buckles), utilitarian objects, tools of different qualities, and minor pieces and functional parts.

The analysis was carried out on an ARL inductively coupled plasma emission spectrometry (ICP) machine in the Metallurgy Laboratory of the Department of Material Science, University of Trento (Italy). The results (Table 1) have a precision of *c.* $\pm$ 1-2% for copper and $\pm$ 5% for elements present at a level greater than 1%, but gradually deteriorating to $\pm$ 50% near the detection limits of each element. The quoted standard deviation is 1%.[24]

The results of the analyses generally reflect the overall situation in the Roman Empire: The lead content is consistent with the manufacturing technique, with noticeably more lead for castings and almost no lead in hammered pieces. Larger castings tend to contain proportionally more lead than smaller pieces. The use of quaternary alloys tends to increase with time, of

24 For detailed discussion on metallurgical aspects, see A. Giumlia-Mair, "Roman copper-based finds from a Slovenian settlement," *BMMA* 25 (1996) 48-63.

Table 1. Analysis of Emona bronzes by inductively coupled plasma emission spectrometry (ICP) (weight percent) (Table: A. Giumlia-Mair.)

N	Object	Inv. No.	Part	Cu	Sn	Zn	Pb	Ni	Fe	Ag	Co	Sb	As
2	vessel	2020	handle	76.8	0.81	14.3	0.31	0.04	0.63	-	0.03	0.04	0.03
3	"	"	rivet	87.2	0.85	2.07	0.31	0.02	0.60	0.01	0.01	0.07	0.05
4	"	"	attachment	78.6	0.50	19.3	0.41	0.41	0.39	0.07	0.10	0.04	-
5	casket	252	handle	75.3	0.24	16.9	0.17	0.02	0.40	1.29	-	0.10	0.70
6	vessel	F1053	handle	73.7	10.3	0.03	3.13	0.07	0.14	0.60	-	0.10	0.10
7	vessel	292	handle	70.1	0.69	21.3	0.20	0.03	1.70	0.02	0.02	0.07	0.02
8	"	"	attachment	74.2	0.58	0.05	0.20	0.03	0.20	-	-	0.06	0.07
9	vessel	1007	handle	83.6	7.68	0.04	0.27	0.06	0.30	-	-	0.02	0.03
10	ring	G2906	attachment	79.7	7.31	0.36	0.29	0.03	0.21	0.03	-	0.46	0.19
11	"	"	chain	90.0	6.88	0.05	0.10	0.01	0.19	0.04	0.03	0.12	0.03
12	"	"	ring	79.6	8.66	0.31	0.16	0.05	0.90	0.04	0.03	-	0.09
13	ring	G4566	chain	82.5	7.92	0.06	0.05	0.03	0.22	0.05	-	0.01	-
14	"	"	attachment	83.6	7.78	0.01	0.04	0.01	0.22	0.06	-	-	-
15	"	"	ring	83.9	8.10	0.13	0.08	0.01	0.26	-	0.01	0.03	0.01
16	ring		chain	92.5	7.21	0.01	0.03	0.01	0.18	0.05	-	0.01	-
17	hinge	F1062	sheet	87.1	0.73	11.4	0.3	0.02		-	-	-	-
18	"	"	rivet	71.1	0.58	0.27	0.24	0.04	0.07	-	-	0.01	-
19	pin	757		76.5	0.66	16.6	0.16	0.02	0.04	0.04	-	0.07	0.04
20	duck pin	2018		75.2	10.5	0.06	0.2	0.01	0.24	0.02	-	0.01	0.08
20a	Belenus	2087	statuette	90.1	2.72	0.01	0.9	0.82	0.10	0.23	0.30	-	-
21	ram	M545	statuette	80.2	6.01	-	11.3	0.06	0.01	0.03	-	0.09	0.04
22	Eros	2480	statuette	84.4	11.4	0.04	3.51	0.02	0.47	0.06	-	0.07	0.11
23	Eros	3070	statuette	86.3	8.5	0.03	3.14	2.00	0.12	-	-	0.01	-
24	goddess	3068	statuette	84.0	6.84	0.01	5.13	0.20	0.30	0.03	-	0.22	0.03
25	Belenus	PN830	statuette	70.2	9.2	0.05	11.8	0.06	0.11	-	-	-	-
26	belt	1139		68.6	0.20	0.04	1.49	0.02	0.27	0.15	-	0.10	0.12
27	fibula	S1508	bow	40.1	1.79	0.19	0.65	0.03	0.25	37.3	-	1.20	3.83
28	fibula		pin	49.4	2.63	0.04	0.77	0.03	0.13	35.1	-	0.80	0.50
29	fibula	G4757	body	78.5	0.20	1.38	4.63	0.04	0.28	-	-	0.04	0.02
30	fibula	G3950	knob	75.0	4.44	0.88	4.13	0.19	0.63	0.20	0.01	0.07	0.83
31	fibula	583	bow	74.2	6.6	1.15	10.2	0.03	0.35	0.05	0.01	0.05	0.21
32	fibula	3961	bow	65.1	4.94	2.85	9.6	0.07	0.34	0.46	-	0.46	-
33	fibula	2046	bow	59.6	6.11	7.93	11.7	0.09	0.67	0.57	0.03	0.74	-
34	brooch	4/6 O	wire	97.5	0.88	0.16	0.20	0.13	0.59	0.25	0.01	0.85	-
35	fibula	5669	tongs	85.8	6.08	1.08	3.23	0.07	0.61	0.59	0.01	0.34	0.50
36	fibula	753	sheet	73.7	1.25	1.72	0.92	0.01	1.00	-	-	0.01	0.01
37	fibula	M291	body	94.3	3.46	0.02	0.08	0.02	0.32	-	-	-	-
38	fibula	1968	tongs	45.6	4.34	0.93	3.90	0.03	0.53	-	0.01	-	-
39	fibula	F1855/oj	pin	76.8	1.13	13.7	0.53	0.06	1.10	-	-	0.02	0.01
40	fibula	3309		78.0	0.69	0.11	0.31	0.01	0.40	-	-	-	0.01
41	fibula	G4596	foot	75.7	0.66	9.87	0.05	0.04	0.45	-	-	0.03	0.01

N	Object	Inv. No.	Part	Cu	Sn	Zn	Pb	Ni	Fe	Ag	Co	Sb	As
42	fibula	F1432	body	69.5	1.04	10.4	0.26	0.02	0.78	-	-	-	-
43	vessel	4760	cast lid	81.3	8.20	0.49	7.68	0.07	0.43	-	-	0.20	0.10
44	horse trapping	1106	sheet	72.4	2.69	13.8	0.32	0.03	0.80	-	-	0.02	0.03
45	"	"	ring	73.4	4.90	17.1	0.50	0.13	1.50	-	-	0.08	-
46	vessel	7	lid	71.9	1.72	11.4	8.50	0.08	0.98	-	-	0	-
47	horse trapping	ST149	pendant	79.9	0.87	16.1	0.06	0.01	0.46	-	-	-	-
48	fibula	AS1502	button	67.9	0.58	14.3	0.50	0.06	0.23	-	-	0.03	-
49	fibula	F694	bow	77.4	0.98	11.2	0.58	0.03	0.79	1.77	0.22	2	-
50	bracelet	4739		76.5	2.12	0.02	1.31	0.06	0.32	-	-	0.01	0.03
51	bracelet	G3673	lion's head	63.8	0.40	8.80	8.60	0.06	0.37	-	-	-	-
52	"	"	ring	79.2	0.83	9.6	0.81	0.03	0.21	-	-	0.03	-
53	bracelet	G1852		82.3	9.2	0.04	0.17	0.08	0.16	-	-	0.02	0.02
54	bracelet	1984		75.5	6.04	2.42	8.20	0.05	0.17	0.02	-	0.03	-
55	belt fitting	3470	sheet	76.3	8.30	0.23	0.44	0.02	0.16	-	-	0.04	0.01
56	"	"	buckle	80.8	4.36	2.02	10.1	0.08	0.65	0.01	-	0.01	0.02
57	"	"	rivet	99.1	0.32	0.10	0.28	0.01	0.09	-	-	0.03	0.03
58	belt fitting	3747	sheet	82.7	2.77	0.03	0.77	0.02	0.38	-	-	0.01	0.03
59	"	"	buckle	80.1	0.14	1.90	2.73	0.06	0.19	-	-	-	-
60	"	"	rivet	84.7	1.25	0.48	0.58	0.04	0.25	0.03	-	-	-
61	belt fitting	G4697	sheet	77.4	3.50	0.37	1.67	0.05	0.73	-	-	-	0.06
62	"	"	buckle	85.4	7.17	0.20	4.85	0.04	0.17	-	-	0.01	0.01
63	"	"	rivet	92.2	2.22	0.07	2.00	0.08	0.11	-	-	0.01	0.02
64	belt fitting	G3718	sheet	76.9	1.59	0.03	2.84	0.04	0.49	-	-	0.01	0.02
65	"	"	rivet	81.9	0.48	0.48	0.26	0.21	0.25	-	-	-	0.04
66	"	"	buckle	70.8	2.16	8.50	6.18	0.07	0.99	-	-	0.02	-
67	belt fitting	3470	plate	82.1	4.23	2.12	10.8	0.07	0.60	0.01	-	-	0.03
68	belt fitting	1839	sheet	75.0	8.50	0.20	4.44	0.05	0.42	-	-	0.02	0.07
69	"	"	buckle	62.1	20.2	5.98	8.9	0.03	0.28	-	-	0.01	0.02
70	"	"	rivet	77.6	2.24	0.22	0.74	0.03	0.75	-	-	0.02	0.02
71	belt fitting	472 a	sheet	69.6	2.89	20.0	0.38	0.03	0.48	-	-	0.03	0.01
72	"	"	rivet	83.3	1.16	10.4	0.12	0.01	0.43	-	-	0.05	-
73	"	"	buckle	69.5	4.20	11.4	6.11	0.27	0.45	-	-	0.01	-
74	pendant	425		75.2	1.88	0.01	10.7	0.05	0.85	-	-	0.02	-
75	ornament	M1733	sheet	69.1	0.09	0.05	1.17	0.08	0.13	-	-	0.01	-
76	"	"	rivet	72.1	0.84	0.05	4.04	0.04	0.15	-	-	0.02	0.02
77	vessel	5217	handle	42.6	4.45	-	6.35	0.02	0.09	-	-	0.01	0.01
78	fibula	40	bow	86.3	8.50	0.17	0.35	0.05	0.25	-	-	0.02	-
79	mirror	G2394	mirror	66.1	20.6	0.05	5.97	0.03	0.49	-	-	0.01	0.01
80	"	"	handle	51.0	13.0	0.05	27.4	0.02	0.12	0.12	-	0.01	-
81	mirror	P872	handle	83.7	9.2	0.08	6.29	0.07	0.50	-	-	-	0.01
82	buckle	P871	pin	77.7	1.71	15.8	1.27	0.05	1.30	0.03	-	-	-
83	bell	2503		70.5	18.5	0.08	3.30	0.03	0.75	-	-	0.02	-

N	Object	Inv. No.	Part	Cu	Sn	Zn	Pb	Ni	Fe	Ag	Co	Sb	As
84	bulla	G3062	sheet	87.4	0.74	0.10	0.10	0.03	0.10	-	-	0.01	0.04
87	surgical instrument	G2023		91.4	6.82	0.05	0.62	0.01	0.32	-	-	0.01	0.03
88	mirror case	G2140		71.6	7.73	0.05	4.73	0.02	0.03	-	-	0.02	0.02
89	mirror case	G4506	front	55.3	8.40	0.38	7.47	0.50	0.37	-	-	-	-
90	"	"	back	67.6	11.2	0.12	10.4	0.03	0.10	-	-	0.04	0.01
91	ladle	G2021	foot	75.3	11.1	0.04	9.1	0.02	0.06	0.02	-	0.01	0.02
92	ladle	G1168	foot	65.5	14.0	0.20	11.7	0.04	0.17	-	-	0.02	0.03
93	ladle	G1168	handle	82.9	8.60	0.03	0.38	0.01	0.45	-	-	0.01	-
94	strainer	9	sheet	87.5	10.3	0.01	0.05	0.06	0.20	-	-	-	0.01
95	"	"	handle	86.2	9.4	0.06	3.67	0.05	0.53	-	-	0.01	-
96	strigil	G1183		71.1	4.51	10.2	4.35	0.03	0.56	-	-	0.04	0.05
97	ladle	G4771		84.5	4.77	7.27	2.73	0.04	0.50	0.01	-	0.02	0.01
98	key	F1616		69.2	5.61	4.34	9.4	0.03	0.26	-	-	0.01	0.04
99	vessel	F1084	lid	59.7	4.92	0.16	20.8	0.02	0.14	-	-	0.01	-
100	dolphin	M14		83.8	5.14	0.13	2.38	0.02	0.34	-	-	-	0.03
101	vessel	5353	lid	65.3	7.79	0.89	11.0	0.03	0.24	-	-	-	0.01
102	key	1986		70.4	5.76	3.04	11.1	0.03	0.22	-	-	0.02	0.03
103	key	5917		70.1	7.42	3.65	8.50	0.03	0.43	0.01	-	0.02	0.02
104	stirrup	2064	strip	72.1	1.45	12.4	3.26	0.05	0.56	-	-	0.01	0.03
105	"	"	button	69.9	0.92	11.2	2.87	0.05	0.54	-	-	0.02	0.03
106	boss	3115		71.8	2.40	9.6	6.68	0.07	0.31	-	-	0.01	0.02
107	boss	M1719		86.8	2.91	3.71	5.13	0.06	0.76	0.01	-	0.01	-
108	vessel	1878A	handle	76.1	6.35	0.06	0.10	0.02	0.78	-	-	0.01	0.01
109	lock	1897A		85.3	8.80	0.03	0.06	0.06	0.30	-	-	0.02	0.02
110	bell	1699A		53.7	6.81	0.90	2.79	0.05	1.30	-	-	0.04	0.01
111	vessel	1819A	handle	75.9	8.20	0.04	3.32	0.05	0.36	0.02	-	0.01	-
112	key	1698A		72.2	4.89	3.21	7.78	0.05	0.49	-	-	0.03	-
113	pendant	1712A		77.4	2.31	0.03	1.44	0.02	0.73	-	-	0.01	-
114	ring	1853A		67.2	0.63	14.6	3.66	0.02	0.24	-	-	0.01	0.01
115	ring	1908A		70.5	0.54	15.2	0.16	0.05	0.43	-	-	-	0.01
116	handle	1853A		64.5	0.75	15.9	1.14	0.15	0.56	-	-	0.02	-
117	spoon	1907A		79.1	0.51	14.3	0.24	0.01	0.48	-	-	0.04	-

course, as the result of the recycling of scrap metal. More elaborate objects of better quality tend to contain more tin, zinc, and lead than do minor objects, and to be made of more refined copper. However, there are also local peculiarities: unalloyed copper is often employed for small objects of personal adornment. The typical local artifacts contain less zinc than is the case in other areas studied. There are very few real brasses, and typical local objects, although finely worked and finished, generally tend to be of 'poor' alloys with low amounts of tin, zinc, and lead. Many decorative artifacts of local production show a tinned surface.

The results of the analyses of small objects of personal adornment (like *fibulae*, pins, and bracelets) are similar to those for comparable objects from other regions of the Roman empire,[25] with widely varying compositions within classes. This might be one of the reasons for the tinning of this kind of object: the wide range of alloys resulted in many different colors, while tinning made them all silvery. There seems to be only one exception, the Aucissa-type *fibulae*, which at Emona are pure brasses, as are the examples analyzed in Bavaria,[26] Britain,[27] and (with one exception) Spain.[28] The statuettes are of leaded bronze, with only one local exception being of leaded copper; none contains zinc in any noticeable amount.

The frequency and types of brass objects re-open the question of a possible specialized production. There are very few classes of objects with higher amounts of zinc. These include horse trappings, with an average zinc content of 15% (which compares well with the analyses of other Roman trappings[29]), buckets and basins (as also the case in the Netherlands[30] and Germany[31]), and casket and furniture fittings, which mostly contain more than 15% zinc and compare well with some examples from Bavaria[32] and from Noviodunum.[33] At Emona, only the local form of casket fittings (rings with chains) was of bronze. However, we need more dated comparisons to be able to say whether the use of brass fittings was a temporary fashion, a local phenomenon, or the prevailing choice, and whether these objects were imported from a specific region.

From a metallurgical point of view, the most interesting piece analyzed is a *fibula* Almgren-type 128a (see Sivec above fig. 1.4) with a very silvery surface and a peculiar composition. The pin contains: copper 49.4%, tin 2.63%, zinc 0.04%, lead 0.77%, nickel 0.03%, iron 0.13%, silver 35.1%, antimony 0.8%, arsenic 0.5%. The body contains: copper 40.1%, tin 1.79%, zinc 0.19%, lead 0.65%, nickel 0.03%, iron 0.25%, silver 37.3%, antimony 1.2%, and arsenic 3.83%. It is clear that in this case we are dealing with a silver imitation or fake, of the sort occasionally found

---

25 P. Craddock, "Copper alloys of the Hellenistic and Roman world," in J. Ellis Jones (ed.), *Aspects of ancient mining and metallurgy* (Bangor 1988) 60; J. Bayley, "The production of brass in antiquity with particular reference to Roman Britain," in P. Craddock (ed.), *2000 years of zinc and brass* (BritMusOccPap 50, 1990) 7-27; S. Rovira Llorens, "La fibula de tipo Aucissa: análisis technológico de algunos ejemplares hispánicos," *Cuadernos de Prehistoria y Arqueología de la Universidad Autónoma de Madrid* 17 (1990) 137-41; J. Riederer, "Metallanalysen römischer Fibeln aus Kempten," in M. Schleiermacher, *Die römischen Fibeln von Kempten–Cambodunum* (Kallmünz 1993) 45-52.

26 Riederer (supra n.25) 47, B I.

27 Bayley (supra n.25) 15.

28 Rovira Llorens (supra n.25) 306.

29 P. Craddock and J. Lambert, "The composition of the trappings from Xanten," *Britannia* 16 (1985) 141-64; R. P. J. Laurenze and P. Craddock, "The Ribchester hoard: a descriptive and technical study," in B. Raftery, V. Megaw, and V. Rigby (edd.), *Sites and sights of the Iron Age* (Oxford 1995) 90-92.

30 M. H. P. den Boersted and E. Hoekstra, "Spectrochemical analysis of the bronze vessels in the Rijksmuseum M. Kam at Nijmegen," *OudMedLeiden* 46 (1965) 118-22.

31 J. Riederer and E. Briese, "Metallanalysen römischer Gebrauchsgegenstände," *JRGZMainz* 19 (1972) 83-88; C. Laurenze and J. Riederer, "Metallanalysen römischer Henkel," *Berliner Beiträge der Archäometrie* (1980) 37-40.

32 Riederer and Briese ibid. 83-88.

33 G. Simion, "Méthodes de datation et de localisation des centres de production des bronzes romains découverts dans la région du Bas-Danube," in Mols *et al.* (supra n.9) 225-26.

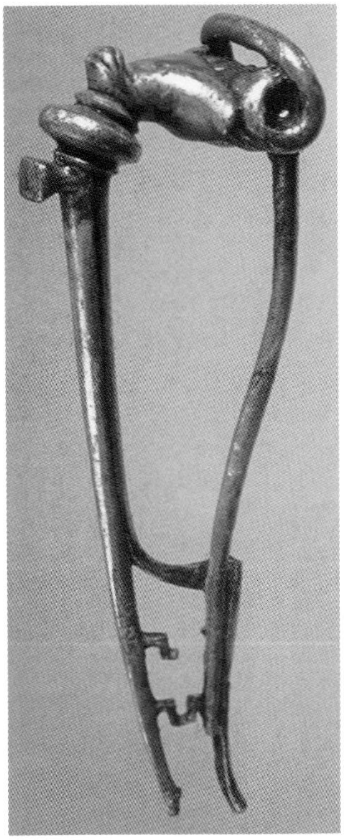

Fig. 3. Fibula, Almgren-type 238a, found at Emona. Roman, 1st c. A.D. Bronze. Mestni muzej Ljubljana (City Museum). (Photo: author.)

in antiquity.[34] In this case, the composition corresponds to the instructions given in ancient alloy recipes in the Leiden and Stockholm papyri.[35] These describe the production of alloys to "deceive even the artisans" and are made of copper, silver, tin, and 'white copper.' This last ingredient is made by mixing copper with 2 drachmas of σανδαράχης τῆς σαπρᾶς τῆς σιδηριζούσης (realgar mixed with stibnite and corrupted by sunlight)[36] and with στυπτηρία σχιστή (possibly As_2O_3).[37] As little as 2% arsenic in copper can produce some inverse segregation and push the silvery eutectoid with 21% arsenic to the surface of the object,[38] giving it the appearance of silver. It has to be noted that the arsenic and antimony content of the pin are noticeably lower than in the body, because they would render the metal fragile and unsuitable for hammering. The presence of tin makes the alloy more elastic and suitable for the spring. Both alloys used for the *fibula* were whitish because of the high silver and tin content, but the drillings of the sample were much more golden than the surface. It is possible that the object was also treated with organic acids (depletion silvering) and burnished to obtain a more homogeneous surface colour, as was done with some Roman *denarii* between A.D. 63 and 260.[39] This *fibula* and perhaps also the very silvery *fibula* from "De Horden" (not analyzed)[40] are possibly not fakes but the kind of cheap objects produced since Hellenistic times by artisans specializing in imitation jewelry for the middle classes, who used, for example, rock crystals coloured with copper salts instead of emeralds, or yellow and white colored copper alloys instead of gold and silver.[41]

Università di Udine, Centro Polifunzionale Gorizia, I-34170

Acknowledgements

The author wishes to thank A. Fuganti and A. Di Corrado, Institute of Material Engineering, University of Trento, for help with the analysis, and A. Oddy, Dept. of Conservation, British Museum, and J. van der Roest, Amersfoort, for information and discussion.

---

34 P. Craddock "The composition of the copper alloys used by the Greek, Etruscan, and Roman civilisations," *JArchSci* 3 (1976) 103 (Cu/As alloy); W. A. Oddy, T. G. Padley, and N. D. Meeks, "Some unusual techniques of gilding in antiquity," in *Proc. 8th int. Symposium on Archaeometry and Archaeological Prospection, Bonn 1978* (*Archaeo-Physika* 10, 1979) 231-33, figs. 1-5 (Ag/Sn alloy, dipped in molten Ag and in electrum).

35 R. Halleux (transl.), *Les alchimistes grecs* I. *Papyrus de Leyde, Papyrus de Stockholm, Fragments de recettes* (Paris 1981) Leid. 4:39; Holm. 3; 4.

36 Cf. Leid. 22: A. Giumlia-Mair, "Argento romano e leghe alchimistiche: tre leghe d´argento da Emona," *ArhVest* 49 (1998) esp. 245-47.

37 Halleux (supra n.35) 172.

38 Cf. P. Budd and B. S. Ottaway, "The properties of arsenical copper alloys: implications for the development of Eneolithic metallurgy," in P. Budd *et al.* (edd.), *Archaeological Sciences 1989* (Oxford 1991) 132-42; N. Meeks, "Surface characterization of tinned bronze, high tin bronze, tinned iron, and arsenical bronze," in S. La Niece and P. Craddock (edd.), *Metal plating and patination: cultural, technical, and historical developments* (London 1993) 267-71.

39 L. H. Cope, "Surface-silvered ancient coins," in E. T. Hall and D. M. Metcalf (edd.), *Methods of chemical and metallurgical investigation of ancient coinage* (RoyalNumSoc Spec. Pub. 8, 1972) 261-78.

40 J. van der Roest, "Die römischen Fibeln von 'De Horden'," *Rijksdienst voor het Oudheidkundig Bodemonderzoek* 38 (1988) 167, 193, Abb. 245.

41 M. Rostovzeff, *The social and economic history of the Hellenistic world* (Oxford 1941) 1222-23.

Die "Trau-Kasserollen": einiges zu den reliefverzierten Kasserollen vom Typ Eggers 151

Richard Petrovszky und Reinhard Stupperich

Die Bronzeindustrie der augusteischen Zeit brachte eine Reihe neuer Gefäßformen auf den Markt. Dazu gehören auch die Kasserollen, deren am wenigsten bekannte Form — die reliefverzierte Kasserolle vom Typ Eggers 151 — innerhalb der Toreutik eine noch sehr umstrittene Stellung einnimmt. Anlaß zur vorliegenden Untersuchung war die Veröffentlichung eines Gefäßes aus Milano, das zu dieser Form gehört, dessen außergewöhnlicher Griff jedoch direkte Beziehungen zu einer Gruppe von Griffschalen und zu einer kleineren Gruppe von Griffen vorweist, die bisher immer als "Spiegelgriffe" interpretiert wurden. Nun stellt sich aber heraus, daß diese "Spiegelgriffe" tatsächlich zu reliefverzierten Kasserollen vom Typ E 151 gehören. Von etwa drei Dutzend erfassten Exemplaren vom Typ E 151 sind nur acht komplette Gefäße, der Rest besteht aus Griffen.

Herstellungstechnik, Form, und Verzierung unterscheiden diese Kasserollen von den anderen Bronzekasserollen der Zeit. Sie sind zweiteilig: ein hohes, zylindrisches Becken mit Fußring, und ein separat gegossener Griff mit üppiger Reliefverzierung. Eine Attasche an der Unterseite des Griffansatzes sorgt für eine verstärkte Haftung am Becken. Die Gestaltung der Griffe ermöglicht, fünf verschiedene Typen zu ermitteln, während die Art der Ausführung die Gefäße bzw. Griffe in zwei klare Gruppen gliedert, die einfache und die "edle" Ausführung.

Entgegen bisheriger Annahme, das Becken sei auf der Drehbank gefertigt, kommen wir zu dem Schluß, daß diese Gefäße durch Guß im Wachsausschmelzverfahren hergestellt wurden. Man hatte nur die Wachsform auf der Drehbank modelliert. Die Griffe wurden ebenfalls gegossen, wofür man verschiedene Gußformen verwendete. Die feinen Unterschiede in der Ausführung sind auf die Nacharbeitung mit Stichel und Punze oder eventuell Feile, aber auch auf Abnutzung und den Erhaltungszustand zurückzuführen.

Betrachtet man die ikonographische Typologie unter dem Gesichtspunkt einer sinnvollen Entwicklung, so stellen sich zwei Grundformen heraus, die sich anhand der Schwanenkopfendungen unterscheiden, und von denen sich die übrigen Formen und Varianten insbesondere durch Vereinfachung und Weglassen von Elementen ableiten lassen. Der primäre Unterschied liegt in der Orientierung der Schwanenköpfe am Griffende. Bei Grundform 1 sitzen zwei nach außen gewendete Schwanenköpfe über dem Brillenmotiv, das ursprünglich nur eine Volute im Schwanenhals bzw. in der Randleiste darstellt. Bei Grundform 2 läuft der Endbogen zum Becken hin in vier umgebogene Schwanenköpfe aus, entspricht also dem der Schwanenkopfkasserollen vom Typ Bornitz.

Auf der Grifffläche finden sich unterschiedliche pflanzliche Motive, meist achsialsymmetrisch angeordnete Blütenkelche in der steifen Art eines Kandelabers, der eine kleine Figur trägt (Amor oder Bacchuskind, selten einmal die Siegesgöttin Victoria), die dann aber auch einfach darüber schwebt, aber auch ein Busch mit Ziege kommt vor oder eine Volutenranke mit Kranich. Die Motive haben mit (bacchischer) Musik, Theater und Bacchus zu tun; der Liebesgott Amor wird ohnehin mit Wein in Verbindung gebracht. Amor mimt auch den Jäger und spielt mit Attributen anderer Götter wie Herakles und Dionysos.

Die Fundorte der Stücke "edler" Ausführung liegen in den verschiedensten Gebieten des Reiches, einige auch außerhalb der Grenzen. Anders dagegen ist es bei den einfachen Kasserollen, deren Verbreitung sich auf den Rhein konzentriert, weswegen man sie auch als "Rhein-Kasserollen" bezeichnen könnte. Die Reliefgriffkasserollen waren insgesamt etwa 40 Jahre im Umlauf. Die Herstellung begann um die Zeitenwende, höchstens einige Jahre früher, die größte Verbreitung fanden sie im zweiten und dritten Jahrzehnt n. Chr. Wahrscheinlich Ende des vierten oder Anfang des nächsten Jahrzehnts wurde dann ihre Fertigung ganz eingestellt.

Unter den etwa 30 Griffen trägt kein einziges Exemplar einen Herstellerstempel, was eine Lokalisierung der Werkstätten erleichtert hätte. Die Indizien auf die Herkunft führen zu dem Schluß, daß die Kasserollen der "edlen" Ausführung ganz allgemein, ohne uns jetzt genauer festzulegen, Erzeugnisse italischer Werkstätten sind. Die Gefäße der einfachen Ausführung sind höchstwahrscheinlich provinzialer Herkunft, und zwar stammen sie aus rheinischen Werkstätten, vielleicht sind sie daher im Zusammenhang mit dem Militär zu sehen.

Historisches Museum der Pfalz, Speyer (R.P.); Universität Mannheim (R.S.)

Der gesamte Aufsatz (Text, Katalog, Tafeln, Karten, und Literaturliste) wurde in der Mannheimer Zeitschrift *Thetis* 5/6 (1999) 7-78 bzw. in der Serie "Mentor" als Bd. 1 (2001) veröffentlicht.

R. Nenova-Merdjanova

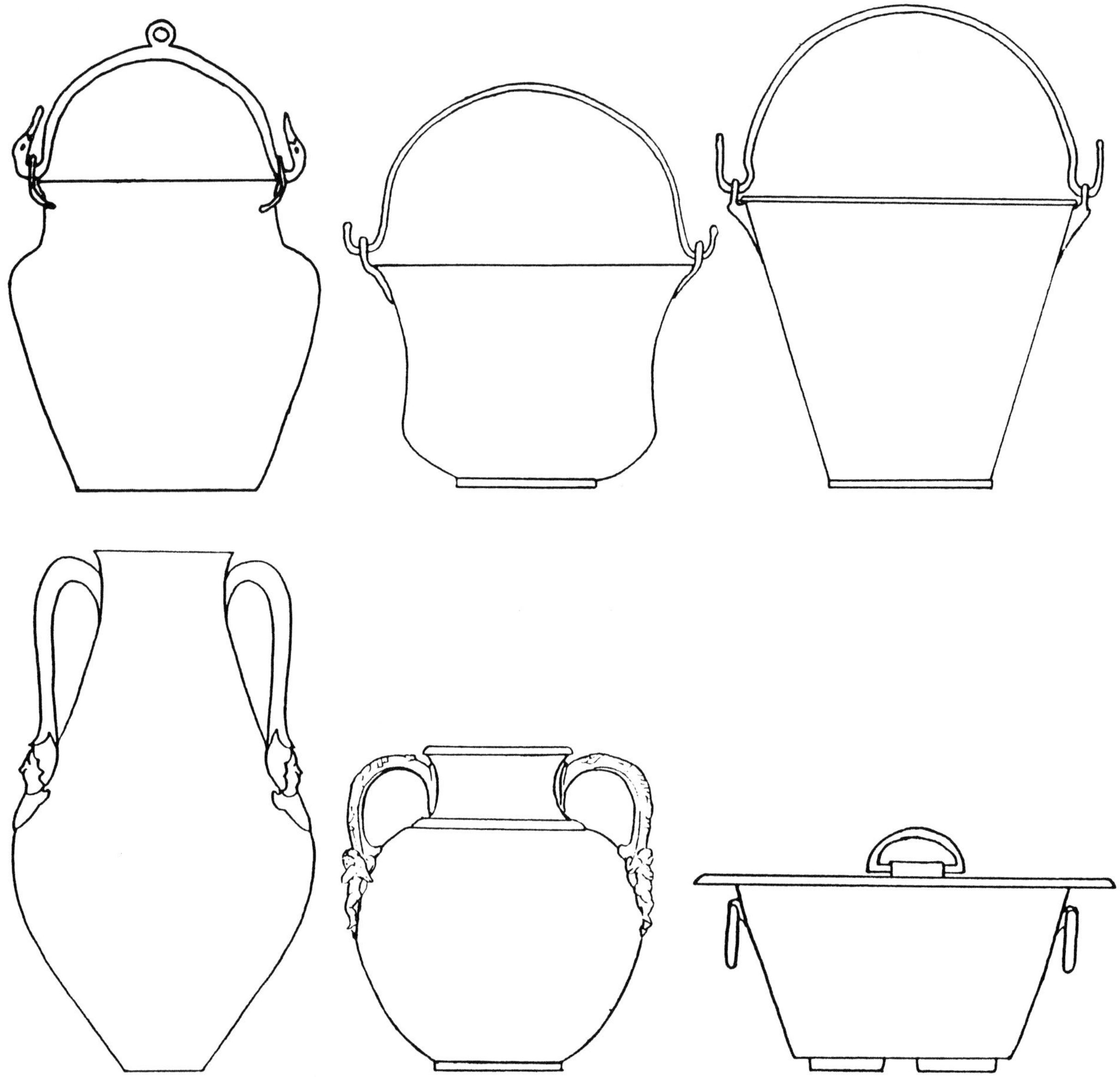

Fig. 1. Bucket with a rounded body and high neck. Fig. 2. Bucket with a U-shaped body. Fig. 3. Bucket shaped like an inverted truncated cone. Fig. 4. Vessel with an elongated curved body. Fig. 5. Vessel with a spherical body. Fig. 6. Basin with ellipsoid cross-section, two handles, and a lid. (All drawings: author.)

Bronze vessels and the toilette in Roman times

Rossitsa Nenova-Merdjanova

Bronze vessels were among the most commonly used objects in Roman everyday life. They were present in most homes in the towns and villas of Italy as well as in the homes of wealthier provincial families. Their ubiquity stimulates questions concerning their function, and this essay attempts to reconstruct the way they were used. Because of the exquisite shape and decoration of some of the most popular kinds of bronze vessels, many have thought that they were used on the dining table for serving food and drink. In reality, the tables of rich Romans were mainly furnished with silver, glass, and clay vessels. The construction of bronze vessels, which differs considerably from that of silver ones, and the relationships between the different types confirm that most were used during the toilette, before the start of the day or at its end.

Washing was the first part of the toilette and the most important, at least as far as men were concerned. For this purpose water was brought from its source in buckets of wood or bronze. Bronze buckets differ according to their date and place of production. In Italy of the 1st c. A.D., buckets with a rounded body and a high neck or out-turned rim[1] were used (fig. 1). They have hinged handles, the ends of which are often shaped like swan's heads. In the 2nd and 3rd c. A.D., buckets with a U-shaped body[2] (fig. 2) were disseminated all around the Roman Empire. Such vessels were produced in the region of the Rhine and in Gaul[3] as well as in Thrace. Buckets from this period could also be shaped like an inverted truncated cone (fig. 3). Buckets with a suitable capacity must have been used for carrying water in the home as well as at the baths. Such a bucket, carried by a bath attendant, is represented on a mosaic from the villa of Piazza Armerina.[4]

In the house, water was kept in amphora-shaped vessels. Two shapes were most popular in Italy and the provinces. The first has an elongated curved body[5] (fig. 4); the second is spherical[6] (fig. 5). Although these vessels' forms are connected in a certain way with the older Greek *hydria*, they must have been used as containers rather than for bringing water from distant sources. This is evident from the shape of the vertically attached handles, which are quite different from the single vertically-attached handle (for pouring) and the two horizontally attached handles (for carrying) of the *hydria* — and are not nearly as practical for lifting and carrying the vessel. These amphora-shaped vessels are often found in pairs, a fact that probably can be explained by the quantity of water needed for the toilette. In Thrace, several of these vessels were found in graves covered with a cloth, most likely to have served as a towel.

Water was also kept in deep basins of ellipsoid cross-section, with two handles, and a lid (fig. 6), that are known mainly from Italy[7] and Moesia.[8] The lid indicates that they were used as containers rather than as basins for washing.

---

1 H. Eggers, *Der römische Import im freien Germanien* (Hamburg 1951) Types 18-23; S. Tassinari, *Il vasellame bronzeo di Pompei* (Rome 1993) Types X1100, X1420, X1612.

2 Eggers ibid. Type 65.

3 H. Willers, *Die römischen Bronzeeimer von Hemmoor* (Hanover 1901) 182-83; id., *Neue Untersuchungen über die römische Bronzeindustrie von Capua und von Niedergermanien* (Hanover 1907) 41.

4 I. Nielsen, *Termae et balnea* Aarhus 1990) 76, fig. 40.

5 Eggers (supra n.1) Type 129; Tassinari (supra n.1) Type A3220; K. Kalcev, "Bronzene Amphoren aus dem Territorium Augusta Trajana (Stara Zagora, Bulgarien)," in J. Ronke (ed.), *Akten der 10. int. Tagung über antike Bronzen in Freiburg, 1988* (Forschungen und Berichte zur Vor- und Frühgeschichte in Baden-Württemburg 45, 1994) fig. 1.

6 T. Schreiber, *Die alexandrinische Toreutik* (Leipzig 1894) fig. 102; Kalcev ibid. figs. 8-10.

7 Tassinari (supra n.1) type T2000.

8 B. Raev, "Die Bronzegefässe der römischen Kaiserzeit in Thrakien und Mösien," *BerRGK* 58 (1978) pls. 29.2, 35.2; R. Nenova-Merdjanova, "Roman precious bronze vessels from Moesia and Thracia," *Archaeologia Bulgarica* 1 (1997) 31, fig. 4.

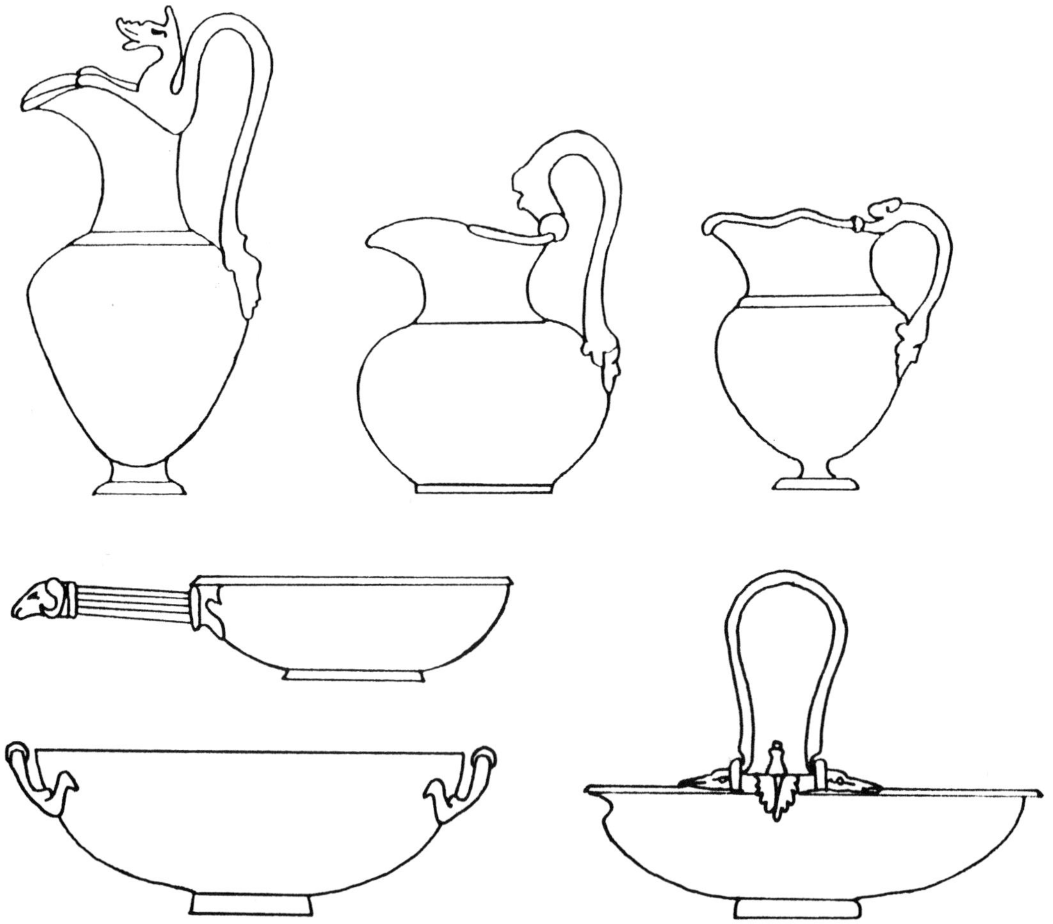

Fig. 7. Jug with projecting mouth. Fig. 8. Jug with trefoil mouth. Fig. 9. Jug with trefoil mouth and high foot. Fig. 10. Bowl with cylindrical handle. Fig. 11. Hemispherical basin with two handles. Fig. 12. Basin with ellipsoid cross-section and two arch-shaped handles. (All drawings: author)

From the various containers, water was collected in jugs of different shapes, but all with projecting (fig. 7) or trefoil mouths[9] (figs. 8-9). From the jugs, water was poured over the hands and collected in a bowl with a cylindrical decorated handle, in most cases ending in a ram's head[10] (fig. 10). These vessels formed a set for washing the hands, used also during meals.[11]

Basins were used for washing the face and legs. They were usually hemispherical, with a soldered round base and two handles[12] (fig. 11) for carrying full vessels in a horizontal position.

Quite a few asymmetrical vessels with an ellipsoid, horizontal cross-section and two tall arch-shaped handles and decorated attachments (fig. 12) have been found in Italy as well as in Thrace.[13] It is easy to pour liquid out of them by holding the handles in one hand and lifting one side of the vessel, holding the projecting rim with the other. With this in mind, we may consider them basins too, though we cannot be certain whether they were used for pouring water or for collecting it.

Semi-ellipsoid basins have been found in several graves from Thrace and Moesia. They were accompanied by jugs with a handle ending in a human foot or two feet, and it is likely that they

---

9 H. Nuber, "Kanne und Griffschale: Ihr Gebrauch im täglichen Leben und die Beigabe in Gräbern der römischen Kaiserzeit," *BerRGK* 58 (1978) Types E, F, G; Tassinari (supra n.1) Types D2300, D2400, E3000; Nenova-Merdjanova (supra n.8) 31, figs. 5-7.

10 Nuber ibid. Types E, F, G; Tassinari (supra n.1) Types H2311, H2312, H2313.

11 On the function of this set of vessels, see Nuber (supra n.9) 96 ff.

12 Tassinari (supra n.1) types S3110, S4111.

13 Ibid. type P2210; Raev (supra n.8) pls. 35.1, 36.4; Nenova-Merdjanova (supra n.8) 33, fig. 11.

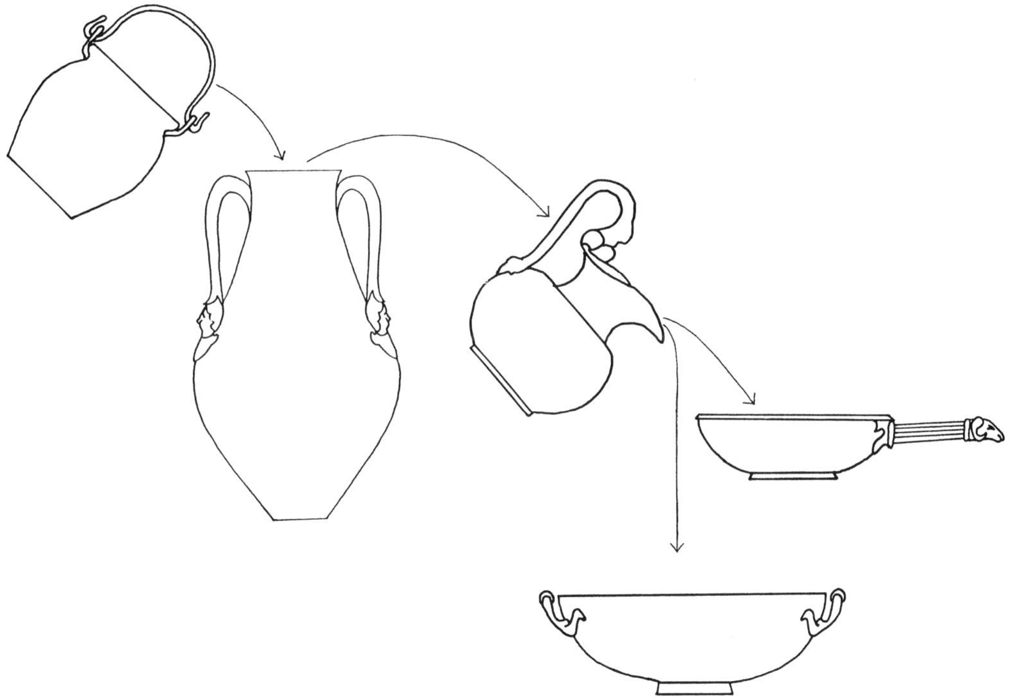

Fig. 13. Sequence for the use of bronze vessels for washing during the toilette. (Drawing: author)

comprise a set for washing the legs.[14] Jugs of this kind are also known from other parts of the empire.[15]

Our reconstruction of how the main shapes were used (fig. 13) is based on evidence of different types. One of the most important consists of burial finds from Thrace and Moesia, an area in which the population had adopted the customs of the classical Mediterranean world long before the Roman invasion. In more than 60 graves in Bulgaria dating from the Roman period, groups with more than a single bronze vessel have been found. In the richest tumulus graves from the necropolis of Chatalka (near ancient Augusta Traiana and modern Stara Zagora, Bulgaria) were found complete sets of vessels for washing.[16] In all the graves, the vessels used for keeping clean were found with toilette caskets with flasks for oil and unguents and, in women's graves, with instruments and beauty products, from combs, pins and *fibulae* to cosmetics and jewels. Most of the metal sticks and small smooth tiles often considered doctors' instruments are actually toilette utensils.

The lamps, lampstands, and *lanternae* in the graves also belonged to objects used while the toilette was being made. This took place in the dark, very early in the morning or just before going to bed.[17] Such objects have been found in all rich Thracian graves.

In many of the graves belonging to both men and women there were folding iron chairs. These were for the master or mistress to sit on, while servants attended them to make their toilette.

Confirmation of the objects used during the making of the toilette comes from silver objects belonging to the late-antique period. At the end of the 4th and the beginning of the 5th c., silver toilette caskets depict detailed representations of the toilette. All of the above-mentioned objects found in Roman graves are depicted on the silver casket of Proiecta from the Esquiline

14 R. Nenova-Merdjanova, "The bronze jugs decorated with a human foot from the Roman provinces Moesia and Thracia," *Archaeologia Bulgarica* 3 (1998) 68-75.

15 See S. Tassinari, "Étude de vaisselle de bronze romaine et gallo-romaine: les pots à anse ornée d'un pied humain," in P.-M. Duval (ed.), *Recherches d'archéologie celtique et gallo-romaine* (Geneva 1973) 130-31.

16 H. Bujukliev, "La nécropole tumulaire thrace près de Catalka, région de Stara Zagora," in *Fouilles et Recherches* 16 (Sofia 1986) figs. 7, 25, 27, 31.

17 J. Carcopino, *Daily life in ancient Rome* (New Haven, CT 1940) 188.

treasure.[18] In the center of the composition, on a chair, sits the mistress sticking a pin into her hair. She is flanked by servants carrying toilette caskets, mirrors, and candlesticks. Vessels corresponding to the bronze Roman-period examples are also represented. Servants carry a bucket, a jug, and a plate with a handle, a big round object that may be a basin, while on the ground is a big vessel for keeping water, similar to the amphora-shaped vessels but without handles.

On the silver toilette casket from the Sevso treasure is a similar scene, with a matron sitting on a chair in the middle.[19] Here we recognize a servant carrying a basin, and a big amphora-shaped container set on the ground.[20] Other servants carry a bucket, a mirror, and toilette caskets.[21]

On a silver bucket from Herculaneum, a bath scene reveals the use of this kind of vessel: An attendant holds in one hand the same kind of bucket and in the other a candlestick. Another attendant brings to her mistress a basin — obviously full of water — holding its two opposed handles to keep it horizontal.[22] Most likely the objects represented are not bronze but silver vessels like those from the Esquiline treasure,[23] yet they can be used to reconstruct the use of Roman bronze vessels, for silver vessels took over the function of the bronze ones in late antiquity, coinciding with the end of the serial, large-scale production of bronze objects, which was never renewed.

Evidence for the rôle of these kinds of vessels in the toilette is found in other sources, such as the wall-paintings in an Early Christian tomb in Silistra, Bulgaria.[24] Here servants approach their masters bearing vessels for washing: a jug and a plate with a handle, a towel, a toilette casket, and cloths. Two candlesticks flank the entrance of the tomb and the composition.

Although certain bronze vessels were used specifically in the baths, such as plates with a flat handle and oil vessels of different shapes, some vessels like the buckets, jug, and plate with cylindrical handle must have been taken to the baths, as is shown on the casket of Proiecta,[25] and especially by women, for whom bathing must have been a more complicated procedure.

All these examples confirm the rôle of specific vessels for the toilette in Roman times and justify removing the most common shapes of bronze vessels from the table in the *triclinium*, where they have been placed by some archaeologists, calling them trays, *oinochoai* (wine jugs), and bowls. Their correct place can be identified as in a casket or on the floor beside the chair and the *candelabra* in the sleeping room, where the master or mistress went to bed, after they had washed away the traces of vanity and fatigue — the same room where they woke up and started the new day by using them again.

Institute of Archaeology, Saborna Str. 2, Sofia-1000

---

18 K. J. Shelton, *The Esquiline treasure* (London 1981) pls. 2-3.

19 M. M. Mango, *The Sevso treasure* 1 (*JRA* Suppl. 12, 1994) fig. 14-25.

20 Ibid. fig. 14-27.

21 Ibid. figs. 14-29, 14-30.

22 L. Pirzio Biroli Stefanelli, *L'argento dei Romani: vasellame da tavola e d'apparato* (Rome 1991) 277, cat. 108, figs. 164-66.

23 E.g., Shelton (supra n.17) pls. 21, 30, 31, 33.

24 L. Schneider, *Die Domäne als Weltbild* (Wiesbaden 1983) pl. 14.

25 Shelton (supra n.17) pl. 6.

A Bacchic bucket of Rhenish origin in The J. Paul Getty Museum

John J. Herrmann, Jr.

A bronze situla was published in the exhibition catalogue (1994) of the collection of Lawrence and Barbara Fleischman of New York City,[1] but the chronology and attribution offered there need to be significantly revised. Seen in its new perspective, the situla raises the question whether bronzeworking in the northern provinces could have influenced traditional classical centers on the Mediterranean.

The situla, which now belongs to the J. Paul Getty Museum, is decorated with figures and ornament that are set off by backgrounds covered with tin plating (figs. 1-2). The vessel is a tall version of a *calathus*, originally a basket shape, but it is clear from the traces of attachments that this vessel was originally equipped with a bucket's handle. The decorative designs were incised into the bronze after casting, using pointed and elongated punches; the contours of the figures are thus made up of rows of dots and dashes. The decoration is arranged in 5 principal bands: from top to bottom, they show discs, a grapevine (without fruit), the triumph of Bacchus, an olive or laurel wreath, and dolphins with a single drinking horn. The figures of the bottom frieze are set off by groups of reserved 'commas' that probably indicate water. The principal frieze shows Bacchus reclining in his chariot pulled by two panthers. Eros rides on, and feeds grapes to, one of the panthers; and a satyr with a *pedum* and goatskin runs ahead of the team holding its reins (fig. 2). In front of the satyr is a sacred pillar, an Agyieus, surmounted by an oval ring and encircled by a fruit-bearing grapevine, which has both grape and ivy leaves.[2] To the right of the Agyieus is a dancing maenad with a *thyrsus* and *calathus*, Pan playing his pipes, and Silenus playing a lyre. Small trees or bushes punctuate the procession, and some reserved 'commas' in the lower part of the frieze may indicate rocks. The Bacchic imagery strongly suggests that the bucket was used for serving wine at a banquet. The bottom frieze may allude to the Tyrrhenian pirates transformed into dolphins by Dionysos.[3]

One of the many artistically pleasing aspects of this rich object is the stylized, cartoon-like drawing of the figures. Their contours are curved into rounded, lobed patterns; they have lively, bouncy poses and are stretched out horizontally. The figures have a gay and ragged effect, enhanced by the drapery that blows out behind them like pennants. Tinning is used within some of the drapery to indicate shadows, a technique that enhances the ragged, insubstantial effect.

The stylized character of the drawing on the bucket initially suggested a late-antique date (late 4th or early 5th c.) and evoked comparison with a well-known group of buckets with incised figural decoration dated to the 5th and 6th c., to be discussed below (figs. 6-8).[4] These late buckets, all of which stem from the Mediterranean area, suggested that the Getty bucket could have been made in Asia Minor. It soon became clear, however, that the origin of the Getty situla lay in an altogether different geographical and chronological setting.[5] The situla is clearly northern provincial in origin and Middle Imperial rather than late-antique in date.

---

1 Now Los Angeles, The J. Paul Getty Museum 96.AC.55; h. 33.5 cm; diam. rim 27.2 cm; diam. base 17 cm: in M. True and K. Hamma (edd.), *A passion for antiquities: Ancient art from the collection of Barbara and Lawrence Fleischman* (Exhib. cat., Los Angeles 1994) 324-27, no. 169 (J. J. Herrmann). Provenance unknown, acquired on the Munich art market.

2 On the Agyieus in the Dionysiac sphere, see V. Fehrentz, "Der antike Agyieus," *JdI* 108 (1993) 182-85, figs. 37, 39.

3 Pointed out to me by A. H. Herrmann.

4 A. Carandini, "La secchia Doria: una 'storia di Achille' tardo-antica," *StMisc* 9 (1963-64) passim.

5 As I already noted in the errata list to *A passion for antiquities* (supra n.1).

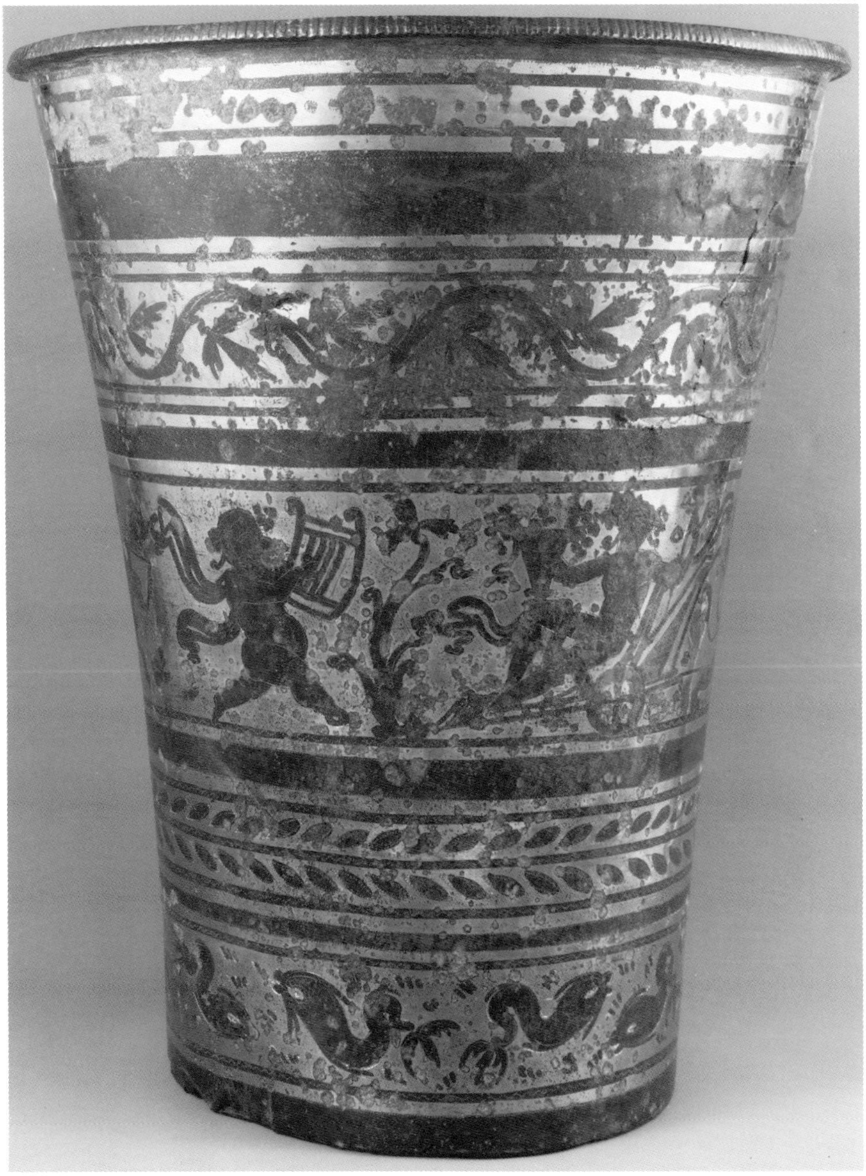

Fig. 1. Situla with tin plating. Roman, 210-230. Bronze, h. 33.5 cm. Los Angeles, The J. Paul Getty Museum 96.AC.55. (Photo: courtesy Museum.)

Bronze vessels with similar incised figures set off by fields of silver, or *Weissmetal*, have been found in considerable numbers in the Rhine and Danube basins and especially in Germanic graves beyond the *limes*. R. Stupperich has gathered these figure-decorated vessels as the Göldenitz Group, which he dates to the first half of the 3rd c. on the basis of numerous well-established archaeological contexts.[6] The drawing on the Getty situla finds its closest parallels in two vessels of the group with the same Bacchic subject-matter; those two had already been linked by H.-J. Kellner and G. Zahlhaas.[7]

The first is a bucket with hemispherical lower body (Hemmoor type), excavated in 1976 as part of a hoard at Kaiseraugst just above Basel (figs. 3-4).[8] The upper of the two friezes has a

6 R. Stupperich, "Die Göldenitz-Gruppe: figürlich verzierte Metallarbeiten des 3. Jhs. n.Chr. mit Weissmetallauflage," in D. Rössler and V. Stürmer (edd.), *Modus in rebus: Gedenkschrift für Wolfgang Schindler* (Berlin 1995) 144-52, pl. 43 (kindly called to my attention by A. Kaufmann-Heinimann.)

7 H.-J. Kellner and G. Zahlhaas, *Der römische Tempelschatz von Weissenburg i. Bay.* (Mainz 1993) 88-95, figs. 11-15.

8 T. Tomasevic-Buck, "Ein Bronzedepotfund aus Augusta Raurica," *BayVgBl* 49 (1984) 152-54, 174-76,

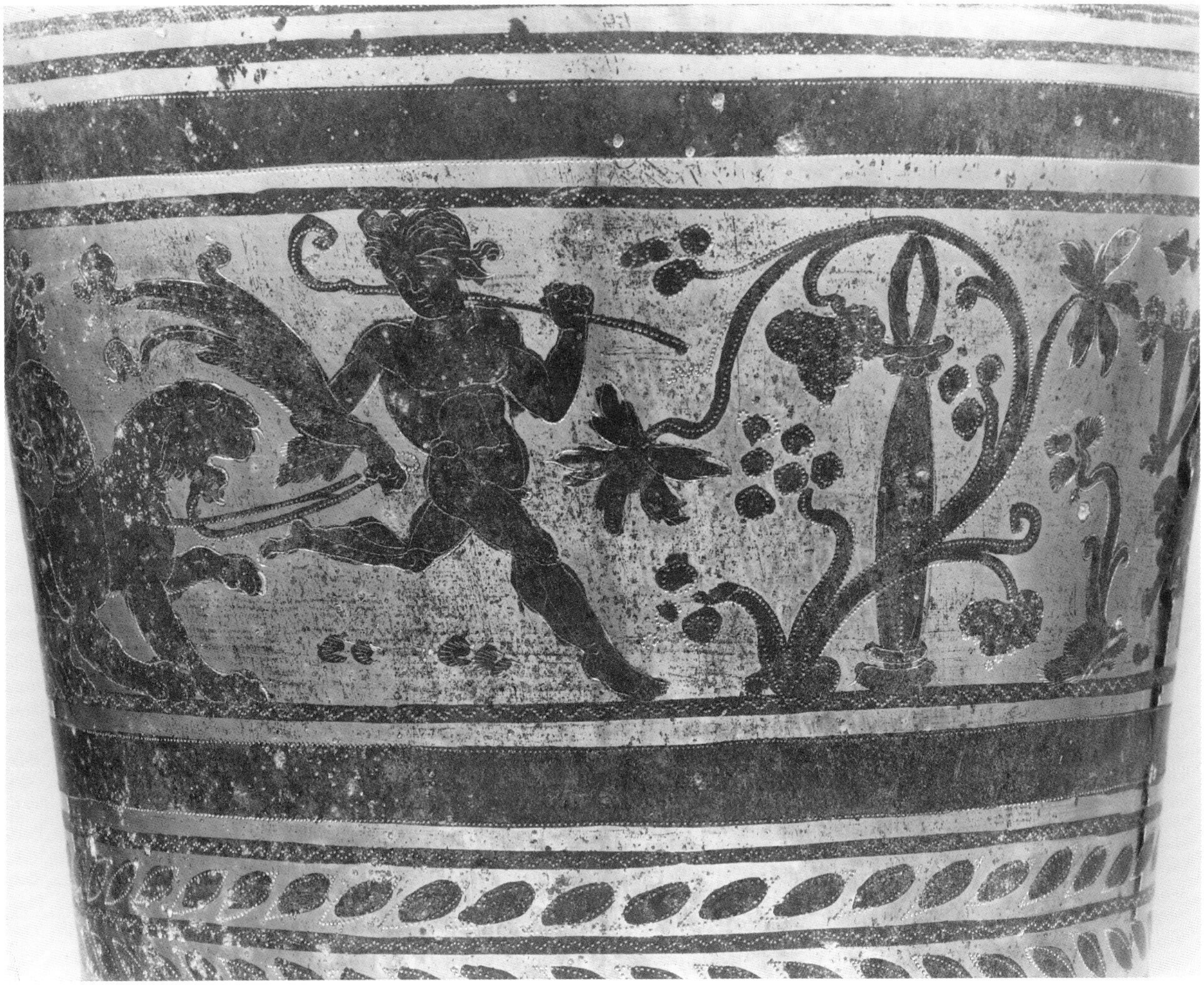

Fig. 2. Detail of fig. 1: satyr and Agyieus.

vine similar to that of band two on the Getty situla but animated by cupids scampering about. In the lower frieze, Bacchus reclines on his chariot pulled by panthers and is preceded by his retinue, very much as on the Getty situla. Not only is the cast of characters basically the same, but the style and technique are also very similar. Bacchus on his chariot seems to replicate the Getty composition exactly, and Silenus re-appears in a similar pose holding the same sort of lyre (figs. 1, 3). The Agyieus is also present on the Kaiseraugst situla, embellished with crossed *thyrsi* and a loaded *calathus* (figs. 2, 4). The curvaceous figures prance ahead with long strides and look back over their shoulders, as on the Getty vessel. On both, the figures seem to be stretched out horizontally. Curving strokes again indicate stones. The Kaiseraugst bucket is described as coated with *Weissmetal*, which recalls the tin on the Getty piece. The Kaiseraugst hoard of vessels, statuettes, and coins was apparently buried in anticipation of one of the Alemannic invasions (A.D. 254 and 260). The similarities with the Getty piece are so great that it is clear not only that the two buckets are more or less contemporary but also that they were produced in the same workshop.

Another member of the Göldenitz Group is a bronze pitcher (without traces of silvering) from Pécs, Hungary (fig. 5).[9] Its short frieze is focused on a drunken Herakles, but the satyr

fig. 3.5, Beilage 3; Kellner and Zahlhaas (supra n.7) 89, 93, fig. 13 a-e; Stupperich (supra n.6) 146-47, Beilage 15.5.

9 Budapest, Hungarian National Museum 62.1902.1: F. Fülep, *Sopianae: the history of Pécs during the Roman era* (Budapest 1984) 70, 202, 205, pl. 34.1; Kellner and Zahlhaas (supra n.7) 89-90, 94-95, figs. 14-15; Stupperich 1995 (supra n.6) 149-50, Beilage 16.4.

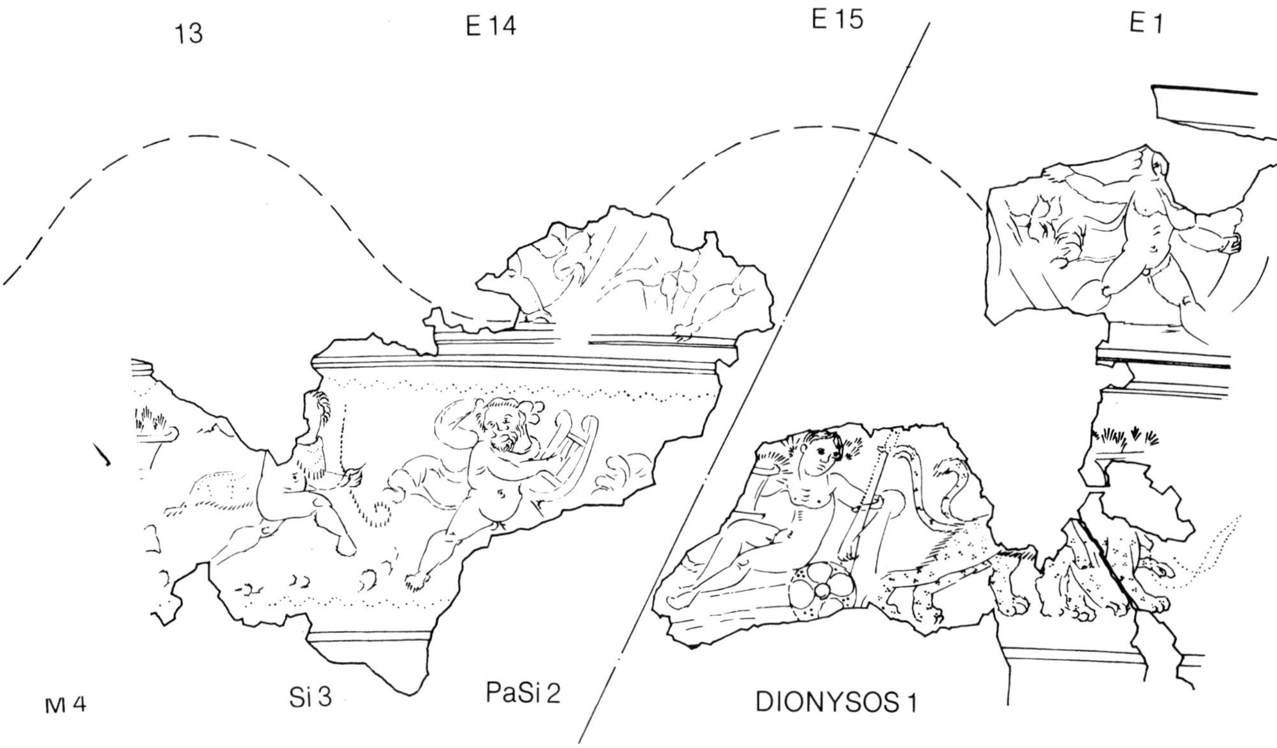

Fig. 3. Situla with 'white metal' plating, from Kaiseraugst: detail of engraving. Roman, 230-250. Bronze, h. (figured zone) 9.2 cm. (Drawing: T. Tomasevic-Buck; from *BayVgBl* 49 [1984] Beilage 3)

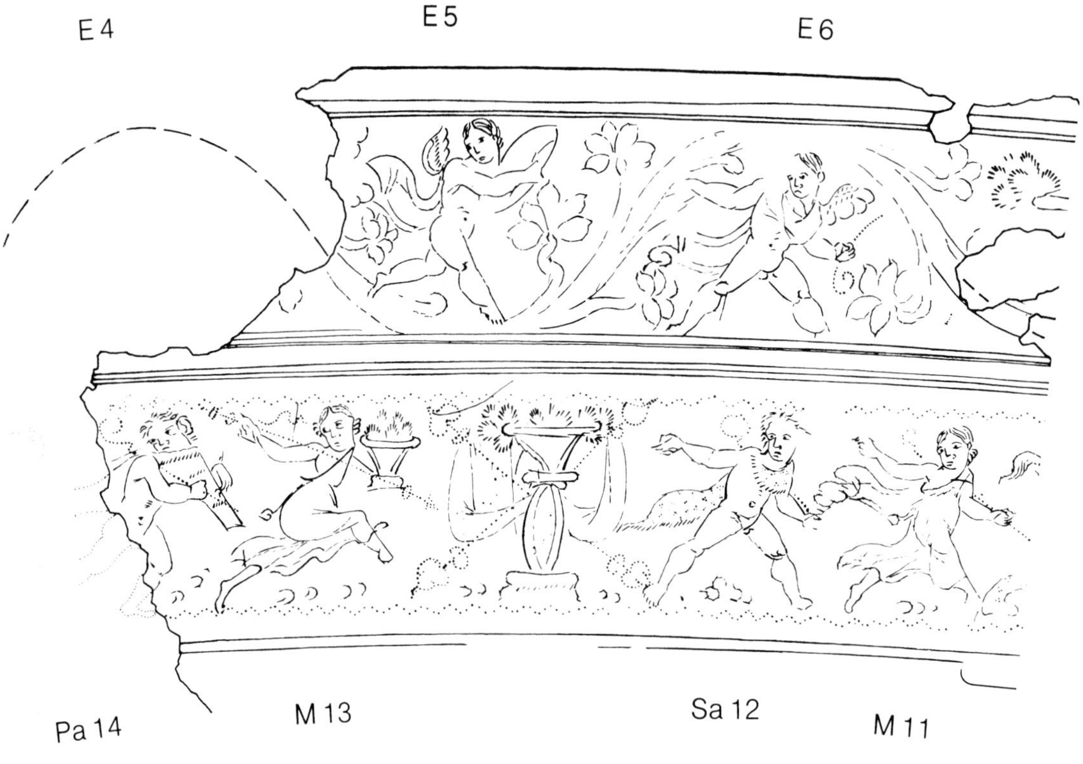

Fig. 4. Additional details of fig. 3.

prancing in from the left with the drinking horn is a brother to the satyr leading Bacchus's panther team on the Getty situla (fig. 2). The long, fluttering cloaks on both vessels are another point of close similarity. The Pécs vessel, which has been dated to the time of Caracalla (211-217), must be another product of the same workshop. The frieze of cupids in a vine scroll on the

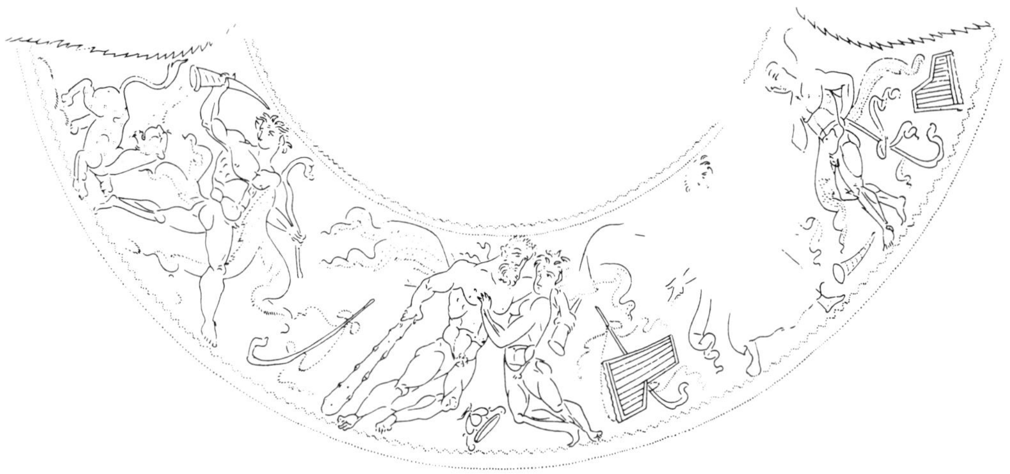

Fig. 5. Pitcher, from Pécs, *c.*215. Bronze, h. 23.8 cm. Budapest, Hungarian National Museum 62.1902.1. (Drawing: H. Ball; from H.-J. Kellner and G. Zahlhaas, *Der römische Tempelschatz von Weissenburg i. Bay.* [Mainz am Rhein 1993] fig. 14)

bucket from Göldenitz, the name-piece of the group,[10] is a stiffer, drier derivative of the cupid frieze on the Kaiseraugst bucket, in which all the cupids have virtually the same pose. This stereotyped approach suggests that the Göldenitz bucket was made in a different, if closely allied, workshop.

The drawing on the other vessels in the Göldenitz Group tends to be more angular and stylized than on these three Bacchic vessels, and it is unlikely that they were produced in the 'Pécs-Getty workshop'. Stupperich, however, has defined the Göldenitz Group as a number of allied workshops. The Pécs-Getty subgroup, then, represents an unusually high quality shop within the association, which Stupperich locates in the upper Rhine valley, perhaps somewhere in the neighborhood of Augst.[11]

The Getty situla appears to date earlier rather than later in the first half of the 3rd c. The bucket itself is a somewhat rare and elegant form. Similar *calathus*-shaped buckets appear in the Weissenburg hoard, which must have been buried in A.D. 233 or shortly before.[12] Like the handles of all the buckets and basins from Weissenburg,[13] the handle of the Getty bucket was fastened to cast attachments that were soldered to the wall of the bucket. In other, presumably later, Rhenish vessels, handles are simply attached to holes in upward projections of a vessel's wall. One should not push the Getty bucket too early, however, because the Kaiseraugst bucket, a product of the same shop, comes from a mid-century hoard and has its handle attached in the simpler, later manner without cast attachment-plates. The Getty situla, therefore, could well have been made in the period 210-230.

The accomplished, curvilinear, lively style of the 'Pécs-Getty workshop' has distinctly Mediterranean parallels and associations. Dolphins with tails that look like grape leaves, as on the Getty bucket, appear on two bronze *paterae* with incised fishing scenes from Italy of mid 3rd- to mid 4th-c. date: one, from Anzio, is in the British Museum,[14] the other is in the Museo Nazionale Romano.[15] In varying degrees, both display the lively, rounded drawing of the Getty situla, albeit in diluted form. In the earlier of the two (from Anzio), a fisherman has a

10 Stupperich (supra n.6) 145, pl. 43, Beilage 14.1.

11 Stupperich (supra n.6) 150.

12 Kellner and Zahlhaas (supra n.7) 108-9, 150 (metal analysis: bronze), pl. 97, no. 55.

13 Ibid. nos. 44-47, 51-55.

14 Walters, *British Museum Bronzes* no. 884; J. W. Salomonson, "Kunstgeschichtliche und ikonographische Untersuchungen zu einem Tonfragment der Sammlung Benaki in Athen," *BABesch* 48 (1973) 72-82, fig. 63; *Spätantike und frühes Christentum* (Exhib. cat., Frankfurt am Main 1983) 620-21, cat. 210 (D. Stutzinger: Tetrarchic or Constantinian); Kellner and Zahlhaas (supra n.7) 90 (mid 3rd c.).

15 Rome, Museo Nazionale Romano: Salomonson ibid. 75-82, figs. 59-62; *Spätantike und frühes Christentum* 621-23, no. 211 (D. Stutzinger).

cross-stepping, backward-looking pose that is a less exuberant version of the poses in the Pécs-Getty group. A bronze plaque in the British Museum with the story of Achilles and Briseis offers another comparable figure style.[16] The plaque, which has been dated to the 4th c., probably comes from the Naples area; and its figures, which are tin-plated, are drawn with lively, curving arcs, making their limbs almost sausage-like, much as on the Getty situla. Lively, cartoon-like drawing can be seen on a votive plaque dedicated to Apollo Praenos in Boston;[17] the Apollo plaque is inscribed in Greek and is roughly contemporary with the Getty situla.

Comparable rounded, stylized drawing can be found in other media in the Mediterranean area as well. Many examples could be cited from Coptic textiles; a 3rd- or 4th-c. roundel with a plump and lively head of Bacchus, now in the Textile Museum, Washington, D.C., has some of the same playfulness.[18]

Bronze vessels of the Pécs-Getty atelier thus present a level of artistic achievement that is similar in character and by no means inferior in quality to Mediterranean incised bronzes. It is possible that an artisan from the Mediterranean moved to the Rhineland to produce this outstanding work. On the other hand, drawings in manuscripts or pattern books may have been enough to inspire talented northerners and keep them in touch with developing empire-wide fashions. The wiggling dolphins with grape-leaf tails are just one of many commonplaces of Roman art present on the Getty vessel (fig. 1), and their basic design could easily have been transmitted via drawings on papyrus or other light, impermanent materials. The artistic sensibility with which these motifs are presented on the Getty situla, however, is far from commonplace.

As Stupperich has observed, analogies between Mediterranean bronzes and the Göldenitz Group in fact raise the opposite question: Could the Rhineland have influenced the Mediterranean production of incised bronzes?[19] There are, to be sure, earlier antecedents for polychrome 'drawing' on bronze in the Mediterranean: lids of doctors' boxes produced in 1st-c. Italy were decorated with figures of Asclepius inlaid with silver, copper, and niello.[20] This kind of polychrome inlay can still be traced in the 4th and 5th c.[21] Inlay, however, was produced in a process that is substantially different from that used in the Göldenitz Group; concavities seem to have been created in the wax model before casting to receive the inlays. In the Getty situla, figures were incised after casting with a series of punches, which produced outlines made up of dots and dashes.

Drawings on bronze similar to the Rhenish works can be ascribed to Mediterranean workshops of the 3rd c. Again, however, the techniques are somewhat different. The bronze plaque of unknown provenance in Boston dedicated (in Greek) to Apollo Praenos may be one of the most securely dated examples: very probably it was made in the first half of the 3rd c. Its drawing was incised into the wax model along with the inscription before casting. Various other bronze plaques of the 3rd and 4th c. of Italian provenance received their figural decoration after casting, but most of the lines seem to have been chased or inscribed, and only a limited use was made of punching.[22] On the other hand, bronze vessels with figure drawings of the late 3rd or

---

16 K. Weitzmann (ed.), *Age of spirituality* (Exhib. cat., New York 1979) 218-19, no. 195 with bibliography (M. Bell).

17 C. Vermeule and M. Comstock, *Sculpture in stone and bronze* (Boston 1988) no. 131; A. van den Hoek and S. Takács, "A bronze plaque to Apollo Praenos in Boston," in C. C. Mattusch *et al.* (edd.), *From the parts to the whole, Part 1* (*JRA* Suppl. 39.1, 2000) 265-71.

18 W. F. Volbach, *Early decorative textiles* (London 1969) 20-21, fig. 7; *Age of spirituality* (supra n.16) 141-42, no. 120 (C. Lindgren).

19 Stupperich (supra n. 6) 152.

20 K. Vierneisel (ed.), *Römisches im Antikenmuseum* (Berlin 1978) 182-83, no. 239; E. Pozzi *et al.*, *Le collezioni del Museo Nazionale di Napoli* (Rome 1986) 214-15, no. 61.

21 See *Age of spirituality* (supra n.16) nos. 76, 77, 94, 137.

22 Ibid. nos. 174, 195, 215, 216.

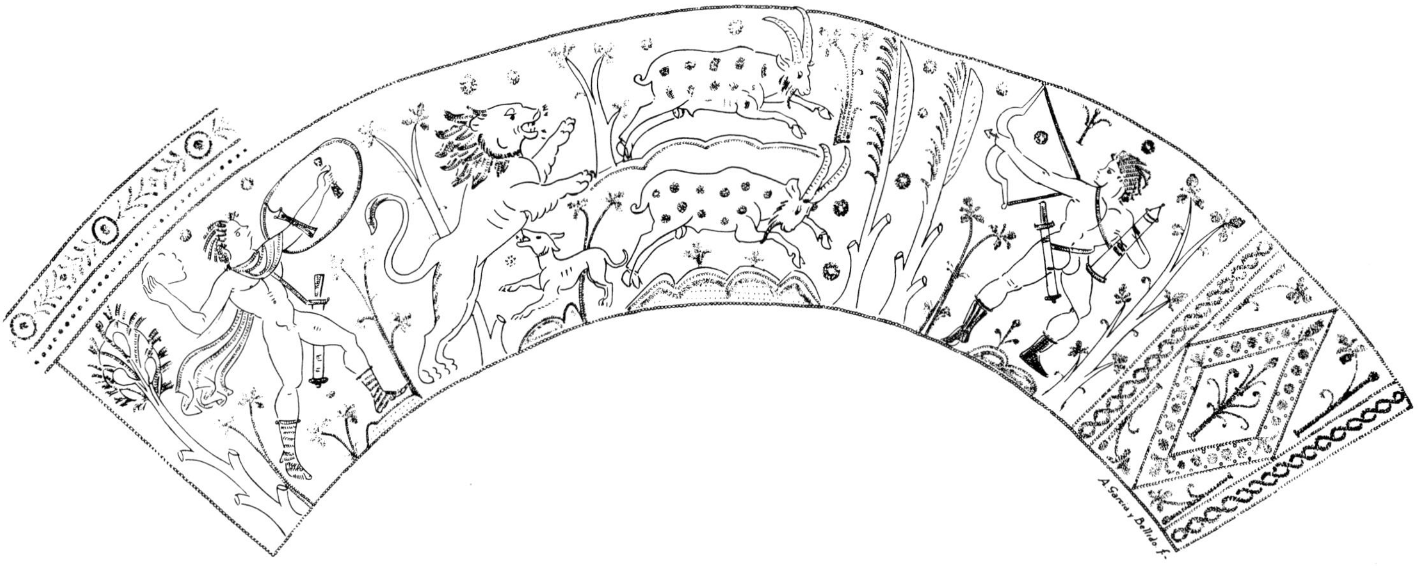

Fig. 6. Situla with 'white metal' plating, from Bueña, 5th or 6th c. Bronze, h. 25 cm. Madrid, Museo Arqueologico Nacional 1.934/118. (Drawing: A. Garcia y Bellido; from *ArchEspArq* 12 [1936]).

earlier 4th c. (i.e., the *paterae* with fishing scenes from Anzio and Rome) make conspicuous use of punches.[23]

Stupperich has pointed out how the activities of the Göldenitz Group were terminated by the Alemannic invasions of the mid 3rd c. Skilled craftsmen may well have fled the frontier areas to more secure locations around the Mediterranean. Most of the incised bronzes of the 3rd and 4th c., as we have just seen, have something in common with the Göldenitz Group, although there are no specific points of contact. It is not impossible that the basic idea of creating drawings on bronze could owe its late-antique popularity to refugee workmen from the Göldenitz Group. One group of late drawings on bronze, however, seems to show specific points of contact with the Rhenish bronzes. As noted by Stupperich, striking analogies with the Göldenitz Group appear in a series of late buckets:[24] one with hunting scenes from Bueña in Spain (fig. 6),[25] another with the story of Achilles and Briseis in the Palazzo Doria, Rome (fig. 8),[26] and a third with crosses enclosed in an arcade, from Zerzevan, now in Istanbul (fig. 7).[27] As in the Göldenitz Group, these situlae have designs rendered with punches and with plant fillers in the backgrounds. The ornamental vocabulary, such as the bands of palm branches interrupted by rosettes seen in the Bueña and Istanbul situlae (figs. 6-7), is similar. The Bueña bucket also has tinned or silvered backgrounds around the figures and plants. These situlae are usually dated to the 5th and 6th c., but the analogies with the 3rd-c. Rhenish buckets are so strong that Stupperich suggested a 4th-c. date for those with non-Christian subject-matter. Since the bucket from Zerzevan is decorated with crosses of Early Byzantine character (fig. 7), this member of the group must date from the 5th c. at least.

In spite of the chronological gap between the Göldenitz Group and the late-antique situlae, points of contact can be established that strengthen their relationship. The Mediterranean situlae all have the shape of a *calathus* or a conical variation on the form. The *calathus* form was not previously known from the Göldenitz Group, but the Getty situla now provides an exam-

23 Salomonson (supra n.14) 75-82, figs. 59-63; *Spätantike und frühes Christentum* (supra n.14) 620-23, nos. 210-11 (D. Stutzinger).

24 Stupperich (supra n.6) 152.

25 A. Garcia y Bellido, "La sítula romana de Bueña," *ArchEspArq* 12 (1936); Carandini (supra n.4) figs. 33-38; J. Arce, *La sítula de Bueña* (Museo Arqueológico Nacional; Catálogos y monografías 6, Madrid 1982); *Los bronces romanos en España* (Exhib. cat., Madrid 1990) 299, no. 258.

26 Carandini (supra n.4); *Age of spirituality* (supra n.16) 219-20, cat. 196 (M. Bell).

27 Carandini (supra n.4) 28-29, figs. 39-40.

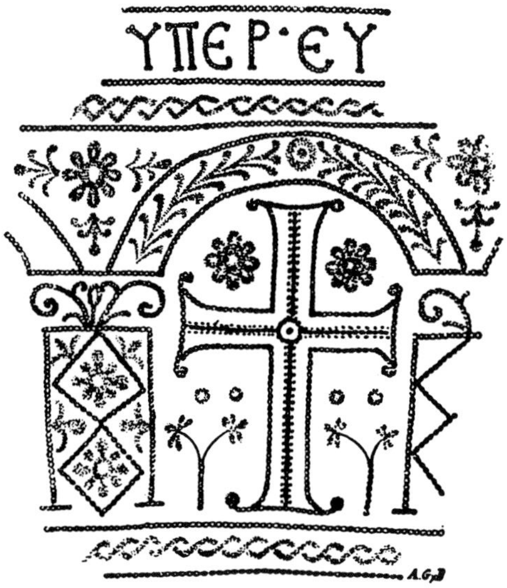

Fig. 7. Situla, from Zerzevan: detail, 5th or 6th c. Bronze, h. 23 cm. Istanbul, Archaeological Museum 852. (Drawing: A. Garcia y Bellido; from *ArchEspArq* 12 [1936]).

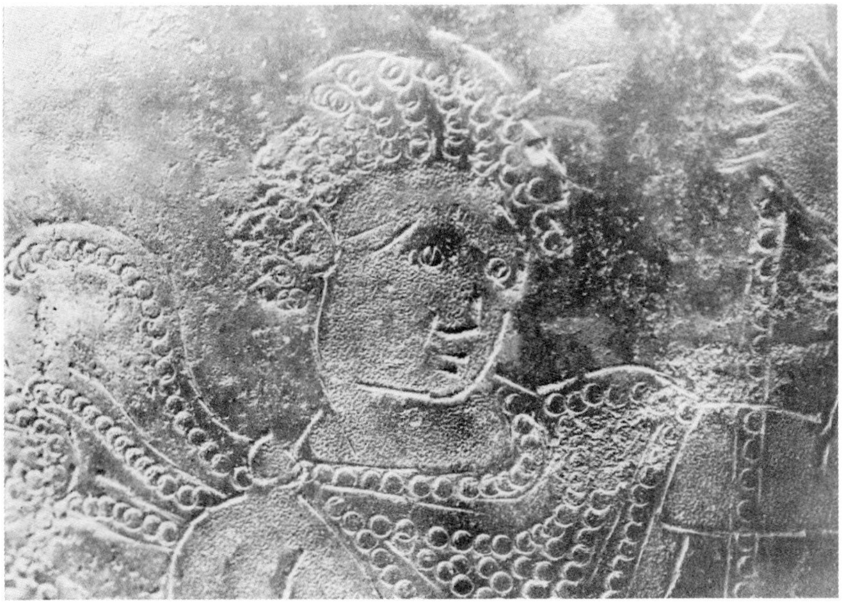

Fig. 8. Situla: detail of Patroclus, 5th or 6th c. Bronze, h. 23.5 cm. Rome, Palazzo Doria. (Photo: A. Carandini; from *StMisc* 9 [1963-64] fig. 25)

ple. The relatively early date of the Getty situla is revealed by its elegant curvature and its tall, slender proportions. The later vessels are lower, wider, and more conical; and their handles are attached to holes in an upward protrusion of the wall of the vessel. The row of reserved dots in the upper frieze of the Getty situla also finds a parallel on the Bueña vessel (below the palm and rosette frieze; figs. 1, 6). Another more subtle element of continuity appears on the Doria and Getty situlae: faces are rendered in generally similar terms, and eyebrows are indicated by an elongated V placed horizontally, an unusual convention that indicates a direct workshop connection between the two (figs. 2, 8). Figures on the Doria situla, of course, have a substantially different look because of the extensive use of a ring punch, a tool that was apparently not used in the Göldenitz Group and is almost certainly a mark of a substantially later period.

Based on available information, then, it seems possible and even likely that craftsmen of the Göldenitz Group transferred their activities to the south, where they had a stimulating effect on certain kinds of bronzeworking. There are few specific traces of their style and techniques in the second half of the 3rd c., but this may simply be due to accidents of preservation. Enough close parallels with Rhenish production turn up in the 4th and/or 5th c. to make it clear that there was a specifically northern contribution to late-antique drawings on bronze. The Getty situla not only emerges as one of the most impressive examples of the Göldenitz Group, but it also provides key evidence for demonstrating the group's durable impact on Mediterranean workshops.

Art of the Ancient World, Museum of Fine Arts, 465 Huntington Avenue, Boston, MA 02115

Römische *Authepsae*, auch ein Instrument der ärztlichen Versorgung?

Teodora Tomasevic Buck

Einleitung

In der Unterstadt von Augusta Raurica (Kaiseraugst, Aargau)[1] hatte ich 1974 eine sehr gut erhaltene Authepsa entdeckt. Es ist erst der dritte Fund einer Authepsa in der Schweiz. Die erste wurde 1874 im Forum Claudii Vallensium (Martigny, Wallis) und die zweite 1910 in Aventicum Helvetiorum (Avenches, Vaud) aufgefunden. Diese Entdeckung hat mich veranlasst, über Jahre hinweg, mich mit diesem aufwendig gebauten antiken "Selbstkocher" zu befassen. Ich stellte fest, dass alle *Authepsae* wohl dem Zweck "selbst" zu kochen dienten, wobei sie sich sowohl in der Verwendung als auch in Form, Bauart und Fassungsvermögen als Flüssigkeitsbehälter grundsätzlich voneinander unterscheiden. Es ist mir ferner gelungen, zwei Hauptgruppen und mehrere Formtypen zu differenzieren.

Definition

Die *Authepsae* sind Metallgefässe, die aus mehreren Teilen gefertigt wurden. Als Fundobjekte sind nur solche aus Kupferlegierung, auch mit Eisenteilen, überliefert. Aus schriftlichen Quellen kennt man auch jene aus Silber.[2] Schon ihre Bezeichnung Authepsa, ein griechisches Wort, wurde auch in der römischen Antike neben dem lateinischen *miliarion/miliarium* benützt und zeigt eine Kontinuität der Verwendung auf. Funde aus Etrurien bezeugen, dass sie bereits im klassischen Griechenland bekannt war. Später jedoch sind hellenistische *Authepsae* auch im römischen Kontext, wie Exemplare aus Pompeji belegen, in den römischen Alltag übernommen worden (Abb. 2.1-3).[3] Die einfache Bedienung und die Möglichkeit, sie auch unterwegs im Reisegepäck mitzunehmen, hat bewirkt, dass sie bis in die Gegenwart als Samowar in Gebrauch geblieben sind.[4]

Typen

Obwohl sich mehrere Autoren bereits eingehend mit den *Authepsae* befasst haben, besteht noch immer keine systematische Übersicht ihrer Formen bzw. Funktionen, um sie einfacher zitieren zu können. Wir wählten die Typenbezeichnung A für mobile und B für stationäre *Authepsae*: mit Hinzufügen der ersten Zahl für den Behältertyp (A1, A2, A3) und der zweiten Zahl für die Fussform (Einzelfuss 1, Standring mit Füssen 2, Piedestal 3, Kompositum 4). Auch neuentdeckte Formen können in dieses System nachträglich mit neuer laufender Nummer hinter dem Buchstaben A oder B eingefügt werden. Unabhängig davon ist für nicht einzuordnende Formen, weil sie aus umgebauten Gefässen in Zweitverwendung als *Authepsae* entstanden sind, die Bezeichnung Typ AV(aria) bzw. BV(aria) vorgesehen.

Wir unterscheiden zwei Grundformen der *Authepsa*, die mobile tragbare, Typ A (Abb. 1.1-11), und die stationäre nicht eingebaute, Typ B (Abb. 1.12). Typ A ist mit dem "Défilé de servi-

---

1 K. M. D. Dunbabin, "Wine and water at the Roman convivium," *JRA* 6 (1993) 116-41. Auf S. 124 gibt sie den Fundort der *Authepsa* aus Augusta Raurica fälschlich mit Augst, statt Kaiseraugst an.

2 *SHA, Heliogab.* 19.3; J. A. Overbeck und A. Mau, *Pompeji in seinen Gebäuden, Alterthümern, und Kunstwerken* (Leipzig 1884[4]) 441; Abb. 237 führt eine *Authepsa* aus Kupferlegierung und Eisen auf, siehe unsere Abb. 1.7.

3 A. Mau, *Pompeii in Leben und Kunst* (Leipzig 1908) 398, Abb. 224; S. Tassinari, *Il vasellame bronzeo di Pompei* (Rom 1993) 347, Inv. 1765, Y 2000; E. Pernice, *Gefässe und Geräte aus Bronze* (Berlin 1925) Taf. 7; *Pompeji wiederentdeckt* (Ausstellungskat., Rom 1994) 207-9, Inv. 6798, Kat. 95.

4 E. Molohowez, *Staraja kuhnja Rossiji [Die alte Küche Russlands]* (Rostov-am-Don 1992) 501, 97 "Der Samowar ... eignet sich besonders für Reisen, im Kriegsfall und Wüstengegenden. Es sind verschiedene Grössen erhältlich, für zwei, drei und vier Personen, mit drei, fünf und sieben Gläser".

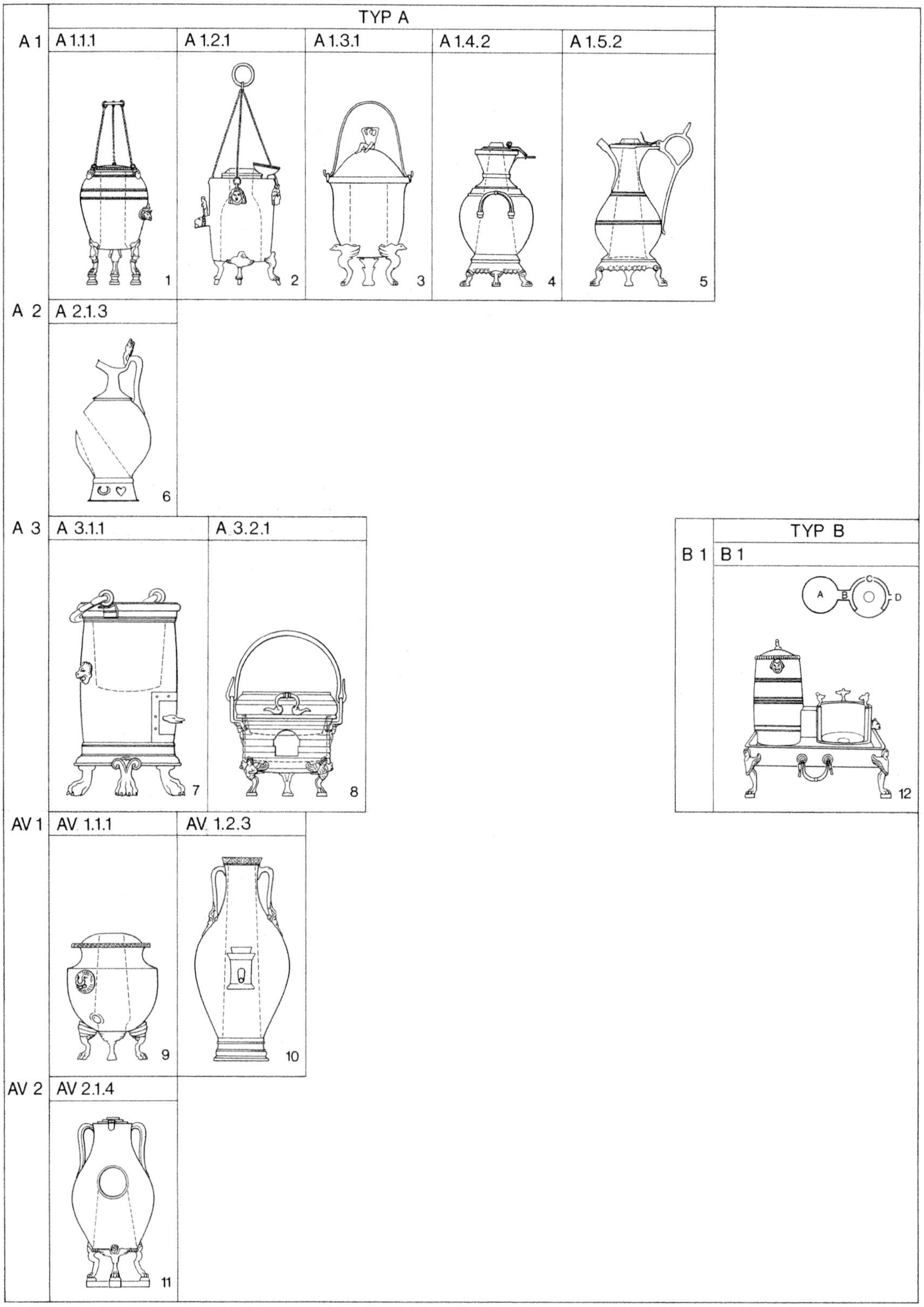

Abb. 1. Typenübersicht der nachgewiesenen *Authepsae*. (Tabelle: Verfasserin; Umzeichnung: E. Weber)

teurs apportant les accessoires d'un banquet?" (Abb. 3) deutlich genug in seiner Mobilität definiert.[5] Die Gruppe der tragbaren Form kann nach ihrer Verwendung in drei Typen A1-3 aufgeteilt werden. Typ A1 mit senkrechtem Heizzylinder (Abb. 1.1-5), in dem man heisse Getränke

5 Mosaikbodenbelag, FO Karthago; SO Musée du Louvre Ma 1796.

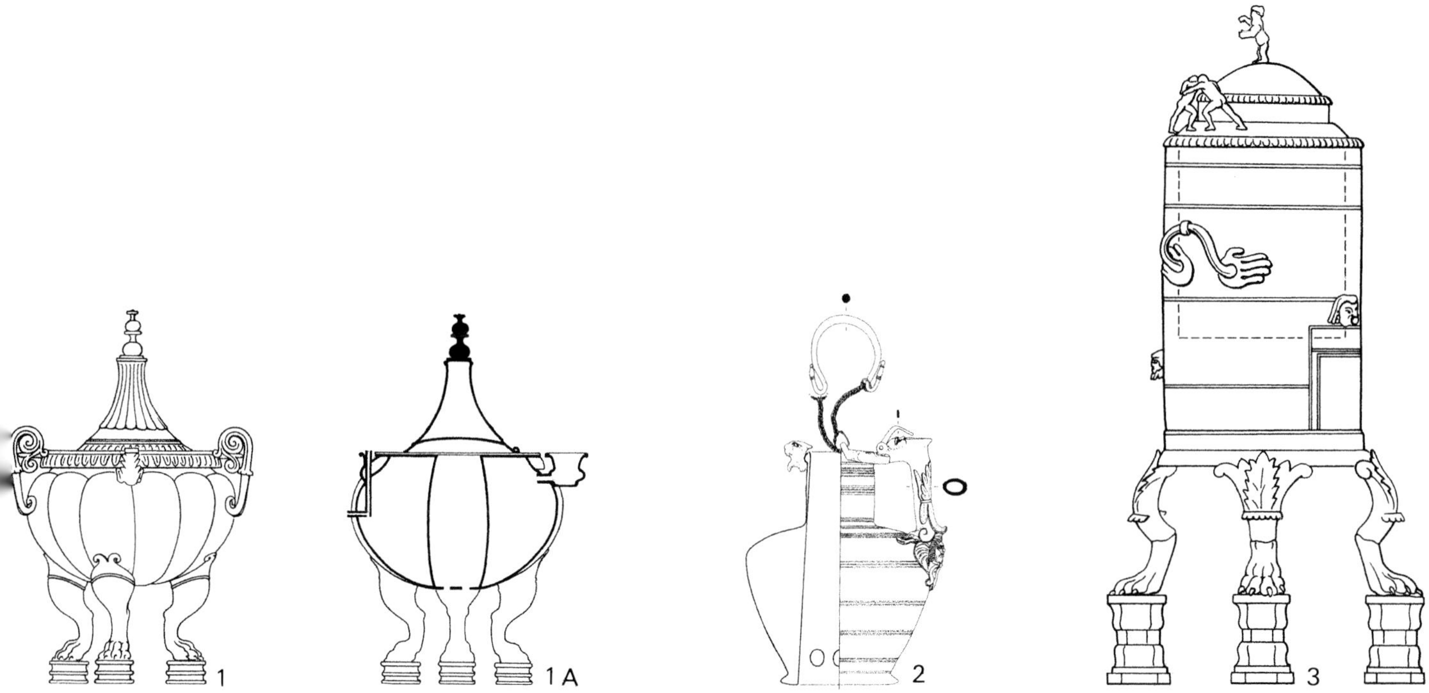

Abb. 2. Pompeji, hellenistische *Authepsae*. 1 Type A1; 2 Type A2; 3 Type A3 (Umzeichnung: E. Weber)

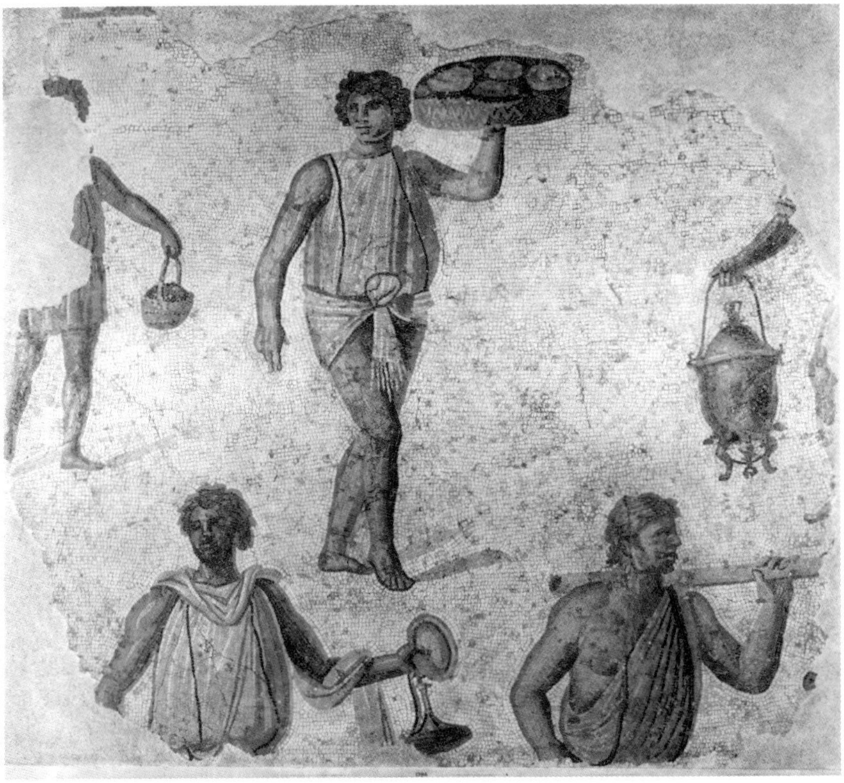

Abb. 3. Karthago, Mosaikbodenbelag mit der Darstellung eines Dieners, der in der rechten Hand eine *Authepsa* Typ A1.3 trägt. Paris, Musée du Louvre Ma 1796. (Foto: Musée)

aufbrühte; Typ A2 (Abb. 1.6) kannenförmig mit schrägem Heizzylinder, wurde als Wasserwärmer, wohl mit Zusatz von duftendem ätherischem Öl, zur persönlichen Toilette sowie an der Tafel genutzt, und Typ A3, ein Kochtopf mit einem (Abb. 1.7) oder mehreren Einsätzen (Abb. 1.8), in dem Speisen zubereitet oder warm gehalten wurde.

Typ A1 hat neben dem Flüssigkeitsbehälter ein senkrechtes zylindrisches (Abb. 1.1-3) oder konisches (Abb. 1.4-5) Heizrohr, das auf einem Rost aufliegt. Der Rost kann in mehreren Varianten vorkommen: von ganz einfachen, in denen man den Boden des Behälters mit mehreren Zuglöchern perforierte, oder aufwendig mit einem Rost versehen. Belegt ist der Rost aus unterschiedlichem Metall, Eisen (Abb. 11.5) oder Röhrchen aus gleichem Metall, Kupferlegierung wie der Behälter.[6] Bei letzterem Typ zirkuliert die zu wärmende Flüssigkeit aus dem Behälter durch die Röhrchen, um sich schneller zu erwärmen. Auch Blech aus Blei wurde als Sieb für aufzubrühende Kräuter verwendet (Abb. 11.3, 5).

Der Behälter des Typ A1 tritt in mehreren Varianten auf: in Fassform Typ A1.1.1 (Abb. 1.1), als Situla Typ A1.2.1 (Abb. 1.2), als Krater Typ A1.3.1 (Abb. 1.3),[7] als Krug Typ A1.4.2 (Abb. 1.4) und in Kannenform Typ A1.5.2 (Abb. 1.5). In der Literatur wird Typ A1.1 auch als Eiform bezeichnet. Um die notwendige Luftzufuhr beim Verbrennen des Heizmaterials (Harzholz, Holzkohle[8]) im Heizzylinder zu gewährleisten, ist der Flüssigkeitsbehälter entweder auf gegossenen, einzeln angebrachten drei Füssen (Abb. 1.1-3) mit Ziffer 1, oder einem Dreifussring (Abb. 1.4-5) mit 2 bezeichnet, montiert. Die beliebtesten Fussformen sind Löwenpranken, die auf separat gegossenen (Abb. 1.1-3) oder mitgegossenen runden Basen (Abb. 1.4-5) ruhen. Ihre Bekrönung ist häufig als mehrblättrige Palmette geformt,[9] aber auch wie eine Erotenprotome (Abb. 5.1; 7.2; 8.1-2) oder Ente (Abb. 1.2)[10] gestaltet. Solch eine mobile *Authepsa* Typ A1 wurde entweder auf drei Ketten getragen, die auf einem Ring befestigt sind (Abb. 1.1-2) und mit kunstvoll gearbeiteten Attachen (Frauenköpfe [Abb. 6.1-3],[11] Masken [Abb. 1.2],[12] etc.) am Behälter oder am Bügel (Abb. 1.3) bzw. Henkel (Abb. 1.4) aufgelötet wurden. Neben Typ A1.5 mit nur einem Henkel ist auch Typ A1.4 (Abb. 11.1) mit zwei oder Variante Typ A1.4 (Abb. 11.2) mit mehreren Henkeln versehen. Ein immer kunstvoll gestalteter Hahn (Rinder/Stierkopf mit Fingerhebel [Abb. 7.1], Negerkopf mit Entenkopfhebel,[13] Löwinnenkopf mit anthropomorphem Hebel [Abb. 1.2],[14] Wildschweinkopf,[15] etc.) ist in der Regel an der unteren Behälterhälfte angebracht. Ein Deckel gehört zur Grundausstattung. Extras trifft man auch in Form von Eingussrezipienten (Krater,[16] Trichter [Abb. 1.2][17]) an. Die Verwendung war vielfältig. Man konnte Wasser wärmen sowie Wein, Kräutertee, etc., in ihnen zubereiten. Ihr Fassungsvermögen ist unterschiedlich, sie kommen in verschiedenen Grössen vor. Ihr Einsatz war sowohl an der Tafel als auch im medizinischen Bereich gefragt. Es sind etwa 15 Exemplare bekannt (Tabelle 1).

Typ A2 (Abb. 1.6) hat einen kannenförmigen Behälter mit Ausguss und Henkel, der auf einem relativ hohen Postament, mit Ziffer 3 bezeichnet, entweder befestigt ist oder aus dem gleichen Stück Blech wie der Behälter geformt wurde. Manchmal ist die Eingussöffnung mit einem Sieb[18]

---

6 Neapel, Museo Nazionale 126 441: A. Mutz, "Eine kleine Authepsa," *JRGZM* 14 (1967) 167-74, Taf. 47.3; L. Pirzio Biroli Stefanelli, *Il bronzo dei Romani* (Rom 1990) 234, 218, Kat. 98.

7 Siehe Anm. 5.

8 Inv. Nr. 8613: *Pompeji wiederentdeckt* (s. o. Anm. 3) 238, Kat. 144.

9 *Greek and Roman metalware* (Ausstellungskat., Baltimore 1976) Kat. Nr. 77, 78; C. S. Lightfoot und M. Yazici, "A Roman tomb-group containing two samovars (*authepsae*) from Kayseri, Turkey," *OpRom* 18.8 (1990) Abb. 10-11. Kayseri Museum, Inv. Nr. 86/11, 86/12-13.

10 *Pompeji wiederentdeckt* (s. o. Anm. 3); Tassinari (s. o. Anm. 3) Inv. Nr. 8613, Y 2200.

11 *Pompeji wiederentdeckt* (s. o. Anm. 3); Tassinari (s. o. Anm. 3).

12 G. di Stefano, "La nave delle colonne," *Archeo* 73 (1990) 115-18.

13 Lightfoot und Yazici (s. o. Anm. 9) Abb. 10.

14 *Pompeji wiederentdeckt* (s. o. Anm. 3) 238-39, Kat. Nr. 144, Inv. Nr. 8613; Tassinari (s. o. Anm. 3) Inv. Nr. 8613, Y 2200.

15 S. Stucchi, *L'agorà di Cirene* 1 (Rom 1965) 325-26, Taf. LIX.3.

16 Mutz (s. o. Anm. 6) Inv. Nr. 126, 441; Stucchi (s. o. Anm. 15) Taf. LIX.3; Pirzio Biroli Stefanelli (s. o. Anm. 6).

17 *Pompeji wiederentdeckt* (s. o. Anm. 14); Tassinari (s. o. Anm. 3) Inv. Nr. 8613, Y 2200.

18 A. Mutz, "Bau und Betrieb einer römischen *Authepsa* (Samowar)," *Ur-Schweiz* 23.3 (1959) 37-48.

TABELLE 1. ÜBERSICHT DER *AUTHEPSAE* ALS FUNDOBJEKTE BZW. DARSTELLUNG AUF MOSAIK; aufgestellt nach Typen A1 (1-15), A2 (16-20), A3 (21-22), AV (23-26), und B (27), mit Angaben über Fundort, Aufbewahrungsort, Höhe, Inv. Nr. und Datierung.

Typ A1

Nr.	Land	Fundort	Aufbewahrungsort	Höhe in cm	Inv. Nr.	Datierung
1	Italien	Pompeji	Neapel, Mus. Nazionale	37.7	8613	1. Jhr.
2	Italien	(?)	Neapel, Mus. Nazionale	40.0	-	1. Jhr.
3	Italien	(?)	Neapel, Mus. Nazionale	42.0	126 441	1. Jhr.
4	Italien	Camerina	Camerina, Mus. Regionale	-	-	Mitte 3. Jhr.
5	Schweiz	Kaiseraugst	Augst, Römermuseum	37.7	74.10376	Mitte 3. Jhr.
6	Bulgarien	Stara Zagora	Sofia, Naz. Museum	45.6	4812	-
7	Bulgarien	Stara Zagora	Sofia, Naz. Museum	47.5	4813	-
8	Bulgarien	Stara Zagora	Sofia, Naz. Museum	44.2	4818	-
9	Türkei	Kayseri	Kayseri, Arch. Museum	35.2	86/9	3. Jhr.
10	Türkei	Kayseri	Kayseri, Arch. Museum	-	86/10	3. Jhr.
11	Türkei	Konya(?)	Stuttgart-Ulbach, Weinbaumuseum	50.0	III.4.047	-
12	Tunesien	Karthago[19]	Paris, Musée du Louvre	-	1796	3. Jhr.
13	Lybien	Cyrene	Mus. in Chahat	55.4	-	Ende 4. Jhr. Anfang 5. Jhr.
14	Lybien	Cyrene	Mus. in Chahat	53.0	-	Ende 4. Jhr. Anfang 5. Jhr.
15	Lybien	Cyrene	Mus. in Chahat	37.0	-	Ende 4. Jhr. Anfang 5. Jhr.
-	Marokko[20]	-	-	-	-	-

Typ A2

Nr.	Land	Fundort	Aufbewahrungsort	Höhe in cm	Inv. Nr.	Datierung
16	Italien	Pompeji	Mainz, RGZM	23.0	0.33874	-
17	Frankreich	Chartres	Chartres	32.0	-	1.-3. Jhr.
18	Schweiz	Avenches	Musée romain	51.0	1910.4986	-
19	Ungarn	Szekszard	Budapest, Nat. Museum	21.2	65/1885	-
20	Magreb	-	Stuttgart-Ulbach, Weinbaumuseum	12.0 n.e.	III.4.002	-

19 Ausgehend von der genauen Darstellung der *Authepsae* Typ A2 (Villa bei Tellaro, Voza [s. o. Anm. 21]) und A3 (Villa bei Marbella, Garcia y Bellido 1969 [s. o. Anm. 24]) an den verschiedenen Darstellungen auf Mosaikböden, haben wir den *Authepsa* Typ A1.3 — ein Krater als Behälter — als einziges, nicht echtes Fundobjekt in die Typologie aufgenommen, noch bevor dieser Typ als Fundgegenstand entdeckt wurde.

20 Seit C. Boube-Piccot in ihrem umfangreichen Werk, *Les bronzes antiques du Maroc* 2: *Le mobilier* (Rabat 1969) Kat. Nr. 419, 612-16, sechs Füsse in Form von Löwenpranken mit verschiedenem Überbau (priapischer Erote, Sirene, Ente, Priap, Sphinx) als "pied et poignée de meubles" veröffentlicht hat, werden in der einschlägigen Literatur diese Objekte als Füsse von *Authepsae* aufgeführt, was von der Autorin mit Recht nie angenommen wurde.

Typ A3

Nr.	Land	Fundort	Aufbewahrungsort	Höhe in cm	Inv. Nr.	Datierung
21	Spanien	Sevilla	Privatbesitz	27.0	-	1. Jhr.
22	Italien	Pompeji	Neapel, Mus. Nazionale	um 1.0	-	1. Jhr.

Typ AV

Nr.	Land	Fundort	Aufbewahrungsort	Höhe in cm	Inv. Nr.	Datierung
23	Italien	-	Neapel, Mus. Nazionale	54.5	-	-
24	Italien	Pompeji(?)	Kassel, Staat. Museen	48.5	Br. 305	1. Jhr.
25	Schweiz	Martigny	Genf, Mus. d'Art et d'Histoire	42.0	13739	Mitte 3. Jhr.
26	Bulgarien	Stara Zagora	Sofia, Nazional Museum	64.0	4810,4811	-

Typ B

Nr.	Land	Fundort	Aufbewahrungsort	Höhe in cm	Inv. Nr.	Datierung
27	Italien	Stabiae, Villa	Neapel, Mus. Nazionale	51.0	-	-

oder Deckel[21] versehen. Der Hauptunterschied zum Typ A1 besteht darin, dass die *Authepsa* Typ A2 einen schrägen Heizzylinder hat, dessen Heizungsöffnung in der Regel in der oberen Hälfte des Behälters, etwa in der Mitte zwischen dem Kannenschnabel und Henkel, ausgespart ist. Sowohl der Behälter, als auch sein Postament sind mit Zuglöchern versehen. Den Behälterinhalt, wohl warmes Wasser, schenkte man ohne Hahnvorrichtung direkt über dem Kannenausguss aus. Seinen Einsatz hat dieser Typ vor allem im Bereich der persönlichen Toilette gefunden, sei es in den Thermen, wie es der Mosaikbelag in den Thermen von Sidi Grib mit seiner "Grande dame à sa toilette" illustriert (Abb. 4),[22] wo 8 für die Toilette als notwendig erachtete Gegenstände (Holzpantinen, Korb mit Bekleidung und Tüchern, Waschbecken, Schmuckkassette, Spiegel, Eimer) abgebildet sind, oder in der Natur, wie das Jagdmosaik aus der Villa Tellaro zeigt.[23] Auf das übliche Bad vor dem Einnehmen eines Mahles verzichtete man bei einem Jagd-Picknick in der Natur, weil keine Thermen vorhanden waren und beschränkte sich auf das Händewaschen mit warmem Wasser, das an Ort und Stelle in der *Authepsa* Typ A2 aufbereitet wurde, ohne auszuschliessen, dass das gewärmte Wasser auch zum Zubereiten von *calda* diente.[24] Dieser Typ ist als Fundgegenstand belegt (Tabelle 1, 16-20).

Typ A3 ist eine *Authepsa miliarion/miliarium*, auch *foculus* genannt, welche sowohl als Selbstkocher, als auch als Wärmehalter diente. Sie besteht aus einem äusseren Behälter, der auf drei Füssen steht und inneren, nicht immer sichtbaren, Einsätzen. Die einfache Variante Typ 3.1 (Abb. 1.7) hat nur einen Einsatz im Gegensatz zum Typ 3.2 (Abb. 1.8), der mit mehreren Einsätzen ausgestattet ist. Der Hauptunterschied zu Typ A1 und A2 besteht darin, dass der Heizzylinder weggelassen wurde. Dieser Typ wurde durch eine Türöffnung an der Aussenwand geheizt. Der Zug brachte den Rauch wohl zwischen der Aussenwand und dem unsichtbaren Behältereinsatz vorbei ins Freie. Dieser Authepsatyp findet sich auch auf dem Mosaik des

21 A. Ferdière und Y. de Kisch, *Gallia* 42 (1984) 271-325; J. D. Joly, "Un *authepsa* romaine à Chartres," *Chartres 1979-1988: 10 années d'archéologie, 20 siècles d'histoire* (Chartres 1989) 69-71.

22 M. Blanchard-Lemée, M. Ennaifer, H. et L. Slim, *Sols de l'Afrique romaine* (Paris 1995) Abb. 116.

23 P. Pelagatti und G. Voza, *Archeologia nella Sicilia sud-orientale* (Neapel 1973) Taf. LIX.

24 Dunbabin (s. o. Anm. 1) 131.

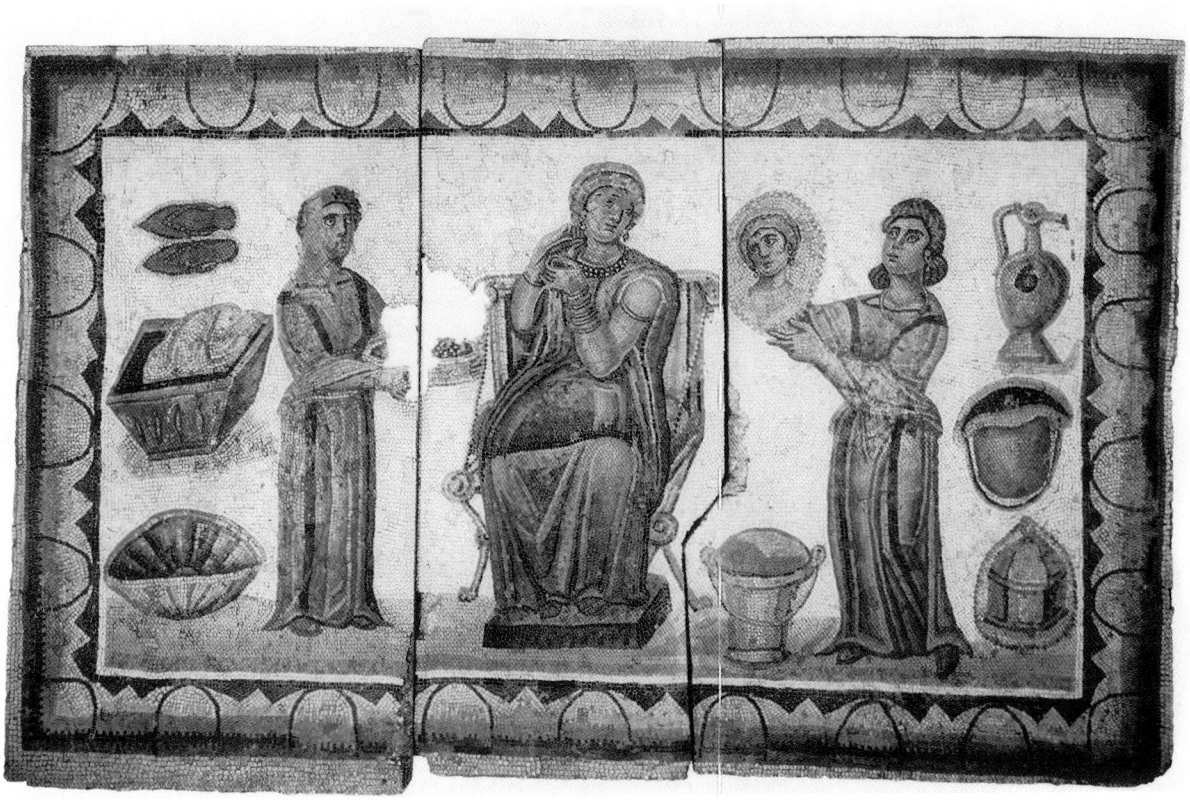

Abb. 4. Sidi Ghrib, Mosaikbodenbelag in Thermen mit der Darstellung einer Domina mit Badeutensilien, darunter eine *Authepsa* Typ A2 oben rechts. Tunis, Musée du Bardo. (Foto: aus M. Blanchard-Lemée, M. Ennaifer, H. et L. Slim, *Sols de l'Afrique romaine* [Paris 1995] fig. 116 S. 162)

Freudenhauses in Ephesus,[25] im Peristyl einer Villa in Marbella,[26] und ähnliche sind aus Pompeji[27] bekannt (Tabelle 1.21-22).

Typ A3.1.1 (Abb. 1.7) *miliarium* hat eine zylindrische, gegen die Mitte der Höhe ausladende Aussenwand aus Eisenblech, die auf drei von Palmettenvoluten gekrönten Löwenpranken ruht. Geheizt wurde die *Authepsa* durch eine kleine Türe, die mit einem Gänsekopfgriff versehen ist. Zwei Löwenkopfattachen sind über Öffnungen angebracht, die für das Entweichen von Rauch(?) gedacht waren. Sie wurden von einem Bügel getragen, der in zwei Ösen am Rand des Zylinders über den Löwenkopfattachen eingehängt wurde. Als Behältereinsatz diente ein Kessel aus Kupferlegierung.[28]

Die Variante Typ A3.2.1 (Abb. 1.8) *foculus* aus Hispalis[29] hat zwischen der Aussenwand und dem Kochbehälter einen zusätzlichen zylindrischen, unsichtbaren Kesseleinsatz mit Horizontalrand, der mit Wasser gefüllt — wie ein *bagno maria* — das Anbrennen des Kochbehälterinhaltes verhindern sollte. Getragen wurde der Selbstkocher auf einem Bügel, der mit zwei kunstvoll gearbeiteten, gegossenen Attachen an der Aussenwand angebracht war. Gleichwohl gegossen waren auch die beiden am Kochbehälter waagrecht angebrachten Henkel. Der *foculus* ruht auf drei Füssen, die mit einer Konsole ausgestattet sind. Löwenpranken auf mitgegossenen Spulenbasen sind von Sphinxen gekrönt. Die Bügelattachen sind als geflügelte Eroten geformt. Die Tür zum Heizen und der Deckel sind nicht mehr erhalten.

---

25 W. Jobst, "Das 'öffentliche Freudenhaus' in Ephesos," *ÖJh* 51 (1976/77) Abb. 21-23.

26 A. Garcia y Bellido, "El mosaico de tema culinario de Marbella," in J. Bibauw (Hrsg.), *Hommages à Marcel Renard* 3 (Bruxelles 1969) 241-46.

27 Overbeck und Mau (s. o. Anm. 2).

28 Ebd.

29 J. J. Storch de Gracia y B. Asensio, "El "foculus" de Sevilla," *Miscelánea arqueológica romana: contactos entres ambas orillas del Estrecho de Gibraltar* (Barcelona 1987) 941-51.

Typ AV(aria) ist eine mobile *Authepsa*, hergestellt aus einem Gefäss in Zweitverwendung. Bei den vier uns bekannten Exemplaren wurden je zwei Amphoren und "Kessel" mit spherischem bzw. flachem Boden zu einem Selbstkocher von Typ AV1 bzw. AV2 umgebaut.

Typ AV1.1.1.1 (Abb. 1.9), eine *Authepsa* aus Martigny[30] (Tabelle 1.25), war ursprünglich als ein "Kessel" mit spherischem Boden und Henkel ausgestattet, wie ein Gefäß aus Pompeji und Ülzen.[31] Der "Kessel" wurde mit einem senkrechten konischen Heizrohr und drei Füssen in Form von Löwenpranken, die von Volutenpalmetten gekrönt sind, ergänzt und so zu einer *Authepsa* adaptiert. Obwohl der eine noch erhaltene Fuss mit wenig Geschick angebracht wurde, so dass man annehmen könnte, der Umbau sei in der Provinz vorgenommen worden, gehört er zur Fussform, die man auch bei anderen *Authepsae* am Golf von Neapel wiederfindet (Neapel, Museo Nazionale 126 441).

Das zweite Exemplar, eine Variante von Typ AV1.1[32] (Tabelle 1.24), hat einen ausladenden Rand, einen flachen Boden und einen Deckel mit einem rundplastischen Kopf als Griff. Das senkrechte Heizrohr ist auch erhalten, hingegen fehlt ein Untersatz, um die Luftzufuhr zu gewährleisten sowie die Vorrichtung zum Tragen. Lötspuren am Behälter zeigen Griffe an.

Bei Typ AV1.2.3 (Abb. 1.10) handelt es sich um eine grosse Amphore aus Augusta Trajana (Abb. 11.4), die mit zwei Behälterkammern bzw. einem Heizzylinder und dementsprechend mit zwei Hähnen ausgestattet wurde. Montiert wurde die Amphore auf einem Piedestal (Form 3), ähnlich wie Typ A2 (Abb. 1.6). Dieser doppelkammerige Selbstkocher ermöglichte unterschiedliche Getränke gleichzeitig zuzubereiten.

Typ AV2.1.4 (Abb. 1.11) ist auch aus einer Amphore entstanden. Das zweihenkelige Gefäss bekam beim Umbau einen getreppten Deckel, welchen man mit einem Scharnier am Behälter befestigte. Es wurde mit einem schrägen Heizzylinder ausgestattet und auf einem Dreifussuntersatz (Form 4, Kompositum) mit Löwenpranken, von geflügelten weiblichen Wesen(?) gekrönt, montiert.[33]

Typ B1 (Abb. 1.12) ist aus den Fundstellen am Golf von Neapel bekannt. Diese stationäre *Authepsa*, ein Beispiel aus einer Villa in der Nähe von Stabiae,[34] besteht aus einem rechteckigen von vier Füssen getragenen Aschenbehälter, der mit zwei gegossenen Henkeln ausgestattet ist. Die Füsse, Löwenpranken, auf die geflügelte Sirenen aufgesetzt wurden, ruhen auf kreisförmigen Spulenbasen. Der Selbstkocher setzt sich aus einem auf den Aschenbehälter montierten fassförmigen Flüssigkeitsbehälter A zusammen, der seitlich mit Attachen verziert ist (Maske) und einem Deckel. Der Deckel weist eine Rundplastik (Merkur) als Griff auf. Der offene doppelwandige Zylinder C, der mit einem plastisch verzierten Hahn D (Löwenkopf) versehen ist, ist in der unteren Hälfte wie kommunizierende Röhren A und B verbunden. Der offene, mit Figuren (Schwäne) geschmückte Zylinder C, hatte zwei Funktionen. Einmal bot er einen Windschutz für das feuernde Brennmaterial, zum anderen zirkulierte in ihm die zu erwärmende Flüssigkeit des Behälters, die sich in dem doppelwandigen Zylinder direkt am Feuer schneller erwärmen konnte.

Herstellung

Die *Authepsae* wurden aus Silbermetall und Kupferlegierung hergestellt. Unsere Beobachtungen begrenzen sich nur auf kaiserzeitliche Exemplare aus Kupferlegierung, weil Selbst-

30 W. Deonna, "Quelque monuments antiques du Musée de Genève III: vaisselle et instruments antiques provenant de Martigny (Valais)," *Genava* 11 (1933) 51-73.

31 Tassinari (s. o. Anm. 3) Regio I, Insula 6, Inv. Nr. 1963, X 2110; *Römer am Rhein* (Ausstellungskat. 1967) 233, Kat. Nr. C 148, Taf. 81.

32 P. Gercke, A. Krug, und R. Lullies, "Zu einer römischen *Authepsa* in Kassel," *JRGZM* 14 (1967) 175-78; U. Höckmann, *Antike Bronzen: eine Auswahl* (Katalog, Kassel 1973) Inv. Nr. Br 305, Kat. Nr. 100.

33 Neapel, Museo Nazionale, ohne Inv. Nr.: Mutz (s. o. Anm. 6).

34 J. B. Ward-Perkins und A. Claridge, *Pompeii A.D. 79* (Exhib. cat., London 1976) Kat. Nr. 159.

kocher aus Silber nur literarisch überliefert sind.[35] Eine weitere Einschränkung geht aus dem Umstand hervor, dass wir alle zitierten Exemplare nicht einer persönlichen Autopsie unterzogen haben und darüber hinaus die Autoren sich selten in ihren Veröffentlichungen über technische Details äussern. Oft sind die einzelnen Objekte ohne Zeichnung nur von einer nicht immer leicht zu deutenden Photographie begleitet. Es hat sich leider auch noch nicht eingebürgert, die einzelnen Teile der *Authepsae* chemisch zu untersuchen.

Allgemein stellen wir fest, dass die aus mehreren Teilen bestehenden *Authepsae* aus Blech bzw. gegossenen Teilen aus Kupferlegierung — mit einer uns bekannten Ausnahme, wo ein Teil der Aussenwand aus Eisen besteht (Abb. 1.7) — zusammengelötet sind; nachgewiesen ist Weichlot.[36] Für Scharniere (Deckel Abb. 11.5 und Abb. 1.7, Türchen[37]) und den Rosteinsatz kann auch Eisen (Abb. 1.5) verwendet werden.

Aus Blech wurden Deckel, Behälter, Zylinderrohr, und Grill gefertigt. Der Grill aus Blech kann mit Aussparungen der Zuglöcher oder Blechröhrchen, die mit dem Behälter verbunden sind, geformt sein.

Aus gegossener Kupferlegierung wurden Attachen an den Tragketten, Hähne, Füsse, Dreifussringe sowie Henkel hergestellt. Die zusätzlichen Verzierungen wie Attachen und Figuren sind selbstverständlich auch gegossen, ohne sich festlegen zu können, ob sie aus Matrizen oder in *cire perdu* Verfahren hergestellt sind.

Attachen und Füsse weisen jeweils minimale Abweichungen voneinander auf, welche möglicherweise nur auf Nachbearbeitung zurückzuführen sind, obwohl sie in der gleichen Form gegossen wurden (Abb. 6-8).

Sowohl der Behälter als auch der Zylinder können unter anderem in zwei Techniken hergestellt sein: aus einem Stück Blech gedrückt oder aus einem Rohr getrieben. Der erste Vorgang ist nicht aus der schriftlichen Überlieferung bekannt, sondern gegenwärtig neu erschlossen,[38] hingegen ist der zweite allgemeines Wissensgut.

Verbreitung

Ausgehend von unserer Typeneinteilung in mobilen Typ A und stationäre *Authepsae* Typ B stellen wir fest, dass beide Gruppen unterschiedlich verbreitet sind. Typ A findet man von der Iberischen Halbinsel bis nach Kleinasien und von Mitteleuropa bis nach Nordafrika, sowohl als Fundobjekt als auch auf Mosaiken und Wandmalereien bildlich dargestellt. Typ B hingegen ist nur als Fundobjekt in der Region um den Golf von Neapel nachgewiesen (Tabelle 1). Neben der erwähnten Funddichte der Typen A und B in Italien sind die übrigen mobilen *Authepsae* jeweils als Einzelfunde zum Vorschein gekommen. Die Ausnahme bilden die vier Exemplare aus Augusta Trajana (Abb. 11.1-4), drei aus Cyrene (Tabelle 1.13-15) und zwei aus dem sog. Battalati Grab in Caesarea Cappadociae (Tabelle 1.9-10).[39] Stellen wir ferner die Typen A1-3 gegenüber, erkennen wir sofort, dass Typ A1 und A2 häufiger als Typ A3 (Tabelle 1) vorkommt. Im Gegensatz zu Typ A3, der einmal in Hispanien und mehrere Male in Italien zum Vorschein gekommen ist,[40] ist die Verbreitung der beiden ersten fast flächendeckend in europäischen und vorderasiatischen Provinzen sowie in Nordafrika.

Die *Authepsae*, insbesondere Typen A1 und A2, die zum erwärmen von Wasser gebraucht wurden, konnten auch die einfache weit verbreitete Deckelkanne Typ Tomasevic-Buck 4 ersetzen.[41] Sowohl Wassersinterspuren an der Innenseite dieser Kannen, als auch die häufig

35 *SHA*, *Heliogab.* (s. o. Anm. 2).

36 L. Lehoczky, Restaurierungsbericht vom 1.11.1994.

37 Overbeck und Mau (s. o. Anm. 2).

38 A. Mutz, "Vom schlichten Rohr zum schönen Krug," *AntW* 9.3 (1978) 31-36.

39 Lightfoot und Yazici (s. o. Anm. 9).

40 Storch de Gracia y Asensio (s. o. Anm. 27). Im Museo Nationale, Neapel.

41 T. Tomasevic Buck, *Ein Bronzedepotfund aus Augusta Raurica* (München 1984) Abb. 3.3a-c, Taf. 31.5.

vorkommenden Reparaturen am Boden durch Ersetzen ganzer Böden zeugen von ihrem intensiven Einsatz als "Wasserwärmer". Typ A3 konnte gleichwohl mit einem gewöhnlichen Kochtopf entweder aus Ton oder aus Metall als Kessel am offenen Feuer eingetauscht werden.[42] Die Tatsache, dass *Authepsae* auch durch einfachere Mittel zu ersetzen waren, bestätigt die allgemeine Auffassung in der Antike, die *Authepsae* seien ein Luxusgut.[43]

Eine *Authepsa* aus Augusta Raurica

Wie schon einleitend bemerkt, wurde in der Unterstadt von Augusta Raurica (Kaiseraugst, Aargau) zwischen 1974 und 1980 wegen des Neubaus einer Unterführung und eines Umschlagplatzes der Bahn eine grossflächige archäologische Untersuchung durchgeführt. Die Bedeutung dieser Ausgrabung ist vielfältig. Zum einen wurde die von uns schon lange gehegte Vermutung über die Gegebenheit einer Ober- und Unterstadt der Kolonie Augusta Raurica auch städtebaulich bestätigt,[44] ferner kam der bis heute bedeutendste Goldfund dieser Stadt, das Goldhalsband,[45] dort zum Vorschein, und nicht zuletzt wurde ein bemerkenswerter, geschlossener Fund mit einer vollständig erhaltenen *Authepsa* hier 1974 entdeckt.

Es handelt sich um zwei relevante Fundkomplexe aus einem Eckhaus, das im nord-west orientierten Unterstadtteil an der Überlandstrasse stand, die zwischen Gallien und Raetien durch Augusta Raurica führte. Zwei Fundkomplexe haben interessantes Material geliefert. Sie sind in bezug auf die Hauseinheit in der sie entdeckt wurden, und betreffend ihrer Verwendung, aussagekräftig. Der eine Fundkomplex FK A5083 wurde in einer rechteckigen Vertiefung, der andere FK A5074 etwa 0.50-0.70 m in höher gelegenem Niveau gefunden.[46] Da sie von ihrer Verwendung her zweifelsohne zusammengehören, legen wir sie gemeinsam, aufgeteilt in Münzen, Instrumente, Geräte und Geschirr, nachfolgend vor:

MÜNZEN [47]

(FK A5083) • ANTONINUS PIUS BIS MARCUS AURELIUS FÜR FAUSTINA II

Dupondius, Rom 145-176

Av.: (FAVST)INA - (...), drapierte Büste n.r. Rv.: (...) Stehende Figur. Stark zirkuliert.

360°, 10.05 g. Inv. Nr. 74.10378, Fund Nr. 619.

• GORDIANUS III.

Antoninian, Rom 241-243

Av.: IMP GORDIANVS PIVS FEL AVG, drapierte gepanzerte Büste mit Strahlenkranz n.r. Rv.: IOVI - STATORI; Jupiter stehend.

RIC IV.3, 25, 84. Sehr geringe Zirkulationsspuren.

180°, 3.60 g. Inv. Nr. 74.10377, Fund Nr. 618.

INSTRUMENTE

(FK A5083) • Skalpelgriff, Kupferlegierung, im Querschnitt quadratisch (Abb. 9.1), L. 9.6 cm, Inv. Nr. 74.10380.

• Skalpelgriff, Kupferlegierung, im Querschnitt achteckig (Abb. 9.2), L. 12.5 cm, Inv. Nr. 74.10381.

(FK A5074) • Ohrlöffelchen aus Bein, L. 6.1 cm, Inv. Nr. 74.6261.

---

42 Dunbabin (s. o. Anm. 1) Abb. 21, 23.

43 Ebd. Anm. 42.

44 T. Tomasevic Buck, "Augusta Raurica und ihre öffentlichen Sakralbauten," *Jahrbuch des Vorarlberger Landesmuseumsvereins* (Bregenz 1988) 43-71.

45 T. Tomasevic Buck, "Ausgrabungen in Kaiseraugst 1980," *JberAugst* 5 (1985) 266-77; E. Riha, *Der römische Schmuck aus Augst und Kaiseraugst* (*Forschungen in Augst* 10, 1990) 67-69.

46 E. Riha, *Römisches Toilettgerät und medizinische Instrumente aus Augst und Kaiseraugst* (*Forschungen in Augst* 6, 1986) 95 (A. R. Furger). Leider war es mir nicht möglich, wie beabsichtigt, an dieser Stelle auch einen Grabungsbericht vorzulegen, weil mir weder Funde, noch die archivierten Ausgrabungsunterlagen meiner archäologischen Untersuchung zugänglich waren.

47 Die Bestimmung der Münzen verdanke ich M. Peter.

GERÄTE

(FK A5083) • Einsatzgewicht mit ausladendem Wulstrand, Standring, und zwei Bodenrillen (Abb. 9.3), Teil eines Schalengewichtsatzes aus Kupferlegierung mit Inschrift EX(actus ad), CA(storis), zwei Unzen (51.703 gr.),[48] Rdm. 3.6 cm, H. 1.5 cm, Bdm. 2.2 cm, Inv. Nr. 74.10382.

• *Authepsa*, Typ A1.1.1 (Abb. 5-8) aus Kupferlegierung. Den fassförmigen Behälter (Abb. 5.1) schließt ein mit Perl- und Eierstab verzierter, gegossener Ring ab. Der Behälter ist in der oberen Hälfte mit drei Doppelrillen gegliedert. Zwischen den Rillen weist er eine etwa 4.6 cm grosse Öffnung auf. Am Boden sind vier Zugöffnungen ausgespart (Abb. 5.3). Das mittlere Zugloch hat einen Durchmesser von ca. 2 cm, das von drei ca. 1.5 cm grossen Öffnungen umgeben ist. In der unteren Behälterhälfte ist der Hahn in Form eines Rinder/Stierkopfes mit einem fingerförmigen Hebel angebracht (Abb. 5.1A). Durch Drehen des Hebels bewegt man den durchlochten Einsatz, so dass die Flüssigkeit ausgelassen wird (Abb. 7.1).[49] Der Deckel ist mit zwei Rillen, die von zwei Doppelrillen eingefasst sind, verziert. Ferner ist der Deckelrand wellenförmig gestaltet (Abb. 5.2). In der Mitte ist eine Schlaufe aus Blech als Henkel in ein rechtwinkliges Loch eingefügt. Der Heizzylinder schliesst mit umgebogenem Rand und breitem ausladendem Fuss ab, der am Übergang von Seitenwand zum Boden des Behälters eingefügt ist (Abb. 5.1A). Die Tragkette ist nur mit zwei der drei Stränge vollkommen erhalten. Die einzelnen Kettenglieder bestehen aus einfachen zusammengelegten und ineinandergeführten, im Querschnitt quadratischen Gliedern. Das einzelne Kettenglied wurde ringfömig ausgestanzt. Die eine Kette zählt 16 und die andere 17 Glieder, die auf einem rundstabigen Ring mit rundstabigen Drahtösen befestigt sind (Abb. 5.1). Mit ähnlichen Ösen sind am anderen Ende der Kette die Attachen angebracht. Ein zusätzlicher Ring, durch die Öse der einen Attache gezogen, diente in Verbindung mit einer nicht mehr erhaltenen Kette zur Sicherung des Deckels (Abb. 6.1). Die drei unterschiedlichen, gegossenen Frauenkopfattachen (Abb. 6.1-3) sind mit einer Aufhängeöse versehen. Die Haare sind in der Mitte gescheitelt, seitlich nach unten gekämmt und die Schläfen von Haaren überdeckt, die unter der Aufhängeöse hochgesteckt wurden. Zwei ausdrucksvolle Augen umrahmen eine klassisch anmutende Nase. Zweimal sind die Lippen stark sensuell geformt (Abb. 6.1-2). Die drei gegossenen ungleichen Füsse (Abb. 7.2; 8.1-2) bestehen aus zwei Teilen: einer Löwenpranke, gekrönt von einem Akanthuskelch, aus dem eine geflügelte Erotenprotome hervorgeht, die sich mit beiden Armen an die Akanthusblätter anlehnt und einer runden, spulenförmigen Basis. Es sind nur zwei (Abb. 8.1-2) nicht identische mit Halbrundstäben und Rillen gegliederte Basen erhalten. Eine mitgegossene Konsole am Rücken der Eroten sichert eine feste Standfläche für die *Authepsa*. Rdm. 14.4 cm, H. 37.7 cm, Bdm. 12.8 cm. Inv. Nr. 74.10376 (Tabelle 1.5).

• Sog. Sturmlaterne aus Kupferlegierung (Abb. 9.4). Es fehlen zwei von drei Trageketten, der Deckel und die aus vergänglichem Material eingesetzte Schutzmembrane (Tierblase?). Bei der Restaurierung wurde an ihrer Stelle ein Plexiglas eingesetzt (auf der Zeichnung gestrichelt angegeben). Das Hauptgerüst bilden drei gegossene senkrechte Pilasterrippen, mit einer Öse versehen, in die mit einem Ring die Tragkette eingehängt war. Von einer der drei Tragketten sind noch 9 Glieder erhalten. Mit jeweils 3 Nieten waren die Rippen an die Membrane und mit je einer an den mit Rillen gegliederten Rand und Boden befestigt (Abb. 9.4A-4B). Der Rand besteht aus einem umgekehrten U-förmig gebogenen Metallstück. Den aussen hochgezogenen Boden und die Rippen hält ein an der Innenseite angebrachter Metallring. Der Boden, aussen mit mehreren Rillen versehen, weist einige konzentrische Vertiefungen auf, die einen guten Halt für das Einsetzen einer Lichtquelle (Kerze, Öllampe, etc.) bieten. Die Laterne ruht auf drei gegossenen Füssen. Rdm. 17.4 cm, H. 21 cm, Bdm. 18.4 cm., Inv. Nr. 74.10375.

(FK A5074) • Augenarztstempel aus grünem Talgstein[50] (Abb. 10.1). Das Plättchen hat eine quadratische Form mit abgerundeten Ecken, so dass sich eine Ansata beim Textabschnitt mit SORICVM (Abb. 10.1B) bildet. Die Schmalseiten des Stempels sind zwischen je zwei Rillen zweimal mit einer bzw. zwei Zeilen beschriftet: C.V.DI.I. (Abb. 10.1A) / C.V.DI.IDIA / SORICVMC (Abb. 10.1B) / CVDI.INAR / DINVM (Abb. 10.1C) / C.V.DI.I. (Abb. 10.1D).[51] Eine der breiten Flächen (Abb. 10.1) ziert die Ritzdarstellung eines Vogels (Rabe?) mit einem Ring im Schnabel, einem Frosch und vielen Ritzstrichen, die sich auch auf der gegenüberliegenden grossen Fläche (Abb. 10.1E) wiederholen. 3 x 3.3 x 0.9 cm, Inv. Nr. 74.6260.

---

48 Das Lesen der Beschriftung verdanke ich H. Lieb.

49 Di Stefano (s. o. Anm. 12) findet sich der Hahn auch in Form eines Stierkopfes, fälschlich "leonina" bezeichnet.

50 Die petrographische Bestimmung verdanke ich V. B. Stern.

51 Lieb (s. o. Anm. 48); Näheres auch H. Lieb, "Nachträge zu den römischen Augenärzten und Collyria," *ZPE* 43 (1981) 207-8.

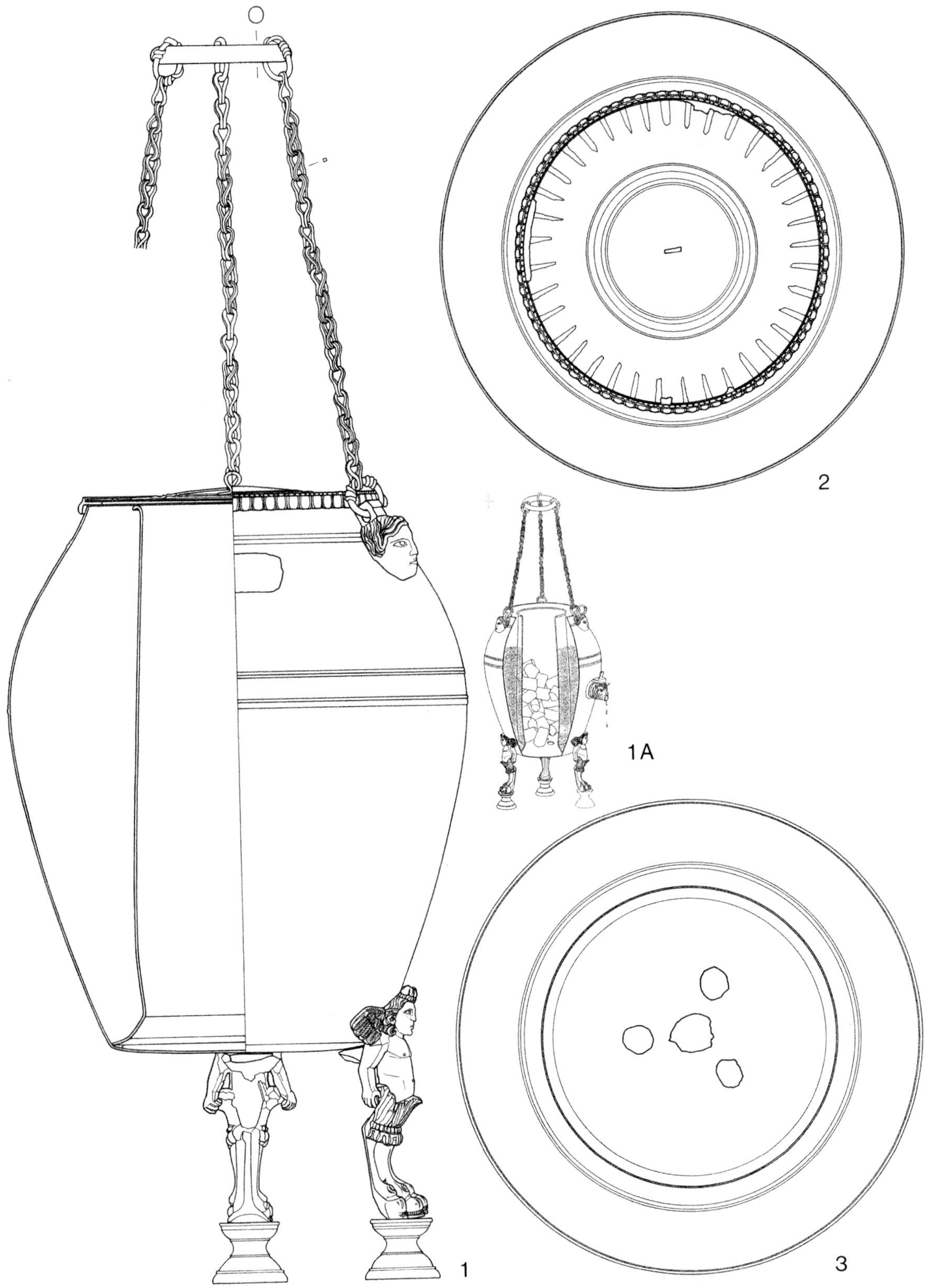

Abb. 5. Kaiseraugst, 1 *Authepsa* Typ A1; 1A Längsschnitt; 2 Ansicht Decke; 3 Ansicht Boden mit Zuglöchern. Augst, Römermuseum. (Umzeichnung: I. Horisberger)

(FK A5083) • Ein kegelförmiges Ende eines Instrumentengriffes(?) gedrechselt aus Bein, L. 4.4 cm, Inv. Nr. 74.10386 (Abb. 9.5). Ohne es näher bestimmen zu können, verweisen wir auf weitere drei ähnliche Exemplare aus Augusta Raurica: Inv. Nr. 66.4463, 77.19420, und FK C00543, Fundnr. 456 (Abb. 9.6-8).[52]

52 Riha (s. o. Anm. 44) führt auf Taf. 10, 82-85, bei Rasiermesser Variante B ähnliche Griffe aus Bronze auf.

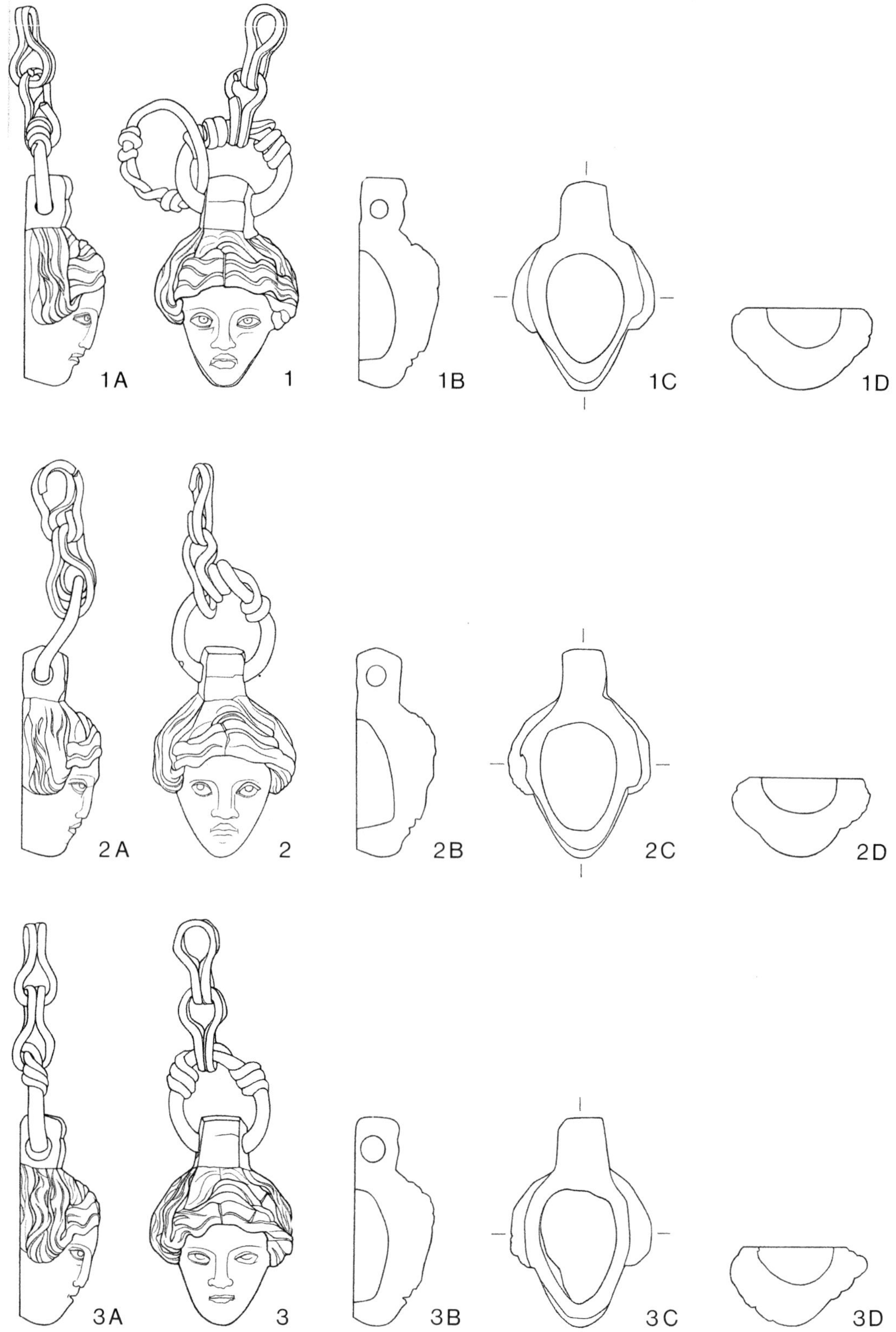

Abb. 6. Kaiseraugst, Kettenattachen: 1A-3A Seitenansicht; 1-3 Ansicht; 1B-3B entsprechender Längsschnitt; 1C-3C Rückansicht; 1D-3D Querschnitt. Augst, Römermuseum. (Umzeichnung: I. Horisberger)

GESCHIRR

(FK A5083) • Bodenscherbe flach, eines Gefässes aus Glas[53] und RS, Napf mit Horizontalrand aus Ton.

---

53 Unser BS ist bei B. Rütti, *Die römischen Gläser aus Augst und Kaiseraugst* (Forschungen in Augst 13, 1991) leider nicht erfasst; vgl. auch Anm. 44.

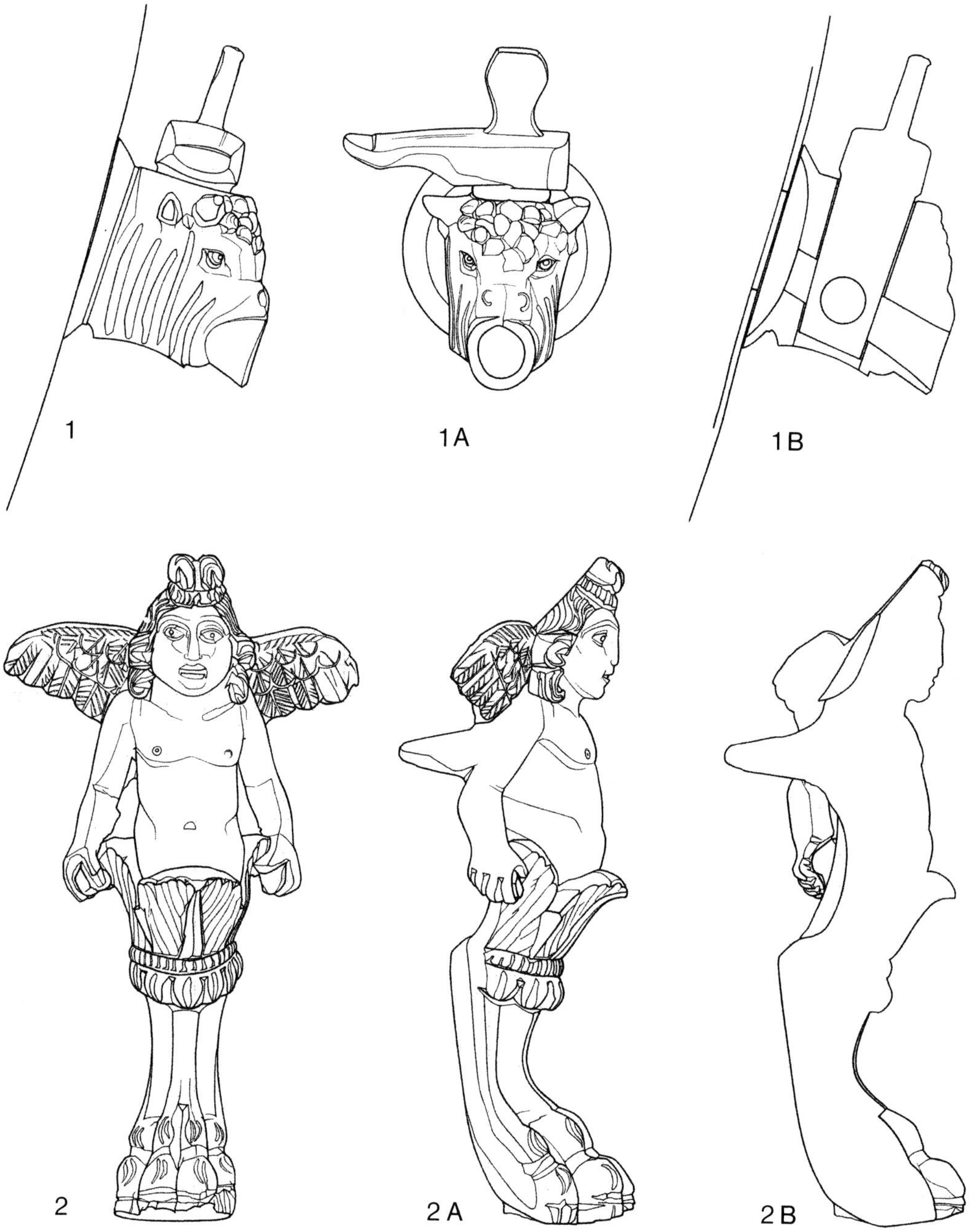

Abb. 7. Kaiseraugst, 1 Authepsahahn mit Hebel, Seitenansicht, 1A Ansicht; 1B Längsschnitt; 2 Authepsafuss, Ansicht, Basis nicht erhalten; 2A Seitenansicht; 2B Längsschnitt. Augst, Römermuseum. (Umzeichnung: I. Horisberger)

Relevant für die Verwendung der *Authepsae* im medizinischen Bereich ist vor allem die Vergesellschaftung der Mitfunde, Münzen, Instrumente und Geräte. Die Münzen datieren den Fund in die Mitte des 3. Jhr. Es handelt sich um den in der Koloniestadt bezeugten Depotfundhorizont, welcher um das Jahr 253 entstanden ist.[54] Von den vier Geräten sind drei, die zwei Skalpelle sicher und das Einsatzgewicht wahrscheinlich im medizinischen Bereich verwendet worden. Das Einsatzgewicht gehört zu einem Gewichtsset, wie wir es aus Mogontiacum (Mainz) kennen. Das vollständig erhaltene Mainzer Einsatzgewichtsset besteht aus 7 Stücken. Das

54 T. Tomasevic-Buck, "Neue Grabungen im Kastell Kaiseraugst," *Studien zu den Militärgrenzen Roms* 3 (Köln 1986) 268-72, Anm. 18.

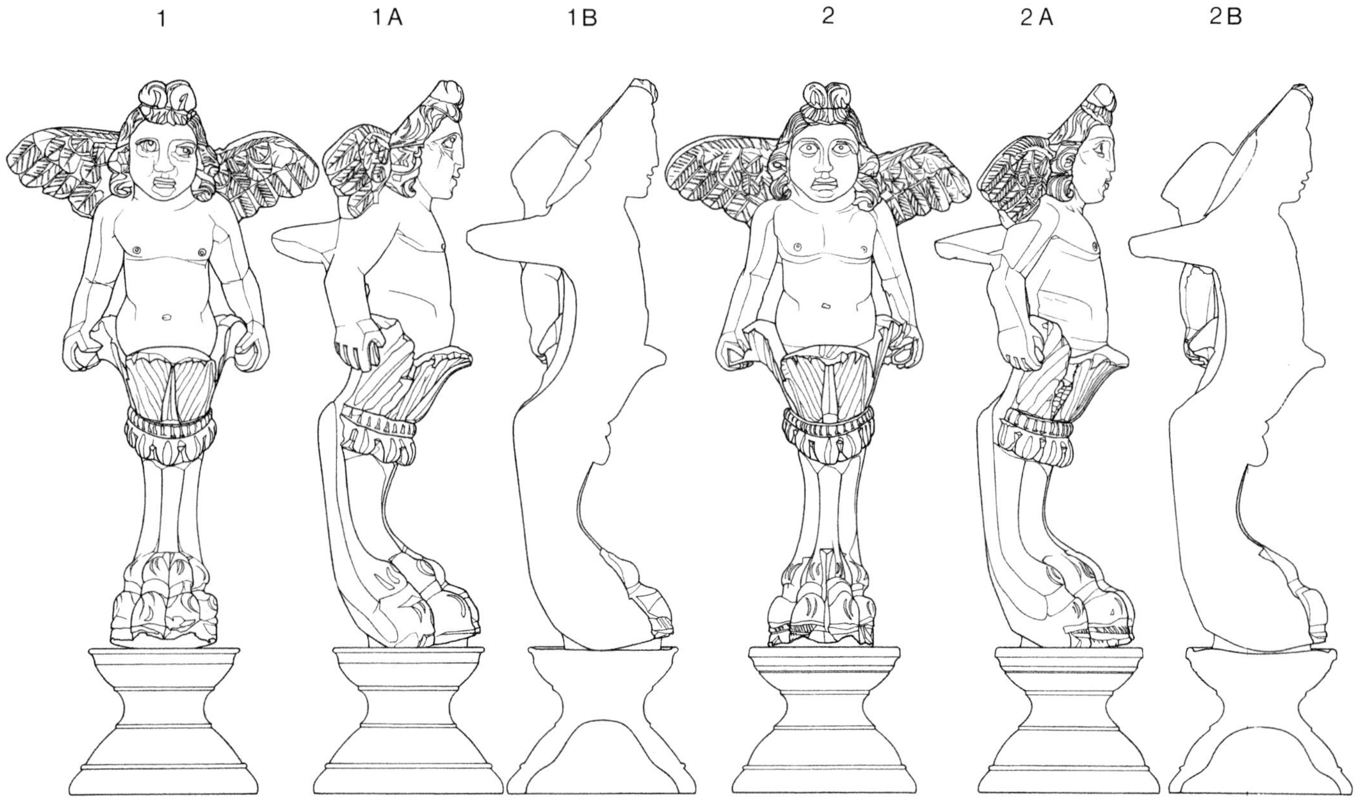

Abb. 8. Kaiseraugst, 1-2 Authepsafussansicht; 1A-2A Seitenansicht; 1B-2B Längsschnitt. Augst, Römermuseum. (Umzeichnung: I. Horisberger)

kleinste Gewicht von 8 g schliesst wie ein Deckel die Reihe des grössten von 320 g ab. Das Letztere weist einen klappbaren Tragbügel auf. Dazwischen sind fünf ineinander geschichtete "Schälchen" von 27, 48, 80, 107, und 163 g, Inv. Nr. R 2263 a-g.[55] Mit Ausnahme des Leichtesten und des Schwersten sind die übrigen in der Form unserem Exemplar zum Verwechseln ähnlich. Was unser Exemplar unterscheidet ist die "Eichung", in der sein Gewicht von zwei Unzen (51.703 g) inschriftlich festgehalten ist. Auf die Frage, wo es auf ein differenziertes Gewicht ankommt, lautet die Antwort: wohl auch bei der Herstellung und Verabreichung von Medikamenten durch den Arzt.

Der Raum, in dem das Gewicht gefunden wurde, befindet sich unter einer gegenwärtigen Überbauung. Ohne zu spekulieren dürfen wir davon ausgehen, dass die Chance, den Gewichtssatz zu komplettieren, grösser gewesen wäre, hätte man den Raum bzw. das betreffende Haus vollständig ausgegraben.

Unsere *Authepsa* gehört zum gängigen Typ A1.1.1, welcher immer den gleichen fassförmigen Behälter und drei Einzelfüsse aufweist. Von Objekt zu Objekt dieses Typs variieren die Attachen, an denen die Tragkette befestigt ist, wie auch der Hahn und die Füsse. Die Füsse insofern als die Konstante — die Löwenpranken — dieselben bleiben, hingegen wechselt ihre Bekrönung von Palmetten[56] zu gewellten Doppelvoluten[57] oder wie bei der unsrigen, zu Eroten und Enten.[58] Keine der uns bekannten Kettenattachen gleicht dem unserem lieblichen Frauenkopf. Der Hahn, ein Rinder/Stierkopf wiederholt sich wahrscheinlich nur bei der sog. leonina.[59] Ihre

55 Die Gewichtsangaben des nicht veröffentlichten Mainzer Einsatzgewichtes verdanke ich der freundlichen Mitteilung von V. Deker.

56 *Greek and Roman metalware* (s. o. Anm. 9); Lightfoot und Yazici (s. o. Anm. 9).

57 Mutz (s. o. Anm. 6) Taf. 47.1-2.

58 *Pompeji wiederentdeckt* (s. o. Anm. 3) Inv. Nr. 8613, Kat. Nr. 144; Tassinari (s. o. Anm. 3) Inv. Nr. 8613, Y 2200.

59 Di Stefano (s. o. Anm. 12).

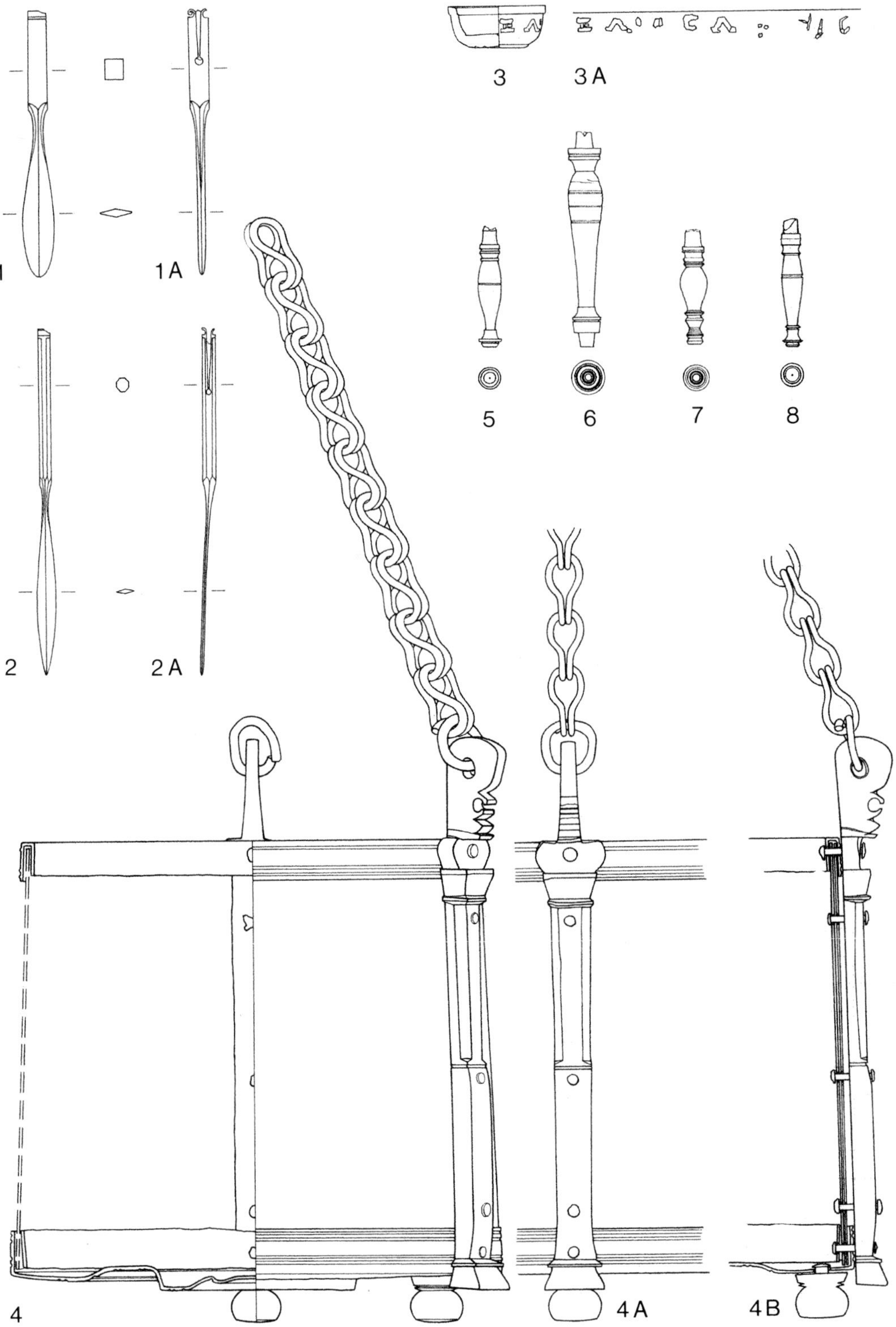

Abb. 9. Kaiseraugst, 1-2 Skalpelle Ansicht; 1A-2A Seitenansicht; 3 Teil eines Gewichtsatzes; 3A Abwicklung der Inschrift; 4 Sturmlaterne; 4A Detailansicht; 4B Detail Längsschnitt; 5 Griff aus Bein; 6-8 Parallelen aus Augusta Raurica zu 5. Augst, Römermuseum. (Umzeichnung: I. Horisberger)

Verwendung Wasser aufzukochen, um *calda*[60] zuzubereiten, schliesst nicht aus, dass sie, wie in unserem Befund auch, Verwendung fand, um Heilkräuter zu Tee oder zu einem Weingetränk aufzubrühen.[61]

60 Dunbabin (s. o. Anm. 1).

61 J. Irmsche und R. Johne (Hrsg.), *Lexikon der Antike* (Wiesbaden 1977-85) 631-32, s. v. Wein.

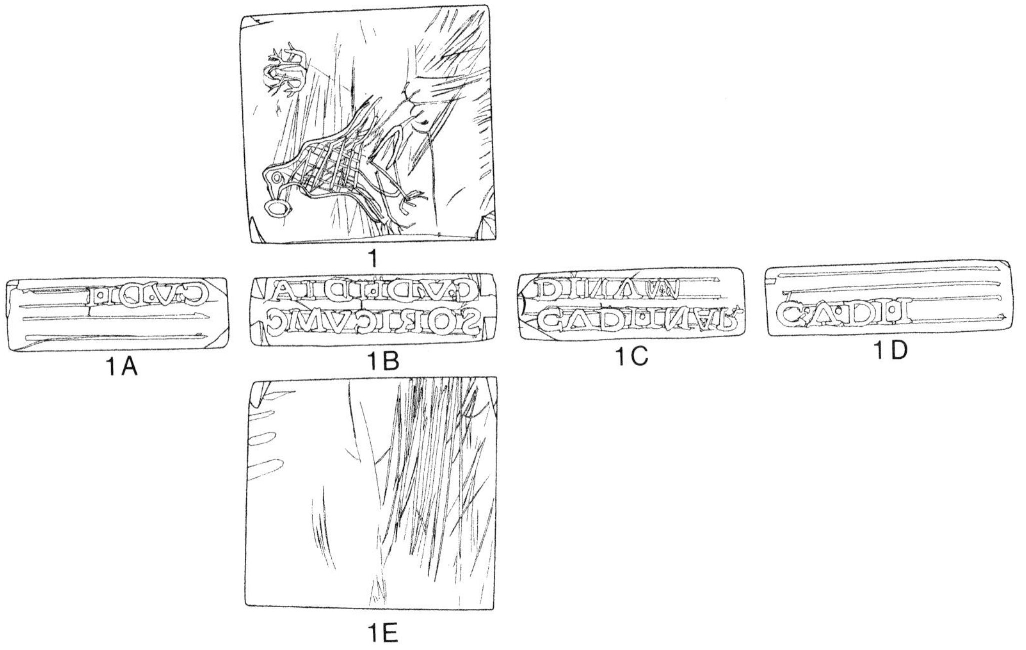

Abb. 10. Kaiseraugst, 1A-E Augenarztstempel. Augst, Römermuseum. (Umzeichnung: I. Horisberger)

Die sog. Sturmlampe war die unabdingbare Utensilie eines Arztes beim nächtlichen Patientenbesuch; waren doch die römischen Städte mit wenigen Ausnahmen nicht beleuchtet.

Der Augenarztstempel gehört, wie Skalpelle und sonstige Metallinstrumente, zur Grundausstattung eines Arztes.

Unsere These, der Befund *Authepsa* gehört zu einer Arztausrüstung, stützt nicht zuletzt auch die Lage des Hauses, aus der sie stammt. Zentral gelegen, zwischen der Ober- und Unterstadt, leicht für jeden Einwohner der Stadt erreichbar und an der Überlandstrasse zwischen Gallien und Rätien für jeden Reisenden, der Arzthilfe benötigte, ersichtlich, ohne Erkundigungen anstellen zu müssen.

Vier *Authepsae* aus Augusta Trajana und eine aus Kleinasien

Die Fundstelle Augusta Trajana (Stara Zagora, Bulgarien) zeichnet sich mit ungewöhnlich vielfältigem und reichem Fundbestand aus. Unter anderem sind vier *Authepsae* anfangs des Jahrhunderts ohne nähere Fundangaben ins Museum gelangt und befinden sich heute in Sofia im Archäologischen Nationalmuseum der Bulgarischen Akademie der Wissenschaften. Es handelt sich um zwei *Authepsae* Typ A1.4.2 und je eine Typ A1.5.2 sowie Typ AV1.2.3.

Eine *Authepsa* Typ A1.4.2 (Abb. 11.1), ein "Zweihenkelkrug" aus Kupferlegierung mit Steilrand, gegliedertem Hals, ausladender Wand, und abgesetztem Boden sowie abgetrepptem Deckel, der mit einer Kette am Deckelwiderlager befestigt war,[62] hat einen senkrechten konischen Heizzylinder. Der Behälter setzt sich aus zwei Stücken, Hals und Seitenwand, zusammen. Der Hahn, der einst an der unteren Hälfte des Behälters angebracht war, fehlt. Der Dreifussring und die beiden unterschiedlichen Henkel sind gegossen. Der Standring ist mit kreisförmigen, von plastischen Zapfen getrennten Löchern verziert. Die Füsse, Löwenpranken, die auf kreisförmigen Plättchen ruhen, enden oben mit stilisierten, verzierten Doppelvoluten. Die in ihrer Mitte gegliederten zwei Henkel sind waagrecht angebracht. Sie sind nicht gleich, sie unterscheiden sich sowohl im Motiv als auch in der Qualität voneinander. Der kanelierte Henkel endet mit zwei fein gearbeiteten Satyrnkopfattachen (Abb. 11.1A), der weniger qualitätsvolle rundstäbige Henkel mit zwei Masken (Abb. 11.1B). Die Masken zierte ursprünglich ein eingelegter, kreisförmiger Haarschmuck. Deckel Rdm. 14.1 cm, Rdm. 12.9 cm, H. 45.6 cm, Bdm. 15.2 cm, Inv. Nr. 4812 (Tabelle 1.6).

Die zweite *Authepsa* Variante, Typ A1.4.2 (Abb. 11.2), ist ein Krug mit Steilrand, ausladendem Hals und

---

62 Auf unserer Zeichnung, die ich dem Standortmuseum dieser *Authepsa* verdanke, ist die Kette nicht dargestellt. Sie war zur Zeit ihrer Veröffentlichung in *Hudozestven bronz ot rimskata epoha [Kunstbronzen der römischen Epoche]* (Sofia 1984) Abb. 319 vorhanden.

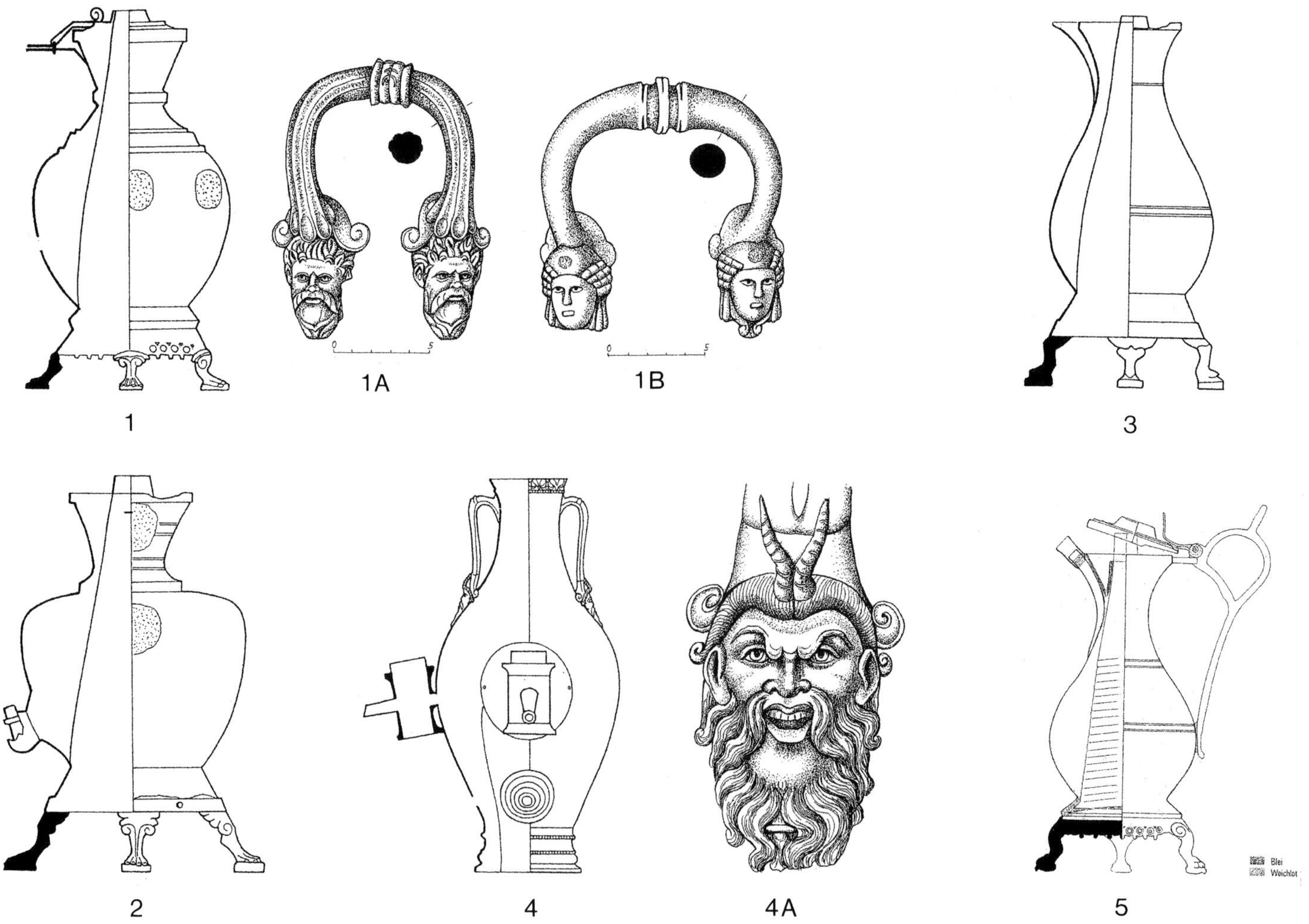

Abb. 11. Stara Zagora, 1 *Authepsa* Typ A1.4, Henkel; 1A Satyrenkopfe und 1B Maskenattachen; 2 *Authepsa* Variante Typ A1.4; 3 *Authepsa* Typ A1.5; 4 *Authepsa* Typ AV1.2; 4A Detail Henkel mit Satyrattache (1-4: Sofia, Archäologisches Museum); 5 *Authepsa* Typ A1.5 Konya (5: Stuttgart-Ulbach, Weinbaumuseum). (Umzeichnung: 1-4 Archäologisches Museum, Sofia; 5 Umzeichnung E. Weber)

Wand, abgesetzten ausladendem Boden sowie einem konisch, senkrechten Heizzylinder aus Kupferlegierung. An der Schulter und am Hals befinden sich Lötspuren, vermutlich von einem senkrecht angebrachten Henkel, wie bei Hydrien. An der unteren Hälfte des Behälters ist die beschädigte Hahnvorrichtung angebracht. Eine dritte Lötspur existiert gegenüber dem Hahn, dort wo das Deckelscharnier des fehlenden Deckels befestigt war. Der Dreifussstandring setzt sich zusammen aus einem schrägen, glattgehaltenen, von zwei Rillen eingefassten Ring mit sorgfältig gearbeiteten Löwenpranken, die auf einem kreisförmigen Plättchen ruhen und oben mit einer Palmette enden. Der Standring weist vier gebohrte Löcher auf. Da sie offensichtlich keine Funktion bei der *Authepsa* hatten, lassen sie die Vermutung aufkommen, dass der Standring in Zweitverwendung eingesetzt wurde. Rdm. 15.3 cm, H. 47.5 cm, Bdm. 20.3 cm, Inv. Nr. 4813 (Tabelle 1.7).

Das dritte Exemplar, eine *Authepsa* Typ A1.5.2 (Abb. 11.3) aus Kupferlegierung, hat eine schlanke Kannenform mit ausladendem Steilrand. Erhalten sind der Flüssigkeitsbehälter mit Ausgussansatz, ein senkrechtes, konisches Heizungsrohr und der gegossene Dreifussring. Der Flüssigkeitsbehälter ist mit drei Doppelrillen gegliedert. Der verlorengegangene Henkel war an der unteren Hälfte des Gefässes — beschädigte Stelle — angebracht. Der Untersatz besteht aus einem schräggeformten, schlichten Ring, ausgestattet mit drei hufförmigen (?) Füssen. Ein perforierter Einsatz aus Bleiblech ist im Kannenhals, wie bei der gleichen *Authepsa* aus der Türkei (Abb. 11.5), eingefügt. Rdm. 12.6 cm, H. 44.2 cm, Bdm. 16.7 cm, Inv. Nr. 4818 (Tabelle 1.8).

Die vierte *Authepsa* Typ AV 1.2.3 (Abb. 11.4) ist eine Amphore aus Kupferlegierung mit steilem, ausladendem Rand, der zu einer *Authepsa* umgearbeitet wurde, indem man das Gefäss der Höhe nach in zwei Kammern geteilt, mit Heizröhre und zwei Hähnen versehen sowie mit einem Postament wie bei *Authepsae* Typ 2, Form 3 ausgestattet hat. Der Rand ist mit einem von Perlstab eingefassten Kymationsband verziert. Der Behälter war mit zwei — am breitesten Wandteil gegenüber angebrachten — Hähnen ausgestattet. Nur ein Hahn, mit zwei Nieten an der Gefässwand befestigt, ist unvollständig erhalten. Es fehlt der Betätigungshebel.

Unmittelbar unter diesem Hahn befindet sich die dritte Öffnung, von einem kreisförmigen Plättchen umrahmt. Die gegossenen zweistäbigen Henkel enden an der Gefässschulter mit einer fein gearbeiteten, lachenden Satyrnkopfattache (Abb. 11.4A). Ein doppeltes Perlband ziert auch den mehrfach gegliederten, mit kleinen Löchern versehenen, Untersatz Form 3. Rdm. 13.1 cm, H. 64 cm, Bdm. 18 cm, Inv. Nr. 4810, 4811 (Tabelle 1.26).

Die *Authepsa* Typ A1.5.2 (Abb. 11.5) stammt aus Kleinasien (Konya, Türkei?) und wurde vom Weinbaumuseum in Stuttgart-Ulbach erworben. Es ist eine Kanne aus Kupferlegierung, mit vier Doppelrillen gegliedert, röhrenförmig ausgebildetem Ausguss und abgetreppt gestaffelt, gearbeitetem Deckel mit kreisförmiger Öffnung sowie senkrechtem konischem Heizzylinder. Wie bei der *Authepsa* aus Augusta Trajana (Abb. 11.3) wurde ein perforierter Einsatz aus Bleiblech im Kannenhals eingefügt, um Kräuter, etc., über den herausquellenden Dampf aufzunehmen. Der Boden weist anstelle von Zuglöchern einen Rost aus Eisen auf. Der Henkel und der dreifüssige Postamentring sind gegossen. Der geschwungene Henkel ist mit einem Widerlager für den Deckel und einer Querverstärkung versehen. Der Standring ist verziert mit perforierten Dreiecken und Kreisen, die von Zapfen getrennt sind. Seine Füsse, als Löwenpranken gestaltet, ruhen auf halbkreisförmigen Basen und sind jeweils von einer Doppelvolute gekrönt. Dem Restaurierungsbericht kann man entnehmen, dass die einzelnen Teile mit Weichlot (Blei–Zinnlegierung) zusammengefügt wurden. Auch über die in der Antike vorgenommenen Reparaturen am Deckel und Ausgusstülle wird berichtet.[63] Deckeldm. 13.4 cm, Rdm. 12.5 cm, H. 50.6 cm, Bdm. 16.7 cm, Inv. Nr . III-4.047 (Tabelle 1.11).

Der Versuch, die vier *Authepsae* vom Balkan und die eine aus Kleinasien in einen breiteren Kontext einzuordnen, zeigt auf, dass im Osten, neben den im Westen bekannten Formen, wie die *Authepsa* Typ A1.1 aus Kayseri[64] auch neue Formen Typ A1.4 (Abb. 11.1) und Typ A1.5 (Abb. 11.2) auftreten, die im Westen noch nicht entdeckt wurden. Die östlichen Exemplare weichen nicht nur in Ihrer Form von jenen aus dem Westen ab, sondern auch in technischen Details. Interessant ist es, dass sich, abgesehen vom Typ AV 1 "Kessel" bzw. AV 2 Amphore (Abb. 1.9-10), auch die Formen Typ A1.4 als Krug oder Typ A1.5 als Kanne, zweifach wiederholen. Ihre Formen und die technischen Details ihrer Herstellung, wie Standring mit drei Füssen, Henkel statt Tragketten mit Attachen und nicht zuletzt die konischen Heizröhren, an Stelle der zylindrischen, zeichnen sie aus. Obwohl sich auch im Osten die Löwenpranken der Beliebtheit erfreuten, taucht ein neuer Fusstyp in Form eines Hufes auf.

Zusammenfassung

Ausgehend vom Fundobjekt, einer *Authepsa*, die in einer Ausgrabung unter eigener Leitung in Augusta Raurica 1974 zum Vorschein gekommen ist und weiteren vier aus Augusta Trajana sowie einer aus der Türkei(?), die mir zur Veröffentlichung zur Verfügung gestellt wurden, entstand der Versuch, nicht nur die 6 *Authepsae* zu veröffentlichen, sondern gleichzeitig auch die bis heute noch fehlende Klassifizierung der verschiedenen Typen vorzunehmen und der Funktion ihres ursprüngliches Benutzungssystems wieder einzuordnen. Die gestellte Aufgabe war insofern leicht zu lösen, als K. M. D. Dunbabin in ihrem Artikel über "Wine and water at the Roman convivium" Grundlegendes über *Authepsae* zusammengetragen hat. Sie ging von dem Phänomen aus, dass der in der griechischen Antike als Weingefäss genützte Krater in der römischen Gegenwart an Bedeutung verlor und wohl wegen anderer Trinksitten die *Authepsa* neuerlich vermehrt Verwendung fand. Sämtliche über *Authepsae* und *milliaria* bekannten literarischen Quellen sowie Aussagen über römischen Umgang mit Wein und Wasser, ferner Zubereitung von *calda*, ein bei den Römern beliebtes warmes Weingetränk, legte sie interpretiert vor. Die Darstellungen der Verwendung der *Authepsa*, sei es auf nielo verziertem Geschirr aus Silber (Sevsoplatte), Mosaiken (häufig), Wandbemalung in Katakomben und Reliefdarstellungen auf Sarkophagen, hat sie gesammelt aufgezeichnet. Uns blieb, neben der Veröffentlichung der *Authepsae*, diese und die anderen bis jetzt bekannten, einzuordnen.

Die *Authepsae* sind mehrteilige Metallgefässe; bekannt sind Exemplare aus Silber, Kupferlegierung und kombiniert mit Eisen. Da die silbernen nur literarisch überliefert sind, haben wir uns nur auf solche aus Kupferlegierung oder mit Eisen ergänzte beschränkt. Eine weitere Einschränkung betrifft auch die Zeitspanne. Wir begrenzten uns nur auf Funde der römischen Kaiserzeit vom 1. bis 5. Jhr. Obwohl man die *Authepsae* schon in Etrurien und im

63 Lehoczky (s. o. Anm. 36).

64 Lightfoot und Yazici (s. o. Anm. 9) Abb. 10.

klassischen Griechenland kannte und als Produkt hellenistischen Kunsthandwerks in der Republik bzw. noch in Pompeji in Gebrauch waren, sind diese nicht berücksichtigt worden.

Wir unterschieden grundsätzlich zwei Gruppen, die mobile tragbare, als Gruppe A bezeichnete, und die stationäre Gruppe B. Bei Gruppe A sind sowohl nach ihrer Funktion, als auch nach ihrer Form bzw. technischen Details, drei Formtypen zu unterscheiden. Typ A1 mit senkrechtem Heizungsrohr, die *Authepsa,* in der Getränke aus warmen Wasser, Wein, Tee etc. aufbereitet wurden. Davon sind funf Varianten bekannt. Typ A2, eine *Authepsa* mit schrägem Heizungsrohr, in der auch Wasser gewärmt wurde und die mit Vorliebe bei der persönlichen Toilette eingesetzt war, ohne auszuschliessen, dass ihre gäbige Kannenform auch bei der Zubereitung von *calda* bei Tisch genützt wurde. Der dritte Typ A3, in dem auch Speisen zubereitet wurden, hat kein Heizungsrohr und dementsprechend keinen Flüssigkeitsbehälter wie Typ A1 und A2, sondern einen oder mehrere Einsätze. Die Feuerung geschah durch ein "Ofentürchen" unter dem Kessel. Neben den drei Standardtypen gab es auch Gefässe, die durch Umbau zu einer *Authepsa* umfunktioniert wurden, Typ AV(aria). Beliebt waren in dieser Kategorie die Amphoren und "Kessel".

In Gruppe B ist nur der Grundtyp B1 vertreten. Es sind kleine Kunsthandwerke mit technischer Höchstleistung. Die *Authepsa* besteht da, neben einem Flüssigkeitsbehälter, aus einem ausgeklügelten Verbindungsteil und Zylinder, alle drei als kommunizierende Röhren verbunden, auf einen Feuer- und Aschenbehälter montiert. Bei dieser Gruppe B wurde viel Wert auf die künstlerische Verzierung gelegt. Nicht selten sind sie mit Relief (Aplicken) und Rundplastik mit und ohne Funktion (Henkel, Hähne, Füsse, etc.) versehen.

Beide Authepsaegruppen wurden mit Kohle bzw. Harzholz beheizt. Da man Flüssigkeit, Wasser, Wein, etc. sowie Speisen auf jedem Feuer wärmen und zubereiten kann, aber nicht ohne anzubrennen längere Zeit warm halten konnte, war die *Authepsa*, insbesondere die mobile Typ A1 – weil handlich, leicht zu transportieren und zu beschicken – ein ausserordentlicher Luxusartikel, wie auch aus den schriftlichen Quellen hervorgeht. Wie selten die *Authepsae* doch waren, illustriert deutlich die Arbeit von R. Mischker, *Untersuchungen zu den römischen Metallgefässen in Mittel- und Westeuropa* (1991). Er erfasste 2158 Gefässe (davon 1455 Gefässorten), die in den Niederlanden, der Bundesrepublik Deutschland (mit den neuen Bundesländern), Österreich, Frankreich, und Spanien entdeckt wurden, und darunter nur eine *Authepsa.*

Die *Authepsa* war in ihrer Funktion nicht auf das Wärmen von Wasser bei der Zubereitung von *calda* beschränkt, sondern sie wurde im medizinischen Bereich als Gerät eingesetzt, wie auch mit Befund in Augusta Raurica belegt. Ferner fand sie bei der persönlichen Toilette Verwendung, wie uns das Mosaik der Thermen in Sidi Grib deutlich vor Augen führt.

Die numerische Typenbezeichnug wählten wir im Hinblick auf die Neufunde, die neue Formen erbringen können, um sie nachträglich leichter einzuordnen.

Schon jetzt zeichnet sich ab, dass die Verbreitung der *Authepsae* typenmässig unterschiedlich ist. Gruppe A, mobile *Authepsae,* findet man von Gallien bis Kleinasien und von Mitteleuropa bis Nordafrika. Vergleich man Sie, sind die "Kocher" Typ A3 selten, hingegen halten sich die "Wasser-Wein-Wärmer" Typ A1 und A2 die Waage. Die im Westen beliebten fassförmigen Selbstkocher Typ A1.1 sind auch im Osten und Nordafrika bekannt. Hingegen sind die krug- und kannenförmigen *Authepsae* bis jetzt nur im Osten (Moesien und Asia Minor) zum Vorschein gekommen. Die stationäre Gruppe B findet man nur am Golf von Neapel, jener klimatisch begünstigten Gegend, in der man sich aus dem aktiven Leben aus Rom gern zum Lebensabend zurückgezogen hat.

Albert-Ludwigs-Universität, Provinzialrömische Archäologie, Glacisweg 7, D-79085 Freiburg

Die Vielfalt der *Authepsae* zu erkennen und auch zu dokumentieren, verdanke ich der Freundlichkeit und dem Wissen meiner Mitstreiter in Sachen Gefässe aus Metall, bei denen ich mich hier für ihre Unterstützung herzlich bedanke: A. Brauer, H. Bujukliev, M. Castoldi, R. Erice Lacabe, P. Gercke, K. Gschwantler, P. Ilijeva, H.-J. Kellner, E. Künzl, C. C. Mattusch, I. Mikl-Curk, A. Milceva-Dimitrova, R. Nenova-Merdjanova, H. U. Nuber, K. Poczy, K. Szabo, S. Tassinari. Auch für die entgegenkommende Erlaubnis, vier Exemplare aus dem Archäologischen Nationalmuseum der Bulgarischen Akademie der Wissenschaften, Sofia, und eine *Authepsa* im Weinbaumuseum in Stuttgart-Ulbach hier vorzulegen, bin ich beiden zu grossem Dank verpflichtet.

Bronze votive *tabulae ansatae* at Summus Poeninus in the Roman Alps

Patrick N. Hunt

Introduction

The Roman *tabula ansata*, a tablet or inscription plate with mostly triangular side handles, is found as a votive form for an epigraphic medium in abundant examples in stone, bronze, ceramic, and even glass or wood.[1] Bronze examples are often among the earliest extant forms, dating to the Julio-Claudian era, although Lepcis Magna has a well-known bilingual (Latin and Punic) stone theater inscription framed by the *tabula ansata* form and dated in the reign of Augustus (*c.*1 B.C.). The Ashmolean Museum, Oxford, has a bronze example, from the Tiberian period, that is double-sided, with chain loops for hanging.[2] L. Keppie finds the earliest reference to the word *ansata* in an inscription dating to Otho,[3] although the first appearance of the form must be significantly earlier (see below).

This paper summarizes pertinent data on the bronze *tabulae ansatae* from the Alpine site of Summus Poeninus, which has produced perhaps the most examples. In the Roman Alps, the arduous and dangerous ascent of the Grand-Saint-Bernard Pass culminated at the temple of Jupiter Poeninus, probably the highest sanctuary in the empire at 8,098 feet.[4] Weather is severe here even in high summer, with snow and dense fog possible on any day of the year. This famous Roman pass connected the Dora Balthea valley in Italy with the upper Rhône valley between Augusta Praetoria (mod. Aosta) and Forum Claudii Vallensium (mod. Martigny or Gallo-Roman Octodurus). The site of the pass over the Pennine Alps was well known in antiquity as Summus Poeninus.[5] The plan (fig. 1) shows the temple site where most of the *tabulae* have been found over two centuries, beginning with the excavations by Canon L. Murith of the famous Hospice du Grand-Saint-Bernard in 1762-64, continuing through the excavations of E. Ferrero and P. Castelfranco at the end of the 19th c., and culminating with the Stanford University project between 1994 and 2000.[6]

Many grateful Romans fulfilled vows for safe passage here with bronze *tabulae ansatae*. Each of the 50 extant *tabulae* may be the complete votive, with no verifiable accompanying sculpture, although numerous small bronzes have also been found at the site and are now in the Hospice Museum collection. The handles of the *tabulae* deliberately evoke an *ansata* form whose function — I suggest as invoking a divine-human contract — and history is still largely unknown despite their appearance on the Arch of Titus in Rome within the "Spoils of Jerusalem" relief.[7] Most of the extant bronze *tabulae* are dedicated to Jupiter Poeninus and use familiar as well as less common votive formulae. T. Mommsen, P. Barocelli, and G. Walser studied the *tabulae* and their informative messages about Roman travelers in the Alps and the

---

1 L. J. F. Keppie, *Understanding Roman inscriptions* (Baltimore 1991) 11, 15, 63-64.

2 *CIL* IX 1456, and see also *ProcSocAnt* 14 (1892) 33.

3 Keppie (supra n.1) 15 n.18; *CIL* X 7852; *TLL* vol. II p. 123; also Keppie pers. comm. 1995.

4 W. W. Hyde, *Roman Alpine routes* (*Memoirs of the American Philosophical Society* 2, Philadelphia 1935) 72.

5 Strab. 4.6.7-12; Tac., *Hist.* 1.70; and the *Peutinger Itinerary, 'In summo Pennino'*; also infra n.6 and below.

6 E. Ferrero and P. Castelfranco, *Scavi nell'area del tempio di Giove Penino, Gran San Bernardo* (*Memorie de l'Accademia delle Scienze di Torino* 1890-94) See also *RE* 21.1 (1951) 1155-62.

7 G. M. A. Hanfmann, *Roman art* (New York 1975) 108, calls the *ansata* forms on the Arch of Titus "placards"; A. Bonanno in M. Henig (ed.), *Handbook of Roman art* (Ithaca 1983) 76, calls them "*tituli*"; B. Andreae, *The art of Rome* (New York 1977) 179, calls them "inscription plates".

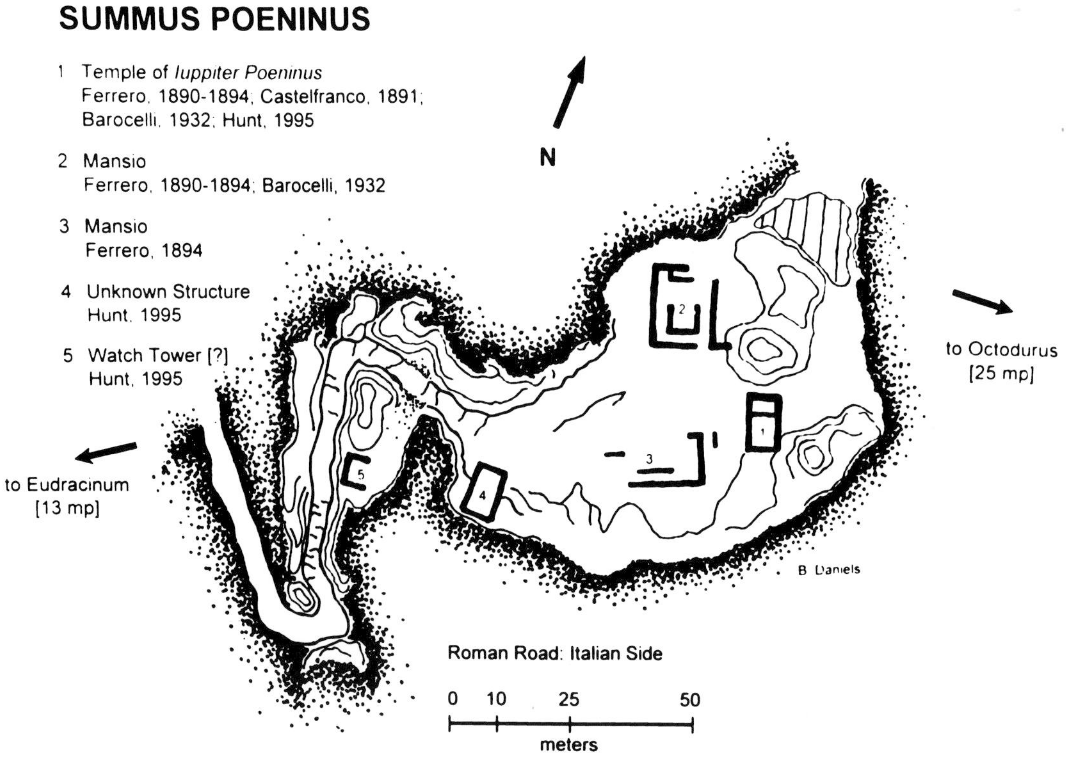

Fig. 1. Summus Poeninus (SP-1996) site plan with route over pass, Via Alpis Poenina. (Map: B. Daniels)

mountain hardships which elicited such vows.[8] There are also other studies of the Summus Poeninus *tabulae*,[9] as well as studies of broader focus where the *tabulae* themselves are not necessarily the primary objects of research and publication.[10] Walser's analysis is the most complete to date, with all 50 votive *tabulae* examined either *in situ* or from early publications of the 7 or 8 specimens now lost. Walser has also published significant texts on Alpine Roman epigraphy, especially military material and milestones, and our debt to him is gratefully acknowledged.

Apart from a single silver-foil *Baum/Blätterform tabula* associated with Jupiter Dolichenus, bronze is the most precious material remaining at the pass. The orthography and *ansata* shapes are usually carefully rendered, with each inscription personalized in formulaic style and with the name of the dedicator given. Although the texts and renderings vary greatly in length and in quality of lettering, these votives are significant not only for their form and content, which tell us much about the Roman presence in the Alps, but also because they were deemed intrinsically precious. In addition to the metal *tabulae ansatae*, several exist on ceramic roof tiles from the temple — including one found in our 1996 season at the Summus Poeninus site, and one found in 1998 at the adjacent Plan de Barasson site.

---

8 T. Mommsen, *Inscriptiones confoederationis helveticae latinae* (*Mitteilungen, Antiquarische Gesellschaft in Zurich* 10, 1854) (Mommsen was also responsible in 1877 for publishing 32 of the tablets in *CIL* V 6863-94); P. Barocelli, *Inscriptiones Italiae* XI.1: *Augusta Praetoria* (Rome 1932); G. Walser, *Summus Poeninus* (*Historia Einselschriften* 46, 1984).

9 Some *tabulae* were originally examined by C. de Loges, *Essais historiques sur le Mont St Bernard* 1 (Paris 1789), in which he published 19 of those found by Murith in the first excavation (1762-64); by L. Murith, *Médailles, inscriptions, statues et autres antiquités du Valais* (*MémSocAntFr* 3, 1821), where he published 23 *tabulae*; by C. Promis, *Le antichità di Aosta* (*Memorie de l'Accademia delle Scienze di Torino*, ser. 2.21, 1864) 30 *tabulae*; and by M. Sauter, *Préhistoire du Valais des origines aux temps mérovingiens* (*Vallesia* 5, 1950) 44 *tabulae*.

10 E. Berard, *Antiquités romaines et du moyen âge dans la Vallée d'Aoste* (*Atti, Società piemontese di archeologia e belli arti* 3, 1881) 119-212; E. Meyer in E. Howald and E. Meyer (edd.), *Die römische Schweiz* (Zurich 1941); and R. Mollo Mezzena, *Documentation sur les cultes aostains* (Aosta 1985) 157-59, 170.

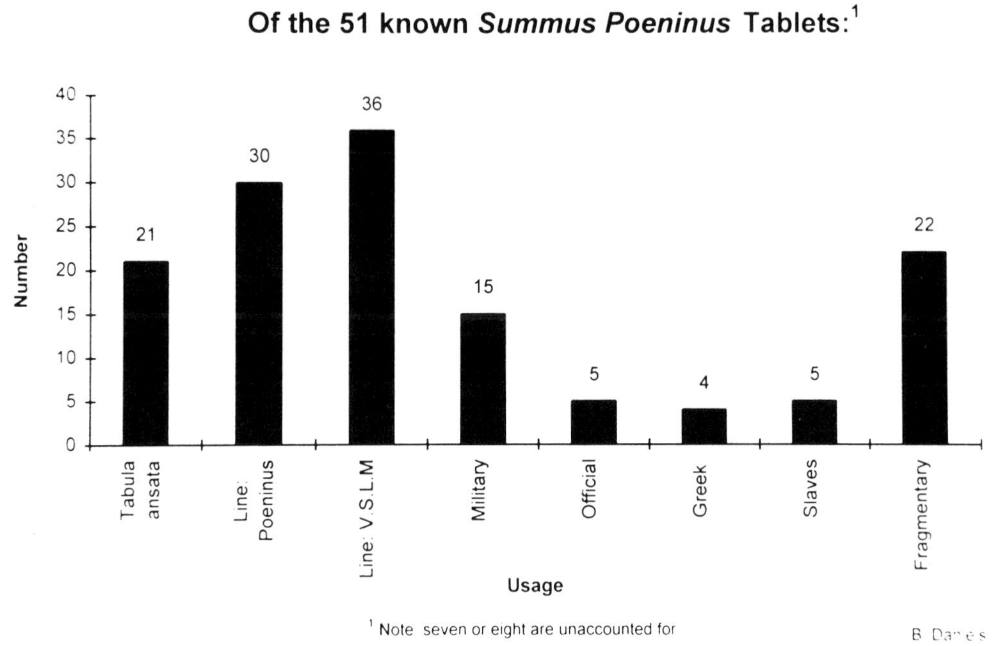

Fig. 2. Summus Poeninus (SP-1996). Full list of extant dedicators of *tabulae*. (Table: B. Daniels)

Analyses of the *tabulae ansatae*

The 51 known bronze *tabulae* from the site have either green corrosion products or black sulfide patina.[11] Twenty-three of the *tabulae* are mostly complete, while 22 are so fragmentary as to make identification as *tabulae ansatae* difficult if not impossible, although several of these probably took the *ansata* form.[12]

The methods of adding texts to the bronze *tabulae* varied. Most (22 out of 41 discernible, or 53%) were probably inscribed with a hand-held iron *stylus* similar to one 22 cm long found in 1996 by the Stanford Project. Some were punched with tiny pricks of awl-like tools, either from the front or rear (14 out of 41, or 31%), and a few were hammered with pre-formed letters or dies from the rear (5, or 12%). It is not yet known where the *tabulae* were inscribed, although the presence of more than 12 iron *styli* in the Hospice Museum collection suggests that the lettering was done locally. It is also possible that tablets were inscribed elsewhere and brought to the site, although this seems less likely given the high numbers of surviving *tabulae*. The inscribed *tabulae* are usually the best, with regular letters and lines, whereas the punched ones are usually the most irregular, with the quality of the hammered examples falling in between.

Several epigraphic formulae are found on the bronze *tabulae*, including the well-known *I.O.M.* for *I[uppiter] O[ptimo] M[aximo]* and *V.S.L.M.* for *V[otum] S[olvit] L[ibens] M[erito]*[13] (36 cases). Three *tabulae* have the shorter epigraphic phrase *ex voto* instead of *V.S.L.M.* Here *I.O.M.* always appears as *I.O.M.P.* with 7 examples of the local *nomen* Poeninus in the dative. Poeninus occurs frequently (figs. 2-3), often with just *Iovi Poenino* (7 *tabulae*), or merely *Poenino* (14 cases) or *Poenino sacrum* (2 *tabulae*). Infrequently the phrase *Pro itu et reditu* (2 cases) appears.

Some discussion of the name Poeninus is needed. The Roman Alpine province of *Alpis Poenina* probably derives from the deity name *Penn*, which may be a Celtic name for a high place

---

11 For helpful discussions of corrosion products, including cuprite (Cu_2O) and chalcocite or copper sulphide (Cu_2S), see A. Beale, "Understanding, restoring, and conserving ancient bronzes with the aid of science," in *The fire of Hephaistos* 69-70, 74-76, 238-39.

12 The fragments were examined *in situ* in 1996 to ensure that none belonged together.

13 *V.S.L.M.* = 'release obtained from [this] vow cheerfully given'.

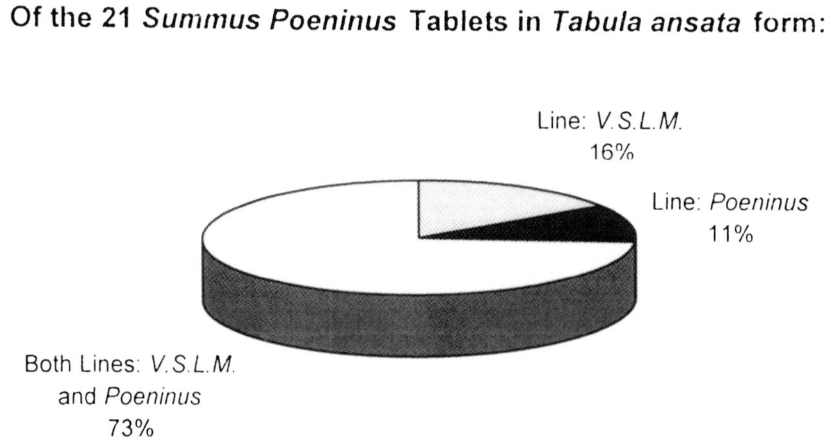

Fig. 3. *Tabulae ansatae* (SP-1996): distribution of formulaic elements and of text. (Chart: B. Daniels)

or peak (as in Scottish *Ben* or the Pennines). The name *Alpis Poenina* and its pass were well-known to Roman writers (Strabo 4.6.7-12; Tacitus, *Hist.* 1.70; Caesar, *BGall.* 3.1; Livy 21.38.9; Seneca, *Ep.* 31.9 ff.; and Varro, in Servius, *ad Aen.* 10.13). The Roman sacred installation in the pass had its antecedent in a Celtic (Salassi tribe) cultic high place for this deity, which the Romans assimilated between 57 B.C., when Julius Caesar's legate Servus Galba defeated the Seduni and Veragri of the Rhône valley (Caesar, *BGall.* 3.1), and 25 B.C., when T. Varro Murena quelled the Salassi (Cass. Dio 53.25.2-5; Suet., *Aug.* 21). Ammianus Marcellinus (1.15.10.9-10), however, incorrectly derived the name Pennine from 'Punic', via the unlikely association with Hannibal's passage in 218 B.C.

There are five variations in the spelling of Poeninus. *Poeninus* occurs 26 times, with single examples of *Peoninus* (obviously a misspelling), *Pyninus, Puoeninus,* and *Phoeninus.* This makes a total of 30 *tabulae* with Poeninus mentioned in some form, but this total could well be higher if all the *tabulae* had complete texts. Only 5 complete *tabulae* — usually the smaller ones under 70 mm in length — have no mention of Poeninus at all. The question of *tabula* size is immediately relevant here: the larger the tablet, the more likely the inclusion of the full deity name (*Iovi Poenino*) or honorific title (*I.O.M. Poenino*). This is particularly likely on the 10 largest *tabulae,* with dimensions between 245 x 145 and 100 x 125 mm.

The *tabula* sizes range from the largest at 245 x 145 mm, with full deity name and title along with dedicator's full name (*praenomen, cognomen, nomen*) and other abbreviated data, to the smallest at 25 x 45 mm, which have only the dedicator's name and no formulae or deity with dative referent. It is also necessary to correlate size and quality of votive tablets with the wealth or importance of the dedicator. The largest is the votive of a wealthy slave-dealer. Other large *tabulae* are votives of a Roman *eques* and of public or military officials. The smallest *tabula* was given by a slave (as were other small *tabulae,* by slaves and poorer Romans). The dates of the votives are more difficult to establish epigraphically, but the probable *terminus post quem* is after the Augustan road was established in 25 B.C. The *terminus ante quem* appears to be A.D. 379, when one may assume that Theodosius destroyed the temple (August., *De civ. D.* 5.26).

Walser has distinguished 4 representative types of dedicators found here:[14] military personnel (at least 15 *tabulae*); officials (at least 5); private servants or slaves (at least 4); and merchants (at least 7) (figs. 2-3). Many Roman armies crossed this pass, from the Julio-Claudians (49 B.C.) to Honorius and Arcadius (A.D. 408), which could account for so many military votives.[15] Roman military personnel attested on the *tabulae* include members (sometimes centurions or other officers) of the following legions and cohorts: *Legio II Italica, Legio III*

14 Supra n.8, 74-79.

15 Hyde (supra n.4) 67-68. C. Wells kindly tells me that this is the most important pass connecting Italy with Gallia, Germania, and Britannia for the Roman military. See also *TIR* Sheet 32 *Mediolanum* (1966).

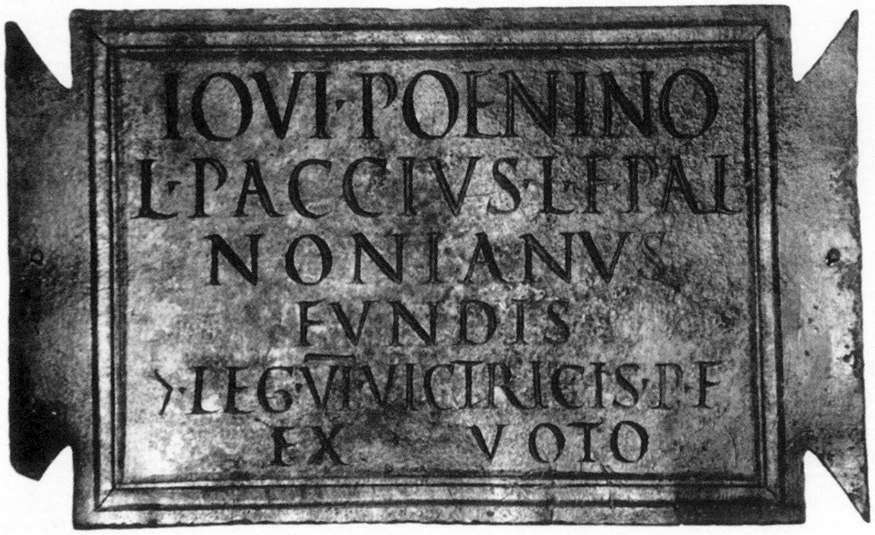

Fig. 4a. *Tabula ansata* (*CIL* V 6881): L. Paccius Nonianus. (Photo: author)

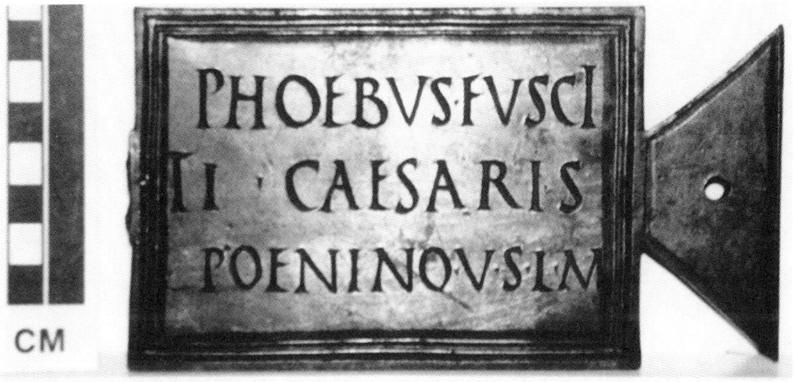

Fig. 4b. *Tabula ansata* (*CIL* V 6884): Phoebus. (Photo: author)

Macedonica, Legio VI [Victrix], (a centurion of) *Legio X [Gemina?], Legio XV [Primigenia?], Legio XXII [Primigenia?], Legio XXX [Ulpia], Cohors V Asturum,* a *cohors tricensima voluntariorum civium Romanorum,* and a *Cohors VIII* of the Praetorian Guard, among others. In light of the cost of offering a bronze votive, we may assume that many in this group were not only of high rank but were also wealthy.

Perhaps the most interesting military *tabula* (*CIL* V 6881) is of the wealthy centurion Lucius Paccius Nonianus of *Legio VI Victrix* (fig. 4a). He is named as son of Lucius the Palatine tribune: *L(ucius) Paccius L(uci) f(ilius) Pal(atina tribu) Nonianus Fundis c(enturio) leg(ionis) VI victricis p(iae) f(idelis) ex voto.* This *tabula,* the second largest (243 x 145 mm), is dated by Walser between A.D. 89 and 122.[16] The calligraphic quality and completeness of this *tabula* is notable; it lacks only the *V.S.L.M.* formula, having instead the shorter *ex voto* formula.

One military tribune and two consular officials are dedicators of *tabulae*: Paullus Vet[tius] Restitu[tus] *trib(unus) mi[l(itum)],* Q. Cassius Facundus *c[om]m(entariensis) co(n)s(ularis),* and Iulius Fortunatus *b(ene)f(iciarius) co(n)s(ularis).*

Private, and probably wealthy, servants or slaves include one Phoebus (fig. 4b): *Phoebus Fusci Ti(berii) Caesaris,* "an underslave of the family of Caesar Tiberius",[17] possibly a Greek slave adopted into the Tiberian *gens*? His votive *tabula* is one of the largest (143 x 78 mm) and has immaculate calligraphy dedicating the tablet to Poeninus with the *V.S.L.M.* formula (*CIL*

---

16 Supra n.8, 110.

17 Mommsen (1854, supra n.8) 10, no. 54.

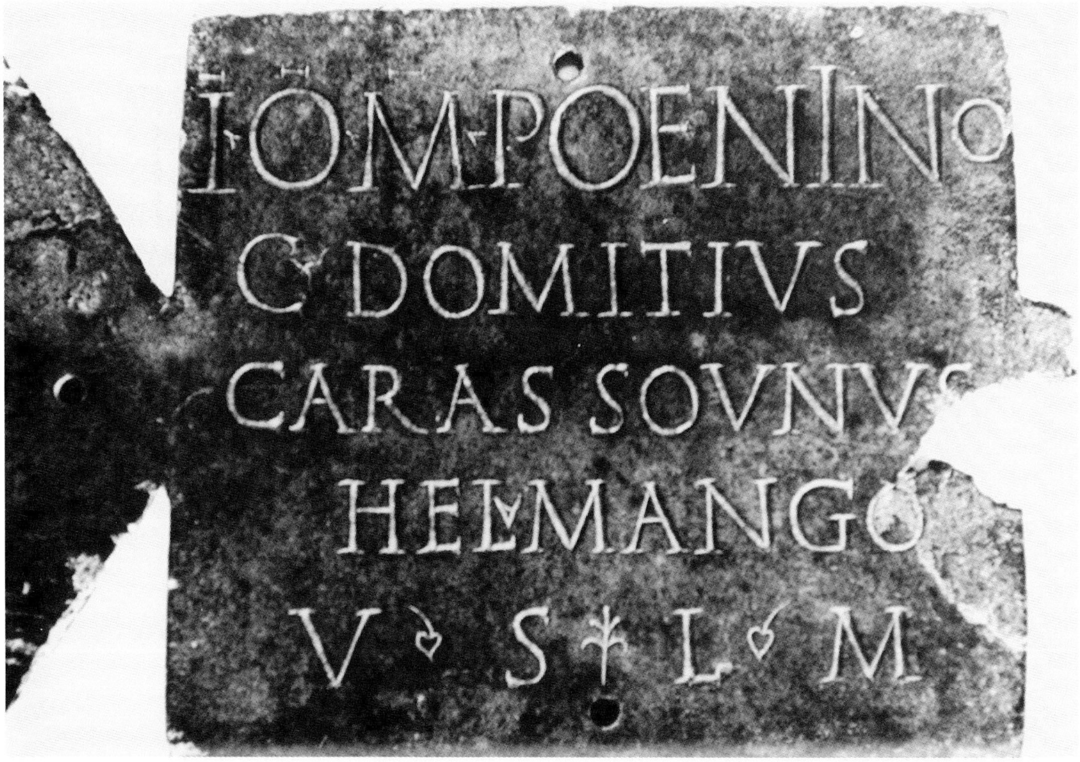

Fig. 5. *Tabula ansata* (Walser 1984, no. 11), found in 1891: C. Domitius Carassounus. (Photo: author)

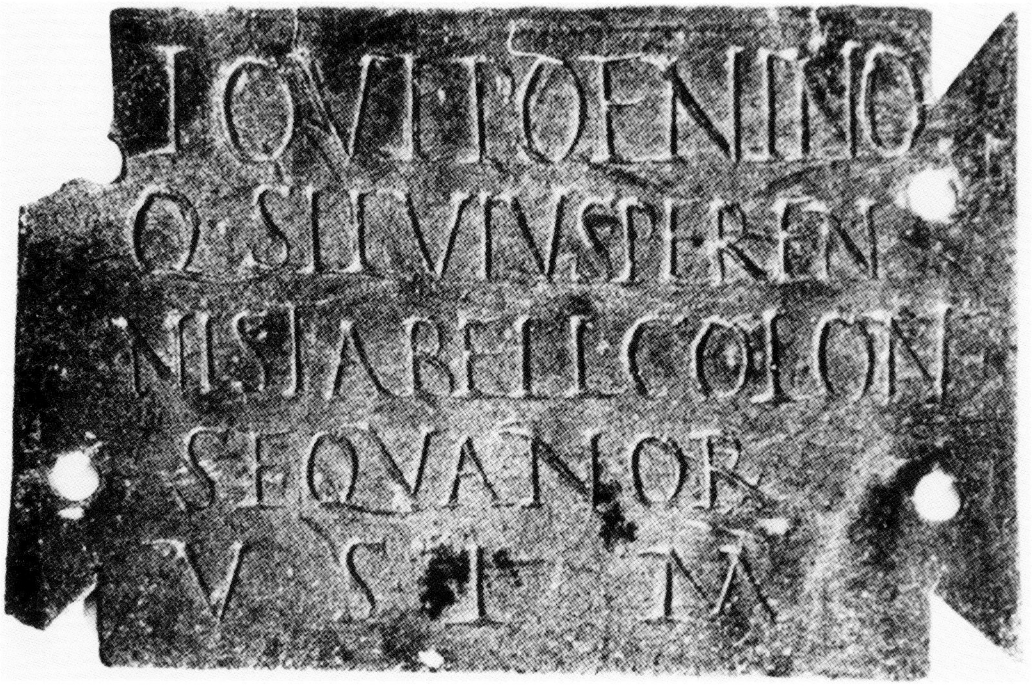

Fig. 6. *Tabula ansata* (*CIL* V 6887): Q. Silvius Perennis. (Photo: author)

V 6884). Another slave dedicator — perhaps poorer as his is the smallest surviving complete *tabula* (45 x 25 mm) — was Puteolanus, slave of Sabinus.

Of private merchants, perhaps the most interesting *tabula* is that of the wealthy slave-dealer Caius Domitius Carassounus: *C. Domitius Carassounus Hel(vetius) Mango* (fig. 5). This *tabula*, the largest of all those surviving (245 x 145 mm), has perfect calligraphic quality with both *I.O.M. Poenino* and the *V.S.L.M.* formula. Maybe it was his gratitude at crossing safely,

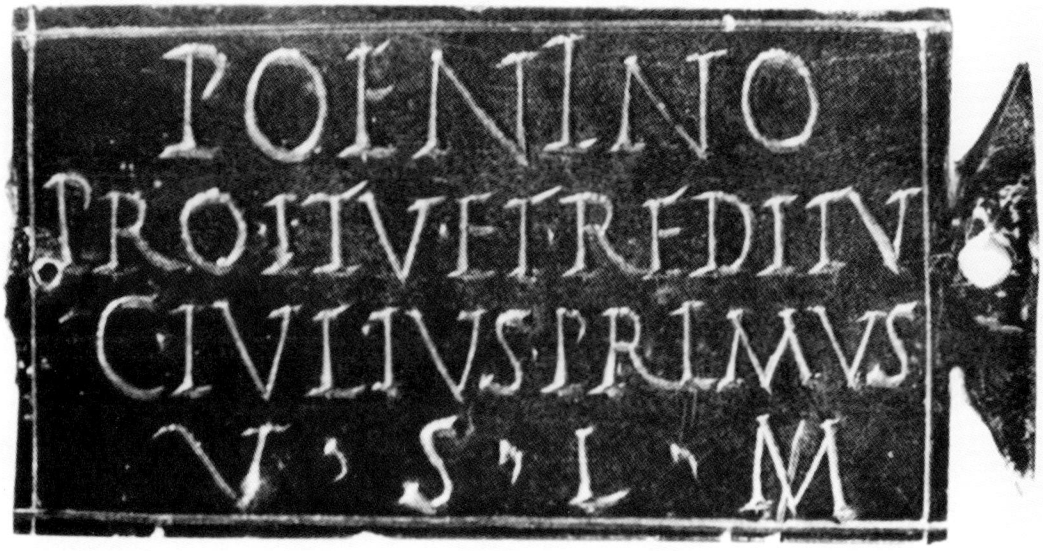

Fig. 7. *Tabula ansata* (*CIL* V 6875): C. Iulius Primus. (Photo: author)

perhaps with his health and valuable human cargo intact, or his hope of doing so, that influenced him to make his vow to the mountain deity with such a large votive.

Two other *tabulae* deserve attention (figs. 6-7). An official of the *cursus publicus*, Quintus Silvius Perennis, and the otherwise unknown Caius Iulius Primus both left interesting *tabulae*. Perennis was a *tabellarius* from the territory of the Sequani (near Besançon): *Q. Silvius Perennis Tabell(arius) Colon(iae) Sequanor(um)*. His 102 x 66 mm votive (*CIL* V 6887) included the standard *Poenino* and *V.S.L.M.* He was sufficiently proud of his station to include it on his votive. As one who may have traveled professionally and widely, he could have been used to hardships in the Alps but would nevertheless have been grateful for safe passage. C(aius) Iulius Primus (*CIL* V 6875) also included the *Iovi Poenino* and *V.S.L.M.* formulas but provided no other details except the poignant wish *Pro itu and reditu*, 'for the journey and the return', perhaps thereby to secure his return journey — hardly surprising since the Alpine fog in this pass can be so thick that one cannot see one's own hand, and one can be easily disoriented. Add to this the precipices, steep icy paths — some Roman gradients are in excess of 19% — and the wind and thunderstorms or the 15 m of snow in a single season (as in 1995), and one can better appreciate the 30-km ascent and descent that the Roman travelers endured, often in the dark.

Details of the small temple (11 x 7 m) are inferred from the rock cuttings, *in situ* marble architectural fragments, and marble ashlar blocks and epigraphic *spolia*, all re-used in the crypts of the 11th-c. Hospice of Saint Bernard, 1 km distant. The temple seems best dated to the Flavian period, as suggested by a probable *VESP* which our project identified in 1995 on a pediment fragment. However, we still need to establish a precise range of dates for the votives. Nor is it certain to what or how the *tabulae* were attached, although most have holes in the handles, and one *ansata* handle in the Hospice collection has a 3-cm iron nail still in place. Wooden temple doors might be a logical place for attachment.

Other questions are why and for how long travelers were in the pass. Were Roman soldiers — the dominant group dedicating votives — stationed here? Or were they simply passing through, like most other travelers? As can be seen from the new site plan (fig. 1, nos. 2 and 3), two *mansiones* (small inns) existed, where private travelers and military or *cursus publicus* officials such as Q. Silvius Perennis stayed, perhaps in separate *mansiones* — one for Roman officials and military, the other for private travelers. Another structure (fig. 1, no. 5) was identified in 1995 as a *specula* or watchtower and excavated in 1999-2000; it would have been manned by a detachment of Roman soldiers who would only guard this pass in summer months since it would usually have been uncrossable during 8-9 months of the year.

Conclusions

Bronze *tabulae ansatae* occur in larger numbers at Summus Poeninus than at any other Roman site of such limited population (at most 90 to 150 people at a time for only 4-5 months a year). Votive messages tell individual stories about fears, aspirations, and aspects of Roman life in a rocky, treeless and vertical landscape where nature seemed often inimical to human life. Thus it was necessary to invoke the Jovian mountain god's protection, using these votives to negotiate safe passage through thunder, icy sleet, snowy cold, or the dangers posed by brigands. Merchants, officials, many soldiers, and other travelers would have been relieved to descend this difficult mountain and head homeward after fulfilling their vows to the god with their votive tablets, expecting the provision of safe passage.

Archaeology Center, Stanford University

Acknowledgements

Acknowledgements are due to F. Wible, Cantonal Archaeologist for Valais, for permission to conduct archaeological research in the Swiss Valais; to R. Mollo Mezzena, Soprintendenza of the Province of Val d'Aosta, for permission to conduct research in Italy in the Val d'Aosta; to Msgr. Abbé Prevôt B. Vouilloz and Prieur B. Gabioud of the Hospice du Grand Saint Bernard and its Museum; to A. Raubitschek for his epigraphical expertise; and to B. Daniels for preparing graphics.

Signaturen Metall verarbeitender Künstler und Kunsthandwerker in der römischen Kaiserzeit

Eberhard Thomas

Die verschiedenen Metall verarbeitenden Künstler und Kunsthandwerker wie etwa die *statuarii*, die *plastae*, die *caelatores* bzw. *toreutae*, die *fabri argentarii*, die *aurifices*, die *vascularii* oder die *cassidarii*[1] haben in der römischen Kaiserzeit zwar anscheinend unterschiedlich häufig, aber immer wieder eigene Werke signiert. Zu fragen ist nach den Beweggründen, die die Künstler und Kunsthandwerker dabei geleitet haben, und welche Aussagen sie mit ihren Signaturen verbanden.

Die einfachste Form, die eigene Arbeit zu kennzeichnen, war die bloße Namensnennung, meist im Genetiv, wobei über die Angabe von *praenomina*, *gentilicia* und *cognomina* auch auf die soziale Stellung eines Herstellers geschlossen werden konnte,[2] was wohl vor allem den aufstrebenden Angehörigen der unteren Schichten, besonders den *liberti* und *libertini* wichtig gewesen sein wird. Als mehr oder weniger Selbständige konnten sie auf diese Weise für ihre Arbeiten werben. Griechische bzw. fremde, d.h. nicht lateinische Namen als *cognomina* erlaubten zudem eine Bestimmung der Herkunft,[3] auf die noch deutlicher aufmerksam gemacht

---

1 Hersteller von Bronzestatuen, Figurenbildner in Erz, Ziseleure/Graveure/Hersteller von Treibarbeiten, Silberschmiede, Goldschmiede, Hersteller von Metallgefäßen, Helmschmiede. Zu den verschiedenen Bezeichnungen und ihrer Bedeutung, vgl. vor allem H. v. Petrikovits, "Die Spezialisierung des römischen Handwerks," in H. Jankuhn *et al.* (Hrsg.), *Das Handwerk in vor- und frühgeschichtlicher Zeit* 1 (Göttingen 1981) 63-132 (= ders., *Beiträge zur römischen Geschichte und Archäologie* 2 [Köln 1991] 87-146). Bei den Handwerkersignaturen ist zwischen der künstlerischen Ansprüchen genügenden und daher aussagekräftigeren Produktion und der Gebrauchswarenherstellung zu unterscheiden. Zu berücksichtigen ist ferner, daß künstlerisch tätige Handwerker im Dienste des Militärs möglicherweise einen anderen Status besaßen, da sie nicht für die Allgemeinheit produzierten. Zu Signaturen auf Waffen bzw. vorzugweise auf Prunkausrüstungen, vgl. etwa R. MacMullen, "Inscriptions on armor and the supply of arms in the Roman Empire," *AJA* 64 (1960) 23-40; G. Ulbert, "GAIVS ANTONIVS der Meister des silbertauschierten Dolches von Oberammergau," *BayerVgBl* 36 (1971) 44-49; J. Garbsch, *Römische Paraderüstungen* (München 1978) 17-18, 49; F. Matz, *Die Lauersforter Phalerae* (*BWPr* 92, 1932); E. Ettlinger und M. Hartmann, "Fragmente einer Schwertscheide aus Vindonissa und ihre Gegenstücke vom Grossen St. Bernhard," *JberProVindon* 1984, 5-46; J. Keim und H. Klumbach, *Der römische Schatzfund von Straubing*[2] (München 1976) 25-31; S. Abdul-Hak, "Les objets découverts à Nawa," *AnnArchSyrie* 4/5 (1954/55) 175-84, Taf. 5-6.

2 Vgl. etwa die Signaturen des Cn. Trebellius Romanus auf spätaugusteisch-frühtiberischen Bronzekasserollen: R. Petrovszky, *Studien zu römischen Bronzegefäßen mit Meisterstempeln* (Buch am Erlbach 1993) 169, 308-10, die des D. Terentius Pamphilus auf tiberischen Bronzegefäßen: Petrovszky ibid. 168, 304-5, oder die des Octavius Faustus auf spättiberisch-claudischen Bronzekasserollen: Petrovszky ibid. 161, 284. Die Art der Namensangabe kann darüber hinaus ungefähre Anhaltspunkte für die Datierung der Tätigkeit eines Künstlers oder Kunsthandwerkers bieten. Mitunter erscheint nach dem Namen im Genetiv die Angabe *officina* oder *fabrica*, vgl. beispielsweise Petrovszky ibid. 238, 247-48; Keim und Klumbach ibid. (s. o. Anm.1) 25-31. Es ist anzunehmen, daß die Werkstattinhaber, vor allem wenn sie auch durch eigene Arbeiten hervorgetreten sind, bestimmenden Einfluß auf die Produkte ihres Hauses genommen haben. Ob dies auch in den Fällen gilt, in denen der Sklave eines Werkstattbesitzers signierte, vgl. etwa Petrovszky ibid. 169, kann nicht gesagt werden. Näher liegt allerdings zu vermuten, daß der Inhaber sich der Fähigkeiten seines Sklaven bediente und sowohl mit dessen als auch mit seinem eigenen Namen werben wollte. Vgl. auch die Signatur *ANTEI·SALONINI·O(fficina) CALVI MELCATORIS* auf einer Silberkasserolle aus Vindonissa: O. Hauser, *Vindonissa* (Zürich 1904) 6-7, Taf. 62.

3 Vgl. z.B. Signaturen auf Bronzegefäßen des C. Accius Euanthus (oder Euanthes?), Mitte 1. Jh. n. Chr.: Petrovszky ibid. 141, 188-89 oder die des C. Atilius Hanno auf Bronzekasserollen tiberischer Zeit: Petrovszky ibid. 154, 164, 292-93. Vgl. ferner G. Behrens, "Römische Fibeln mit Inschrift," in ders. (Hrsg.), *Festschrift Paul Reinecke* (Mainz 1950) 1-12 zu signierten Fibeln. Das Urteil von H. Solin, *Beiträge zur Namenforschung* 5 (1970) 300, es sei "völlig unzulässig, aus der Etymologie auf die

wird, wenn wie etwa im Falle der Signatur des Oktavios Menodoros griechische Buchstaben verwendet wurden.[4]

Nachdrücklicher wird auf die Urheberschaft verwiesen, wenn der Name im Nominativ erscheint und *FECIT* hinzugesetzt ist.[5] Oder *EΠOEI* wie auf einem der beiden augusteischen Silberbecher aus dem Fürstengrab von Hoby,[6] die ein *XEIPICOΦOC* signiert hat, ein Grieche, der als Sklave oder Freigelassener einen Namen trägt, der auf Fähigkeiten bezogen werden kann:[7] der mit den geschickten Händen. In Griechisch steht die Signatur auf der Rückseite des Achilleus-Bechers, auf einem Pfeiler, der den Wagen des Priamos halb verdeckt. Auf dem Philoktet-Becher wird die Signatur in lateinischer Umschrift wiederholt, vor dem Kopf des durch einen Schlangenbiß verwundeten Philoktet. Diese Umschrift ist als Lesehilfe für den germanischen Empfänger des Becherpaares, das ein Diplomatengeschenk gewesen sein dürfte, interpretiert worden. Man fragt sich jedoch, warum der Künstler bei einem römischen Auftraggeber — am Boden beider Becher ist der Name Silius eingeritzt, möglicherweise der Befehlshaber des obergermanischen Heeres zwischen 14 und 21 n. Chr. — und einem germanischen Empfänger überhaupt in griechischer Sprache signiert hat. Ist dies nicht vielmehr Ausdruck eines gewissen Selbstbewußtseins, mit dem der Künstler vor die Öffentlichkeit tritt und seine Arbeit als griechisches Qualitätserzeugnis ausweisen will? Chirisophos nutzte dabei offensichtlich — wie Oktavios Menodoros und auch andere Griechen — die vielfach belegbare Hochschätzung, die Silbergefäße von griechischen Meistern wie Mentor, Mys oder Kalamis bei Römern genossen.[8] Als griechischer Toreut suchte er, sich mit seinen signierten Werken bewußt in diese Tradition einzureihen.

Traditionsbewußt gibt sich auch der Künstler, der eine nach dem Doryphoros des Polyklet gearbeitete augusteische, in der Villa dei Papiri zu Herculaneum gefundene Bronzeherme mit der im Wortlaut altem griechischen Brauch folgenden Signatur *AΠOΛΛΩNIOΣ APXIOY AΘH–*

ethnische Herkunft zu schließen", dürfte kaum in jedem Fall zutreffen. Vgl. auch weniger apodiktisch ders., *Beiträge zur Kenntnis der griechischen Personennamen in Rom* 1 (Helsinki 1971) 146.

4 Kanne mit Reliefdekor, Silber, vergoldet, augusteisch: E. Künzl, "Das Gebet des Chryses (Homer, *Ilias*, 1. Gesang): Griechisches Epos und römische Politik auf der vergoldeten Silberkanne des Octavius Menodoros," *JRGZM* 31 (1984) 365-84. Vgl. z.B. auch die Signatur des Euporos auf einem mit einem Domitiansbildnis versehenen Spiegel: M. Taddei, "On a silver mirror with a portrait of Domitian from northern Iran," *EastWest* 17 (1967) 41-50, Abb. 1-3; B. Cämmerer, "Badisches Landesmuseum: Neuerwerbungen 1968," *JbBadWürt* 6 (1969) 282-84, Abb. 8; M. R.-Alföldi, "Silberspiegel mit Domitiansporträt in Karlsruhe," in *Festoen: Festschrift A. N. Zadoks-Josephus Jitta* (Groningen) 15-22, Taf. A 1-2; E. Künzl, "Quod sine te factum est hoc magis archetypum est? (Martialis 8,34)," *AKorrBl* 8 (1978) 314-15, Abb. 4.

5 Vgl. beispielsweise den frühkaiserzeitlichen zum Silberschatz von Boscoreale gehörenden Mänaden-Spiegel des M. Domitius Polygnos, eines Freigelassenen griechischer Herkunft: A. Heron de Villefosse, "Le trésor de Boscoreale," *MonPiot* 5 (1899) 88-99, Nr. 21, Taf. 19; Künzl ibid. 314-15, Abb. 2, oder die ebenfalls frühkaiserzeitliche Pigna, den riesigen bronzenen Pinienzapfen in Rom, den der Freigelassene P. Cincius Salvius an drei Stellen signiert hat: W. Amelung, *Die Skulpturen des Vaticanischen Museums* 1 (Berlin 1903) 898, Taf. 119; Helbig[4] I, Nr. 478.

6 K. Friis Johansen, "Hoby Fundet," *Nordiske Fortidsminder* 2 (1923) 119-39; C. Vermeule, "Augustan and Julio-Claudian court silver," *AntK* 6 (1963) 33-40; V. H. Poulsen, "Die Silberbecher von Hoby," *AntPl* 8 (1968) 69-74, Taf. 42-55; E. Künzl, "Der augusteische Silbercalathus im Rheinischen Landesmuseum Bonn," *BJb* 169 (1969) 364-65, 376; id. 1978 (supra Anm. 4) 314-15, Abb. 3; *LIMC* I.1 (1981) 154, s.v. Achilleus Nr. 687 (A. Kossatz-Deißmann), I.2 (1981) 127; E. Künzl, "Romanisierung am Rhein—germanische Fürstengräber als Dokument des römisches Einflusses nach der gescheiterten Expansionspolitik," in *Kaiser Augustus und die verlorene Republik* (Ausstellungskat. Berlin [Mainz 1988]) 569-71; C. W. Müller, "Das Bildprogramm der Silberbecher von Hoby. Zur Rezeption frühgriechischer Literatur in der römischen Bildkunst der augusteischen Zeit," *JdI* 109 (1994) 321-52.

7 Zur Namenskategorie, vgl. H. Solin, *Die griechischen Personennamen in Rom: Ein Namenbuch* 1 (Berlin 1982) 789-90.

8 Vgl. Künzl 1978 (supra Anm. 4) 311-17.

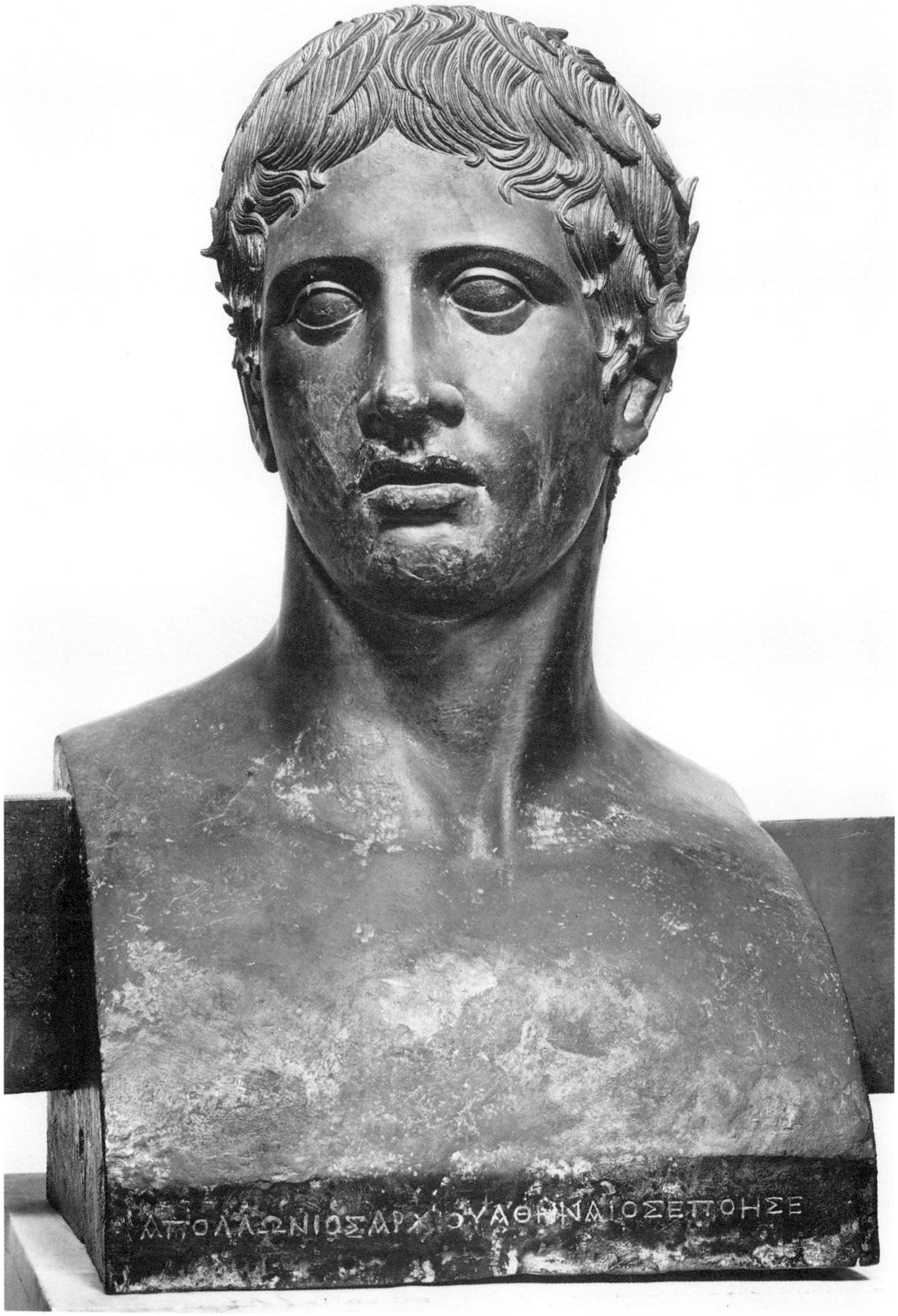

Abb. 1. Herme des Apollonios. Bronze, h. 54 cm. Neapel, Museo Nazionale Archeologico 4885. (Foto: Archäologisches Institut der Universität zu Köln, Forschungsarchiv für *Antike Plastik*)

ΝΑΙΟΣ ΕΠΟΗΣΕ ("Apollonios, der Sohn des Archias, aus Athen, hat es gemacht") versehen hat (Abb. 1).[9] Neben seinem eigenen Namen nannte er den Vatersnamen; dies wird nicht nur als Hinweis auf bestimmte Verwandtschaftsverhältnisse und als genauere Bestimmung der Person zu werten sein, sondern es sollte damit wohl vor allem auch auf die künstlerische Abkunft und die Qualität der Ausbildung verwiesen werden, d.h. Söhne gedachten auf diese Weise vom Ruf der Väter oder einer Werkstatt- bzw. Familientradition zu profitieren.[10] Als wesentlich wurde

---

9 M. R. Wojcik, *La villa dei Papiri ad Ercolano* (Rom 1987) 171-73; D. Kreikenbom, *Bildwerke nach Polyklet* (Berlin 1990) 81-94, 174, Taf. 172-75.

10 Apollonios scheint aus einer über Generationen tätigen attischen Bildhauerfamilie zu stammen. Vgl. E. Loewy, *Inschriften griechischer Bildhauer* (Leipzig 1885) Nr. 144, 230, 341, 545, siehe auch Nr. 336. Zu Kunsthandwerkerfamilien, vgl. auch Petrovszky (supra Anm. 2) 384; in diesen Fällen bietet der

auch die Angabe der Heimat des Künstlers angesehen: Apollonios bezeichnet sich als Athener, was lediglich heißen kann, daß er aus Athen stammt, nicht daß er auch dort ansässig und tätig war. Sinn der Angabe scheint hauptsächlich gewesen zu sein, ein Werk als Qualitätsarbeit zu kennzeichnen, Kunstkreis und Kunstrichtung zu charakterisieren und sich von der außerattischen Konkurrenz abzugrenzen.[11] Im Hinblick darauf, daß es sich um eine Kopie handelt, ist zu fragen, ob sich Apollonios ausschließlich der geleisteten handwerklichen Arbeit rühmen wollte[12] oder ob er sich des Werks des Polyklet im Sinne eines Zitats bediente, und zwar in der Weise, wie man in der antiken Schriftstellerei mitunter zu zitieren pflegte, nämlich in Ehrerbietung vor dem zitierten Autor und dessen Werk, aus dem die Entlehnung stammte, und in dem Bewußtsein, daß das gebildete Publikum den Zitierten auch ohne Namensnennung erkannte. Schon indem er eine Teilkopie bietet, aber wohl auch in Einzelheiten der Formengebung beweist der Künstler eine gewisse, den klassizistischen Geschmack der Zeit treffende Eigenständigkeit,[13] die er selbstbewußt durch seine Signatur unterstreicht.

Über die Bezeichnung der Herkunft hinaus konnte offensichtlich auch die des Werkstattstandortes von Wichtigkeit sein: Auf einem im frühen 2. Jh. n.Chr. entstandenen, kunstvoll gemusterten Bronzesieb liest man neben dem abgekürzten Herstellerstempel auf der Griffscheibe unter dem Rand als Lochmuster *L·CASSIVS·AMBROSIVS·FECIT·IN·CIRCO·FLAMINIO*.[14] Möglicherweise aus derselben Werkstatt stammt nicht nur auf Grund von Gemeinsamkeiten in Gefäßform und -dekoration, sondern auch im Hinblick auf die Ortsangabe in der Inschrift das Bronzesieb des Freigelassenen M. Ulpius Eufrates.[15] Beiden Kunsthandwerkern war daran gelegen, auf den Herstellungsort und vielleicht auch auf ein zugehöriges Ladenlokal in Rom, im Viertel um den Circus Flaminius aufmerksam zu machen.

Auf den Wirkungsort weist auch Felicio hin, von dem wahrscheinlich im dritten Viertel des 1. Jh. n.Chr. ein schüsselförmiges Bronzesieb in Pompeji gearbeitet wurde; daß er das überaus reiche Lochmuster aus Rosette, Blattranke, Palmetten, Wasservogel, Blütenkelchen, und Spiralranke ausgeführt hat, betonte er sowohl durch die Wortwahl als auch die Wortstellung: *PERTVDIT·POMPEIS·FELICIO*.[16] Er legte offensichtlich Wert auf die Kennzeichnung und Beachtung seiner besonderen kunsthandwerklichen Fähigkeit. Entsprechend wird gelegentlich eine Berufsbezeichnung dem Namen hinzugefügt: *CELATVS AERARIVS FECIT* ist beispielsweise an einer der Nebenseiten der Basis für eine Bronzestatuette des Mars zu lesen (Abb. 2-3).[17]

Gentilname den entscheidenden Hinweis.

11 Zur Angabe des Herkunftsorts (oder Werkstattstandorts?), vgl. etwa auch die auf spätantiken aus Silber gearbeiteten Platten angebrachten Signaturen des Pausylypos aus Thessaloniki, V. von Gonzenbach, "Achillesplatte," in H. A. Cahn und A. Kaufmann-Heinimann (Hrsg.), *Der spätrömische Silberschatz von Kaiseraugst* (Derendingen 1984) 225-307, und des Euticius aus Naissus: F. Baratte, "Euticius-Platte," ibid. 188-93.

12 Vgl. A. J. B. Wace, "Design and execution," *ASAtene* 8-10 (1946-48) 119-20.

13 Zur Frage der Umsetzung eines griechischen Vorbildes in die eigene — zeitgenössische — Formensprache, vgl. z.B. R. Wünsche, "Der Jüngling von Magdalensberg," in J. A. Schmoll gen. Eisenwerth *et al.* (Hrsg.), *Festschrift L. Dussler* (München 1972) 62-68.

14 R. Noll, *Das Inventar des Dolichenusheiligtums von Mauer an der Url (Noricum)* (Wien 1980) 80-82, Taf. 28-30; Petrovszky (supra Anm. 2) 107-8, 147, 217-18, Abb. 15, Taf. 4.40.

15 M. Bucovala, "Vase romane de bronz descoperite la Dervent, Jud. Constanta," *Pontica* 5 (1972) 121-36, Abb. 5-9; Noll ibid. 82, Beil. IX; Petrovszky (supra Anm.2) 107, 180, 342-43. Zu den Werkstattstandort betreffenden Angaben, vgl. etwa auch Ettlinger und Hartmann (supra Anm.1) 7, 36-43.

16 J. Sieveking, "Erwerbungen der Sammlungen München 1916-17: K. Museum antiker Kleinkunst 1917," *AA* 1919, 28-30, Abb. 3-4; K. A. Neugebauer, *Bronzegerät des Altertums* (Bielefeld 1927) 9, Taf. 27.2; Noll (supra Anm. 14) 82, Beil VIII; Petrovszky (supra Anm. 2) 108-9, 180, 343 Taf. 4. Nicht Felix, sondern Felicio, so daß die Schlußfolgerung von R. Petrovszky, "Bermerkungen zu Stempeln auf Bronzegefässen," in *Specimina Nova Universitatis Quinqueecclesiensis* (1991) 74 entfällt.

17 R. A. Smith, *A guide to the antiquities of Roman Britain* (London 1922) 89, Taf. 8; P. Salway, *The illustrated history of Roman Britain* (Oxford 1993) 417, 462; *CIL* VII 180. Zudem ist in Verbindung mit der Signatur angegeben, daß der Künstler sich an den Materialkosten beteiligt hat, somit wahrscheinlich

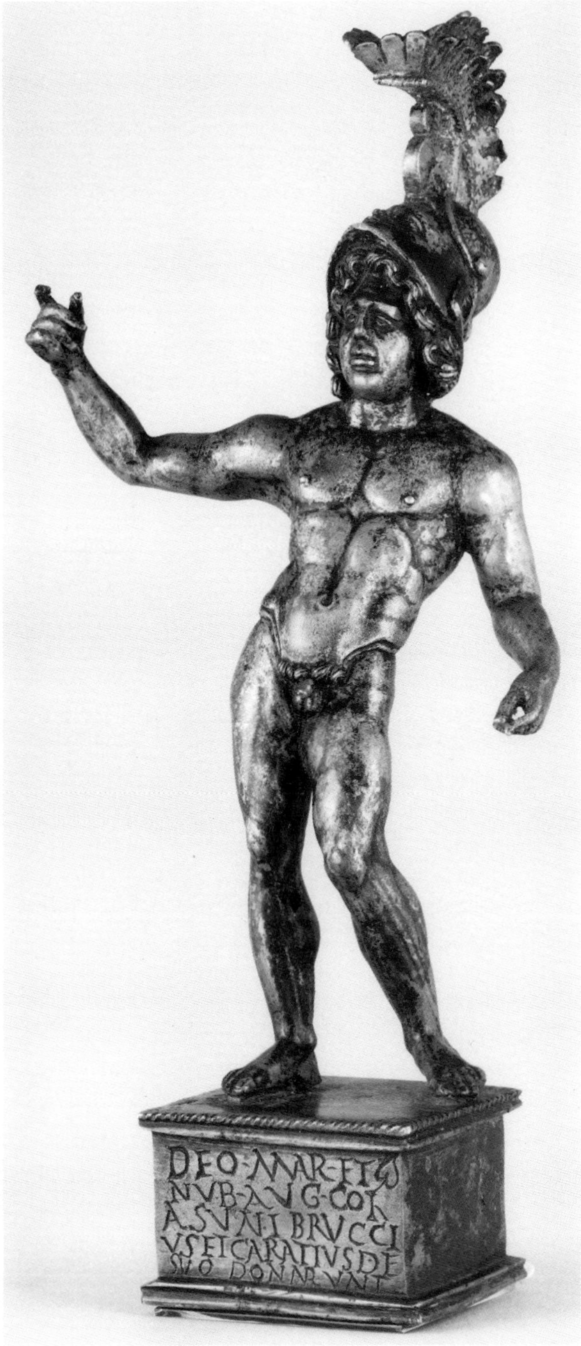

Abb. 2. Statuette des Celatus, Vorderseite. Bronze, h. 27 cm. London, British Museum OA 248. (Foto: courtesy Trustees of the British Museum)

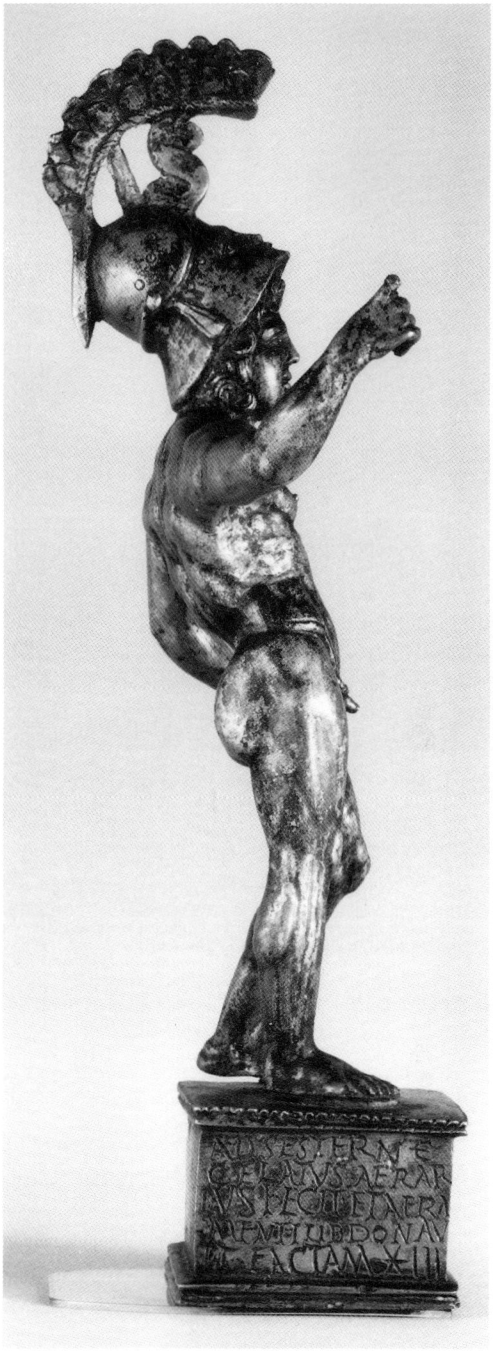

Abb. 3. Statuette des Celatus, Nebenseite. London, British Museum OA 248. (Foto: courtesy Trustees of the British Museum)

Ähnliche Beweggründe werden den im 2. Jh. n.Chr. tätigen Thekenbeschlägehersteller Gemellianus bewogen haben, sein Erzeugnis in der Signatur zu benennen: *THECAM GEMELIANVS F(ecit)*.[18] In anderen Signaturen desselben Meisters wird noch deutlicher als in den Fällen

als Sklave an der Stiftung seiner in der Weihinschrift an der Basisvorderseite genannten Herren, den Colasuni Bruccius und Caratius beteiligt war. Vgl. z.B. auch die Berufsbezeichnung in der Signatur *ROMVLIANVS ARTI(fex) FEC[I]T* auf einem Statuettensockel aus Bronze: M. Hörig und E. Schwertheim, *Corpus Cultus Iovis Dolicheni (CCID)* (Leiden 1987) 163-64, Nr. 253, Taf. 49.

18 L. Berger, "Die Thekenbeschläge des Gemellianus von Aquae Helveticae und verwandte Beschläge," in *Handel und Handwerk im römischen Baden* (Baden 1983) 13-42.

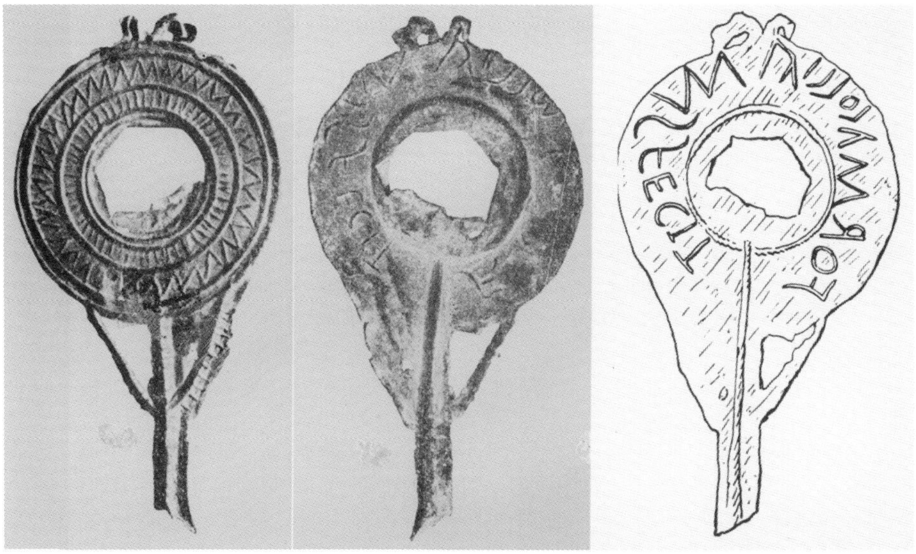

Abb. 4. Spiegelrahmen des Lollianus. Blei, l. 10,4 cm. Bucuresti, Muzeul National de Istorie al României 16610. (Foto: nach *Dacia* 3 (1959) 418, Abb. 1.7 a-b; 429, Abb. 6.3)

des Felicio, des M. Ulpius Eufrates oder des L. Cassius Ambrosius der Herstellungsort hervorgehoben: *AQVIS HE(lveticis) GEMELLIANVS F(ecit)* ("In Aquae Helveticae [Baden in der Schweiz] hat es Gemellianus hergestellt"). Es ist sicherlich mit Recht vermutet worden, "daß Gemellianus diese Art von Beschlägen [für Messerscheiden] mit Schaft, Ortband und heller aufscheinendem Blech eingeführt, gewissermaßen erfunden und dies mit seiner Signatur zum Ausdruck gebracht habe."[19] Ein Grund für die Änderung der Signatur könnte darin bestanden haben, daß es Gemellianus, nachdem seine mit durchbrochenen Metallbeschlägen verzierten Messerscheiden, die er vielleicht zunächst nur als ein an einem Kurort erwerbbares 'Souvenir' angeboten hat, einmal eingeführt waren, wichtiger erschien, zwecks überregionalen Vertriebs ausdrücklich auf den Produktionsort hinzuweisen.[20] Daß es sich um einen gefragten Markenartikel handelte, beweisen nicht nur die in verhältnismäßig großer Zahl erhaltenen Stücke, sondern auch Nachahmungen. Der sichere Nachweis der Imitation eines Gemellianus-Thekenbeschlages gelang mit einem in Niederbayern gefundenen Gußformfragment aus Ton.[21] Es konnte gezeigt werden, daß zur Anwendung der Technik des direkten Wachsausschmelzverfahrens von einem Original eine Form für ein Wachsmodell abgenommen worden war. Mit dem Nachguß ist die Herstellung einer vom Original nicht oder kaum zu unterscheidenden Kopie gegeben und der Tatbestand der Fälschung erfüllt.[22]

Möglicherweise um solchen Praktiken vorzubeugen und einen deutlichen urheberschaftlichen Hinweis in einer auf größere Stückzahl gerichteten Produktion zu geben, ist auf ins 3. Jh. n.Chr. datierten aus Blei gearbeiteten Spiegelrahmen, die bei Sucidava im Süden der Provinz Dakien gefunden wurden, die Inschrift *FORMA(m) LOLLIANVS FECIT* angebracht (Abb. 4)[23]: Von Lollianus stammt die Form bzw. das Modell und damit der zugrundeliegende Entwurf.

Über die aufgeführten Einzelfälle hinaus sind ferner regionale Unterschiede und zeitbedingte Veränderungen bei den kaiserzeitlichen Signaturen zu beobachten: Beispielsweise

19 Ibid. 30, eingeschränkt: id., "Thekenbeschläge aus Aventicum," in *Arculiana: Festschrift H. Bögli* (Avenches 1995) 132-33.

20 Anders Berger (supra Anm. 18) 30.

21 T. Fischer, "Die Gußform eines Thekenbeschlags aus Pocking, Kr. Passau," *Germania* 71 (1993) 539-43. Vgl. auch die von Berger (supra Anm. 18) 30 vermutete Nachahmung im Beschlag von Friedberg (Hessen), der sich durch seine geringere Größe und in den Buchstabenformen von den übrigen Stücken unterscheidet. Darüber hinaus hat es den Anschein, daß *Thecae* des Gemellianus bis ins fortgeschrittene 3. Jh. n.Chr. weiter produziert worden sind. Vgl. Berger (supra Anm. 19) 132.

22 Auch wenn es einen rechtlich abgesicherten Markenschutz nicht gab. Vgl. dazu S. von Schnurbein, *Das römische Gräberfeld von Regensburg* (Kallmünz Opf. 1977) 62-63, mit Anm. 245; Fischer ibid. 542-43.

23 D. Tudor, "Le dépôt de miroirs de verre doublé de plomb trouvé à Sucidava," *Dacia* 3 (1959) 415-32, Abb. 1.7 a-b, 6.3; vgl. auch die Signatur des Brutus, Tudor ibid. Abb. 3.19 a-b, 6.4.

konnte im Hinblick auf die Bronzegefäßherstellung des 1. und 2. Jhs. n.Chr. festgestellt werden,[24] daß die signierenden campanischen, norditalischen, gallischen und niedergermanischen Meister sowohl in der Art der Abfassung als auch der Anbringung und in der äußeren Form der Stempel voneinander abweichen, wobei mitunter einerseits die Spezialisierung auf bestimmte Gefäßformen, andererseits ein gewisser Verdrängungswettbewerb eine Rolle gespielt haben können; denn die gallischen Hersteller beginnen im dritten Viertel des 1. Jhs. n.Chr. mit den seit augusteischer Zeit führenden italischen zu konkurrieren und erringen schließlich eine marktbeherrschende Stellung.

Im Gegensatz zu den Bronzegefäßen sind frühkaiserzeitliche Arbeiten aus Silber auffallend selten signiert worden. Mit guten Gründen hat man dies mit dem seinerzeitigen Käuferverhalten zu erklären gesucht,[25] d.h. mit der mehrfach überlieferten, aber sicherlich kaum zu befriedigenden Nachfrage nach alten griechischen Originalen: Nicht durch eine Signatur gekennzeichnete Werke konnten leichter als antik durchgehen; denn nur Kenner werden in der Lage gewesen sein, zwischen alten und zeitgenössischen Arbeiten zu unterscheiden. Die wenigen erhaltenen Signaturen ließen andererseits keinen Zweifel über den Zeitpunkt der Entstehung der Arbeiten aufkommen, d.h. die fast ausnahmslos griechischen Meister dürften mit der Absicht die Inschriften angebracht haben, bewußt vom Ruf der griechischen Toreutik zu zehren und ihren Kunstwerken einen gewissen Rang zuzuweisen.[26]

Aber nicht nur auf dem Gebiet der Silberschmiedekunst, sondern auch in anderen Kunstgattungen und Zweigen des Kunsthandwerks, in denen Metalle verarbeitet wurden, scheint es lohnend gewesen zu sein, sich in der Signatur als Meister griechischer Herkunft und das eigene Werk als griechische Qualitätsarbeit auszuweisen. Dies würde die verhältnismäßig große Zahl griechischer Namen und Beinamen oder die gänzlich griechischen Signaturen, vor allem im 1. Jh. n.Chr. im lateinischen Westen des Imperium Romanum erklären.

Die stets deutlich sichtbare Anbringung der Inschriften, die mitunter unübersehbar in Darstellungen oder Ornamente eingefügt sind, zeigt, wie wichtig kaiserzeitlichen Künstlern und Kunsthandwerkern die Kennzeichnung ihrer Werke war. In der Mehrzahl der Fälle haben sie ihr Werk ohne weitere Erläuterungen für sich sprechen lassen, d.h. nur ihren Namen angegeben. Ausführlichere Signaturen mit über die Namensnennung hinausgehenden Angaben betreffen Hinweise auf künstlerische Abkunft, auf den Herstellungsort, auf eine besondere Fertigkeit bzw. auf das ausgeübte Handwerk, auf ein spezielles Produkt oder auf die Qualität.[27] Von zusätzlichen Informationen wird man sich eine bessere Werbung für das eigene Erzeugnis und damit verbunden Marktvorteile versprochen haben. Bei künstlerisch anspruchsvolleren Arbeiten wird neben den Aspekt der Reklame der der Mehrung des Ruhmes getreten sein, was einerseits auf ein ausgeprägtes Selbstbewußtsein bei Künstlern und Kunsthandwerkern schließen läßt, andererseits ein Publikum voraussetzt, das bereit war, künstlerische Leistungen und damit Künstler und künstlerisch tätige Handwerker nicht nur anzuerkennen, sondern auch entsprechend hoch zu schätzen.

Archäologisches Institut der Universität zu Köln, Albertus-Magnus-Platz, D-50923 Köln

Die hier vorgelegten Überlegungen stehen im Zusammenhang mit einer Neubearbeitung und Ergänzung bzw. Erweiterung von J. Overbeck, *Die antiken Schriftquellen zur Geschichte der bildenden Künste bei den Griechen* (Leipzig 1868), bei der zunächst die antiken Schriftquellen zur bildenden Kunst und zum Kunsthandwerk der römischen Kaiserzeit behandelt werden sollen.

---

24 Petrovszky (supra Anm. 2) 181-83.

25 Künzl 1978 (supra Anm. 4) 311-17.

26 S. o. die Bemerkungen zu den 'homerischen Bechern' des Chirisophos.

27 Mit der Inschrift SORS MERCVRI(i) auf Bronzegefäßen etwa der Cipii: Petrovszky (supra Anm. 2) 149-50, scheinen die Hersteller überdies selbstbewußt ihre Waren als 'Spitzenerzeugnisse' angepriesen zu haben. Vgl. A. Carandini, "Alcune forme bronzee conservate a Pompei e nel Museo di Napoli," in *L'instrumentum domesticum di Ercolano e Pompei nella prima età imperiale* (*Quaderni di cultura materiale* 1, 1977) 165; *CIL* III 6017.9; G. Henzen, "Marchi di fabbrica," *BdI* 1859, 229 mit Anm.1.

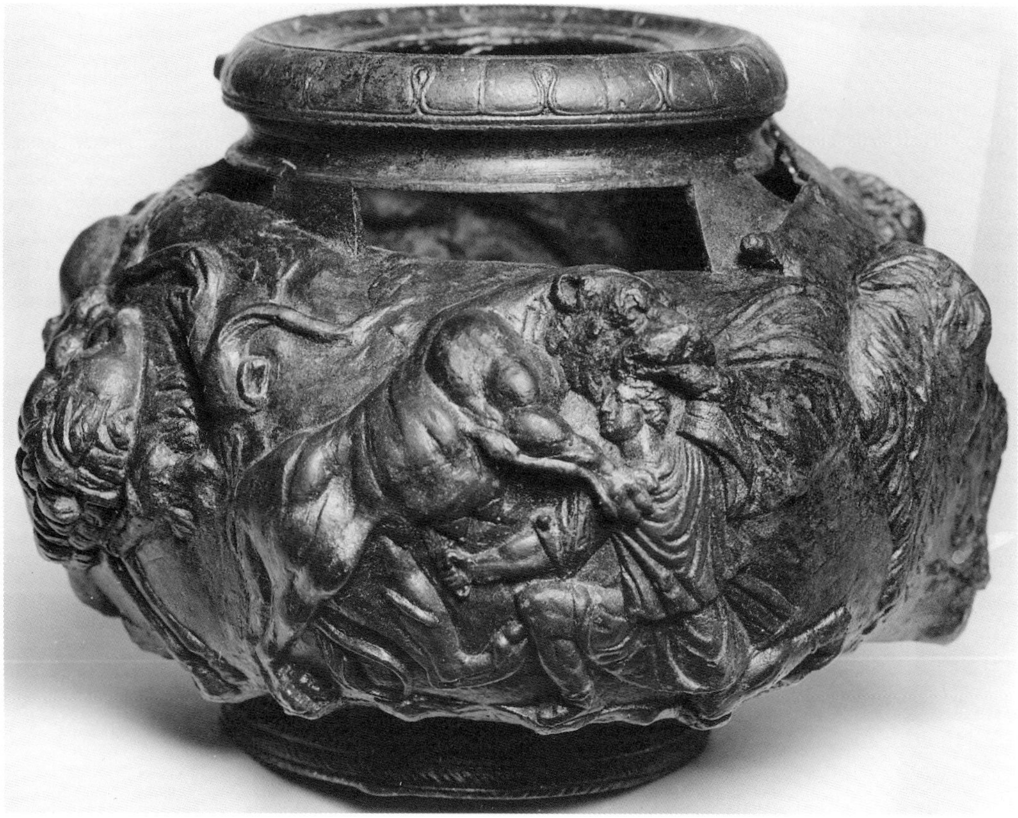

Fig. 1. Vessel found at Emona. Roman, probably 4th-5th c. A.D. Bronze, h. 0.135 m. Ljubljana, City Museum 5971. (Photo: courtesy C. Narobe)

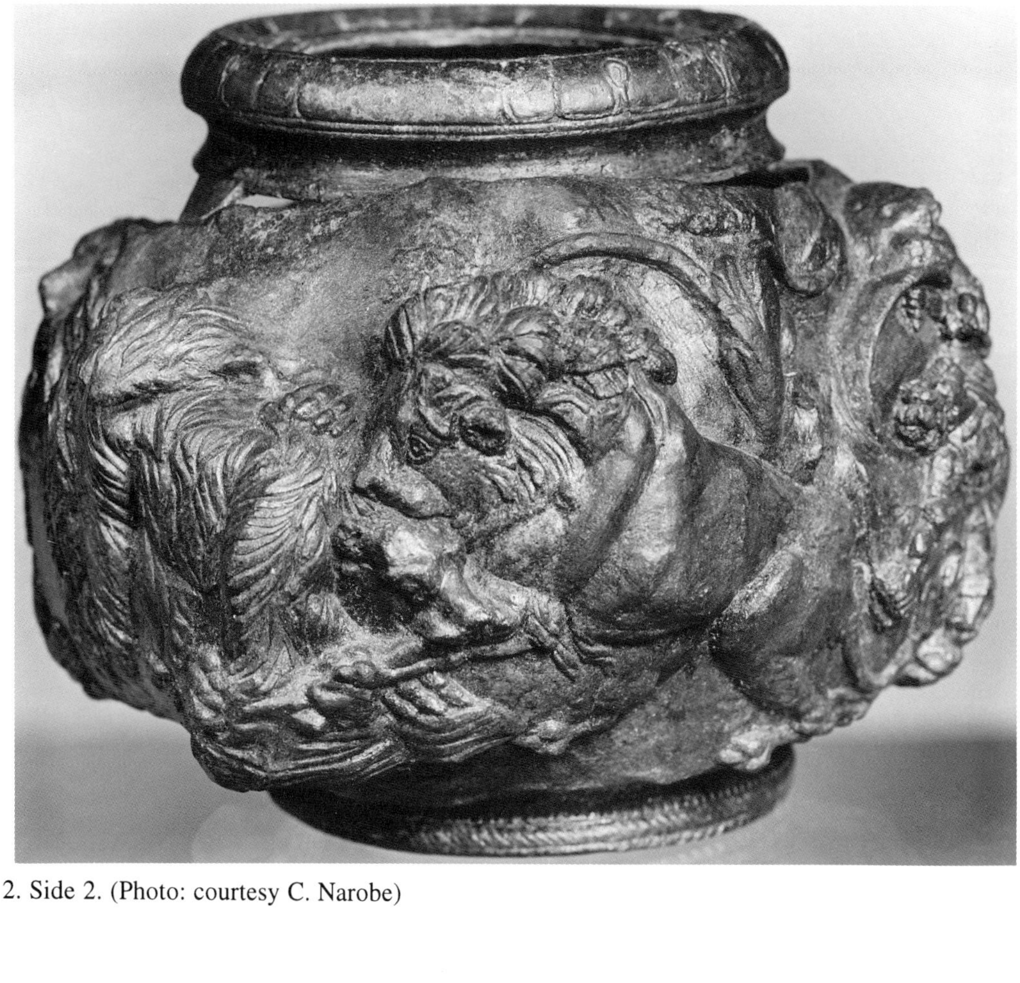

Fig. 2. Side 2. (Photo: courtesy C. Narobe)

The figural vessel from Emona

Ljudmila Plesničar Gec

Because of its location between the Julian Alps, Pannonia, the Adriatic, and the Balkans, Slovenia had long been a melting pot of various peoples and cultures. The Amber Road passed through this territory, connecting the Baltic to the Mediterranean, while the many valleys and rivers linked central Europe to Greece and the East to northern Italy.[1]

Several bronze vessels, some dated even to prehistoric times like the situla from Vače, have been found in this region.[2] The Roman vessels have been published by D. Breščak.[3] Most of these were found in large urban settlements, such as Neviodunum, Emona, Celeia, Poetovio, Nauportus, and Pretorium Labicorum, presumably the result of the greater purchasing power of those living in towns and because the towns had easy connections with important cultural centers. The few examples of Roman vessels with figural elements seem to have been imported from Gaul, the Rhine area, and S Italy, whereas the simpler vessels made of sheet metal have been attributed to N Italian, Pannonian, or local workshops.

The nearly spherical bronze vessel with a figural frieze found in 1977 at Emona is a particularly fine example of toreutic art. It was excavated in the débris of the latest building phase, in one of the oblong entrance halls of house 35.[4] The lack of stratigraphy does not permit its precise dating and the only possible starting points are its workmanship, stylistic elements, and comparisons to other pieces. The vessel was heavily damaged, but has been restored at the Römisch-Germanisches Museum, Mainz. The mouth was found detached and inside the pot, while the body gave the impression of having been cut below the top, leaving a somewhat wavy cut edge. However, the original shape cannot have been much different: the vessel is a rather massive casting, so it could not be adapted to a different form without damaging the relief, and all the figures are perfectly preserved.

The vessel (h. 0.135 m, diam. 0.16 m) is almost spherical and 0.3-0.4 cm thick; on the inside it was only summarily smoothed. The evenly shaped, thickened mouth shows two opposed small holes (diam. 0.5 cm) for attaching a handle (now lost). The edge of the mouth is decorated with fish scales and emphasized with semicircular and vertical incisions. The diameter of the mouth opening is 5.6 cm. The ring-shaped base (diam. 9.5 cm) is ornamented with hatched incision and a row of oblique cuts. The relief protrudes sharply directly over the foot (cf. fig. 6 below).

The body of the vessel is covered with figures of animals and men fighting each other in a continuous chain (fig. 5 below). It is not possible to distinguish where the decoration begins or ends. The figures are represented in high relief and their bodies positioned so as to fill the rather low space around the vessel. The narrowing upper part is filled with wavy vegetation, which covers every possible space. In fact, a flat surface probably would have diminished the expressive value of the actions in the complex relief. Each scene is independent but is still an integral element of the tightly-packed contorted figures forming the composition.

The chief scene shows a man fighting a lioness (fig. 1). The enraged animal leaps from the left and attacks a kneeling man wearing a *chiton* with its right paw and fangs. The man is stab-

---

1 J. Šašel, "Tisočletju pred rimsko zasedbo," in *Keltoi-Kelti in njihovi sodobniki na ozemlju Jugoslavije* (Ljubljana 1983) 11 n.3; id., "K zgodovini Emone v rimskih napisih in literaturi," *Zgodovina Jubljane, Kronika* (Ljubljana 1984) 35-45.

2 F. Stare, *Prazgodovinske Vače* (Ljubljana 1954); J. Kastelic, *Situla z Vač* (Ljubljana 1956).

3 D. Breščak, *Antično bronasto posodje Slovenije* [Roman bronze vessels in Slovenia], *Situla* 22.1 (1982).

4 L. Plesničar-Gec, *Antična posoda iz Emone s figuralnim prizorom* [The figural vessel from Emona], *Situla* 22.2 (1982).

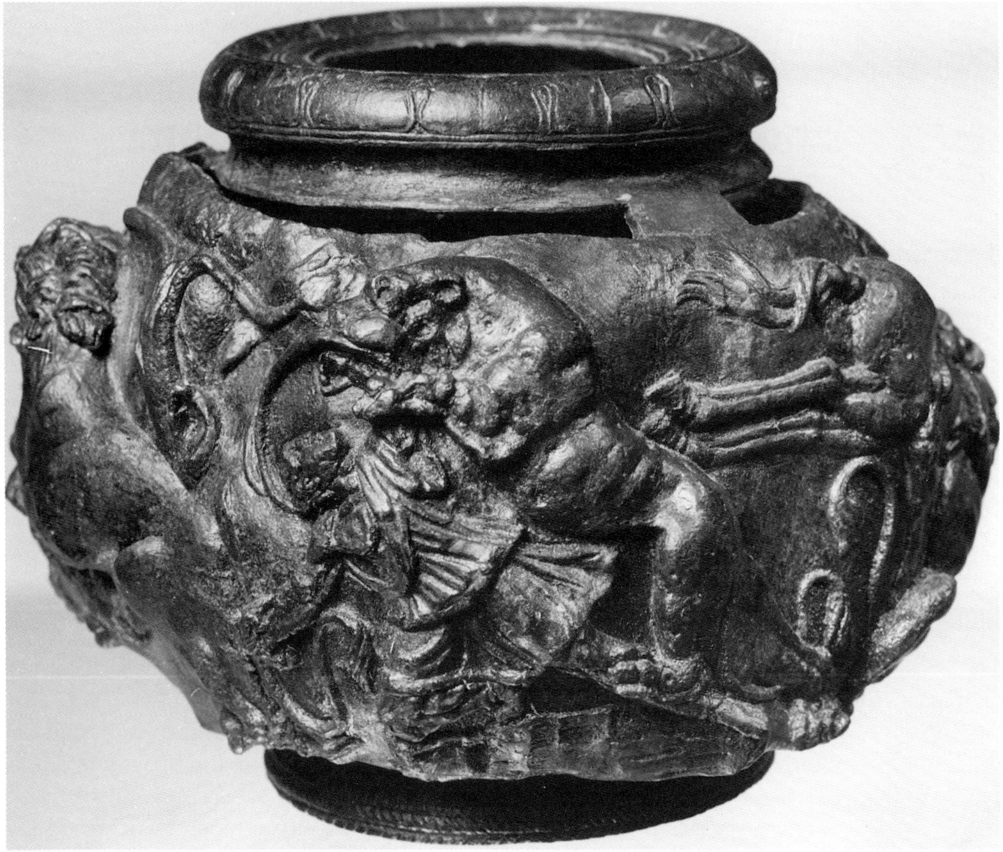

Fig. 3. Side 3. (Photo: courtesy C. Narobe)

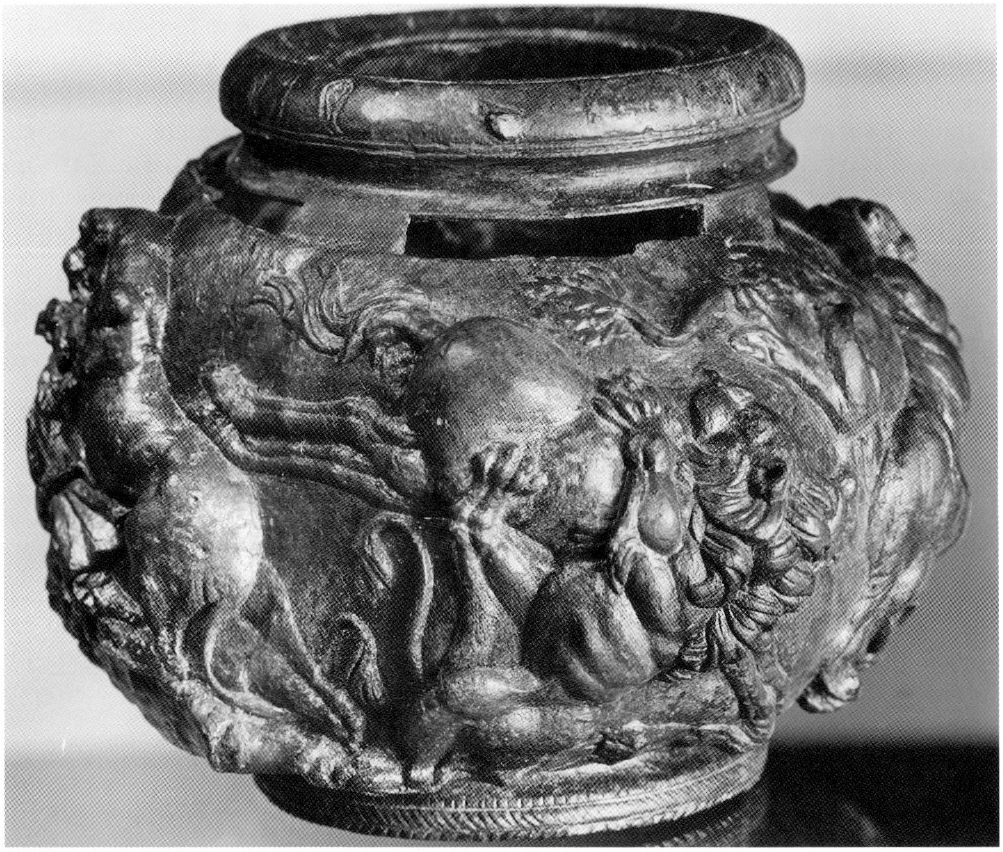

Fig. 4. Side 4. (Photo: courtesy C. Narobe)

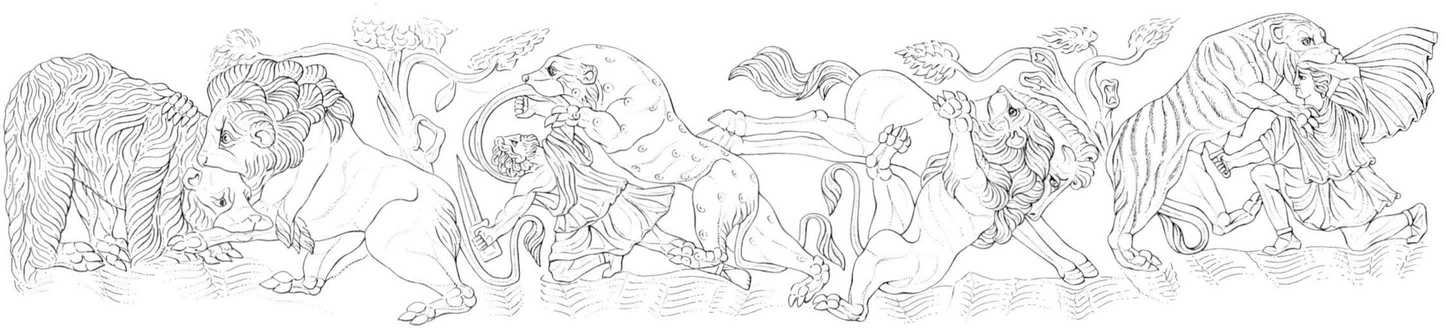

Fig. 5. Roll-out drawing of the figural frieze. (Drawing: D. Lunder Knific)

bing the lioness in her belly with the sword in his right hand. The head, flexed muscles, and open mouth of the lioness are rendered with great expressiveness, but the figure of the man is oddly rigid, creating a sharp contrast to the realistically tensed beast. His richly draped *chiton* as well as his strained arm and leg muscles are accurately rendered. The scene is framed by the waving *chlamys*, held by the left hand of the fighter, which also creates a counterpoint to the line of the lioness's tail, curved downward between her legs on the opposite side.

A lion and a bear are fighting in the second scene (fig. 2). The lion's head, mane, and body are represented in high relief. The lion bites the bear in the neck and pushes it down with its paws, so that the bear's front legs are bent. The artist tried to smooth the surface below the bear's front legs after casting but he did not completely succeed. The lion's head with its curly mane and the strained position of its body are the most expressive parts of the scene. The bear's body and the lion's head show some cold working.

In the next scene a man is fighting a spotted leopard (fig. 3). The man, wearing a *chiton*, falls to his right knee. He holds a sword in his right hand and a shield in his left to protect his head. The head is tilted backward and his extended limbs show strained muscles. The folds of his *chiton* are defined by cold working. The leopard's head and its left paw, clawing the man's left arm, are plastically rendered. The spots on the leopard's fur are represented by small circles punched on the body.

The fourth and last scene (fig. 4) shows a lion grabbing a running horse with its front paws and biting into its shoulder. The tension of the muscles is very well rendered, underlining the dramatic moment. The central feature here is the lion's head in high relief, while the exquisite body of the horse, with its extended legs and streaming tail, closes the composition. In this scene too every empty space is filled and rounded off with details, such as the lion's tail turned up between the stretched hind legs of the horse, and the fan-shaped leafy branches of the exotic trees filling the upper parts of the four scenes. Here the artist's *horror vacui* manifests itself: he wanted at all costs to fill up all empty space between the frieze and the mouth of the vessel.

Questions may be raised about the origin of the vessel, its purpose, and its date. The workmanship required exceptional skill which probably did not exist in local workshops. Some parallels can be found in the NW provinces, in the area of Gaul, particularly for some ornamental elements, such as the fish-scale ornament. A bronze vessel from Borsu (Bois-et-Borsu, Liège), found in a grave in the 19th c., is very similar in shape and size. Its high relief represents hanging grapes and erotes carrying fruit on trays.[5] Another parallel is a vessel found in a grave dated to the 1st c. A.D. at Bakar (Volcera or Raparia) on the N coast of Dalmatia. It is very well preserved and still has its lid. The frieze shows four trees with acorns and, between them, four fleeing animals: a stag, a bull, a dog, and a bear. The relief is more modest but the theme is close to that of our vessel.[6] A further parallel is a bronze bowl from Panticapaeum,

---

5 G. Faider-Feytmans, *Les bronzes romains de Belgique* (Mainz 1979) pls. 152-53.

6 F. Hoffiller, "Antične bronsane posude iz Hrvatske i Slavonije u Narodnom Muzeju u Zagrebu," *Vjesnik Hrvatskoga arheološkoga Društva* n.s. 7 (1903) 98-123 at 122; S. Ljubič, "Arkeologičko izkapanje u Bakru," *Vjesnik Hrvatskoga arheološkoga Društva* 4.1 (1882) p. 7 pl. 4/52.

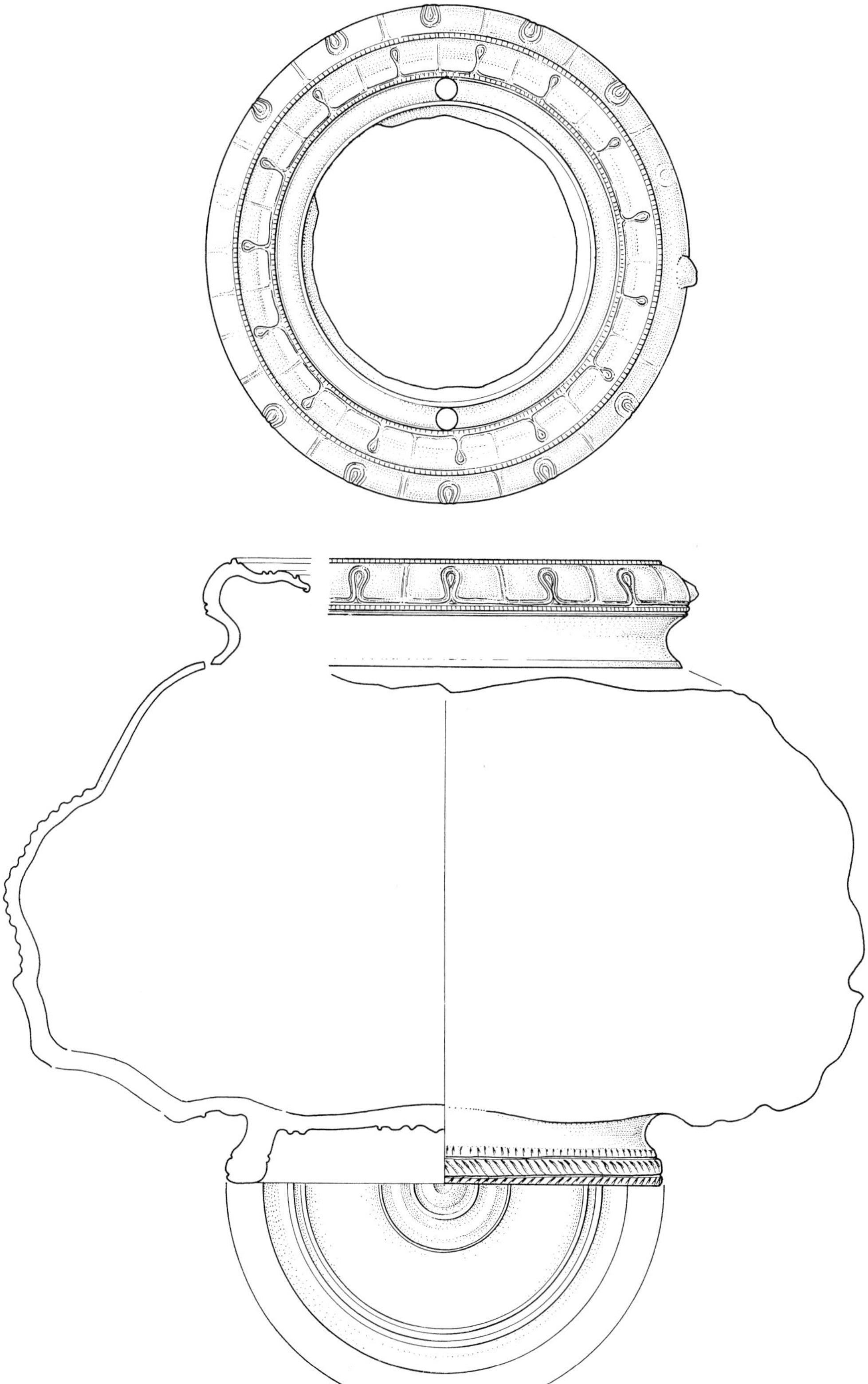

Fig. 6. Profile drawing. (Drawing: D. Lunder Knific.)

now in the Museum of Fine Arts, Boston. It represents two pairs of erotes holding the ends of floral garlands and flying above the waves of the sea.[7] Another relief-decorated vessel shows

7 Comstock-Vermeule, *Bronzes* 344-45, no. 483; E. Babelon and J.-A. Blanchet, *Catalogue des bronzes anti-*

dancing erotes or *genii* between trees very similar to those on the frieze of our vessel, except that their tops end with snake's heads; it was found in 1898 at Tongeren (Limburg) along with a coin of Faustina the Elder that may point to a date around A.D. 140.[8] Charles-Picard considered it a replica of an Alexandrian motif circulating as drawings in the Empire.[9] A similar motif with a tree in the shape of a snake and with four tunic-clad figures can be seen on a vessel of unknown provenance now in the Museum of Lyon; it is dated to the 1st or 2nd c.[10] A fragmentary vessel from Nijmegen can also be considered as belonging to this group. Its subject is the most similar to that of our bowl.[11] A naked man and a man wearing a tunic are fighting with cudgels against several running bulls and goats. The decoration at the mouth and the frieze elements are closely comparable to those of our frieze, although some differences can be found in the theme and in the expressiveness.

The scenes on the vessel from Emona are clearly linked to *venationes,* hunts and fights against wild animals. From its theme, the vessel cannot be closely dated. The human figures are rendered with elements of Hellenistic expressiveness, suggesting that the vessel could have been made either in the 1st c. A.D., or, more probably, in a period of classical renaissance, perhaps at the time of Constantine the Great or his sons. This was also a period of resurgence for Emona. The Roman bronzes from Emona, including this vessel, have been analyzed by A. Giumlia-Mair (see below), and her analysis supports the suggestion that this vessel may date to the 4th or 5th c.[12]

Mestni Muzej Ljubljana, Gosposka 15, 1000 Ljubljana, Slovenia

Technical appendix

Alessandra Giumlia-Mair

The heavy cast vessel from Emona with relief decoration of men and beasts fighting was found in three pieces and with some fragments missing. It was restored at Mainz, but there were doubts about the original shape, and for this reason the mouth was re-attached to the body only with broad bands. It was thought that the vessel could have been broken and restored with a new mouth and/or base in antiquity.

A simple analysis of the metal clarified these questions. Three samples — from the mouth, the body, and the base — were taken with a 0.8-mm jeweler's drill and analyzed by inductively coupled plasma emission spectrometry (ICP) in the Metallurgy Laboratory, Department of Materials Science, University of Trento. The results (Table 1) show that all three parts have the same composition and therefore belonged originally to the same vessel.

TABLE 1. ANALYSES OF BRONZE SAMPLES
BY INDUCTIVELY COUPLED PLASMA EMISSION SPECTROMETRY (ICP) (WEIGHT %)

	Cu	Sn	Zn	Pb	Ni	Fe	Ag	Co	Sb	As
Body	68.6	6.31	12.4	5.05	0.06	0.70	1.51	0.51	0.80	0.37
Base	67.8	5.73	11.7	7.39	0.03	0.52	0.53	0.13	0.24	0.37
Mouth	65.3	6.01	12.2	8.65	0.03	0.58	0.87	0.27	0.58	0.20

ques de la Bibliothèque Nationale (Paris 1895) 577, no. 1423.

8 Faider-Feytmans (supra n.5) pls. 129-30.

9 C. Picard, "Propos et documents concernant la toreutique alexandrine," *RA* 1961.

10 S. Boucher, *Bronzes grecs, hellénistiques et étrusques des musées de Lyon* (Lyon 1970).

11 M. H. P. de Boerstad, *The bronze vessels* 5 (Nijmegen 1956) pl. 17.310a-310c.

12 A. Giumlia-Mair, "Roman copper-based finds from a Slovenian settlement," *Bulletin of the Metals Museum* 25 (1996) 48-63.

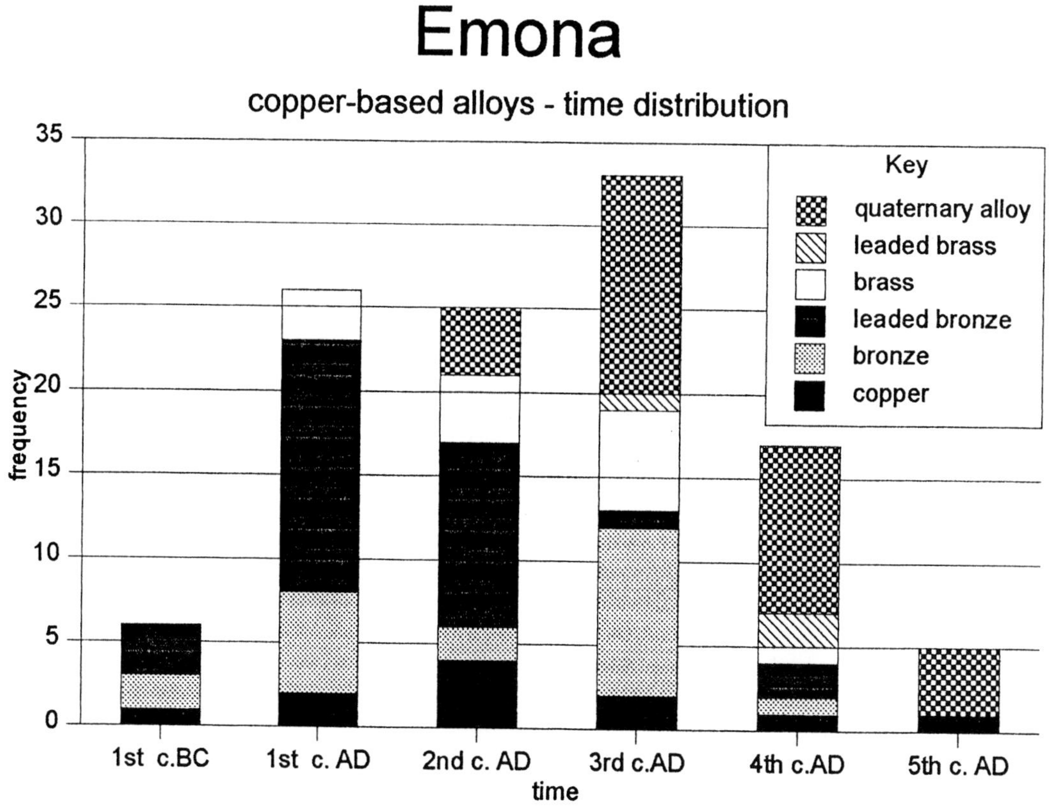

Fig. 7. Distribution of copper-based alloys found at Emona between the second half of the 1st c. B.C. and the 5th c. A.D. As the discovery of the objects was haphazard and the selection limited, the chart does not reflect the real relationship between time and alloys. Nevertheless, it provides an idea of what the proportions might have been. (author.)

The analyses thus allayed any doubts about the original shape of the vessel, but the composition re-opened the question of its date. The vessel had been tentatively dated to the Hellenistic period by the excavators. It is made of a quaternary alloy with a high zinc content, but from earlier work[13] we know that alloys containing zinc were not in use before the 1st c. B.C., except for some natural brasses.[14] Brass became common throughout the Roman empire only in the 1st c. A.D., after the introduction of brass *dupondii* in the coinage of Augustus. Brass with a high zinc content (i.e., freshly made brass) was used only for coins and a few other items. As recent scientific research in France, Britain, and Germany has shown,[15] brass was normally diluted with copper and lead. However, analyses carried out on N Gallic material[16] seem to indicate that there were also regional differences, with a much wider use of brass in that area, doubtless because of the proximity of the calamine mines. In later Roman times, quaternary alloys containing copper, tin, zinc, and lead become increasingly common. Their origin is the

---

13 P. Craddock, "The composition of the copper alloys used by the Greek, Etruscan, and Roman civilisations 3: the origins and early use of brass," *JArchSci* 5 (1978) 1-16; id., "Copper alloys of the Hellenistic and Roman world: new analyses and old authors," in J. Ellis Jones, *Aspects of ancient mining and metallurgy* (Bangor 1988) 58-60; R. Jackson and P. Craddock, "The Ribchester hoard: a descriptive and technical study," in B. Raftery, V. Megaw, and V. Rigby, *Sites and sights of the Iron Age* (Oxford 1995) 75-102.

14 Listed in Craddock 1978 ibid. 2-3.

15 J. Condamin and S. Boucher, "Recherches techniques sur des bronzes de Gaule Romaine 4," *Gallia* 41.1 (1973) 157-78; J. Bayley, "The production of brass in antiquity with particular reference to Roman Britain," in P. Craddock (ed.), *2000 years of zinc and brass* (BritMusOccPap 50, 1990) 7-27; J. Riederer, "Metallanalysen römischer Bronzen," in *Toreutik und figürliche Bronzen in römischer Zeit: Akten der 9. Tagung über antike Bronzen, Berlin 1980* (Berlin 1984) 220-25.

16 E. Rabeisen and M. Menu, "Métaux et alliages des bronziers d'Alésia," in *Recherches gallo-romaines* 1 (Paris 1985) 141-82.

random melting of scrap. Such alloys have many advantages: the normally low tin content improves resistance to corrosion and malleability; zinc improves ductility and hardness and deoxidizes the alloy; lead lowers the melting point of the alloy, and the addition of up to 2% lead increases fluidity and improves casting. Quaternary alloys soon became the standard Roman alloy, suitable for many purposes. The only variation encountered is in the lead content, which is moderate in hammered pieces (a technical device to avoid too frequent annealing), but much higher in cast pieces.

Quaternary alloys were not used for two classes of objects. One is large statuary, which is always of leaded bronze, even in the case of hurriedly produced statues such as the horse from Augsburg.[17] This is rather surprising as there is no special metallurgical reason for excluding zinc from big castings. The second class of objects without any noticeable zinc is mirrors.[18]

The composition of vessels from Emona varies depending on their manufacturing technique and on their shape and size. For example, larger vessels tend to contain proportionally more lead. However, vessels containing zinc in noticeable amounts are few and all belong to the class of buckets and basins.[19] The vessel with the wild beasts relief is the only vessel from Emona made of a high-lead quaternary alloy which also has a high zinc content.

The chart (fig. 7) illustrating the frequency of the different alloys in the period between the 1st c. B.C. and the 5th c. A.D. shows that quaternary alloys were more common at Emona in later periods. In general, quaternary alloys of this type became common for all vessel shapes in Late Roman times and in the Early Middle Ages.[20] The composition of this particular vessel thus seems to indicate a rather late date, in the 4th or 5th c.

Università di Udine, Centro Polifunzionale, Palazzo Alvarez, Via Diaz 5, I-34170 Gorizia

---

17 See Giumlia-Mair below pp. 92-94.

18 N. Meeks, "A technical study of Roman bronze mirrors," in S. T. A. M. Mols *et al.* (edd.), *Acta of the 12th int. Congress on Ancient Bronzes, Nijmegen 1992* (Nijmegen 1995) 179-93.

19 See Sivec above and Giumlia-Mair p. 193.

20 Craddock (supra n.13) 61.

Entella Tablets VI (254-241 B.C.) and VII (20th c. A.D.?)

William T. Loomis

One of the most sensational additions to our knowledge of the ancient world in the past 20 years has been the corpus of (so far) 9 bronze inscriptions known as the Entella Tablets, so-called because all but one of them record decrees of Entella, a small *polis* in the interior of western Sicily. These tablets have been sensational for four reasons. First, they cast light on a subject that had previously been very obscure — the internal history of Sicily in the Hellenistic period. Second, there has been an illicit aura about the tablets, stemming from allegations that they were unearthed in clandestine excavations near the Mafia stronghold of Corleone. Third, the texts of the tablets, although published, continue to be shrouded in mystery: a) the present location of the tablets has never been disclosed (with the exception of the most recently published tablet IX); b) prior to 1992, photographs of only two of the tablets (VIII and IX) had been published; and c) most texts therefore depended entirely on transcriptions made by an unnamed British scholar, tantalizingly referred to as the *Anglicus interpres*. Finally, the date of the inscriptions has been controversial: suggestions have ranged from the middle of the 4th c. to the end of the 3rd c. B.C., or even (in one case) to the 2nd c. A.D.

In December 1991, two inscribed bronze tablets were given to the Harvard University Art Museums. After preliminary cleaning and research, they turned out to be Entella Tablets VI [= *SEG* XXX, 1122] and VII [= *SEG* XXXII, 914]. The Museum made full disclosure to the Italian archaeological authorities, at whose request the tablets were transferred, in February 1996, to the Museo Archeologico, Palermo.

Tablet VII, however, is a modern fake. This is clear not only from defects in its Greek text but also from its nearly uniform thickness, the absence of corrosion, and the composition of its metal alloy — nearly 100% copper, as shown by electron beam microprobe analysis.

Three new clues offered by Tablet VI (the now certain dating formula in ll. 1-3, the present tense of the participle συνοικιζόντων in ll. 8-9, and the letter shapes), together with interlocking references in the other genuine Entella Tablets and evidence from other literary and epigraphical sources, indicate that the Entella decrees were issued at some point during the latter part (254-241 B.C.) of the First Punic War.

The Entella Tablets offer a unique perspective. We now see Sicily through local, rather than Roman or Carthaginian, eyes. At this early date, the Roman presence is not dominant, and there is no hint that it will be permanent. Instead, the citizens of Entella and the other Sicilian cities are, all too briefly, enjoying the diversity and genuine autonomy of Greek *polis* life.

54 West Cedar St., Boston, MA 02114-3302

For a full publication, see W. T. Loomis, *HSCP* 96 (1994 [1997]) 127-60.

Hercules and Antaeus: Giambologna and Renaissance artists wrestling with antiquity

Yvonne Korshak

A boldly designed ancient bronze sculpture of Hercules and Antaeus, familiar to Renaissance artists through a marble copy now in the Cortile of the Pitti Palace Museum in Florence[1] (fig. 1), had a significant, and somewhat surprising, influence in the development of artistic ideas during the Renaissance. In the work Hercules, his legs broadly spaced and feet firmly based, lifts Antaeus in a wrestling bodyhold from behind. The head of Antaeus and the lower legs of both figures are restorations of the 16th c.

Antaeus was the son of Poseidon and Gaia whom Hercules encountered in Africa and whom he defeated by wrestling.[2] The well-known idea that Hercules had to *lift* Antaeus in order to separate him from his mother, Earth, although universally accepted in the Renaissance, was not originally a part of the ancient conception. The antagonists are shown fighting on the ground, for example, in the representation on a late Archaic red-figure calyx crater by Euphronios.[3] Earlier Greek art is replete with images of wrestling postures, and Hercules is shown in many of these as he wrestles with Antaeus and others. In Archaic and Classical works, however, he is never shown lifting Antaeus as he does in the Pitti Palace sculpture, although wrestling lifts achieved by a bodyhold from behind appear early in Greek art, as on a black-figure amphora in Munich.[4]

In the Hellenistic and Roman epochs, Hercules is always shown lifting Antaeus, and the pose is that of the bodyhold from behind.[5] The new uniformity of conception suggests the influence of a famous and defining model. In light of the large scale and dramatic power of the Pitti Palace marble, it is tempting to hypothesize that it is a copy of the paradigmatic work. Specific comparisons between the marble and other Hellenistic and Roman representations of Hercules and Antaeus, however, show significant contrasts among them and with the Pitti Palace marble.[6]

The earliest example to date of an image in which Hercules seizes Antaeus in a bodyhold from behind is a diobol of Tarentum of the 3rd c. B.C. (fig. 2).[7] In contrast to the Pitti Palace marble, Antaeus's left leg swings behind Hercules's right leg, his left arm is bent at a 90° angle, his back does not press against Hercules's face, and the heads are nearly at the same height.

---

1 The sculpture was in the Belvedere of the Vatican from 1503, but the inspiration Mantegna drew from it for a Hercules and Antaeus in the Ducal Palace in Mantua reveals that it was known to artists at least as early as 1474. Sent to Florence in 1560, the sculpture was placed in the Palazzo Pitti in 1564. It is discussed by H. Möbius in "Vier hellenistische Skulpturen," *AntP* 10 (1970) 39-47, figs. 1-10; Möbius dates the copy to the early 2nd c. A.D. For a summary of its history in the Renaissance, see also P. P. Bober and R. O. Rubinstein, *Renaissance artists and antique sculpture* (Oxford 1986) 172-74.

2 Pind., *Isthm.* 4.52-55; cf. *Isthm.* 9.105-8.

3 Paris, Musé du Louvre G 103: P. E. Arias and M. Hirmer (transl. and rev. B. B. Shefton), *A history of Greek vase painting* (London 1962) pls. 108-11; E. N. Gardiner, *Athletics of the ancient world* (Oxford 1930, repr. Chicago 1980) fig. 201.

4 Gardiner ibid. fig. 164; Y. Korshak, *Frontal faces in Attic vase painting of the Archaic period* (Chicago 1987) fig. 40.

5 U. Hoff, "The sources of 'Hercules and Antaeus' by Rubens," in F. Philipp and J. Stewart (edd.), *In honour of Daryl Lindsay: essays and studies* (Melbourne 1964) 73 nn. 5-6, lists Hellenistic and Roman representations.

6 Möbius (supra n.1) 47 discusses generally a Lysippan model for the head of Hercules.

7 *A catalogue of the Greek coins in the British Museum: Italy* (London repr. 1983) no. 376; O. E. Ravel, *Descriptive catalogue of the collection of Tarentine coins formed by M. P. Vlasto* (London 1947) pl. 42, nos. 1442-44; R. Vollkommer, *Herakles in the art of classical Greece* (Oxford 1988) 22, no. 164.

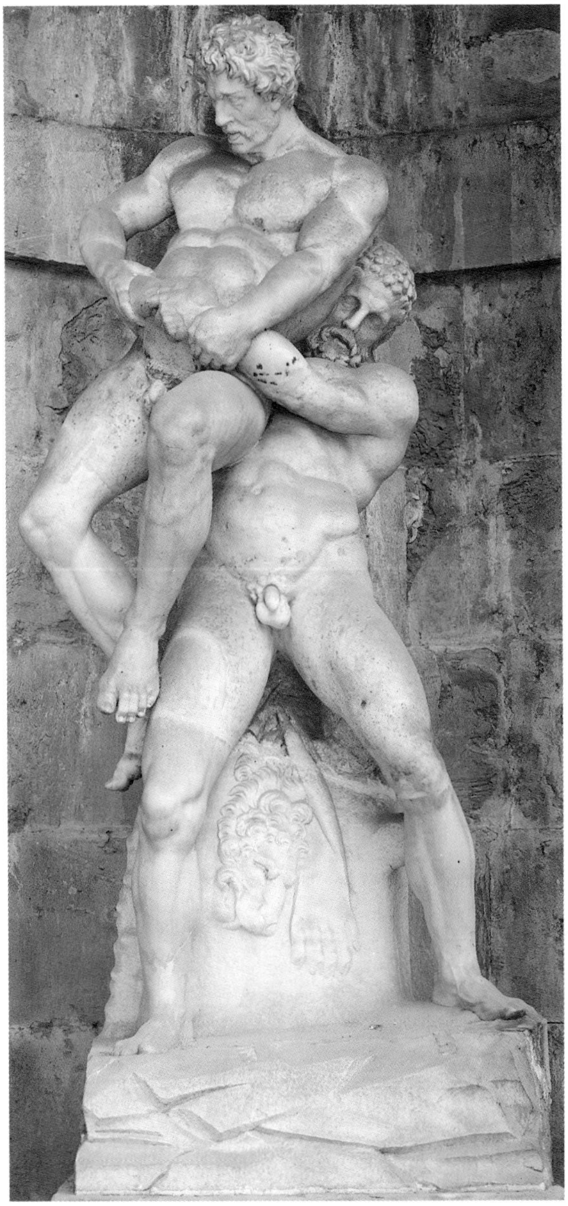

Fig. 1. Hercules and Antaeus. *c*.A.D. 200. Marble, h. 193.2 cm. Florence, Palazzo Pitti. (Photo: DAI Rom, neg. 56.1374)

As is generally the case in subsequent ancient representations, on the Tarentine coin Hercules looks more like his counterpart in the Pitti Palace sculpture than does Antaeus.[8]

The dynamic relationship between the two fighters on a representation on a sarcophagus from Athens of the 2nd c. A.D.[9] contrasts significantly to that of the Pitti Palace sculpture. Notably different is the forward thrust of Antaeus's body: on the sarcophagus, the Giant is not merely trying to break Hercules's grip around his abdomen but he also lunges as if to run away. Here, too, as on the Tarentine coin (which it does not otherwise resemble), the back of Antaeus does not press against the side of Hercules's face. On three Roman coins — of Caracalla, Antoninus Pius, and Geta Caesar — Antaeus's back is pressed against the front of Hercules's face (causing Hercules the powerful lift from his right shoulder); and in the latter two, instead of throwing himself into the lift, Hercules turns the lower part of his body away from Antaeus.[10] Although these images differ among themselves, thereby making it hard to define a classical paradigm, they agree in representing the grip from behind.

The earliest text describing the vitality that Antaeus receives from contact with the Earth, which forces Hercules to lift him upward, is that of Apollodorus in the 2nd c. B.C. This account does not, however, inform us about whether Hercules's hold was taken from behind — as we see it in the Pitti Palace sculpture — or from the front.[11] Diodorus, in the 1st c. B.C., reporting that Hercules killed Antaeus by wrestling with him, does not describe the struggle;[12] Hyginus, writing probably in the 2nd c. A.D., gives only a brief mention of the contest.[13] Lucan, writing in the 1st c. A.D., narrates the background and the final contest in more detail. In his account of the ultimate struggle, he reports that Hercules, standing between Earth and her son because he has come to realize the source of his antagonist's strength, and 'holding his breast already tight/in torpid chill and for a long time did not trust his enemy to the earth.'[14] Hercules is lifting Antaeus,

---

8 Pausanias 9.11.4, reports that on the pediments of the temple in the sanctuary of Herakles at Thebes, Praxiteles carved Herakles's labors, substituting Herakles and Antaios for the Stymphalian birds. The sculpture, not known otherwise, cannot be evaluated.

9 Athens, National Museum: P. B. Jongste, *The twelve labours of Hercules on Roman sarcophagi* (Rome 1988) cat. 12, fig. 60.

10 Hoff (supra n.5) figs. 45, 46, and 47 respectively.

11 Apollod., *Bibl.* 2.5.11.

12 Diod. Sic. 4.17.4-5; 4.27.3.

13 Hyg., *Fab.* 31.1-3.

14 Luc. 4.652-53: *Alcides medio tenuit iam pectora pigro / Stricta gelu terrisque diu non credidit hostem.* ('Alcides [Hercules] was in between them [Earth and Antaeus], holding his [Antaeus's] breast already

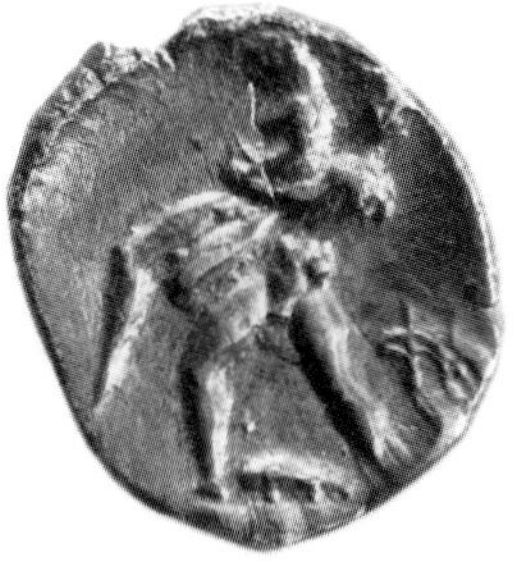

Fig. 2. Diobol. Tarentum, 3rd c. B.C. London, British Museum. (Photo: courtesy Trustees of Museum)

and the phrase 'gripped the breast', in the context of a lift, implies that Hercules has a bodyhold on him from behind. In the attempt to reconcile the written description with visual renderings, the word 'breast' (*pigro*) is problematic, because in the Pitti Palace sculpture and in other renderings in art (compare the Tarentine diobol, fig. 2) Hercules's grip is close to waist-level. The lift requires a grasp near the opponent's center of gravity, and, indeed, photographs of modern wrestlers lifting opponents in the bodyhold from behind demonstrate that the grip is made near the waist.[15] Lucan, one must conclude, did not really understand the lift he described and had not observed it closely in art or in life.

Philostratus Lemnius (2nd to 3rd c. A.D.), within the conceit of describing a painting, explains the hold much as we see it in the Pitti Palace sculpture. He writes, 'So Heracles, at a loss how to deal with Earth, has caught Antaeus by the middle just above the waist, where the ribs are, and set him upright on his thigh, still gripping his arms about him; then pressing his own fore-arm against the pit of Antaeus's stomach, now flabby and panting, he squeezes out his breath and slays him by forcing the points of his ribs into his liver.'[16] In sum, although classical writers provide ample evidence of "one fighting with the strength of Earth, the other with his own,"[17] only Philostratus provides a clear description of the hold.

In striking contrast to classical artists, those of the Italian Renaissance consistently represent Hercules grasping Antaeus in a bodyhold taken from the front, beginning with the representation on the Porta della Mandorla in Florence (1391-1405).[18] Other Quattrocento examples include Hercules and Antaeus in a manuscript by Pietro Andrea Bassi of *c.*1435,[19] in Leonardo Da Besozzo's Crespi Chronicle of *c.*1440,[20] on Filarete's bronze door for St. Peter's Basilica (1445),[21] and in Antonio Pollaiuolo's sculpture dated to the 1470s (fig. 3) as well as in his paintings.[22] Hercules and Antaeus became a popular and signifying Renaissance theme,[23] and the front-to-front struggle is seen in almost all subsequent compositions, such as that atop Tribolo's Fountain in the Villa di Castello near Florence (1559-60) where, by a striking conceit, in place of the last breath Hercules squeezed out of him, water gushes from Antaeus's mouth.[24]

Why, for depictions of Hercules and Antaeus, did the Renaissance select overwhelmingly the front-to-front lift rather than the bodyhold taken from behind? We have seen that the classical literary basis for visualizing the lift from behind during the Renaissance is not strong, the best account of it being in the Greek text of Philostratus. Another reason may be that, although trained wrestlers use both holds, the front-to-front posture is more often observed in

---

tight / in torpid chill and for a long time did not trust his enemy to the earth.') *Lucan, the Civil War* (transl. S. H. Braund; Oxford 1991) 80.

15 For photographs, see W. A. Martell, *Greco-Roman wrestling* (Champaign, IL 1992) fig. 3.9e and *passim;* the grip is also around waist-level in the bodyhold taken from behind, fig. 3.3a.

16 Philost., *Imag.* 2.21.38-44 (Loeb edn.).

17 Luc. 636-7: ... *telluris viribus ille, / Ille suis.*

18 L. D. Ettlinger, "Hercules Florentinus," *Mitteilungen des Kunsthistorischen Instituts in Florenz* 16 (1972) 124-28, figs. 3-5.

19 P. A. Bassi (transl. W. K. Thompson), *The labors of Hercules* (Barre, MA 1971) 67, with facsimile ills. from a manuscript in the P. Hofer collection, Harvard University.

20 Ettlinger (supra n.18) fig. 15.

21 J. Pope-Hennessy, *Italian Renaissance sculpture* (London 1985) 318-19, pl. 108, fig. 115.

22 F. Hartt (rev. D. G. Wilkins), *History of Italian Renaissance art* (4th edn., Englewood Cliffs, NJ 1994) fig. 323. The Uffizi painting is a small version of a larger lost painting that Pollaiuolo made for the Medici Palace; see Ettlinger (supra n.18) 128-29.

23 Ettlinger ibid.

24 J. Pope-Hennessy, *Italian High Renaissance and Baroque sculpture* (2nd edn., London 1985) 359-60, fig. 92; the cast was made by Ammanati.

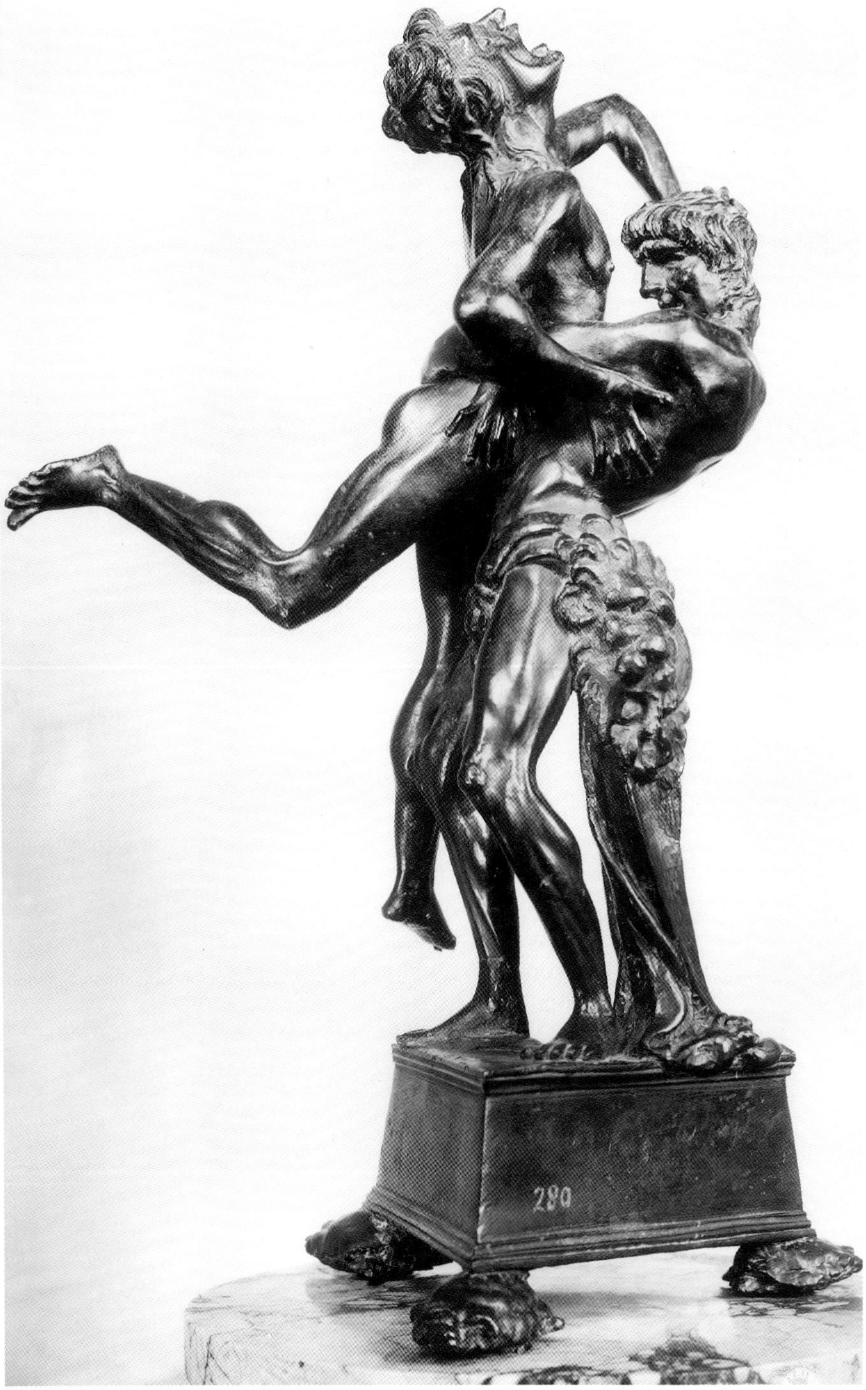

Fig. 3. Antonio Pollaiuolo, Hercules and Antaeus. Italian, *c.*1470. Bronze, h. (with base) 45.2 cm. Florence, Bargello Museum. (Photo: Art Resources, NY)

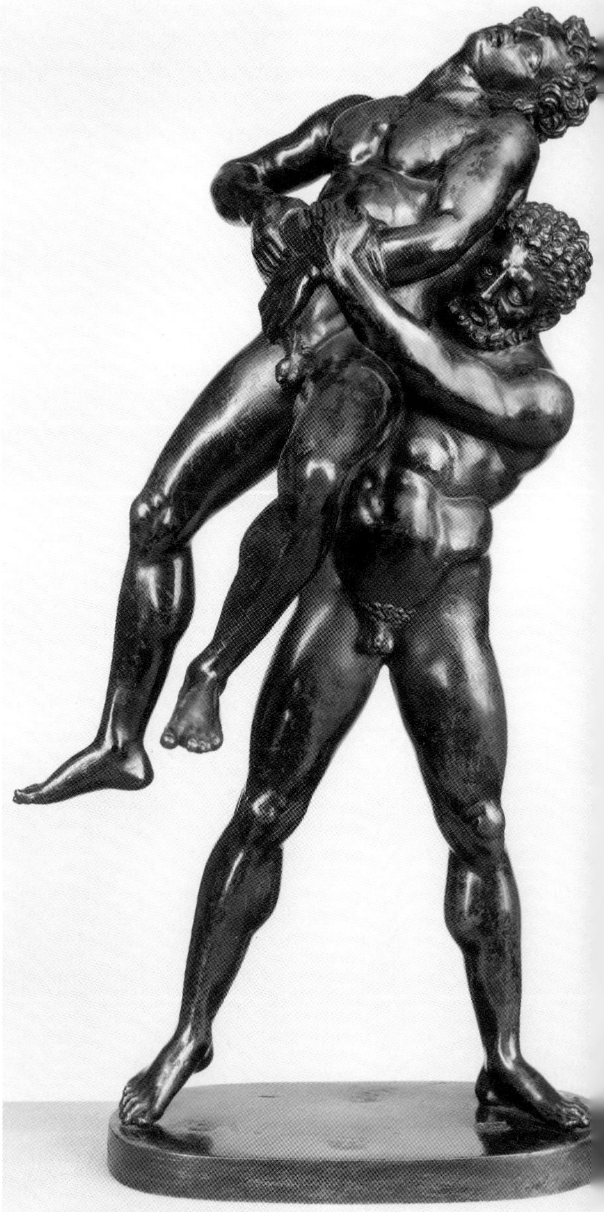

Fig. 4. Antico, Hercules and Antaeus. Italian, *c.*1500. Bronze with silver inlay, h. (with base) 40.7 cm. London, Victoria and Albert Museum A37-1956. (Photo: courtesy Board of Trustees of V&A)

scenes of life — combat or victory — as when a triumphant athlete is lifted by a teammate.[25] Pollaiuolo's early success in capturing the full drama of the agonistic encounter through the front-to-front composition was surely an important factor in its influence on subsequent works. Tribolo's fountain, with the expressive silhouette of Pollaiuolo's design enlarged and viewed against the sky, would have supported its paradigmatic status.

---

25 For a photograph of Dwight Gooden lifted by a member of his team after pitching a no-hitter in baseball, see the *New York Times*, May 19, 1996.

Another explanation may lie in a possibly subliminal desire to evade the homoerotic suggestion of the hold achieved from behind, as seen in homosexual subject-matter such as Michelangelo's *Rape of Ganymede*.[26] This position may have seemed particularly indecorous because of the allegorical elevation of Hercules in the Renaissance. This elevation is perhaps the chief reason for the turning away from the bodyhold from behind. Since antiquity, it had always been possible to understand Hercules as 'standing for something', and the foundations of the Renaissance conception of Hercules were humanist analyses of the many ancient interpretations of his deeds. These analyses resulted in an abstraction of the hero, so that, as G. K. Galinsky writes, he became a symbol of "virtue in all its aspects — physical, moral, spiritual, and even intellectual."[27] Antaeus, conversely, came to represent everything opposite, a view that, as M. A. Jacobsen has observed, was already developed by Coluccio Salutati in *De laboribus Herculis*, incomplete at his death in 1406.[28] One feels that if the ancients had not introduced the view that Hercules had to lift Antaeus from the earth, the Renaissance Neo-Platonists would have had to invent it, so perfectly does the episode lend itself to their views. Landino wrote around 1470: '... Hercules, that wise man cannot destroy him [Antaeus] so long as he clings to the earth: that is, so long as we desire earthly and corruptible things; but only if he is lifted to the divine.'[29]

Even in antiquity, when Hercules's combat with Antaeus was viewed in terms of values such as civilization *versus* barbarism, as in Euphronios's image, the antagonists were shown facing one another. The iconography of moral opposites underlying Renaissance representations requires awareness — consider the Renaissance insistence on Hercules as 'wise'. To be morally meaningful, a struggle demands knowledge of the opposite value and requires a face-to-face confrontation.

What, then, was the influence of the ancient marble statue of *Hercules and Antaeus* in the Pitti Palace?[30]

Two artists active in the Quattrocento, who were both particularly archaeological in their approach to antiquity, based their representations of Hercules and Antaeus on the ancient sculptural group: Mantegna in a fresco in the Camera degli Sposi of the Ducal Palace in Mantua (1468-74),[31] and Antico in a bronze sculpture with inlaid silver eyes, cast probably *c.*1500 (fig. 4).[32] Antico's Hercules and Antaeus differs from the ancient model particularly in the areas that were lacking in that — the legs of both figures and the head of Antaeus. Through a series

---

26 Fogg Museum of Art, Cambridge, MA: C. De Tolnay, *Corpus dei disegni di Michelangelo* 2 (Novara 1976) cat. 344 *recto.*

27 G. K. Galinsky, *The Herakles theme* (Oxford 1972) 185-230 discusses Hercules as an *exemplar virtutis* in the Renaissance (the quotation is on p. 197).

28 Salutati (ed. B. L. Ullman), *De laboribus Herculis* (Zurich 1951); for Salutati, Antaeus represents vice because *anti* in Greek means "contrary" and "equal", p. 325; his text reflects Lucan's account. Cf. M. A. Jacobsen, "A note on the iconography of Hercules and Antaeus in quattrocento Florence," *Source* I.1 (1981) 16-17. Jacobsen's analysis of Neoplatonism in Pollaiuolo's Hercules and Antaeus, a response to Ettlinger (supra n.18), gains support from the observation that a statue primarily created *all'antica,* might have shown the hold from behind.

29 C. Landino (ed. M. Lentzen), *De vera nobilitate* (Geneva 1970) 108. The translation is that of Jacobsen ibid. 17.

30 For views of the group before restoration, see M. H. L. Netto-Bol (ed.), *Die römischen Skizzenbücher von Marteen van Heemskerck* 2 (Soest 1975) pl. 59; and F. Caroli, *Lorenzo Lotto* (Florence 1975) 208, *Portrait of Andrea Odoni*, in Hampton.

31 M. Cordaro, *Mantegna la camera degli sposi* (Milan 1992) 62. Cf. A. Mezzetti, "Un 'Ercole e Anteo' del Mantegna," *BdA* 63 (1958) 232-40, and M. J. Zucker, *Early Italian masters* (The Illustrated Bartsch 25, New York 1984) 188-90 for Mantegna's school. Antico's use of inlaid silver eyes is taken up by B. Cohen, below p. 272.

32 D. Chambers and J. Martineau (edd.), *Splendours of the Gonzaga* (Exhib. cat., London 1981) cat. 55; see fig. 48 for Antico's later cast of the group, in the Kunsthistorisches Museum, Vienna.

of modifications, Antico represents a later moment in the narrative: past all struggle, the mighty Antaeus has gone limp. This sculpture should be linked with other notable examples of the limp heroic nude, such as Mars in Botticelli's painting Venus and Mars,[33] as a significant precursor of Michelangelo's remarkable exploration of the theme of the limp heroic male nude in figures such as Adam in the Sistine Chapel and the Dying Slave in the Louvre.

Michelangelo drew several versions of Hercules and Antaeus in connection with a marble sculpture of the subject that was to have been placed before the entrance to the Palazzo Vecchio as a pendant to the marble David but that was never realized. In a sheet now in the Ashmolean Museum (*c.*1525), he represented Hercules and Antaeus twice, struggling front to front and clutched together.[34] Although I proposed that the symbolic purification of Hercules led to an avoidance of the homosexual suggestion of the back-to-front posture, in these drawings Michelangelo demonstrates the close alignment of the front-to-front wrestling posture with a passionate embrace. It is interesting, in the light of his front-to-front representations of Hercules and Antaeus, that Michelangelo drew the ancient group in the Pitti Palace on a small sketch on a sheet now in the British Museum,[35] and again on a sheet of 1525-35 in the Teyler Museum, Amsterdam, where he modified it by adding female breasts to the "Antaeus" figure.[36] The definition of the female breasts is very insistent in the drawing on the *verso* of this sheet, traced from the *recto*. Thus, Michelangelo, like others of the period, while familiar with the ancient sculpture, seems not to have considered it seriously as a model for his conception of Hercules and Antaeus, but instead found a new iconography for his drawing.

Giambologna's sculpture of Hercules and Antaeus (late 1570s) is a purposeful hybrid of the antique and Renaissance models. As seen in the cast in the Kunsthistorisches Museum, Vienna,[37] Hercules is modeled after his namesake in the Pitti Palace group (but reversed); Antaeus, however, is derived from Pollaiuolo's sculpture, perhaps through the medium of Tribolo's fountain, and (also reversed) is squeezed in a bodyhold from the front — a striking example of the Renaissance resistance to the bodyhold from behind for Hercules and Antaeus.

This leads us to consider the rôle played by the Pitti Palace sculpture in one of the most innovative and influential sculptures of the later 16th c., Giambologna's three-figure group, Rape of the Sabine Woman (1583), in the Loggia dei Lanzi, Florence (fig. 5). In developing the figure of the young man lifting the woman, Giambologna took inspiration from the Hercules lifting Antaeus in the Pitti Palace sculpture, a figure that he knew well, for he had already based *his* Hercules lifting Antaeus on Hercules in the ancient work.[38] The composition of Giambologna's monumental sculpture is so complex that the connection between it and the Pitti Palace Hercules and Antaeus is not immediately apparent: the subject differs and although the motif in Giambologna's work involves a lift, we do not see a clear representation of the female figure seized either from behind or from the front — an important point of a sculpture composed with the intent of eluding any single comprehensive view. Thus, full understanding of the link between the Pitti Palace sculpture and the Florence Rape of the Sabine Woman requires a consideration of the evolution of the sculptural composition. First in this development comes Giambologna's two-figure Rape of the Sabine Woman (1579) in the Museo e Gallerie Nazionali di Capodimonte, Naples, in which the lift is from behind but the woman is seated on the male's

---

33 Hartt (supra n.22) fig. 348.

34 De Tolnay (supra n.26) cat. 237 *recto*.

35 Ibid. cat. 236 *recto*.

36 Ibid. cat. 238 *recto* and *verso*, with questioned attribution.

37 C. Avery, *Giambologna: The complete sculpture* (Oxford 1987) cat. 76, pl. 141, after a design of 1578 executed in silver, p. 109.

38 Pope-Hennessy (supra n.24) 52, noting several classical references in the sculpture, proposed that the figure of the young man and the torsion in woman's body originated in the Farnese Bull, now in Naples. Möbius (supra n.1) suggested a relationship between the Pitti Palace sculpture and Giambologna's *Rape of the Sabine Woman*.

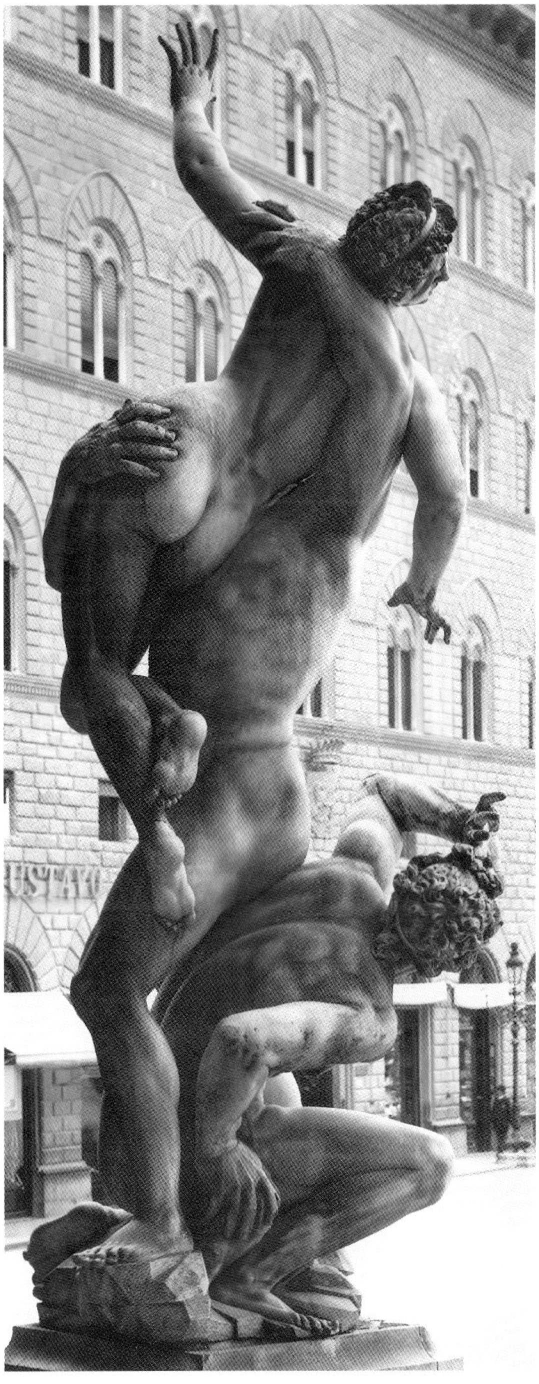

Fig. 5. Giambologna, Rape of the Sabine Woman. Italian, 1583. Marble, h. *c.*410 cm. Florence, Loggia dei Lanzei. (Photo: Art Resources, NY)

arms.[39] While hindsight allows us to understand this sculpture as a starting point for the artist's sculpture in the Loggia dei Lanzi, its conception is fundamentally different because, although the lift is from behind, the woman is seated on the man's arms. Thus, it cannot be considered a study for the monumental sculpture but rather as an initial idea for treating the subject.[40] Giambologna clearly did have the composition of the Loggia dei Lanzi marble in mind, however, when he created two wax sketches (now in the Victoria and Albert Museum) with a new motif: the female figure is no longer seated but is in the extended posture seen in the monumental sculpture. In these models, it is clear that she is grasped by the male in a bodyhold from behind.[41] In what is probably the first model, with two figures, the woman's back and hips are pressed against Hercules's neck and chest; in the latest, with the third figure now at the base, she twists her back away from full contact with his chest but is still grasped from behind.

With this development in mind, we can now arrive at a full appreciation of the rôle played by the ancient Hercules and Antaeus group as models in the development of Giambologna's Rape of the Sabine Woman. The influence of the Hercules of the Pitti Palace marble on Giambologna's Hercules lifting Antaeus and on the artist's subsequent series of male figures that culminate in the youth in the Florence Rape of the Sabine Woman is clear. We can now understand, further, that through his study of Hercules's hold on Antaeus from behind, Giambologna was able to find his way toward unifying his ambitious, monumental, and complex three-figure group through the continuous form of the Sabine and to imbue it with the serpentine flow of movement so desirable in the Mannerist aesthetic. Combining three figures into a cohesive group was "an idea that had obsessed Michelangelo, without

39 Avery (supra n.37) cat. 87, pl. 79. *The Rape of the Sabine Woman* in Vienna's Kunsthistorisches Museum, cat. 88, pls. V, 144, is closely related but probably slightly later.

40 C. Avery and A. Radcliffe (edd.), *Giambologna 1525-1608: Sculptor to the Medici* (London 1978) 105, question whether he even had the three-figure group in mind at that point.

41 Avery (supra n.37) cat. 196, pl. 78 (two figures) and cat. 197, pl. 80 (three figures). For early notice of the wax models as preliminary studies, see E. Dhanens, *Jean Boulogne* (Brussels 1956) 237; J. Pope-Hennessy, *Catalogue of Italian sculpture in the Victoria and Albert Museum* 2 (London 1964) 468-69.

his ever having been permitted to realize it."[42] Giambologna was able to fulfill the artistic project set by his mentor: the key lay in Hercules's powerful lift in the Pitti Palace sculpture. Michelangelo's drawings with the transformed gender of Antaeus may also have suggested the pose for Giambologna's sculpture of a man violently lifting a woman.[43]

The fluidity of Giambologna's Rape of the Sabine Woman, with its unbroken flow of movement and multiple points of view that mask its classical heritage, are innovative aspects of the composition, recognized with great enthusiasm for their originality at the time,[44] and appreciated for their power and innovative creativity ever since. The model of the ancient sculpture of Hercules and Antaeus in the Pitti Palace enabled Giambologna to find that his way to that goal.

In the work of Giambologna and in that of other artists, Hercules, having undergone a creative transformation as a perfected hero, faced his moral opposite and antagonist, Antaeus, head on. Thus, for the most part in the Renaissance, the hero and the ancient group parted ways. But the ancient sculpture of Hercules and Antaeus did not gasp its last breath. It too lived on through the process by which art perennially responds to the vitality of antiquity, through creative transformation.

Department of Art and Art History, Adelphi University, Garden City, NY 11530

---

42 Avery and Radcliffe (supra n.40) 15.

43 De Tolnay (supra n.26) 56, following P. Squellati, proposed that the drawing may be a "Rape of the Sabine Woman" and may have inspired Giambologna's group.

44 Bartolomeo Sermartelli, *Alcuni composizioni di diversi autori in lode del ritratto della Sabina* (Florence 1583); e.g., S. Lorenzo Giacomini Tebalducci, 23: "Mira i tre volti, che affetti, e sensi di viui / Mostrano in un sol marmo espressi da nuovo Lisippo."

Antico's bronze busts: precious metal and the invention of Renaissance "antiquities"

Beth Cohen

Pier Jacopo Alari-Bonacolsi, called Antico, was the preeminent sculptor employed by Gonzaga courts in Mantua and its territory from the 1470s until his death in 1528. Prominent among his Gonzaga patrons during the cinquecento was Isabella d'Este, the first woman in Western history to collect classical antiquities. The artist's Renaissance nickname derived from the classicizing nature of his work as a restorer of antiquities and goldsmith as well as a bronze sculptor.[1]

Antico has been praised for his sophisticated craftsmanship in producing the first multiples of bronze statuettes in Renaissance Italy indirectly cast by the lost wax process.[2] His small bronzes were often miniature reflections of extant ancient statues, occasionally of large bronzes, such as the Spinario (fig. 1), but usually of marble statues, such as the Apollo Belvedere in the Vatican.[3] Generally viewed as a master of bronze reductions, Antico has been judged a figure of lower stature than, for example, the inventive "antiquizing" Paduan sculptor Andrea Briosco, called Riccio.[4] Relatively late in his career, however, Antico shifted his attention from the production of small bronzes — i.e., medals, plaques, and statuettes — to the life-size, classicizing busts with which he was surely occupied during the 1510s and 1520s.[5] In this short study, I will call attention to these important monumental bronzes (figs. 2, 4) by considering the light they shed on a highly significant, yet often overlooked, aspect of Antico's artistic contribution: his translation into bronze of classical images known to the Renaissance in Roman marbles. My final focus will be the contrasting eyes on Antico's bronze portraits (figs. 2-5), which are distinctive in terms of both their antiquizing aesthetic and their technology (see Appendix below).

Although Antico's bust of Bacchus and his bust of "Ariadne" in the Kunsthistorisches Museum, Vienna, were obviously conceived as characters from classical mythology,[6] most of his large bronzes appear to have been intended as historicizing portraits of classical personages. These *portraits*, however, need not resemble an ancient image of their intended namesake, and

1 The major studies are A. H. Allison, "The bronzes of Pier Jacopo Alari-Bonacolsi, called Antico," *JKSW* NF LIII/LIV, 89/90 (1993-94) 35-310 [hereafter Allison, *Antico*] and H. J. Hermann, "Pier Jacopo Alari-Bonacolsi, gennant Antico," *Jarhbuch der Kunsthistorischen Sammlungen des Allerhöchsten Kaiserhauses* 28 (1909-10) 201-88 [hereafter Hermann, *Antico*]. For Gonzaga patronage: D. Chambers and J. Martineau (edd.), *Splendours of the Gonzaga* (Exhib. cat., London 1981) particularly 46-49 (A. Radcliffe) and 132-40, 170-71 [hereafter *Splendours*]. The following exhibition catalogues were not available to me during the preparation of this article: V. Krahn (ed.), *Von allen Seiten schön: Bronzen der Renaissance und des Barock* (Berlin 1995) and S. Ferino-Pagden, *Isabella d'Este: Fürstin und Mäzenatin der Renaissance: "La prima donna del mondo"* (Vienna 1994), but references to the latter have been inserted in the notes.

2 R. E. Stone, "Antico and the development of bronze casting in Italy at the end of the Quattrocento," *MMAJ* 16 (1981-82) 87-116.

3 Allison, *Antico* (supra n.1) 108-16; A. Legner, "Anticos Apoll vom Belvedere," *StädelJb* NF 1 (1967) 102-18. For the ancient statuary: F. Haskell and N. Penny, *Taste and the antique: the lure of classical sculpture, 1500-1900* (New Haven 1981) and P. P. Bober and R. O. Rubinstein, *Renaissance artists and antique sculpture: a handbook of sources* (London 1986).

4 For the common view of Antico: R. J. M. Olson, *Italian Renaissance sculpture* (London 1992) 139-40.

5 See Allison, *Antico* (supra n.1) passim. Little consensus of opinion exists regarding the chronology and attribution of the more than a dozen large bronze portraits associated with Antico (e.g., fig. 2), his workshop, and his followers (e.g., fig. 4).

6 Allison, *Antico* (supra n.1) 244-46, figs. 207-9; 254-57, figs. 214-16; Hermann, *Antico* (supra n.1) 277-79, pls. 44-45.

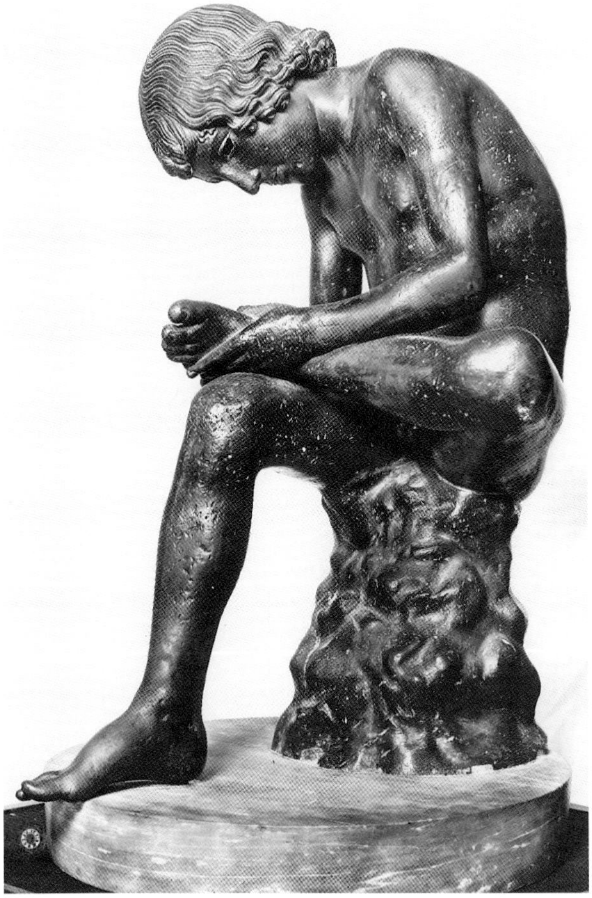

Fig. 1. Spinario. Hellenistic or Roman. Bronze with copper inlay, h. 0.73 m. Rome, Musei Capitolini, Palazzo dei Conservatori. (Photo: Alinari/Art Resource, NY)

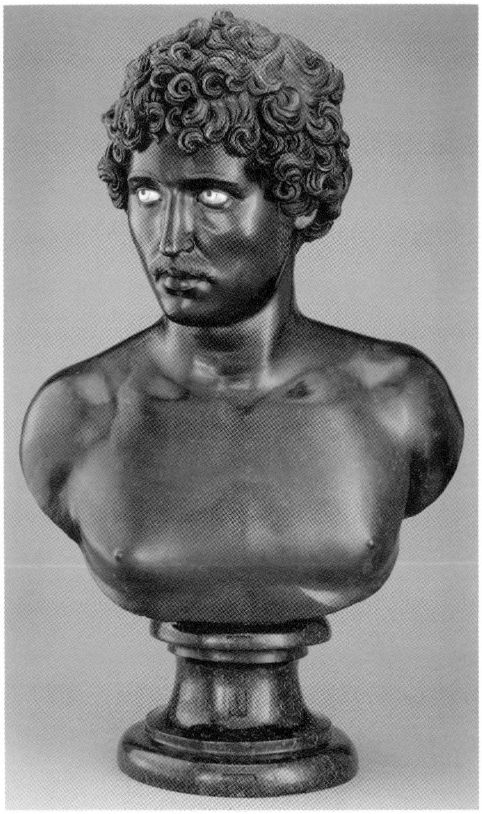

Fig. 2. Antico (Pier Jacopo Alari-Bonacolsi), "Young Marcus Aurelius." Italian, *c.*1520. Bronze with silver inlay, h. 0.547 m. Los Angeles, The J. Paul Getty Museum 86.SB.688. (Photo: courtesy Museum)

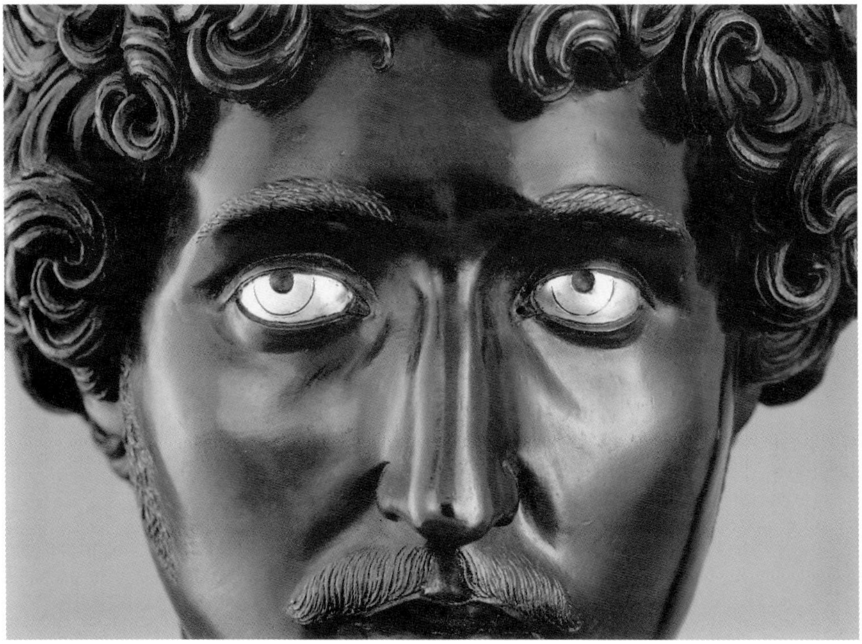

Fig. 3. Detail of bust in fig. 2. (Photo: courtesy Museum.)

without documentation their Renaissance identifications are not always self-evident: witness the probable "Cleopatra" in the Museum of Fine Arts, Boston, or the Portrait of a Young Man in the collection of the princes of Liechtenstein at Vaduz, which has been called Hercules, Scipio Africanus, Antinoos, and Alexander the Great.[7] Antico's sophisticated busts were designed to satisfy the taste of his Gonzaga patrons, in a typically Renaissance process described by A. H. Allison:

> ... it can be presumed that it was seldom, if at all, that the simple desire for the reproduction of a famous antiquity motivated a commission ... While in some instances the antique work may have suggested the idea, the most likely procedure, after the *concetto* of the patron, or of his or her advisor, or proposed by Antico himself, would first have been the selection, variation, or creation of an appropriate motif — not solely from antique art and literature but also from more modern sources.[8]

While Antico's portraits do not appear to be dry, archaeological copies, K. Fittschen has, nevertheless, attempted to demonstrate that "... Antico was concerned above all with a careful and effective reproduction of antique models,"[9] by assessing the associations of these large Renaissance bronzes with Roman portraiture. He believes that close ancient marble prototypes (which may no longer be preserved) existed for all the bronze busts in the Renaissance. The so-called "Young Marcus Aurelius" (fig. 2) in the J. Paul Getty Museum, for example, appears to have been based on a Roman marble bust of an unknown young man now in the Hispanic Society, New York, rather than on the corresponding imperial portrait type.[10] The "Cleopatra" is related to a portrait type of Augustus's wife Livia as Ceres.[11] The autograph Antoninus Pius in the Metropolitan Museum of Art and the workshop example in the Musée du Louvre are clearly related to the familiar Roman portraits of the emperor.[12] The later cast of a bust of Faustina, Antoninus Pius's wife, also in the Louvre, brings to mind the fact that a Roman marble bust of the empress, once owned by Mantegna, was acquired by Isabella d'Este.[13] The "Portrait of a Roman Imperial Man" (fig. 4) in the Walters Art Museum, a 16th-c. bronze bust by a follower of Antico, imitates an ancient portrait type now identified as the Greek comic playwright Menander.[14] Finally, the bronze head of Augustus in the Seminario Vescovile, Mantua, attributed to Antico by Allison, is still preserved alongside its Roman marble prototype.[15]

This review of classical portraits associated with Antico's large bronzes is significant here because these ancient *prototypes* are sculptures in marble. Thus Antico's original intention in producing his bronze portraits must have gone beyond "a careful and effective reproduction of antique models". With his bravura translation of an emblematic classical genre from incompletely preserved Roman marbles into resplendently-finished Renaissance metal sculpture, Antico created a horse of a different color: the *bronze* portrait bust *all'antica*.

In the humanist environment of the Gonzaga court, Antico would have gleaned from literary sources not only the preeminent position of bronze in classical sculpture generally but also this

---

7 Ibid. 240-43, figs. 204-6; 246-51, figs. 210-11; Hermann, *Antico* (supra n.1) 279, pl. 46; *Die Bronzen der Fürstlichen Sammlung Liechtenstein* (Exhib. cat., Frankfurt 1986) 257-61.

8 Allison, *Antico* (supra n.1) 56.

9 K. Fittschen, "The bronze bust of the 'Young Marcus Aurelius' by Antico and its antique model," *GettyMusJ* 18 (1990) 126.

10 Ibid. 113, 118-20, figs. 2a-d. I would like to thank P. Fusco, formerly of the Getty Museum, for permitting me to examine the "Young Marcus Aurelius".

11 Fittschen (supra n.9) 120, figs. 7-8; Allison, *Antico* (supra n.1) 242.

12 Fittschen (supra n.9) 120.

13 Allison, *Antico* (supra n.1) 287-88; *Splendours* (supra n.1) 170, no. 122.

14 Fittschen (supra n.9) 121, 125, figs. 12-14; W. S. Sheard, *Antiquity in the Renaissance* (Exhib. cat., Northampton, MA 1979) 69-70.

15 A. H. Allison, "Four new busts by Antico," *Mitteilungen des Kunsthistorischen Institutes in Florenz* 20 (1976) 213, 220, 222, figs. 13-14. For the prototypes of these busts: Fittschen (supra n.9) 121, 123. I would like to thank G. Manzoli for permission to see the works in the Seminario Vescovile, Mantua, and A. H. Allison for help pertaining to the Mantua sculptures.

medium's original, specific rôle in commemorative portraiture, as recorded, for example, by Pliny (*NH* 25.2.9-10):

> Nor must we pass over a rather new invention, that of setting up portraits in libraries, if not of gold or silver at least of bronze, of those immortal spirits who speak to us in these places; in fact, even portraits of those whose looks were never modeled are made, and our sense of longing gives birth to faces which have not been recorded ...[16]

Pliny pointedly refers to ancient historicizing portraits of esteemed individuals fabricated specifically in costly materials, in precious metals or bronze. The classical association of commemorative portraiture with expensive metals was not lost on Antico. His fabrication of classicizing *bronze* busts must have contained an element of 'one-upmanship': 'Surely my classic portraits in lustrous metal are finer and more valuable than the battered, marble antiquities collected by the Gonzaga!'

Antico's large bronzes should not be confused with the cinquecento copies and fakes of antiquities that follow.[17] His impressive bronze portraits presage the post-antique vogue for the classicizing bust in Western art. Significantly, they include some of the earliest Renaissance sculptures in the round that imitate the artfully curved form of a Roman portrait bust rather than presenting a slice of upper body in the Florentine quattrocento manner.[18]

Beyond cross-fertilization by classical texts and marble prototypes, Antico's sophisticated bronze portraits must also have been inspired by extant bronze sculpture.[19] However, the nature of the influence of ancient bronzes on Antico's large bronzes is somewhat difficult to recognize.[20] For this consummate craftsman during the latter half of his career, these antiquities appear to have served as an aesthetic and technical guide for formulating evocations of the classical bronze original in Renaissance terms rather than as a source of specific models. This must have been the case, in part, because classical sculpture in bronze, an eminently convertible material, rarely survives. Unlike other genres of antiquities, our current breadth of knowledge of ancient bronze statuary could not have been achieved through examples known in the Renaissance. The present corpus has been enriched by many chance discoveries — particularly examples salvaged from the sea over the past century.[21] In fact, most of the famous bronzes from Italy that we think of as venerable were discovered after Antico's lifetime,[22] and the modern acquaintance with *bronze* Roman portraits has been altered immeasurably by the excavation of Pompeii and Herculaneum since the 18th c.[23] Since Antico died in 1528 and appears not to have frequented

---

16 Translation: J. J. Pollitt, *The art of ancient Greece: sources and documents* (Cambridge 1990) 91.

17 E.g., I. Favaretto, "La fortuna del ritratto antico nelle collezioni venete di antichità: originali, copie e 'invenzioni,'" *BdA* 79 (1993) 65-72; K. Fittschen, "Über einige römische Porträts in Venedig: antike Vorbilder und neuzeitliche Nachahmungen," in *Venezia e l'archeologia* (*RdA* Suppl. 7, 1990) 203-8, pls. 43-49; P. C. Bol, "Archäologische Anmerkungen," *StädelJb* NF 11 (1987) 171-78; K. Fittschen, "Sul ruolo del ritratto antico nell'arte italiana," and E. Paul, "Falsificazioni de antichità in Italia dal Rinascimento alle fine del xviii secolo," in S. Settis (ed.), *Memoria dell'antico nell'arte italiana* 2 (Turin 1985) 383-412, 413-39.

18 T. E. Martin, "Michelangelo's Brutus and the classicizing portrait bust in sixteenth-century Italy," *Artibus et Historiae* 27 (1993) 67-83; id., *The portrait busts of Alessandro Vittoria* (Ann Arbor, MI 1988) 41-43. I am grateful to D. Lewis of the National Gallery of Art, Washington, for this reference. For Florentine busts: I. Lavin, "On the sources and meaning of the Renaissance portrait bust," *ArtQ* 33 (1970) 207-26.

19 I will deal elsewhere with Renaissance sources, e.g., Mantegna's bronze self-portrait: J. Martineau (ed.), *Andrea Mantegna* (London 1992) 89-90 (A. Radcliffe).

20 Supra nn. 3, 17; generally the focus is the influence of ancient marbles or decorative arts rather than bronze statuary.

21 Mattusch, *Greek bronze statuary* 1-9; Mattusch, *Classical bronzes* passim.

22 E.g., the *Idolino* was not found until 1530: Haskell and Penny (supra n.3) 240-41.

23 C. C. Parslow, *Rediscovering antiquity: Karl Weber and the excavation of Herculaneum, Pompeii, and Stabiae* (Cambridge 1995).

Rome after the 1490s,[24] this Mantuan court sculptor's knowledge of bronze antiquities was indeed limited.

In considering Antico's Renaissance evocation of the visual appearance of classical bronzes, it is important to take into account how he chose to reference the rare examples with which he was familiar. In this context, one telling metallic detail, characteristic of the bronze portraits by Antico and his circle, deserves special attention: the contrasting eyes (see Appendix; figs. 2-4). In general, the eyeballs were cast in bronze as an integral part of these portraits' heads, and variations in color were achieved by means of the treatment of the surface and/or thin silver inlays. For example, on Antico's Antoninus Pius in New York, the eyes appear to have golden-hued unpatinated irises surrounded by inlaid silver whites.[25] The portrait bust of a "Roman Imperial Man" in Baltimore (fig. 4) has eyes with silver whites and darkly patinated irises. Several of the bronze heads of Roman emperors in Mantua, attributed to Antico by Allison, still exhibit contrasting eyes with pale whites and dark pupils.[26] Both Antico's Portrait of a Young Man in Liechtenstein and his "Young Marcus Aurelius" in Los Angeles (figs. 2-3) have eyes with entirely silvered whites and irises. Antico's bust of "Ariadne" in Vienna has light eyes (originally unpatinated or gilt) with a plastic indication of iris and pupil.[27] Contrasting eyes were not common on large Renaissance bronzes outside of the Mantuan milieu.[28]

These striking metallic coloristic effects can best be understood in light of the treatment of eyes on ancient sculpture. Of course, Antico was readily familiar with small bronze antiquities enlivened by contrasting eyes inset in silver.[29] And he often employed silver eyes on his own bronze statuettes, such as his reduced versions of the Apollo Belvedere in the Liebieghaus, Frankfurt, and of the Spinario in the Wrightsman collection, New York.[30] In his characteristic appropriation of this signal detail Antico departed from other Renaissance masters of the small bronze *all'antica*, such as Riccio, who did not commonly use silver for eyes.[31]

But what would Antico have known specifically about eyes on large ancient bronzes? The surprisingly few, famous specimens known in Italy by roughly the first quarter of the cinquecento display several types of handlings for the eyes:

1) The eyes are cast as part of the head, with the iris and pupil delineated in plastic detail. The gilt Marcus Aurelius Equestrian, which may well have always been visible, displays this type of handling for the eyes of both rider and horse. This handling also occurs on the head of Constantine in the Palazzo dei Conservatori, also always above ground, and on the gilt Horses of San Marco, which were taken to Venice from Constantinople in the 13th c.[32]

---

24 Allison, *Antico* (supra n.1) 37, 39, records a trip in 1497 to Rome; cf. Hermann, *Antico* (supra n.1) 206-7.

25 Allison, *Antico* (supra n.1) 252, fig. 212.

26 Allison 1976 (supra n.15) 218, describes the four Seminario Vescovile heads as having silver irises or pupils (cf. Allison, *Antico* [supra n.1] 230-34), and two as possibly having copper whites. A definitive statement would require prior cleaning, but dark pupils and pale whites suggest silver whites and bronze pupils (cf. fig. 4).

27 Allison, *Antico* (supra n.1) 246, fig. 210; 254, fig. 214. While Allison describes them as unpatinated, according to M. Leithe-Jasper, in Ferino-Pagden (supra n.1) 357, the eyes of the *"Ariadne"* are gilt; see the color reproductions on 359-60. I have not examined the eyes of this bust since beginning the present study.

28 On a bronze portrait of Ludovico Gonzaga with silver eyes in Berlin: A. Radcliffe, in *Splendours* (supra n.1) 117. Cf. the "silvered" eyes on Donatello's *Reliquary Bust of San Rossore* in the Museo Nazionale di San Matteo, Pisa, and the inlaid eyes on the horse of his *Equestrian Statue of Gattamelata* in Padua: J. Pope-Hennessy, *Donatello: sculptor* (New York 1993) 71, 204 and 72, fig. 63; 75, fig. 64; 205, fig. 197. I shall discuss elsewhere Donatello's rather different use of silver inlay as well as of gilding.

29 E.g., *The gods delight* 139, no. 22; 299, no. 54; 316, no. 59; 350, no. 69; 359, no. 72.

30 Allison, *Antico* (supra n.1) 109 and fig. 42; 112 and fig. 46; 113, 211, 213, fig. 170.

31 *Natur und Antike in der Renaissance* (Exhib. cat., Frankfurt 1985) 460, no. 160.

32 Haskell and Penny (supra n.3) 252-55, 236-40; A. Oliver, "Honors to Romans: bronze portraits," in *The fire of Hephaistos* 138, 154, fig. 10.

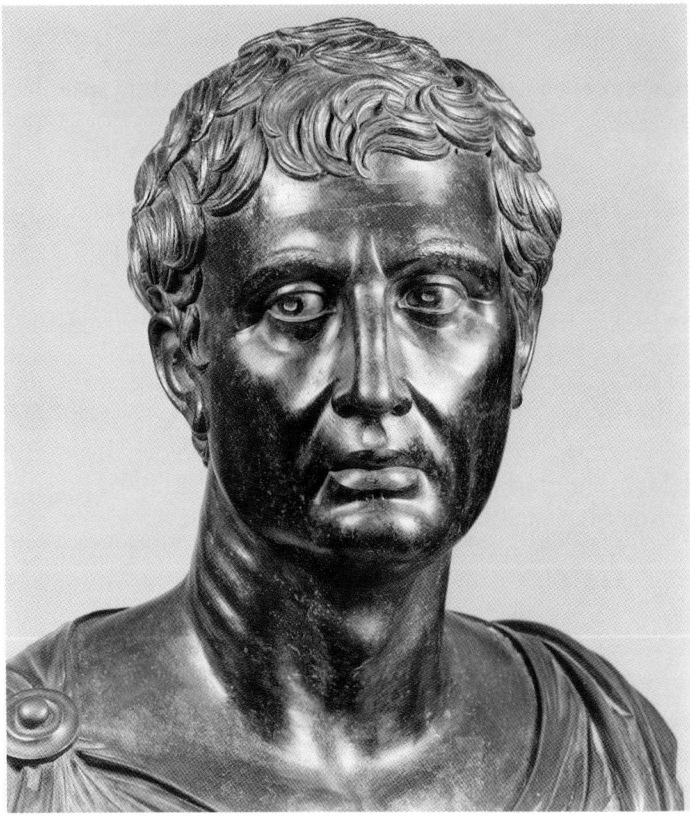

Fig. 4. Follower of Antico, "Portrait of a Roman Imperial Man". Italian, 16th c. Detail of bronze bust with silver inlay, h. 0.51 m. Baltimore, The Walters Art Museum 27.419. (Photo: courtesy Museum)

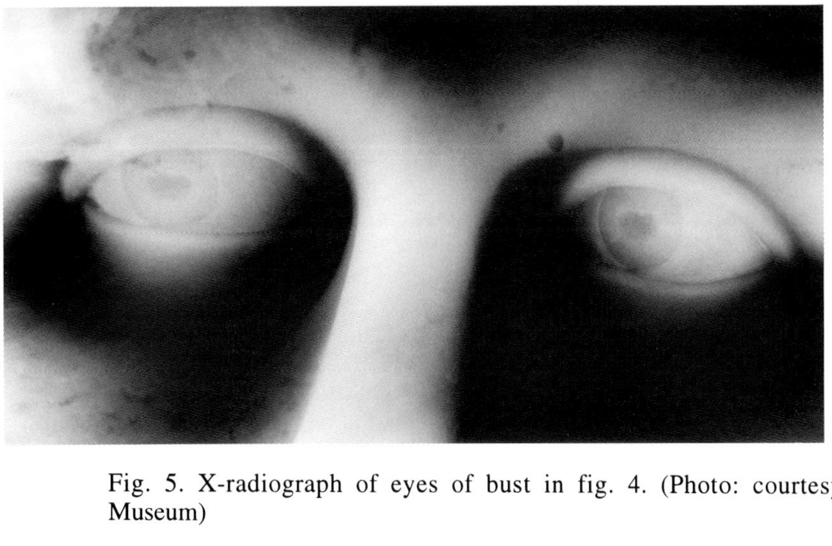

Fig. 5. X-radiograph of eyes of bust in fig. 4. (Photo: courtesy Museum)

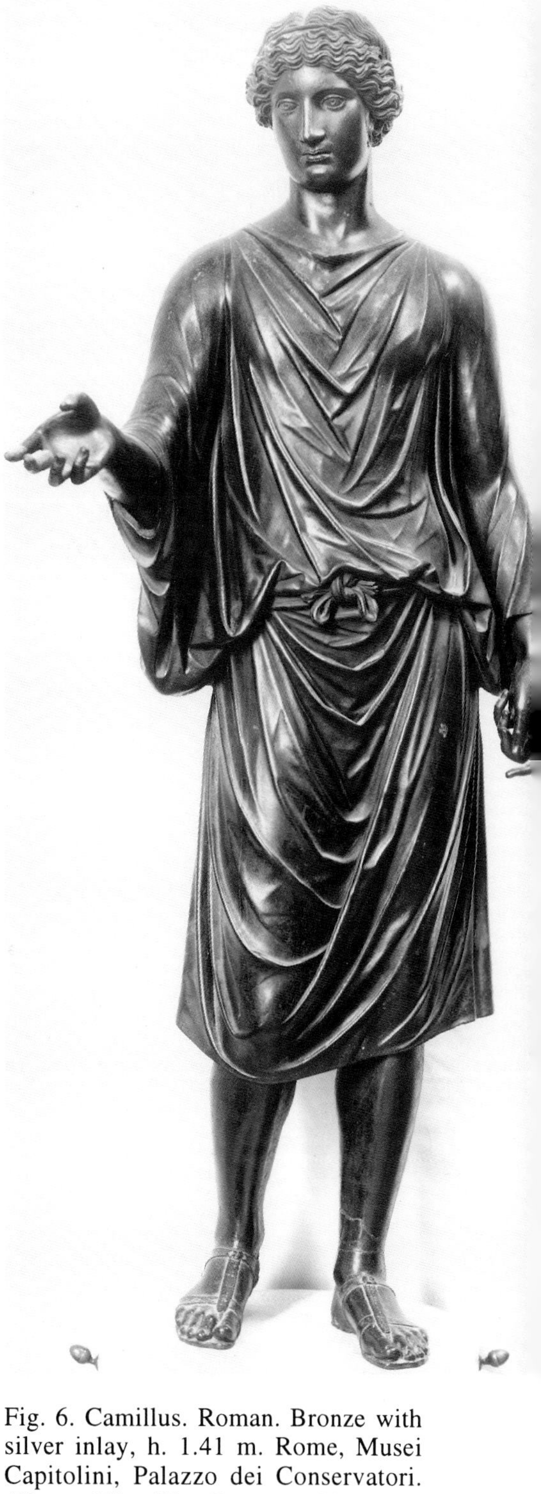

Fig. 6. Camillus. Roman. Bronze with silver inlay, h. 1.41 m. Rome, Musei Capitolini, Palazzo dei Conservatori. (Photo: Alinari/Art Resource, NY)

2) The eyes are inlaid with sheets of silver.[33] This handling, of obvious importance for Antico, cannot be documented widely among large ancient bronzes known to have existed in his life-

---

33 C. C. Mattusch, in *The fire of Hephaistos* 222-23, no. 22; 237-42, no. 25; 262-63, no. 31; 274-81, no. 35; 293-96, no. 39; 298-301, no. 41; 318-20, no. 46. The examples in this catalogue do not appear to have been

time. The Roman portraits with silver eyes that might have been preserved at that time have not been specifically identified. Significantly, silver eyes do occur on the Early Imperial bronze statue of a Camillus (fig. 6) in the Palazzo dei Conservatori, Rome, believed to be female (the Zingara) and displayed in the same room as the Spinario in the Renaissance.[34] Knowledge of the ideally beautiful classicizing head of the Camillus, then regarded as a masterpiece, could well lie behind such works by Antico as the "Ariadne" in Vienna and the Portrait of a Young Man in Liechtenstein, which also has silver eyes.[35]

3) A third type of large ancient bronze extant in the Renaissance originally had naturalistic inset eyes composed of non-metallic materials, e.g., ivory or marble for the white, and colored stones such as quartz and obsidian for iris and pupil, not to mention bronze lashes. Yet most of the large ancient bronzes, whether Greek, Roman, Etruscan, or Italic, found on Italian soil outside Pompeii and Herculaneum through the 19th c. that originally had naturalistically inset eyes, have lost their insets; now they have only empty, gaping eye sockets.[36] Examples known during Antico's lifetime include the famous Spinario (fig. 1), first recorded in 1165.[37] How such ancient bronze statuary with lost eye insets should be restored may be common knowledge for modern archaeologists, but it was not for Renaissance artists.

The first large ancient bronze with preserved inset eyes found in Italy appears to be the so-called "Lucius Junius Brutus" in the Conservatori, an Italic portrait head with naturalistic insets of ivory and dark cobalt smalt. That the Brutus's colorful preserved eyes were indeed a rarity may be deduced from the comments of early observers. The head was first documented in 1556 and was probably drawn by Heemskerck in the 1530s, but it does not appear to have been found early enough to have been seen in Rome by Antico.[38]

One of the earliest restorers of (marble) antiquities, Antico surely would have reconstructed the missing eyes of ancient bronze statuary in his mind's eye. However, based on his knowledge of bronze statuettes and a rare, well-preserved large find like the Camillus (fig. 6), he must have thought that the lost eyes, such as those of the Spinario (fig. 1), had been made of precious metal which contrasted in color with the darkened bronze face. Like all Renaissance artists, he incorrectly presumed that the surfaces of classical bronzes, rather than being a natural golden hue, had originally been intentionally patinated to create the dark colors in which they had been preserved. In assessing the impact of Antico's attentive observation of classical antiquities, it is also important to bear in mind that he could have seen traces of paint defining the eyes on some ancient marbles, such as the Roman prototype for the attributed bronze head of Augustus in Mantua.[39] The missing eyes, silver eyes, and painted eyes of antiquities that Antico knew would have fostered his use of contrasting metals, e.g., silver alone, or in conjunction with patinated or unpatinated bronze, for eyes on his large Renaissance bronzes. However, he chose never entirely to inset colorful naturalistic eyes into open eye sockets.

Antico's selective use of metallic colors was limited to golden and silvery hues. Although he surely knew of copper inlays on classical bronzes, like the red lips of the Spinario (fig. 1), Antico did not employ them. And while he was aware of fully gilt ancient bronzes, such as the

---

known in Renaissance Italy.

34 Haskell and Penny (supra n.3) 167-69; Bober and Rubenstein (supra n.3) 224-25.

35 For the Liechtenstein bust's silver eyes interpreted as an attribute of Alexander the Great: Allison, *Antico* (supra n.1) 55.

36 E.g, A. Romualdi and G. De Marinis, *Itinerario Laurenziano nel Museo Archeologico di Firenze* (Florence 1992) 9, 12, 13, 14: Medici-Riccardi horse protome, Minerva of Arezzo, Idolino, Arringatore, Chimera of Arezzo.

37 Haskell and Penny (supra n.3) 308-10; Bober and Rubenstein (supra n.3) 235-36.

38 Haskell and Penny (supra n.3) 163-64; B. Andreae, *The art of Rome* (New York 1977) 42, fig. 15 (color). See M. Scalini, *L'arte italiana del bronzo, 1000-1700* (Milan 1988) 63 and fig. 248 for the restoration of the "Brutus" into a bust and the possible association of the latter with Ludovico Lombardo.

39 Allison, *Antico* (supra n.1) 231, figs. 194-95.

equestrian statue of Marcus Aurelius, he did not entirely gild the surfaces of his own bronze sculptures. His finest works in bronze subscribe to a variegated jewel-box aesthetic in which their Renaissance patinated surfaces are enhanced by details illuminated in once-gleaming precious metal: shining eyes in silver and bronze, partial gilding for draperies and wreaths on large bronzes and for hair, sandals, and special attributes on small bronzes. A striking contrast of metallic tones may thus be considered Antico's aesthetic signature. The selective coloristic handling of free-standing bronze sculpture, inspired by ancient practices, had not previously been a widespread Renaissance phenomenon.

To conclude: beyond a knowledge of classical texts and marbles, Antico's fabrication of bronze pseudo-antiquities depended on his intense study of real bronze antiquities. Yet, in creating new works comparable to ancient bronzes, Antico actually invented his own distinctive aesthetic. He created opulent visual effects with an economy of means worthy of his masterfully cast bronzes, the likes of which had been unknown since classical antiquity. Antico's resplendent bronzes must literally have been eye-catching apparitions in Renaissance North Italy. They are archaeologically antiquizing in a way Renaissance sculpture usually is not, yet they were conceived neither as simple copies nor as intentional fakes, but rather as objects suitable for display alongside meticulously restored genuine antiquities in courtly humanist settings, like the Grotta of Isabella d'Este.[40]

New York Academy of Art, 111 Franklin Street, New York, NY 10013

Appendix
Observations on the eyes of Antico's bronzes

Beth Cohen and Richard E. Stone

In Renaissance Italy, although oil gilding was common, no convenient metallurgical technique for coating the surface of bronze with silver had as yet been developed. The silver of the eyes on large bronzes by Antico and his workshop (figs. 2-4) consists of thin (*c.*1-2 mm) sheets, cut to shape and mechanically inserted over the cast bronze eyeballs so that they remain in place securely without soldering. The basic technique can be observed in an x-radiograph of the eyes on the bust in the Walters Art Museum (fig. 5),[41] which shows that the whites of the eyes are obviously denser than the pupils — an indication of a layer of silver of an appreciable thickness. Yet there are no signs of air trapped by molten solder (solder-porosity). The edges of each silver sheet were fit into a beveled undercutting running around the eye socket beneath the lid. These thin sheets were then hammered and burnished over the underlying bronze surface. They were generally cut to fit around the diameters of the busts' raised bronze irises (figs. 4-5) or of their recessed bronze pupils (figs. 2-3). Sometimes the outlines of the irises and/or pupils were engraved on the surface of the silver (figs. 2-3).

The recessed pupils on large bronze heads by Antico and his workshop have conical or hemispherical concavities (figs. 2-5); they are often said once to have been inlaid with precious or semiprecious stones.[42] This scenario is unlikely. If they were inlaid with semiprecious stones (rock crystal) or glass paste, these inlays would have been cut in the form of cylinders and inserted into straight-sided, flat-bottomed cavities. Moreover, this method, which gives a good mechanical fit, would need the least amount of adhesive and be consonant with other forms of inlay (cf. *pietra dura*). The later confusion about the conical holes is related to a knowledge of diamond brilliants, which were not yet being cut in the early 1500s.

---

40 *Splendours* (supra n.1) 48, and C. M. Brown and A. M. Lorenzoni, "The Grotta of Isabella d'Este," *GBA* 89 (1977) 155-71 and *GBA* 91 (1978) 72-82. For the Grotta of Isabella d'Este and its contents: *Splendours* (supra n.1) 48; C. Brown, *La grotta di Isabella d'Este: un simbolo di continuità dinastica per i duchi di Mantova* (Mantua 1985) and now also Ferino-Pagden (supra n.1) 145-74, 263-88.

41 B. Cohen would like to thank the following staff members of the Walters Art Museum for their special help: J. Spicer, for permission to study and publish the Baltimore bust; D. K. Strahan, for taking the x-radiograph of the Baltimore bust (fig. 5) and for examining and discussing the sculpture with her; also Q. Gregory, J. Lauffenburger, and E. D. Reeder.

42 For stones or inlays in the pupils, see, e.g., Allison, *Antico* (supra n.1) 231, 233, 234; Sheard (supra n.14) nos. 68-69.

Replication and restoration: ancient bronze techniques and the construction of the figure in cinquecento painting

Leatrice Mendelsohn

"di pezzo in pezzo la figura si forma" (Giorgio Vasari)

Although numerous ancient works were known throughout the Middle Ages, dismembered statues, discovered or rediscovered and identified in the 16th c., exerted renewed influence on painting practice with far-reaching effects on cinquecento style. Despite considerable scholarly interest in Renaissance attitudes toward ancient sculpture, including recent studies documenting collections of antiquities known to Renaissance artists, the influence of ancient bronzes on painting practice has not been studied.[1] Existing studies, concentrating primarily on marble sculpture, focus either on the re-interpretation of motifs or on reconstructions of lost statues based on surviving fragments (e.g., the Belvedere Torso or the Laocöon). The basic assumption of this paper is that methods of sculptural replication and the use of casting by-products in the painting workshop of the cinquecento were crucial for the development of the Maniera style. To this end we shall consider the relationship between the replication of sculptural fragments and the repetition in paintings of a limited corpus of limbs based on them. It is hoped that the observations made here will begin to address the larger question of the intentions behind the quotation of body fragments in cinquecento painting.

In Dolce's 1557 dialogue on painting entitled L'Aretino, "maniera" (style) is defined pejoratively as "[that] in which you constantly see forms and faces resembling one another."[2] This Venetian critique must be read in connection with the definition of "bella maniera" in the 1550 edition of Vasari's *Lives* where "frequently copying the most beautiful things and from those most beautiful hands, heads, bodies, or legs, adding them together to make a figure of as many beauties as are possible, and employing them in every work for all the figures ..." is considered the source of style.[3] In Florentine terms, "maniera" not only justifies repetition but is also one of

---

1 R. Harprath and H. Wrede (edd.), *Antikenzeichnung und Antikenstudium in Renaissance und Frühbarock: Akten des int. Symposion, 1986 Coburg* (Mainz 1989); P. P. Bober and R. Rubinstein, *Renaissance artists and antique sculpture: a handbook of sources* (London 1986); D. Blume, "Zur Technik des Bronzegusses in der Renaissance," in H. Beck and D. Blume (edd.), *Natur und Antike in der Renaissance* (Exhib. cat., Frankfurt am Main 1985) 18-23, ills. 1-11; M. Cristofani, "Per una storia del collezionismo archeologico nella Toscana granducale 1: i grandi bronzi," *Prospettiva* 17 (1979) 4-15; C. De Benedictis, *Per la storia del collezionismo italiano: fonti e documenti* (Florence 1991); A. M. Massinelli (ed.), *Bronzetti e anticaglie dalla guardaroba di Cosimo I* (Florence 1991); A. Nesselrath, "I libri di disegni di antichità, tentativo di una tipologia," in S. Settis (ed.), *Memoria dell'antico nell'arte italiana* 3 (Torino 1986) 87-147; R. Quednau, "'Imitatione d'altrui': Anmerkungen zu Raphaels Verarbeitung entlehnter Motive," in *De arte et libris: Festschrift Erasmus* (Amsterdam 1984) 349-67; S. Danesi Squarzina (ed.), *Roma: centro ideale della cultura dell'antico nei secoli XV e XVI* (Rome 1989) [essays by A. Marino, S. Borsi, A. Uguccioni, G. Schweikhart *et al.*]; and recent catalogues of exhibitions of the Farnese collection.

2 "Dialogo della pittura," in P. Barocchi (ed.), *Trattati d'arte del cinquecento fra manierismo e controriforma* I (Bari 1960) 196. C. H. Smyth, *Mannerism and maniera* (Locust Valley, NY 1962; rev. edn. Vienna 1992) 114 nn. 35 and 44, was the first to connect these criticisms with a definition of *maniera*. Repetition of Michelangelo's poses was for a long time thought to be the source of 'decline' of painting in the cinquecento, but antique sources were rarely mentioned as a criticism or cause of mannerism.

3 See Smyth (supra n.2) 114. "La maniera venne poi la più bella dall'aver messo in uso il frequente ritrarre le cose più belle, e da quel più bello, o mani o teste o corpi o gambe, aggiungnerle insieme e fare una figura di tutte quelle bellezze che più si poteva, e metterla in uso in ogni opera per tutte le figure, che per questo si dice esser bella maniera": in R. Bettarini and P. Barocchi (edd.), *Giorgio Vasari: le vite de' più eccellenti pittori, scultori, e architettori: nelle redazioni del 1550 e 1568* (Florence 1966-87) IV testo.

its distinctive characteristics. By the second decade of the 16th c., figural images repeating formulaic patterns are marked by a heightened exactitude of detail in the hair and the extremities, what Vasari calls "minuzie dei fini".[4] These are given special attention because, for Vasari, beauty is in the details ("in ogni minima cosa").[5] Vasari, and Alberti before him, recommended ancient statues as preferred models, as supplements and even as substitutes for nature.[6] Both authors focus upon the extremities as modules for the creation of proportionally harmonious figures and as conveyors of the aesthetic quality of "grazia" (grace).[7] It is not coincidental that the two most frequently mentioned qualities of the "maniera," repetition and attention to detail, are also characteristics of ancient bronzes.

Still more significant for painters is the discussion of the method of combining separate body parts to make a figure, which forms the core of the definition of style in the *proemio* to Part III of Vasari's *Lives*.[8] This additive method had already been described in the technical introduc-

---

4 The citation follows Vasari's reference to Verrocchio's restoration of an antique Marsyas for the Medici and is part of a contrast he makes between the imitation of antiquity in his own day and quattrocento practitioners: "... mancando loro pure una fine et una estrema perfezzione ne' piedi, mani, capegli, barbe, ancora che il tutto delle membra sia accordato con l'antico et abbia una certa corrispondenza giusta nelle misure; ché s'eglino avessino avuto quelle *minuzie dei fini* che sono la perfezzione et il fiore dell'arte, arebbono avuto ancora, una gagliardezza risoluta nell' opere loro ...": Bettarini and Barocchi (supra n.3) 5. Ettlinger, cited in Smyth (supra n.2) 37 and 122 n.102, believed that this attention to detail stemmed from competition with ancient literary description and was the source of the debate on the "paragone". On the restoration of the Marsyas, see F. Caglioti, "Due 'restauratori' per le antichità dei primi Medici: Mino da Fiesole, Andrea del Verrocchio, e il 'Marsia rozzo' degli Uffizi, Part 1," *Prospettiva* 72 (1993) 17-42; Part 2, *Prospettiva* 73-74 (1994) 74-96.

5 "... aveva bisogna d'una invenzione di tutte le cose e d'una certa bellezza continuata *in ogni minima cosa*" (italics mine): Bettarini and Barocchi (supra n.3) 5; this phrase appears in both editions of the *Lives*.

6 Alberti, *De pictura*, in C. Grayson (ed.), *On painting and On sculpture* (London 1972) 100-1. Unlike Vasari, Alberti cautioned against repeating poses in the same painting (Bk. II, 40).

7 "... in assessing the proportions of a living creature we should take one member of it by which the rest are measured. The architect Vitruvius reckons the height of a man in feet. I think it more suitable if the rest of the limbs are related to the size of the head, although I have observed it to be well-nigh a common fact in men that the length of the foot is the same as the distance from the chin to the top of the head. Having selected this one member, the rest should be accommodated to it, so that there is no member of the whole body that does not correspond with the others in length and breadth .... all the members should fulfil their function according to the action performed, in such a way that not even *the smallest limb* fails to play its appropriate part, ... so that the members of the dead appear dead down to *the smallest detail* and those of the living completely alive ... A picture in which the attitudes and movements of the bodies differ very much among themselves is most pleasing of all." (Bk. I 36, 37: ibid. 74-77, italics mine.)
It is with these phrases in mind that the reader must approach Alberti's emphasis on dimension and finish (*dimensio* and *finitio*) in his later treatise "On sculpture," addressed to painters as well as sculptors. These two "powers", as Alberti calls them, permit the sculptor to "record the outlines and the position and arrangement of the parts of any given body in accurate and absolutely reliable written forms so that ... he can again at will situate and arrange that same body in that very same place in such a way that no part of it, not even the *smallest*, is not placed exactly in space where it ordinarily stood." The purpose of which is: "... *to make something like it of the same size or smaller or a hundred cubits large, or even ... as big as Mount Caucasus* ..."Alberti concludes that "... as in all bodies different forms result from changes in the bending and stretching of limbs and the position of the parts, ... we must treat of the means which enable us to portray these things with constant method and, as I have said, these are: *dimensio* and *finitio*" (*De statua*, ibid. 124-25; italics mine.) Alberti makes clear that modular parts are necessary for replication. Beyond this, he is asserting that all figures must depend on a common system of measurement. It is understood that this system ensures beauty.

8 Barocchi and Bettarini (supra n.3) IV, 3-13. In a review of P. L. Rubin, *Giorgio Vasari: art and history* (New Haven 1995) in the *New York Review of Books*, October 5, 1995, C. Hope proposed that Vasari is not the author of the proemios to the *Lives*. The question of authorship is beyond the scope of this paper, but a change in author would not substantially alter my argument.

tion to Part I where, in both the 1550 and 1568 editions of the *Lives*, contemporary bronze casting procedures were outlined.[9] Writing about both small and large terracotta *models* to be used in casting large-scale figures in metal or bronze, it is stressed that "they must be brought to that perfection which is the result of study and skill."[10] The next step is to make a *gesso* mold from the modello, "part by part".[11] Speaking of the construction of the piece mold, the author says:

> Thus piece by piece the figure is formed and the head, the arms, the torso and the legs, up to the last thing, in such a way that the negative of that statue, that is, the form encased is imprinted into the hollow with all the parts and every minute thing which appears in the *modello*.[12]

While this is a straightforward description of a known process, it cannot be accidental that the same phrases and vocabulary used in the technical *proemio* to Part I are repeated in the theoretical *proemio* to Part III to prove that contemporary artists surpassed antiquity. The importance Vasari gives to body parts in speaking about style may depend on a comparison Quintilian makes, when speaking of 'arrangement' in oratory, between the body and a statue cast in separate parts:

> For the fact that all the limbs of a statue have been cast does not make it a statue: they must be put together; and if you were to interchange some one portion of our bodies or those of other animals with another, although the body would be in possession of all the same members as before, you would none the less have produced a monster ... even a slight dislocation will deprive a limb of its previous use and vigor.[13]

A harmonious 'arrangement of parts' in statuary is therefore comparable to a well-constructed piece of oratory.

A similar parallel can be drawn between the lost-wax process of casting as a reproductive method and the evident repetition of body parts on a limited number of torsos in cinquecento paintings. Paintings which exhibit these stylistic characteristics were most often produced in workshops using assembly-line methods. The figures in these paintings were composed of separate fragments taken from ancient statues. When, in bronze casting, the indirect method is used, then the separate pieces, corresponding to the divisions of the figure in the molds, survive after the molds are used. These surviving pieces could then serve as models for limbs to be attached to a number of antique torso fragments. The results provide the variation of poses Alberti advised. The segmented approach to sculpture translates into a convenient pictorial formula, one with a built-in system of proportion derived from antiquity. Thus, a practical link appears to exist between techniques of ancient bronze casting as they were known and practiced by Renaissance sculptors and the widespread use of ancient fragments in painting workshops.[14]

---

9 Barocchi and Bettarini (supra n.3) I, 96-98.

10 Ibid. I cap. XI: "Come si fanno i modelli per fare di bronzo le figure grandi e picciole" (97 ff.).

11 Ibid. I, 97: "... cominciano poi con gesso da fare presa a formare sopra questo modello parte per parte, facendo addosso a quel modello i cavi d'i pezzi."

12 "... e così di pezzo in pezzo la figura si forma, e la testa, le braccia, il torso e le gambe per fin all'ultima cosa, di maniera che il cavo di quella statua, cioè la forma incavata, viene improntata nel cavo con tutte le parti et *ogni minima cosa* che è nel modello": ibid. I Cap. XI, 97, 11-15, from the *proemio* to Part I. The importance Vasari gives to the wax model was reinforced by its literary use as a metaphor. The conceit of the wax impression appears in Dante's *Commedia* as a metaphor for reproduction, as in *Purgatorio* X.45 and in the proemio to *Paradiso*. The source of this idea is Aristotle's *Nichomachean Ethics*, translated in 1537 by Benedetto Varchi and cited in his "Due Lezzioni" (1549) to which Vasari contributed a letter on the *paragone*. See L. Mendelsohn, *Paragoni: Benedetto Varchi's 'Due Lezzioni' and Cinquecento art theory* (Ann Arbor, MI 1982) Appendix.

13 Quint., *Inst. Or.* 7, *Pr.* 2-1.1 (Loeb transl. H. E. Butler, vol. III, pp. 3-4). Discussing the organization of the points of a legal argument, "arrangement" is defined as "the distribution of things and parts to the places which it is expedient that they should occupy" [7.1.1-4] This would seem to argue against the interchangeability of parts; however, the Renaissance artist would have believed that he was selecting the appropriate parts to re-assemble, as in the case of a piece-mold.

14 The Roman technique of casting bronze in sections and assembling the parts mechanically or by the use of fusion welding was revived in the Renaissance: B. Bearzi, "Le fusioni artistiche in bronzo nell'anti-

The new pictorial aesthetic reflects a desire to incorporate sculptural properties into painting through the emulation of sculptural processes as well as their products.

A veritable corpus of famous fragments known to the Renaissance is repeatedly cited in paintings of the period. Ancient fragments, referred to at the time as "anticaglie",[15] appear in paintings as ostentatiously as any line of Cicero quoted in a Renaissance dialogue.[16] Most renowned were the fragments of destroyed ancient colossi. These were either bronze or thought to derive from Greek bronzes. For both sculptors and painters, the fragment became a synecdoche, useful for mathematically reconstructing the entirety of the original while also signifying the perfection of the lost work.[17] Information about these fragments was disseminated through engravings, Renaissance drawing notebooks, and written descriptions which had survived from antiquity.[18] A drawing by von Heemskerck records the scattered body parts of colossi on the Capitol surrounding the marble statue of Hercules, famous as a copy of a Greek bronze by Lysippos.[19] Another drawing by Francesco da Hollanda documents the colossal bronze hand and head now in the Palazzo dei Conservatori, along with fragments of a marble colossus — a foot, a head, part of an arm, and a hand.[20] Displayed in the Middle Ages outside the Lateran near the globe it was thought to have once held, the bronze hand (fig. 1) was associated with the colossal bronze head (fig. 2), at the time considered a portrait of Commodus or Nero.[21] In the 16th c., the hand was transferred to the Capitol along with other fragments of colossi, where its new setting augments its earlier meaning: the imperial infuses the Christian.[22]

---

chità," *La metallurgia italiana* 2 (1949) 62-66; E. Formigli *et al.*, "Indagini sulle techniche di esecuzione di un torso bronzeo romano dei Musei Vaticani," *Bolletino Musei e Gallerie Pontificie* 10 (1990) 5-24.

15 Vasari's use of the term included architectural fragments as well as body parts (*Vite* 5.81, cited in *Vocabolario degli Accademici della Crusca* 1 [Florence 1863] 546). By 1863, the term was used pejoratively.

16 The parallel between words and limbs is an extension of Quintilian's discussion of rhetorical ornament in the *Inst. Or.* 4.3.2-3. M. Baxandall was among the first to compare texts on rhetoric and texts about images in *Giotto and the orators* (Oxford 1971). Alberti's *Istoria* consisted of bodies, members, and their parts (*De pictura* II.35). Among the ancient texts Baxandall cites (p.103) is the *Imagines* of Philostratus who, in his *proemio*, talks about the relationship between limbs. Baxandall distinguishes clearly between the 15th-c. theorists and those of the cinquecento of whom we speak.

17 On the detached limb as synecdoche, cf. H. W. Janson, "The right arm of Michelangelo's *Moses*," in A. Kosegarten and P. Tigler (edd.), *Festschrift Ulrich Middeldorf* (Berlin 1968) 211-47. On the creative resurrection of the whole based on the evidence of the fragment, see esp. T. M. Greene, "Resurrecting Rome: the double task of the Humanist imagination," in P. A. Ramsey (ed.), *Rome in the Renaissance: the city and the myth* (New York 1982) 41-54, esp. 43, 44, 45.

18 Bober and Rubenstein (supra n.1) App. I, 451-70; Nesselrath (supra n.1) 87-147.

19 Bober and Rubenstein (supra n.1) 164-65, 216-17, figs. 129a, 130. On Heemskerck, see E. Filippi, *Maarten van Heemskerck: Inventio urbis* (Milan 1990). On the Resting Hercules, see M. G. Barbarini, "Reflessioni sulla fortuna dell'Ercole Farnese nella scultura dal XVI-XIX secolo," in P. Moreno (ed.), *Lisippo: l'arte e la fortuna* (Exhib. cat., Rome 1995) 440-47.

20 Bober and Rubenstein (supra n.1) 216-17, figs. 183, 183a (de Hollanda). See also the illustrated *Codex Escurialensis*: H. Egger, *Codex Escurialensis. Ein Skizzenbuch aus der Werkstatt Domenico Ghirlandaios* (Vienna 1905-6) L.5, 15,f.31v, showing a colossal hand holding a globe and a colossal head, both exhibited on columns. The bronze head was originally displayed in this way at the Lateran.

21 Rome, Palazzo dei Conservatori, Sala dei Bronzi 2; Head 0.77 m; l. left hand 1.5 m; globe 0.76 m. The globe was at one time placed on top of an obelisk. Cf. Vasari, *Vite* (supra n.3) II, 798. On the identification as Nero, see below n.34. The portrait has more recently been considered Constans I: H. Stuart Jones (ed.), *A catalogue of the ancient sculptures preserved in the municipal collections of Rome: the sculptures of the Palazzo dei Conservatori* (Oxford 1926) 173, no. 7, pl. 60. For other identifications, see M. Winner, *Zeichner sehen die Antike: Europäische Handzeichnungen 1450-1800* (Exhib. cat., Berlin-Dahlem 1967) vol. 2, pl. 1; K. Fittschen and P. Zanker, *Katalog der römischen Porträts in den Capitolischen Museen und der anderen Kommunalen Sammlungen der Stadt Rom 1: Kaiser- und Prinzenbildnisse* (Mainz 1985) 152-55, no. 123, pls. 153-54 (Constantine?); *Da Pisanello alla nascita dei Musei Capitolini: l'antico a Roma àlla vigilia del Rinascimento* (Exhib. cat., Milan 1988) no. 67, 218 ff.

22 The hand and globe together signified not only Sol Justiciae or Regisole but also Roma Caput Mundi: see

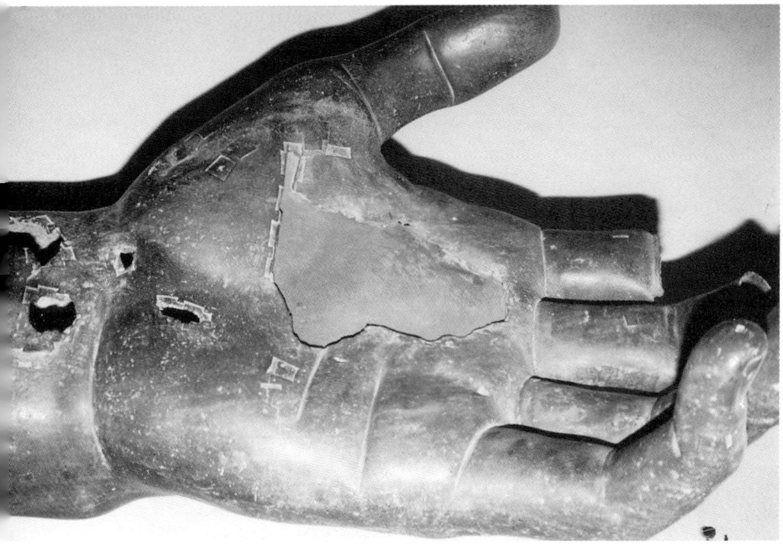

Fig. 1. Colossal left hand. Bronze, h. 1.50 m. Rome, Palazzo dei Conservatori, Sala dei Bronzi 2 inv. 1070. (Photo: E. Gabbai)

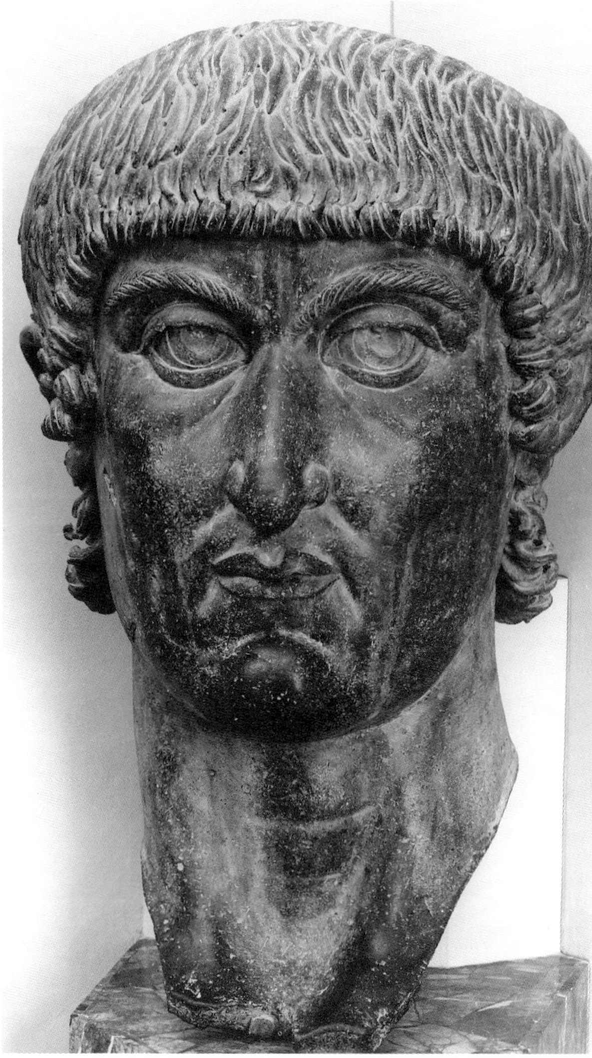

Fig. 2. Colossal head. Bronze, h. 0.77 m. Rome, Palazzo dei Conservatori, Sala dei Bronzi 2 inv. 1072. (Photo: A. Bracchetti; courtesy Museum)

The colossal hand and head appear in both Renaissance painting and sculpture. The bronze head provides the basic construct for the formation of the ruler portrait-type. Signs of its influence are clearly visible in Andrea del Verrocchio's equestrian portrait of Bartolomeo Colleoni in the 15th c. and in Benvenuto Cellini's bronze bust of Cosimo I de' Medici in the 16th c.;[23] both evoke the imperial ruler in the telling details of the eyes and eyebrows. A Chatsworth drawing of Pope Leo X by Giulio Romano superimposes the qualities of a colossal statue on a contemporary papal persona.[24] Though transformed, the fragment retains references to its antique meaning in its new pictorial context, however altered by intervening works.

A. Marino, "Idoli e colossi: la statuaria antica sulla piazza del Campidoglio da Sisto IV a Leone X," in Danesi Squarzina (supra n.1) 237-47.

23 Illustrated in J. Pope-Hennessey, *Cellini* (New York 1985) pls. 117-19, the last showing the details of the eyes and eyebrows. The influence of the bronze head as a model must also have been felt in Michelangelo's destroyed colossal bronze of Julius II in Bologna.

24 Inv. 38: M. Jaffé, *A great heritage: Renaissance and Baroque drawings from Chatsworth* (Exhib. cat., New York 1995). According to Jaffé, it was J. Shearman who suggested that it was originally intended for the colossal statue of Leo X commissioned by the Conservatori (now in Sta. Maria in Cosmedin). The drawing has at different times been attributed to Michelangelo, Sebastiano del Piombo, and Raphael. It

Compared to those in marble, the number of ancient works in bronze available to Renaissance artists was relatively small. Possibly their very rarity was a factor in the estimate of the high value of bronze statues. Pliny had emphasized the high esteem in which they were held in antiquity, in part because of the material value of bronze, in part because of the skill necessary for their production, but also because of their sheer size, durability, and most of all their beauty. However, the very scarcity of surviving examples caused the durability of bronze with respect to marble to play a lesser rôle in its valuation during the Renaissance than it had in antiquity.[25] Michelangelo saw one of his two known bronzes, the colossal statue of Julius II, melted down to make a cannon, while the other, a David, is entirely lost.[26] A desire to produce works of colossal size equaling those of antiquity, largely in bronze, was stimulated by the desire of Medici patrons in both Rome and Florence to validate their Etruscan ancestry.[27] This revival of bronze statuary was given new impetus by the discoveries of two bronzes statues. In 1530, a bronze statue of a youth known as the Idolino was unearthed in Pesaro; in 1552, in Arezzo, the bronze Chimera, a hybrid monster, was immediately identified as Etruscan and restored by the Medici.[28] The Idolino was actually found in pieces and was heavily restored. Thus, although it has been referred to as of Early Imperial style, it is probably either "a learned classicistic re-elaboration from the Augustan period ... or a classical archetype ... or a Late

---

is of some interest that the statue of the Chimera was notably placed in the Sala di Leo X of the Palazzo Vecchio, as explained by Vasari in the *Raggionamenti*, not only because of its Leonine appearance but also for its reference to Tuscan–Etruscan Medici origins.

25 *NH* 34.40-41 (and most of all for its beauty).

26 The colossal bronze seated portrait of Julius probably resembled the later Moses and was, I believe, based upon the remains of a marble statue of Zeus, now divided in two, one half in the Vatican Museums, the other in the Museo Nazionale Archeologico, Naples. The surviving pieces reflect an original described by Pliny. The same source must have inspired Michelangelo's seated Dukes in the Medici Chapel in Florence. The lost bronze David sent to France is discussed in F. Cagliotti, "Il David bronzeo di Michelangelo," in *Ad Alessandro Conti* (Pisa 1996) 85 ff.; and id., "Il perduto 'David Mediceo' di Giovanfrancesco Rustici e il 'David' Pulszky del Louvre," *Prospettiva* 83-84 (July-Oct. 1996) 80-101 (n.9 for bibliography on the Michelangelo). The lost Sleeping Cupid, executed in marble, was described by Paolo Giovio and Michelangelo's biographer Condivi in 1553 as "un Dio d'Amore, d'eta di sei anni in sette, a giacere in guisa d'uom che dorma"; the many existing marble copies reflect an original in marble but undoubtedly based on an ancient bronze similar to one now in the Metropolitan Museum of Art (Greek, 3rd-2nd c. B.C.; Rogers Fund, 1943, 43.11.4). For bibliography, see P. Barocchi (ed.), *Giorgio Vasari: la vita di Michelangelo* (Milan 1962) I 16, 15; II 144-45 n.126; IV 2098; G Agosti and V. Farinelli (edd.), *Michelangelo e l'arte classica* (Exhib. cat., Florence 1987) 43-47; on the variants: M. Hirst, *The young Michelangelo* (Exhib. cat., London 1994) 24-28; H. and A. S. Wohl (edd.), *The life of Michelangelo by Ascanio Condivi* (Baton Rouge 1976) 127 n.31.

27 Pliny, *NH* 35.43, 152. See G. Cipriani, "Il mito etrusco nella Firenze repubblicana e medicea nei secoli XV e XVI," in *Ricerche storiche* 5 (1975) 257-309; S. Bertelli, "Egemonia linguistica come egemonia culturale e politica nella Firenze cosimiana," *Bibliothèque d'humanisme et renaissance* 38 (1976) 249-383 and the discussion in Cristofani (supra n.1).

28 "Mandarmi anche la chimera, con quelle lettere Hetrusche et anche di tale inscriptioni se costi se ne trovano ovvero nel regno delli vostri padroni, ch'io vi prometto": an excerpt from the 1570s correspondence of Jacopo Strada and Jacopo Dani, secretary to Cosimo I in 1573-74, cited by R. O. Rubenstein, "A codex from Dosio's circle (BNCF NA 1159) in its mid-sixteenth-century context," in *Antikenzeichnung* (supra n.1) 12. The Chimera was found "fuori Pa. S. Laurentino" along with other "anticaglie" and, as Cellini wrote, "una quantità di piccole statuette"; it was brought immediately to the Palazzo della Signoria. It is usually said, but without documentation, that the restoration of the tail and two feet on the left side was the work of Cellini: A. Del Vita, "Dove fu trovata la Chimera di Arezzo?" *RömMitt* 25 (1910) 293-97. The important documents are presented in Cristofani (supra n.1), whose dates I use. He identifies at least 20 bronzes now in the Museo Archeologico, Florence, with those recorded in the Medici inventory of 1589, exhibited in the Tribuna of the Uffizi by Francesco I de' Medici. For additional bibliography, see Pope-Hennessey (supra n.23) 225 n.26. Both the Chimera and the Arringatore are discussed by B. S. Ridgway, "Roman bronze statuary — beyond technology," in *The fire of Hephaistos* 125-26.

Hellenistic eclectic invention."[29] In the words of L. Beschi, the Idolino does not present a "typical problem of a copy" but rather is the result of "a process of eclectic construction".[30] The Chimera and Idolino were restored according to cinquecento taste: the Idolino under the supervision of Girolamo Genga (architect and painter), the Chimera by Benvenuto Cellini (sculptor), artists who were not primarily restorers but whose works influenced painting style.[31] The Chimera and the Idolino (both found in the 1530s) are now displayed in the Museo Archeologico, Florence, along with two other major bronzes from the Medici collection: the Minerva (found in 1541) and the Arringatore (found in 1556, acquired in 1566). The discovery of so many large bronzes in the mid cinquecento cannot have been entirely accidental; the finds must have been due to a deliberate campaign of archaeological digs. The documents concerning their discovery indicate that bronzes held a special place in Medici collections and were prized for different reasons than marble statues. The Idolino and the Chimera became instant models for painters, exemplifying the skill of ancient "bronzisti".[32] If the Idolino became a model of ideal proportions, the Chimera signified deviation from the norm, artistic freedom (*fantasia*). Both stylistic modes — the canonical and the inventive — were associated in the Renaissance with ancient bronzework. Even though marble was the preferred medium (in large part because of Michelangelo's influence), greater exactitude in the superimposition of detail upon idealized forms made bronze rather than marble the sculptural model of choice for many Renaissance painters. This dual and often contradictory skill was identified most with the sculptor Lysippos, about whom Pliny wrote:

> Lysippos is said to have contributed greatly to the art of bronze statuary by representing the details of the hair and by making his heads smaller than the old sculptors used to do, and his bodies more slender and firm, to give his statues the appearance of greater height. He scrupulously preserved the quality of 'symmetry' (for which there is no word in Latin) ... and he used commonly to say that, whereas his predecessors had made men as they really were, he made them as they appeared to be. A peculiarity of this sculptor's work seems to be the minute finish maintained in even *the smallest details*.[33]

In the cinquecento, sculptural models begin to take precedence over the human in the construction of painted figures. The use of models in painting workshops was conveniently appropriated from sculptors, especially in cases where a single shop dealt in multiple media. While Michelangelo is known to have preferred marble over bronze for both aesthetic and philosophical reasons, he also made terracotta models that were highly prized. Their appreciation may be due to Pliny, who singled out for its remarkable likeness the preparatory clay model for the colossal bronze statue of Nero by Zenodorus.[34] Michelangelo's contemporaries preserved his preparatory models (*bozzetti*) in wax and terracotta, later casting some of them in bronze — for

---

29 "... [U]n processo di construzione eclettico," quoted on p. 16 of L. Beschi, "L'Idolino: storia, critica, fortuna," in M. Iozzo (ed.), '... *Qual era tutto rotto': l'enigma dell'Idolino di Pesaro, indagine per un restauro* (Exhib. Cat., Florence 1999) 7-19. Based on chemical analysis, the right hand through the wrist, the right leg almost to the knee, and the left foot and inner thigh are demonstrably Renaissance additions. See the diagrams in Iozzo ibid. pp. 90, 91, 95.

30 Ibid. 16.

31 As Beschi notes, it is difficult to discover a single ancient model for the Idolino. Probably the missing parts were based on a combination of fragments. The similarity of the replaced left hand to the left hand of Michelangelo's marble David as well as its similarity to a wax model attributed to him now in the Casa Buonarroti, leads one to speculate on the impact of cinquecento sculptural style on incomplete antiquities. Michelangelo's reputation as "equal to the ancients" permitted the limbs of his statues to be substituted for missing parts of works such as the Idolino.

32 On the Idolino as a model for painters, see C. H. Smyth, who speaks of Bronzino's "predilection for neo-Greek ideals" in *Bronzino as draughtsman: an introduction* (Locust Valley, NY 1971) 56 n.39; figs. 6-7. The notion of the statue's 'Greekness' was perpetuated by the inscription on it composed by Pietro Bembo, suggesting it was Delian.

33 *NH* 34.65 ff. (italics mine).

34 *NH* 34.46. On possible identification of this statue with the Capitoline bronze Head, see supra n.21.

example, an unexecuted river god intended for the New Sacristy Tombs.[35] Terracotta and bronze replicas of body parts from other statues in the Chapel survive in collections of the Casa Buonarroti (Florence), the Victoria and Albert Museum, and elsewhere.

Preparatory models used for marble sculpting, however, should not be confused with casting models. Lost-wax casting permits replication of like statues in bronze, with or without variations, using the master mold taken from an original model.[36] Re-use of a basic model with adaptive variations is possible when the indirect casting technique is employed.[37] In these cases, the *modello* in wax or terracotta may therefore be considered the original. A small-scale model in bronze for the 16th c. statue of Perseus by Cellini was probably cast after a surviving wax model as a test, but the full-size final cast was probably done using the direct lost-wax casting process, and for this we have no *modello*.[38] Along with Cellini's writings, these examples provide additional information about Renaissance casting methods.[39] In her study of classical bronzes, C. Mattusch promotes the idea of mass-production of figures facilitated by the lost-wax process.[40] Regardless of whether the lost-wax casting was direct or indirect, and in spite of a tendency for major bronze monuments made in Florence to be cast in one piece, influence of the Roman method of assembling separately cast segments of large-scale statues, a method revived in the Renaissance, was unquestionably felt in the conception of the painted figure.[41] The depiction of the human body as a construct of parts results from the influence of casting methods on painters, especially piece-molds and their by-products.

---

35 Preserved because they were thought to reflect the hand of the master, not all of these surviving models are actually by Michelangelo; some are casts taken from copies or rejected *bozzetti*. A waxed terracotta model attributed to Michelangelo, now in the Victoria and Albert Museum, and the river god, now in the Casa Buonarroti, appear to be original *bozzetti* (rather than casts). A *bozzetto* must, however, be distinguished from the final *modello* from which the mold was made: see C. Avery, "'La cera sempre aspetti': wax sketch models for sculpture," *Apollo* 119 (1984) 166-76. Bibliography on Michelangelo's models is scarce and outdated: L. Goldscheider, *A survey of Michelangelo's models in wax and clay* (London 1962), remains the major source, supplemented by an article by I. Lavin, "*Bozzetti* and *modelli*: notes on sculptural procedure from the early Renaissance through Bernini," in *Stil und Überlieferung in der Kunst des Abendlandes* [Akten des 21. Int.. Kongresses für Kunstgeschichte, Bonn1963] 3 (Berlin 1967) 93-103. These early overviews are updated in P. D. Weil, *Bozzetto-modello: form and function in Orfeo Boseli, Osservazioni della scoltura antica* (Diss., Florence 1978) 113-34. A Ph.D. dissertation on the subject of sculptor's models has recently been completed by J. O'Grody (Case Western Reserve Univ. 1999).

36 R. E. Stone, "Antico and the development of bronze casting in Italy at the end of the Quattrocento," *BMMA* 16 (1982) 87-116 and Blume (supra n.1).

37 Stone ibid. 94 ff. and Blume (supra n.1). At the same time, a cautionary word is in order. Stone (pers comm. 1997) believes we have "no evidence of 'indirect' casting in Florence" and no surviving casting models from its use. Bronzes which formerly were thought to be made using 'indirect' methods should be reconsidered as 'direct'. When speaking of small-scale bronzes, however, especially those from Mantuan and Paduan workshops, Stone points out the importance of the use of piece-molds and separate castings: R. E. Stone, "Technical note," in B. F. Davidson, *Severo and the sea-monsters* (New York 1997) 29-31.

38 Now in the Victoria and Albert Museum; R. Stone, pers. comm. 1997. Cf. Cagliotti (supra n.26) 83-84, figs. 1, 4, 9, 14, 19, 22 for the Louvre bronze after a *bozzetto* attributed to F. Rustici rather than Michelangelo.

39 B. Cellini, "The treatise on sculpture," in C. R. Ashbee (transl.), *The treatises of Benvenuto Cellini on goldsmithing and sculpture* (New York 1898; 1967) 114-18, on the model; G. Somigli, *Notizie storiche sulla fusione del Perseo* (Milan 1958). The Perseus, however, was cast in one piece.

40 *Classical bronzes* 129-39 and 18-19. On bronze technique, see ead., "The preferred medium: the many lives of classical bronzes," in *The fire of Hephaistos* 20-26, fig. 3, 22-23.

41 Although the attachment of the leg of Holofernes in Donatello's *Judith* has been shown not to have been cast separately, the cast was made in stages from body parts *modeled* separately: M. Leoni, "Considerazioni sulla fonderia d'arte ai tempi di Donatello: aspetti technici del gruppo della Giuditta," in L. Dolcini (ed.), *Donatello e il restauro della Giuditta* (Exhib. cat., Florence 1988) 54-57. See photographic details in L. Dolcini (ed.), *Verrocchio's Christ and St. Thomas* (Exhib. cat., New York 1993) 98.

According to Radcliffe, it was only after the mid-16th c. that sculptors' models were systematically preserved.[42] Significantly, this new habit approximately coincides with the criticisms of painters based on their excessive use of repetitive poses.[43] The increase in the value of models in wax and clay at this time may be due, in part, to the contemporaneous re-use of casting models for the replication and restoration of marbles. In the cinquecento, it was considered necessary to render whole any sculptural fragments to be placed on view, and techniques used to restore both marble and bronze statues necessarily involved the replication of ancient fragments.[44] Body parts could be replicated by taking casts from original bronze or marble fragments.[45] The technique of taking plaster casts from ancient bronzes is mentioned by Pliny,[46] and casts of the 1st c. A.D. from Baiae provide concrete evidence of this practice.[47] Casting from bronze was revived in the 16th c. by Primaticcio who copied marble antiquities for François I.[48] As a technique, it was more appropriate for replicating bronzes in bronze than for copying marble statues in bronze.[49] In addition to serving as models, Roman marbles were often used as direct replacements in restorations, but it was usually easier to attach a *gesso* or stucco copy covered with marble dust[50] than to replace a missing limb with a marble.[51] The reproduction of limbs to restore missing parts of antiquities must have contributed to the ubiquity of fragments.

---

42 "The model and the marble in the Renaissance" and "Multiple production in the fifteenth century: Florentine stucco Madonnas and the della Robbia workshop," in A. Radcliffe *et al.*, *The Thyssen-Bornemisza collection: Renaissance and later sculpture: with works of art in bronze* (London 1992) 10-15, 16-23. Full-scale models of wax and terra-secca used in sculpture workshops exist from the late quattrocento, but contemporary documents on the use of models for carving large-scale sculpture are rare and few have survived. On this, see J. Myssok, "Bildhauerische Konzeption und plastisches Modell in der italienischen Skulptur des Quattro- und Cinquecento," in *Kunstchronik* (July 1998) 7, pls. 317-21.

43 Dolce, "Dialogo della pittura," in Barocchi (supra n.2) I, 196 and Smyth (supra n.2) 115 nn. 35 and 36, 121 nn. 89 and 98. For criticism of Perugino by Vasari for the same flaws: ibid. 114 n.35.

44 On sculpture restoration in the cinquecento, see L. Dolcini, "Per una storia del restauro delle sculture, posizioni teoriche fra XVI e XIX secolo," *Quaderni dell'Opificio delle Pietre Dure e Laboratori di Restauro di Firenze: restauro del marmo; opere e problemi* (Florence 1986) 12-16.

45 For discussion of marble restoration techniques in a manuscript of 1650 (Rome, Biblioteca Corsiniana, Vetus n.1391 coll. 36F 27), see Weil (supra n.35); Vasari, "Life of G. della Porta," in Bettarini and Barocchi (supra n.3).

46 *NH* 35.153, referring to Lysistratos of Sikyon, the brother of Lysippos, who 'invented a method of molding copies from statues.'

47 On the Baiae casts: C. Landwehr, *Die antiken Gipsabgüsse aus Baiae* (Berlin 1985) and Ridgway (supra n.28) 122-37.

48 See Vasari as in n.19 and F. Haskell and N. Penny, *Taste and the antique: the lure of classical sculpture, 1500-1900* (New Haven 1981) 1-6; J. Montagu, *Roman baroque sculpture: the industry of art* (New Haven–London 1989) 151-72, esp. 161-62. Some replicas were cast from copies rather than being taken from the originals. This was certainly the case with small-scale replicas. An example of a cast copy, hollow but weighted, is the *Spinario* by A. Gagini, executed in Messina in 1500 and now in the Metropolitan Museum of Art (inv. 32.121). My attention was drawn to this work by S. Settis. On Primaticcio's casts, see J. Cox-Rearick, *Royal treasures: the collection of Francis I* (New York 1995) 319-54.

49 Surviving bronze replicas made in the Renaissance are rare. One example is the standing male known as the *Magdalensberg Youth*, now in the Kunsthistorisches Museum, Vienna, a 16th-c. cast after a Roman original found in 1502 (inv. VI 1; h. 1.835 m). That this statue was Renaissance rather than ancient was discovered only in 1983. The Renaissance cast was made in one piece. The statue bears a strong resemblance to the Idolino: A. Bernhard-Walcher *et al.* (edd.), *Meisterwerke aus der Antikensammlung des Kunsthistorischen Museums in Wien* cat. 15, fig. 54; 38.

50 Dolcini (supra n.44) 13.

51 Restoration in the 16th c. is not as well documented as in later periods. On those by Lorenzetto for the gardens of Cardinal della Valle, see Vasari (*Le Vite* (G. Milanese [ed.], Florence 1906) 579: "... e di sopra nelle dette nichie pose alcune statue pur antiche e di marmo, le quali sebbene non erano entere per essere quale senza testa quale senza braccia, ed alcuna senza gambe, ed insomma ciascuna con qualche cosa meno, l'accomodò nondimeno benissimo, avendo fatto rifare a buoni scultori tutto quello che

Evidence of the influence of bronze-casting techniques on painting is found in two kinds of testimony. The first, as we have seen, comes from ancient and Renaissance literary sources. The second is the visual evidence of drawings made after antique fragments. Of the two methods of recording antiquities, the literary is the more reliable. Although drawings are visually more convincing, the interpreter must exercise caution since it is difficult to detect falsification. Ancient fragments copied in notebooks composed for diverse motives often re-appear as complete statues in the preparatory drawings of painters; subsequently, in the final pictorial execution, the fragments are absorbed into the finished figure. Drawings of incomplete or damaged antiquities more accurately reveal workshop practices precisely because they permit us to recognize the fragments. Their ostentatious assemblage derives, then, not from theory but from the painter's workshop use of *gesso*, terracotta, wax, or bronze fragments.

Gian Giorgio Trissino's *I ritratti*, published in Rome in 1524, and Lucian's *Eikones*, on which it depends, advises the use of sculptural models for assembling images of perfect female beauty.[52] Lucian's description of how to make a portrait of Panthea, a beautiful courtesan, reverses the method traditionally attributed to Zeuxis, who derived his ideal image from the 'best parts of five Crotonian women'. Panthea's body is made, instead, from the body parts of five famous Greek statues:

> ... the hands, the graceful wrists, and the supple tapering of the fingers shall come from Our Lady in the Gardens, an Aphrodite by Alcamenes.[53]
>
> ... from them all I shall make a combination as best I can and shall display to you a single "icon" that comprises whatever is most exquisite in each ... combine and unite them as harmoniously as possible, retaining at the same time that composite effect and the variety.[54]

Unlike sculpture, an impression of unity can easily be achieved in painting even though parts from different statues are assembled to form a new whole. Nevertheless, in many *maniera* paintings, body parts remain visibly distinct and separable. Their very separateness recalls each limb's prior function and encourages the viewer to recall its former context. The recognition of a citation depends on memory reinforced by repetition. Two engravings depicting Bandinelli's workshop in Rome as recorded by Aneas Vico and Agostino Veneziano[55] tell us that three-dimensional *modelli* were drawn by masters and their students from a variety of different positions.[56] Constant drawing to reinforce memory was suggested by Vasari as an aid to the painter

---

mancava." On Cellini's restorations: A. Conti, *Storia del restauro e della conservazione delle opere d'arte* (Milan 1988) 32-42.

52 Lucian's description, utilized by Boccaccio, appears in his *Essays in portraiture* (transl. A. M. Harmon, Loeb edn. vol. 4, 257-95). See E. Mattioli, *Luciano e l'umanesimo* (Naples 1980) and W. Hirdt, *Gian Giorgio Trissinos Porträt der Isabella d'Este: ein Beitrag zur Lukian-Rezeption in Italien* (Heidelberg 1981). Firenzuola, writing on women's beauty in the 16th c., needed only four women from whom to extract his ideal parts. Addressing specific women living in Prato in the mid 16th c., and citing ancient authorities such as Homer, Cicero, and Livy, as well as modern authors, he explains: "I will take from each one of the four of you and do as Zeuxis .... The magnificent M. Giovan Giorgio Trissino probably learned portraiture from the same Zeuxis or from Lucian, who created his beautiful woman from the many beautiful parts he gathered from the best statues of the most renowned sculptors of his day. In the same way I will try to make from four beautiful women a perfect beauty" (from Agnolo Firenzuola, "Dialogo ... delle bellezze delle donne," in L. Scala and L. Domenichi [edd.], *Prose* [Florence 1548] I, 56r-108v; cf. K. Eisenbichler and J. Murray [edd.], *On the beauty of women* [Philadelphia 1992] 13ff.)

53 Lucian, *Essays* (ibid.) 267-68, identified by the editor with the Roman *Venus Genetrix.*

54 *Ikones* 5-6, 267. Lucian considers the statue created to be a portrait of her body alone, not her soul.

55 Both prints represent drawing students in a workshop setting and both depend on a drawing by Bandinelli. The Vico inscription reads *Baccius Bandinellus invent., Enea Vigo Parmegiano Sculpsit* and *Accademia 1531* (Rome, Gabinetto delle Stampe, Gabinetto Fotografico Nazionale E53569). See J. Spike (ed.), *The illustrated Bartsch* 30 (New York 1985) 68-69. See also the engraved self-portrait of Bandinelli of 1548 with small-scale models around him. On Bandinelli's bronzes and the engraving, see Massinelli (supra n.1) 43-50, figs. 34-37.

56 It is not possible to determine the materials of the statuettes in the engraving, but they resemble the small-

who, like the restorer, required a repertoire of limbs to provide spare parts for incomplete bodies. Methods for acquiring such a repertoire were derived from rhetorical practice.[57]

Drawings from the Renaissance document the stages of a similar transformation from the sculptural to the pictorial. Such drawings served a wide variety of purposes — from recording and documenting antiquities to testing hypothetical re-creations of lost works to playfully recombining body parts, up to and including their final re-assembly into finished, painted figures. A silverpoint drawing *c.*1500 of a female torso based on an incomplete statue of a Venus type, attributed to Francesco Granacci, shares the page with a detailed drawing of a hand (fig. 3).[58] That incomplete female torsos were completed in drawings and paintings from the 15th c. on is self-evident. In this drawing, a torso, probably from the Medici collection, provides the raw armature onto which a variety of arms and legs in different poses could be attached. The torso represented in the Granacci drawing can be found repeated in drawings by other artists, in small statuettes, and in paintings where it is re-united with its lost members (or, as in the case of restored statues, with members not originally meant for it). What appears to be a reduced *gesso*, probably cast from a mutilated marble in the Medici collection (perhaps the very example in the Granacci drawing), can be seen in the background of a portrait of Cosimo I de' Medici by Agnolo Bronzino, now in Ottawa (fig. 4).[59]

The isolated hand on the Granacci sheet to the left of the torso is instructive; it depends on a type known from Greek bronzes, for example, the hand of the bronze youth (fig. 5) in the Metropolitan Museum of Art. That a similar bronze hand was known to Florentine artists in the 15th c. is attested to by its similarity to the hand of Donatello's Amorino-Atys, dependent in its form and technique on an ancient bronze.[60] This hand, with its raised index and little fingers, is found in numerous Quattrocento paintings and drawing notebooks of the period. By the second quarter of the 16th c., this type of hand is supplanted by a more robust type, closer to Roman marble fragments but also to Michelangelo, who by then is as a mediator for antiquity.[61]

---

scale bronze copies of ancient works made in the Renaissance as well as descriptions of small figurines found during Renaissance excavations. The limb fragments in the engraved 'studio' could have been either *gesso* or marble but may have also occasionally have been bronze: Massinelli (supra n.1) figs. 34-35.

57 Quintilian was cited on this subject by Erasmus in *De copia* (i.1.4,9): "Once we have carefully committed the theory of memory, we should frequently take a group of sentences and deliberately set out to express each of them in as many versions as possible, as Quintilian advises, using the analogy of a piece of wax which can be moulded into one shape after another ... We shall find it particularly useful to '*thumb the great authors by night and day*' especially those who were outstanding in the rich style, such as Cicero, Aulus Gellius, and Apulius. We must keep our eyes open to observe every figure of speech that they use, store it in our memory once observed, imitate it once remembered, and by constant employment develop an expertise which we may call upon instantly." (Italics: author.)

58 See the discussion of this drawing in *Il giardino di San Marco: maestri e compagni del giovane Michelangelo* (Exhib. cat., Florence 1992) cat. 9: Florence, Gabinetto dei Disegni e delle Stampe degli Uffizi 190E, 47-48: "Studio da una statua antica di Venere" (Andrea De Marchi).

59 I would like to thank K. Johnston (Museum of Fine Arts of Canada) for allowing me to examine the painting after its cleaning and for providing access to archival files.

60 The most recent discussion of the statue is found in A. Rosenauer, *Donatello* (Milan 1993) 179, cat. 42 with bibliography. The drawing of an isolated hand on the same sheet as Bronzino's drawing of the Christ Child (Smyth, *Bronzino* [supra n.32]) depends on a bronze similar to the one used as a model for the Atys's left hand of Donatello's *Atys*.

61 Compare, for example, the frequently illustrated late 15th-c. page of hands sometimes attributed to Leonardo da Vinci (Windsor RL 12615 and 12616) with a page by Francesco Morandini: Gabinetto dei Disegni e delle Stampe degli Uffizi, Florence n. 4279F, one of a group of pages probably once belonging to a notebook called "Studies from the sixteenth century and the antique," in A. Giovanetti (ed.), *Francesco Morandini detto Il Poppi: i disegni, i dipinti di Poppi e Castiglion Fiorentino* (Florence 1995) 36, cat. 40.

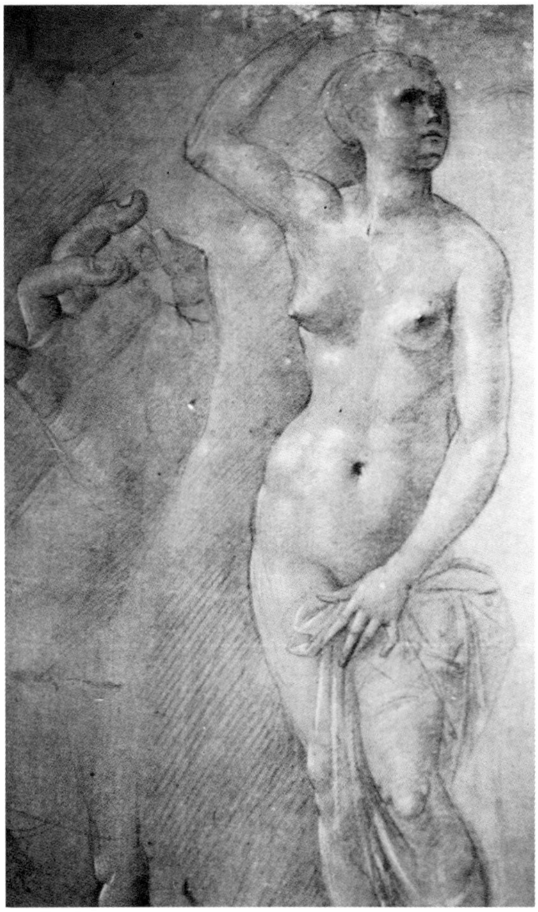

Fig. 3. Francesco Granacci, Study of an antique statue of Venus, *c.* 1500. Silver point, white highlighting, prepared paper salmon tinted, 275 x 192 mm. Florence, Gabinetto dei Disegni e delle Stampe degli Uffizi 190E. (Photo: courtesy Soprintendenza dei Beni Artistici, Florence)

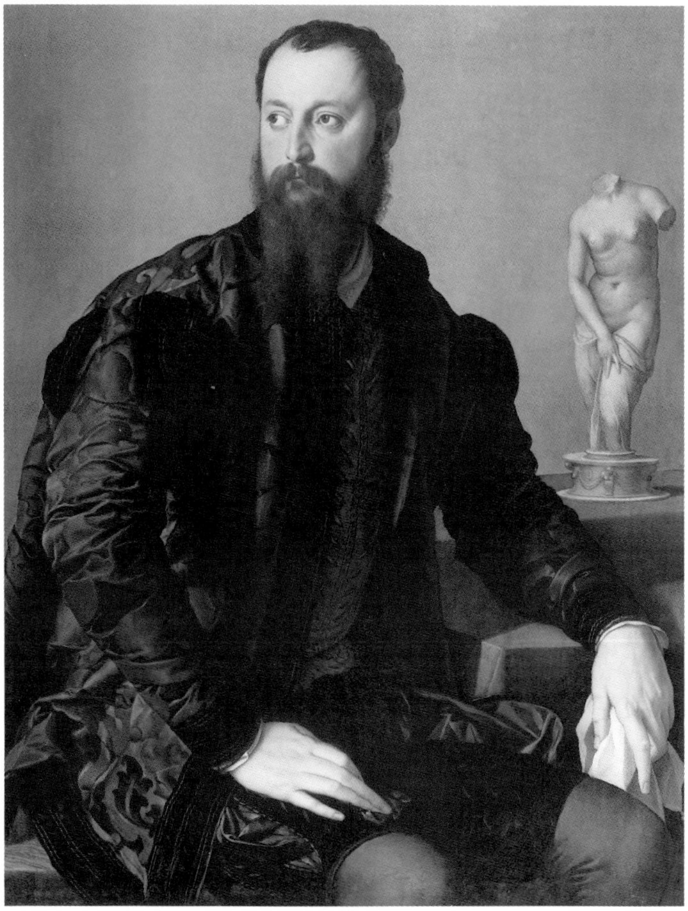

Fig. 4. Agnolo Bronzino, Portrait of a gentleman (detail of statue), 1550-55. Oil on panel, 115 x 83 cm. (Photo: courtesy National Museum of Fine Arts, Ottawa)

Use of three-dimensional sculptural fragments by 16th-c. painters is most evident in drawings by Francesco Morandini, known as Il Poppi (fig. 6).[62] Sheets of Poppi's drawings, apparently used as workshop patterns, depend on a limited repertoire of body parts. How the drawings functioned is immediately apparent when they are compared with his finished paintings. As a less than major painter whose works imitate the styles of artists such as Beccafumi and Rosso Fiorentino, Poppi's drawings enable us to visualize the mechanics of a mid 16th-c. *bottega*, uncontaminated by the anomalies of a genius or innovator. Drawings of feet, heads, and hands appear isolated in groups, viewed from different perspectives, from which the painter could select those appropriate for his painted subjects.[63] Clearly, this piecemeal method was not invented by Poppi. But while this technique is noticeable in earlier Florentine paintings, the ostentatious citation from antiquity is not.[64] In the paintings of Bronzino, especi-

62 Giovannetti ibid. fig. 25 (where the model is clearly a hollow cast), fig. 32 (where the statue's broken limbs are completed), fig. 40 (studies of hands apparently taken from Michelangelo's sculpture in the New Sacristy but ultimately based on antique fragments).

63 Ibid. figs. 39 hands; 40, 41, 90 feet; 25-28, 81-86 heads; 89 leg. Interestingly, arms are shown as fragments attached to torsos but not isolated.

64 R. Lieberman pointed out to me the detachment of hands from arms in Andrea Castagno's fresco of the *Last Judgment* in Sant' Apollonia, Florence. The pictorial technique of applying hands separately was common in the quattrocento and its effects are not always harmonious.

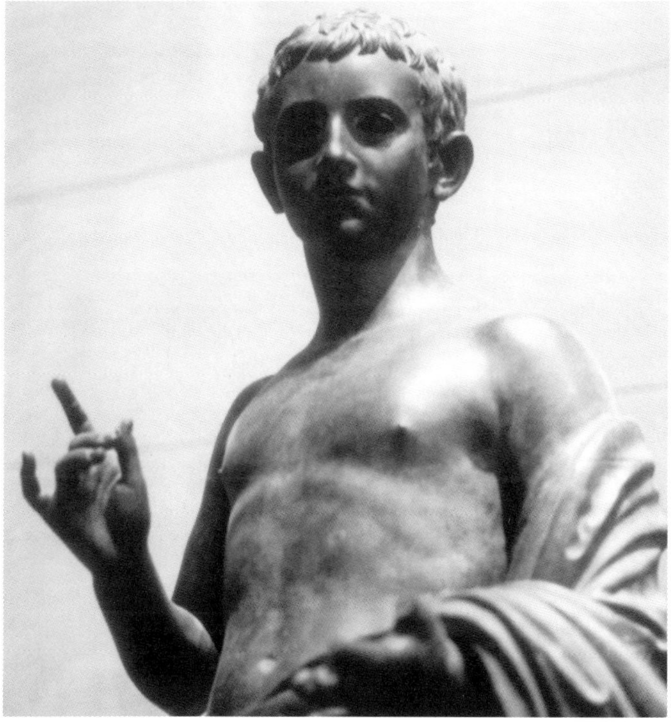

Fig. 5. Statue of youth, perhaps Gaius or Lucius Caesar. Bronze, h. 1.22 m. New York, The Metropolitan Museum of Art, Rogers Fund, 1914, 14.130.1. (Photo: author)

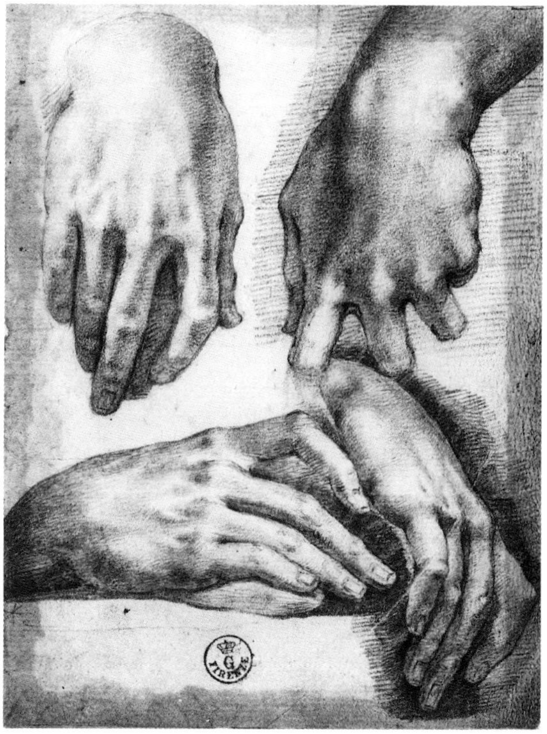

Fig. 6. Francesco Morandini, called Il Poppi, Sheet from a drawing notebook, 129 x 96 cm. Florence, Gabinetto dei Disegni e delle Stampe degli Uffizi 4279F. (Photo: courtesy Soprintendenza dei Beni Artistici, Florence)

ally his portraits, bodies are similarly constructed in segments. Following Lucian's method for constructing an ideal woman, heads, necks, and hands are attached separately to elaborately costumed torsos in his depictions of men as well as of women. Although the effect of the painted hands is to simulate marble, the artist and his audience were probably aware that many of the originals from which they derived were bronze and possibly Greek.[65] In his 'carved' signature piece ("Bronzo") as well as in his style, the painter acknowledged his debt to the sculptor Lysippos.[66] Other artists and other workshops using similar sculptural models produced paintings in which figures, like variations on a theme, resemble one another and those by other painters. Gradually, during the course of the 16th c., painters utilizing the bronze techniques of assemblage, reconfiguration, and repetition of body parts, forged a unified *maniera*.

303 West 66th St., 14JE, New York, NY 10023

I would like to thank G. Bonsanti, C. H. Smyth, and R. Stone for invaluable advice at earlier stages in the preparation of this manuscript.

---

65 The painted hand of Eleonora of Toledo in her official state portrait resembles the hand type of the *Venus Felix* recorded in the papal collection in 1509, installed in the Belvedere Court by 1528, and visible there when Bronzino visited Rome about 1548.

66 The artist signed his name "Bronzo" as if carved in stone in his *Holy Family* now in Vienna. In the same painting Bronzino used the same type of antique bronze or marble *Sleeping Cupid* as Michelangelo did, as a model for the Christ child. For the preparatory drawing, see Smyth, *Bronzino* (supra n.32) fig. 1. For the aspects of Lysippos that Bronzino admired see the quote from Pliny, *NH* 33.65 ff. (supra p. 279).

Late 19th-early 20th c. replicas, imitations and falsifications(?) of brooches from the Pyrmont spring: a light and scanning electron microscopic approach

Wolf-Rüdiger Teegen

During restoration work in the fall of 1863 at the famous mineral springs of Pyrmont (Germany), about 300 brooches, three Roman coins, an enameled skillet, and two wood ladles were discovered. Approximately 253 objects (244 of them brooches) could be identified amd 228 (222 of them brooches) were preserved. The finds belonged to a spring and tree shrine, dating to the first half of the first millennium A.D. (before *c*.450). I presented some of the Roman objects at the 10th International Bronze Congress in Freiburg in 1988.[1] I studied the complete find for my doctoral thesis, submitted to the University of Göttingen in 1995.[2] In the present paper I shall deal with late 19th- and early 20th-c. replicas and imitations of some brooches from the find.

The excavator R. Ludwig stated in his first reports that replicas had been made of the finest objects.[3] Production of the so-called Quellnadeln ("brooches of the spring") can be traced from 1865 to the present, almost continuously. Generally they were sold as souvenirs to tourists at the baths. In 1911/12 the C. Haegemann foundry at Hannover produced replicas of 23 of the most important brooch types of the Pyrmont find for the museum of the Prussian province of Hannover.[4] They are very well made (see below). Total reflection X-ray fluorescence analysis was carried out on two of the replicas. In both cases, a zinc-rich brass was used, probably the same alloy.

Analysis of weights and measurements indicates that the cast replicas are only a little shorter and lighter than the originals. This was probably caused by shrinkage of the moulds. On the basis of the most important measurements and the weight, a principal components analysis (PCA) was undertaken. The PCA revealed, in part, differences between original and replicas similar to those obtained from brooches produced by the same craftsman (fig. 1).

Detailed analysis of the brooches published by E. aus'm Weerth in 1869 led to the conclusion that not all of his examples were ancient.[5] This could be proven for a type with "perldraht" applications where the original was preserved. For another type the same could be hypothesized by metal and wear analysis. A few of the 1911/12 replicas were also published as originals, a strong indication of the fine quality of the modern brooches.

Taking full account of the new facts, we placed special emphasis on the detection of non-antique objects in the group. A total of 27 *fibulae* was identified as being of dubious authenticity. Detailed study gave the following results: 8 of 27 objects are probably originals, 14 are replicas, and in 5 cases a decision was not possible. The degree of certainty was expressed with mathematical symbols (Original, Recent, ≥, >, n.d.) (Table 1).

---

1 W.-R. Teegen, "Neues zu zwei provinzial-römischen Bronzeobjekten des Pyrmonter Brunnenfundes. Ein Arbeitsbericht," in J. Ronke (ed.), *Akten der 10. int. Tagung über antike Bronzen, Freiburg 1988* (Forschungen und Berichte zur Vor- und Frühgeschichte in Baden-Württemberg 45, 1994) 411-16.

2 W.-R. Teegen, *Der Pyrmonter Brunnenfund* (Diss. Univ. of Göttingen 1995); and id., "Studien zu dem kaiserzeitlichen Quellopferfund von Bad Pyrmont," *Reallexikon der germanischen Altertumskunde Ergänzungsbd.* 20 (Berlin 1999).

3 Cf. R. Ludwig, "Germanische Alterthümer und römische Münzen in den Stahlquellen von Pyrmont," *Pyrmonter Wochenblatt* 22.11.1863 (14. Jg., Nr. 93, 1863) 1-3; id., "Germanische Alterthümer und römische Münzen in den Mineralquellen zu Pyrmont," *Archiv für Balneologie* 3 (1864) 1-4. See also R. Ludwig, "Der Fund von Pyrmont," *BJb* 38 (1865) 47-60.

4 H. Hahne, "Vermehrung der Sammlungen I: Historische Abteilung 1: Vor- und frühgeschichtliche Sammlung," *Jahrbuch des Provinzial-Museums zu Hannover 1911/1912* (1912) 3-7.

5 E. aus'm Weerth, "Römische Gewandnadeln 1: Aus der Sammlung des verstorbenen Herrn Dr. Fritz Hahn zu Hannover," *BJb* 46 (1869) 45-49.

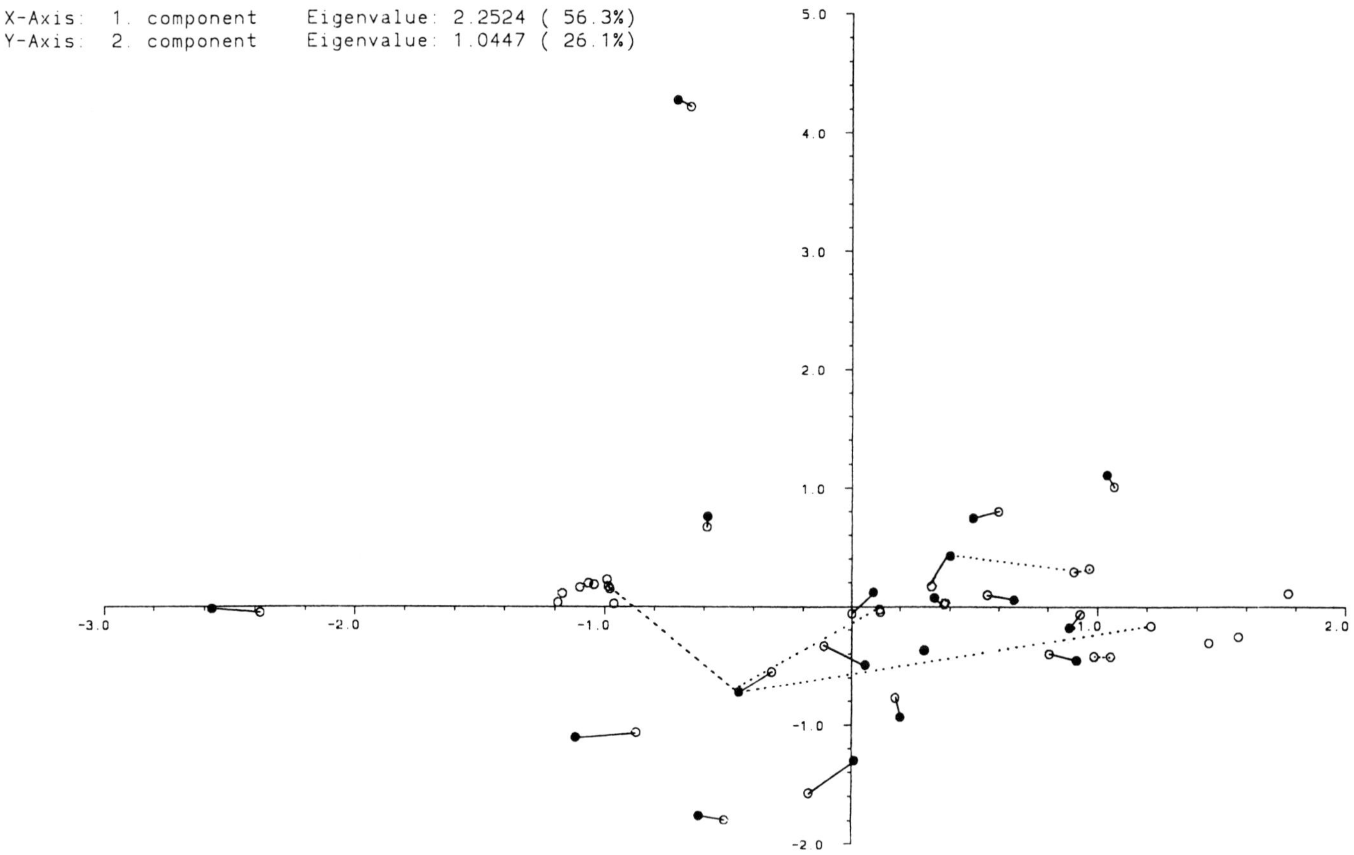

Fig. 1. Pyrmont spring find. Principal component analysis (PCA) of the most important measurements and weights of brooches. Black dot = original; circle = replica or imitation. A bold line connects an original and its replica or imitation. The dotted line connects some different types of imitations or replicas. (author).

TABLE 1. DEGREE OF CERTAINTY OF AUTHENTICITY OF DUBIOUS BROOCHES IN THE PYRMONT SPRING FIND (N=27).
O = Original, R = Recent (replica or imitation), n.d. = not determined

O	O>R	O≥R	O=R	R=O	R≥O	R>O	R
n: 3	5	–	1 (n.d.)	4 (n.d.)	1	4	9

The following criteria were used: 1) shape and style, 2) parallels in the Pyrmont spring find and/or in the literature, 3) traces of wear, 4) manufacturing traces, 5) repairs, 6) metal analyses, 7) corrosion, 8) documentary sources, and 9) other information. All criteria could not be applied to all the 27 brooches. Special attention was given to traces of wear, handling, and the way in which repairs were carried out. Study of the data from metal analyses led to the conclusion that their usefulness for detecting non-ancient objects was limited. This is particularly true if the analyses did not reveal an extremely high content of zinc or show the presence of unusual trace elements or a very high content of some elements.

It must be stated here that neither the replicas nor the dubious objects were free inventions of the (modern) craftsmen. All objects have more or less similar parallels in other finds of the Roman Iron Age and the Early Migration period. There is no evidence of real falsifications. On the contrary, in all reports published before 1870 the authors described the presence and good quality of the replicas. Unfortunately there is no graphic documentation, and the institutional records of museums (Stuttgart, Braunschweig) possessing replicas from Pyrmont lack iconographical data. As the objects themselves were destroyed in World War II, direct examination was not possible.

To detect dubious objects and determine authenticity, a multi-factorial model gives the greatest chance for obtaining good results. However, a decision was not possible in every case.

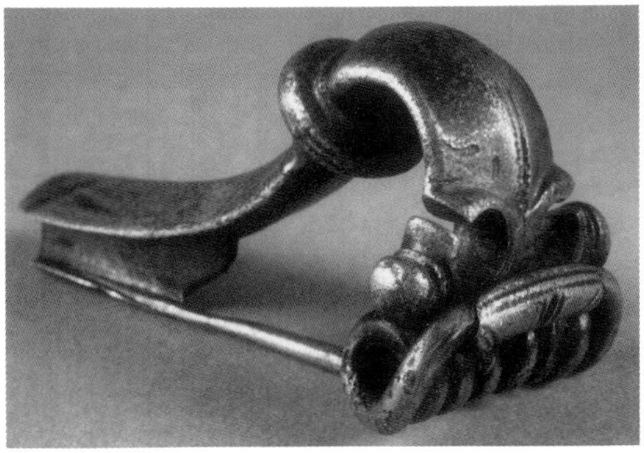

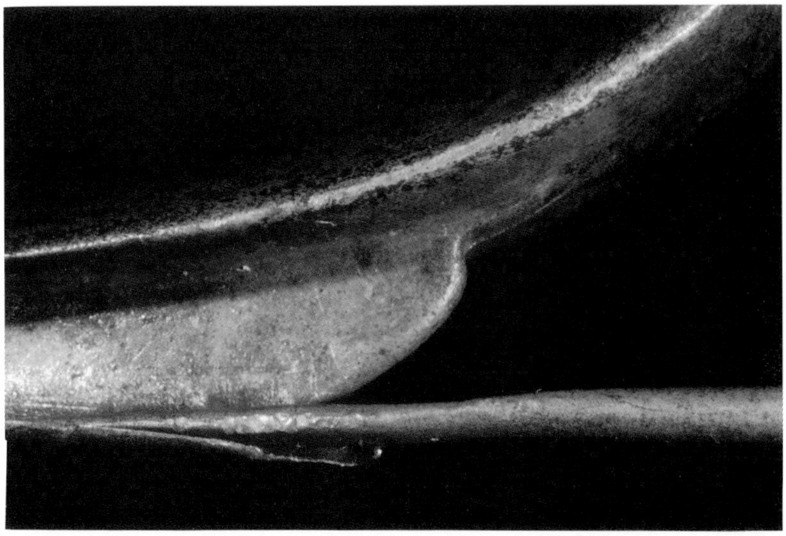

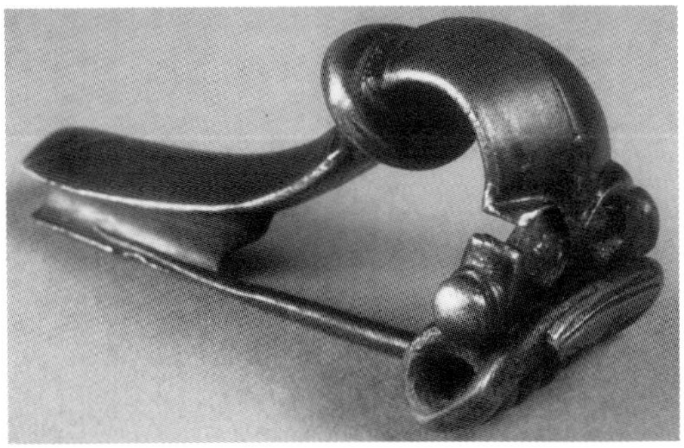

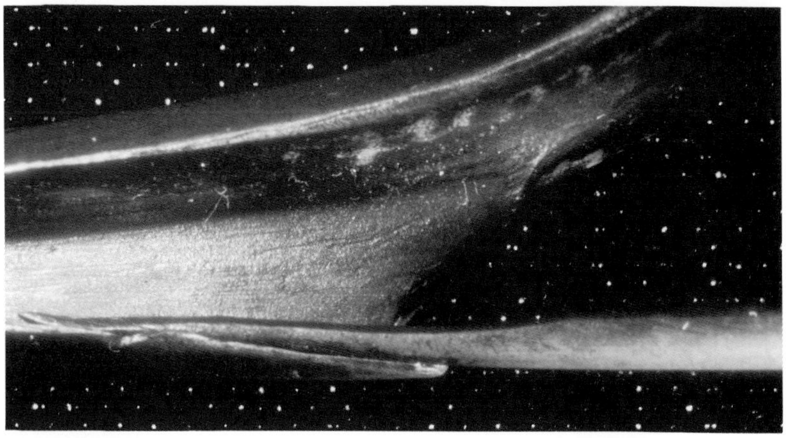

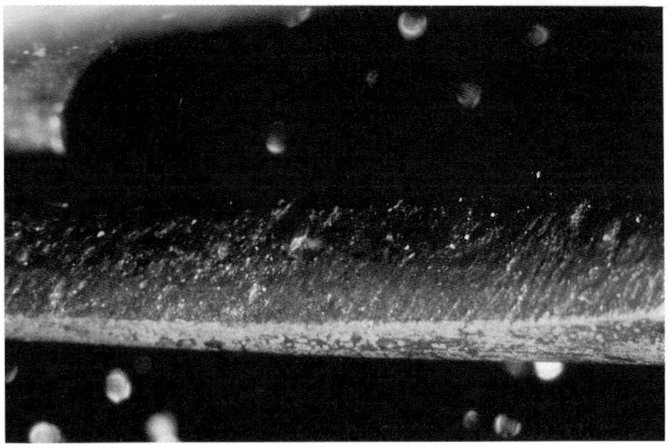

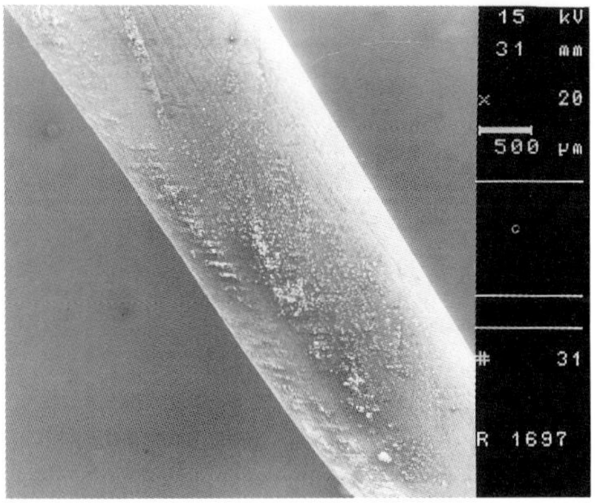

Fig. 2 (top left). Original eye-brooch (Almgren III,45), cat. no. 26. First half of the 1st c. A.D. L 57.5 mm. Bad Pyrmont, Museum im Schloß. (Photo: C. S. Fuchs)

Fig. 3 (top right). Original eye-brooch (Almgren III,45), cat. no. 26: close-up view of the extremely worn catchplate and needle. (Photo: author)

Fig. 4 (center left). Cast replica of eye-brooch cat. no. 26 (Almgren III,45) = replica no. 5, produced in 1911/12. L 56.8 mm. Hannover, Niedersächsisches Landesmuseum Hannover, Urgeschichtsabteilung. (Photo: C. S. Fuchs)

Fig. 5 (center right). Cast replica of eye-brooch cat. no. 26 (Almgren III,45) = replica no. 5: close-up view of catchplate and needle. (Photo: author)

Fig. 6 (bottom left). Cast replica of eye-brooch cat. no. 26 (Almgren III,45) = replica no. 5: close-up view of the needle with traces of filing. (Photo: author)

Fig. 7 (bottom right). Cast replica of eye-brooch cat. no. 26 (Almgren III,45) = replica no. 5: SEM photograph of the needle with traces of filing. (Photo: I. Hettwer-Steeger)

This is particularly true in cases where parallels are still not known. In the following, I will show some specific differences between one original and a very good replica. The study was carried out by light and scanning electron microscopy in the Institute of Anatomy, Göttingen University. The insights could also be applied to dubious pieces.[6]

We are well informed about the general difference in jewelry techniques between ancient and recent objects, for example by E. Formigli's book *Oreficeria etrusca e romana*.[7] Here I will show some special criteria that deal with traces of wear. These kinds of traces have rarely been studied in ancient jewelry.[8]

The test object was a very worn eye-brooch, type Almgren III,45 (fig. 2).[9] This type is characteristic of the first half of the 1st c. A.D. in central Europe. A copy was made in 1911/12 by the Haegemann foundry for the provincial museum at Hannover. The traces of wear on the original are extreme and led to the conclusion that the brooch was used for more than one generation. This fact also has consequences for chronology. Precise chronology does not seem to be possible with (very) worn objects. The needle of the brooch is much reduced, particularly in the area in front of the catchplate (fig. 3).[10] This could also observed but on a lesser scale near the spring case. The ornament on the top of the bow is missing, and the end of the foot is rounded. The holder of the external chord is destroyed at the edges. This was probably caused on the inside by movement of the external chord during handling and on the outside from wear by textiles. The catchplate and turnover are also much reduced.

These important alterations, caused by handling and by textiles over a long period, were copied by the craftsman in the Haegemann foundry (figs. 4-5). He saw all the critical details, but he did not understand their significance. On the top of the needle are traces of filing (figs. 5 and 7). The holder of the external chord looks like a block. SEM analysis of the catchplate shows traces of wear under higher magnification; they are probably the result of the handling of the brooch over the last 80 years by the museum staff and by researchers like myself.

Replicas of traces of wear by filing (cf. figs. 6-7) or by other techniques are, as in our case, visible only with magnifying glasses or with a microscope. They are a very strong indication of a non-antique object. Without sensitivity to such traces and their significance, detection would be difficult.

Universität Leipzig, Historisches Seminar, Ritterstrasse 14, D-04109 Leipzig

The support and help of the following individuals and institutions is gratefully acknowledged: the directors of the museums of Bad Pyrmont (D. Alfter), Hameln (N. Humburg), and Hannover (G. Wegner) gave permission for study. C. S. Fuchs, Institut für Denkmalpflege, Hannover, made excellent colour photographs. H.-J. Kuhn and M. Schultz gave permission for use of the technical equipment of the Institute of Anatomy, I. Hettwer-Steeger made excellent SEM photographs, and C. Maelicke corrected my English manuscript. Travel funds were kindly made available by Dr.(†) and Mrs. A. J. Barthelmes (Tulsa, OK). To all the above I am highly indebted. This paper is dedicated to the memory of the late Dr. Barthelmes.

---

6 I used a simpler method for my doctoral thesis.

7 E. Formigli, *Tecniche dell'oreficeria etrusca e romana: originali e falsificazioni* (Florence 1985).

8 For my thesis I undertook a first light and scanning electron microscopic study.

9 Typology after O. Almgren, *Studien über nordeuropäische Fibelformen der ersten nachchristlichen Jahrhunderte mit Berücksichtigung der provinzialrömischen und südrussischen Formen* (2nd edn., Mannus-Bibliothek 32, Leipzig 1923).

10 The English terms used to describe component parts of the brooches derive from M. E. Snape, *Roman brooches from North Britain: a classification and a catalogue of brooches from sites on the Stanegate* (BAR 235, Oxford 1993) 2, fig. 1.

BRARY